THE
URBANIZATION
OF OPERA

THE URBANIZATION OF OPERA

*Music Theater in
Paris in the
Nineteenth Century*

ANSELM GERHARD

TRANSLATED BY
Mary Whittall

THE UNIVERSITY OF CHICAGO PRESS
Chicago and London

ANSELM GERHARD is professor of musicology at the University of Bern, Switzerland.

The University of Chicago Press, Chicago 60637
The University of Chicago Press, Ltd., London
© 1998 by The University of Chicago
All rights reserved. Published 1998
Printed in the United States of America
07 06 05 04 03 02 01 00 99 98   5 4 3 2 1

ISBN (cloth) : 0-226-28857-9

Originally published as *Die Verstädterung der Oper:
Paris und das Musiktheater des 19. Jahrhunderts,*
© 1992 J. B. Metzlersche Verlagsbuchhandlung und Carl
Ernst Poeschel Verlag GmbH in Stuttgart.

Library of Congress Cataloging-in-Publication Data

Gerhard, Anselm, 1958–
    [Verstädterung der Oper.   English]
    The urbanization of opera : music theater in Paris in the nineteenth
century / by Anselm Gerhard ; translated by Mary Whittall.
        p.   cm.
    Includes bibliographical references and index.
    ISBN 0-226-28857-9 (alk. paper)
    1. Opera—France—Paris—19th century.   2. Opera—Social aspects.
I. Title.
ML1727.8.P2G3813   1998
782.1'0944'36109034—dc21   97-46199
                                                            CIP
                                                            MN

♾ The paper used in this publication meets the
minimum requirements of the American National Standard
for Information Sciences—Permanence of Paper for
Printed Library Materials, ANSI Z39.48-1992.

CONTENTS

Preface to the English-Language Edition   ix
Acknowledgments   xiii
Chronology   xv

INTRODUCTION
1

Urban Experience and Reception History   4
Conventions and Genre History   8
The Kaleidoscope and the Theory of Reflection   13

CHAPTER ONE
Realities of a Metropolis
17

A Place for Dreams   21
Operas for a New Public   25
Managing the Opéra   33
Artists as Capitalists   36

CHAPTER TWO
Victor-Joseph Étienne de Jouy, a Hermit in the City
41

"The Hermit of the Chaussée d'Antin"   41
Sensual Enchantment   44
Contrasts   50
A Mirror   56

CHAPTER THREE

Rossini and the Revolution
63

Le Siège de Corinthe   63
Guillaume Tell   65
"A Veritable Revolution"   68
Stories from History   71
The Unhappy Ending   76
The Emancipation of the Chorus   82
"The Firstborn of Liberty"   90
"What a Picture!"   94
The Indecisive Hero   100
The Retreat of the Princess   105
Melancholy   111
Silence   114

CHAPTER FOUR

Eugène Scribe, an Apolitical Man of Letters
122

La Muette de Portici   122
An Apolitical Man of Letters   124
Opera and Revolution   127
"The Well-Made Play"   134
The Mélodrame   140
Mime   145
Panorama   150

CHAPTER FIVE

Meyerbeer and the Happy Medium
158

Les Huguenots   158
Color   162
Character   170
The Obedient Daughter   177
The Fleeting Moment   182
Shock   197
Music in Space   202
The Happy Medium   206

CHAPTER SIX

Victor Hugo, the Illustrious Poet as Librettist

215

La Esmeralda 215
Two Conceptions of Dramaturgy 217
The City in Opera 220
Fear of the Mob 227
Voyeurism 232
The Power of Fate 238

CHAPTER SEVEN

Meyerbeer and Reaction

247

Le Prophète 247
A Pamphlet 250
Dreams and Visions 260
Memory 268
Mother and Son 277
Demagoguery 284
Suicide 289
Magic Fire 298
Mosaic 303

CHAPTER EIGHT

The Composer as Librettist

318

The Librettist's Martyrdom 318
"La Parola Scenica" 324
The Ideal Collaborator 327
Librettos from Stock 335

CHAPTER NINE

Verdi and an Institutional Crisis

342

Les Vêpres siciliennes 342
Regular Miracles 345
Tête-à-Tête 349
Invocation 359
The Powerless Father 361
Spleen 366
Farewell 373
Decline 377

CHAPTER TEN

The International View
388

Nationalism and Cosmopolitanism 388
Mythology 395
The Legacy of Grand Opéra 402

CHAPTER ELEVEN

Verdi and Interior Space
409

Un ballo in maschera 409
"Profound Observations" 412
Concision 419
Masquerade 426
The Chorus as Scenery 436
The Longing for Interior Space 440
Horror 446
Past and Future 453

Bibliography 457
Index of Titles of Operas and Plays 493
Index of Names 498

PREFACE TO THE
ENGLISH-LANGUAGE EDITION

Every author must experience pleasure and satisfaction at the appearance of his or her book in a language other than that of the original. In the specific case of this book, which concerns itself with the aesthetic and perceptual premises of grand opéra (so-called), the nature of the subject matter adds something directly to the pleasure, for an international perspective is one of the implicit strands of this study of certain fundamental questions of opera in the nineteenth century, relating in particular to the French and Italian traditions, but undertaken within a hermeneutic tradition characteristic of German-language *Geisteswissenschaft*. However, almost six years have passed since the original German manuscript was completed, so that a brief preface to the English edition seems called for.

Six years, after all, is a relatively long time, given the speed with which academic research in the field of opera has advanced in the last years of the waning twentieth century. On the other hand, it is quite a short period not only in relation to the length of the book's genesis (it grew out of a dissertation started in 1982) but also in view of the most recent studies of Parisian grand opéra. Important research initiatives, especially contributions to a better knowledge of the outstanding composer in the genre, Giacomo Meyerbeer, were undertaken during the 1990s, but their outcome is still awaited. A series of three conferences—under the general rubrics "Giacomo Meyerbeer" (Thurnau, September 1991),[1] "Meyerbeer and Dance" (Thurnau, September 1995), and

---

1. Report by Manuela Jahrmärker, *Die Musikforschung* 45 (1992): 285–86.

"Meyerbeer's Theater" (Salzburg, July 1996)[2]—produced some extremely promising papers which have yet to be published, but even more significant are two major projects that will have a profound effect on future Meyerbeer studies, in that they will make all the essential sources available for the first time: the Meyerbeer-Institut in Thurnau, in partnership with Verlag G. Ricordi & Co. Munich, has announced the first volumes of a critical edition of selected operas,[3] to appear by the end of the present millennium, and meanwhile a study group at the Philipp University in Marburg an der Lahn, led by Sabine Henze-Döhring, has resumed work on the edition of Meyerbeer's letters and diaries, publication of which was interrupted in 1985.[4]

Apart from these initiatives, and the publication of the critical edition of Rossini's *Guillaume Tell* edited by M. Elizabeth C. Bartlet,[5] I am not aware of any fundamentally new directions in research into French nineteenth-century opera, unless an exception is to be made for James H. Johnson's *Listening in Paris*, which includes a cursory look at some grands opéras in the course of depicting the process that led to the modern practice of listening to music in theaters and concert halls in reverent silence. Unfortunately, however, the account of the "operatic rebirth and the return of grandeur," focusing too narrowly on the year 1831, is one of the weaker passages of this highly ambitious study, and furthermore it concludes with an assessment of Meyerbeer that cites, without any comment whatever, judgments tainted by antisemitic prejudice against a composer who, in Johnson's words, "defied all musical pedigree."[6] It is thus probably safe to say, with a few modifications registered in the annotation, which has been updated for the English-language edition, that the attempt to interpret Parisian grand opéra on the premises of fundamentally altered perceptual structures has not been superseded by anything published since 1992.

A reviewer of the German edition remarked that one reason why it lacked a "résumé" was probably because it would have to be "formulated

2. Report by Stephanie Schroedter, *Die Musikforschung* 50 (1997): 91–92.

3. Three have been announced to start with: *Robert le diable*, ed. Wolfgang Kühnhold; *Le Prophète*, ed. Matthias Brzoska; and *Les Huguenots*, ed. Milan Pospíšil and Marta Ottlová.

4. Volume 5, covering the years 1849–52, is expected to be published in 1998.

5. Chapter 3 in this English-language edition of my book has been revised to take account of this edition.

6. James H. Johnson, *Listening in Paris: A Cultural History*, 253; see also the review by Maribeth Clark in *Cambridge Opera Journal* 8 (1996): 77–81.

at best in Benjaminian paradoxes."[7] That is a very flattering interpretation of the fact that in the current state of research I had no alternative but to leave unanswered questions raised by my own work—along with many questions to which it attempted to formulate answers. In one particular instance, I regret very much having overlooked, at the time of writing, a monograph that appears at first sight to have nothing to do with opera. Gerhart von Graevenitz's ambitious essay describing myth in terms of a "habit of thought" is not uncontroversial, specifically in the sections dealing with operatic history,[8] but it expounds the fascinating thesis that some essentially mythic qualities of Wagner's music-dramas were already present in librettos by Scribe (in the structuring of which Meyerbeer had a decisive hand). A more detailed and qualified expansion of this bold hypothesis would make it possible to interpret the antirationalist tendencies in *Le Prophète* in a wholly new context, and thus simultaneously to relate this opera first performed in Paris in 1849 more closely to the subsequent development of German opera. Nevertheless, after long hesitation, I decided against modifying the concluding paragraphs of my seventh chapter to take account of Graevenitz's thesis—it would have created a new and different book, in which I would also have had to develop afresh the idea of irony as a central premise of Meyerbeer's dramaturgy, affected as it was by his pessimistic view of history.[9]

I contented myself instead with a critical rereading of the complete text of my book, taking particular pains to correct all the errors and omissions that had come to my notice, and to incorporate the secondary literature up to the end of 1996. I was helped in this prolonged task by the exceptional care and consideration shown me by the publisher of this edition and the translator. I would like to express particularly warm thanks to Mary Whittall not only for undertaking the work but also for her patience in the face of all the last-minute modifications. Insofar as her version not only reproduces the argument of the German original faithfully—as it seems to me—but also adds some quite unlooked-for flashes of wit in places, I regard it as a piece of exceptional good luck that the publisher entrusted the work to such an experienced translator.

7. Gerrit Walther, "Bürger zwischen Hof und Hot-Club," *Archiv für Sozialgeschichte* 35 (1995): 395.

8. See the chapter "Richard Wagner: Europäischer Synkretismus und mythologisches Gesamtkunstwerk," *Mythos*, 46–89; and Dieter Borchmeyer, "Wagner-Literatur—Eine deutsche Misere," 46–52.

9. But see my article on Meyerbeer in *Metzler Komponisten Lexikon* (Stuttgart, 1992).

I would also like to extend very cordial thanks to Kathleen Kuzmick Hansell of the University of Chicago Press, whose careful study of the text has contributed to the correction of inaccuracies in a number of places, while her positive engagement has greatly assisted the appearance of the book in this form. It goes without saying that all remaining errors and faults of judgment are solely the responsibility of the author, and it will only be an added satisfaction to him if this translation plays a part in ensuring that as many as possible of these are corrected soon in the light of much more research into the fascinating history of French opera in the nineteenth century.

ACKNOWLEDGMENTS

The work on this book was started within the framework of the research project "Giuseppe Verdi und die Situation der italienischen Oper in den 1860er Jahren" (Giuseppe Verdi and the situation of Italian opera in the 1860s), led by Professor Carl Dahlhaus and sponsored by the Stiftung Volkswagenwerk. Much of the text was written during research visits to Parma (1982–83) and Paris (1983–85), and in its first form was accepted in September 1985 as a dissertation at the Technische Universität Berlin, with the title "Großstadt und Große Oper: Motive der 'Grand Opéra' in Verdis *Les Vêpres Siciliennes* und ausgewählten Pariser Opern von Rossini und Meyerbeer." During the period 1989–90 I substantially revised and expanded the text, in particular adding the chapters about Victor-Joseph Étienne de Jouy and Verdi's *Ballo in maschera*. This version was published in German in 1992, with the title *Die Verstädterung der Oper: Paris und das Musiktheater des 19. Jahrhunderts*.

It was during the process of revision that news came of the death of Carl Dahlhaus, to whom the work owes so much. Dahlhaus was the first musicologist to take up Walter Benjamin's view of Paris as "the capital city of the nineteenth century" and put it to use in the field of music history, and that is far from being the only stimulus he gave my work. In offering me the chance to take part in the Verdi research project he promoted the circumstances that enabled me to take the work begun under his supervision as a dissertation to its conclusion as a published book. I cannot now express my thanks to him in person, but I can thank the Stiftung Volkswagenwerk (Hanover) for its support in the years 1982–84, without which I would not have been able to work in Italy and France unencumbered by financial worries.

To the pleasure of concentrated work among the inexhaustible resources of the Bibliothèque Nationale in Paris was added that of working in numerous other institutions, where I received unstinting help from librarians, many of whose names I never learnt. I am glad to thank by name Martine Kahane and Nicole Wild, librarians at the Bibliothèque de l'Opéra in Paris, for their assistance in the search for elusive sources and material suitable for reproduction in the case of some of the illustrations. I am especially grateful to Marisa Di Gregorio Casati, Lina Ferretti Rè, and Daniella Negri Mazzola, all of the Istituto Nazionale di Studi Verdiani in Parma, who made me welcome for fifteen months and to Uwe Schweikert, who did not hesitate to accept the German version of the book for the music list of Metzler-Verlag, Stuttgart, and saw it through production with great enthusiasm.

For stimulating discussion, important advice, constructive criticism, and patient encouragement, I owe thanks not only to Professor Pierluigi Petrobelli (Parma and Rome), director of the Istituto Nazionale di Studi Verdiani, and Dr Barbara Beyer (Berlin), my colleague on the Verdi research project, but also to many other professors and colleagues, especially Lorenzo Bianconi (Bologna), Sieghart Döhring (Thurnau), Michael Fend (London), Ludwig Finscher (Wolfenbüttel), Klaus Hortschansky (Münster), Friedrich Lippmann (Rome), Laurenz Lütteken (Marburg an der Lahn), Jean Mongrédien (Paris), and Angelo Pompilio (Bologna), and last but not least my friends Virginia Bernal (Maubourguet) and Balthasar Müller (Baeriswil).

A. G.

CHRONOLOGY

1826 The Bourbon King Charles X has reigned in France since 1824, George IV in Great Britain since 1820, Frederick William III in Prussia since 1797. Italy has long been broken up in small states. Beethoven (b. 1770) is composing his last string quartets, Schubert (b. 1797) his String Quartet in G major, Op. 161. Weber (b. 1786) dies in London, after the première of *Oberon*. Rossini (b. 1792), manager of the Théâtre Italien since 1824, gives up the post. Premières: *Olimpie* (revised version) by Spontini (b. 1774) and *Le Siège de Corinthe* (T: Soumet and Balochi, M: Rossini), both at the Opéra, *Margherita d'Anjou* (revised version) by Meyerbeer (b. 1791) at the Théâtre de l'Odéon.[1] Jouy (b. 1764) publishes his *Essai sur l'Opéra français*, Lamennais (b. 1782) his *De la Religion considérée dans ses rapports avec l'ordre politique et civil*, which has a decisive influence on the foundation of Christian socialism. With *Robert le diable*, Scribe (b. 1791) begins his many years of association with Meyerbeer. Delacroix (b. 1798) exhibits his *Greece on the Ruins of Missolonghi* in aid of the Greeks in their war of independence. The new stock exchange, the Bourse, is opened in Paris; the first aniline dyes are produced in Berlin.

1827 Beethoven dies in Vienna, Liszt (b. 1811) returns to Paris after years of touring, the first performance of Mendelssohn Bartholdy's (b. 1809) overture to *A Midsummer Night's Dream* is given in Stettin. Goethe (b. 1749) coins the expression "world literature," Manzoni (b. 1785) publishes the last volume of *I promessi sposi* in Milan, Hugo (b. 1802) publishes his verse drama *Cromwell* and its polemical preface in Paris. The première of *Moïse et Pharaon* (T: Balochi and Jouy, M: Rossini) is given at the Opéra. The *Revue musicale*, the first regular French musical periodical, founded by Fétis (b. 1784), begins publication in Paris. Halévy (b. 1799) becomes professor of harmony at the Conservatoire, Pixérécourt (b. 1773), celebrated as a very successful author of *mélodrames* retires

---

1. When no town is named, the theater referred to is in Paris. The following abbreviations are used: M = music, T = text.

as director of the Opéra-Comique, Ingres (b. 1780) finishes *The Apotheosis of Homer.*

1828 Schubert dies in Vienna. Premières: *La Muette de Portici* (T: Scribe and Delavigne, M: Auber) and *Le Comte Ory* (T: Scribe and Delestre-Poirson, M: Rossini) at the Opéra, Marschner's (b. 1795) *Der Vampyr* in Leipzig. In Paris, Habeneck (b. 1781) conducts Beethoven's Third Symphony at the opening concert of the Société des concerts du Conservatoire, Deburau (b. 1796) makes his début as Pierrot at the Théâtre des Funambules, Delacroix shows *The Death of Sardanapalus* at the Salon. The first horse-drawn omnibuses begin to provide public transport in Paris.

1829 The Greco-Turkish War ends with Greek independence. Mendelssohn Bartholdy conducts the St. Matthew Passion in Berlin (the first performance since Bach's death), the first complete performance of Goethe's *Faust*, Part 1, is given in Brunswick. Balzac (b. 1799) begins *La Comédie humaine*. Gossec (b. 1734) dies in Paris, and Auber (b. 1782) takes his place in the Académie Française. The première of *Guillaume Tell* (T: Jouy and Bis, M: Rossini) is given at the Opéra. Rossini leaves for Bologna immediately afterwards, and visits Paris rarely during the next twenty-six years. Véron (b. 1798), medical man, pharmacist, and entrepreneur, founds the *Revue de Paris*.

1830 A French expeditionary force seizes Algiers and starts the colonization of Algeria. In July the Bourbon monarchy is brought down by an opposition composed of bourgeois liberals and proletarian street-fighters, and Louis-Philippe of Orléans is proclaimed king of the French. Premières: *Anna Bolena* by Donizetti (b. 1797) in Milan, Berlioz's (b. 1803) *Symphonie fantastique* in Paris, *Fra Diavolo* (T: Scribe, M: Auber) at the Opéra-Comique, Hugo's *Hernani* at the Comédie-Française. Catel (b. 1773) dies; his place in the Académie Française goes to Paër (b. 1771). A performance of Auber's *La Muette de Portici* in Brussels plays a role in the secession of the new kingdom of Belgium from the United Netherlands. Stendhal (b. 1783) publishes *Le Rouge et le noir*, and Pushkin (b. 1799) *Eugene Onegin*. The rue de la Paix and the rue Vivienne are the first streets in Paris to be lit by gas.

1831 A revolt by textile workers in Lyons is suppressed with bloodshed. Paganini (b. 1782) gives his first concerts in Paris, to great acclaim. Heine (b. 1797) moves to Paris in May, and Chopin (b. 1810) arrives there in September. Premières: Weber's *Euryanthe*, in the version by Castil-Blaze, and *Robert le diable* (T: Scribe, M: Meyeerbeer), both at the Opéra; Bellini's (b. 1801) *Norma* in Milan. Delacroix's *Liberty leading the People* is shown at the Salon. Schumann (b. 1810) publishes *Papillons*, his Op. 2, Hugo publishes his novel *Notre-Dame de Paris, 1482.* Hegel (b. 1770) dies in Berlin. Faraday (b. 1791) discovers electromagnetic induction in London.

1832 A cholera epidemic breaks out in Paris. Chopin gives his first public concert in Paris. Verdi (b. 1813) is refused entry to the Milan Conservatory. Goethe dies in Weimar, Scott (b. 1771) at Abbotsford. The première of Hugo's *Le Roi s'amuse* at the Comédie-Française ends in an unprecedented uproar. A canal linking the Rhine and the Rhône is opened.

1833 Premières: *Gustave III, ou Le Bal masqué* (T: Scribe, M: Auber) at the Opéra, Marschner's *Hans Heiling* in Berlin. Reicha (b. 1770) publishes his textbook, *Art du compositeur dramatique*. Offenbach (b. 1819) comes to Paris to continue his education. In Paris, the Jockey Club is founded to promote equestrian sports, and asphalt is used to cover a road surface for the first time, on the Pont-Royal. In Göttingen, Gauss (b. 1777) and Weber (b. 1804) set up the first electromagnetic telegraph, over a distance of 1500 metres.

1834 Renewed unrest among workers in Paris and Lyons is brutally suppressed by the government, as recorded by Daumier (b. 1808) in his lithograph *Rue Transnonain, 15 April 1834*. Mozart's *Don Giovanni* is given at the Opéra in the version by Castil-Blaze, and a revival of *Robert Macaire* enables the popular actor Lemaître (b. 1798) to repeat his success in the title role. Musset (b. 1820) publishes his drama *Lorenzaccio*. The first number of the *Neue Zeitschrift für Musik*, co-founded by Schumann, appears in Leipzig. Boieldieu (b. 1775) dies; Reicha is elected to his place in the Académie Française.

1835 Censorship is reintroduced in France, and the satirical journal *La Caricature* is banned. Bellini dies in Puteaux near Paris. Premières: Donizetti's *Lucia di Lammermoor* in Naples, *La Juive* (T: Scribe, M: Halévy) at the Opéra, Bellini's *I Puritani* at the Théâtre Italien. Büchner (b. 1813) finishes *Dantons Tod* in Strasbourg. The introduction of steam-powered cylindrical presses in France, making it possible to print between 3,000 and 7,000 copies an hour, increases the circulation of newspapers.

1836 The Arc de Triomphe de l'Étoile is finished after many delays. Louis Bonaparte, Napoleon's nephew, attempts his first coup d'état in Strasbourg. Premières: *Les Huguenots* (T: Scribe, M: Meyerbeer) and *La Esmeralda* (T: Hugo, M: Bertin) at the Opéra, *Le Postillon de Longjumeau* by Adam (b. 1803) at the Opéra-Comique, *The Government Inspector* by Gogol (b. 1809) in St Petersburg. Reicha dies in Paris, and Halévy takes his place in the Académie Française, to which Scribe is also elected. *La Presse* begins publication, the first Paris newspaper to be sold in single copies, as well as by subscription.

1837 Queen Victoria (1819–1901) is crowned in London. The first stretch of railway-line in France, from Paris to Saint-Germain-en-Laye, is opened. Büchner dies in Zurich, Pushkin in St Petersburg, Le Sueur (b. 1760) in Paris; Carafa (b. 1787) is elected to the Académie Française in Le Sueur's place. Coal-production in France exceeds 2 million metric tons in a year for the first time (for comparison: in 1990, 89 million metric tons were produced in the United Kingdom, and, in the United States, 861 million).

1838 Chopin goes to Mallorca with George Sand (b. 1804). Premières: *Guido et Ginevra* (T: Scribe, M: Halévy) and *Benvenuto Cellini* (T: Wailly and Barbier, M: Berlioz), both at the Opéra. Daguerre (b. 1787) experiments with photography in Paris. Steamships begin to ply regularly between the British Isles and North America.

1839 Arriving in Paris, Wagner (b. 1813) dreams of having a work staged at the Opéra. Gounod (b. 1818) is awarded the Prix de Rome. Paër dies in Paris; Spontini is elected to his place in the Académie Française. Véron buys the daily newspaper, *Le Constitutionnel*. Verdi's first opera, *Oberto, Conte di San Bonifacio*, has its première in Milan, the French star tenor Nourrit (b. 1802) commits suicide in Naples.

1840 Frederick William IV is crowned King of Prussia. In Paris, Napoleon's remains are reinterred in the church of Les Invalides in a solemn ceremony, and a column is erected in the Place de la Bastille to commemorate the victims of the revolution of 1830. France follows other countries in making laws to limit the hours worked by children. Paganini dies in Naples. Premières: *Les Martyrs* (T: Scribe, M: Donizetti), *La Favorite* (T: Royer and Vaëz, M: Donizetti), both at the Opéra, *Judith* by Hebbel (b. 1813) in Berlin. Le Creusot-Schneider revolutionizes French steel production with the introduction of the drop hammer. Great Britain introduces the world's first adhesive postage stamps.

1841 Work begins on military fortifications around Paris, the line of which corresponds roughly to the present-day Boulevard périphérique. After years of discord, Spontini is dismissed from the post of Generalmusikdirektor in Berlin, and Meyerbeer is appointed in his place. Premières: Schumann's First Symphony in Leipzig, Weber's *Le Freyschütz* (adapted by Berlioz) and *La Reine de Chypre* (T: Saint-Georges, M: Halévy), both at the Opéra. Hugo is elected to the Académie Française, Schinkel (b. 1781) dies in Berlin. The first experiments with electric street-lighting are made in Paris, along the Seine embankment.

1842 A law which to a large extent privatizes railway construction in France encourages yet greater stock exchange speculation. Premières: Rossini's *Stabat mater* in the Théâtre Italien, Wagner's *Rienzi, der letzte der Tribunen* in Dresden, Verdi's *Nabucodonosor* (better known as *Nabucco*) in Milan. Cherubini and Stendhal die in Paris; Cherubini is succeeded by Auber as director of the Paris Conservatoire, and by Onslow (b. 1784) in the Académie Française. In Paris Comte (b. 1798) publishes the *Cours de philosophie positive*, and serialization of Sue's (b. 1804) novel *Les Mystères de Paris* begins in the *Journal des débats*. Poe (b. 1809) publishes his first crime stories in Philadelphia. The church of La Madeleine in Paris is dedicated after nearly 80 years in the building.

1843 Premières: *Charles VI* (T: C. and G. Delavigne, M: Halévy) and *Dom Sébastien, roi de Portugal* (T: Scribe, M: Donizetti), both at the Opéra, Donizetti's *Don Pasquale* at the Théâtre Italien. Hölderlin (b. 1770) dies in Tübingen. In

Paris Berlioz publishes his *Grand Traité d'instrumentation et d'orchestration moder-nes*, and the first French illustrated magazine, *L'Illustration*, appears, with the (for the time) exceptionally large print-run of over 13,000 copies for the first issue. Marx (b. 1818) arrives in Paris, where he meets Engels (b. 1820).

1844 Nodier (b. 1780), one of the major French romantic writers, dies in Paris. The composer Berton (b. 1767) dies in Paris, and his place in the Académie Française is taken by Adam. Pixérécourt dies in Nancy. The court architect, Hittorf (b. 1792), finishes the suburban Parisian church of Saint-Vincent de Paul.

1845 The première of Wagner's *Tannhäuser* takes place in Dresden. Johann Strauss the younger (b. 1825) composes his first waltz. Mérimée (b. 1803) publishes his story *Carmen*. Turgenev (b. 1818) comes to Paris with the singer Pauline Viardot (b. 1821). After a first telegraph line from Paris to Rouen is opened, work starts on a system to serve the whole of France.

1846 Premières: Berlioz's cantata *La Damnation de Faust* in the Opéra-Comique, Hebbel's *Maria Magdalene* in Königsberg. Jouy dies in Saint-Germain-en-Laye, the mime Debureau dies in Paris. French coal production surpasses five million metric tons in one year for the first time.

1847 Mendelssohn Bartholdy dies in Leipzig. Premières: *Jérusalem* (T: Royer and Vaëz, M: Verdi) at the Opéra, Verdi's *Macbeth* in Florence, Flotow's (b. 1812) *Martha* in Vienna. Meyerbeer travels from Paris to Berlin by rail for the first time (the last gaps in the service having been filled in 1846): he spends more than 40 hours in the train, over four days.

1848 Revolutionary unrest forces Louis-Philippe to abdicate in February, but in June the Provisional Government suppresses further demands from the workers with extreme harshness (at least 3,000 dead). Louis Bonaparte is elected president of the republic in December. Liszt moves to Weimar and gives up the career of a traveling virtuoso for good, while Brahms (b. 1833) makes his solo debut in Hamburg. Donizetti dies in Bergamo, Chateaubriand (b. 1768) dies in Paris. Wagner publishes *Der Nibelungen-Mythos als Entwurf zu einem Drama*, Marx and Engels publish the Communist Manifesto, Baudelaire (b. 1821) publishes the first French translation of a story by Poe.

1849 Chopin and Habeneck die in Paris, Poe dies in Baltimore, Nicolai (b. 1810) dies in Berlin, two months after the première of his opera *Die lustigen Weiber von Windsor*. The Opéra stages the première of *Le Prophète* (T: Scribe, M: Meyerbeer). Courbet (b. 1819) causes a stir at the Salon. Verdi spends over six months in Paris. Postage stamps are introduced in France.

1850 Liszt gives the première of Wagner's *Lohengrin* in Weimar, the Bach-Gesellschaft is founded in Leipzig, the Benedictine monks of Solesmes begin research into Gregorian chant. The *Neue Zeitschrift für Musik* publishes Wagner's polemic *Das Judenthum in der Musik*, under a pseudonym. In Paris, Balzac dies, and Nadar opens a photographic studio.

1851 Louis Bonaparte outflanks all his political opponents in a coup d'état. Hugo flees to Brussels to escape arrest. Daguerre dies in Bry-sur-Marne, Spontini dies in Maiolati, and Thomas (b. 1811) takes his place in the Académie Française. Wagner publishes *Oper und Drama*. The Great Exhibition, precursor of all world fairs since, opens in London. Verdi's *Rigoletto* has its première in Venice.

1852 Louis Bonaparte holds a referendum which confirms him as Emperor Napoleon III. Onslow dies in Clermont-Ferrand; his place in the Académie Française goes to Reber (b. 1807). Verdi sees a performance of a new play by Dumas fils, *La Dame aux camélias*, in Paris. Hachette opens the first bookstalls on French railway stations, with specially published new editions, and the first department store in the world, Le Bon Marché, opens in Paris.

1853 The prefect of Paris, Haussmann, launches his radical program of re-designing the city. Three Verdi premières take place: *Il trovatore* in Rome, *La traviata* in Venice, and *Louise Miller* (a French version of *Luisa Miller*) at the Opéra. Véron begins publication of his memoirs, *Mémoires d'un bourgeois de Paris*.

1854 France enters the Crimean War, and her forces besiege Sebastopol. Liszt publishes his B minor Piano Sonata, Brahms his F minor Sonata, Op. 5. *L'Étoile du Nord* (T: Scribe, M: Meyerbeer) has its première at the Opéra-Comique. Halévy becomes secretary of the Académie Française, and his place as *académicien* is taken by the minor opera composer Clapisson (b. 1808). Hanslick (b. 1825) publishes *Vom Musikalisch-Schönen* (*On Beauty in Music*) in Leipzig. In Paris, 400 omnibuses, using 3,278 horses, carry nearly 100,000 passengers a day, and aluminum is produced on an industrial scale for the first time in the suburb of Javel.

1855 Rossini returns for good to Paris, where life is dominated by the Universal Exposition. Premières: *Les Vêpres siciliennes* (T: Scribe and Duveyrier, M: Verdi) at the Opéra, Offenbach's *Ba-ta-clan* at the newly opened Théâtre des Bouffes-Parisiens. Bruckner (b. 1824) becomes organist of Linz Cathedral.

1856 The Peace of Paris ends the Crimean War, to Russia's detriment. Schumann dies in Endenich, Heine and Adam die in Paris, and Berlioz is elected to Adam's place in the Académie Française. Thomas becomes professor of composition at the Conservatoire, Smetana (b. 1824) becomes a piano-teacher in Gothenburg.

1857 The Société Chimique de France is founded in Paris. Verdi's *Il trovatore* is done in French (as *Le trouvère*) at the Opéra, and his *Simon Boccanegra* has its première in Venice. Baudelaire publishes *Les Fleurs du mal*, and Flaubert (b. 1821) *Madame Bovary*. Bizet (b. 1838) wins the Prix de Rome. Sue dies in Paris. Ibsen (b. 1828) becomes director of the Norske Teatret in Christiana (now Oslo).

1858 Napoleon III and Cavour make a Franco-Italian pact in Plombières. After Orsini's failed attempt to assassinate Napoleon III, repression intensifies in France. The first transatlantic telegraph link is established. Berlioz completes *Les Troyens*. Offenbach's *Orphée aux enfers* has its première at the Théâtre des Bouffes-Parisiens. Musorgsky (b. 1839) abandons the career of an army officer.

1859 With French assistance, Piedmont-Savoy takes Lombardy by force from Austria. A French consortium starts the construction of the Suez Canal. The Académie des Sciences sponsors a competition to find uses for steam power in warships. The first electrical accumulator is developed in France. The suburbs between the outer ring of boulevards and the line of the present-day Boulevard périphérique are incorporated into the city of Paris. Premières: Meyerbeer's *Le Pardon de Ploërmel* at the Opéra-Comique, Gounod's *Faust* at the Théâtre-Lyrique, Verdi's *Un ballo in maschera* in Rome, Brahms's First Piano Concerto in Hanover. Delacroix exhibits at the Salon for the last time; his work is derided. Nadar takes the first aerial photographs of Paris from a hot-air balloon. Wagner finishes *Tristan und Isolde* in Lucerne, Tchaikovsky (b. 1840) completes his law studies in St Petersburg, Dvořák his study of the organ in Prague. Dostoyevsky (b. 1821), exiled for political reasons, is granted an amnesty and allowed to return to St. Petersburg. Darwin (b. 1809) publishes *On the Origin of Species by means of Natural Selection, or the Preservation of Favoured Races in the Struggle of Life*.

INTRODUCTION

"Grand Opera" is a suspect expression. "Opera," on its own, already suffers the reputation of being the most grandiose of all theatrical genres, and to preface it with "grand" makes it sound wholly inordinate and overbearing. The average operagoer is happy to use the term indiscriminately for almost all opera of the nineteenth century, and even some from the twentieth. During the twentieth century, however, grand opéra, often distinguished by the French é, as in this book, came to be used by scholars as the generic name for the format of musical drama associated with the Paris Opéra, which began to take shape around 1830;[1] in the end, admittedly, the term as such says nothing specific about what distinguishes the operas by Rossini, Auber, Meyerbeer, or Verdi that were first performed at the Opéra from other works: Rossini's *Guillaume Tell* and Meyerbeer's *Les Huguenots* are neither more grandiose nor of larger dimensions than, say, Verdi's *Otello* or Wagner's *Tannhäuser*.

Yet the odium of being specious and coarse-grained clings to them, and to many other operas to which the label "grand opéra" has been attached. There is a tacit implication that shady "talents" who fell short of "genius"—chief among them the Jewish millionaire's son, Giacomo Meyerbeer—deliberately set out to make a commercial killing from an artistically naive mass public by every conceivable means at their disposal. Lavish sets, the quality of illusion made possible by new lighting techniques, sumptuous costumes, titillating ballets holding up the action, bloodthirsty plots, recherché orchestrations, were allegedly more

1. See Becker, "Die historische Bedeutung der Grand Opéra," 151.

important in these works than "true art" or "profound" feeling. This polemic is as old as the works now classified as constituting the genre of grand opéra, and since Richard Wagner came up with the pithy phrase "effects without causes," in his antisemitic diatribe *Jewry in Music*, there has probably not been a single music-lover, critic, or composer who has remained wholly unaffected by the influence of such (prejudicial) judgments.

One thing is almost always overlooked, however: these accusations have been made against operas of all kinds since the hybrid genre itself first came into existence. Even if it is true, as it probably is, that they have been made more frequently against the genre of so-called grand opéra than any other, they still apply in the first instance only to the practice of mixing art for the eyes with art for the ears. Every opera, be it Mozart's *Die Entführung* or Wagner's *Parsifal*, makes a more penetrating impression on the spectator than a string quartet or the recital of a poem; it is not by chance that in the Romance languages opera is known, without a trace of pejorativeness, as *spettacolo* or *spectacle*.

Can we then simply ignore the aesthetic charges laid against grand opéra? The criticisms of Meyerbeer are tainted by antisemitism, the polemics against an operatic form which was created by composers of heterogeneous origins and which attained to international standing always contained an element of chauvinist nationalism: if they are set aside, is anything left that deserves to be taken seriously? Is Wagner's rallying cry of "effects without causes" nothing more than "a bon mot which is an example of the very thing itself"?[2] Perhaps a little more than that. The effect that operas like Auber's *La Muette de Portici*, Rossini's *Guillaume Tell*, or Meyerbeer's *Le Prophète* have on the audience is distinctively different from that of most earlier lyric dramas. Where people are expected to be enchanted by Gluck's *Armide*, thrilled by Mozart's *Don Giovanni*, and moved by Beethoven's *Fidelio*, they are overwhelmed by a grand opéra, and their ability to view the spectacle on the stage with detachment is drastically reduced. In consistently associating musico-dramatic form with tragic outcomes, opera for the first time laid claim to the aesthetic standing of tragedy. Consequently the aspirations of such productions increased by leaps and bounds, not only with respect to staging and performance, but also to the music itself. Up to the 1820s the composition of an opera was a matter of a few weeks, possibly months, but during the rest of the century spending years on one work

2. Miller, "Große Oper als Historiengemälde," 72.

became the rule, first in the case of the eccentric Spontini and his *Olimpie*, which flopped in Paris in 1819, then with Meyerbeer, and later, finally, with Wagner and Verdi.

It seems clear enough that changes like that were the external signs of more profound changes which were early symptoms of a new approach to musical drama. That new approach has continued to influence perceptions of musical drama ever since, and is responsible for the claims to totality embodied in the expression "music theater." Such aesthetic distinctions say nothing about the intrinsic quality of the works in question, however: consideration of whether Meyerbeer's *Le Prophète* is artistically more convincing than Wagner's *Götterdämmerung*, or whether Verdi achieved a more "authentic" expression of high art in *Aida* than Meyerbeer did in *Les Huguenots*, is irrelevant when the primary function of aesthetics is understood to be the recognition of structures of perception, rather than the legitimation of value judgments. Only if we take a new look at grand opéra, through eyes free of old prejudices, will we see the artistic achievement behind the commercial success of certain works, and start to understand the changes separating the musico-dramatic works composed in the middle decades of the nineteenth century from operas of the seventeenth and eighteenth centuries.

As in other areas, the period of around 1800 can be regarded as transitional, marking a historical divide during which concepts, modes of perception, genres, and aesthetic expectations transformed themselves into what we can recognize as those of our own time.[3] This general historical convention needs to be modified in opera's case already in that the transitional period extends up to around 1830. Many operas composed after it are still in the standard repertory, while earlier operas—like those of Handel and Gluck, or the numerous settings of Metastasio's librettos—cannot be performed nowadays without some kind of mediation. Certain operas dating from the transitional period— Mozart's Da Ponte operas, Beethoven's *Fidelio*, and Weber's *Der Freischütz*—belong to the core repertory of most opera houses, but all of these, either because of their content or for the formal reason that they intersperse the musical numbers with spoken dialogue, are in the "comic opera" tradition, where "bourgeois" tendencies began to have an effect far sooner than they did in "serious" opera. It is hardly surprising that epoch-making changes occurred later in an area of the arts

3. See Koselleck, introduction to *Geschichtliche Grundbegriffe*, xv.

which, if only for material reasons, was the preserve of the larger royal courts than they did in, for instance, the realm of ideas or less prestigious artistic genres.

Urban Experience and Reception History

What concept can we use to define the changes occurring in the early years of the nineteenth century? The catch-phrase "bourgeoisification" looks as if it might serve, since we are clearly considering tendencies that run parallel to those which made the bourgeoisie the socially dominant class. After the middle-class victories of the revolutions of 1789 and 1830, the operagoing public in France, like other sections of society, was no longer dominated by the court but brought together a paying public of bourgeois, aristocrats, and a "citizen king" on an equal footing. The kind of theatrical actions concerned solely with the doings of princes gave way to dramas in which crowned heads shared the stage with nobodies, and success was no longer measured by the reaction of the court and leading intellectuals but by the box office.

But on further thought the term "bourgeoisification," together with the concept of economic and social history underlying it, proves so vague as to express virtually nothing. The word "bourgeois" itself has such a multitude of applications that it lacks all analytical precision, which makes it ill-suited to the task of denoting what is specifically new about modern forms of theater, including dance, mime, and gesture.[4] This is all the more true in the case of the history of opera, where tendencies toward "bourgeoisification" can be observed from the early seventeenth century onward, alongside all the court traditions: the first opera house not under the control of a royal family but open to everyone who could afford the admission price was opened in Venice in 1637, and there are good reasons for regarding what developed in Venice, rather than the Florentine experiments of around 1600, as the decisive experience allowing us to distinguish between court entertainments and the art form that came to be known as opera.[5] Conversely, some "prebourgeois" circumstances persist even in the last years of the twentieth century: even if theaters in today's European constitutional monarchies are no longer financed out of the budget of the royal household, as was usual in the nineteenth century, there are still opera houses which call themselves "royal."

4. See Eichberg, *Leistung, Spannung, Geschwindigkeit,* 256.
5. See Bianconi, *Music in the Seventeenth Century,* 161 ff.

Political and economic upheavals therefore seem far less significant than profound alterations in the models of perception to which the product and its reception conformed and to which bourgeois, proletarian, and aristocrat alike were exposed. Of course these developments cannot be considered in isolation from the economic context, but numerous anomalies rule out any notion of a one-way current of cause and effect. The scene in Wagner's *Das Rheingold*, for example, where the clamor of a large number of smiths hammering on their anvils in Alberich's Nibelheim is transformed into musical structures, is regularly interpreted as a symbolic reflection of the rhythms of machine production, yet it was actually composed in a country where industrial development lagged far behind France or England. Not only that, but the use of anvils as percussion instruments, which Wagner took to a new extreme in this scene, had precedents in operas written for Paris by Kreutzer and Spontini forty years earlier. Verdi's *La traviata*, too, the first opera to take the contemporary reality of urban society as the setting for a tragedy, was not composed for a worldly, modern metropolis but was first performed in Venice, by then a provincial backwater in a remote corner of the Habsburg Empire. The consciousness and the experiences of people living in that era were influenced by economic change, certainly, but also by the Revolution of 1789, by the wars of the following twenty-five years, and perhaps even more strongly by the stress and confusion of life in a large city: a phenomenon that invaded every area of sensual experience.

The reality of the experience of everyday life in the metropolis, which will be outlined in chapter 1 of this book, had been subject to a steadily more rapid process of transformation ever since the mid-1780s, and the process of assimilation to city ways had led the French author Nicolas Rétif de la Bretonne to coin the verb *urbaniser* ("to urbanize") as early as 1785.[6] Rétif's neologism is only one among many instances which prove that the effects of "urbanization" were exhibited earlier in literature than in the other arts, and it was in literature that the dominant formal genres were shaken to the core and thrown into the process of crisis and dissolution of which Heinz Brüggemann has written.[7] Besides the recipients, it was primarily the author as producer who was affected, especially after the period of art rooted in the exhausted ancien

6. Note dated 25 November 1785, in Rétif de La Bretonne, *Mes Inscripcions*, 138. The German language had to wait until the early twentieth century for the noun "Verstädterung." (An English traveler used the verb "urbanize" as early as 1642, as a synonym for "refine," or "polish," but that is an earlier view of the city.—Trans.)

7. See *"Aber schickt keinen Poeten nach London!,"* 16.

régime had come to the end acclaimed by Heine.[8] "The subjective authorial ego, confident in its special literary mode of perception, and in
its individual linguistic and stylistic competence," Brüggemann observes, was increasingly replaced by "the objective, observed world of
everyday life as the channel of expression and organizing principle."
This development was by no means confined to the first half of the
nineteenth century; rather it was completed "only in the literary avant
garde of the twentieth century, in association with the possibilities
opened up by the cinema."[9] But if investigation of literary descriptions
of the metropolis leads us to acknowledge the significance of cinematic
techniques for the later development of new artistic forms and genres,
at the same time it seems quite reasonable to look for earlier forms of such
modes of perception in the genre from which cinema has inherited so
much. My thesis is, therefore, that it was only under the extreme pressure
exerted by new modes of perception, and the expectations springing from
them, that the operas composed for Paris in the middle decades of the
nineteenth century developed new forms and conventions that have
nothing to do with the historical predecessors of grand opéra.

At first sight, a large number of these characteristics still appear
nothing out of the ordinary today, for the majority of the models of
perception that came into existence after 1800 have scarcely changed.
They continue to apply not merely in opera, now an antiquarian genre,
but specifically in film also. To that extent it is not surprising that—with
a few exceptions[10]—they have not been taken into account by music
historians; literary and social historians, too, have not so far followed
the lead given in the fragmentary studies by Walter Benjamin, who attempted to explain not only the poetry of Charles Baudelaire[11] but also
the entire phenomenon of the "capital city of the nineteenth century"[12]
on the basis of the confusions of the metropolitan experience.

It is only in recent years that the alteration of perceptual structures
has impinged more frequently on literary and social history. Richard
Sennett's exciting study *The Fall of Public Man* (1977) describes how the
always precarious relationship between private and public life, and between the individual and society, was fundamentally changed in London

8. See "Französische Maler" [1831], in Heine, *Sämtliche Schriften*, 3:27–87 (esp. 72).

9. *"Aber schickt keinen Poeten nach London!,"* 21.

10. See Dahlhaus, *Nineteenth-Century Music*, 125–28; Döhring, "Multimediale Tendenzen," 497–500.

11. See Benjamin, *Charles Baudelaire*.

12. See Benjamin, "Paris—the Capital of the Nineteenth Century," in ibid.

and Paris under the pressure of the new conditions of city life, but
Sennett's disquiet at the destructive narcissism of our time leads him to
represent the development exclusively as a history of decline.[13] Consciousness of time, as a central category of all human perception, is the
theme of a compendium published in 1980, which, in the chapters devoted to the nineteenth and twentieth centuries, explains the growing
dominance of linear and dynamic consciousness of time as another consequence of city life.[14] Finally, works of literature are increasingly being
examined for the ways of seeing that underlie them.[15]

There has been a series of pioneering studies of the changes in the
meaning of fundamental historical concepts and terms, in which historians have systematically identified the challenges presented to all the historically oriented branches of scholarship by the upheavals of the period
around 1800. The traditional models of processualized history can no
longer serve the apprehension of the modern era "breaking free of the
continuity of an earlier mode of time," as Reinhart Koselleck describes
it.[16] Traditional formal categories are inadequate as tools for interpreting what was unique and new about the works of art representing that
breach of continuity within a traditional genre; similarly, the conditions
and causes of the upheaval are not adequately explained by applying to
them the word "bourgeois," with its misleading suggestion of an unbroken continuity from the preindustrial and prerevolutionary bourgeoisie.[17] Koselleck has argued not only that "experience and expectation
are two categories appropriate for the treatment of historical time because of the way that they embody past and future" but also that they
are especially fruitful when applied to an epoch in which "the difference
between experience and expectation is increasingly enlarged."[18]

The terms "space of experience" and "horizon of expectation," used
by Koselleck and those literary scholars with an interest in reception
aesthetics, thus lend themselves to a survey of works of art in which the
transition from the ancien régime to our modern age can be seen taking
place. Moreover, they serve better than other categories to do justice to

13. The tendency to regard the eighteenth century wholly uncritically as a Golden
Age of urban living is even more pronounced in Sennett's more recent book, *The Conscience
of the Eye* (1990).

14. Wendorff, *Zeit und Kultur.*

15. See, for example, Brüggemann, *"Aber schickt keinen Poeten nach London!"*

16. In "Historia Magistra Vitae," *Futures Past,* 27.

17. See Eichberg, *Leistung, Spannung, Geschwindigkeit,* 256.

18. "'Space of Experience' and 'Horizon of Expectation': Two Historical Categories,"
Futures Past, 270, 284.

the peculiarities of an artistic genre that depended more than any other on the economic and social prosperity of its time.[19] They have been criticized for good reasons admittedly,[20] and if this study uses them it is primarily because without them it seems impossible to break away from the evolutionary models that still predominate in music history. Organic terms like "birth," "development," and "decline," or less controversial ones like "tradition" and "innovation,"[21] are not well suited to describing the kind of ostentatious, large-scale operas regarded both in their own time and later as revolutionary, in which "innovations" were transformed into "traditions" overnight, as their influence was immediately reflected in new works. The evolutionary imagery associated with the course of Germano-Austrian instrumental music during the nineteenth century is also inappropriate, for purely structural reasons, to the discussion of operas already exhibiting signs, at least, both of a teleological formal dynamic and of the technique of an uninterrupted progress determined by purely musical structural principles, which Wagner later used in his music dramas. Whatever may have happened to the symphony in Beethoven's hands, operatic dramaturgy was still governed by discontinuities until well into the nineteenth century.[22] Lotman's comparison of the painting and the drama of the early nineteenth century can be extended to the opera of the period too: it shows the same tendency "to present a distinct articulation of the spectacle in separate, synchronically arranged, fixed 'cross-sections,' each of which, like a picture, was given a scenic frame, and was itself arranged according to the strict rules of composition for figures on a painted canvas."[23]

CONVENTIONS AND GENRE HISTORY

If—as I propose in the previous section—the "space of experience" of grand opéra's creators and public alike was stamped by the reality they experienced in the modern big city, overshadowing all other aspects of experience, for the reconstruction of their "horizon of expectation" it is convenient to turn once more to the immanent characteristics of the genre. Early Parisian grand opéra descends from the established form of opera with exalted subject matter and elevated musical aspirations, known in France as *tragédie lyrique* and in Italy as *opera seria*, and strictly

19. See Bianconi, "Perché la storia dell'opera italiana?," 40–44.
20. See Anz, "Erwartungshorizont," 398–408; Grimm, *Rezeptionsgeschichte*, 144–47.
21. See Bianconi, "Perché la storia dell'opera italiana?," 44.
22. See Bianconi, introduction to *La drammaturgia musicale*, 48.
23. Lotman, "The Stage and Painting as Code Mechanisms," 165–66.

distinguished from forms with lower aesthetic pretensions like *opéra comique* and *opera buffa*. But while in Italy the stages of the transition from the opera seria of the eighteenth century to the *melodramma romantico* of the 1830s ran smoothly on the whole, despite the differences of subject matter, in the case of France it is possible to point to a relatively exact caesura. One might get away with using the eighteenth-century designation opera seria for a work with a tragic ending like Rossini's *Otello* (1816), or even Donizetti's *Lucia di Lammermoor* (1835), but no one would dream of calling Meyerbeer's *Les Huguenots* a tragédie lyrique. And whereas before the French Revolution numerous tragédies lyriques were performed for the first time at Fontainebleau or Versailles before passing into the repertory of the Opéra in Paris, the notion that the idyllic seclusion of a royal palace would have been an appropriate venue for the premières of works like *Les Huguenots* and *Le Prophète*, or Verdi's *Un ballo in maschera* and *Don Carlos*, with their vivid portrayal of city ways and attitudes, verges on the preposterous. After a brief outline of the typical characteristics of a tragédie lyrique, therefore, I propose to describe what it is that so profoundly distinguishes a thoroughly urbanized grand opéra from its ancestors.

"Convention" is a particularly useful category for this purpose. That may appear paradoxical, when the object is to distinguish something older—that is, more conventional—from something modern. But unlike tradition and innovation, in the light of categories of reception aesthetics convention has its own specific meaning. Lorenzo Bianconi, in a methodological sketch setting the word alongside its etymological cousin "invention," has defined conventions as the determining factors of every communication that takes the form of a theatrical performance. It is in the nature of theater that it works on the eye first and foremost, rather than the ear, which is far less susceptible to conventionalized patterns. In addition to the historical and legal sense of the word, "convention" denotes a tacit agreement between stage and audience and between author and public.[24]

It is possible, therefore, to define some of the essential aspects of grand opéra without necessarily relativizing their novelty at the time. Its conventions include a tragic ending, a hero incapable of making crucial decisions, and above all the *tableau*—the large-scale, set-piece choral scene, in which the chorus typically plays the role of a destructive mob. These are matters of form and content simultaneously, and the newly formed relationship of soloists and chorus reflects what Brüggemann

24. See Bianconi, "Perché la storia dell'opera italiana?," 44.

calls the "indissoluble, enforced association" of the individual and the crowd.[25] The primary goal of the present book is to identify and analyze constantly recurring stereotypes of that kind, usually by dint of looking at one individual opera at a time. Occasionally, to be sure, comparisons will be made between analogous scenes from different works, but not in order to determine the elements of "original" creativity, that is, the contribution of authorial invention to the individual work; still less with the object of demonstrating that one composer was influenced by an earlier work by another composer. Rather, comparison will be used to bring out contrasts, and so make specific characteristics shared by operas composed at different times stand out more distinctly.

This is a different procedure from the one favored by musicologists, who like to use metaphors borrowed from biology—generation, flowering, and decay—to describe the evolution of a genre; any instances which prove hard to integrate into the process are "mutations."[26] It can hardly be an accident that grand opéra refuses to lend itself to such treatment.[27] Only two comprehensive accounts of the genre have been published to date, one of which views its artistic manifestation primarily as a function of its creators' commercial interests,[28] while the other regards it as fulfilling the propaganda purposes of the supposedly all-powerful state.[29] As yet, this area of research lacks clear perspectives.[30] The present survey may help if it establishes orderly outlines on which future research can improve, making corrections and inserting new salient points, until a picture of grand opéra emerges in which the genre is defined "neither normatively *ante rem*, according to universal criteria of realism, nor merely *post rem*, by nominalist classifications [but] *in re*, as a historical concretization with relatively constant, common characteristics."[31]

French grand opéra is not an entirely self-sufficient genre, however: although there are many differences it remains too closely connected to its French precursors for that, and above all it is bound up with the

25. See *"Aber schickt keinen Poeten nach London!,"* 191.

26. For a critique of the generic metaphor see Arlt, "Einleitung," 80.

27. Heinz Becker, in "Zur Frage des Stilverfalls," perhaps provides an exception, but significantly he fails to justify the metaphors on the basis of actual operas.

28. Crosten, *French Grand Opera.*

29. Fulcher, *The Nation's Image.* For a critique of the method adopted by Fulcher see my review in *Neue Zeitschrift für Musik* 149, no. 3 (1988): 57–58.

30. For a more detailed description of research in the period 1945–87, see Gerhard, "Die französische 'Grand Opéra' in der Forschung."

31. Krauss, introduction to the section "Gattungssystem und Gesellschaftssystem," in *Bildung und Ausbildung in der Romania,* 1:38.

Italian and German opera of its own time. Of the two, the connection to German opera, which emancipated itself from its origins in Singspiel only gradually during the nineteenth century, is certainly the less important. Clearly, *Der Freischütz*, which was particularly well received in Paris, and the other romantic operas of Carl Maria von Weber exerted an influence—and not only on the work of Meyerbeer, who was educated in Germany. After 1830, however, almost all the traffic was in the other direction, from France to Germany.

The ways in which opera composition developed in Italy and France were more intimately interconnected, however, not only in the persons of prominent composers from Piccinni and Gluck, through Cherubini, Spontini, Rossini, and Meyerbeer, to Verdi, but also in the repeated instances where the French adopted Italian conventions of form and subject matter. This gives grounds for supposing that some traits of French spoken drama made their way into French opera only after considerable delay, and by way of a detour through Italy, where musical theater had the status and function of an almost nonexistent spoken theater and thus absorbed innovations directly. On the other hand, during the second half of the century, Italian opera came increasingly under the influence of French grand opéra;[32] this was confused with the influence of Richard Wagner at the time—and the confusion persists.

It is regrettable but necessary that the simultaneous development of Italian and German opera can be referred to only in exceptional cases in the present book: necessary because otherwise the narrative would ramify into boundless complexity. Nevertheless, the last chapter deals with Verdi's *Un ballo in maschera*, and therefore touches on Italian opera in the 1850s. This has been done in order to avoid depicting the later stages in the development of grand opéra as a history of decline. There is no mistaking the fact that in works like Meyerbeer's *Prophète* and Verdi's *Vêpres siciliennes* the dramaturgical conception is barely equal to the task of preventing the action from breaking up into its contradictory elements, and yet the following years do not see a proliferation of epigonal, artistically inferior imitations but a disparate development in which elements from grand opéra are transmuted in new associations and contexts.

Of course it would be possible to call Meyerbeer's last opera, *L'Africaine* (1865: the process of revision before performance was completed after his death), as principal witness to the genre's ability to survive forty years after its first appearance. Or one could cite Verdi's *Don Carlos*,

---

32. See Roccatagliati, "Opera, opera-ballo e *grand opéra*."

composed for the Paris Opéra only a short time later, in 1867, as the last example of a French opera in which the political and the private dramas are closely intertwined,[33] and which retains its popularity to the present day, were it not that proper understanding of that work also demands reference to Verdi's earlier, Italian operas. One might equally well point to Hector Berlioz's attempt, in *Les Troyens*, to refashion the historicizing elements of grand opéra in the service of a national-cum-mythological vision—a vision doomed to failure when set before an audience (and the work was not performed complete until the twentieth century). On the other hand, the genre of *drame lyrique*, which came into being around 1860,[34] might be regarded as the successor to grand opéra, for study would discover points of agreement as well as differences. And of course, if one adopted the teleological concepts that Richard Wagner introduced into his version of the history of opera and turned them against their progenitor's idiosyncrasies, one could interpret Wagnerian music drama as the heir and fulfillment of grand opéra.[35]

If, instead of any of those possibilities, this book ends by considering an opera by Verdi which was first performed in Rome in 1859, it is not simply because the libretto of *Un ballo in maschera* is a version of one by Scribe which Auber had previously set for Paris, making for an intimate connection with grand opéra, but rather because it is only in the new version that the dramaturgical potential of Scribe's text is realized to the full, in a form which proved to have considerably more importance for the subsequent development of European opera than *Les Troyens*, *L'Africaine*, or *Don Carlos*. In spite of their fundamental differences from grand opéra, the operas that Verdi wrote after 1860, right up to *Otello* (1883), successfully continue to deploy characteristics that originated in grand opéra, without simultaneously altering the relationship of author and public as radically as did Wagner's music dramas. A position where Verdi's later works are in prospect is therefore a more effective standpoint than the alternatives from which to judge the extent to which present-day understanding of opera is still affected by elements typical of French music theater in the middle decades of the nineteenth century.

33. See Beyer, "Selbstverständigung und Verselbständigung."
34. See Schneider, "Drame lyrique."
35. See Laudon, *Sources of the Wagnerian Synthesis*.

The Kaleidoscope and the Theory of Reflection

The urban space of experience exerted a strong influence on the forms of spectacle with which grand opéra attempts to combine a wide range of perceptual stimuli in one visual image. This influence becomes especially clear in the generous scale of opening and closing scenes, which act as reminders of the contemporary popularity of the true-to-life images created by the magic lantern and, later, the panorama. The latter invention, patented in 1787, had made it possible to project a multiperspectival picture on a curving wall that was "so artful in its artifice . . . that the spectator believes that he has not a painting of nature but the real thing in front of him."[36] Neither the panorama and the diorama which was a later development of it, nor grand opéra confined itself to depicting nature, admittedly; both forms of spectacle aspired to the realistic reproduction of everyday life in Paris.[37]

It is not only the "realistic" aspirations of early nineteenth-century spectacle which prompt the thought that social reality is being reflected here. The theory that works of art reflect the social conditions of the time of their creation has fallen into complete discredit nowadays, due to all too shortsighted applications of a "theory of reflection" which dwindled to a textbook aesthetic theory.[38] Now scarcely anyone is aware that it did not originate with Lenin or even Karl Marx, but in fact, it was in an essay published in 1805 that the royalist political theorist Bonald described tragedy as a "faithful mirror of human life and society."[39] This was nothing new as an observation about lower genres like comedy, but in applying it to tragedy Bonald began a development in which the mirror metaphor was "promoted to a central topos of literary-theoretical speculations concerned with all genres as a matter of principle."[40] As will emerge in chapter 2, which discusses the librettist Jouy, although Bonald had intended to express his disquiet at the state of contemporary tragedy, his meaning was soon misunderstood and the metaphor was adopted in the discussion of operatic aesthetics in the following decade.

That is not the only reason why it is legitimate to examine the forms taken by nineteenth-century French opera in order to find out the

---

36. Oettermann, *Das Panorama*, 41.
37. Ibid.; see also Willms, *Paris: Hauptstadt Europas*.
38. See Karbusicky, *Widerspiegelungstheorie und Strukturalismus*, 92–93.
39. "miroir fidèle de la vie humaine et de la société"; Bonald, "Observations morales sur quelques pièces de théâtre" [1805], in *Mélanges littéraires et philosophiques*, 1:109–45 (p. 136).
40. Schöning, *Literatur als Spiegel*, 20–21.

LES PRODIGES MERVEILLEUX DU KALOÏDOSCOPE
où Le Joujou de la Cour des Fontaines au Palais Royal

1   The newly invented kaleidoscope was put on show in public places in Paris in the early 1820s. This undated print by Louis-François Charon (1783–1839) makes it clear that only the more affluent classes had access to the modish toy.

extent to which they reflect contemporary realities, whether unconsciously or with a deliberate intention of depicting them accurately. Opera's aesthetic aspirations set a limit to the investigation, however. The panorama might confine itself to the representation of—usually—historical events, in as exact and deceptively lifelike a manner as possible, but in Parisian operas of the time such naive realism was constantly overruled and the "real world" was subsumed in phantasmagorias. Grand opéra never renounced its poetic ability to transcend the everyday world despite all the realistic detail of sets and costumes, and despite the inordinate number of successive images, the relative importance of which was never clear to anyone on either side of the proscenium arch. In distancing itself from the panorama in this way, however, opera grows closer to a structure of perception exemplified in another invention of the early nineteenth century.

In 1817, the Scottish physicist David Brewster patented an instrument which he called a kaleidoscope. Similar in appearance to a telescope, it was equipped with interior mirrors and loose chips of colored glass; each time the instrument was shaken the pieces of glass presented themselves to the viewer's eye in a new pattern. Brewster's prophecy of a future for it as a "popular instrument for the purposes of rational amusement"[41] was fulfilled at a breathtaking speed. The craze spread across Europe, and it was all the rage in Paris for three or four years.[42] It survives today as a child's toy, small enough to hold in the hand, but in its early days it was also often "gigantic, and demonstrated in the open air to an astonished paying public."[43] A print made about 1820, with the title *The marvellous Prodigies of the Kaloïdoscope, or, The Toy in the Fountain Court of the Palais Royal* (see fig. 1),[44] shows that at first the public was almost entirely made up of adults from the upper social class. The new word entered their vocabulary, gaining the additional meaning of a rapidly changing succession of sensations and impressions when a new periodical was launched in June 1818 under the title *Kaléidoscope*, with the editorial pronouncement that "the physical world and the moral world are but two huge kaleidoscopes."[45] Finally Balzac, in 1826, boasts of having contrived a "veritable moral kaleidoscope with its millions of inflexions" in his depiction of a particular area of contemporary Parisian society.[46] Similarly, the kaleidoscope, the craze of the 1820s, provides this study of grand opéra with a metaphor for the confusing multiplicity of the genre's motives and conventions, even if it also entails the risk of the narrative fragmenting.

The treatment of individual aspects in chapters focusing on individual works or particular librettists does not avert that risk altogether, especially as the works considered here do not enable every development of grand opéra, still less every aspect of French opera's progress toward modern music theater to be illustrated. As always when an author has to be selective, readers will raise objections. Here, the finger may be pointed at the decision to banish Auber and Halévy to the sidelines, although they were the only two native French composers of the day to be successful at the Paris Opéra. My own opinion is that the essential qualities of works like Auber's *Muette de Portici* and *Gustave III, ou Le Bal*

41. Brewster, *A Treatise on the Kaleidoscope*, 7.

42. "il fit fureur . . . pendant les trois ou quatre années qui suivirent"; Allemagne, *Histoire des jouets*, 285.

43. Groeber, *Kinderspielzeug aus alter Zeit*, 86; see also Brewster's letter to his wife, late May 1818, in Gordon, *The Home Life of Sir David Brewster*, 97.

44. See Allemagne, *Histoire des jouets*, 289.

45. "le monde physique et le monde moral ne sont que deux grands kaléidoscopes"; [Hus], *Le Kaléidoscope philosophique et littéraire* 1, no. 1 (1818): 1.

46. "[un] véritable kaléidoscope moral, avec ses millions de désinences"; *Physiologie du mariage, ou Méditations sur le bonheur conjugal* [1826], in *La Comédie humaine*, 11:903–1205 (p. 1046).

masqué are sufficiently well displayed by analysis of their librettos, while Auber's regularly overrated music, as well as Halévy's *La Juive*, Donizetti's operas for Paris, and even large parts of Meyerbeer's *Robert le diable* do not contribute anything decisively new to conventions which originate in opéra comique[47] or Italian opera in the style of Rossini.

In the end, like the thesis chosen as starting point in heuristic anticipation, the selection will stand or fall by results: by the success of this attempt to present a convincing new view of grand opéra. Inevitably, given the present state of research in the subject, it is impossible to illuminate every single aspect with equal clarity, and one assessment or another of earlier or contemporary developments in other operatic forms may well not stand up to critical scrutiny. Nevertheless, it is the author's hope that his examination of certain questions will contribute not only to a better understanding of grand opéra but also to the study of the historical genre of opera itself as a whole.

47. See Everist, "The name of the rose," 240.

~ 1 ~

REALITIES OF
A METROPOLIS

The Paris Opéra: commissioned by Napoleon III and designed by Charles Garnier, it rears majestically at the top of the avenue de l'Opéra where it seizes the attention of every visitor to Paris. The opulence of the architectural style seems to epitomize the spirit of the nineteenth century, as well as forming an imperishable monument to the institution of opera itself. Even though the Palais Garnier lost the privilege of staging opera when the new Opéra de la Bastille opened its doors in 1990 it continues to be known as the Grand Opéra, the name synonymous in music history with a particular type of French opera in the middle years of the nineteenth century.

Yet the image which has gone round the world on millions of picture postcards is deceptive in this respect: none of the works that belong in the category of grand opéra were composed for the Grand Opéra, which did not open its doors until 1875. This lexical anomaly is overshadowed by another: by the time the avenue de l'Opéra was completed in 1877, the city of the early nineteenth century, the Paris of grand opéra, lay buried beneath it. Today only the neighboring streets give any idea of what the city looked like, even in its busiest quarters, up until the middle of the nineteenth century. The generally uniform façades running down either side of this exceptionally wide and imposing street have nothing in common with the rabbit-warren of crowded alleys where the Parisians for whom the works of grand opéra were written lived their lives until Napoleon III and Prefect Haussmann carried out their radical program of town planning reforms.[1] While it may be pos-

1. Pinkney, *Napoleon III and the Rebuilding of Paris.*

2   A photograph by Charles Marville, taken around 1874, shows the scale of destruction necessary to drive the avenue de l'Opéra through the old center of Paris, to form a new axis running from the Comédie-Française to the Palais Garnier. The picture shows the junction of the rue d'Antin and the rue Louis-le-Grand, with the new opera house dimly visible in the background.

sible to see something of the spirit of an industrial age in the repetitive character of the façades, the Paris of the era before 1850 cannot really be called an "industrial city."

It is true that Paris was the second largest city in Europe, after London, but the growth in the size of the French capital's population was not directly related to the Industrial Revolution. That expression belongs in the economic history of Great Britain, and extreme caution should be used in transferring it to French circumstances. Industrialization on the British model was introduced to France only after 1850 and proceeded very slowly, so that large areas of French economic output were still governed by preindustrial forms even at the end of the nineteenth century. Furthermore, the major French industrial centers were dispersed all over the country, far from Paris.

The doubling of the population of Paris in the first half of the century was therefore due only in small measure to any increase in employment in the industrial sector. Then as now, the majority of Parisians earned their livings in the "tertiary sector": in trade, in administration and government, and in "services" (people work in "service industries" now; they were "in service" then).

In terms of international economics, the importance of Paris was founded above all on its banking and credit services. The building of the Paris Stock Exchange—the Bourse—was completed in 1827 and rapidly became one of the most important institutions in European finance. With its two triumphal arches, it constitutes one of the few prominent architectural monuments of the early part of the century to survive today. From a mere thirty-eight securities officially listed in 1830, by 1841 two hundred and sixty share-prices were being fixed every day.[2] Even contemporaries like Heinrich Heine regarded the banker and the speculator as the representative figures of the July Monarchy, and Balzac made the name of a fictional bank the title of one of the tales, *La Maison Nucingen*, in his *Comédie humaine*. Clearly, citizens who were ready to take the risks involved in stock-market speculation were the real winners of the July Revolution: one of their gains being the self-confidence that made them the leading social class alongside the aristocracy, which never recovered fully from the first French Revolution, in spite of the fifteen-year restoration that had followed the defeat of Napoleon I in 1815. But it was not only at the Bourse that everything revolved around money: the mentality of a financially bullish bourgeoisie transformed the whole of society. Balzac pinpointed cold-blooded financial interest as the common factor in all his "scenes of Parisian life":

> [In Paris] genuine emotions are the exception; they are broken by the play of interests, crushed between the cogs of this mechanical world. Virtue is slandered here, and innocence sold; passions have given way to ruinous tastes and to vices. Everything is sublimated, analyzed, bought and sold. It is a bazaar where everything has its price: the calculations are made in broad daylight and without shame. Humanity has only two forms, the deceiver and the deceived; the victor is whoever can subjugate civilization and bend it to his will.[3]

2. See Jardin and Tudesq, *La France des notables*, 1:213.

3. "[A Paris] les sentiments vrais sont des exceptions; ils sont brisés par le jeu des intérêts, écrasés entre les rouages de ce monde mécanique; la vertu y est calomniée, l'innocence y est vendue; les passions ont fait place à des goûts ruineux, à des vices; tout se sublime, s'analyse, se vend et s'achète; c'est un bazar où tout est coté; les calculs se font au grand jour et sans pudeur; l'humanité n'a plus que deux formes, le trompeur et le trompé; c'est à qui s'assujétira la civilisation, la pressurera pour lui seul." Davin, introduc-

Paris the modern city inevitably struck Balzac and his contemporaries as a wholly new life experience, but that was not solely because it was "really a revelation of the human psyche fully emancipated from stable obligations, feudal contacts, traditional ties."[4] The purely physical experience of life in a big city was at least equally important, not that it had been transformed in any fundamental way, but the immense growth in the size of the population had meant some extraordinary changes. The number of people inhabiting the area of fractionally over 34 square kilometers enclosed within the city's toll barriers swelled from approximately 550,000 in 1801 to one million in 1846.

We must remember, too, that, until "Haussmanization" began in 1855, producing the broad new boulevards along which traffic was to circulate henceforward, the only streets which served the growing population for the movement of people (now conveyed on the Métro) and wheeled traffic alike had become far too narrow for either purpose. The widest north–south axes were the rue Saint-Denis, the rue Saint-Martin, and the rue Saint-Jacques, all of them one-way streets today, and relieved of through traffic. The first relatively wide street in an east–west direction was the rue de Rivoli, linking the Palais Royal and the Hôtel de Ville, and that was constructed only in 1848.

We can obtain some idea of how people experienced the realities of life in the French capital from the literature of the time, especially the novels of Balzac, although even their amplitudinous portrayal of Parisian life around 1830 finds room only in the margins for non-aristocratic and non-bourgeois society. As the French historian Louis Chevalier demonstrated in a pioneering study,[5] the more affluent were well aware of the misery of the steadily growing proletariat. Poverty among the masses came to be equated with criminal tendencies, and the omnipresent fear of crime, which could no longer be connected with particular places and a few professional criminals, actually became an essential ingredient in upper-class perception of metropolitan realities, as the runaway success of Eugène Sue's journalistic novel *Les Mystères de Paris* (1844) illustrated. And behind this fear of criminality lay a more profound fear that the fragile social order would be overthrown, for it rested on injustice, and the wealthy never forgot that. After the hunger

---

tion to Balzac's *Études de moeurs au XIXe siècle* [1834], 103. Although attributed to Félix Davin, this introduction was probably co-written by Balzac; see the editors' comment, 103, n. 2.

4. Sennett, *The Fall of Public Man*, 155.

5. Chevalier, *Classes laborieuses et classes dangereuses à Paris pendant la première moitié du XIXe siècle* (1958).

riots in Lyon and Paris, especially in 1832 and 1834, no one could remain ignorant of the fact that the revolutionary potential of the poor,
whose violence had been to the advantage of bourgeois financiers and
aristocratic liberals alike during the July Revolution of 1830, was now
directed against them. An explosive unrest fermented behind the façade
of a liberal regime, although it was vented in leaderless and poorly organized uprisings until 1848.

A Place for Dreams

One place where the unrest was palpable every day was the theater. Audiences in the first half of the nineteenth century did not sit wrapped
in the passive silence that became prevalent in the second half,[6] and
interaction between performers and public was still possible. The turbulent behavior of the audience in the "gods" of the Théâtre des Funambules and the improvisations with which Frédérick Lemaître directly involved the spectators in his playing of Robert Macaire—both
depicted in Marcel Carné's legendary film Les Enfants du paradis—are
only two outstanding examples of the reality of some Parisian theaters
in the 1830s. These were undoubtedly theaters that drew their audiences from the petty bourgeoisie and the proletariat, audiences which
even after 1850 were "pushed to the incontinence of tears by the unhappiness of some stage heroine at the hands of a traitor."[7]

Even the elite audiences who attended the Comédie-Française
reacted with a lack of restraint that was closer to the popular theater
of the day than to today's temples of high art. The fistfights between
liberals and conservatives at the first performance of Victor Hugo's Hernani (1830) entered theater history, and even at the sole performance of
Hugo's Le Roi s'amuse (1831) the audience behaved in a way that would
be inconceivable today, chorusing politically militant songs like the Car-
magnole and the Marseillaise.[8] This was at the Théâtre de l'Odéon, where
the audience was as bourgeois as at the Comédie-Française but included
a larger percentage of students, and the incident was evidently nothing
unusual there.[9]

Things were different at the Opéra, in many respects. In the early

6. See Sennett, The Fall of Public Man, 206.
7. Pierre Véron, Paris s'amuse (Paris: Lévey Frères, 1874); cited in Sennett, The Fall of
Public Man.
8. See Krakovitch, Hugo censuré, 18.
9. Ibid., 88.

eighteenth century, it is true, the audience's custom of joining in whole choruses and arias evoked this irritated comment from a British visitor:

> This Inclination of the Audience to Sing along with the Actors, so prevails with them, that I have sometimes known the Performer on the Stage do no more in a Celebrated Song, than the Clerk of a Parish Church, who serves only to raise the Psalm, and is afterwards drown'd in the Musick of the Congregation.[10]

On other occasions, "a particular phrase or high note beautifully performed could rouse the audience to demand that the little phrase be immediately sung again; the text was interrupted and the high note hit once, twice, or more."[11]

By around 1830, however, audiences at the Paris Opéra had already arrived at a state of passivity which did not spread to other theaters until much later. The exceptions, like the disturbances that forced the sixth performance of Bertin's *La Esmeralda* to be abandoned in 1846, and the legendary *Tannhäuser* row of 1861, were few and far between.[12] Restrained behavior in the theater became a sign of sociological change in the audience, which aspired to differentiate itself from a working-class audience by this gentility. Singers were not applauded until the end of the aria, just as later it became customary not to applaud between the movements of a symphony.[13] This is one of the many indices which support Adorno's thesis that the opera in the nineteenth century performed some of the functions of the cinema in the twentieth.[14] If interaction between screen and audience is impossible in motion pictures for technical reasons, it had been reduced to insignificance in the opera much earlier.

On the other hand, the opera's social function as the theater for a self-consciously distinct elite was not comparable to the cinema at all, as the next section of this chapter will demonstrate,[15] even if parallels can be drawn between grand opéra and the film industry in matters of production. Like all the theaters in Paris and its suburbs (there were

10. Joseph Addison, in *The Spectator*, 3 April 1711; cited in *The Spectator*, Donald F. Bond, ed. (Oxford: Clarendon, 1965), 1:122–23.

11. Sennett, *The Fall of Public Man*, 206.

12. See Pistone, "L'Opéra de Paris au siècle romantique," 33–34.

13. See Sennett, *The Fall of Public Man*, 206.

14. "Bürgerliche Oper" [1955], in Adorno, *Gesammelte Schriften*, 16:24–39 (p. 29).

15. Adorno himself modified his thesis shortly before his death. See Wangermée, "Introduction à une sociologie de l'opéra," 74–76.

twenty-seven others in 1834),[16] the Opéra gave its audiences the opportunity to forget their mundane existence and dream vividly as they watched the theatrical illusion.[17] And the Opéra was as keen as every other theater to exploit each new technical invention in order to perfect the illusion.

The difference between the Opéra and the other theaters lay above all in material conditions. It enjoyed a larger budget than any other theater in Europe: in addition to receiving the highest state subvention, it charged the highest seat-prices. Moreover, protective mechanisms existed by which it was shielded from unwelcome competition. It was the only theater in Paris licensed to give performances of works in the French language which were furnished with unbroken musical accompaniment from start to finish and included ballet as a fundamental element in the entertainment.

At the moment in history when the available means were drawn on systematically, in order to create a "spectacle" in which the (sung) word was no longer of primary significance, opera was on the threshold of an aesthetics of effect characterized by great expense and the interrelationship of text, visual image, and music. This is what Adorno refers to when he writes that opera shares with film

> the massiveness of the means, which was applied teleologically in the material of the opera, as it is in film, and gave opera a similarity to the modern cultural industry from at least the middle of the nineteenth century onward, if not earlier. Meyerbeer, for one, had appropriated wars of religion and events of great historical significance to serve his ends, and in doing so neutralized them, in that nothing of the substance of the conflicts remained, and the Catholics and Huguenots caught up in the massacre of St. Bartholomew are marveled at as if in the Panopticon. Film, especially technicolor, made this its canon.[18]

One topic explored in the following chapters, accordingly, will be grand opéra's tendency deliberately to discount the public's knowledge of literature, just as "the modern cultural industry" does: it was no longer necessary for the audience at an opera to be familiar with classical mythology or to have read the libretto beforehand in order to follow the action.

---

16. See Krakovitch, *Hugo censuré*, 288–89.
17. See Bab, *Das Theater im Lichte der Soziologie*, 222.
18. Adorno, "Bürgerliche Oper" (see above, n. 14), 29–30.

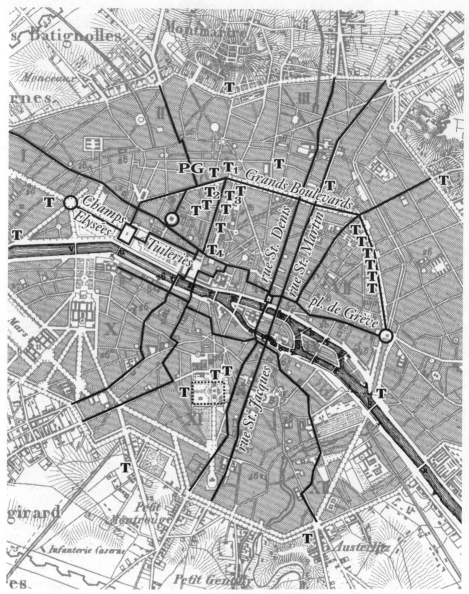

3 No fewer than twenty-eight theaters were in regular business in Paris in 1834. They are indicated by the letter T in this plan, adapted from one published in a modern standard work on theater censorship, *Hugo censuré*, by Odile Krakovitch. The drawing shows clearly the relatively peripheral position of the Opéra (T1), and the cluster of popular theaters along the north-eastern section of the ring of boulevards that gave a whole theatrical genre its name. Other theaters marked individually on the plan are the Théâtre Italien (T2), the Opéra-Comique (T3), and the Comédie-Française (T4); PG marks the site of the future Palais Garnier.

OPERAS FOR A NEW PUBLIC

What was the Paris Opéra like before it moved into the Palais Garnier? For more than fifty years the institution known officially, up to 1848, as the Académie Royale de Musique, and from 1852 onward as the Théâtre Impérial de l'Opéra, staged its productions in the Salle Le Peletier, a theater erected in great haste just outside the inner ring formed by the *grands boulevards*, north of the junction of the Boulevard des Italiens and the Boulevard Montmartre. It owed this position, a peripheral one in comparison with that of theaters such as the Théâtre Italien, the Opéra-Comique, or the Comédie-Française, to the fact that the Duc de Berry, the nephew of King Louis XVIII and heir presumptive to the French throne, was assassinated on the steps of the previous opera house, close to the Comédie-Française, on 13 February 1820. Evidently the authorities could not stomach the idea that any reminder of the atrocity should survive: before the year was out the old theater, which stood where the Square Louvois now is, was torn down and the institution forced to move to its new home.

The Salle Le Peletier, which opened on 16 August 1821, could hold an audience of nearly two thousand.[19] It already broke with the tradition of an all-box theater, as would the Salle Garnier in its turn. In a refurbishment undertaken in 1831, when some of the larger boxes were divided,[20] the front section of the partitions between the boxes was removed, so that spectators who wished to conceal themselves from the gaze of the rest of the audience had to retreat to the rear of their box, which they could cut off altogether by drawing a curtain. There were already seats in the front and rear sections of the pit, the so-called *stalles de l'amphithéâtre* and *stalles de l'orchestre*, to which only males were admitted; these were among the most expensive seats in the house, and even the *parterre*, the area of standing room which lay between them, was more expensive than seats in boxes in the uppermost of the four tiers.

The compromise between the concept of an auditorium as a place where the spectators could withhold themselves from the stares of other people and the one with which we are more familiar today, where members of the audience want, if anything, to be seen, is most obvious in the new form of seating called a *baignoire:* literally, "bathtub." In this, the

19. Lasalle, *Les treize salles de l'Opéra* (p. 238), gives a figure of 1,954 seats; Palianti, *Petites Archives des théâtres de Paris* (p. 5), gives 1,905; the seating plan in the guidebook *Paris, son histoire, ses monuments, ses musées . . .* (inserted after p. 240) designates only 1,811; see also Gourret, *Histoire des salles de l'Opéra de Paris*, 144.

20. See Véron, *Mémoires*, 3:181.

4 A contemporary lithograph by Rousseau and Courvoisin, showing the architecturally nondescript façade of the opera house in the rue Le Peletier, the home of the Paris Opéra from 1821 to 1873.

grouping of the seats in units of four or five, which still had something of the traditional box about it, was completely disfunctional: there was no private space at the back to which patrons could retire for intimate or mundane conversation, but only the door, which, together with the low walls between the individual *baignoires*, was the only thing preventing assimilation into the wholly open area of stalls (*stalles*) in the parterre or pit, which was no longer the preserve of the poorer members of the audience that it had once been.

Performances took place at the Opéra only three times a week, on Mondays, Wednesdays, and Fridays from 1817 onward,[21] although the director had the power to open the doors on Saturdays and Sundays as well during the winter. There was no summer break: the première of Rossini's *Guillaume Tell*, for example, took place on 3 August 1829.[22] This, in itself, constitutes a fundamental difference from the way things had been organized for over a century in Italy, where performances of opera were restricted to specific seasons (*stagioni*). The most important season ran from 26 December to Shrove Tuesday, and others might occur in the spring or summer, or during a trade fair in a particular city, but no opera house remained open all year long.[23] One or more productions were prepared for each season, and as a rule each was performed every night until the première of the next one. It was rare for a production to be revived in a later season.

While the Paris Opéra follows the stagioni system nowadays, in the nineteenth century its program resembled the repertory system customary in German- and English-speaking countries today. New productions were favored in the period following their first performances, but were interspersed with repetitions of works already in the repertory, to which the new work was added if it was a success.

The Opéra's privilege, going back to Louis XIV and renewed by Napoleon I in 1807, whereby it was the only theater permitted to give works in the French language with music throughout, was challenged repeatedly during the nineteenth century: by the Théâtre Royal de l'Odéon (1823–28), the Théâtre des Nouveautés (1827–31), the Théâtre de la Renaissance (1838–41), and the Opéra-National (1847–48).[24] None of these enterprises lasted long. The first to exhibit staying power

21. See Pistone, "L'Opéra de Paris au siècle romantique," 29.

22. Up until 1829, concerts were performed during Holy Week instead of opera; see Ritterman, "Les Concerts spirituels à Paris," 84, 90.

23. See Rosselli, *The Opera Industry in Italy from Cimarosa to Verdi*, 3–4.

24. See Prod'homme, "La Musique et les musiciens en 1848," 165–69; for more precise data see Wild, *Dictionnaire des théâtres parisiens au XIXe siècle*.

opened in 1851 as the Opéra-National and changed its name to Théâtre-Lyrique in 1852. Here the premières of Gounod's *Faust* (1859), Bizet's *Pêcheurs de perles* (1863), and Berlioz's *Troyens à Carthage* (1863) were given, among others.[25] The Théâtre-Lyrique and its predecessors were rivals not only to the Opéra itself but also to two other theaters which would count as opera houses by today's definition. The Opéra-Comique, where spoken dialogue instead of sung recitative was obligatory, was devoted entirely to this *genre mineur* which had evolved as an independent form during the eighteenth century. The Théâtre Italien, treasured by conservative music-lovers as the home of pure singing, put on nothing but Italian (or very occasionally German) opera in the original language. The Théâtre Italien closed during the summer, and from November to April it opened on alternate nights to the Opéra, on Tuesdays, Thursdays, and Saturdays,[26] while the Opéra-Comique, which had become the preserve of a middle-class public,[27] played almost every night throughout the year.

What was the social profile of the audience at the Opéra? It is almost impossible to answer the question precisely because the only records are of the names of subscribers, and even these cannot always be identified with complete certainty now. It appears that after 1830 approximately one-third of the subscribers were members of the nobility,[28] and a comparison of the only two subscription lists to include addresses, thus permitting reliable categorization, suggests that between 1833/34 and 1866/67 the proportion of rentiers and financiers grew at the expense of the liberal professions, which were not notably well paid, and, above all, of officers.[29] But even when we allow for the methodological uncertainties inherent in the use of such statistics, they still apply only to a minority of operagoers—those entered in the subscription lists—and it is impossible to find out anything more certain about the purchasers of tickets for individual performances.

Comparison of admission prices gives a clue, nevertheless, to the Opéra's standing among other Parisian theaters. By this criterion, it was at the top, alongside the Théâtre Italien, charging 10 francs for the most

25. See Walsh, *Second Empire Opera*.

26. See *La Musique à Paris en 1830–1831*, 58.

27. See Sibille, "Physiologie du spectateur," 139; Huebner, "Opera audiences in Paris," 216.

28. Huebner, "Opera audiences in Paris," 208, gives 32 percent "subscribers with noble titles" as the figure for 1833/34, and 33.9 percent for 1866/67; Marschall, "L'Opéra et son public de 1848 à 1852," 384, speaks of 38 percent for the period 1854–57.

29. See Huebner, "Opera audiences in Paris," 208, 211–14.

expensive single ticket, and 2.50 francs for the cheapest, in both 1830 and 1854.[30] The Comédie-Française and the Opéra-Comique came next, with the most expensive seats varying between 6.60 francs and 8 francs. No other theaters had seats costing more than 5 francs, later 6 francs. The cheapest venue of all was the Théâtre des Funambules, where the highest admission price was 75 centimes.

These figures do little to support the thesis of a heterogeneous public advanced by Catherine Join-Dieterle in one of the few studies of audience structures at the Opéra.[31] The picture Join-Dieterle paints, of a "fusion of publics" and of the existence of proletarian operagoers, does not stand up to cool critical examination. The documentary evidence for her case is drawn partly from material that does not relate to audiences at the Opéra, and partly from aristocratic memoirs. In the eyes of aristocratic audiences, which had had the Opéra largely to themselves up to 1830, even the invasion by wealthy bourgeois amounted to a social mélange, as an anonymous complaint from 1835 reveals:

> The latest blow to the Opéra was dealt by the present Director. Never has this theater been so close to disaster. Not only has M. Véron ruined art in the house, but he must also suffer the reproach of having robbed it of its dignity. The showplace of the aristocracy is today the rendezvous of the bourgeoisie; the boxes are still rented by people of good breeding, but the shop and the factory have already invaded the galleries and the amphitheater.[32]

This confirms, from the standpoint of an aristocrat, that Véron, director of the Opéra from 1831 to 1835, had succeeded in opening its doors to a new public. Véron, a versatile entrepreneur who applied the new techniques of advertising to pharmaceuticals as well as to newspapers

30. Following a small reduction under Véron's directorship, 9 francs was the highest price charged in 1834, 1844, and 1847; see ibid., 219; Bréant de Fontenay and Champeaux, *Annuaire dramatique*, 194.

31. "L'Opéra et son public à l'époque romantique," esp. 30, 33. The example given of a proletarian operagoer is especially absurd, representing a misinterpretation of a passage at the beginning of Balzac's tale *La Fille aux yeux d'or*, which refers to a former laborer, now employed in trade, who supplements his meager income by regular appearances as a member of the Opéra chorus.

32. "Le dernier coup porté à l'Opéra l'a été par le Directeur actuel. Jamais ce théâtre n'a été si près de sa ruine. Non seulement Mr Véron a perdu l'art à ce théâtre; on a encore à lui reprocher d'avoir ôté à l'Opéra sa dignité. Ce spectacle de l'aristocratie est aujourd'hui le rendez-vous de la Bourgeoisie; les loges seules sont encore louées par les quelques gens comme il faut, mais la boutique et l'industrie ont déjà envahi les galeries et l'amphithéâtre." Cited in Derré, "Les Théâtres parisiens en 1835 vus de Vienne," 337. See also Saint-Mars, *Mémoires des autres*, 2:210.

and to opera houses, was completely frank about his reasoning in his memoirs:

> I said to myself, "The July Revolution is the triumph of the bourgeoisie: this victorious bourgeoisie will want to cut a dash and be entertained. The Opéra shall be its Versailles, it will flock there to take the place of the banished court and nobility."[33]

The correctness of this calculation is confirmed not only by Véron's own proud testimony, but also by a report published in 1835, under the title of "The Physiology of the Theatre-Goer," which, unlike the anonymous complaint cited in the previous paragraph, expresses approval of the mingling of classes that were formerly kept apart.

> [The Opéra] is of course the theater of the aristocracies of money and of blood, which are beginning to mix so well with one another that before long it will be hard to distinguish between them. It is the theater of fortunate people who do not notice the mud, thanks to their carriages, and who come to the theater at least as much in order to be seen as to see, if not more so.[34]

Of course it is not beyond the bounds of possibility that a laborer, one of those whose average daily wage was 2.49 francs in 1854 (more than it had been in the 1830s),[35] would occasionally treat himself to a 2.50-franc seat at the Opéra. But the fact that in the Paris of 1854 over 100,000 men had to manage on less than 2 francs a day, and over 75,000 women on less than 1 franc a day,[36] means that an outing like that would have been wholly atypical, both of the working class and of the make-up of the Opéra audience.[37] For the really poor, even a visit to the Thé-

---

33. "Je m'étais dit: 'La révolution de Juillet est le triomphe de la bourgeoisie: cette bourgeoisie victorieuse tiendra à trôner, à s'amuser; l'Opéra deviendra son Versailles, elle y accourra en foule prendre la place des grands seigneurs et de la cour exilés." Véron, *Mémoires*, 3:171.

34. "[L'Opéra] est naturellement le théâtre de l'aristocratie, de l'aristocratie d'argent et de la nobiliaire, qui commence à se mêler si bien avec l'autre qu'on ne pourra bientôt plus les distinguer; il est le théâtre des gens heureux, qui ne s'aperçoivent pas de la boue, leurs équipages aidant, et qui viennent au théâtre au moins autant pour se montrer que pour voir, si non davantage." Sibille, "Physiologie du spectateur," 138.

35. See *Paris, son histoire, ses monuments, ses musées*, 599; see also Huebner, "Opera audiences in Paris," 218–20.

36. See *Paris, son histoire, ses monuments, ses musées*, 600.

37. It is also possible, of course, to interpret all this as a refusal to mix with another social class; even today, some historians prefer to think of the proletariat as responsible for its own disadvantages. See Pistone, "L'Opéra de Paris au siècle romantique," 40.

âtre des Funambules (where the cheapest seat cost 20 centimes)[38] must have been a rare luxury.

It is far more likely, on the other hand, that the change observed by so many witnesses in the Opéra's audience after 1830 was hastened by the way some conservative members of the aristocracy and other elitist contemporaries reacted to the influx of the moneyed bourgeoisie. There is evidence that after the July Revolution class-conscious nobles developed a preference for the more intimate Théâtre Italien,[39] where attendance was almost exclusively by subscription,[40] while another sector, with artistic and intellectual pretensions, turned to concertgoing, which offered an increasingly diverse spectrum. A detailed study of concerts in Paris shows that the performances of Beethoven under Habeneck, put on under the aegis of the Société des concerts du Conservatoire after 1830, had the reputation of a fashionable venue for this elite, on account of the artistic quality,[41] while even more exclusive musical activities were pursued in private salons, where, for example, Chopin concentrated his activities.[42]

Another piece of evidence that contradicts the surprisingly persistent thesis of a "democratic" opera house, accessible to the middle and working classes alike,[43] is the share of the total number of seats that was taken by subscribers from the beginning of the July Monarchy onward.[44] Only thirty-one subscriptions were sold in 1830, the last year before Véron took office as director, but Véron and his successors managed to increase the number until subscriptions accounted for no less than 40 percent of the total box-office takings by 1864.[45] This at last made up for the shortfall the Opéra suffered in 1831 when a levy imposed in its favor on all other theaters was abolished.[46] Even if financial necessity was the essential motive for this evolution from a court theater, enjoying a royal privilege and granting free access to over five hundred people,[47] to a modern theater eager to recruit subscribers, the growth in the number of sub-

38. *La Musique à Paris en 1830–1831*, 41.

39. See Join-Dieterle, "L'Opéra et son public à l'époque romantique," 33; Wild, "Le spectacle lyrique," 44.

40. See Huebner, "Opera audiences in Paris," 211.

41. See W. Weber, *Music and the Middle Class*, 69–75; Nectoux, "Trois Orchestres parisiens en 1830," 471–505.

42. See W. Weber, *Music and the Middle Class*, 49–50.

43. See H. Becker, "Französische Grand Opéra," 162, 173.

44. See Pistone, "L'Opéra de Paris au siècle romantique," 30–32.

45. See Huebner, "Opera audiences in Paris," 210.

46. Ibid., 214–15.

47. Ibid., 214.

scriptions was also flattering to the self-esteem of those regular operagoers. Undoubtedly, it was to them that Véron referred when he wrote of the wealthy bourgeoisie which chose to make the Opéra its home.[48] Then as now, the turnover among the irregular attenders who occupied the cheaper seats made no difference to the fact that the regular operagoers, who knew each other socially, regarded themselves as *the* Opéra audience.

It was possible to take out subscriptions to single seats, but the typical subscriber had his personal box, which gave him the opportunity to indulge in other forms of ostentation. He had to take the whole box, but then he could have it fitted out to suit his own taste, invite friends and acquaintances to share it, or receive visits from other operagoers during the course of a performance.

The subscription prices reveal an order of precedence among the boxes. At the head came the proscenium boxes in the first and second tiers: in 1854 one with ten seats cost 10,000 francs for the year, and one with eight seats 8,100 francs. The higher the tier, the lower the price of the box, but central ones were always dearer than those at the sides. The cheapest was still as much as 2,100 francs, for which the subscriber had a year's access to a box with six seats in the fourth tier, at the side.

Such prices bore virtually no relation to the salary of a director of a hospital, which lay between 2,400 and 5,500 francs a year,[49] but they were within the reach of any of the fifteen lawyers who practiced at the Tribunal de commerce, who earned at least 30,000 francs a year,[50] and would be a trifle to the possessor of a large capital fortune. Studies of the register of deaths have revealed that twenty-one people in every thousand who died in 1820 left a fortune of between 100,000 and 200,000 francs, while three in every thousand left more than 500,000 francs (in 1847 the figures were twenty-eight and eight respectively).[51]

The triumph of the property-owning bourgeoisie, reflected in this growth of large fortunes, is regarded by historians as the outstanding result of the "liberal" capitalism of the reign of Louis-Philippe. In Balzac's novels, too, whenever the question of a "suitable" marriage is addressed, it is repeatedly made clear that money is the primary mark of distinction within the "bourgeoisified" society of the day. The change in the composition of the audience at the Opéra was thus only a consequence of the shift of power from one class to another that was made

48. "la bourgeoisie riche fit élection de domicile à l'Opéra"; *Mémoires*, 6:247.
49. See *Paris, son histoire, ses monuments, ses musées*, 551.
50. Ibid., 588.
51. See Daumard, *Les Bourgeois de Paris au XIXe siècle*, 23.

manifest in the July Revolution of 1830. There are countless indices of a fundamental transformation of French opera which can be grouped under the rubric "bourgeoisification," and summarized in the quip that the Opéra entered *l'âge d'argent* in 1831: at once a silver age and an age of money.[52]

The change was exhibited in externals, too. For example, the time at which performances began was steadily put back to a later hour, from 5 P.M. before 1793, to 5:30 between 1793 and 1799, to 6 between 1799 and 1803, and to 7 after 1803. In 1831 the idea of one fixed time was abandoned altogether, and performances began at 7, 7:30, or 8, according to their lengths.[53] Obviously these alterations were made to accommodate a public which—unlike the aristocrats of the ancien régime—did not spend the earlier part of the day at leisure but in the pursuit of business or other professional duties.

MANAGING THE OPÉRA

The most striking example of the transformation of the Paris Opéra, however, was the organizational reform carried out after the July Revolution. Until then it had been administered as a court theater pure and simple, both under Napoleon I and during the Restoration. The role of the director was merely to carry out instructions covering even the smallest matters of detail given him by the *Maison du roi*, the ministry in charge of the royal household. The responsible official within the ministry, the *directeur des beaux-arts* (the Vicomte de La Rochefoucauld-Doudeauville from 1824 onward), thus had a much greater influence on the Opéra's affairs than his subordinate, the director. The last director under this regime was Émile-Timothée Lubbert, who held the post from 12 July 1827 to 1 March 1831.

From the financial point of view, this was a disastrous way to conduct business. By today's standards, it may seem highly commendable that the "normal" subvention during the Restoration amounted to at most 50 percent of the Opéra's total income. But the amount of state subvention required rose steadily during the late 1820s until in 1828 it reached the record high of 1,016,919 francs, almost exactly 60 percent of the total budget: and that was generally recognized as intolerable.[54]

This development was not the least of the reasons why the new re-

52. Lan, *Mémoires d'un chef de claque*, 151.

53. See Castil-Blaze, *Mémorial du Grand Opéra*, 59.

54. See Gourret, *Ces Hommes qui ont fait l'Opéra*, 220. The following account is based on Gourret's study.

gime decided to privatize the Opéra with effect from 1 January 1831. In a leasehold agreement dated 28 February 1831,[55] management was transferred for six years to Louis-Désiré Véron, an entrepreneur who, after studying medicine, had made a fortune from a balsamic chest-rub patented in his name but appears to have had no previous experience of running a theater.[56] To raise the deposit required by the government he formed an association with the Spanish banker, and friend of Rossini, Marie-Alexandre Aguado. The lease specified Véron's obligations in such matters as the minimum number of first performances of new works to be staged per annum, and the number of orchestral musicians and chorus singers to be employed, and it also made him answerable to a supervisory committee at the ministry of the interior, but for the rest the management of the Opéra as a business was left to him.

Véron proved to have a good eye for what the new public wanted. Among his many innovations, lavish productions and new stage-effects took priority, and he was lucky enough to be able to stage the world premières of three exceptionally successful operas: *Robert le diable* by Meyerbeer and Scribe in 1831 (secured for the Opéra by his predecessor but not performed), Auber's *Gustave III, ou Le Bal masqué* in 1833, and Halévy's *La Juive* in 1835. As a result, he was the first director of the Paris Opéra since Lully to conclude his term of office with an overall profit.

This fact is often mentioned in isolation in histories of music, as evidence of the success of a purely capitalist style of management. It is too easily forgotten that Véron continued to receive substantial subsidies from the state, although these were due to be reduced from an annual sum of 810,000 francs to 670,000 francs. The intended reduction was much to the state's advantage, and was probably the crucial reason behind the decision to privatize. Under Véron's successors, too, the proportion of subvention was kept at a lower level than it had been under the Restoration, although it never fell below 620,000 francs, or one-third of the total budget.

Véron retired early, in August 1835, after another cut in subsidy led him to recognize that running the Opéra at a profit was likely to be far more difficult in the future. In fact, all his successors, after making gains initially, ended up with substantial deficits which had to be met by the state. There were four more directors between 1835 and 1856, all of whom found it a hard task.

55. The contract is printed in full in ibid., 263–67, and in Véron, *Mémoires*, 3:173–78.
56. See Godlewski, "L'étonnante carrière du Docteur Véron," 35.

Véron's immediate successor in 1835 was the set designer and producer Charles-Edmond Duponchel, who allowed his partner Aguado to bear the financial risk alone and contented himself with a fixed salary and a small share of the net profits. After running into difficulties, he formed an association with Léon Pillet on 1 June 1840, but before long the two men had quarreled, and Duponchel retired in October 1841.

Of all the Opéra's directors in the nineteenth century, Pillet was the least successful. The problems caused by unforeseeable events like Aguado's death in 1842, and his widow's withdrawal from the undertaking, were compounded by errors of judgment. As the lover of the singer Rosine Stoltz, he showed her such inordinate favoritism that he alienated other singers and the public as well in the end. In addition, with regard to arrangements for forthcoming premières, he fell afoul of not only the most successful librettist of the age but also the most successful composer. Both Scribe, who blamed Pillet for the continual postponement of *Le Duc d'Albe*, which Donizetti began but never finished, and Meyerbeer, who insisted on choosing the cast for the première of his latest opera, *Le Prophète*, refused to work again with Pillet after 1845.

A huge burden of debt and a press campaign against himself and Rosine Stoltz combined to force Pillet to retire in October 1847.[57] The direction was taken up again by Duponchel, now in association with Nestor Roqueplan. Duponchel retired from all forms of work in opera in November 1849, however, leaving Roqueplan in sole command. A dandy and well-known socialite, and an exemplary opportunist, Roqueplan contrived to keep his feet through all the political upheavals experienced between 1848 and 1852, but in the process he ran up debts for the Opéra totaling almost a million francs. In the light of this managerial catastrophe, Napoleon III did not simply force Roqueplan to resign; instead, he decided to close down the "enterpreneurial regime, under which bad engenders bad,"[58] and took the Opéra back under the wing of the royal household after twenty-three years.

Once again, the Opéra was under the day-to-day management of a ministerial bureaucracy and the director's powers were severely restricted. The minister of state for the Imperial Household, Achille Fould, made himself responsible for performance schedules, for ex-

---

57. See Deux Amis des Beaux-Arts, *Académie royale de musique*; and a series of reports and counter-reports published in *La France musicale* 10 (1847): "Compte-rendu de M. Pillet" (pp. 44–46, 49–50, 57–59); "La Vérité sur l'Opéra: Réponse au mémoire de M. Léon Pillet" (pp. 65–70); "Réponse à notre réponse au mémoire de M. Léon Pillet" (pp. 78–79).

58. "[le] régime de l'entreprise, où le mal engendre le mal"; [Troplong], "Rapport de la commission chargée d'examiner la situation de l'Opéra," 2.

ample. That may be the reason why Roqueplan resigned on 6 November 1854, in spite of having been appointed as first "established" director only on 30 June. His successor, François Crosnier, did not last long either, resigning in June 1856. He was followed by Alphonse Royer and, in December 1862, by Émile Perrin, who finally took on the direction again as a private entrepreneur on 1 May 1866. But even this return to the leasehold arrangement that had existed under the July Monarchy did not mean that the Opéra was run on private capital in any real sense. It continued to receive state subventions, which were now as high as 920,000 francs a year.

ARTISTS AS CAPITALISTS

If the relationship between the directors of the Opéra and the state was a mixed one, in which subsidies and a system of control by the state overlaid the elements of free capitalism, on the other hand the Opéra's relations with composers and librettists were governed purely by capitalist conventions from 1831 onward. The procedures observed under the Restoration were swept away for good.

Before 1830, as a rule, librettos were examined by a jury appointed by the ministry, which was required to assess, among other things, whether the work was "fit for the stage of the Académie," and its subject "interesting." More than that, the matter of whether or not the style of the text could be regarded as "suitable for music" was decided by the jury's vote, even before it was established what composer might be interested in setting it to music.[59] This ponderous system, which went back to the priority of the literary element in tragédie lyrique, made the collaboration between composers and librettists all the harder, but in any case it was increasingly often set aside from 1825 onward.[60] Rossini, for example, who was a protégé of La Rochefoucauld, had an almost completely free hand in the planning of his operas.

From 1831, the first step in the preparations for a new opera was the agreement of a contract between the Opéra management and a libret-

59. See the minutes of the meetings of the *jury d'examen des poëmes:* F-Po, Archives de l'Opéra, AD 23 (December 1 1803 to December 12 1821) and AD 25 (January 16 1822 to December 15 1824); Vauthier, "Le Jury de lecture et l'Opéra sous la Restauration"; Ozanam, "Recherches sur l'Académie Royale de Musique," 360.

60. See Ozanam, "Recherches sur l'Académie Royale de Musique," 375. A register of librettos received (F-Po, Archives de l'Opéra, AD 24) was kept only from 16 May 1816 to 28 April 1825 and from September 1828 to 1 April 1830, while there are substantial gaps in the records for the intervening period, now held variously in the Archives Nationales and the Bibliothèque de l'Opéra.

tist. This set out the date of delivery and the fee, as well as penalties in the case of late delivery of the libretto or delay of the first performance. In theory, still, it was only when the management had taken delivery of the libretto that it would choose a composer, but that was no longer the practice. It was not only in the case of Meyerbeer, who drove an exceptionally hard bargain, that contracts between the Opéra and the composer and between composer and librettist were drawn up at the same time as the one with the librettist; sometimes there was a joint contract between all three parties as well.[61] That was already an indication of the new importance attached to the composer; the shift in the relative positions of composer and librettist was acknowledged to be complete in 1852, when Verdi signed a contract for a new opera with the management before he had even spoken to the librettist of his own choice—Scribe—about a possible subject.

The financial terms which librettists and composers sought and obtained, together with the fees paid to singers, illustrate the Opéra's exceptional standing. In the case of a major opera in four or five acts, as a rule both composer and librettist received 250 francs for each of the first forty performances, and 100 francs for each subsequent performance—in other words, they profited directly from the work's success. To these performance royalties can be added the prices they could expect for the sale of the publishing rights of the score, the piano-vocal score, and the libretto: thus Donizetti had 16,000 francs from the publisher Schonenberger for *Les Martyrs* in 1840,[62] Meyerbeer received 24,000 francs for *Les Huguenots* from Schlesinger,[63] and for *Le Prophète*, as he noted with evident pride in his diary, his fee was "the largest ever paid to date," namely 44,000 francs.[64] After 1840, single premiums were also often paid in addition to the royalties for individual performances, according to the author's market value: thus Scribe rarely settled for a premium below 5,000 francs,[65] while Meyerbeer got as much as 19,000 francs for *Le Prophète* in 1849.[66]

Without more detailed research, it is hard to say what difference sums like that made to the annual income of the most successful composers of grand opéra, such as Meyerbeer, Auber, or Halévy. It is easier

61. See, for example, the contract between Pillet, Scribe, and Meyerbeer, dated 20 December 1842, in Meyerbeer, *Briefwechsel*, 3:747.

62. See Rosselli, "Verdi e la storia della retribuzione del compositore italiano," 16.

63. See Meyerbeer, *Briefwechsel*, 2:679.

64. "den größten, den man bis jetzt bezahlt hat"; entry for 5 June 1849, ibid., 4:488.

65. See *Paris, son histoire, ses monuments, ses musées*, 250.

66. See H. Becker, *Giacomo Meyerbeer in Selbstzeugnissen*, 97.

in the case of the outstanding librettist of their age, however, for Scribe kept scrupulous records of all his earnings from his literary endeavors. Between 1830 and 1850 his annual income (not counting the yield on invested capital) varied between 100,000 francs and 180,000 francs, and in 1855 it rose to the record height of 232,070 francs.[67] Scribe spent something in the region of 100,000 francs annually from this huge income,[68] and the rest went to swell his capital, which amounted finally to two million francs.[69] Yet Scribe was left far behind by Meyerbeer, who at the end of 1857 calculated his fortune as 1,205,732 talers, equivalent to almost four-and-a-half million francs.[70]

Beside sums like those—in Scribe's case, admittedly, only a relatively small proportion came from his activities on behalf of the Opéra and Opéra-Comique—the terms which leading singers could demand appear almost modest, yet they were still very advantageous. The star tenor Adolphe Nourrit received 30,000 francs a year to begin with,[71] 40,000 francs later, and his fee for a brief appearance in a private salon was 500 francs.[72] While the annual salary paid to the soprano Laure Cinti-Damoreau during the 1830s never exceeded 60,000 francs, in the 1850s the less highly regarded Sophie Cruvelli earned as much as 100,000 francs.[73] An explosion of the top fees had led to exceptional rates becoming the norm, according to a contemporary guidebook: "It should be remembered that a singing artist of any merit will not expect to earn less than 25 or 30,000 francs per annum."[74]

When such sums are compared with the 12,000 francs that Duponchel asked for as his (very good) annual salary as director of the Opéra,[75] or the 3,000 francs (later reduced to 2,200) paid annually to the first concertmaster of the orchestra,[76] we are drawing close to the kind of

67. F-Pn, n.a.f. 22573, fol. 140–140v.

68. See Scribe's Livres de dépenses for 1840–50 and 1850–60, ibid., 22575 and 22576.

69. See Williams, "The well-made play," 1911.

70. Meyerbeer's accounts book 1857/58 (Staatsbibliothek Preußischer Kulturbesitz, Berlin, Musikabteilung, N. Mus. Nachl. 97, X/48); cited in H. Becker and G. Becker, *Giacomo Meyerbeer, Weltbürger der Musik*, 169, cat. no. 270. The calculation is based on the customary exchange rate at that date, the silver standard, whereby one taler (equivalent to 3 marks) was reckoned at 16.7 grams pure silver, and one franc at 4.5 grams.

71. See Véron, *Mémoires*, 3:262.

72. See Vier, *La Comtesse d'Agoult et son temps*, 1:341–42.

73. See Lasalle, *Les treize salles de l'Opéra*, 268.

74. "Il est juste de se rappeler qu'un artiste chantant, de quelque mérite, ne peut pas se résigner à gagner moins de 25 ou 30,000 fr. par an"; *Paris, son histoire, ses monuments, ses musées*, 261.

75. See Gourret, *Ces Hommes qui ont fait l'Opéra*, 127.

76. See Nectoux, "Trois orchestres parisiens en 1830," 474–75.

differentials that exist in the twentieth-century entertainment industry. But while immense fees for famous singers had been normal since the eighteenth century,[77] and the annual maximum fee of 15,000 francs set at the Paris Opéra under the Restoration[78] was an exceptional divergence from that rule, paying such generous rewards to composers and librettists was an innovation which in time also improved the social standing of composers (but not that of librettists) in Italy and other countries.[79]

The explanation for this new recognition of artistic work had nothing to do with a newly fashionable cult of genius. What lay behind it was a capitalist way of thinking, in the light of which artistic and industrial products alike were forms of property, and which therefore treated both an opera text and an opera performance as goods for sale. This standpoint is characterized in Victor Hugo's complaint in the preface to Le Roi s'amuse, where he puts the damage done to his rights of ownership by the play's banning after its first performance on the same footing as the attack on artistic and political freedom which the ban also represented: "The ministerial suppression of a play is an assault on liberty by censorship, and an assault on property by confiscation."[80]

In 1791, France had been the first state to pass a copyright law in the modern sense, giving writers and composers not only material protection in respect of their works but also, and more importantly, rights in respect of the content. In contrast to the practice in Italy, in France the composer of an opera—once he was sufficiently well established— could forbid others to make any alterations to his work in performance. This allows us to assume recognition in nineteenth-century France of a concept of an opera as a "work in itself," whereas no such concept existed at the same period in Italy, where works were adapted to the given circumstances in any performance.

Consequently, it is possible for a study of French grand opéra to be centered on composers and on individual works, in a way that would be quite inappropriate for the history of opera at other times or in other countries. The example of Meyerbeer, who was prepared, and could afford, to pay a penalty of 30,000 francs in order to prevent Les Huguenots being staged before he thought the production was ready, is admittedly an extreme case, even in the circumstances of France. Nevertheless,

77. See Rosselli, The Opera Industry in Italy from Cimarosa to Verdi, 59–65.
78. See Véron, Mémoires, 3:167.
79. See Rosselli, "Verdi e la storia della retribuzione del compositore italiano," 15.
80. "La suppression ministerielle d'une pièce de théâtre attente à la liberté par la censure, à la propriété par la confiscation"; Théâtre complet, 1:1324.

after 1830 there was a general tendency to look upon the composer as the most important among an opera's authors.

In 1825, on the other hand, the librettist Jouy could still postulate that "the poet is incontestably the primary and the most important author of an opera."[81] True, the very use of the word "incontestably" betrays that Jouy, the proponent of a classicist aesthetics, was aware that the librettist's preeminence was under threat.[82] But the profound consequences that the changes since 1830 would have for the composer are made clear only in 1852, in a letter Verdi wrote while he was negotiating a contract with the director of the Théâtre Italien in Paris, in which he saw fit to specify that the librettist should be paid by the theater and not by himself.[83]

Today, we take so much for granted the absolute preeminence of the composer, which was established once and for all by Meyerbeer in France and by Verdi in Italy, that we ought to look first at the French tragédie lyrique as it existed before their time, with its concept of the primacy of the literary element. Only then will we be able to assess the radical changes which took place in this and other areas of opera when modern music theater began, in Paris around 1830.

81. "Le poète est incontestablement le premier et le plus important auteur d'un opéra"; Jouy, *Essai sur l'Opéra français*, 233 (p. 65 in the 1987 modern edition). Throughout, citations will be made to both editions of the *Essai*.

82. See Ellis, *Music Criticism in Nineteenth-Century France*, 27–29.

83. Letter to Benjamin Lumley, 14 February 1852, in Verdi, *I copialettere*, 135.

✥ 2 ✥

VICTOR-JOSEPH
ÉTIENNE DE JOUY,
A HERMIT IN THE CITY

"The Hermit of the Chaussée d'Antin"

Victor-Joseph Étienne de Jouy may scarcely seem to deserve a chapter to himself in any history of French opera, even if he was one of the outstanding librettists in the two decades immediately preceding the emergence of grand opéra as a discrete form. Although he was a highly successful author in his heyday, his name had already been forgotten by the middle of the nineteenth century, and is no better known today. Yet a closer look at his work is well worthwhile, for in its many facets it provides tangible examples not only of the possibilities and contradictions of French opera at the beginning of the nineteenth century but also of forward-looking experiments with new theatrical forms.

Jouy was born Victor-Joseph Étienne in Versailles in 1764. He entered the army in 1781, spent three years in the French colony of Guiana and then four years in India and Ceylon, before returning to France in 1790. He was an impulsive adventurer, and during the Reign of Terror fell under suspicion of being an enemy of the people; threatened with a sentence of death, he fled to Switzerland in 1793. After the fall of Robespierre he rejoined the French army, but was dismissed in 1795 under suspicion—probably unwarranted—of collaborating with the British enemy.[1]

It was only after his military career was over that he began to write, under the name of de Jouy. His first play appeared in 1798 and was followed, first, by numerous vaudevilles, and then by tragedies on a

---

1. On Jouy's life, see primarily Comeau, "Etienne Jouy."

41

5 This sketch of the set of Act III of *La Vestale*, designed by Pierre-Luc-Charles Cicéri (1782–1866) for a revival of the work in 1821, reveals the influence of a long tradition of landscape painting with classical subjects. Although it was 14 years since the opera's first performance, even a designer alert to all the innovations, in terms of spectacle, taking place in the popular theater of the day could not cast off the conventions associated with the classicist categories underlying Jouy's libretto.

grand scale, which marked scarcely any advance on the dramas of Voltaire on which they were modeled. He had greater success with his opera librettos; following *Milton*, written for Spontini in 1804, he worked with the leading Parisian composers of the time. Among the most important of his texts are two more that he wrote for Spontini, *La Vestale* (1807) and *Fernand Cortez* (1809/1817), *Les Abencérages* for Cherubini (1813), and finally *Guillaume Tell* (1829), written at the end of his career and set to music by Rossini.

He was elected to the Académie Française in 1815. His contemporaries knew him best as the author of a regular column in the *Gazette de France*, in which he regaled readers with his everyday observations on urban life in Paris, from 1811 onwards. A collection was later published in book form under the title *L'Hermite de la Chaussée d'Antin, ou Observations sur les moeurs et les usages français au début du XIXe siècle* (The Hermit of the Chaussée d'Antin, or, Observations on French manners and customs at the beginning of the nineteenth century). They strike the modern reader as inconsequential and often naive, but they have an important place in the early history of literary assimilation of the phenomenon of the modern metropolis. Jouy's predecessors in depicting the confusing and manifold impressions of city life had tended to impose limits on themselves in the manner of the *Tableau de Paris* by Louis-Sébastien Mercier (1781–89), in which the view of Paris purports to be one contained within a metaphorical picture frame (a similar device was used by E. T. A. Hoffmann in *Des Vetters Eckfenster*, published in 1822, which affects to record what an invalid sees from his window). Jouy was one of the first writers to abandon that convention, and, schooled by his travels in exotic lands, examined the Parisian "natives" as if with the eye of an ethnologist exposing himself directly to the perceptual demands of the unfamiliar. He never aspired to the probing analyses and systematic classifications attempted in the *physiologies* fashionable after 1830; the attraction of his journalism, which might anachronistically be called "reportage," lies in the artlessness of his associations and his ingenuous style. The inhabitant of the Chaussée d'Antin regarded himself as belonging to the metropolis, even if he had adopted the role of an observer. At the same time, his adopted persona of a hermit, living in what was then still an outer suburb on the northwestern periphery of Paris, separated him from the amorphous throng of the city's inhabitants, and so enabled him to exploit the tension between the individual and the mass. It was a tension that was to demand ever new resolutions in the future development of French opera.

SENSUAL ENCHANTMENT

It must be admitted that the literary impressions which had shaped Jouy all dated from the eighteenth century. He had grown up in the intellectual atmosphere in which definitions and ideas about future developments were constantly discussed by prominent adherents of the Enlightenment and the Encyclopedists. One of their favorite topics, debated vehemently and incessantly, was the future style of French opera, and even though these discussions scarcely survived the maelstrom of the French Revolution, Jouy preserved a general theoretical interest in aesthetic questions. At a date when the flow of contributions to the discussion of the aesthetics of opera had amazingly all but ceased, he actually produced one.[2] His *Essai sur l'Opéra français* of 1826 can be regarded as the last of a long line of publications to address the subject, not as a composer, from the inside, nor from the perspective of the burgeoning profession of musical journalism, but from the standpoint of the "men of letters, whose ignorance of music was complete, and who considered that art only as an accessory of poetry."[3]

Certainly, this normative treatise contains no trace of any effort to find aesthetic justifications for the artistic beliefs of the time. The careful observer of the changing face of city life shows himself here to be entrenched in a classicist aesthetics, going back further even than the position reached during the second half of the eighteenth century. At the start of the *Essai* Jouy gives a definition of opera that derives directly from the previous century, as a "spectacle wherein the citizen may forget his troubles in a sweet enchantment."[4] His ideal character for a style of opera whose primary function is to bewitch the senses is—in the middle of the 1820s—still Armida, the sorceress from Tasso's epic poem *La Gerusalemme liberata* (1575), although, after an *Armide* from Lully (1686) and another from Gluck (1777), French opera had long been forced to look elsewhere for subject matter.

No synopsis of either *Armide* can express the special character of a traditional eighteenth-century tragédie lyrique, and the primary requirements of a classicist operatic aesthetics, as vividly as Jouy does in a rapturous account, in which the figure of the enchantress Armida melds

2. See Gerhard, "Incantesimo o specchio dei costumi," 47–51.

3. "littérateurs, dont l'ignorance en musique était complète, et qui n'ont considéré cet art, que comme un accessoire de la poésie"; Fétis, Review of Castil-Blaze's *De l'Opéra en France*, 472.

4. "Spectacle, où dans un doux enchantement le citoyen chagrin oublie"; Jouy, *Essai*, 228 (1987 ed., 63)

with the Muse of Opera herself. Jouy paraphrases the action of the five acts (Lully and Gluck set the same libretto) in his picturing of Armida "in a magic place where all nature is subject to her laws. . . . Presently, her eyes heavy with languor and voluptuousness, she sits down in a cool grove perfumed with flowers, where the light is gentle and tinted by all the colors of the rainbow; the zephyr rocks the waters and the foliage with harmonies." This idyll is contrasted with scenes in which "all at once the clamor of war is heard; the Muse rises, casts off her garlands and replaces the coronet of roses about her head with a casque; she flies to the battle and wraps herself in all the splendor of glory." But the illustrious sorceress's heroic combat is disturbed by Eros: "Love has betrayed her vows, victory slips from her courageous grasp; her eyes, grown wild, summon up infernal powers and compel them to serve her vengeance; at her command torrents are unleashed, volcanos erupt, cities tremble, and dread fills every heart." The conflict between heroic, martial glory and human passion is heightened in a dispute between the sorceress and the infernal deities, in which, finally, the idyll gains the upper hand, without the need of intervention from any deus ex machina: "But the terrible storm raised for an instant by passion is quelled by the first smile of love; calm returns, the air clears, Armida has disarmed Hades, and her peaceful triumph is prepared amid sports and festivities."[5]

Jouy regarded the purpose of opera as being to enable the audience to forget their everyday circumstances by transporting them to a realm of mythological fantasy.[6] It is only logical, therefore, that he devoted an entire section of his book to "the marvelous," although it was more than

5. "dans un séjour magique où la nature entière est soumise à ses lois . . . Tantôt, les yeux pleins de langueur et volupté, elle s'assied sous un frais bocage qu'embaume le parfum des fleurs, qu'éclaire un jour douteux et nuancé par les teints variées de l'écharpe d'Iris: le zéphir anime les eaux et le feuillage d'un ton harmonieux." "Tout-à-coup un bruit de guerre se fait entendre; la muse se lève, détache ses guirlandes, remplace par un casque la couronne de rose qui paraît sa tête; elle vole au combat, et s'entoure de tout l'éclat de la gloire." "L'amour avait trahi ses voeux, la victoire échappe à son courage; son regard, devenu farouche, évoque les puissances infernales et les contraint à servir à sa vengeance; à sa voix les torrents se déchaînent, les volcans s'ouvrent, les cités frémissent, et l'épouvante est dans tous les coeurs." "Mais l'orage terrible, que les passions ont un moment soulevé, s'apaise au premier sourire de l'amour; le calme renaît, l'air s'épure, Armide a désarmé l'enfer, et son triomphe paisible se prépare au milieu des jeux et des fêtes." Ibid., 230–31 (1987 ed., 64–65).

6. Jouy's opinion was shared by a former solo dancer of the Opéra who is better known as the author of an aesthetic treatise; see Deshayes, *Idées générales sur l'Académie Royale de Musique*, 25, 35.

sixty years since this central category of classicist operatic aesthetics had been dismissed by Encyclopedists such as Diderot and Rousseau;[7] Friedrich Melchior Grimm was especially brusque, condemning it as "so vapid, tedious, and ridiculous that there is nothing that would amuse children."[8] For all the extreme conservatism of his fundamental views, Jouy had some sense of the realities of the 1820s. Even if he was not prepared to cast aside an outdated aesthetic theory, some of the details and unresolved contradictions in the *Essai* expose the real aesthetic problems that French opera faced in the years of radical change between 1789 and 1830. He went into the question of the marvelous in such detail solely in order to demonstrate how this poetic quality could be added to "the brilliance of the spectacle" without detracting from "the interest of the action."[9] However, although it was still occasionally to find a use in nineteenth-century opera, the marvelous had long outlived its function as a central category in French dramatic theory, and between his search for a theoretical justification for it and the more realistic observation that classical mythology or pastoral idyll could not possibly deliver an operatic plot capable of holding the interest of a public that read the novels of Sir Walter Scott, Jouy lost his way.

French opera had been in this very plight for some considerable time. Ever since the foundation of the Paris Opéra in 1672, tragédie lyrique had always been defined by reference to its counterpart, *tragédie en prose*. That made it hard to assign opera the status of a genre in its own right, with the potential for independent development. Under a system in which catharsis, the tragic ending, historico-political subject matter, and the calculated unfolding of a tragic conflict toward a catastrophe were the preserve of spoken drama, tragédie lyrique was necessarily confined to the task of bewitching audiences with fabulous subjects, and having recourse to a deus ex machina if dramatic probability prevented the obligatory happy ending by any other means. Admittedly, from 1789 onward French opera had tried to free itself from this straitjacket by stages, by drawing subject matter from sources other than classical mythology and the epics of Tasso and Ariosto, and, in isolated cases such as Piccinni's *Didon* (1783) and Cherubini's *Médée* (1797), experiments had even been made with tragic endings.

7. See Angermüller, "Reformideen von Du Roullet und Beaumarchais als Opern-librettisten," 236.

8. "si plat, si ennuyeux et si ridicule qu'il n'y a pas de quoi amuser les enfans"; *Correspondance littéraire*, 1:463 (article of 15 May 1756).

9. "l'éclat du spectacle"; "l'intérêt de l'action"; Jouy, *Essai*, 233 (1987 ed., 66).

Even though Voltaire's plays were repeatedly adapted as operatic librettos,[10] including *Sémiramis*, set as a tragédie lyrique by Charles-Simon Catel (1803), and *Olimpie*, Spontini's last opera for Paris (1819), tradition was too strong for a more radical departure to be conceivable for the time being. Voltaire is known solely for his prose now, but his plays were highly successful in their day and were accepted into the French classical canon because he never fundamentally abandoned the dramaturgical principles of his models, Racine and Corneille. While Catel and his librettist, Philippe Desriaux, ventured to keep the tragic ending of *Sémiramis* in their opera, thereby breaking one of the strictest rules of the genre, Spontini opted to end *Olimpie* with an apotheosis in the form of one of the large-scale divertissements, with multiple choruses and ballets, which had been the staple fare of French opera since Lully's day. He had done the same in *Fernand Cortez*, which he wrote with Jouy in 1809, at Napoleon's request. Other authors of operas which drew their subject matter from relatively recent history were as little ready as Spontini and Jouy to abandon the divertissement, which always served to transport tragic events on to the plane of the marvelous, and to resolve the convolutions of the plot in a final imposing tableau. That resolution is proclaimed in the very title of Le Sueur's biblical opera *La Mort d'Adam et son apothéose* (1809); in Manuel García's *La Mort du Tasse* (1821), too, the death of Tasso, after an action centered on the poet rather than any characters or events of his invention, is represented as an ascent into immortality with a concluding tableau glorifying him. Even in operas that did not look to classical mythology for their subjects, such as Catel's *Les Bayadères* (1810) and Spontini's hugely successful *La Vestale* (1823)—both on librettos by Jouy—or Berton's *Virginie, ou les Décemvirs* (1823) and the pasticcio opera *Pharamond* (1825), which put the religious practices of India, Rome, and Gaul on the stage, the human aspects of the plot always took second place to the sublime and the marvelous elements inseparable from the religious framework.

As will be discussed in more detail later, in connection with Rossini's *Siège de Corinthe*, this kind of conception had grown unsustainable by the end of the 1820s. And while Jouy admitted as much indirectly in his *Essai*, his sometime collaborator Jean-Toussaint Merle declared in 1827, with unsurpassable clarity, that the time for radical change in French opera had arrived.

10. See Ridgway, "Voltairian bel canto."

It is important to persuade them [poets and playwrights] that these Aga-
memnons, Aeneases, Anacreons, Alcibiadeses, and Aristippuses are no
longer very dramatic personages, least of all at the Opéra, and that these
eternal families of Greeks and Trojans, whose misfortunes and pleasures
have filled our stages for over a century, are the reason why the Opéra,
for all its right royal expenditure, is known throughout Europe as the
most boring spectacle in the world. . . . I think it is time that all this Roman and mythological frippery was relegated to the warehouse.[11]

Merle suggested fairy tales and stories from the *Bibliothèque bleue*, a popular collection of ballad-like tales,[12] as sources worth exploring for more
suitable subject matter, and in so doing pointed the way that was to lead
from Meyerbeer's *Robert le diable* (1831) to Gounod's setting of *La Nonne
sanglante* (1854). Jouy's *Essai* shows him to be more flexible than his fundamental allegiance to "mythological frippery" might have allowed, for
he cites several times historical subjects such as those which had been
tackled by another librettist as early as the 1770s.[13] It is true that he uses
some rather tortuous reasoning to claim them for his aesthetic maxims, asserting that they were already intrinsically sufficiently marvelous
and, "if I may so express myself, possessed of a truth sufficiently fabulous for them to dispense with all supernatural intervention."[14] Although he robbed historical subjects of a good deal of their particular
quality by speaking of them thus, grand opéra proved him right, with
its historical subject matter and what Jouy himself, in another context,
acknowledged as typical of the age, namely its "highly pronounced tendency toward political grandeur."[15]

The aging librettist's only self-deception lay in his association of that
tendency with patriotism. Parisian audiences did not look to the Opéra

11. "Il est important de leur [les poëtes] persuader que les Agamemnon, les Énée, les
Anacréon, les Alcibiade et les Aristippe sont aujourd'hui des personnages peu dramatiques,
sur-tout à l'Opéra, et que ces éternelles familles de Grecs et de Troyens, dont les malheurs
et les plaisirs occupent notre scène depuis plus de cent ans, sont cause que l'Opéra, avec
une dépense toute royale, passe en Europe pour le spectacle le plus ennuyeux du monde.
. . . Je crois qu'il est temps de reléguer dans les magasins toute la friperie romaine et
mythologique." *De l'Opéra*, 20–21.
12. See Bollème, *La Bibliothèque bleue*, 7–26.
13. Barnabé Farmian de Rosoi's librettos *Henri IV ou la bataille d'Ivry* and *La Réduction
de Paris sous Henri IV* were set by Martini and Bianchi respectively (1774, 1775); see also
Rosoi's *Dissertation sur le drame lyrique*, 36–37, 44.
14. "si j'ose m'exprimer ainsi, d'une vérité assez fabuleuse, pour se passer de toute
intervention surnaturelle"; Jouy, *Essai*, 235 (1987 ed., 66).
15. "tendance fortement prononcée vers la grandeur politique"; "Discours préliminaire," *Oeuvres complètes*, 1:1–28 (p. 25).

or any other institution to confirm a patriotism they scarcely felt: what they wanted first and foremost was to be swept off their feet by stage effects and grandiose spectacles. The creators of grand opéra more often found the subject matter of their most successful operas in foreign history, or in the darkest periods of French history, than in the celebration of "the great themes of our national history," as recommended by Jouy.[16] Operas that made a deliberate appeal to the reawakening spirit of French nationalism, like Halévy's *Charles VI* (1843), Mermet's *Roland à Roncevaux* (1864), or the same composer's *Jeanne d'Arc* (1875), remained rare exceptions, and their success was even rarer.

As Jouy himself recognized, the nineteenth-century public preferred entertainment that put "situations alternatively passionate, tender, and terrifying"[17] on the stage. But when their object was to glorify "the prodigious achievements of the genius of patriotism"[18] how should composer and librettist set about painting terrors? Jouy had been in that situation himself when he was working on the text for Spontini's *Fernand Cortez*, which was intended to enlist the Opéra to provide propaganda in support of Napoleon's Spanish campaign.[19] In the "anecdotal notes" with which he accompanied the text of that libretto in his *Oeuvres complètes*, Jouy wrote:

> I thought it my primary duty to present the spectator with a natural exposition, and compel him to pity the fate of the Spanish prisoners, in order to soften the odious aspects of their victory later on. That was my subject's principal stumbling block. I was perhaps successful in avoiding it; I do not flatter myself that I surmounted it. Between the sympathy inspired by the temerity and audacity of the conquerors and that felt for the miserable fate of the conquered, the soul remains uncertain and, as it were, suspended.[20]

So the librettist had become unsure of his métier to the extent that he was prepared to admit that when a drama depicts warfare, the audience

16. "les grands traits de notre histoire nationale"; *Essai*, 250 (1987 ed., 75).

17. "situations alternativement passionées, douces [et] terribles"; ibid., 233 (1987 ed., 66).

18. "les prodiges que le génie du patriotisme a opéré"; ibid., 250 (1987 ed., 75).

19. See Gerhard, "*Fernand Cortez* und *Le Siège de Corinthe*," 105–8; Gerhard, "'Une véritable Révolution,'" 21–23.

20. "Je crus devoir présenter d'abord au spectateur une exposition naturelle, et le forcer de plaindre le sort des prisonniers espagnols, pour affaiblir ensuite l'odieux de leur victoire. C'était là le principal écueil de mon sujet. Je l'ai peut-être évité; je ne me flatte pas de l'avoir franchi. Entre l'intérêt qu'inspire la témérité audacieuse des vainqueurs et celui qui s'attache au malheur des opprimés, l'âme reste comme incertaine et comme suspendue." Jouy, *Fernand Cortez* [1817], *Oeuvres complètes*, 19:57–108 (p. 106).

will be moved to spontaneous pity for the losers, and consequently the victory of the other side will seem abhorrent, at least if it is represented as a good outcome. There was no way to avoid that, if the centuries-old convention of the "happy ending" was to be observed. Jouy himself defended the convention with such rigor that he even qualified his admiration for Piccinni's *Didon* of 1782, one of the few tragédies lyriques to end tragically.[21]

Jouy's successors were not always in a position to choose subjects that ended with victory for those who were oppressed at the start—as happens in Jouy's own libretto for *Guillaume Tell*. The logical alternative for a generation that felt little respect for other maxims of tragédie lyrique was acceptance of the tragic ending, which also offered a means of meeting the ever-growing requirement for harsh contrasts, in that the final scene of the opera could bring together the bloody fate of the victims and the triumph of the detested victors.

Contrasts

Another indication of Jouy's sensitivity to the needs of contemporary audiences is his recognition that "those oppositions, those contrasts for which painting and musical poetry thirst" were an essential strength of every successful libretto.[22] His discussion of the uses of contrast is one of the most modern aspects of his *Essai*. Right at the start, he distances himself from eighteenth-century aesthetic maxims by asking for "strongly contrasted characters" and "varied scenes,"[23] where Diderot, in his essay on dramatic poetry, had decreed that "contrast in style is bad."[24] Jouy also regards it as necessary "to project characters strongly and let them stand out" against their situations[25]—but Diderot, too, on the same page of his essay, conceded that characters might be contrasted with their situations.

More than any other concept, the changing attitudes to contrast illustrate how French opera in the nineteenth century developed new forms of spectacle step by step, under the pressure of new perceptual expectations. While contrast was exclusive to painting at the start of the

21. See *Essai*, 245–46 (1987 ed., 72–73).
22. "ces oppositions, ces contrastes dont la poésie musicale et la peinture sont avides"; ibid., 241 (1987 ed., 70).
23. "caractères fortement contrastés"; "des tableaux variés"; ibid., 233 (1987 ed., 66).
24. "le contraste est mauvais dans le style"; Diderot, "De la Poésie dramatique," 348.
25. "d'y opposer et d'y prononcer fortement les caractères"; *Essai*, 242 (1987 ed., 71).

eighteenth century,[26] it was gradually admitted in discussion of musical aesthetics during the last thirty years of the century. Rousseau had a short article under the heading "contrast" in his dictionary of music, but did not go below the musical surface. His definition is summed up in the sentence: "There is a contrast in a piece of music when the movement passes from slow to quick or from quick to slow; when the diapason of the melody passes from flat to sharp, or from sharp to flat; when the air passes from sweet to bold, or from bold to sweet."[27] It was not until 1794 that a musician developed ideas of musical contrast which went beyond Rousseau.

André-Ernest-Modeste Grétry, who enjoyed all-round success in the 1770s and 1780s as the classic exponent of French opéra comique, devoted an entire chapter of his memoirs to the subject of contrasts, and though it is hard to find any sign that he ever applied his advanced theories in his works, he writes so eloquently that it is instructive to read the first part in full.

> It is by contrasts, above all, that sensibilities are moved; something which has not touched us at all will produce a multitude of effects upon us if it is presented again with contrasts that reveal its value. An idea does not strike our imaginations forcibly if it is not accompanied by its contrast, as bodies on which light falls are accompanied by shadow. The artist comprehends better than other men the contrasts that strike the senses. Much has been said of Poussin's painting, *The Dance of Arcadian Shepherds*, and the sublime contrast which it presents: there is a tomb beside the place where they dance, and on the tomb is inscribed: "I, too, was a shepherd in Arcady."
>
> During our Revolution, I was struck by many contrasts that will not be erased from my imagination, and which are—given the circumstances of the time—more striking and also more horrible than the contrast in Poussin's painting. During that time, the horror of which will echo down the centuries under the name of "The Terror," I was returning toward evening from a garden in the Champs-Élysées; I had been invited to enjoy the sight of the most beautiful lilac tree in flower that one could ever hope to see. It was toward evening, as I say, and I was returning alone, and I would have been enjoying the scent of a thousand flowers, and the most majestic sunset, had not public misfortunes afflicted my soul with the most somber sorrow.

26. See Kambartel, "Kontrast" I, *Historisches Wörterbuch der Philosophie*, vol. 4, coll. 1066–67.

27. *A Dictionary of Music*, 92.

I was close to the place de la Révolution, formerly de Louis XV, when my ear was struck by the sound of instruments; I advanced a few paces; there were violins, a flute, a tambourine, and I could distinguish the dancers' joyful cries. I was reflecting on the contrasts of the scenes of this world when a man passing by me drew my attention to the guillotine: I raised my eyes and saw at a distance its fatal blade fall and rise again, twelve or fifteen times in succession. Country dances on one side of me, streams of blood flowing on the other, the scent of flowers, the gentle influence of spring, the last rays of the setting sun which would never rise again for those unhappy victims . . . these images have left indelible traces. . . .

Let us recall another contrast, but one which cannot be well appreciated except by a musician. A king, as we know, is a man like any other; but the habit of seeing him surrounded by pomp and grandeur makes him a being who overawes us, if reflection does not overcome our proclivities.

The military cortège which conducted Louis XVI to the scaffold passed beneath my windows, and the march in $\frac{6}{8}$, with drums marking its skipping rhythm, so ill-suited to the funebral nature of the occasion, affected me by its contrast and made me tremble.[28]

28. "C'est par les contrastes sur-tout que la sensibilité est émue; une même chose qui ne nous a point affectés, si elle se représente avec les contrastes qui la font valoir, produit sur nous des effets multiples; une idée ne se présente pas fortement à notre imagination, si son contraste ne l'accompagne; de même l'ombre accompagne les corps éclairés. L'artiste saisit mieux qu'un autre homme les contrastes qui frappent les sens. On a souvent parlé du tableau du Poussin *(La danse des bergers d'Arcadie)*, et du contraste sublime qu'il présente; un tombeau est à côté du lieu où l'on danse; sur ce tombeau est écrit: Et moi aussi je fus berger d'Arcadie.

"Pendant notre révolution, j'ai été frappé de plusieurs contrastes qui ne peuvent s'effacer de mon imagination, et qui sont, vu les circonstances des temps, plus frappans, mais plus horribles que le contraste du tableau du Poussin. Dans ce temps, dont l'horreur passera aux siècles à venir sous le nom du "temps de la terreur," je revenois vers le soir d'un jardin situé dans les Champs-Élysées; on m'y avoit invité pour jouir de l'aspect du plus bel arbre de lilas en fleurs qu'on pût voir. Vers le soir, dis-je, je revenois seul, et j'aurais joui du parfum de mille fleurs, d'un soleil couchant des plus majestueux, si les malheurs publics n'eussent affecté mon âme de la tristesse la plus sombre.

"J'approchois de la place de la Révolution, ci-devant de Louis XV, lorsque mon oreille fut frappée par le son des instrumens; j'avançai quelques pas: c'étoient des violons, une flûte, un tambourin, et je distinguai les cris de joie des danseurs. Je réfléchissois sur les contrastes des scènes de ce monde, lorsqu'un homme qui passoit à côté de moi me fit remarquer la guillotine; je lève les yeux, et je vois de loin son fatal couteau se baisser et se relever douze ou quinze fois de suite. Des danses champêtres d'un côté, des ruisseaux de sang qui coulent de l'autre, le parfum des fleurs, la douce influence du printemps, les derniers rayons de ce soleil couchant qui ne se relevera jamais pour ces malheureuses victimes . . . ces images laissent des traces ineffaçables. . . .

The source of the idea is rammed home: the composer, whose wife was a painter,[29] speaks first, following Diderot, of the contrast to be found in a famous painting from the 1630s by Poussin,[30] before coming to his main theme; the transition from the description of the colors of the spring evening, a genre scene in words, to the sober remarking of "the sound of instruments" can be said to reproduce the act of assimilating a category that originated in the aesthetic theory of painting. In spite of the very personal character of his account of his experiences in the year 1793, he leaves no room for doubt concerning the general validity of his new perception of contrasts. It is only the contrast by which an idea is accompanied that allows the idea itself to stand out in full clarity, just as these contrasts had become indispensable if his contemporaries' sensibilities were to be touched.

The novelty of Grétry's view is not only evident in this radical departure from the earlier aesthetic theory that affects were sufficient unto themselves; the text itself puts the idea in a direct relationship with perceptual expectations of the years after 1789. The terrifying upheavals following the French Revolution had sensitized people to the perception of "unprecedented shocks,"[31] and so it was now only a question of time before these new impressions would be reproduced in works of art, for the artistic intensification of experiences would allow unforgettable horrors to be domesticated.

It is possible, therefore, to regard Cherubini's *Médée*, first performed at the Opéra-Comique in 1797, as a first reflection of those horrors in French opera. One contemporary critic did so, at all events, asserting in his review that there had never been a subject so well suited to musical "terrorism." That neologism had made its debut in the vocabulary of political discourse only in 1794,[32] and its use in the discussion of a work of art was anything but accidental: having disconcerted his readers with

---

"Rappelons un autre contraste, mais qui ne peut être bien senti que par l'artiste musicien. Un roi, nous le savons, est un homme comme un autre; mais l'habitude de le voir environné de la pompe et de la grandeur, en fait un être qui nous impose, si la réflexion ne nous détournoit de nos préjugés.

"Le cortège militaire qui conduisit Louis XVI à l'échafaud, passa sous mes fenêtres, et la marche en $\frac{6}{8}$, dont les tambours marquoient le rhythme sautillant, en opposition au lugubre de l'événement, m'affecta par son contraste et me fit frémir." Grétry, *Mémoires*, 2:139–42.

29. See Charlton, *Grétry*, 172.
30. See Panofsky, "'Et in Arcadia ego,'" 364, n. 48.
31. "chocs inopinés"; Grétry, *Mémoires*, 2:143.
32. See Heuvel, "Terreur, terroriste, terrorisme," 120.

it, the conservative critic embarked on a polemic against the "triumph of barbarism," and posed a rhetorical question: "Can it be true that we have fallen so low that we must be astonished to be pleased, and harrowed to be moved? That only murder and conflagration will delight our eyes, and only dissonances and diminished sevenths please our ears?"[33]

For all that, an assimilated form of the "terrorist" aesthetics is to be found in Jouy's journalism. In his column of 28 May 1812, having developed the concept of contrast from an analogy with painting, just as Grétry did, he went on to give an example of it in a description of the rue de Richelieu at night, evoking the noisy "concourse of market-gardeners' carts carrying vegetables to market and carriages going to or returning from the Opéra ball."[34] He explained that the contrast of work and pleasure had given him the idea of the framework in which to unite his observations. Some months later, on 11 November 1813, in a description of a public execution in the square outside the Hôtel de Ville, he used the contrast between that "spectacle" and the one to be seen at the Opéra to make his scene all the more vivid.

> I happened to take note of . . . the strange contradiction . . . between extreme good manners and savage curiosity, of which people in the mass, and above all the inhabitants of this capital city, provide examples at all times. Indeed, how different would be the impression of us borne away by two foreigners, one of whom had seen Parisians only at the Opéra, and the other only while crossing the city and passing along the quays on a day when there was an execution in the place de Grève![35]

33. "terrorisme musical"; "triomphe de la barbarie"; "Serait-il donc vrai que nous en fussions à ce point humiliant, qu'il faille nous étonner pour nous plaire, nous déchirer pour nous émouvoir; qu'on ne puisse plus charmer nos yeux que par des meurtres et des incendies, et nos oreilles que par des dissonances et des septièmes diminuées!" L.C. [Ange-Étienne-Xavier-Poisson de La Chabeaussière], "Spectacles: Médée au Théâtre de la rue Feydeau," *La Décade philosophique, littéraire et politique* 18 (1797): 555–57 (my thanks to David Charlton for bringing this review to my attention); on the reviewer's identity see Kitchin, *Un Journal "philosophique,"* 291, 237–44.

34. "concours des charrettes des maraichers qui portaient des légumes à la Halle, et des carosses qui allaient au bal de l'Opéra ou qui en revenaient"; Jouy, "Paris à différentes heures," *Oeuvres complètes*, 2:173–81 (p. 174); see also Comeau, "Etienne Jouy," 169–70.

35. "J'ai eu l'occasion de faire remarquer . . . cette étrange contradiction . . . d'une extrême politesse et d'une curiosité féroce, dont le peuple, et principalement celui de cette capitale, offre à tout moment l'exemple. En effet, quelle idée différente emporteraient de nous deux étrangers, dont l'un n'aurait vu les Parisiens qu'à l'Opéra, et l'autre qu'en traversant la ville, le long des quais, un jour d'exécution en place de Grève!" "Une Exécution en Grève," *Oeuvres complètes*, 3:299–308 (p. 299).

In fact, in spite of the unaccustomed harmonies and subject matter to which Cherubini exposed his audience, French opera of around 1800 provides scarcely one example of contrast as drastic as the one described by Jouy. A number of commentators, admittedly, professed to discover comparable things in earlier operas. Madame de Staël, for example, writing in 1810, referred to the "contrast of the joyous airs . . . and the Queen's stifled groans" in Gluck's *Alceste*,[36] and another writer, in 1813, mentioned the simultaneous choruses in Act I of Piccinni's *Iphigénie en Tauride*.[37] One can add "the metrically opposed double choruses" in Grétry's *Colinette à la cour, ou La double épreuve* (1782) and his *La Caravane du Caire* (1783),[38] and, of course, the dance scene in the first finale of Mozart's *Don Giovanni* (1787). But the earliest foretaste of the blatant, uncompromising way in which grand opéra would in the future systematically force musically and dramatically opposed structures into a common framework comes in a scene in an opera by Cherubini with a libretto by Jouy, *Les Abencérages, ou l'Étendard de Grenade* (1813): a large-scale number for double chorus in Act I, Scene 6, expresses simultaneously the rejoicing of the Abencerages, led by their general Almanzor, and the grim vows of the defeated Zegries to be revenged.[39]

Jouy had obviously already grasped the forward-looking character of a technique that would be perfected after 1830, above all by Meyerbeer and Berlioz,[40] although when he described it in his *Essai* as the "return in combination of several contrasted motifs" he was thinking only of instrumental forms like the overture.[41] Once again, the sixty-year-old *académicien* shrank from the consequence which would have had him appreciate, for instance, the macabre and blasphemous play with opposing melodies in the fourth movement of Berlioz's *Symphonie fantastique* as much as he did the contrast between the "extreme good manners and savage curiosity" of the different sectors of Parisian society attending the Opéra and a public execution. Nevertheless, Jouy confirms the direct association between the new familiarity with dramatic contrasts and the confusions of turbulent political events in recent history when he admits, at the end of the preface to the edition of his complete works,

36. "contraste des airs joyeux . . . et des gémissements étouffés de la reine"; *De l'Allemagne*, 3:377.
37. See Martine, *De la Musique dramatique en France*, 48.
38. Charlton, *Grétry*, 275.
39. See Mongrédien, "A la Découverte des Abencérages," 16.
40. For examples before Berlioz, see Bockholdt, *Berlioz-Studien*, 57–63.
41. "[le] retour combiné de plusieurs motifs en contraste"; *Essai*, 270 (1987 ed., 85).

that the epochs already labeled "Revolution," "Empire," and "Restoration," during which his works had come into being, "were more fertile, perhaps, in tableaux and contrasts than almost all those which make up our previous annals."[42]

A MIRROR

Jouy's gift for observation, trained by life in the Paris of his time, overruled all classicist principles even in his aesthetic theories. That same inclination, which was the foundation of his newspaper column (Comeau calls it "leitmotivic"),[43] had also by his own admission guided him in his dramatic works, and came in useful when he was writing librettos too: "Even in the operatic genre, which would seem to be more of a stranger to the spirit of observation than any other, I applied myself to capturing and differentiating the manners of the divers people that I placed upon the stage."[44] Jouy does not even try to resolve the unavoidable contradiction between the primacy of the marvelous and so realistic a mode of observation, between the elevated character of an exclusive artistic genre and the immediacy of everyday behavior. It is true that the only instances he gives of operas he wrote in accordance with that principle were those in which the "divers people" were distinctly exotic: the Indian inhabitants of Benares in *Les Bayadères*, Catholic knights and Islamic inhabitants of the Moorish Spain of 1480 in *Les Abencérages*, Spanish conquistadores and native Mexicans of 1519 in *Fernand Cortez*, and finally the Gauls of pre-Christian France in *Velleda*, a libretto never set to music. But even if that kind of exoticism could not serve indefinitely as a substitute for the marvelous that could no longer be taken for granted in the tragédie lyrique, Jouy's actual choice of words suggests the observation of the manners of people in real life, and not necessarily living in faraway places.

Jouy clearly had no notion of the far-reaching changes that general application of the "spirit of observation" might unleash in French opera,

42. "ont été plus fécondes peut-être en tableaux et en contrastes que presque toutes celles dont se composent nos précédentes annales"; "Discours préliminaire," *Oeuvres complètes*, 1:27. For another contemporary view on contrast, as the principal trait of the nineteenth century, see Duvergier de Hauranne, "Du Mélange du comique et du tragique," *Le Globe* 3 (January–August 1826): 385.

43. "Etienne Jouy," 138.

44. "Dans le genre de l'opéra même, qui semble plus étranger que tout autre à l'esprit d'observation, je me suis appliqué à saisir et à nuancer les moeurs des divers peuples que j'ai mis en scène." "Discours préliminaire," *Oeuvres complètes*, 1:26.

6 The aesthetics of "the marvelous" continued to dominate at the Opéra until 1826, and even exotic subjects were confined within the limits of a distinctly stereotyped classicism, as this engraving by Drouot illustrates. It shows the stage and auditorium on the opening night of the Salle Le Peletier, 16 August 1821. The stage is set for a scene in Catel's *Les Bayadères* (1810), with a libretto by Jouy.

but he did point out the consequences for costumes and scenery, urging that truth could never be too faithful, or fidelity too strict.[45] In insisting that the set-designer "cannot receive too deep an impression of, so to

45. "on ne peut apporter une vérité trop fidèle, une fidélité trop sévère"; *Essai*, 280 (1987 ed., 90).

speak, the local color"[46] he was still cautious in his use of the term which literary and musical historians associate nowadays, first and foremost, with Victor Hugo's preface to his play *Cromwell*, published two years later.

That famous aesthetic manifesto owes its reputation to the exaggeration with which Hugo stated his case and pressed his universalist claims: its importance as a turning point in the French theater, and hence as a milestone in the history of literature, has been exaggerated. For all the revolutionary verve of its style, very little of its content was really new. History as a source of subject matter for the stage had been urged as long ago as the 1770s, by Louis-Sébastien Mercier and Barnabé Farmian de Rosoi.[47] The concept of local color had been introduced by the classicist historian of literature Jean François de La Harpe in 1772,[48] and in the striving for "characteristic details"[49] Mercier and Rosoi had used it of literature.[50] As has recently been shown,[51] this new expression was associated with the music of operas as early as 1788,[52] after Grétry, in several of his works, had given the first examples of how dramatic compositions can be provided with local color.[53]

The development of local color to become one of the central categories of grand opéra will be followed in a later chapter. At this juncture it is enough to say that the search, from around 1800 onward, for the most precise local color possible is only a symptom of a new understanding of the arts, in which even the elevated genres of tragedy and opera are understood as expressions of contemporary reality, supplanting the older axiom that art is the mimetic imitation of nature.[54] The metaphor of literature as a mirror is associated especially with Stendhal and the novel, but it was current in the 1820s and '30s among many commentators, who took it up at first in order to express a certain

---

46. "[il] ne peut trop s'empreindre pour ainsi dire de la couleur locale"; ibid., 281 (1987 ed., 90).

47. See the discussion above in this chapter, and also Mercier, *Du Théâtre*, 144.

48. See Malakis, "The first use of 'couleur locale,'" 98.

49. "détails caractéristiques"; Mercier, *De la Littérature et des littérateurs*, 119; see also Temple-Patterson, "Poetic genesis," 128.

50. See Mercier, *Mon Bonnet de nuit*, 2:146 (also Temple-Patterson, "Poetic genesis," 144); Rosoi, *Dissertation sur le drame lyrique*, 44.

51. See Charlton, *Grétry*, 197–98.

52. See Le Vacher de Charnais, *Costumes et annales des grands théâtres de Paris*, 3ème année, 3(i):100–101.

53. See Charlton, *Grétry*, 172, 229–40, 312–15.

54. See Iknayan, *The Concave Mirror*, 3.

disquiet at the state of the arts in post-Revolutionary France. When the vicomte de Bonald described tragedy as a "faithful mirror of human life and society,"[55] he neither justified nor explained the metaphor, as if he referred to a well-known, traditional maxim. But, as Udo Schöning points out, the simile traditionally referred to comedy or the novel, and Bonald extended the usage in applying it to tragedy.[56] He went on in the same breath, however, to assert that tragedy "consists in the revolt of the passions and the triumph of reason."[57] It would therefore be completely wrong to interpret Bonald's dictum as an aesthetic maxim, for when we look more closely, it appears that his normative understanding of drama directly contradicted his recognition, in a later essay, that literature is an expression of the political and religious constitution of a society—an opinion he called fundamental.[58] Bonald was a convinced royalist, and what he said was in no way intended to be a hint to playwrights, but was simply a diagnosis of an additional symptom of the need to restore the ancien régime. In his view, the function of drama was not to portray events—that was history's role—but to be a school for society: "If history shows us all too often order disturbed by human passions, and virtue succumbing to the onslaught of crime, tragedy ought to restore order, and redress history."[59]

It was the next generation, that of Stendhal and Hugo, which resolved the contradiction between social reality on the one hand and moral and aesthetic pretension on the other, by dispensing with any mention of political order at all and thus turning the mirror metaphor into a defense against the charges of immorality and glorification of ugliness.[60] Jouy was still a long way from that liberal consensus when he remarked in the preface to his complete works that his oeuvre as a whole would be found to offer "the most direct reflection of the manners, customs, sentiments, and opinions that stirred France during the three

55. See above, introduction, n. 39.

56. See Schöning, *Literatur als Spiegel*, 35.

57. "consiste dans la révolte des passions et le triomphe de la raison"; Bonald, "Observations morales sur quelques pièces de théâtre" [1805], *Mélanges littéraires et philosophiques*, 1:109–45 (p. 136).

58. "Du Style et de la littérature" [1806], *Mélanges littéraires et philosophiques*, 1:284–349 (pp. 284 and 304, n. 1).

59. "Et si l'histoire nous montre trop souvent l'ordre troublé par les passions humaines, et la vertu succombant sous l'effort du crime, la tragédie doit rétablir l'ordre, redresser l'histoire"; "Observations morales sur quelques pièces de théâtre," *Mélanges littéraires et philosophiques*, 1:118.

60. See Heitmann, *Der Immoralismus-Prozeß gegen die französische Literatur*, 261–62.

great epochs in which they were written."[61] Much earlier than that, however, in an article published in 1815, he had already demonstrated how far his own position was from that of Bonald's rigorous moralism: "The theater is neither a school nor a painting of manners; but it can be considered as their mirror, in the sense that it is a place where manners are concentrated and reflected, and where the play of passions, prejudices, and public opinion can be more conveniently observed."[62] Practitioner of many trades that he was, Jouy abstained from commenting on how these ideas might relate to his opera librettos: it would in fact have been hard for him to bridge the gap between the conception of the spoken theater outlined in that sentence and his advocacy, for opera, of a theater "where everything speaks to the senses and the heart, where nothing is addressed to reason."[63] Like many of his contemporaries, he was convinced that music, with its supranational character, was not one of the arts that could be expected to be an expression of any one society.[64] All the same, he could hardly have denied that his librettos, too, reflect manners, customs, feelings, and opinions, for he himself had pointed out what the representation of "divers peoples" in them owed to conscientious observation.

The later chapters of this book will explore the extent to which that claim holds good in examples of grand opéra, from Rossini's *Guillaume Tell* (with libretto by Jouy) to Verdi's *Vêpres siciliennes* and *Ballo in maschera*. It is scarcely surprising that many of the features characteristic of both the librettos and their musical realization disclose themselves only after closer examination of contemporary manners, for much that was commonplace in nineteenth-century culture has long since vanished. What may be found more surprising is the direct influence of contemporary manners on the forms of spectacle cultivated in grand opéra,

61. "le reflet le plus direct des moeurs, des habitudes, des sentiments, et des opinions qui ont agité la France pendant les trois grandes époques où elles ont été écrites"; "Discours préliminaire," *Oeuvres complètes*, 1:27.

62. "Le théâtre n'est ni l'école ni la peinture des moeurs; mais il peut en être considéré comme le miroir, dans ce sens que c'est dans ce lieu qu'elles se concentrent, qu'elles se réfléchissent, et qu'on peut y observer plus commodément le jeu des passions, des préjugés, et de l'opinion publique." "Guillaume le franc-parleur, No. LIX," *Gazette de France*, 28 June 1815; also in Jouy, *Oeuvres complètes*, 5:280–89 (pp. 283–84).

63. "où tout parle aux sens et au coeur, où rien ne s'adresse à la raison"; *Essai*, 245 (1987 ed., 72).

64. See, for example, Lahalle, *Essai sur la musique*, 56; for the contrary view, however, see Ortigue, *De la Guerre des dilettanti*, 58; see also Brzoska, *Die Idee des Gesamtkunstwerks*, 142–53.

even if we allow for the fact that a number of composers for the Paris Opéra had very probably reflected on the close connection between their works and the change in perceptions and attitudes. It is true that Rossini, in 1856, long after he had retired from composing operas, replied confusedly that he didn't know, when the German composer Ferdinand Hiller asked him if he held political circumstances responsible for the predominance of the taste for tragedy and extravagant emotions in Italy at that time.[65] Meyerbeer, on the other hand, still active and more cosmopolitan than Rossini, was in no such doubt in 1852, when he replied to Jean F. Schucht, his future biographer: "You ask me if I have ever felt an inclination to follow Mendelssohn's example and set classical tragedies, by Sophocles for example, to music. My answer, simply, is no: works like that and their subject matter are too remote from the spirit of our time, they do not lend themselves to today's music."[66]

To back his view, Meyerbeer could refer to a lecture given in 1847 by Robert Griepenkerl, a German writer on music who held him in particularly high esteem and praised *Les Huguenots* as "the highest point to date in the developing progress of the operatic ideal. . . . Snatched hot from the issues of the present day, [*Les Huguenots* contained] the essence of the greatest concerns of our time."[67] This enthusiastic opinion was developed in positively Hegelian terms, with reference to the opera's conformity to "the laws of the perspectivist development of the World Spirit."[68] Griepenkerl was in no doubt of art's mission to be the "imprint and mirror image" of the universals of the time,[69] and he was equally sure of the relationship between his new operatic aesthetics and perceptions of events in world history at the turn of the century:

65. See "Plaudereien mit Rossini," in Hiller, *Aus dem Tonleben*, 2:1–84 (p. 48).

66. "Sie fragen mich, ob ich nicht auch Neigung gehabt, wie Mendelssohn, antike Tragödien, z. B. des Sophoklos, in Musik zu setzen. Ich sage einfach: nein, dergleichen Werke und Sujets liegen unserem Zeitgeiste zu fern und eignen sich nicht für unsere heutige Musik." Meyerbeer's letter to Schucht, 12 December 1852, in Schucht, *Meyerbeer's Leben und Bildungsgang*, 379. I am unable to pursue Heinz Becker's arguments (in his introduction to Meyerbeer, *Briefwechsel und Tagebücher*, 1:41–42, and in many later publications) against the authenticity of the letters quoted by Schucht, because the only available sources are secondary ones.

67. "die bis dahin letzte Spitze der fortschreitenden Entwicklung des Opernideals . . . das heiß herausgeholt aus den Fragen des gegenwärtigen Tages, den eigentlichen Kern der größesten Beziehungen unserer Zeit [birgt]"; Griepenkerl, *Die Oper der Gegenwart*, 25–26 (*NZM*, 103).

68. "den Gesetzen perspectivischer Entwicklung des Weltgeistes"; ibid., 29 (*NZM*, 104).

69. "Abdruck und Spiegelbild . . . des Universalgehaltes der Zeit"; ibid., 5 (*NZM*, p 98).

If it was still possible at the time of the first French Revolution for the German artist to ignore the volcanic eruptions of those events, and, in his solitary chamber, to scoff at this slash across the reckoning of a century, if it was possible in Germany to go on dreaming even when Napoleon's cannon were plowing our fields—it is not possible any longer.[70]

This same connection between art understood as "reality, vitality, present existence"[71] and the roar of the cannon in his own lifetime was expressed far more succinctly by Verdi in 1870. While working on *Aida* he referred to current events, unprompted and matter-of-factly, without a trace of awareness that there might be any incongruity between his words and the ambience of ancient Egypt which both the libretto and the first production were to attempt to reconstruct with meticulous exactitude. In order to give his librettist inspiration for the chorus of priests in the celebrated triumph scene in Act II, for which he himself had sketched a text on the lines of "we have conquered with the aid of divine providence," he laconically recommended reading what the king of Prussia—who was to be proclaimed as the first Hohenzollern German emperor within six months—was expressing about Prussian victories in the war being waged at that very time against France: "See King William's telegrams."[72]

70. "War es zur Zeit der ersten französischen Revolution in deutscher Kunst noch möglich, sich den vulkanischen Stößen dieses Ereignisses zu entziehen und in einsamer Kammer diesen Riß durch die Rechnung eines Jahrhunderts zu verachten; war es in Deutschland möglich, selbst da noch zu träumen, als Napoleons Kanonen unsere Aecker pflügten—so ist dieses jetzt durchaus nicht mehr möglich"; ibid., 7 (*NZM*, 98).

71. "Wirklichkeit, Lebendigkeit, gegenwärtiges Dasein"; ibid., 6 (*NZM*, 98).

72. "Vedi i telegrammi del re Guglielmo"; Verdi's letter to Antonio Ghislanzoni, 8 September 1870, *I copialettere*, 644.

·: 3 :·

ROSSINI AND
THE REVOLUTION

LE SIÈGE DE CORINTHE

TEXT
Luigi Balocchi (1766–1832) and Alexandre Soumet (1788–1845)

MUSIC
Gioachino Rossini (1792–1868)

FIRST PERFORMANCE
Paris, Académie Royale de Musique, 9 October 1826

PLACE AND DATE OF THE ACTION
Corinth, August 1458

CHARACTERS
Mahomet II (bass); Cléomène, leader of the Greeks and Pamyra's father
(tenor); Pamyra (soprano); Néoclès, young Greek soldier (tenor); Hiéros, aged
guardian of the catacombs (bass); Adraste, Cléomène's confidant (bass); Omar,
Mahomet's confidant (bass); Ismène, Pamyra's confidante (mezzo-soprano)

SYNOPSIS

ACT I
First setting: the entrance hall of the Governor's Palace. Cléomène has sum-
moned his troops to discuss the danger to the city, which is besieged by a Turkish army under Mahomet. The mood is pessimistic until first Néoclès and then
Hiéros encourage their fellow Greeks to vow to resist to the death (No. 1. *Introduction*, "Ta noble voix, seigneur"). Cléomène's plan to marry his daughter Pamyra to Néoclès meets with her refusal, for she has exchanged vows of love with
a certain Almanzor in Athens; there is no time to dwell on this emotional tangle,
however, for the men are called to defend the city against a new Turkish attack;
all Cléomène can win from Pamyra is a promise to kill herself rather than fall

63

into Turkish hands (No. 2. *Scène et trio:* "La Grèce est libre encor" / "Disgrâce horrible!").

Second setting: the marketplace in Corinth. Turkish troops gradually advance to the city's heart (No. 3. *Marche et choeur,* "La flamme rapide") and Mahomet praises their victory (No. 4. *Récit, air et choeur,* "Qu'à ma voix la victoire s'arrête!" / "Chef d'un peuple indomptable"). Some of the Greeks have barricaded themselves in the citadel, but Cléomène is brought before Mahomet as a prisoner; Pamyra comes to plead for her father, and is amazed when she recognizes in Mahomet the man she knew as Almanzor (No. 5. *Scène et final,* "Nous avons triomphé" / "Ah! L'amant qui m'enchaîne"). Cléomène tries to force her to admit publicly that she is betrothed to Néoclès, and curses her when she refuses, but she also resists Mahomet, who has her carried away by force.

ACT II

Mahomet's tent in the Turkish camp. Faced with the immediate prospect of marriage to Mahomet, the distraught Pamyra implores her dead mother to help her, and suddenly sees a gleam of hope for her country (No. 6. *Récitatif, air et choeur,* "Que vais-je devenir?" / "Du séjour de la lumière"). Although she loves Mahomet, she cannot share his tender feelings (No. 7. *Scène, duo et choeur,* "Rassure-toi . . . mon pouvoir t'environne" / "Que vois-je! ô ciel!") and watches the festivities put on in her honor in a state of confusion. After a bridal chorus (No. 8. *Ballade et choeur,* "L'hymen lui donne") and dances *(1er air de danse, 2e air de danse)* the ceremony culminates in a prayer to the Prophet (No. 9. *Hymne,* "Divin prophète"), which is interrupted by guards bringing in Néoclès, who has recklessly attempted a one-man attack on the Turkish camp. To save his life, Pamyra pretends he is her brother; she finally decides not to marry Mahomet, in spite of his angry threats, but to rejoin the Greeks, as the defenders of the citadel (visible in the distance) renew their resistance (No. 10. *Final,* "Il est son frère!").

ACT III

The catacombs of Corinth. Néoclès has escaped; he hears Pamyra and other Greek women praying for their country (No. 11. *Récit et prière,* "Avançons . . . oui, ces murs . . ." / "O toi que je revère") and feels renewed courage (No. 12. *Air,* "Grand Dieu! faut-il qu'un peuple"). Cléomène enters, and Néoclès begs him to pardon Pamyra, but it is only when she announces her astonishing decision to marry Néoclès after all that her father's anger is assuaged (No. 13. *Scène et trio,* "Cher Cléomène . . ." / "Céleste providence"). The two men are about to throw themselves into the fighting but are restrained by Hiéros who, in view of the hopelessness of the Greek position, administers a solemn oath to all the Greeks to die rather than be slaves, and, in a vision, foretells the rebirth of the Greek nation (No. 14. *Récit, scène et choeur,* "Je viens de parcourir" / "Fermez-vous tous vos coeurs à d'indignes alarmes?"). After the Greeks have left to fight their final battle, Pamyra addresses a last prayer to Heaven for mercy (No. 15. *Récit et prière,* "L'heure fatale approche . . ." / "Juste ciel! Ah! ta clémence"). Mahomet's army has massacred all the Greeks without mercy and set the city on fire; as he enters and tries to seize her by force she stabs herself (No. 16. *Final,* "Mais quels accents se font entendre!")

EDITIONS: The full score published by Troupenas in Paris in 1827 is available in many libraries in a reprint (*Early Romantic Opera* 14 [New York: Garland, 1980]); the piano-vocal score also published in 1827 is extremely rare.

RECOMMENDED RECORDING: The first (and, at the time of writing, only) recording of *Le Siège de Corinthe* was issued in 1992. It was recorded live at the Teatro Carlo Felice, Genoa, directed by Paolo Olmi with Marcello Lippi, Dano Raffanti, Luciana Serra, Maurizio Comencini, and Armando Caforio in the principal roles, and Vito Martino, Francesco Facini, and Francesca Provvisionato as the confidant(e)s. It has its weak points, especially in the declamation, but as a whole it gives a convincing impression of Rossini's first French opera.

GUILLAUME TELL

TEXT

Victor-Joseph Étienne de Jouy (1764–1846) and Hippolyte Bis (1789–1855)

MUSIC

Gioachino Rossini

FIRST PERFORMANCE

Paris, Académie Royale de Musique, 3 August 1829

PLACE AND DATE OF THE ACTION

the Swiss canton of Uri, July and August 1308.

CHARACTERS

Guillaume Tell (baritone), Arnold Melcthal (tenor), and Walter Furst (bass), Swiss confederates; Melcthal, Arnold's father (bass); Jemmy, Tell's son (soprano); Gesler, governor of the cantons of Schwyz and Uri (bass); Rodolphe, captain of Gesler's archers (tenor); Ruodi, a fisherman (tenor); Leuthold, a shepherd (baritone); Mathilde, a princess of the house of Habsburg, designated to govern in Switzerland (soprano); Hedwige, Tell's wife (mezzo-soprano)

SYNOPSIS

ACT I

Bürglen, outside Tell's house. While the Swiss peasants sing of the beauty of the day, and a young fisherman dreams of his sweetheart, Tell alone mourns the state of his oppressed homeland. All the others are looking forward to a wedding and welcome old Melcthal who has come to give a blessing to three happy couples (No. 1. *Introduction*, "Quel jour serein le ciel présage!"). Arnold obviously does not share the general mood of rejoicing, and is about to slip away to meet his beloved, Mathilde, when Tell starts to question him and wrests from him a promise to fight for their country (No. 2. *Récitatif et duo*, "Contre les feux du jour" / "Où vas-tu?") But Arnold stands apart during the blessing of the

bridal couples (No. 3. *Marche, récitatif et choeur,* "Sur nos têtes le soleil brille" /
"Ciel, qui du monde es la parure") and makes his escape when the sound of
Gesler's hunting horns indicates that Mathilde is nearby. The festivities continue with a bridal chorus (No. 4. *Choeur dansé,* "Hymenée, ta journée"), dances
(No. 5. *Pas de six*), and an archery contest won by Jemmy (No. 6. *Choeur dansé,*
"Gloire, honneur au fils de Tell!"). Suddenly Leuthold bursts on to the scene:
he has killed one of Gesler's men, who was attempting to rape his daughter, and
now begs for help in his flight from the other soldiers. The fisherman refuses
to row him away over the dangerous mountain torrent, but Tell is willing to
take the risk, and the chorus prays to God to protect the pair (No. 7. *Final 1er,*
"Dieu de bonté"). By the time the Austrians arrive Tell and Leuthold are in
safety; the soldiers make furious threats, in the hope of at least discovering the
name of Leuthold's savior. Old Melcthal encourages the Swiss not to betray Tell
and the enraged Austrians drag him away, leaving the Swiss to express their
anger helplessly.

ACT II

The high plateau of the Rütli. Gesler's men are hunting while Swiss herdsmen can be heard in the distance, driving their cattle down to the valley (No.
8. *Choeur de chasseurs et de Suisses,* "Quelle sauvage harmonie"). Mathilde, in love
with Arnold, remains alone behind the hunt and admits how much she prefers
simple nature to the glitter of the court (No. 9. *Récitatif et romance,* "Ils s'éloig-
nent enfin . . ." / "Sombre forêt"). Arnold arrives and the couple confess their
love to each other. He is so much in love that he is even ready to join the Austrian army to show himself worthy of her (No. 10. *Duo,* "Oui, vous l'arrachez à
mon âme"). Hearing footsteps, Mathilde flees, and Arnold finds himself confronting Tell and Walter who have followed him and now question him; at first
he defends his decision to join the side of the woman he loves, but when he
learns that the Austrians have killed his father he at last embraces the cause of
Swiss freedom (No. 11. *Trio,* "Quand l'Helvétie est un champ de supplices").
He joins in the secret meeting convened in the mountains by representatives of
the cantons Unterwalden, Schwyz, and Uri, and takes part in the solemn oath
they make to rid their homeland of Austrian tyranny (No. 12. *Final 2e,* "Des
profondeurs du bois immense").

ACT III

First setting: a ruined chapel near the fortress of Altdorf. Arnold has come to
bid Mathilde a last farewell; she grieves for the hopeless situation and renounces
her love with a heavy heart (No. 13. *Scène et air,* "Arnold, d'où naît ce désespoir?" / "Pour notre amour plus d'espérance").

Second setting: the marketplace at Altdorf. Gesler orders a celebration of Austrian rule and, setting up his hat as a trophy, he forces the Swiss to bow before
it (No. 14. *Marche et choeur,* "Gloire au pouvoir suprême!"). While soldiers force
Swiss women to dance with them, some Tyrolese sing a song from their homeland (No. 15. *Pas de trois et choeur tyrolien,* "A nos chants viens mêler tes pas!";
No. 16. *Pas de soldats*). Tell enters with his son Jemmy, and is the first Swiss to
refuse to pay homage to the governor's hat; the furious Gesler orders his arrest
(No. 17. *[Final 3e] Quatuor et choeur,* "C'est là cet archer redoutable"). When

Tell tries to send his son away, the vindictive governor intervenes and forces the horrified father to prove his skill at archery by placing an apple on the boy's head and commanding Tell to shoot at it (*Scène et final*, "Je te bénis en répandant des larmes" / "Qu'ai-je appris? sacrifice affreux!"). Although Tell brings off the shot without touching Jemmy, he is not released because he frankly admits that a second arrow which he took from his quiver was intended to kill Gesler if the first had hit the boy. Mathilde comes on the scene at this moment and manages to secure Jemmy's freedom, but the angry soldiers drag Tell away in chains while the Swiss curse them.

ACT IV

First setting: Melcthal's house. Arnold recognizes that Tell's arrest means that he must lead the Swiss. After a moment of quiet reflection the confederates arrive and he rouses them to vengeance against the oppressors (No. 18. *Récitatif, air et choeur,* "Ne m'abandonne point, espoir de la vengeance!" / "Asile héréditaire").

Second setting: a rock above the Lake of Lucerne, Tell's house in the background. Hedwige is filled with anxiety for her husband's life. At this very moment, in spite of a severe storm, Tell is being brought across the lake by boat. He manages to free himself, jumps on land and shoots Gesler dead (No. 19, *final 4e,* "Suivez-moi, suivez-moi!"). The rising of the other confederates, meanwhile, has been successful; Arnold, having taken Altdorf, comes to Tell's house and all sing in praise of their regained liberty.

EDITIONS: The full score as published in the *Edizione critica delle opere di Gioachino Rossini* (Critical Edition of the Works of Gioachino Rossini), section I: Opere, vol. 39, edited by M. Elizabeth C. Bartlet (Pesaro: Fondazione Rossini, 1992) reconstructs the version given on 14 August 1829, the last performance of the work before Rossini left for Italy. The appendixes of this edition include all the material cut before the première, the original version of Act IV, material cut by Rossini after the première, and material for the versions of 1831 (Paris) and 1840 (Bologna). The critical edition also contains a volume of texts which include the draft version of the libretto by Jouy and Solomé's production book *(mise-en-scène)* for the first production. The full score published by Troupenas in Paris in 1829, available in many libraries in a reprint (*Early Romantic Opera* 17 [New York: Garland, 1980]), does not represent any version actually performed in Paris; while it contains most of the numbers composed for Act IV but cut before the première, it does not have a ballet which was performed at the première. The piano-vocal score, corresponding to the Troupenas edition, was frequently reprinted and many copies survive.

RECOMMENDED RECORDING: only one recording of a performance in the original French language can be recommended, and that follows the complete text of the Troupenas edition. It was made in 1973 under Lamberto Gardelli, with Gabriel Bacquier (Tell), Nicolai Gedda (Arnold), and Montserrat Caballé (Mathilde). Though there are weaknesses in the balance between individual voices it gives an excellent impression of this monumental work.

"A Veritable Revolution"

On 9 October 1826 the Paris Opéra for the first time gave the première of a work by Gioachino Rossini, who until then had pursued his successful career only in Italian opera. The traditional aesthetic of tragédie lyrique was in decline by that date and, like politics and literature, opera was beginning to be affected by the tendencies now associated with the "year of revolution"—1830—as well as the cultural phenomenon known as Romanticism. In this situation the première was anticipated with especially keen excitement, for *Le Siège de Corinthe* was Rossini's first opera with a libretto in the French language. It was not really a new work (it reused parts of *Maometto II*, written by Rossini for Naples in 1820) but nevertheless many observers recognized this première as a revolutionary event in the history of French opera. One of the first people actually to use the word "revolution" in association with it was La Rochefoucauld, the minister responsible for the Opéra, who reported to the king in a letter of 20 October that "*Le Siège de Corinthe* is a veritable revolution in French opera."[1]

"Revolution" is a strange word to come from the pen of an aristocrat who desired more ardently than other members of the government of Charles X to see the ancien régime fully restored and all the consequences of the revolution of 1789 swept from the face of the earth. But if La Rochefoucauld—well known for his moral rectitude—was unshakable in his political opinions, at the same time he clearly believed that it was the function of the arts to progress, step by step, to new heights. It was only natural, therefore, that he should connect Rossini's arrival on the scene of French opera with the last major advances in its history: the new dramaturgy of Rameau's works of the 1730s and 1740s, and the overwhelming success of Gluck's "reform operas" in the 1770s. Both of those developments had been controversial from the first and led to the publication of mountains of pamphlets. The word "revolution," coined in connection with astronomy and apparently first applied to the arts in 1755,[2] was bandied about in these prints—in Chabanon's obituary for Rameau in 1764, and in a pamphlet by Marmontel in 1777—several decades before it became a reality in politics;[3] when a collection of the most important of the pamphlets to do with the Gluck/Piccinni controversy was published under the title *Mémoires pour servir à l'histoire de la*

1. See La Rochefoucauld-Doudeauville, *Mémoires*, 9:248.
2. See Méhégan, *Considérations sur les révolutions des arts;* admittedly, the word appears only in the title.
3. See Vendrix, "La Notion de révolution," 71–73.

révolution opérée dans la musique par le M. le Chevalier Gluck, the word was used as a matter of course to designate the effect of Gluck's reforms. So it is likely that it came unbidden to La Rochefoucauld in 1826, without carrying any political implications, when he thought fit to proclaim the end of the age of Gluck and his followers; the words he uses in his letter to the king ("une véritable révolution opérée à l'Opéra français") suggest that he was familiar with the title of the 1781 collection.

It has to be said that the minister was promoting his own interests when he placed so high an estimate on the success of *Le Siège de Corinthe* and set Rossini on the same level as Gluck. It was La Rochefoucauld who had forged an enduring bond between Rossini and Paris when he appointed the then thirty-two-year-old composer to be director of the Théâtre Italien in 1824,[4] and he proved his unconditional admiration for him by his forbearance when Rossini failed to meet his contractual obligation to write French operas at regular intervals.

Rossini's reputation could hardly have failed to reach even those who did not venerate him as enthusiastically as La Rochefoucauld and the novelist Stendhal. It is no exaggeration to call him the most successful opera composer of his day, even the most successful composer of any kind, when we consider that Beethoven's reputation was slow to spread outside Austria and Germany. He achieved what no composer before him had done, in subsuming the regional differences of Italian schools of opera within his style, and his works were constantly before the public, in opera houses all over Europe and even the Americas, from Lisbon to Odessa and St. Petersburg, from London through Vienna to Corfu and Malta, and from New York to Buenos Aires. He was compared to the greatest military conqueror of the age already in his own lifetime,[5] and Edward Dent endorsed the comparison a century later:

> Rossini has been called the Napoleon of music, and the comparison is not altogether absurd, for Rossini too conquered the world and did not enjoy his conquest long, though he survived his age, as Napoleon did at St Helena. Before Rossini, Italian music had always been local and provincial, Neapolitan or Venetian; Rossini made it Italian and universal.[6]

Rossini was, admittedly, not the first composer to continue in Paris a career which had started in Italy, but unlike Lully, Piccinni, Paër, or Spontini, he did not arrive in the French capital until long after his op-

4. See Janet Johnson, "Rossini e le sue opere al Théâtre Italien," 232–36.
5. See "Filosofia della musica" [1836], in Mazzini, *Scritti*, 8:117–65 (p. 138); Vitet, *Études sur les beaux-arts*, 1:80.
6. *The Rise of Romantic Opera*, 116.

eras had made his name throughout Europe. Consequently he could get away both with making the Parisians wait two years before a première of any kind was seen at the Opéra, and with giving them reworked versions of two earlier Italian works—*Le Siège de Corinthe* was followed in 1827 by *Moïse et Pharaon*, another piece originally composed for Naples—before at last producing a work composed expressly for Paris: *Guillaume Tell*, first performed in 1829.[7]

Even if belief in the revolutionary significance of *Le Siège de Corinthe* owed something to hyperenthusiasm, it survived Meyerbeer's great triumphs and was still maintained long after the opera itself, along with *Moïse et Pharaon*, had disappeared from the repertory.[8] (Only in the twentieth century did opinion change, when historians allowed themselves to be influenced by Wagner's version of events and selected instead Auber's *Muette de Portici* as the first work of the new era in French opera.) What one critic wrote, at the time of the première of Rossini's second French opera, *Moïse et Pharaon*, on 26 March 1827, could have been said fifty years later: "Whenever we have had occasion to mention *Le Siège de Corinthe* we have said that the work would mark the dawn of a new era for the Académie Royale de Musique."[9]

What was it about *Le Siège de Corinthe* that made people regard it as revolutionary? As will be shown in more detail below, its subject matter breaks with the conventions of tragédie lyrique, and Rossini's numerous musical innovations introduced things never heard before in the Paris Opéra. But the astonishing reaction it produced is best explained by a look at French opera in the years immediately before 1826. A crisis had built up which in the last analysis was nothing more than the expression of the unsolved aesthetic problems of an outmoded genre. No composer of international rank had worked at the Opéra since Spontini's departure for Berlin in 1820. Paër, Boieldieu, Hérold, and Auber preferred, with rare exceptions, the more flexible genre of opéra comique. The Académie Royale de Musique was abandoned to conservatives like Berton, Kreutzer, and Reicha, who lived up to the opera house's official title with works that looked steadfastly back to Gluck. Not even the most patriotic of their contemporaries could any longer close their eyes to

7. See Bartlet, "Rossini e l'Académie Royale de Musique."
8. See Dauriac, *Rossini*, 62–63; on the question of historical periods, see Lajarte, *Bibliothèque musicale du Théâtre de l'Opéra*, and Bloom, "A review of Fétis's *Revue musicale*," 76–77.
9. "Chaque fois que nous avons eu occasion de parler du *Siège de Corinthe*, nous avons dit que de cet ouvrage daterait une ère nouvelle pour notre académie royale de musique"; *L'Étoile*, 28 March 1827, p. 4; see also *Le Globe* 5 (1827–28), p. 211, and Véron, *Mémoires*, 1:262.

the sorry state of academic petrifaction into which tragédie lyrique had fallen. Music-lovers were all of one mind and flocked to the Théâtre Italien, where Rossini's Italian opere serie were hailed with delight. It was the Querelle des Bouffons of the 1750s all over again, with Italian opera once again luring Parisian audiences away from their French rivals. But it must have been an additional blow to French national pride that on this occasion the Italians took the lead not only in the light genre of opera buffa but also in the far more prestigious field of serious opera on the grand scale.

Rossini's transfer of compositional techniques from Italian opera seria to a genre that had been closed to more recent Italian influences until then was not a very surprising step for him to take in this situation. Already in the overture of *Le Siège de Corinthe* those famous Rossinian crescendos are heard that were completely without precedent in the context of a French tragédie lyrique. And both here and in *Moïse et Pharaon* one year later Rossini resorted to typically Italian solutions to problems of musico-dramatic structure and form.

But although a large amount of the music of *Le Siège de Corinthe* is recycled from *Maometto II*, an opera seria composed six years earlier, it represents "a veritable revolution" from the standpoint of Italian opera, too. In the following pages three particularly prominent elements in the opera will be used to show how it not only overthrows every tradition of French tragédie lyrique but also adds something wholly new to Rossini's oeuvre. For an understanding of the third of these, the new role of the chorus in his French operas, we shall also have to look in some detail at the first entirely new work that he composed for Paris, *Guillaume Tell*, with a libretto by Victor-Joseph Étienne de Jouy, first performed in 1829, and we shall do that in the second half of this chapter.

STORIES FROM HISTORY

The subject of *Le Siège de Corinthe* is an incident from modern history: Rossini and his librettists, Balocchi and Soumet, depict the last hours of Corinth before it fell to the Turks in 1458. Radicals like Mercier and Rosoi had raised a demand for historical subject matter as long ago as 1770, and Jouy had repeated it more recently, but this was the first time that a successful French opera appeared to meet the demand without the prompting of the government of the day for its own propaganda purposes. A closer look at Rossini's opera of 1826 does show, admittedly, that in many respects the historical element so essential to later grand opéra is only hinted at here, and that while it is present in the libretto it scarcely informs the musical realization of the events. Nevertheless, Balocchi, Soumet, and the composer, who undoubtedly had a voice in the choice of subject, struck a contemporary nerve with a theme that corresponded exactly to the new perceptual expectations of a society undergoing change.

The era stretching from the Revolution of 1789 to the fall of Napoleon had left traces in France which the restoration of the Bourbons in 1815 had been unable to erase. In a mere twenty-six years, the country had witnessed the end of a thousand-year-old monarchy, the death on the scaffold of a king who had once reigned by "the grace of God," the rise of a Corsican army officer to be the first emperor of France, and his subsequent fall, not once but twice. Less than two years had passed between the moment when Napoleon ruled almost all continental Europe and the entry of foreign troops into Paris for the first time in four hundred years.

It is not surprising that such upheavals, during which new structures proved to be even less durable than the old ones, resulted in a new sense of the impermanence of historical events, and, indeed, a new sensitivity toward history and its capacity for arousing passions.[10] A new historical awareness came into being at the beginning of the nineteenth century, as was very clearly described by Arnold Hauser (though he failed to provide a proper definition of the crucial term "romanticism" and underestimated the significance of class barriers, which continued to exist):

> Historicism, which was connected with a complete reorientation of culture, was the expression of deep existential changes and corresponded to an upheaval which shook the very foundations of society. The political revolution had abolished the old barriers between the classes and the economic revolution had intensified the mobility of life to a previously inconceivable degree. Romanticism was the ideology of the new society and the expression of the world-view of a generation which no longer believed in absolute values, could no longer believe in any values without thinking of their relativity, their historical limitations. It saw everything tied to historical suppositions, because it had experienced, as part of its own personal destiny, the downfall of the old and the rise of the new culture.[11]

The contours of this slow development only became visible in retrospect, and it is a far from straightforward matter to map it in any great detail. It is only very rarely goal-directed and is full of contradictions,

---

10. See Koselleck, *Futures Past*, 149.
11. Hauser, *The Social History of Art*, 661–62.

which modern historians have identified in the light of established models from the history of knowledge, where, as Wolf Lepenies has remarked, it is "scarcely possible to arrive at a precise chronology of temporalizing and spacializing tendencies," for any attempt to do so comes up against the fact that development in different disciplines is not simultaneous, and more especially the fact "that at the same time and in one and the same discipline there can be observed both processes of temporalization and denaturalization and tendencies toward de-historicization and renaturalization of temporal concepts."[12] And even if very little precise research has been published as yet in the field of the general history of mentalités, such principles probably apply with equal validity to the new interest in history shown by the forerunners of the modern entertainment industry, namely the novel calculated to reach a mass readership and the theater.[13]

The greatest significance attaches to the historical novel in the first instance, for its intention, Eberhard Lämmert writes, was "the restitution of collective historical experience as the means of preserving history as 'story.'"[14] It was possible to represent history as something that could be experienced collectively in retrospect, thus avoiding raising the fearful question "What will happen next?" As Lämmert says:

> The subject matter available [to the historical novel] is an area of history that can be contained within limits, in two respects: firstly, the history is past, and therefore can be surveyed as a whole, in retrospect, and secondly it can be referred to the present situation both as prehistory and as a parallel or contrasting mirror—either way, as something settled.

The prime examples of this new genre were the novels of Sir Walter Scott, which reached France from 1816 onward and had the same enormous success as elsewhere. Even if a critical distancing became apparent after 1827, among discriminating readers and critics,[15] it failed to trickle down to the general reading public, who continued during the 1830s to relish entertainment of a kind that kept them turning the pages and, above all, allowed them to identify with the characters and situations. The total numbers of editions of Scott in French translation rose from approximately 200,000 volumes in 1824, to 1.5 million in 1830, and to 2 million in 1840.[16]

12. Lepenies, *Das Ende der Naturgeschichte*, 120–21.
13. See Schalk, "Über Historie und Roman," 41; and Gerbod, "La Scène parisienne."
14. "Zum Wandel der Geschichtserfahrung," 509.
15. See Massmann, *Die Rezeption der historischen Romane Sir Walter Scotts*, 80.
16. Ibid., 11.

It is tempting to see a direct connection between the popularity of Scott's work and the new interest in the representation of historical subjects manifested in French opera from the time of Rossini's *Siège de Corinthe* onward.[17] But however much Scott's narrative technique may have contributed to individual librettos by Eugène Scribe, whose work was first performed at the Paris Opéra in 1828, it would be wrong to regard Scott as the sole source of a new form of spectacle which was to revolutionize that institution. As Jouy's *Essai* of 1826 shows, it was only a matter of time before the repeated demand for historical subjects met with some response. At the same time, the earliest operatic adaptations of works by Scott—Rossini's Neapolitan opera seria *La donna del lago* (1819)[18] and Auber's French opéra comique *Leicester* (1823)[19]—largely ignored the historical authenticity for which the novels strove, and concentrated on the romantic coloring instead. In that respect they are aligned with the genre of opera that, in the early years of the century, had responded to the challenge of the "Ossianic" poetry of Macpherson.[20]

In fact, the stage of the Paris Opéra had been the scene of some not very successful experiments at depicting events from modern history in the 1780s and '90s,[21] followed in 1809 by *Fernand Cortez*, which was produced at Napoleon's command and written according to his own personal specifications. This idealized representation of the conquest of Mexico by a magnanimous general was intended as propaganda on behalf of the Emperor's Spanish campaign, but after a few performances it became clear that the "ambiguities" inherent both in the libretto, by Jouy and Esménard, and in Spontini's music obscured the intended effect.[22] Although the opera was later so thoroughly overhauled that it was possible to stage it again after the Bourbon restoration,[23] it remained a very rare example of operatic representation of events from less than three centuries before the date of composition. Other operas written to glorify Napoleon, such as Le Sueur's *Le Triomphe de Trajan* (1807), took their subject matter from those seemingly inexhaustible sources, Roman history and classical mythology. Many other operas produced in Paris

17. See Finscher, "Aubers *La muette de Portici*," 88–89.
18. See Ambrose, "*La donna del lago.*"
19. See Mitchell, *The Walter Scott Operas.*
20. See Ambrose, "Walter Scott, Italian opera and romantic stage-setting," 64–66; Jahrmärker, *Ossian;* Wessel, *Die Ossian-Dichtung,* 133–44, 172–83.
21. See Bartlet, "The new repertory at the Opéra," 108.
22. See Joly, "Les Ambiguités de la guerre napoléonienne."
23. See Gerhard, "*Fernand Cortez,*" 94–97; on the prehistory of the revision of 1817, see also Joly, "Gli elementi spettacolari nel *Fernand Cortez,*" 74–79.

between 1815 and 1826 did the same. The only exceptions to the rule were operas set in Gaul (France, that is, at the time of the Roman Empire) and the isolated case of García's *La Mort du Tasse* (1821), which presented a mystically transfigured portrait of the sixteenth-century poet.

Rossini, however, did not need a royal command to break new ground in *Le Siège de Corinthe*, the subject matter of which had no less contemporary relevance in the late 1820s than the conquest of Mexico had had in 1809. The struggle of the Greeks to regain the independence they had lost in the fifteenth century was followed with great sympathy in Paris. As in 1458, in the episode from which the opera takes its name, so too in real life in 1826 Greek soldiers were facing a Turkish army led by a general called Mahomet. In one respect—the decision to connect the plot with the siege of Corinth in 1458—the libretto ignores the procedures that would later be taken for granted in grand opéra where history formed the basis of the plot. For Rossini and his colleagues it was clearly good enough to transpose the events of his six-year-old opera *Maometto II*, which centered on the Turkish conquest of the Venetian colony of Negroponte, in northern Greece, to a place which could stand as the epitome of Greek culture in the eyes of an audience whose philhellenism was sincere but lacked the foundation of familiarity with historical detail. In its representation of the merciless massacre of the population of Negroponte in 1470, *Maometto II* corresponds reasonably well to the historical facts, even to the presence of real people like Paolo Erisso and Alvise Calbo among the defenders;[24] but those events bore little resemblance to the fall of Corinth, apart from the bald fact of the involvement of Mehmet II. In reality, after a protracted siege and negotiations about the ways and means of the surrender, Corinth capitulated on 6 August 1458 without bloodshed.[25]

Although Rossini and his librettists may have regarded concrete historical events as interchangeable within certain limits, *Le Siège de Corinthe* nevertheless already provides a model of the way that French grand opéra would later deal with selected episodes from modern European history. In the dramatic representation of the bloody conflict between the Greeks and the Turks, the perspective changes repeatedly, showing first one side and then the other, before the Greeks are annihilated in the final scene, in which, too, the fictional love affair of the Greek girl, Pamyra, and the Turkish general, Mahomet, comes to its apparently inevitable end. This basic pattern was to dominate French

24. See Babinger, *Mehmed der Eroberer*, 300–302.
25. Ibid., 168–69.

opera in the coming decades. Even when operas were set in classical antiquity, like Donizetti's *Les Martyrs* (1840), or had "romantic," folk- or fairy-tale plots, like Meyerbeer's *Robert le diable* (1831), they were invested with historicizing elements, for in a single step Rossini and his librettists had established the convention of a plot based on the bloody confrontation of two hostile nations or races, with a fictional love affair between two people from those opposing sides, so that not only did the historical episode end with the defeat or even massacre of one of the hostile groups, but also the love interest was irrevocably doomed.

Even if the form in which such episodes reached the stage bore only the faintest resemblance to any historical "truth," the pattern conformed to the expectations of an audience which had ceased to believe in indestructible institutions, after having lived through historical developments as a process of collective experience. The survivors of the 1789 Revolution had grown skeptical, and no longer looked to historical subject matter for the sublime elements, subsuming the fate of individuals, which had been invoked in the heroic epics and propagandizing spectacles of the years immediately following 1789, and even, still, in *Fernand Cortez*. In opera as elsewhere, the heroic interpretation of history yielded to a disillusioned view, which could not separate the fate of the individual from the remorseless processes of the apparently invincible might of history.

The Unhappy Ending

With the disappearance both of traditional ideas of heroism and of the convention of a celebratory divertissement at the end of a work, it became imperative to find an ending appropriate to an opera with historical subject matter representing the enmity between two parties. Jouy had already encountered this difficulty in writing the libretto of *Fernand Cortez* in 1809: he called it the "principal stumbling block,"[26] and admitted that he had only avoided and not surmounted it. A little less than twenty years later, in his *Essai*, he was still true to the classical convention of the happy ending and declared that "the dénouement of every opera should be sudden, unforeseen, true to life, and happy,"[27] but for the young Rossini, and for all his contemporaries influenced by their reading of historical novels, the question of the appropriate dénouement presented itself with new urgency.

26. See above, 49.
27. "Le dénouement de tout opéra doit être prompt, imprévu, vraisemblable et heureux." Jouy, *Essai*, 245 (1987 ed., 72).

7   This watercolor of the set for Act III of Rossini's *Siège de Corinthe* is by the designer Cicéri's pupil Auguste Caron. All the conventionality of the columnar classicist architecture has been stripped from it in this scene of destruction.

So another of the experiments that Rossini undertook in *Le Siège de Corinthe* was a new kind of ending, again deserving the epithet "revolutionary." In ending with the heroine's suicide, as in *Maometto II*, Rossini uncompromisingly broke with a convention disregarded only rarely and in exceptional circumstances in tragédie lyrique. Not content with that, however, Rossini went further in the new Parisian version of his opera and intensified the final scene so greatly that his French librettists explicitly disowned it: in the published libretto they gave it an ending fundamentally different from the one in the first edition of the score.

Only a comparison of the closing scene of *Maometto II* with those two versions of the corresponding scene in *Le Siège de Corinthe*[28] reveals how radically the opera as it was finally performed in Paris differed from all precedents and possible models, even though its setting in the cata-

28. For a synoptic printing of the two versions of the Paris text, see Gerhard, "*Fernand Cortez*," 107–8; and idem, "'Une véritable révolution,'" 22–23.

combs *("les tombeaux de Corinthe")* appeared to adhere to the convention
of a place below ground, the *luogo sotterraneo* established by Metastasio.
Both Pamyra and her "forerunner" Anna in *Maometto II* resolve the conflict between patriotic duty and love for Mahomet, who has in both
cases subjugated their homeland, by stabbing themselves. However, in
the original Italian version of 1820 the suicide, enacted on stage in the
audience's sight, is the dominant event of the whole final scene. In the
Italian libretto it was the subject of a tragic monologue in recitative,[29]
from which Rossini fashioned a large-scale farewell aria for the prima
donna, with only a brief chorus to follow it. Although the published
libretto of the French opera does not provide for a bravura scene of that
kind, Pamyra's suicide comes at the end of a closing ensemble which
would still have given the composer the opportunity to put his heroine
in the musical foreground and depict the contrast of her feelings with
the confusion reigning in the breast of her lover, Mahomet, and also
with the sight of Corinth going up in flames in the background. But
although the version performed on the first night appears to have conformed to the libretto,[30] the ending in the published score is different,
with the suicide marginalized, taking place while the Turkish soldiers
ruthlessly put all Greeks to the sword. The manuscript production book
(livret de mise en scène) prescribes: "Through the flames and the ruins,
the Musulmans are seen pursuing the Greeks and slaughtering them
furiously" *(A travers les flammes et les décombres, on voit les musulmans poursuivre les Grecs et les égorger avec rage),*[31] but although this document includes all the important details of the staging, it does not mention Pamyra's suicide, and in the first printed edition of Rossini's score, too,
her last words to Mahomet—"Listen to our wedding hymns, behold
our nuptial torches" ("Entends les chants de notre fête; vois les flam-
beaux de notre hymen")—occupy only five bars or four seconds of music, which, in the context of a highly unusual operatic finale, scarcely
register as a decisive event.

Everything about this finale is unusual: not only Pamyra's part but
also that of the chorus is kept to a minimum. The singing breaks off
on the unresolved dominant with the Greeks' final invocation of their
fatherland, sung "at a distance" *(dans le lointain).* But even before that

29. See Cagli, "L'edizione critica dell'opera lirica," 25–26.

30. Until now, this version had to be reconstructed from the performance materials
(F-Po, Mat. 19 [239]). The edition of *Le Siège de Corinthe* forthcoming in the Edizione
critica delle opere di Gioachino Rossini will make use of that material. I am indebted to
Elizabeth Bartlet for drawing this particular substantial variant to my attention.

31. F-Po, C. 4895.

the vocal parts are treated as wholly secondary in their importance for the musical structure, which is dominated by an incessantly repeated, eight-bar, unison figure in the orchestra. The mechanical rigidity of this figure is made even more unnatural by the repetition in every bar of the dynamic marking ($f \implies$) which destroys every conceivable sense of musical continuity. This drastic musical device makes it plain to every ear that the suicide of one person no longer has any significance amid the general carnage. The uncontrollable hordes overwhelm the individual, and the human voice is swamped by the machine-like orchestra, which has a postlude lasting some eighty seconds, longer than the whole of the first part of the finale when voices are still singing.

It is not surprising that this unconventional formal device was not repeated until 1855, when Verdi tried something similar in *Les Vêpres siciliennes*, once again overruling the librettist's intention. The problem that Rossini and his collaborators ran into here is all too obvious: the role of the vocal soloists has been a crucial constituent throughout the opera until the very end, when they are suddenly made to appear superfluous.

The last two sentences in the manuscript production book give us a clue to understanding this unusual conception: "The entire stage is on fire! The curtain falls on this horrifying tableau" *(Tout le théâtre est en feu! Le rideau baisse sur cet horrible tableau)*. The relentlessness of the drive toward the unhappy ending makes a more realistic staging possible for the first time. It was no longer a question of attempting "to soften the odious aspects" of the victory, as Jouy had tried to do in *Fernand Cortez*. The producer was given a free hand to represent all the horrors of warfare: indeed, the phrase "this horrifying tableau" might stand as the motto for the closing scenes of the majority of nineteenth-century operas after 1826.

It is true that Rossini's extremely reductive music did not go so far as to elevate the ugliness in beauty, as Victor Hugo was to recommend in the preface to *Cromwell* a year later,[32] but it followed contemporary examples in allowing ugliness the right to exist on the stage in the name of truth.[33] It was an early manifestation of a new aesthetics of horror,[34] especially as Rossini went farther than any composer who followed him at the Paris Opéra, in that he did not provide a single appeasing element to counter the effect of the wholesale massacre. With this drastic inten-

32. *Théâtre complet*, 1:409–54.
33. See Grobert, *De l'Exécution dramatique*, 232.
34. See Bohrer, *Die Ästhetik des Schreckens*.

sification of the unhappy ending he darkened the previously idyllic landscape of opera with the horrors that were part and parcel of the experience of the audiences of the 1820s. What Grétry had been able to
express in words, in his vivid description of the execution of Louis XVI,
but not in his music, was achieved here by Rossini in its full force: the
artistic representation of horror.

The proof that this new style of operatic finale conformed to the
perceptual expectations of contemporary audiences lies in the fact that
Rossini's experiment was repeated in almost all later operas: by 1830 the
traditional happy ending, the *lieto fine*, had become the exception. After
1826 the happy ending was not only rare, as a matter of statistics, but it
also put a strain on the immanent dramaturgy of those works that had
one. The final acts of Rossini's *Moïse et Pharaon*, his *Guillaume Tell*, and
Meyerbeer's *Robert le diable* all reveal the difficulties. In the case of *Moïse
et Pharaon* they led the composer to write two radically different versions of the closing scene,[35] while the degree to which the happy ending
of *Guillaume Tell* conflicted with the dramaturgy of the first act will become clear later in this chapter. Meyerbeer, too, had problems in constructing a convincing happy ending for *Robert le diable:* with barely a
month to go before the première he contemplated having the Archangel
Michael appear in an aerial machine.[36] Even though he abandoned this
recourse to the long obsolete device of the deus ex machina, he only
managed to bring about the *lieto fine* by means of an abrupt change of
scene at the end of Act V, which flooded the final tableau in visionary
light and obviously derived from the compromise found in the endings
of Rodolphe Kreutzer's *La Mort d'Abel* (1810, 1823), García's *Mort du
Tasse* (1821), Reicha's *Sapho* (1822), and above all the first version of
Spontini's *Olimpie* (1819): in all of these an apparently inevitable tragic
ending is transformed into nothing less than an apotheosis. This entailed an element of unreality, which is exaggerated in the case of Meyerbeer's opera by the orchestration, especially the arpeggios emanating
from two harps placed in the wings.

Even if the introduction of the unhappy ending into French opera
can be explained in terms of changes in the attitudes and expectations
of the audience, the timing of it and, above all, the suddenness with
which the new convention took hold after 1826 are surprising. A com-

35. See Gerhard, "L'eroe titubante," 121–24.
36. See Meyerbeer's pocket diary, 28 October 1831, *Briefwechsel*, 2:150; see also Frese,
Dramaturgie der großen Opern Giacomo Meyerbeers, 30; Rieger, "Eugène Scribe et l'anticipation," 116.

parison with Italian opera seria, in particular, in which final scenes involving murder and suicide had become steadily more common since
1788, prompts the question as to why "tragic" endings remained almost
unknown during the much more turbulent revolutionary and Napoleonic years in France, only to make an appearance at a time of relative
political stability. One possible answer, that in the 1820s Parisian operagoers no longer needed escapist reassurances, does not explain why the
lieto fine, an obvious symptom of the dominance of court patronage in
the lyric theater, began to lose ground in Italy, politically one of the
most backward countries in Europe, nearly forty years earlier.

This question about the gradual disappearance of happy endings
from Italian opera has only recently been formulated, and it will not be
easy to find an answer,[37] but the new preference for unhappy—indeed,
horrifying—endings in French opera can only be explained in connection with changed perceptions of characters that we will explore
presently. The difference between the "hero" in grand opéra and his
counterpart in librettos of the Metastasian school is comparable to the
difference Arnold Hauser described between the heroes of bourgeois
and classical tragedy. In classical tragedy (and Metastasian opera) the
hero is presented as "an independent, autonomous intellectual entity,"
but in bourgeois tragedy and grand opéra he is one who "instead of
controlling concrete reality . . . is himself controlled and absorbed by
it."[38] In other words, French opera introduced the tragic ending—previously reserved, with very few exceptions, for spoken drama—at the
very moment when tragedy in the strict sense was no longer possible.
The fact that the generation of around 1830 would no longer have accepted that opera was inferior to spoken tragedy in aesthetic rank is
even more important with respect to the future history of European
opera. Both in appropriating the "tragic" ending and in returning to the
five acts of classical French tragedy, as Scribe did in *La Muette de Portici*
(1828), French opera staked its claim to a seriousness of purpose which
had previously been accorded only to spoken drama.[39] In doing so it
created an essential precondition for the recognition, over the course of
the nineteenth century, of musical drama as an independent artistic
genre equal in rank to spoken drama.

37. See Gerhard, "Republikanische Zustände," 28–29.
38. Hauser, *The Social History of Art*, 583.
39. See Labussek, *Zur Entwicklung des französischen Opernlibrettos*, 57.

THE EMANCIPATION OF THE CHORUS

With the exemplary heroes of the seventeenth and eighteenth centuries giving way to protagonists driven by an all-powerful fate to a death which hunted its victims down indiscriminately and *en masse*, the chorus's function in opera also had to be redefined. This was all the more necessary for an opera in which the importance of the soloists had dwindled almost to invisibility, as in the last scene of *Le Siège de Corinthe*. It is not surprising, therefore, that the modernity of Rossini's first French opera was brought home to his contemporaries most strikingly by a large-scale choral scene, the "benediction of the flags" in the middle of Act III. Almost all the critics singled out the sensational effect of this key scene;[40] even one who was hostile to Rossini in general, and later dismissed *Guillaume Tell* as a "tedious spectacle," was moved to write: "The benediction of the flags and the finale in *Mahomet* is an action, a drama in itself; such music will never bore anyone."[41]

What is the reason for this scene's sensational success? The audience sees "the catacombs of Corinth, lit by many fires" *(les tombeaux de Corinthe, éclairés par des feux multipliés)*, where the Corinthians have barricaded themselves. Hiéros, the guardian of the catacombs, enters and announces that the military situation is hopeless. In spite of that, he administers an oath to the Greeks to fight to the last man, and he blesses their flags. In a vision anticipating events of the 1820s, he sees the Greeks shaking off slavery five centuries hence, and in the ensemble which follows all present pray for "an undying death" ("trépas immortel"—that is, a death whose fame will be immortal). While in terms of its musical structure this ensemble ("Répondons à ce cri de victoire") remains within the traditional framework of an Italian *aria con cori*, the passage preceding it displays revolutionary novelty. The text in this passage all too obviously owes much to models in French opera of the 1790s,[42] but there it would have been set as a rhythmically uniform chorus; here it is recitative.

Traditionally, the chorus was only expected to take part in self-

---

40. See Hector Berlioz, "Théâtre de l'Opera: Reprise du *Siège de Corinthe*," *Journal des débats politiques et littéraires*, 5 November 1838, p. 1; Escudier and Escudier, *Rossini*, 192; see also the excerpts from reviews of 1826 in Radiciotti, *Gioacchino Rossini*, 2:64–65.

41. "spectacle ennuyeux"; "La bénédiction des drapeaux et le finale dans *Mahomet* est une action, un drame; pareille musique n'ennuiera jamais aucun de nous"; Gail, *Réflexions sur le goût musical en France*, 62.

42. See Bartlet, "The new repertory at the Opéra," 131.

contained numbers, but here the assembled Corinthians exchange dialogue with their spiritual leader, Hiéros:

> *(Tous les guerriers se prosternent, ainsi que les femmes)*
> HIÉROS
> Fermez-vous tous vos coeurs à d'indignes alarmes?
>
> CHOEUR GÉNÉRAL
> Oui, tous, nous le jurons.
>
> HIÉROS
> Guerriers, reviendrez-vous avec ou sur vos armes?
>
> CHOEUR
> Oui, tous, nous le jurons.
>
> HIÉROS
> Saurez-vous mourir pour la patrie en larmes?
>
> CHOEUR
> Oui, tous, nous le jurons.
>
> HIÉROS
> Au nom de Dieu qui vous inspire,
> Je bénis vos fronts glorieux;
> J'attache à vos drapeaux les palmes du martyre,
> Levez-vous pour mourir; je vous ouvre les cieux.
> (*Le Siège de Corinthe*, Acte III, scène 6)[43]

ᵔ ᵔ ᵔ

(All the warriors and the women prostrate themselves)
HIÉROS: Do you all close your hearts to unworthy terrors?
CHORUS: Yes, we all swear it.
HIÉROS: Warriors, will you return with your arms or on them?
CHORUS: Yes, we all swear it.
HIÉROS: Will you lay down your lives for your sorrowing country?
CHORUS: Yes, we all swear it.
HIÉROS: In the name of God who inspires you, I bless your glorious brows; I fix the martyr's palms to your banners, arise ready to die; I open the heavens for you.

Throughout this passage, the chorus makes its replies in the same style of dramatic recitative as Hiéros's questions, so that it constitutes an equal partner in the dialogue, singing in a unison all the more effective for the daring modulations. This is the first time since the 1790s, when political propaganda prompted various experiments in French opera,

43. Cited from the full score published in 1829. In the published libretto, the chorus's reply is always only "Oui, tous."

that an operatic scene satisfied a demand formulated at that time by the librettist of a tragédie lyrique first performed in 1793: "In this work, as in the tragedies of the ancients, the chorus is in the forefront, because the principal charcters being only the representatives or the proxies of the People, it is the People who must dominate, for everything relates to them."[44]

The chorus thus becomes one of the dramatis personae, able to assume an active role in what occurs on the stage. Earlier in 1826 a commentator had complained about the neglect of the chorus and the absence of ensemble in productions at the Opéra: "It's a rare event when nothing falls flat. Sometimes the chorus members are a motley gathering, with faces and deportment unworthy of them, sometimes their costumes are not new or sumptuous enough for the production."[45] But within just three years the situation changed fundamentally, as the references to *La Muette de Portici* and *Guillaume Tell* show in this passage from the memoirs of Nestor Roqueplan, published after his own term as director of the Opéra from 1847 to 1854:

> Previously, the chorus used to line up in two blocks, to left and right, and stood still, both men and women, without participating at all in the action taking place within the circle of singing tailor's dummies. The new styles of production gave movement to each and every one of them, swords to draw from scabbards, daggers to flourish in the air, arms to throttle the first person to cross their paths, legs to carry them at the run to liberate Naples or Switzerland.[46]

Admittedly, it is only in this visual aspect that Rossini's operas and Auber's work of 1828 can be equated. It is true that Auber's writing for chorus in *La Muette de Portici* also broke new ground, but the very com-

---

44. Barouillet, *Fabius*, iii (preface); cited after Bartlet, "The new repertory at the Opéra," 138.

45. "L'Opéra manque presque toujours d'ensemble; il est rare que quelque chose n'y cloche. Tantôt c'est une réunion de choristes d'une figure, d'une tournure ignobles, tantôt ce sont des costumes qui ne sont pas assez nouveaux ni assez brillants pour la représentation." [Aldeguier], *Le Flâneur*, 149.

46. "Autrefois, les choeurs se plaçaient sur deux rangées, à droite et à gauche, et restaient immobiles, hommes et femmes, sans prendre aucune part à l'action qui se consommait dans le cercle de momies chantantes. Les systèmes nouveaux de mise en scène ont donné, à tout ce monde, du mouvement, des épées pour les tirer du fourreau, des poignards pour les brandir en l'air, des bras pour étrangler le premier sujet, dans l'occasion; des jambes pour courir à la délivrance de Naples ou de la Suisse." *Les Coulisses de l'Opéra*, 38.

parison with that piece highlights the novelty of what Rossini developed in *Le Siège de Corinthe*. The means Auber employed originate, for the most part, in opéra comique and remain within the traditional framework of that genre. The chorus either sings in self-contained choral numbers or joins in arias and ensembles in a purely accompanimental function; and, although it contributes to many more of the musical numbers than any one soloist does, it takes little part in the action.[47] There is one passage where it participates in a recitative-like construction, but only in order to comment on the protagonist; the effect, if any, is to underline how unimportant the chorus is compared with him.

> CHOEUR
> Masaniello paraît: quel sombre ennui l'accable;
> Qui l'afflige, amis?
> (*La Muette de Portici*, Acte II, scène 1)[48]

CHORUS: Here comes Masaniello: what trouble weighs on him? Who causes him distress, friends?

Rossini, by contrast, casts the chorus as an active partner of the soloists in all three of his serious Paris operas,[49] and took the technique that he used for the first time in *Le Siège de Corinthe* considerably farther in the finale of Act II of *Guillaume Tell*. Whereas in the earlier opera the chorus only responds to questions put to it by a soloist, in *Tell* the chorus itself twice puts questions for soloists to answer.[50] The ensembles that end the "benediction of the flags" on the one hand and the "Rütli oath" on the other also differ in significant ways: in the scene in *Le Siège*, the chorus does not join in until after the soloists have presented the complete text, which is not much of an advance on the traditional aria con cori, where the chorus joins in the refrain, and an early version of the libretto of *Tell* envisaged this same procedure for the Rütli scene.[51]

As set to music, however, the chorus joins in after Tell has sung only two bars proposing the oath ("Jurons, jurons, par nos dangers"), and it repeats the oath *together* with the other soloists. Everyone on stage then sings together in octaves the melody of the second half of the oath, al-

---

47. See Walter, *"Hugenotten"-Studien*, 197.

48. Cited from the full score of 1829. In the published version of Scribe's libretto, significantly, the words are ascribed to "a fisherman."

49. With reference to *Moïse et Pharaon* see Azevedo, *G. Rossini*, 261.

50. For further examples, see Gerhard, "'Sortire dalle vie comuni,'" 199–200.

51. For a description of this version, see ibid.

8a, 8b   Placing this lithograph by Antoine Jean Weber of Carl Steuben's painting *The Oath of the Three Swiss* (1824; destroyed during the 1848 attack on the
Palais-Royal) beside a lithograph by Célestin Deshayes showing the scene of the
Rütli Oath in Rossini's *Guillaume Tell* (opposite page) gives a clear illustration of
how much the opera's Act II finale was influenced by the painting.

though its wide intervallic leaps are far greater than the octaves common in choruses of this type and would be easier for a soloist. The text
of this passage is a threat to traitors ("Si parmi nous il est des traîtres")
which could be a conscious paraphrase of the chorus "Si dans le sein de
Rome il se trouvait un traître" in Méhul's *Horatius Coclès* (1792).[52] Rossini sets off the "monophonic" vocal writing against a pointed, dotted
rhythm and extravagant harmonies, heightening the melodic uniformity
at the end of the act by means of a tightly woven canonic web.

This scene was also singled out for praise by almost all the critics.[53]

52. See Bartlet, "The new repertory at the Opéra," 153.
53. See Berlioz, "*Guillaume Tell* de Rossini," 343 (cited in Radiciotti, 151); Azevedo,
G. Rossini, 289.

Many commentators remarked on the way it was staged, too,[54] with a tableau that made no attempt to disguise its debt to a painting that had been the biggest hit of the 1824 Salon, *The Oath of the Three Swiss* by the history painter Carl Steuben (see pls. 8a and b).[55] The oath-taking scene had become a popular subject in painting during the revolutionary period, thanks to David and others; enhanced by the means of music theater, it was a potent expression of the new political power of the people, as later composers discovered, not least Meyerbeer in Act IV of *Les Huguenots.*

But in *Guillaume Tell* the added emphasis on the chorus is a feature of the dramaturgy as a whole, and not just the finale of Act II. This becomes very clear if the score is compared with the early draft of the

54. See the reviews in *Revue musicale* 4 (1828): 542, and 5 (1829): 569.
55. See *Explication des ouvrages,* 171.

libretto, mentioned above, which dates from December 1828.[56] As I have described in detail elsewhere,[57] Rossini made fundamental and comprehensive changes during 1829, which resulted in a complete inversion of his librettists' conception.

For one thing, he drastically reduced the importance of soloists. On the Swiss side, Tell himself is left as the only significant character apart from "the people" and the sentimental tenor-hero, Arnold. The draft libretto, on the other hand, also made major characters of Tell's wife, Hedwige, and their son, Jemmy, as well as presenting a large number of secondary figures in some detail. Leuthold, whom Tell rescues in the Act I finale, was set to reappear as a soloist in the oath-taking in Act II and again in Act IV, where he would have joined in a quartet with Mathilde, Hedwige, and Jemmy: instead, Rossini wrote the number as a trio for three women's voices (and cut it before the first performance). In Act I, old Melcthal would have joined Tell in trying to persuade his son to take up the cause of liberation; again, Rossini scaled things down, from a trio to a duet. In the celebrated trio of Act II, Arnold is challenged by Tell and by Walter, who also joins in the oath, but in the draft libretto two further characters took part in this scene, Werner, another solo oath-taker, and a certain Ulrik: Rossini dispensed with them altogether. Nothing remains of the active part Jemmy should have played in the rising against Gesler, which would have been the principal matter of the third and fourth acts, except for the report that it is he who gave the signal for the revolt—by setting his parents' house on fire! Rossini did set the aria Jemmy was to have sung to reassure Tell ("Ah, que ton âme se rassure") before his father takes aim at the apple on his head, but cut it during rehearsals for the première, as he had earlier cut, without composing, Hedwige's aria in the last act ("O spectacle inhumain").

By concentrating on a small number of major characters in this manner, Rossini completely destroyed the formal equilibrium of the draft libretto. This would have given each of the five principals an aria, but Rossini used none of them in the final version, where there are only two arias (Mathilde's "Pour notre amour plus d'espérance" in Act III, and Arnold's "Asile héréditaire" in Act IV) and a single-movement *romance* ("Sombre forêt") for Mathilde in Act II. Characteristically for the Paris

56. This draft libretto was published in 1992, subsequent to the appearance of the German edition of the present book. See "Commento critico, Testi," in Edizione critica delle opere di Gioachino Rossini, sec. 1: Opere, vol. 39: *Guillaume Tell*, ed. M. Elizabeth C. Bartlet, 9–105.

57. See Gerhard, "'Sortire dalle vie comuni'"; see also Bartlet, preface to Gioachino Rossini, *Guillaume Tell*, xxxix (cited hereafter as Bartlet, Preface).

Opéra, even Mathilde's Act III aria was cut at later performances of this première run;[58] so too was the "prière" newly written for Hedwige in Act IV.[59]

Such a dearth of solo numbers is surprising even today, and must have seemed revolutionary to an audience accustomed to the steady succession of recitatives and arias. No composer, not even Rossini himself, had attempted such a drastic reduction in the amount and importance of solo singing before that date, and no composer of French or Italian opera went any further down that path during the nineteenth century—not even Meyerbeer, who was constantly looking for new ways to replace the traditional strophic aria he had inherited.

Obviously, Rossini knew exactly what he was doing when he decided to disappoint the audience's expectations so thoroughly, for he was equally uncompromising in the steps he took to expand the role of the chorus in his last opera. Thus in Act I he systematically excised all the passages where the chorus was to have repeated the words of soloists at the end of an arioso or an ensemble, and instead wrote new, larger, self-contained numbers that were wholly choral. The first two scenes contain four large-scale choruses, in which the Swiss successively hail the beauty of the day, the signal for the end of the day's work, the virtues of work, marriage, and love, and finally the echo from the mountain. It made a disastrous impression when compared with the exemplarily concise and well-contrasted dramaturgy of *La Muette de Portici*, seen a year earlier.[60] Berlioz, in his review of the score of *Tell*, deplored the monotony of so many choruses in succession as "an awkward blunder," without considering what reasons Rossini might have had for choosing such an unusual procedure.[61]

The only reason he could have had was an uncompromising determination to create a completely new kind of relationship between protagonists and crowds, soloists and chorus. Plainly, his absolute priority in this opera was to represent the Swiss people as the decisive element, not merely a picturesque background for an intrigue revolving around private individuals. Like all his contemporaries, Rossini had been made

58. See Bartlet, Preface, xxxix.

59. See Bartlet, "Staging French *Grand opéra*," 634; Gerhard, "'La prière qui nous paraît être d'un pittoresque achevé.'"

60. See "Erinnerungen an Auber" [1871], in R. Wagner, *Gesammelte Schriften*, 9:42–60 (p. 45); Pendle, *Eugène Scribe*, 417–19; Finscher, "Aubers *La muette de Portici*," 101.

61. See Berlioz, "*Guillaume Tell* de Rossini," 337 (in Radiciotti, 141); cited here in the translation by Oliver Strunk, *Source Readings in Music History*, 5:68–86 (p. 73). See also Fétis, "Académie Royale de Musique: Première représentation de *Guillaume Tell*," 36.

to recognize the crowd's new role as a protagonist. In the attempt to create a new musico-dramatic form encompassing this recognition, however, he resorted to a conception that had typified the enthusiastic depiction of crowds around 1800. By 1829, in literature and in life, that view had been superseded by an ever greater consciousness of the crowd's destructive potential. Fear of the crowd (which will be the central topic of a later chapter) was already an active theme in Scribe's libretto for *La Muette de Portici*, although opera had to wait for Meyerbeer as the first composer to muster the technical means to represent it convincingly in music. Rossini's depiction of the crowd, by contrast, still betrays something of the continuing fascination that stirred foreign observers of the French Revolution of 1789 to sympathetic admiration. Like the poets and writers who were the first to turn their gaze upon the urban mob, Rossini selected a festive occasion[62] as the form of spectacle best suited to the portrayal of a freedom-loving nation. The whole of the first act of *Guillaume Tell* is conceived as a celebration, not only of the marriage of the three couples but also of the Swiss people in its harmonious relationship with the natural world. As in the political metaphors current during the revolutionary period, so too in this opera we find once again "the old fairy-tale motive of the pact between the free human being and nature."[63]

"THE FIRSTBORN OF LIBERTY"

Old-fashioned and structurally maladroit as the conception of *Guillaume Tell* may be, it is at all events eminently political. Even if today we find Rossini rather behind his times in painting that unknown entity, the crowd, in such radiant colors, and imbuing it with the virtues of the exemplary heroes of operas of a bygone era, in the context of the 1820s it was an unmistakably progressive political statement. Charles X's reactionary government was becoming increasingly repressive, and intellectual circles in the French capital were in ferment. Support for the liberal opposition was growing, and one sign of it was the interest theater audiences showed in subjects that could be related, to a greater or lesser degree, to the idea of revolution. Surprisingly, what had been very strict theatrical censorship was actually relaxed in 1828,[64] and the performance of plays on such subjects increased. As the discussion of *La*

62. See Brüggemann, *"Aber schickt keinen Poeten nach London!,"* 90.
63. Ibid., 77.
64. See Treille, *Le Conflit dramatique*, 22; Hallays-Dabot, *Histoire de la censure théâtrale*, 276–78; Finscher, "Aubers *La muette de Portici*," 89; and Krakovitch, *Hugo censuré*, 36–37.

Muette de Portici in chapter 4 will show, there were many different ways to approach the topic of revolution. And of course the fact that Rossini's three serious operas for the French stage all deal with oppressed peoples' struggles for liberty does not in itself amount to proof of pro-revolutionary sympathies.

In fact Rossini did not restrict himself to giving such opinions an airing in his operas. He was directly engaged in the philhellenic movement, in which at first only the liberal opposition made common cause with the Greeks in their War of Independence. On 28 April 1826 he took part in a fund-raising concert in aid of the Greek cause,[65] which, as Stendhal reported in the British press, provided the upper social classes with their first opportunity in twenty-six years to show their opposition to the government.[66] The grounds of their opposition are abundantly clear from the words of the *Chant grec* with which the concert ended. The final chorus of Philarète Chasles's text goes:

> Fils des héros, marchez! déjà le clairon sonne!
> Vers les monts de Phylé j'entends l'airain qui tonne!
> Et l'écho de l'Hemus vingt fois a repété
> Ce cri des nobles coeurs: liberté! liberté![67]

> ♪ ♪ ♪

> March, sons of heroes! Already the trumpet is sounding!
> Over toward the hills of Phyle I hear the clamor of bells!
> And the Haemus mountains have echoed twenty times
> this cry of noble hearts: Liberty! Liberty!

The censors forbade the use of that inflammatory word "liberty" in Rossini's first French opera, *Le Siège de Corinthe*, the première of which took place exactly six months later.[68] All the same, it could hardly have been interpreted as a work supporting the pro-government political right wing, although that too was now coming round to the Greek cause, in the name of "Christianity."[69] In Rossini's depiction of the Greeks' battle for freedom from the Turks besieging Corinth, the religious opposition of Islam and Christianity is scarcely an issue at all, and the Turkish gen-

---

65. See Pichois, *Philarète Chasles*, 1:259–61.

66. See the article of 20 May 1826, for *The New Monthly Magazine and Universal Register*, in Stendhal, *Courrier anglais*, 3:69–99 (pp. 71–73).

67. The text is given in full in Pichois, *Philarète Chasles*, 1:261; see also Amandry, "Le Philhellénisme en France," 26, 35, 37.

68. See Prod'homme, "Rossini and his works in France," 124; Gerhard, "La 'Liberté'—inadmissible à l'Opéra."

69. See Dimopoulos, *L'Opinion publique française*, 70.

eral Mahomet is represented as a calculating but cultivated politician, not a bloodthirsty barbarian.

But if *Le Siège de Corinthe* contains direct allusions to contemporary politics, they are less easily perceived in *Guillaume Tell* (or in *Moïse et Pharaon* or *La Muette de Portici*, for that matter). Nevertheless, the story of Tell was not a random choice. In the 1820s the common view of Switzerland was the one propagated by Philarète Chasles (the poet of *Chant grec*), who also happened to be Jouy's private secretary at the time. He published a "brief history" of Switzerland in 1825, in which, wasting no time, he apostrophized the Swiss on the very title page (in German) as "the firstborn of liberty," while the section on Tell's assassination of the tyrant ends with the stirring words: "An example for all nations!"[70]

To regard the deeds of the "firstborn of liberty" as an example to emulate was necessarily an expression of some degree of opposition to the regime in power. That is equally true of *Guillaume Tell* itself; Heine's quip that Rossini's music was better suited to the Bourbon restoration[71] certainly does not apply to this opera. Rossini, who chose the subject in preference to others suggested to him by Jouy,[72] was apolitical, it is true, insofar as he never made an outright statement about his political opinions and was capable of arranging his business with Charles X's government to his own very good advantage. And once he had settled the dispute about his pension with the administration of the July Monarchy, he appears to have been content, for all the republican ideas he had absorbed as a child, with the life of a law-abiding and docile citizen.[73]

Nevertheless, he was well aware that *Guillaume Tell* was not an apolitical opera. We have his fervent declaration, in a letter written in 1864, that "I embellished the word liberty in my *Guillaume Tell* in a manner intended to show how much I love my country and the noble ideals which adorn it."[74] There is also, for what it is worth, the evidence of the conversation he is reported by Michotte to have had with Richard Wagner in 1860. To a question about the oath-taking scene in Act II of the opera, Rossini allegedly replied:

70. "die Erstgebohrnen der Freiheit"; "Exemple pour les nations!" Chasles, *Resumé de l'histoire de Suisse*, title page; 13.

71. *Über die französische Bühne: Vertraute Briefe an August Lewald* [1837], in *Sämtliche Schriften*, 3:335.

72. See Pichois, *Philarète Chasles*, 1:180–83, and 2:142–44.

73. See Radiciotti, *Gioacchino Rossini*, 3:35.

74. "ho vestito la parola libertà nel mio Guglielmo Tell a modo di far conoscere quanto io sia caldo per la mia patria e pei nobili sentimenti che la investono"; letter to Filippo Santocale, 12 June 1864, *Lettere*, 271 (also in Rognoni, *Gioacchino Rossini*, 316).

That scene, in fact, was profoundly modified to my specifications, and not without trouble. I composed *Guillaume Tell* at the country home of my friend Aguado, where I was spending the summer. There my librettists were not at hand. But Armand Marrast and [Adolphe] Crémieux (parenthetically, *two future conspirators* against the government of Louis-Philippe), who were also staying at Aguado's in the country, came to my assistance with changes in the text and the versification which I needed in order to work out, as I had to, the plan of *my own conspirators* against Gesler.[75]

In the present state of our knowledge, it appears doubtful that Armand Marrast and Isaac-Adolphe Crémieux had any hand in the libretto, yet it is remarkable that a report composed in the reign of Napoleon III laid such stress on the libretto's revolutionary elements in this way.[76] Marrast and Crémieux were indeed active in their opposition to the monarchy, even after the July Revolution of 1830 brought the "citizen king" Louis-Philippe to the throne. Marrast was forced to spend years in exile in Great Britain, but eventually became mayor of Paris, after the revolution of February 1848.[77] Crémieux became minister of justice in the provisional revolutionary governments of both 1848 and 1870.[78]

But the two acknowledged librettists of *Guillaume Tell* were also known opponents of the Bourbon monarchy. Jouy had served a one-month prison sentence in 1823, for criticizing the politicization of the administration of justice under Louis XVIII, and Hippolyte Bis had

75. Michotte, *Richard Wagner's Visit to Rossini*, 64–65. This report was not published until after Rossini's death and has always attracted skepticism. The critique published by Elizabeth Bartlet in her preface to *Guillaume Tell* (Edizione critica, sec. I, 39:xxvii–xxviii) is especially damning, yet I cannot bring myself categorically to dismiss Michotte's account as pure fiction, for that conclusion rests essentially on the implicit hypothesis that the version of the libretto dating from late 1828 reflects Jouy's text before any revisions by other hands (see Bartlet, Preface, xxv). But there is no foundation for this hypothesis in the sources, while the remarks reported by Michotte gain some support from Rossini's statement that the libretto was "not . . . yet complete" in his letter of 7 August 1828 to Count Neipperg (cited in Bartlet, Preface, xxiii), and from his telling Gaetano Conti, in a letter of July 1828, that he was going to spend the latter part of the summer with Aguado (Rossini, *Lettere*, 43–45).

76. Furthermore, if Michotte wanted to create a Rossini "myth" (one to which the image of a Rossini who read critically and even corrected the various versions of his libretto would have been irrelevant), it is hard to see how he could have thought it enhanced by dragging in two names that had long been forgotten by the date at which he published his story.

77. See Ambert, *Portraits républicains*, 157–225.

78. See Posener, *Adolphe Crémieux*.

been in trouble with the police as early as 1816, for distributing anti-Bourbon leaflets.[79]

With such a pedigree, it is not surprising that Rossini's last opera is wholeheartedly sympathetic toward the Swiss insurgents and depicts their Habsburg rulers as cruel tyrants of the blackest hue. It is true that, like most nineteenth-century operas, it starts by focusing on the emotional state of an individual, but Tell's sufferings are purely political not personal. This is even more emphatically the case in the opera than in Schiller's play, which, to this day, is referred to as the primary source of the libretto, while it was in fact only one of many.[80]

"What a Picture!"

The emphasis on political events in *Guillaume Tell* is very strong, and as long as Rossini and his librettists stuck to the convention of weaving a love-interest into the political texture, they had to find new means to join the personal and the political plausibly—or, in formal terms, to sustain the relationship between soloists and chorus. Comparison of the different versions of the first scene of Act I sheds a clear light on Rossini's efforts to organize that relationship in a new way. In all the versions, from the draft libretto to the form the opera took at its première, the curtain rises on an idyllic picture of rural life. The printed version of the libretto gives the following scene indication:

> *La scène se passe à Burglen, canton d'Uri; à droite se trouve la maison de Guillaume Tell; à gauche débouche le torrent de Schachental, sur lequel un pont est jeté; une barque est attachée au rivage. Des paysans entourent de verdure des cabanes destinées à trois nouveaux ménages; d'autres se livrent à divers travaux agrestes. Jemmy s'essaie à tirer de l'arc, Guillaume, pensif et appuyé sur sa bêche, est arrêté au milieu d'un sillon. Hedwige assise près d'un chalêt assemble les joncs d'une corbeille et regarde alternativement son époux et son fils.*

   ு   ு   ு

The scene is set at Bürglen in the canton of Uri; to the right is the house of William Tell, to the left the mouth of the Schachental torrent. There is a bridge over the river and a boat is tied to the bank. Some peasants are spreading greenery as decoration around the chalets where three newly

79. See Gerhard, "'Sortire dalle vie comuni,'" 196.
80. Ibid., 186, n. 6; recent proponents of the theory that Schiller's play was the librettists' main source are Ulrich Weisstein, in "Der Apfel fiel recht weit vom Stamme," and Gilles de Van, in "Les sources littéraires."

married couples are to live; others are engaged in various rustic tasks. Jemmy practices drawing his bow. Tell, thoughtful and leaning on his spade, has stopped digging in mid-row. Hedwige, sitting near one of the chalets, is making a basket, and looks alternately at her husband and her son.

In the opening Andante grazioso the chorus sings appreciatively about the beauty of the festive day that is dawning, and gives thanks to the Creator ("Quel jour serein le ciel nous présage!"). With its regular periodic structure and its only slightly expanded da capo form, it is the sort of opening chorus found in many operas of the 1820s. By then it had become the rule to frame an opening scene with a choral number, and that is what was provided for in the draft libretto and realized in the score.

However, there are substantial differences in detail between the draft libretto and Rossini's realization. The librettists followed the opening chorus with a dialogue in recitative between Tell and his wife. Hedwige was to be the first soloist heard, asking Tell if she was right to think she saw tears in his eyes ("Dans tes yeux obscurcis ne vois-je point des larmes?"). But Tell was to give his wife only a brief reply before a second chorus ("Du plaisir messagères") brought the scene to a close. Only then, in a scene *without* chorus, would the soloists have discussed Tell's mood at greater length. The key word "rest" ("repos") in the text sung by the chorus as it left the stage would have both indicated the motive for the departure and triggered Tell's vehement reaction:

> *Scène Deuxième (Guillaume, Hedwige, Jemmy)*
> GUILLAUME
> Le repos? . . . insensés!! Gesler vous le dénie,
> En vain les empereurs, les rois
> Redoutés dans la Germanie,
> Par leurs sermens ont consacré nos droits;
> Un gouverneur plus puissant que les lois
> De son joug, de sa tyrannie,
> Fait peser sur nos fronts toute l'ignominie.
>
>
> *AIR*
> Monts sourcilleux de l'Helvétie,
> Forêts, fleuves de ma patrie,
> Vous frémissez de nos affronts;
> L'esclavage est partout, il habite vos cimes,
> Vos sombres profondeurs, vos vallons, vos abîmes,
> L'air même que nous respirons!

Scene 2 (Tell, Hedwige, Jemmy)

TELL: Rest? . . . fools! Gesler gives you none. In vain have emperors and kings feared in Germany assured our rights through solemn vows; a governor more powerful than the laws makes his yoke, his tyranny, bear down on us with all its ignominy. *Aria:* Lofty mountains of Helvetia, forests and rivers of my homeland, you tremble at our wrongs; slavery is everywhere, in your peaks, your somber depths, your valleys, your abysses, the very air we breathe!

This solo of the traditional kind would have separated the opera's eponymous hero from the mass of the chorus, just as the aria following his recitative would have placed him musically in the center.

Rossini composed something drastically different. The solo scene as such is cut, and its dramatic function of establishing Tell's discontent is accomplished within a much longer opening scene. The first chorus is followed immediately by a second closed musical number, instead of recitative, as a young fisherman sings of his sweetheart in a barcarole rhythm (in the printed libretto, the cast list gives his name as Ruodi, but he is not referred to by name in the text). It is his dreamy contentment that unleashes Tell's reaction:

> GUILLAUME *à demi-voix*
> Il chante son ivresse,
> Ses plaisirs, sa maîtresse;
> De l'ennui qui m'oppresse
> Il n'est pas tourmenté.
> Quel fardeau que la vie!
> Pour nous plus de patrie!
> Il chante, et l'Helvétie
> Pleure sa liberté.
> (*Guillaume Tell*, Acte I, scène 1)

TELL *(mezza voce):* He sings of his joys, his pleasure, his sweetheart; the sorrow oppressing me does not torment him. What a burden is life! We have no homeland! He sings, while Helvetia weeps for her lost liberty!

Tell's *a part* carries on the $\frac{6}{8}$ meter of the Andantino, but contrasts strikingly with it in matters of musical detail: the fisherman's C major yields to a gloomy C minor, and the accompanying harp chords to dramatic string tremolos. Nevertheless, the musical number preserves its unity, for Rossini does not change the meter or tempo, or the key-note C; and after Tell's solo he has the fisherman sing a second stanza of his barcarole in C major, and then extends the conclusion with a vocal quartet, with Tell repeating the last four lines of his aside, and Jemmy and Hedwige commenting. By this means he sets out the contrasting feel-

ings of two different characters in a single movement, which he simultaneously integrates into the larger frame of the score's opening number,
titled *Introduction*. The chorus has remained on stage and the quartet is
followed by an additional group of choral movements.

The next two choruses, "On entends des montagnes le signal du repos" and "Aux chants joyeux qui retentissent," are separated by another
aside disclosing the frame of mind of another principal character. In a
solo lasting less than ten seconds Rossini has the tenor, Arnold, reveal
his envy for the three couples being married that day—"Des amants!
des époux! Ah! quel penser m'assiège! . . ."—and thus his own unhappy love.

Once again, this solo adopts the meter and tempo of the preceding
chorus, yet contrives a marked contrast in musical detail. Arnold's despairing outburst breaks up the syntactic structure of the text (which
has consisted of complete sentences until now), the metrical regularity
of the music (above all by the prolonged second syllable of the word
"époux"), and its melodic and harmonic framework: where the music
for chorus alternates between E minor and G major, Arnold's interpolation is harmonically quite indeterminate, and where the former is purely
diatonic the solo includes two exposed tritone leaps. The twelve bars
shine a spotlight on the indecisiveness of Arnold's character. For the
time being, however, the interpolation is not pursued. A dialogue between Tell and old Melcthal, Arnold's father, leads to the next chorus
("Aux chants joyeux"); another song of praise for the Swiss landscape
("Près des torrents qui grondent") concludes the *Introduction*.

Modern audiences, familiar with later works of grand opéra and
above all with cinematic techniques, will take this method of singling
out individuals by spotlighting them during the course of a large-scale
scene of exposition in their stride. But in fact the *Introduction* in *Guillaume Tell* is nothing less than the start of a revolution in musical dramaturgy. For all the developments in form and content since the beginning
of the century, opera had not yet fully shaken off the baroque conventions of symmetry and formal equilibrium that underlie, for example,
the static concluding tableau of a tragédie lyrique. After the intervention of a deus ex machina or some other unexpected event makes the
happy ending possible, the action comes to a halt. There is one last
scene in which the chorus, the ballet, and the soloists all assemble for
the performance of a large-scale divertissement: in a lavish tableau, choral and dance movements alternate, contrasting in style but all focusing
on the purpose of this scene, which is the celebration of the restoration
of order. This model underwent changes, in Spontini's operas for Paris,

for example, but such divertissements remained much closer to baroque festivals with their ceremonial succession of ritualized acts of homage than to any form of spectacle that evolved during the nineteenth century. Even if the individual musical movements gradually acquired greater individual worth, the underlying structure was still that of a central perspective directed toward a focal point occupied by a triumphant victor or a happily united royal or noble couple.

An opera often began, however, with only a simple chorus or a more extensive aria, until the composers and librettists of Italian opera seria began to experiment with new techniques of exposition, following the trend of the time as evinced in other theater genres. In opera, too, the move resulted in a more consistent dynamism in the evolution of the dramatic action. Not enough research has been published as yet to enable us to follow that development in detail, but after 1815, at all events, large-scale opening scenes, going beyond the simple schema of "chorus—*sortita* of the hero or heroine—chorus," became more common in Italian opera. The credit for leading this development may belong to Meyerbeer, who began his career working in northern Italy; at least, that appears to have been the opinion of the librettist Gaetano Rossi, of whom Meyerbeer thought highly enough to consult him late in life over the revision of *Les Huguenots*.

When Rossi was working on *Semiramide* for Rossini in 1823—the first time they had collaborated since *Tancredi* in 1813 (both operas were based on plays by Voltaire)—he constructed the opening scene as a differentiated succession of choruses, contrasting ensembles, and brief, "spotlit" utterances for individual soloists, but dispensed altogether with any self-contained solo numbers.[81] Proudly he reported to Meyerbeer: "I have done an Introduction in the style of Meyerbeer . . . A spectacle, an imposing tableau."[82] And in Meyerbeer's last Italian opera, *Il crociato in Egitto*, which had its première the following year, also in Venice and with a libretto by Rossi, the two took their lust for experiment a step further: the stage directions for the opening scene specify the numerous movements of highly varied groups of soloists and choruses about the stage in the most precise detail, and culminate in the pithy command: "All is motion."[83]

81. See Henze-Döhring, "'Combinammo l'ossatura. . . ,'" 126.

82. "Feci un'Introduzione, alla Meyerbeer . . . : Una pompa, un quadro imponente"; Rossi's letter to Meyerbeer, 28 October 1822, in Meyerbeer, *Briefwechsel*, 1:446.

83. "Tutto è azione." See Viale Ferrero, "Luogo teatrale e spazio scenico," 90. On Rossi and Meyerbeer's collaboration in this opera, see also Everist, "Meyerbeer's *Il crociato in Egitto*," 215–21.

The *Introduction* of *Guillaume Tell* falls some way short of that radical standard of dynamism and is static for long stretches at a time, but it nevertheless provides the prototype of what was to become a norm in Parisian grand opéra: individual principal characters present themselves against an imposing background which is dominated musically by the chorus. The first, brief solo is not given to one of the principals but to a singer who will play no significant part in the coming drama—the unnamed fisherman in *Tell* is a representative of the crowd. The brief solo interjections of the principals, on the other hand, serve as musical spotlights which differentiate them within the crowd.

It has become customary to use the term "tableau" for this dramaturgical device,[84] but it is misleading on several counts. The French word is already very imprecise in its basic meaning of "picture," and in the narrower context of the theater it meant originally nothing more than a new setting, a change of location within an act.[85] Then, around 1800, in connection with the new theatrical genre of *mélodrame*, it acquired the more specialized meaning of a wordless spectacle at the end of an act which, like the newly fashionable tableau vivant, enabled the audience "to take in at a single glance the moral state of each character."[86] But although dramatists resorted to pantomime increasingly often, it did not contribute significantly more to the drama than eighteenth-century conventions that brought together multifarious, well-contrasted visual elements on the operatic stage in one grandiose stage "picture."[87]

There had been "tableaux" in that sense in French opera since Rameau at least, and the sumptuously dressed divertissements at the end of Spontini's operas also fulfilled the requirements of a worn-out terminology. What distinguishes the new type of scene described here is the chance it provides to focus briefly on individual characters, and switch between the overall view and the close-up. (Michael Walter, writing on *Les Huguenots* in German,[88] suggested a new expression for the type: "Großszene"—something like "super-scene" or "megascene"; it loses

84. The usage appears to go back to Bernard van Dieren, "Meyerbeer," 160.

85. See Walter, *"Hugenotten"-Studien*, 151; see also Pougin, *Dictionnaire historique et pittoresque*, p 699.

86. "de ressaisir d'un coup-d'oeil l'état moral de chaque personnage"; A!A!A!, *Traité du melodrame*, 47. See Brooks, *The Melodramatic Imagination*, 61–62; Sala, "Dal *Mélodrame à grand spectacle*," 185–86; and Wild, "La Musique dans le mélodrame," 600.

87. "Tableau" had been long established in a sense closer to one meaning of "table": the display of elements of knowledge in a spatial arrangement. See Foucault, *The Order of Things*, 74–75.

88. *"Hugenotten"-Studien*, 151.

the unwanted associations of "tableau" but is not really any more precise.) This multiperspective style of scene-setting radically widened the centrally focused perspective of operatic tradition as, once again, a small detail in Act I of *Guillaume Tell* illustrates.

In scene 6 Hedwige invites old Melcthal to bless the three bridal couples. The draft libretto provided for the blessing to take the form of recitative, but Rossini inserted another choral number ("Ciel, qui du monde es la parure"), in which the villagers ask for heaven's blessing on the couples. Only Arnold stands aside, unable to join in the general rejoicing:

> ARNOLD *à part*
> Ils vont s'unir . . . quelle souffrance!
> Ils vont s'unir . . . pour moi plus d'espérance!
> Quels maux j'endure . . . fatal amour!
> (*Guillaume Tell*, Acte I, scène 6)[89]

> ♪   ♪   ♪

ARNOLD *(aside):* They are to be married . . . how I suffer! They are to be married . . . there is no hope for me! What ills I endure . . . doomed love!

Rossini composed these interjections, however, in the form of brief parlando repetitions that do not break up the musical structure of the chorus. The passage does not amount to much on the page, but is highly effective on stage: the juxtaposition of general celebration and one person's despair destroys the integrity of the rustic idyll, and Arnold's position as an onlooker, detached from the traditional framework, is crystallized when he finally emits a cry that is absent from the printed libretto and disrupts the ceremonial character of the scene: "What a picture!" ("Quel tableau!").

THE INDECISIVE HERO

With the interjections that have just been described, Rossini again underlines an essential trait of Arnold's character—one already made apparent in his first short solo. The opera's young lover stands to one side, unhappy and unable to play any part in the rites taking place before his

89. Cited from the revised version in Rossini's autograph score; the printed libretto lacks these interjections, while the performance material at the Paris Opéra reveals that in the first performances Arnold sang: "Ils vont s'unir . . . Qu'ils sont heureux! / Ils vont s'unir . . . Le Ciel bénit leurs voeux. / Ivresse pure! . . . ô chaste amour!" (They are to be married . . . how happy they are! / They are to be married . . . heaven blesses their vows. / Pure ecstasy . . . o chaste love!).

eyes, unable to suppress his private emotions as other lovers publicly celebrate their wedding. His despair demands to be expressed, over and over again, and he cannot control his feelings.

This is the first instance in serious French opera of the sentimental character who is well on the way to losing all faith in himself. To those familiar with the nineteenth-century operas remaining in the repertory today there is nothing surprising about the fact that one of the central characters in an opera is a sentimental lover who gives his subjective state absolute priority over external events and finds himself constantly unable, or able only very reluctantly, to make the decisions demanded of him by the objective situation. All the great tenor roles in grand opéra and even in Verdi's late Italian operas represent, with minor variations, a hero who is undecided and ill-equipped to make decisions.[90]

Such characters were unknown, however, in either Italian opera seria or French tragédie lyrique before *Guillaume Tell*. The only precedents were in a mixed genre of the period around 1800, the *melodramma eroicomico*, which, as Helen Geyer-Kiefl has noted, "questioned the traditional role of the young hero by putting his manly *virtus* in doubt, at least temporarily."[91] Although such "heroicomic" characters were found repeatedly in Italian opera buffa and French opéra comique from 1770 onward, Rossini's earlier operas contain no examples of heroes afflicted with this kind of human weakness. However young the lovers may have been in his Italian operas and the earlier Paris works, they were always confident of their own feelings and able to make the decisions appropriate to virtuous heroes when the moment came. Malcolm, in *La donna del lago*, is always prepared to risk his life in a duel for his Elena, and Aménophis, in *Moïse et Pharaon*, wastes no time in fruitless despair when his beloved decides to leave Egypt with the Israelites, but issues a call to arms. Similarly, in Spontini's *Fernand Cortez*, the hero is both a victorious general and a magnanimous lover.

It was a new departure, therefore, when the usually young heroes of the melodramma eroicomico took the stage, as Geyer-Kiefl puts it, "no longer sovereign, sublime, and ideal, but . . . plagued by doubts, worries and anxieties, and . . . exposed helplessly to unforeseen events and emotions."[92] This "relativization of the traditional hero,"[93] under the mingled influences, seemingly, of the *comédie larmoyante* and the bourgeois "novel of development" *(Entwicklungsroman)*, is a trait, not only of

90. See Gerhard, "L'eroe titubante," 114–20.
91. *Die heroisch-komische Oper,* 184.
92. Ibid.
93. Ibid., 185.

the paradigm of melodramma eroicomico, Paër's *Sargino, ossia L'allievo dell'amore* (1803), but also of the conception of Arnold in Rossini's last opera.

The character is unmistakably intended to appear weak and insecure from the first moment. In the two large-scale duets involving him in Acts I and II, Rossini makes clear through musical means how his hero avoids making necessary decisions, and how the decisions he actually does make do not correspond to his own cherished intentions. In Act I, in "Où vas-tu?," Tell tries to force his young compatriot to reveal what is in his heart. Their opening exchanges are accompanied by the orchestra in an unvarying E-flat major, and at the end the tonality is confirmed by an eight-bar pedal-point on the dominant, in the accompaniment. It seems that Arnold cannot avoid giving Tell his answer in E-flat major, but Rossini switches to the remote key of G-flat major by a chromatic shift, which shows that Arnold is still rapt in an interior monologue, dreaming of his beloved.

Something similar happens at the end of this duet. Tell has succeeded in convincing Arnold that he must join the struggle for Swiss liberty. This time Rossini has the orchestra reinforce the dominant of E-flat major for a full twenty-three bars, and after a last hesitation on Arnold's part the concluding section of the duet actually begins in E-flat major, as the lover yields to the call of patriotic duty. Admittedly, the text of this section is as half-hearted as its music. While the orchestra thumps out a march rhythm, Arnold sings, aside, of his love for Mathilde, indulging in the most lyrical ornamentation. True, he adopts the orchestra's march rhythm in the second eight-bar period, but his protestation remains as noncommittal as could be conceived. He leaves the matter of whether or not he will personally take part in the struggle for liberty wide open, and curses tyranny in only the most general terms ("Haine, malheur à nos tyrans!"). What Arnold's promises are worth is revealed before long: when he hears the sound of Gesler's hunting horns again, he is unable to resist them any longer, and he flees to join the enemy and his beloved.

That is where he is when next seen, soon after the start of the second act, in conversation with Mathilde. Now he is even ready to meet her wishes and fight on the side of the oppressors. But once again Rossini shows in the music how incapable Arnold is of making a definitive decision. In the third part of the duet with Mathilde, as in the last part of the duet with Tell in Act I, a long pedal-point on the dominant builds up: the trumpets repeat the same fanfare rhythm on the dominant, which remains unresolved for thirty-four bars, and it is to this accompaniment that Mathilde and Arnold wax enthusiastic about "fields of glory" ("champs de la gloire"). But once again, Arnold is only strong in intention, the orchestra breaks off on the dominant chord of C major, and after a general pause listeners are left in no doubt as to the lovers' true concern.

Now they are accompanied by clarinet, bassoon and strings. As they sing "Dans celle qui t'aime / que j'aime," the dotted rhythms seem forgotten, and the chromatic evasions in the melodic writing show once again how undecided both characters really are. It is true that they have announced a decision, which is confirmed in the duet's stretta, and Arnold's resolution is strong enough to let him defend it in the first part of the next number, his trio with Tell and Walter, but the music has already betrayed that this will not necessarily be his last word.

Sure enough, he starts to waver again before long, when Walter tells him of his father's death. His final change of mind is announced in the second part of the trio (Andantino)—yet his immaturity and capacity for self-destruction are spotlighted once more in the recitative that follows.

ARNOLD
Grand Dieu! que faire?

GUILLAUME
Ton devoir.

ARNOLD
Il faut mourir?

GUILLAUME
Il faut vivre.
(*Guillaume Tell*, Acte II, scène 4)

ARNOLD: Great God! What shall I do? TELL: Your duty.
ARNOLD: Must I die? TELL: You must live.

In this exchange, the clash between an active, decisive hero, who admits to no emotions unless they are related to his actions (and who therefore, like Moses in *Moïse et Pharaon*, whom he resembles in many respects, does not get to sing an aria), and a weak, indecisive hero of the new type is encapsulated in the difference of *one* word: "die" and "live."

It would undoubtedly be consistent with Arnold's character as unfolded in the first two acts of the opera, and pinpointed in his choice of that one word "mourir," that his indecisiveness would lead him to a personal catastrophe. This creates the situation where the "psychologically motivated" heroes of contemporary tragedy become incapable of decisive action in the drama,[94] and the end of almost all the later "indecisive heroes" in grand opéra—the King in Auber's *Gustave III, ou le Bal masqué*, Raoul in Meyerbeer's *Huguenots*, Fernand in Donizetti's *Favorite*, Henri in Verdi's *Vêpres siciliennes*, and the same composer's Don Carlos—is either death or terminal despair. The few who escape catastrophe, like Robert in Meyerbeer's *Robert le diable* or Énée in Berlioz's *Troyens*, have supernatural influences to thank for it rather than their own willpower.

The fact that Arnold does arrive at a *lieto fine*, and can join in the general rejoicing of the Swiss at the end as the victorious liberator of Altdorf, is not due to his character, as revealed in the first two acts, but rather to the sheer necessity of a happy ending imposed by the tradition of the William Tell legend. Such contradictions also betray, however, that Rossini was not ready to cast off the traditional heroic elements of serious opera. True, there are places where his depiction of Arnold's character conforms to what Sir Walter Scott described in terms of "a thing never acting but perpetually acted upon,"[95] and one student of Scott's work elaborates this, saying: "The passive, inactive, indeterminately outlined heroes of Scott's novels are deliberately fashioned so as to direct the reader's attention away from themselves and toward the scene unfolding before him."[96] This "perspective function" of individual characters had not yet been developed, however, to the stage where it became a component in "a unified conception of representational technique, derived from painting,"[97] as it was to be in Meyerbeer's historical panoramas, but is simply placed here alongside other characteristics which still acknowledge the exemplary nature of the classical hero.

The spectator is bound to feel the awkwardness in the dramatic development of *Guillaume Tell* when Arnold takes the stage at the start of Act IV as one of the Swiss rebels' military leaders, with an aria conceived when the composition of the music was already in train,[98] and the inconsistency needed to be smoothed over. In the draft libretto, as late as Act III, Arnold was still represented as a person incapable of making a responsible decision,[99] but in Rossini's score Arnold's participation in the events of Act III is reduced to an absolute minimum. He does not

94. See Schlaffer, *Dramenform und Klassenstruktur*, 107–8.
95. *The Fortunes of Nigel*, 290; see also Welsh, *The Hero of the Waverley Novels*, 30–41.
96. Tippkötter, *Walter Scott*, 107.
97. Ibid., 108.
98. On the role the tenor Adolphe Nourrit may have played in writing this aria, see Bartlet, Preface, xxviii; and Johnson, "Rossini in Bologna and Paris," 73, 78.
99. For a more detailed discussion, see Gerhard, "'Sortire dalle vie comuni,'" 206–10.

appear at all in the big scene in the marketplace at Altdorf, and in the first scene of the act, a meeting with Mathilde, he does no more than put in an appearance. There is only a bald hint in the trio in Act II that Arnold will undergo this astonishing change from unhappy lover to heroic freedom-fighter, and adding more psychological depth to the process seems to have been as far beyond Rossini as it would have been for him to create the modern hero, driven by an all-powerful fate, who was to inhabit the worlds of both grand opéra and the plays of Victor Hugo.

The Retreat of the Princess

If we consider Rossini's last opera from the vantage point of the entire history of the genre to date, we can see that the counterpart to the "indecisive hero," Arnold, is not the boldly drawn hero of popular legend, William Tell, whose emotions hardly qualify for expression in the form of solo arias, nor the Swiss people as a group, although elevated to the role of a dramatis persona, but the female protagonist, Mathilde. It is true that she takes less part in the visible action than the omnipresent Tell, but the role of this Habsburg princess is the one most abundantly provided with solos. Although Rossini often dispenses with the conventions of opera seria in these numbers, Mathilde is the only person in this exceptional work whose music gave audiences of the 1820s what they had learnt to prize in Rossini's Italian operas. Lyrical melodies, in which solo orchestral instruments pick up the vocal line, as in the *romance*, "Sombre forêt," at the beginning of Act II or in the middle section of the duet following it, alternate with passages in which the orchestra is confined to the subordinate role of accompanying soaring vocal lines, as in the Allegro which concludes that same duet. The last section of the duet, in particular, is unmistakably indebted to the formal model, established in Italian opera, of the aria in several sections, culminating in a final cabaletta; in contrast, Mathilde's aria at the beginning of Act III ("Pour notre amour") departs from such conventions, with its unusual succession of an Allegro agitato at the start and a slower (Moderato) final section.[100] Yet even here Rossini marks the ending of individual sections with elaborate vocal cadenzas, and gives his soloist ample opportunities for the ornamental *fioriture* so beloved of French connoisseurs of Italian opera, which are otherwise encountered in *Guillaume*

100. See Döhring, "Formgeschichte der Opernarie," 549–51.

Tell only in Arnold's aria (and in the trio for women's voices, composed for the fourth act but cut before the first performance).

It is certainly no accident that Mathilde's lover, Arnold, is only allowed to display such vocal artistry when he has conquered his indecisiveness and discovered the strength of purpose that audiences could take for granted in earlier operatic heroes. In Mathilde's music, too, the artifice and beauty of such vocal technique corresponds to the sublime character of the Habsburg princess, whom we can regard as one of the last representatives of an older, aristocratic conception of the operatic heroine. Like the Queen of Babylon in Rossini's Italian opera *Semiramide*, Mathilde is noble even when she is wrong. Although Semiramis is guilty of having incited the murder of her husband, and Mathilde—when all is said and done—is implicated in Gesler's oppressive regime, the composer and his librettists refrain from using musico-dramatic means to represent these encumbrances as negative traits. Before long Meyerbeer would be denouncing the elementary wickedness of characters like Saint-Bris in *Les Huguenots* and Oberthal and the Anabaptists in *Le Prophète*, and Verdi would make the blind hatred of Azucena in *Il trovatore* the outstanding feature of one of his principal female characters, but before 1830 serious opera observed the rule that the nobility were noble.

An illustration of just how far respect for the legitimate rule of aristocratic characters in principal roles might go is found in *Le Siège de Corinthe*, in the scene where Mahomet first appears on the stage: entering Corinth as conqueror, the Turk is at first represented as an enlightened and art-loving sovereign. The librettists put into the mouth of the man who will shortly be responsible for ordering the ruthless massacre of the Greeks words indistinguishable in tone from anything used at an earlier date to flatter legitimate kings or the self-crowned emperor, Napoleon.

> MAHOMET *à ses guerriers*
> Qu'à ma voix la victoire s'arrête!
> Guerriers, relevez-vous; au sein de ces remparts,
> Respectez ces palais, ces prodigues des arts;
> Je veux y graver ma conquête,
> Je veux, à la posterité,
> Qu'ils recommandent ma mémoire:
> Sans les arts, frères de la gloire,
> Il n'est point d'immortalité.
> *(Le Siège de Corinthe*, Acte I, scène 6)

* * *

MAHOMET *(to his soldiers):* Let the victory halt here at my command! Soldiers, put up your arms: within these ramparts respect these palaces, these prodigies of art; I wish to engrave my conquest on them, I wish to leave them to posterity in commendation of my memory: without the arts, glory's brothers, there is no immortality.

Only in the conclusion of this address do the librettists seem to recall that Mahomet is a violent, barbarian tyrant who has destroyed a Christian city:

> Chef d'un peuple indomptable
> Et guidant sa vaillance,
> Je vais à ma puissance
> Soumettre l'univers.

     ꝑ   ꝑ   ꝑ

> Leader of an invincible race, the helmsman of its valor, I shall make the universe submit to my might.

It is true that the ferocity of Mahomet's "invincible" warriors has the upper hand in *Le Siège de Corinthe,* and that in *Guillaume Tell,* too, the Austrian soldiers are guilty of bloody excesses. But even during the sadistic ritual when their commander makes Tell fire at the apple balanced on his son's head, Gesler's brutality and cruelty are represented only in the text and stage action, and not by any musical means. Neither Rossini nor his librettists granted Gesler an aria, although they actually had a precedent in the great aria "Non jamais, non, qui jamais eut pensé" in Grétry's *Guillaume Tell* (1791), the first adaptation of the Tell story for the lyric stage. That was an opéra comique, however, and in a serious opera it was still impossible, even in 1829, to allow the personification of villainy as much prominence as the other principals who are either noble or at least capable of nobility.

But it is not only in its ambivalence toward villainy that Rossini's *Guillaume Tell* still looks over its shoulder at conventions of earlier serious opera; there is another respect in which the role of Mathilde, too, is nearer to the traditions of opera seria and tragédie lyrique than to grand opéra. Throughout the eighteenth century, opera turned frequently to tales dominated by larger-than-life women for its subject matter. Mythological sorceresses like Armida and Alcina, priestesses of ancient Greece like Iphigenia, queens like Dido and Semiramis throng the librettos of Quinault and Metastasio up until the early years of the nineteenth century. Undoubtedly there were more operas named for a male hero than for a heroine: nevertheless, from the perspective of the nineteenth century, it is astonishing to see how often the operatic stage was dominated by women who, moreover, did not primarily provide a passive point of reference at the heart of the work, as the objects of male passions, but took imperious command to drive the action forward. Once again, Rossini's *Semiramide* can be cited as a late example of a tradition whose force can still be felt in the role of Mathilde, but there it is close to the end of its run.

At the start of the third act, Mathilde has come to realize that everything stands in the way of her love for Arnold, and with a heroic gesture she accepts the inevitable and tells Arnold to give her up. Although the two lovers take leave of each other "forever" ("pour toujours"), it cannot possibly be the last word, for it is one of the most unassailable canons of operatic convention that lovers are united by the end in one way or another. Sure enough, as the action continues, the audience realizes that at some point Mathilde, Habsburg princess or no, has become converted to the justice of the Swiss cause. At the end of Act III she takes Tell's son Jemmy under her wing to protect him from any further atrocities at Gesler's hands, and in Act IV (in the version of the opera as it was first performed) she comes out on the Swiss side. The conversion is not motivated in any very convincing way: Mathilde comes on stage in the Act III finale only after Tell has shot the apple, and without any explanation in the text of how she has heard of what is going on. Neither at this juncture nor in Act IV does she have a solo in which to tell the audience about her decision. It is clear that Jouy and Bis were aware of this weakness at an early stage, for in the draft libretto, in the Act IV finale, they provided for a choral number, corresponding to the one with which the opera actually ends, to be preceded by a large-scale aria for Mathilde. In this the princess would have explained the reasons for her renunciation of her royal rank and her decision to throw in her lot with Arnold, and finally asked Swiss women to accept her as one of their own.

The text of that aria is all too idyllic—"Oh, my dear comrades, I wish to assist your labor in the fields . . ." ("O mes chères compagnes, je veux dans vos campagnes aider votre labeur")—but besides the risk of the ridiculous, dramaturgically it would have been wholly ineffective within the context of the opera's unusual finale. It is true that in Italian operas of the time it is quite common for the final scene to be deliberately constructed to culminate in a last bravura aria for the prima donna, but it is always matched by something equally spectacular in the staging: Anna's final aria in Rossini's *Maometto II*, for example, culminates in her suicide. In Mathilde's case, however, there is no call for a psychological explanation of something which is history by now, and it would lack all dramatic tension. To that extent, it is not surprising that Rossini cut it and did not put anything in its place. It was not a wholly satisfactory move, for it leaves Mathilde's development as vague as that of her lover Arnold, but it has the advantage of not befogging the dramaturgical issues with halfhearted compromises.

And it is clear that Rossini was less and less inclined to make compromises as his work on this opera advanced. After the decision to cut Mathilde's closing aria had been taken, the librettists still wanted to bring the affair between Arnold and Mathilde to a satisfactory conclusion of some kind, however perfunctorily. In a brief recitative which was set by Rossini, and included in the first performances, they provided Arnold with the opportunity to express his surprise at finding Mathilde at the Tells' house:

> ARNOLD
> Vous ici, Mathilde?
>
> MATHILDE
>   Oui, c'est moi:
> Des fausses grandeurs détrompée,
> Ton égale je te revois;
> Et m'appuyant sur ton épée,
> Jusqu'à la liberté je m'élève avec toi.
>
> ARNOLD
> Pourquoi ta présence, ô mon père!
> Manque-t-elle au bonheur de l'Helvétie entière?
> (*Guillaume Tell*, Acte IV, scène 11)

> ✒   ✒   ✒

ARNOLD: You here, Mathilde?
MATHILDE: Yes, it is I. No longer dazzled by false greatness, I rejoin you as your equal; and supported by your sword I aspire to liberty with you.
ARNOLD: O my dear father, why is your loss the only shadow on Helvetia's happiness?

But in a last revision, undertaken after the première, Rossini decided to do without even this unsatisfactory last word. The fact that it was out of all proportion to the importance of the love interest in the first three acts actually made its perfunctoriness worse, as some early reviews pointed out.[101] Instead, something completely unprecedented happens: although the two lovers are on stage, and although nothing stands in the way of their love any more, they take no notice of each other; Arnold thinks of his father, in two lines of recitative retained from the text quoted above, and then the final chorus begins.

101. See Bartlet, Preface, xxxvi.

A number of different reasons can be advanced for this unusual ending, tied up as it is with the many unresolved contradictions: the anomaly of a pair of lovers made up of an indecisive hero of the new type and
a heroic princess of the old school; the presentation of character now by
psychological weaknesses and now by noble strengths; the conflicting
demands of the primacy of the political issues in the historical subject
matter and the conventional overemphasis on the love interest; and the
need to reconcile a traditional *lieto fine* with the skepticism of Rossini
and his generation.

The gradual reduction of Mathilde to a state of such speechlessness
that she has not a single word to utter in the opera's finale, gives notice,
in fact, of the final eclipse of the concept of the sovereign female protagonist described above. For the time being active heroines continued to
appear in Italian opera—Bellini's Norma, and Donizetti's Anne Boleyn
and Lucrezia Borgia, to name only the most obvious examples—but
they vanished almost entirely from grand opéra. True, *La Muette de Portici* and *La Juive* both feature a princess as well as their eponymous heroines, but Elvira and Eudoxie are audibly indebted to older Italian models, and their standing in the drama is secondary. Their roles, like those
of their socially inferior rivals in love, already herald the advent of the
new type of passive heroine, a phenomenon that will be examined in
more detail in chapter 5, with reference to Meyerbeer's *Huguenots*. That
opera, the first to present fully fledged the new type of recognizably
"bourgeois" heroine, also contains the last major example of an aristocratic heroine in the person of Marguerite de Valois. As in Rossini's
Guillaume Tell, the vocal presence of this princess is so greatly reduced
that, as Milan Pospíšil suggests, it can be taken as a symbol of the decline of royal power illustrated by the events of 1572. After the failure
of her attempt to reconcile Catholics and Huguenots, Marguerite is
condemned to ever-increasing passivity; from that of a major soloist in
Act II, her role in Act III shrinks to a recitative and a few interjections
in an ensemble for the quarreling parties. Finally, in the last act "the
Queen is robbed of the first essential of an operatic role, namely the
chance to sing," and although she witnesses the catastrophe in the last
scene, there is no musical reaction to her presence on the stage.[102]

Against this background, the curious treatment Rossini deals out to
the principal female role in his last opera can be read as a sign that the
days of sovereign royal power were numbered, and with it the relative
freedom of action enjoyed by princesses in an otherwise patriarchal so-

---

102. Pospíšil, "Die Stellungnahmen zur Revolutionsproblematik," 500–501.

ciety, not only in the legendary Switzerland of the early fourteenth century but also in grand opéra, and, not least, in the expectations of the
operagoing public.

MELANCHOLY

While the unusual way in which Rossini breaks off the story of his pair
of lovers lends itself to interpretation as a reflection on the gradual decline in importance of the roles of royalty and nobility, arguably it also
makes a fundamental statement about the possibility of a happy ending. As in the last finale of *Le Siège de Corinthe*, the fate of two individuals seems to dwindle to a matter of no importance when set against
immense events involving a whole nation. Yet in spite of this uncompromising concentration on the triumph of the Swiss revolt, Rossini
modified the *lieto fine* of the libretto in such a way as to allow skeptical
undertones to be heard alongside the expressions of joy at the restoration of liberty. As well as including a big aria for Mathilde to set the seal
on the love story, the draft libretto also eliminated all causes for sorrow
that could have clouded the general rejoicing. Even old Melcthal would
have reappeared in the finale: not butchered by the Austrians after all,
but only falsely reported dead, and liberated by his son when the castle
at Altdorf was stormed. And in both the draft libretto and in a new version of the finale which Rossini made for a three-act abridgment, re-
quested by the Opéra management in 1831,[103] the work closed with a
triumphant final chorus in which the opera's most rousing melody was
reprised.

The draft libretto of December 1828 provided for a repeat of the
oath on the Rütli with which Act II had closed, and at the end of the
third (last) act of the 1831 version, the chorus of rejoicing Swiss sang
the following lines, to the tune of the famous Allegro vivace from the
overture, transposed to C major:

> CHOEUR GÉNÉRAL
> Des bois, des monts, de la cité,
> Aux cieux où Melcthal est monté,
> Qu'un cri, qu'un seul soit répété:
> Victoire et liberté!
> (*Guillaume Tell* [1831], Acte III, scène 7)

∻   ∻   ∻

---

103. On this version see Gerhard, "L'eroe titubante," 125–27.

CHORUS: From the woods, from the peaks, from the city, to the heavens where Melcthal has gone, let one cry, one alone, be repeated, victory and liberty!

But in the original version of the opera approved by Rossini, as performed at the première in 1829 and, with cuts, in the immediately following weeks, things are very different; even the word "victory" is not to be found in the text, and the final chorus takes the form of a prayer:

> Liberté, redescends des cieux,
> Et que ton règne recommence!

> ∕   ∕   ∕

Liberty, come down from heaven and let your reign begin again!

This Allegro maestoso does not begin with the trumpet fanfares that launch the final chorus in the 1831 version but with harp arpeggios, string tremolos, and a solemn melody in the horns. Trumpets do not enter until eighteen bars before the end, and then they are only required to play long, sustained notes which add very little to the musical texture. In his choice of this instrumentation and the key of C major, Rossini was reverting to a pattern used by French opera composers in the years immediately following 1794 as a stereotype for the evocation of natural virtues garlanded with piety.[104] The naively affirmative character of this model from the revolutionary period undergoes a fundamental modification in *Guillaume Tell*, admittedly, for the whole chorus is affected by the C minor coloring of Arnold's melancholy reflection ("Pourquoi ta présence, ô mon père . . ."), which immediately precedes it. After two bars at the start establishing C major as the home key, the music modulates incessantly, and at the first cadence it confirms not C major, as expected, but C minor, which is scarcely the most appropriate tonal goal for a hymn to liberty. C major is not reached until after another progression, and with noticeable effort, at the end of Tell's solo, at the moment when the chorus enters, but it is then abandoned once more. The grandly proportioned final climax culminates in a *deceptive* cadence on A minor; the very brief final cadence in C major yields at last what the ear has been waiting for, but it is unable to expunge the memory of the repeated excursions into related minor keys. So the impression is left of delusion, and of doubt as to whether liberty is really within the grasp of all mankind.[105]

Here Rossini delivers a modification of the *lieto fine*, which seems in

---

104. See Charlton, "Orchestration and Orchestral Practice," 470–74.
105. This is discussed in more detail in Gerhard, "L'eroe titubante," 127–28.

this particular case to owe less to traditional tragédie lyrique than to the "rescue" operas of the revolutionary period (cf. Beethoven's *Fidelio* and its ending with the release of a whole castle-ful of political prisoners).[106] The finale of *Guillaume Tell* takes up that by now outmoded tradition and at the same time it represents the most recent operatic trend, leading away from the older tradition of the happy ending, and pioneered by Rossini himself in the horrifying ending of *Le Siège de Corinthe*.

Something similar affects the allegorical role of natural phenomena in this finale: in the expansive and detailed orchestral representation of a storm on the lake which precedes Tell's assassination of the tyrant Gesler, Rossini followed models from eighteenth-century French opera,[107] but at the same time his ending suggests something far beyond those earlier works in which the calming of the waves is matched by the return of general happiness. Certainly, with the storm having cleared the air, the sun breaks through the clouds and shines brightly over the closing tableau, so that nature herself appears to adorn the triumph of the principle of liberty, yet this final scene is anything but a genre picture, sufficient unto itself. In Schiller's play, the first and last scenes are superficially similar to those in Rossini's opera but are made to correspond to each other as idylls, before and after the action; Rossini's last scene, on the other hand, does not make the slightest musical reference to the vanished idyll of the first.[108]

It is true that the triadic motive in the orchestral accompaniment to the final chorus uses the traditional, Swiss, alphorn melody which had been made known to the outside world by Rousseau as the *ranz des vaches* (a generic title, applicable to this and other airs sung by herdsmen as they drove the cattle to or from the mountain pastures), and had come to be regarded in France as *the* archetypal Swiss folk melody.[109] But although Rossini had adapted other authentically Swiss tunes in the horn calls in Act I, thus creating a "folk" atmosphere, there is no attempt to revive it in the finale. The chorus at the end of the opera is neither simple nor celebratory: not designed to relieve the tensions of a dramatic peripeteia, in the manner of the divertissement of older operatic tradition, nor an uplifting depiction of landscape, absorbing humanity, all divisions healed, into the sound-world of nature. Uncommonly short, perhaps the most striking thing about it is its nostalgic, visionary

106. See Pendle, *Eugène Scribe*, 418.
107. See Dent, *The Rise of Romantic Opera*, 69, 124; Charlton, "Orchestration and Orchestral Practice," 460.
108. Edler, "'Glanzspiel und Seelenlandschaft,'" 82.
109. See Vander Straeten, *La Mélodie populaire*.

quality, evoking another element that had become firmly associated with the Swiss national character in the mind of the average French person in the eighteenth and early nineteenth centuries. Swiss mercenaries, serving far from their homeland in other countries' armies, had repeatedly been observed to manifest severe symptoms of *mal du pays*, or homesickness, and that had led to Swiss examples being cited in every attempt to define that elusive ailment.[110] Thus Rousseau wrote in his dictionary of music that the *ranz des vaches* "was so generally beloved among the Swiss [mercenaries] that it was forbidden to be play'd in their troops under pain of death, because it made them burst into tears, desert or die, whoever heard it; so great a desire did it excite in them of returning to their country."[111] And in the article "nostalgia" in the supplement of Diderot's *Encyclopédie*, Albrecht von Haller defined it as a "melancholy caused . . . by the discomfort of being among strangers whom we do not love."[112] By representing this emotion in *Guillaume Tell* not only as something experienced by an individual but also as forming the basis for a grandiose political allegory, however, Rossini paints a picture of the restoration of liberty as a utopia, executed in the sad knowledge that utopias are unattainable. That is precisely the definition of the word "melancholy" (admittedly not the most common sense in which it is used) given in Diderot's *Encyclopédie:* "Melancholy is the customary sense of our imperfection."[113] And that, too, seems to be exactly what Delacroix discerned, when he said of *Guillaume Tell*, "Rossini . . . brushed in the broad outline of a few landscapes where you can almost smell the air of the mountains, or rather you can sense the melancholy that grips the soul when face to face with the great spectacles of nature."[114]

Silence

Guillaume Tell, composed when Rossini was thirty-seven years old, was his last work for the theater. In spite of the obligations set out in his contract with the Opéra, and in spite of repeated announcements of new

110. See Ernst, *Vom Heimweh;* Frigessi Castelnuovo and Risso, *A mezza parete*, esp. the opening chapter.

111. *A Dictionary of Music,* s. v. "Music," 92.

112. "[une] mélancholie causée . . . par l'ennui d'être avec des étrangers que nous n'aimons pas"; see Ernst, *Vom Heimweh,* 116; Starobinski, "La Nostalgie," 1516.

113. *"Mélancolie,* c'est le sentiment habituel de notre imperfection": opening sentence of the article in question; see Schalk, "Der Artikel 'mélancolie.'"

114. Delacroix's diary, entry for 24 December 1853, *The Journal of Eugène Delacroix,* 217.

plans, the once so prolific Rossini did not write another opera in the remaining thirty-nine years of his life. The decision created a sensation. It baffled his contemporaries and continues to exercise posterity.

What made him suddenly abandon his career at its height? Most of those who deplored the move at the time had an answer ready. Once Rossini had won the lawsuit he brought against the new government of Louis-Philippe to make it continue to pay him the annuity of 6,000 francs which he had had from the civil list of the previous king, Charles X,[115] he was able to live in relative comfort without needing to earn any additional income from new compositions. He succeeded, that is, in converting the annuity paid him by the ancien régime in order to tie him to the French crown as an old-fashioned court composer into the means whereby, paradoxically, he could live like a capitalist rentier after the July Revolution.

Rossini himself actually encouraged the spread of the popular image, surviving to this day, of a contented idler, dedicated to a life of luxury and avoiding all obligations. One of his letters refers to his "natural tendency toward indolence,"[116] and he did nothing, at least, to contradict the impression of a dedicated gourmet.[117] Undoubtedly, there were times, even before 1829, when he had found it hard to drive himself to work. Reports in the contemporary press indicate that it was only the pressure of the imminent première that forced him to finish the full score of *Guillaume Tell*.[118] Furthermore he had a sickly (if not hypochondriac) constitution that made him seek rest increasingly after 1830,[119] and there is also the possibility that he felt offended to some extent by Louis-Philippe's government's attempt to block his annuity.[120]

But behind such external causes and any physical problems lay concealed "a profoundly painful dejection," that can probably be held responsible for Rossini's gradual "cessation of interest in the outside world" and above all for "the inhibition of all activity"; the words in quotation marks are Freud's terms, setting out the modern psychia-

115. For a more detailed discussion see Ozanam, *Recherches sur l'Académie Royale de Musique*, 347–49; Kern, "Meister der Verhandlungstaktik," 17.

116. "[una] naturale inclinazione alle pigrizia"; see Radiciotti, *Gioacchino Rossini*, 2:203; Dumas, "Un Dîner chez Rossini." Translations of Rossini's Italian in this section are by Kathleen K. Hansell.

117. See Radiciotti, *Gioacchino Rossini*, 3:26–27; Périgord, "Dédicace à M. Rossini."

118. See Gerhard, "'Sortire dalle vie comuni,'" 217–18; the reports in the contemporary Italian press derived from one published in *Revue musicale* 4 (1828): 423–24.

119. See Radiciotti, *Gioacchino Rossini*, 2:204, and 3:8.

120. This "secret cause of Rossini's silence" was floated by the critic Louis Desnoyers in *Le Siècle*, 28 February 1847; see also Desnoyers, *De l'Opéra en 1847*, 69.

tric definition of melancholia.[121] The "lowering of the self-regarding feelings to a degree that finds utterance in self-reproaches and self-revilings," which Freud also diagnosed, is reported of Rossini too. One contemporary account describes an explosive revelation of his private thoughts, in which he blamed "fate" for the early halt to his operatic career: "At times, when he was angry, the maestro would pace excitedly up and down the room, smite his brow, and, cursing his unhappy fate, exclaim, 'Anyone else in my position would have killed himself, but I . . . I am a coward, and I don't have the courage to do it!!'"[122]

The psychological difficulties were, however, inseparable from objective problems which every French opera composer had to face after 1830. The operatic revolution that Rossini had helped to start in Paris was kept in motion by Meyerbeer, primarily, but also by Halévy, and it was possible to interpret Rossini's retirement as a reaction to the immense success of those two composers. At all events, most contemporaries inclined toward that view, regularly trotting out the antisemitic anecdote which many attributed to Rossini, to the effect that he was waiting to start a new work "until the Jews had finished their Sabbath."[123]

Meyerbeer's sensational successes in the early 1830s made it incontrovertibly clear to everyone that it was no longer possible to write a ranking opera in only a few months. Rossini himself had spent more than a year on *Guillaume Tell*, whereas he had written up to five operas a year in the early part of his career. Bellini, too, took increasingly long to finish each of his Italian operas, and almost two years separated the premières of his last two works, *Beatrice di Tenda* (March 1833) and *I Puritani* (January 1835). Only composers who were regarded, up to 1840 at least, as second-rate—such as Donizetti, Mercadante, Verdi, Auber, or Halévy—continued to produce work at the rate of one or more a year, yet that had been the norm up to 1825, apart from the sole exception of Spontini.

Rossini would, therefore, have had to work harder than ever to respond to Meyerbeer's successes with work of equal stature, but addition-

121. See Freud, *Mourning and Melancholia*, 244.

122. "Talvolta l'alterato Maestro girava per la camera a passi concitati, battevasi la testa, e imprecando *contro la sorte a lui avversa*, esclamava: *Un altro nel mio stato si ammaz-zerebbe, ma io . . . io sono un vile, e non ho il coraggio di farlo!! . . .*" Branca, *Felice Romani*, 201–2.

123. "J'attends que les juifs aient fini leur sabbat"; Boigne, *Petits mémoires de l'Opéra*, 302–3. The authenticity of the anecdote is doubtful, however: see Radiciotti, *Gioacchino Rossini*, 2:449. In another version of the story the quip is ascribed to the librettist Castil-Blaze: see Pailleron, *François Buloz et ses amis*, 52.

ally he found himself confronting certain fundamental technical problems. We have already looked at several examples in *Guillaume Tell* of the insoluble contradictions he had encountered in the dramaturgical conception of a large-scale opera. In all three of his serious French operas, the disproportionate concentration on the role of the "people" came into conflict with the demands of a genre in which the concentration on soloists remained a central constituent, however unnaturalistic it might be. In the particular case of *Guillaume Tell*, furthermore, it had proved virtually impossible to reconcile the purely political motivation of the Swiss uprising with the dominance of personal emotions customary in opera and Rossini's emphasis on a love interest, even a freely invented one. The highly unusual pair of lovers suffered from the clash between fundamentally different conceptions of an operatic hero, and the decision to give a happy ending to the lovers' story ultimately contradicted the presentation of the male lover as a new-style, romantic protagonist, guided solely by his emotions.

Rossini obviously knew that he had struck out on entirely new paths in his last opera. A few weeks before the première, an Italian theatrical periodical contained the following report from its Paris correspondent: "This music is said to be a completely new departure; the author makes no secret of having wanted to transform himself; a simple style, severe ideas—that is what we can expect in *Guillaume Tell*."[124] Keen innovator that he was, the composer can hardly have been unaware that those "severe ideas" were at odds with older aesthetic categories in which he himself still had faith, and furthermore that they could only be realized at the cost either of the work's own integrity or of generally accepted aesthetic conventions.

All the same, it appears that after 1830 Rossini did contemplate developing more fully the intentions realized only halfheartedly in *Guillaume Tell*, and writing another opera about a nation's struggle for liberty, in which there would be no love interest. He is reported to have said, looking back on a projected opera about Joan of Arc:

> I was offered two or three different Joans of Arc. In one she was beloved,
> in another she was in love: I understood neither the one nor the other.
> What role has love to play in the legend of this heroine? I observed that

124. "Questa musica dicesi sortire tutt'affatto dalle vie comuni; l'autore non nasconde che egli ha voluto metamorfosizzarsi; stile semplice, idee severe, ecco ciò che vi offrirà senza dubbio il Guglielmo Tell"; from a report dated 4 July 1829, published in *Cenni storici intorno alle lettere, invenzioni, arti, commercio e spettacoli teatrali*, 23 July 1829, p. 174, which clearly goes back to a French source that I have been unable to trace (see the different translation in Radiciotti, *Gioacchino Rossini*, 2:101–2).

when there is no love it is necessary to invent it, and so I replied: No, there are better things to do. When a subject does not offer the public the fascination of love, one should put it aside and forget it. And that's what I did.[125]

He was probably right in recognizing that an opera in which none whatever of the principal characters was involved in a love affair would never get off the ground in the nineteenth century. The historical operas of Meyerbeer and Halévy (which did not appeal to him) would indirectly have confirmed his view. Their subject matter posed problems for the composers and librettists very similar to those Rossini encountered in *Guillaume Tell*. It was necessary to rethink the relationship between soloists and chorus, to consider the juxtaposition of traditional and modern conceptions of the protagonists, to create a single framework in which to accommodate historical events and fictional love interest.

As will be shown in the following chapters, Rossini's successors, aided and abetted by the experienced Scribe, worked hard to find compromises that would enable them to solve these problems without having the contradictions become all too obvious. They achieved it only by enlisting the new ideas that Rossini had already tried out, in a framework incorporating technical virtuosity and the aesthetic principle of the *juste milieu* or happy medium. Viewed from the standpoint of Rossini's *Guillaume Tell*, their solutions can justly be reproached with a lack of artistic "rigor."

That appears to be the estimate at which Rossini himself arrived, to judge by the isolated and often contradictory comments he passed in the years following 1830. For example, he wrote in 1853, to a Turinese nobleman who had sent him a libretto:

> I have always been too fond of naturalness and the spontaneous situations that constitute the essence of art, and which have been renounced of late in favor of the paltry pleasures of surprise and astonishment. Heaven preserve me both from entering such a path and from opposing the freedom of others to travel it beyond all human limits. If I ventured to give advice, it would be to return to natural limits instead of forging ahead into that realm of fantasy and witchcraft from which modern philosophers say they

125. "Mi si offrirono due o tre Giovanne d'Arco. L'uno la faceva amata; l'altro la faceva amante; io non comprendevo nè l'una nè l'altra. Che ha da fare l'amore nella leggenda di questa eroina? Mi si osservò che, quando l'amore non c'è, bisogna inventarlo ed allora io risposi: No v'ha di meglio a fare. Quando un argomento non offre per il pubblico il fascino dell'amore si mette da parte e non ci si pensa più. —E così ho fatto." Cited without a source in Radiciotti, *Gioacchino Rossini*, 2:198, n. 2.

have labored so hard to free a too credulous humanity. Stupendous contradiction! inoculate music today with the plague from which it is claimed
to have been cured. What extraordinary cowardice! to trust once again
the ravings of that rationalism whose propagators Italy claims to serve
so unwillingly.[126]

Rossini obviously enjoyed playing the part of the traditionalist in retirement, spurning every form of progress and lamenting the Good Old
Days. He repeatedly bewailed the waning of classical bel canto,[127] and
the decline of opera seria as a whole. But it is difficult to take all he said
at face value when one reflects that he himself had tried to break away
from tradition and create something wholly new in his last operas.

His contempt for progress is credible only insofar as it refers to a
certain form of technical progress, connected with "rationalism," that
he regarded as inimical to art and evidently diagnosed in Meyerbeer. He
did not hesitate, for example, to associate Meyerbeer's music with the
railway, which he detested, but which most people viewed as the symbol
of technical advance: "How can anyone listen to music after having his
eardrums pierced by the whistle of a locomotive? One is condemned to
hear nothing but Meyerbeer for the rest of one's life!"[128] Rossini probably knew about Meyerbeer's habit of composing on long journeys, for
the latter had freely revealed, to the guests at a salon in 1844, how he
went in search of inspiration:

> There are two things I cannot stop myself doing (he said): one is suffering
> from sea-sickness if I spend a single hour on a steamship, and the other
> is composing music if I travel in a coach for an hour . . . it is *irresistible*
> then. If I am in a coach I have to write, for ideas come to me from all
> sides. I hear sounds, I see an orchestra playing before my very eyes . . . I
> have to jot those ideas down on a piece of paper, for otherwise it would

126. "Io sono stato sempre troppo amico della naturalezza e della spontaneità delle
situazioni che costituiscono l'essenza dell'arte, a cui da qualche tempo si è rinunciato pel
meschino piacere della sorpresa e dello sbalordimento. Il cielo mi guardi e di entrare in
codesta via e dal contrastare ad altri la libertà di correrla fuori d'ogni umano confine. Se
dovessi dare un consiglio sarebbe quello di rientrare nei limiti del naturale, anzichè inol-
trarsi nel mondo delle stravaganze, e delle diavolerie da cui dicono i filosofi moderni d'aver
tanto affaticato per liberarne la troppo credula umanità. Stupenda contradizione! inocu-
lare oggi in musica la peste da cui si pretendeva averne guarito. Insigne viltà! ricreditare i
delirii di quel razionalismo, ai propagatori del quale l'Italia dice di servire tanto a malin-
cuore." Silvestri, *Della vita e delle opere di Gioacchino Rossini*, 348.
    127. See Michotte, *An Evening at Rossini's*; Lippmann, "Rossinis Gedanken," 290.
    128. "Comment écouter de la musique après qu'on a eu les tympans percés par le
sifflet de la locomotive? On est comdamné à ne plus pouvoir entendre que du Meyerbeer
pour le restant de sa vie!" Cited in Villemessant, *Mémoires d'un journaliste*, 3:74.

torment me horribly . . . Sometimes, even, if I am being pressed for
something new, I take a little journey—for it never fails me . . .[129]

Of course this statement, reported at second hand, and probably greatly
exaggerated, especially with regard to the last point in it, refers expressly
to travel by mail-coach, to which Meyerbeer had been accustomed all
his life—quite literally, for his mother was on her way to have her baby
at her parents' house in Frankfurt an der Oder, when she went into labor
and gave birth in a village somewhere between Berlin and Frankfurt (not
identified with complete certainty to this day), and the coach rocked the
baby as in a cradle when the journey was resumed. Meyerbeer traveled
constantly, and had no difficulty in adapting his working habits to long
train journeys as the railway network expanded;[130] indeed, he thought it
deserved a note in his diary when such a journey was "wholly unfruitful
as regards music."[131] The fact that Meyerbeer was so completely at ease
with the latest, mechanical mode of transport does something to clarify
Rossini's otherwise puzzling comparison, especially if one is prepared to
charge Meyerbeer's style with a certain artificiality and systematic striving for technical perfection and calculated effects. That was precisely
what Rossini objected to: as he wrote to a Hungarian admirer in 1854,
"excessive science sterilizes art and diminishes the pleasure of the heart
in exact proportion as it increases the property of the brain."[132]

There is another respect in which parallels can be drawn between
the railways and grand opéra. In chapter 5, in the section "Shock," I
shall discuss Scribe's pandering to "the paltry pleasures of surprise and
astonishment" by recourse to "unworthy subjects, even atrocious
crimes"—as Rossini put it in another passage in the letter cited in the

129. "Je ne puis m'empêcher de faire deux choses (dit-il), c'est de souffrir du mal de
mer si je suis une heure seulement sur un bateau à vapeur, ou bien, de composer de la
musique si je roule une heure en voiture . . . c'est alors *irrésistible* – si je suis en voiture, il
faut que j'écrive, car les idées me viennent de tous côtés; j'entends des sons, je vois une
orchestre jouer devant mes yeux . . . il faut que je jette ces idées-là sur un morceau de
papier, car autrement cela me tourmenterait horriblement . . . Quelquefois, même, si on
me presse de faire une nouvelle composition, j'entreprends un petit voyage—car cela ne
manque jamais de me réussir." Maria L'vova's letter to Wiktor Każyński, late May or early
June 1844, in Każyński, *Notatki*, 87–88.

130. See, for instance, Meyerbeer's diary, entry for 31 October 1847, *Briefwechsel*,
4:332.

131. "in musikalischer Hinsicht ganz unfruchtbar"; Entry of 12 September 1848,
ibid., 443.

132. "L'eccessiva scienza isterilisce l'arte e diminuisce il piacere del cuore a misura
che fa preponderare le virtù del cervello"; cited in Radiciotti, *Gioacchino Rossini*, 3:133; on
the source see ibid., 2:337.

previous paragraph.[133] Scribe worked on the assumption that members of the audience had overcome their anxieties about crime, rather as those who traveled by rail in its early days were thought to have suppressed their subliminal fear of accidents.[134] According to Michotte, Rossini refused to travel by train,[135] and during the 1850s he set his fear of railways to music in a piano-piece, drawing on all the resources of tone-painting to depict a derailment in which two lives were lost.[136]

It was only by thus adopting the pose of a simultaneously cynical and naive satirist that Rossini was able to react musically to the needs and fears of audiences from a rapidly changing urban population. The success of Meyerbeer's operas had evidently led him to the conclusion that there was no longer a place for operas like *Guillaume Tell* in a society distracted by a constant succession of new perceptual demands, that rejected melancholy,[137] and sought the luxuries technical progress could bring.

133. "soggetti indigni anzì delitti atroci"; cited ibid., 2:201.

134. See Schivelbusch, *The Railway Journey*, 129–30.

135. See Michotte, *Richard Wagner's Visit to Rossini*, 23.

136. "Un petit train de plaisir comico-imitatif," in Rossini, *Péchés de Vieillesse*, vol. 6 (*Album pour les enfants dégourdis*), No. 9. On the date of composition see Gossett, "Rossini e i suoi *Péchés de Vieillesse*."

137. See Lepenies, *Melancholie und Gesellschaft*, 277.

~: 4 :~

EUGÈNE SCRIBE,
AN APOLITICAL
MAN OF LETTERS

LA MUETTE DE PORTICI

TEXT
Eugène Scribe (1791–1861) and Germain Delavigne (1790–1868)

MUSIC
Daniel-François-Esprit Auber (1782–1871)

FIRST PERFORMANCE
Paris, Académie Royale de Musique, 29 February 1828

PLACE AND DATE OF THE ACTION
Naples and Portici, a nearby fishing village, July 1647

CHARACTERS
Masaniello, Neapolitan fisherman (tenor); Fenella, his sister (mute,
a dancer); Alphonse, son of the Viceroy of Naples, Count d'Arco (tenor);
Elvire, betrothed to Alphonse (soprano); Piétro, Borella, and Moreno, Masa-
niello's companions (all basses); Lorenzo, Alphonse's confidant (tenor);
Selva, the Viceroy's officer (bass); Lady attending Elvira (soprano)

Synopsis

ACT I
The gardens of the viceregal palace in Naples. Even while receiving congrat-
ulations from the populace on his imminent marriage to Elvire, Alphonse thinks
of Fenella, whom he has seduced and has now sent soldiers to find (No. 1. *Introduction et air,* "Du prince, objet de notre amour" / "O toi! jeune victime"). Elvire
enters, in her bridal procession (No. 2. *Choeur,* "Mais du cortège qui s'avance" /
"Du prince, objet de notre amour"), and expresses her happiness (No. 3. *Air,*

"Plaisirs du rang suprême" / "À celui que j'aimais"). Dances from her Spanish homeland are performed in her honor (*1er et 2e airs de ballet*, Guarache et Boléro), but are interrupted by Fenella, fleeing from soldiers, who begs Elvire to protect her and describes her plight (No. 4. *Scène et choeur*, "Dans ces jardins, quel bruit se fait entendre?" / "O Dieu puissant! Dieu tutélaire!"). Elvire promises to help her, then enters the church for the wedding. As the bridal couple leave the church, Alphonse is horrified to see Fenella and cannot stop her recognizing him and identifying him as her seducer; Fenella makes her escape in the general confusion (No. 5. *Finale*, "Ils sont unis").

ACT II

The seashore at Portici. While the fishermen cheerfully prepare for their day's work (No. 6. *Choeur*, "Amis, le soleil va apparaître"), Masaniello broods on the tyrannical regime of the Viceroy, but only reveals his feelings obliquely in an allegorical fisherman's song (No. 7. *Barcarolle*, "Amis, la matinée est belle"). When Piétro arrives to tell him of his fruitless search for Fenella, Masaniello's anger breaks out and the two friends vow to fight to the death in their pursuit of revenge (No. 8. *Duo*, "Mieux vaut mourir que rester misérable!"). Fenella appears and for the first time tells her brother of her debauching; when Masaniello learns that her seducer is of high rank his patience is at an end and he summons all the fishermen to storm Naples (No. 9. *Finale*, "Venez, amis, venez partager mes transports").

ACT III

First setting: a room in the viceregal palace. Alphonse's insistent pleading wins Elvire's forgiveness for his infidelity (No. 10. *Duo*, "N'espérez pas me fuir" / "Écoutez-moi, je vous supplie").

Second setting: the marketplace in Naples. Traders offer their wares (No. 11. *Choeur du marché*, "Au marché qui vient de s'ouvrir") and young people dance (*3e air de ballet*, Tarantelle). One of the palace guards recognizes Fenella and tries to seize her, inadvertently sparking a bloody uprising, in the course of which Masaniello and his followers, after a prayer for divine assistance, take the city (No. 12. *Finale*, "Non, je ne me trompe pas").

ACT IV

Masaniello's cottage in Portici. After the victory Masaniello asks God's help in controlling the bloodlust of his comrades-in-arms, which Fenella also describes when she enters; her brother sings her to sleep (No. 13. *Air et cavatine*, "Spectacle affreux, jour de terreur" / "O Dieu! toi qui m'as destiné" / "Du pauvre seul ami fidèle"). Piétro comes, seeking Masaniello's approval for further acts of vengeance; Masaniello invites the fishermen into the inner room, so as not to disturb Fenella, with the result that it is she who opens the door when Alphonse and Elvire arrive, imploring shelter from the marauding crowd (No. 14. *Choeur et cavatine*, "Mais on vient. C'est Piétro" / "À nos sermens l'honneur t'engage" / "Arbitre d'une vie"). Masaniello enters and assures the fugitives of his hospitality; though angry he feels bound by his word and gives them free passage, even when Piétro has told him Alphonse's identity (No. 15. *Scène et choeur,* "Des étrangers dans ma chaumière!" / "Du transport qui m'anime"). While Neapolitans hail Masaniello as their new ruler, Piétro and his adherents swear revenge for what they regard as an act of betrayal (No. 16. *Marche et choeur,* "Honneur, honneur et gloire!").

ACT V

The entrance hall of the viceregal palace, with Vesuvius visible in the background. At the end of a frenzied orgy Piétro celebrates the rebels' victory and tells them he has given Masaniello poison (No. 17. *Barcarolle,* "Voyez, du haut de ces rivages"). A counterattack by the Viceroy's troops sends the people back to Masaniello, but in his drugged state he is no longer capable of leading them, and, as Elvire recounts to the terrified Fenella, he is killed by the bloodthirsty mob after saving the princess from certain death; after placing Alphonse's hand in that of Elvire, Fenella throws herself in despair into the crater of Vesuvius as it erupts (No. 18. *Finale,* "On vient! silence, amis!").

EDITIONS: The full score published by Troupenas in Paris in 1828 is available in many libraries in a reprint (*Early Romantic Opera* 30 [New York: Garland, 1980]); the piano-vocal score was frequently reprinted and is also widely available.

RECOMMENDED RECORDING: The only recording was made in 1986 in Monte Carlo under the direction of Thomas Fulton, with Alfredo Kraus, John Aler, and June Anderson in the principal roles. Apart from two cuts, in the first-act ballet and in the chorus No. 11, this serves as an introduction to the complete text of the work.

AN APOLITICAL MAN OF LETTERS

Eugène Scribe, the most successful French librettist of the nineteenth century, can be regarded, unlike Rossini, as typical of the liberal social order under which grand opéra flowered. Born in the same year as Meyerbeer, 1791, and only a few months before Rossini, he seems wholly a man of the nineteenth century: the aesthetic maxims of the French Enlightenment which were so dear to Jouy meant as little to him as the conventions of Italian opera seria in which Rossini, and Meyerbeer too, had been raised. He lived in Paris all his life, and the commercial class into which he was born was to prove one of the social strata which made it "the capital city of the nineteenth century"—and not in economic terms alone. He showed exceptional diligence as a student, and appeared set for a career in the law, which would have helped him up the social ladder, but before completing his studies he turned to the theater, where he scored his earliest successes in vaudeville. He quickly made his mark as a librettist of innumerable opéras comiques from 1813 onward. In spite (or perhaps because) of the attention he attracted for his substantial innovations in that genre, however, he had some difficulty getting his foot in the door of the Opéra. *Le Comte de Claros*, a three-act libretto which he wrote together with Germain Delavigne, on a subject evidently borrowed from the romancero genre, was accepted by the Opéra management in 1823, but it was never performed—indeed, probably never composed.[1] It was not until the successes of around 1830, therefore, that Scribe emerged without a rival as the most important living French librettist in the serious as well as the comic field. Eventually his librettos were set by every contemporary composer to make a mark in Paris, from Auber, Donizetti, Halévy, and Meyerbeer to Gounod, Verdi, and Offenbach. Throughout his life, Scribe continued to write for the Opéra-Comique and the numerous boulevard theaters that catered to popular tastes, but after his spectacular successes at the Opéra he even had plays produced at the Comédie-Française, thus earning a rare distinction from the two institutions that between them effectively held exclusive title to the traditions and prestige of the highest in French art. With works like *Le Verre d'eau* (1840), which went on being performed until into the twentieth century, he became the leading representative of bourgeois comedy in France, and in recognition of his status he was elected to the Académie Française in 1836.

All the same, the go-getting wordsmith aroused controversy even in his lifetime. Few critics denied themselves the pleasure of poking fun at the awkward locutions or lines in less than perfect taste that can be found in almost all his texts—and, busy as he was, he occasionally transferred lines almost unaltered from one work to another. Even those contemporaries who were ready to acknowledge without envy that he possessed a sure sense for complex and exciting dramatic construction seem to have found something rather dubious about the circumstances in which he produced his dramas, for Scribe's title pages often acknowledged one or even two co-authors, making no secret of the fact that some were not all his own work, and provoking the sardonic comment that the Académie Française should have given him a bench rather than a single chair.[2] With such practices, Scribe was about as far removed as it was possible to be from the image of the artist popularized by the contemporary Romantic movement as someone who unwaveringly pursued a poetic ideal, driven only by his own unique, personal inspiration. His immense dramatic oeuvre—the posthumous complete edition ran

1. See entry no. 260, 1 May 1823, in the receipt book of the Jury de lecture (F-Po, Archives, AD 24) and the minutes of the jury session on 28 May 1823 (ibid., AD 25, pp. 99–100).

2. See Matthews, "Eugène Scribe," 88; Koon and Switzer, *Eugène Scribe*, 26.

to no fewer than sixty-eight volumes—was geared to meet the immediate needs of the different kinds of Parisian theater. Quite clearly the value of his works in capitalist terms meant more to him than any idealistic concepts: once a year, with the exactitude of an accountant, he recorded how much he had earned from their performances, and in 1830 he gave this meticulously kept ledger the significant title "The Fortune of a Man of Letters, or, What I earned by my pen and by my labors, from 25 August 1810, the day of my leaving the Collège Sainte-Barbe, to . . . . 18. ., the day of my death."[3]

His idea of himself was determined by the value system of the ascendant bourgeoisie, which had found the doorway leading to wealth and esteem in commerce. Balzac, who was slightly younger than Scribe, provided an exemplary account of that culture in his *Histoire de la grandeur et de la décadence de César Birotteau.* The first commandment was accurate bookkeeping, and so the successful dramatist, Scribe, wrote down in his "books of personal expenditure" not only his occasional disbursements on various mistresses but even annual records of the tips he gave his servants, in a cashbook reserved for them alone.[4] When the "value" of a literary activity that eventually earned Scribe a total of almost 6 million francs[5] could be measured financially and documented to the last detail like that, political and artistic ideals alike faded into insignificance. Totting up the balance for the year 1830 in his ledger, he wrote:

> There has been a great revolution. I neither deplore nor approve its causes. I have never concerned myself with politics but only with literature, and it is from that standpoint alone that I shall examine the consequences of a change which may do me more harm than good.[6]

For us, it is surprising to see a typical member of the mercantile and commercial class distancing himself so sharply from the July Revolu-

3. "Fortune d'un homme de lettres ou Registre de ce que j'ai gagné par ma plume et par mon travail depuis le 25 août 1810, jour de ma sortie du collège Sainte-Barbe jusqu'au . . . . 18. ., jour de ma mort." F-Pn, n.a.f. 22573, fol. 1.

4. F-Pn, n.a.f. 22572 and 22574.

5. In the appendix of the ledger referred to in the text, under the heading "Received from my work" ("J'ai reçu de mon travail"), a "general recapitulation" lists income amounting to exactly 5,786,276 francs for the years from 1811 to Scribe's death on 20 February 1861 (F-Pn, n.a.f. 22573, fols. 139v–140v).

6. "Une grande révolution vient d'éclater. Je n'en blâme ni n'en approuve les causes. Je ne me suis jamais mêlé de politique, mais de littérature, et c'est sous ce dernier rapport seulement que j'examinerai les conséquences d'un changement qui doit m'être plus nuisible qu'utile." Ibid., fol. 53; cited without source in Bonnefon, "Scribe sous l'Empire et sous la Restauration," 368.

tion. The accession of the "citizen king" Louis-Philippe within a few days of the fall of the reactionary Charles X had made it obvious to everyone that the bourgeoisie could expect to profit from the change and the more liberal economic order it had introduced. In addition to that, any author who had had to struggle incessantly with the petty interference of the censors throughout the 1820s[7] ought to have been delighted with the Charte constitutionelle of 7 August 1830, by means of which censorship was suspended for the first time in the history of the French theater—if only for a few years.[8]

But Scribe appears to have opted for the complacent position of an "apolitical" citizen as early as 1830, seeking to persuade himself that business and the theater had nothing to do with politics, and behaving as though the decision to adopt an antipolitical stance was not itself political.

OPERA AND REVOLUTION

It is only against the backdrop of this ambivalence toward all political realities that we can understand how a libretto by Scribe came to be involved in an event that brought the histories of music and politics into contact with each other in a quite extraordinary way. The government of the United Netherlands had arranged for a gala performance of *La Muette de Portici* by Auber and Scribe to be given in Brussels on 25 August 1830 as part of the celebrations for the fifty-ninth birthday of King William I. In connection with this event, a revolution began that led to the secession of the southern part of the Dutch kingdom and the foundation of Belgium as an independent state.

Histories of music have repeatedly exaggerated the importance of the links between this celebrated performance of *La Muette* and the Belgian revolution—as if the sight of the Neapolitan insurrection on the stage was the thing that first gave the spectators the idea of taking up arms against their Dutch rulers. Close examination of the historical events leaves no room for doubt that the opera performance, as the principal event of the royal birthday celebrations, had been chosen several days beforehand to be the spark for the uprising:

> Although from the evidence at hand, *La Muette* in itself did not, after all, spontaneously incite or initiate the Belgian revolution of August, 1830 (the spirit of the period notwithstanding), but was deliberately used as a

7. See Krakovitch, *Hugo censuré*, 36–38.
8. Ibid., 7.

point of departure according to a previously conceived and carefully but apparently flexibly prepared plan, there is no doubt that its daring subject-matter (rooted in actual history) and its musical—and particularly, its dramatic and scenic—treatment contributed considerably to the success of the plan. The musical drama may, in fact, have drawn into action innocent spectators who might otherwise have remained aloof from the hysteria of the night.[9]

This raises the question, much discussed in recent years,[10] of why Scribe and Auber's dramatic treatment of the historical subject came to have such a revolutionary impact, and how great its influence really was. Scribe's choice, in 1825, of the 1648 uprising of Neapolitan fishermen as the subject for a drama was not remarkable in itself, in view of the newly fashionable interest in historical narrative. The surprising thing was that, although he had still not had any of his works put on at the Opéra, he did not offer the subject to a boulevard theater or the Opéra-Comique, but to the tradition-bound Académie Royale de la Musique, where customarily persons of humble origins trod the boards only in attendance on those of higher rank. It was no secret, however, that tragédie lyrique was in crisis, and while La Rochefoucauld, as minister responsible for the Opéra, sought to rejuvenate the repertory by offering commissions to Rossini, a composer of Italian opera seria who had until then only worked outside France, Scribe and his co-author Delavigne saw an opportunity to obtain the entrée to France's leading theater by proposing a new kind of subject matter.

In the full awareness that they were setting aside accepted conventions of French serious opera, they arrived at a product the novelty of which would seem to guarantee the interest of the public; but at the same time they could not avoid offending the sensibilities of the guardians of traditional taste, the members of the Opéra's literary jury, who were the first people to examine librettos that were submitted. In the minutes of a meeting held in October 1825, when they studied the libretto in a first draft (possibly the work of Delavigne for it is in his handwriting),[11] the jury's doubts about the uncommon nature of the opera are combined with concrete suggestions for its improvement. It is a lengthy document that shows how strong was the jury's tendency still to consider a libretto purely as a work of literature, and how completely blind its members were to spectacular aspects that could be far more

9. Slatin, "Opera and revolution," 56.
10. See the references cited below, notes 15 and 17–26.
11. See Schneider, introduction to *La Muette de Portici*, 4.

effective in the theater than wordy descriptions. They singled out certain improbabilities in the love interest, for example, and were particularly exercised by the absence of any explanation for the muteness of the eponymous heroine: they could imagine someone who had lost the power of speech as the result of an accident, or someone born deaf-mute, but they could not understand a heroine who simply was what she was. And of course they were upset by the "very sad, distressing impression" made by the unhappy ending, and wanted the authors "to find means to soften, if possible, this painful catastrophe."[12]

On the other hand, surprising though it may seem, they raised no objections to the revolutionary subject matter and its political implications. That aspect was not raised until the censors saw the libretto in August 1827, although by then it had been rewritten, with the depiction of the popular uprising greatly watered down. Luckily for Scribe and Delavigne, however, the individual censors were not in full agreement. Jean-Louis Laya protested against the "deplorable" idea of combing history books for the "vilest and most obscure scoundrels" with the intention of making heroes of them, and disputed the authors' right "to denature [history] in order to exalt vice or crime, and bring virtue or innocence low." Such moral considerations hardly touched his colleague René-André-Polydore de Chazet who, although he saw "the grave impropriety of putting a revolution on the stage," emphasized the great skill with which the subject was addressed. This attitude, in which the rigid aesthetic judgments of the ancien régime can be seen giving way already to the liberal belief in the *juste milieu*, carried the day and the censors' concluding report approved the libretto of *La Muette de Portici* for performance on condition that a few small alterations were made.[13]

This is especially surprising in view of the subsequent events in Brussels, for Scribe and Delavigne depict the leader of the revolutionaries with obvious sympathy. The fisherman Masaniello takes up arms (in the final version) for the sole reason that his mute sister, Fenella, has been

12. "impression bien triste, bien pénible"; "à chercher les moyens d'adoucir, s'il se peut, cette douloureuse catastrophe." From the document accompanying Louis-Simon Auger's letter to La Rochefoucauld, 24 October 1825, F-Pan, O³ 1724 (II). See also Mongrédien, "Variations sur un thème," 110–11.

13. The separate reports by Laya, dated 4 August 1827 ("l'idée ... déplorable que d'aller chercher dans l'histoire les plus vils et les plus obscurs scélérats pour les transformer en héros"; "dénaturer [l'histoire] pour exalter le vice ou le crime, et flétrir la vertu ou l'innocence"), and Chazet, dated 8 August 1827 ("le grave inconvénient de mettre une révolution en scène"), are with the censorship documents, F-Pan, F²¹ 969, while the concluding report is with the Opéra documents, F-Pan, AJ¹³ 1050. See also Mongrédien, "Variations sur un thème," 111–14.

dishonored. Later he even allows the Viceroy's son to go free, because the sacred laws of hospitality are stronger than his desire for vengeance. His aristocratic counterpart, Alphonse, on the other hand, is presented as the seducer of an unprotected maiden, Fenella. At the same time Scribe and Delavigne did not take the side of the oppressed, but, showing "the fine, delicate touch of a skillful painter well versed in all the secrets of his art" that the censors praised,[14] they ensured a thoroughgoing depoliticization of the explosive material by concentrating on the complexities of the personal relationships, and furthermore so distributed light and shade that the faults of the governing class are excusable but those of the ravening crowd are not. Their libretto is at bottom unambivalently antirevolutionary. While Alphonse is shown to be aware of his faults and troubled by his conscience, and displays the self-doubt typical of the "indecisive hero," the revolutionary mob is an epitome of brutality and murderous blood-lust. The opera ends, therefore, with the crushing of the rebels who have poisoned their own leader, Masaniello, in blind rage. The final chorus, in particular, added only in August 1827 when the censors were considering the libretto,[15] makes it plain that

> the death of the insurgents is meant to be regarded as atonement for their uprising. The eruption of Vesuvius, into which Fenella throws herself, shows how even nature abhors the injustice carried out by an unbridled, revolutionary mob . . . which now—at the sight of the powers of nature allied to the old and new authorities—prostrates itself . . . and begs for mercy: "Grâce pour notre crime! / Grand Dieu! protège-nous ! / Et que cette victime / Suffise à ton courroux!" ["Mercy for our crime! / Great God, protect us! / And may this one victim / assuage your wrath!"], sensing that punishment is inevitable the moment the volcano starts to rumble . . . It is the good nobles who—purged by the past—survive into the future with their power restored to them.[16]

Goethe, aged eighty-two, was in no doubt about the opera's antirevolutionary tendency, commenting, "The whole opera is, in fact, a satire upon the people; for, when it makes a public matter of a fisher-girl's amour, and calls the prince a tyrant because he marries a princess, it appears as absurd and ridiculous as possible."[17] Certainly, impartial

---

14. "la touche fine et délicate d'un peintre habile qui connaît bien tous les secrets de son art." F-Pan, AJ[13] 1050.

15. See Schneider, introduction to *La Muette de Portici*, 7; on the date, see idem, *Chronologisch-thematisches Verzeichnis*, 1:227–28.

16. Rieger, "*La Muette de Portici* von Auber/Scribe," 355–56.

17. Eckermann, *Conversations with Goethe*, 397.

reading of the whole libretto can lead to no other conclusion than that the representation of a revolution in such terms offered no threat whatever to a reactionary regime. Naivete on the part of the authorities, therefore, was not the reason why the opera was staged more than once in politically delicate circumstances.[18] The King of the Netherlands had expressly insisted on its performance on 25 August 1830, even though an earlier performance had unleashed anti-Dutch reactions,[19] and it had actually been given in Paris in May 1830 on the occasion of a state visit by the King and Queen of Naples.[20]

What the literary-minded French censors and Goethe in his study both overlooked, however, is that a libretto is not designed to be read in silence. In the course of an actual performance in the theater, "the ideological structure of the libretto as a whole breaks away from the viewpoint of the individual recipient, and the separate parts . . . acquire a relative autonomy, which makes relativization harder for the audience in the context of the opera as a whole."[21] Thus, in combination, the text and music of the celebrated duet in the second act ("Mieux vaut mourir que rester misérable"—"Better die than remain in misery") took on an exhortatory character capable of being received out of context by an audience already charged with revolutionary sentiments. In its refrain, "Amour sacré de la patrie," Scribe and Delavigne quoted the first line of the sixth verse of the *Marseillaise*, and the strongly marked rhythms of Auber's music also invoked successful models of revolutionary music, with an effect reinforced here by a technique plainly borrowed from Rossini, of fortissimo emphases on unstressed beats of the bar.

The revolutionary effect of this antirevolutionary opera is exemplified in this refrain. The majority of the accounts of the famous performance in Brussels in 1830 mention that it was this duet, above everything else, that provoked the demonstrations of revolutionary enthusiasm.[22] Revolutionary-minded German students sang it as a battle-hymn, while audiences in Frankfurt am Main in 1831 were said to have demanded encores of this number at every performance, and to have gone on to exchange blows with members of the city militia.[23] In Paris, too, where the première had taken place without incident, the opera was later associated with revolutionary events: after the successful outcome

18. See Finscher, "Aubers *La Muette de Portici*," 104, n. 34.
19. See Slatin, "Opera and Revolution," 47.
20. See Muret, *L'Histoire par le théâtre*, 2:290.
21. Rieger, "*La Muette de Portici* von Auber/Scribe," 357–58.
22. See Slatin, "Opera and Revolution," 53–54.
23. See Finscher, "Aubers *La Muette de Portici*," 99.

9   This drawing by the Belgian illustrator Louis Titz (1859–1932) purports to
have been based on a sketch by an eye-witness (see Colenbrander, *De afscheiding
van België*, 14) of the uproar that broke out among revolutionary sympathizers
in the audience at the Brussels performance of *La Muette de Portici* on 25 August
1830. Significantly, Titz selects the barnstorming duet "Amour sacré de la
patrie" from Act II as the epitome of the five-act work, and thus supports the
one-sided interpretation of Auber's opera as the invocation of revolutionary
sentiment.

of the July Revolution, it was performed repeatedly with the action broken off at the end of Act IV, with Masaniello in triumph, and Act V
replaced by the singing of the *Parisienne*.[24]

Yet in different political circumstances Auber's opera was the occasion of demonstrations of Bonapartist and patriotic sentiment—as in
Paris shortly before the outbreak of the Franco-Prussian War in
1870[25]—and it was reported of a performance in Copenhagen that loyal
Danes rose to their feet during the famous duet and shouted "Long live
the King!"[26]

In their different ways, these incidents in the opera's checkered and
contradictory reception history confirm the thesis that the key to its
extraordinary emotional effect lay in the music.[27] At the time of its earliest performances, one critic, Stefan Schütze, showed more acumen than
most in recognizing the part the *music* played in the dramaturgy:

> The thing that gives the opera as a whole its unique constitution is—
> the dominance throughout of the *affects*, which here and there, it is true,
> successfully express heroic sentiments, but leave the music with too little
> time and too little repose for that representation of inner states which is,
> when all is said and done, the principal purpose and aim of opera. . . .
> Thus the composer has often, even when it was unnecessary, followed the
> *principle of excitement* which predominates in the text.[28]

The strongly marked rhythms evoking the bellicose dynamic of revolutionary songs in the Act II duet are found in almost every other number
in the opera as well, even in an aria in which Masaniello communes with
God, at the beginning of Act IV, and in the contemplative ensemble
"Je sens qu'en sa présence," which comes at the end of the same act, in
a dramatic situation where time seems suspended. This use of strong
pulses in the slow passages of large-scale ensembles was very common
in nineteenth-century opera in general, but other composers modified

---

24. See Muret, *L'Histoire par le théâtre*, 3:16.

25. See Rieger, "*La Muette de Portici* von Auber/Scribe," 353.

26. See Longyear, "*La Muette de Portici*," 45.

27. See Finscher, "Aubers *La Muette de Portici*," 101; Borchmeyer, *Die Götter tanzen
Cancan*, 57–59.

28. "Wodurch nun aber die ganze Oper ihre eigentümliche Beschaffenheit erhält,
ist—das durchgängige Vorherrschen der *Affekte*, die hier und da wohl mit Erfolg zum
Ausdruck des Heroischen führen, aber der Musik zur Darstellung innerer Zustände, wie
dies doch bei Opern hauptsächlich Ziel und Zweck ist, zu wenig Zeit und zu wenig Ruhe
lassen. . . . Der Komponist ist also oft sogar da, wo es nicht nötig war, dem *Prinzip der
Aufregung* gefolgt, das im Texte herrscht." Schütze, "Ueber die Stumme von Portici," 30
and 33.

the effect by combining it with particularly smooth melodic lines. Auber, for his part, gives this Andante as insistent a forward impetus as the chorus "Honneur, honneur et gloire" sung in homage to Masaniello in the Act IV finale: this melody (already heard in the Overture) also possesses a strong pulse and has the "terrible élan" of a military quick march.

The "principle of excitement" affects more than certain musical details: it underlies the whole formal conception of the opera, which is as far removed from Rossini's works of the same period as can be imagined. Of course the leading soloists in *La Muette de Portici* have extended arias with separate, musically contrasted sections, but Auber fails to use the form to delineate character with precise nuances or to highlight psychological conflict. It is only the text that reveals Alphonse's indecisiveness: there is none of the musical expression of inner conflict that Rossini brings off in *Guillaume Tell*. In Alphonse's entrance aria, and in Elvire's which follows it, Auber contents himself with juxtaposing emotions in a schematic fashion that can only be described as wooden. For the rest, short-breathed forms like the barcarole cavatina dominate the opera, which has by far the shortest text of any of Scribe's five-act librettos.

This shortness of breath, underlining the "principle of excitement," is not without a positive aspect. The concision and drastic compression praised by Wagner[29] constitutes the decisive element distinguishing Scribe's first work for the Opéra from every other French opera, especially those by Rossini. It is only when *Guillaume Tell* is compared with *La Muette de Portici* that we can understand what a disastrous effect the succession of choral numbers in Rossini's first act, deplored by Berlioz,[30] or the epic breadth of the entrance of one group of Swiss patriots after another in the finale of the second act must have had.

Two diametrically opposed dramaturgical conceptions meet head-on here, and it is not surprising that the one that prevailed after 1830 was the one that Scribe did more than anyone else to shape, in which the rapid succession of contrasting dramatic events seems to encapsulate something of the breathless excitement of life in a large city.

"THE WELL-MADE PLAY"

In the course of writing numerous pieces for the Opéra-Comique and the boulevard theaters, Scribe had developed an infallible sense for a

29. *Erinnerungen an Auber* [1871], in *Gesammelte Schriften*, 9:45.
30. "*Guillaume Tell* de Rossini," 337 (in Radiciotti, 141).

precise mechanism of plot construction and the colorful details that heighten dramatic tension. When he began to write for the Opéra as well, therefore, he was able to introduce into the tradition-bound and artistically distinct genre of serious opera elements that satisfied new perceptual needs with fast-moving and exciting librettos. Heedless of the aesthetic conventions of tragédie lyrique, he wrote dialogue mixing the elevated verse of classical tragedy with modern colloquial forms, and he dispensed with the limited range of locations deemed suitable for the action of earlier operas. Of course his librettos continued to have scenes set in royal palaces and temples (and churches), but they also astonished spectators with scenery of an unvarnished realism that must have been almost intolerable to conservative champions of the theater as the seat of the "marvelous." When Swiss shepherds and fisherfolk were depicted on the shore of the Lake of Lucerne in Rossini's *Guillaume Tell*, even if the principal characters were no longer restricted to members of the upper classes, the location itself could still be accommodated within the classical definition of a *locus amoenus*. In Act IV of *La Muette de Portici*, on the other hand, Scribe set the interior of a poor fisherman's cottage before his audiences. In the second scene of Act III of the same opera, the direction "a large square" ("grande place") appears to conform to the convention of setting major public events in public squares, but the square in question is a marketplace, and Scribe's detailed specifications of Neapolitan traders selling their fruit, flowers, and fish divest the scene of all public grandeur or formality.

We will return to what Franz Liszt disapprovingly called Scribe's "superabundance of picturesque motives"[31] in a later chapter, to discuss it in the different context of *Les Huguenots*. One of its effects was to blur the differences between the historical subjects of Scribe's serious operas and the subjects of his other works, which, almost without exception, were set in the present. Although historical characters were now seen on stage for the first time in garments that nodded to historical realism rather than in "timeless" costumes, their circumstances and their all too human ways of reacting to them brought them nearer to the prosaic present, whereas once they had been set apart as exemplary, larger-than-life figures. Nothing distinguishes Scribe's procedures when working on the libretto of a grand opéra from those he had developed during his years of writing for the popular theater. The crucial thing for him was not the conjunction of politics, morals, and emotions that had been at the center of classical French tragedy and most serious opera of the

31. "Ueberfülle von pittoresquen Motiven"; "*Die Stumme von Portici* von Auber," 28.

eighteenth century, but the constantly changing configuration of different characters in carefully delimited scenes, which he always began by
outlining in a couple of sentences. Only after he had discussed this first
outline of the plot with his collaborators and the composer did he proceed to work up the text, and it was an unavoidable consequence that he
neglected psychological differentiation of individual characters in favor
of the precise calculation of the mechanism of the plot.

Since the early twentieth century, for want of a more exact term,
dramatic construction in emulation of Scribe's technique has been described by the phrase "well-made play."[32] American scholars, in particular, have tried to define this as exactly as possible, but identifying its
essential characteristics has inescapably involved some measure of oversimplification. Stephen Sadler Stanton attempted a definition, in the
mid-1950s, with a list of six essential "structural features,"[33] but since
then Patti Gillespie has pointed out that their strict application would
exclude well over two-thirds of Scribe's own output, while one less strict
would embrace "a wide variety of plays which no one seems to mean
when using the term *well-made*."[34] Nevertheless, running the six features
in question over texts like that of *La Muette de Portici* enables us to recognize the things which Scribe's plays, vaudevilles, and operatic librettos have in common, and also to pinpoint the differences between his
dramaturgy and the conventions prevailing in French and Italian opera
in the early years of the nineteenth century.

When the curtain rises on the first act of *La Muette de Portici* to show
the cast making ready for the marriage of Alphonse and Elvire, with
the prince guilt-stricken over his love affair with Fenella, the situation
provides the basis for the first of Stanton's six features, namely "a
delayed-action plot whose point of attack occurs at the climax of the
story of which it is a part and whose central character struggles to overcome obstacles (usually to love and marriage)." Scribe turns the high-
born male protagonist of earlier operas into an indecisive hero, who
scarcely allows political considerations to affect him at all, and moral
ones only to the extent that they have a bearing on the state of his own
emotions. The crucial obstacle to Alphonse's marriage, his illegitimate
liaison with the mute fisher-girl, Fenella, is not directly mentioned in
this opening scene, any more than are his father's dynastic plans, to further which the Viceroy has arranged the marriage with Elvire and had

32. "la pièce bien faite." See Longyear, "Le livret bien fait," 175.
33. "English Drama," 41–42.
34. "Plays: Well-complicated," 20, n. 4.

Fenella thrown into prison. Those matters have been banished to the prehistory of the opera, and this device for delaying the plot's "point of attack" sets Scribe's libretto midway between operas like Gluck's *Armide* or Spontini's *Vestale*, in which the exposition takes place on stage, and others such as Verdi's *Trovatore*, which has so long and complex a prehistory that modern "opera guides" have to give it more space than they do to the actual events of the drama. Fenella's unexpected entrance in scene 4 helps the audience to grasp the prehistory in a condensed form, and at the same time, by means of this visible confirmation of the vague hints dropped by Alphonse, Scribe sets an effective match to the fuse of his "delayed-action plot."

Even before Fenella begins to convey her sad story to Elvire, the experienced operagoer will have realized that the mute is the princess's rival in love, and will be waiting impatiently for it to dawn on Elvire, too, so that she can confront Alphonse with his perfidy. As in most plays and comic operas this process relies on Stanton's second feature: "a pattern of increasingly intense action and suspense, carefully prepared by exposition which establishes certain facts for the spectator and causes him to anticipate each significant event."

Scribe prepares the climax of the dramatic complications in Act IV in a very similar manner. At this point the audience—and Fenella— know that the fugitives to whom Masaniello has given shelter are Alphonse and Elvire, but Masaniello himself does not. Inevitably he finds out, but that discovery is only a first high-point, and it leads on to a sequence of further amazing twists in the plot. His assurance of hospitality carries more weight for Masaniello than his vow of vengeance, and the prince and princess are saved, contrary to expectation. Masaniello's comrades-in-arms have no sympathy for this act of generosity, and they vow to be revenged on him, taking him for a new oppressor. The act does not end with a premonition of Masaniello's fall, however, but with his triumph, after another surprising twist of fate: the principal inhabitants of Naples arrive at the cottage to pay homage and hand him the keys to the city. Instead of a simple peripeteia, like the end of Act III of *Guillaume Tell*, Scribe unfolds "a teeter-totter arrangement of incidents to create successive ups and downs in the fortunes of the hero caused by his conflict with one or more opponents and leading to his ultimate triumph or failure"—the third of Stanton's structural features.

The first peripeteia comes in this large-scale act-finale, as Piétro recognizes that the fugitive Masaniello is sheltering is none other than Alphonse. This will have greater consequences for Masaniello's future than Alphonse's, for it provides the jealous Piétro with a welcome opportunity to discredit the hitherto unassailable leader of the rebellion in the eyes of the bloodthirsty mob. By saving the prince from the murderous vengeance of the revolutionaries, Masaniello appears to have succeeded in preventing further bloodshed, but in reality his hours are numbered, and in the final tableau of Act IV the conspirators who will poison him in Act V are already making their preparations. Although the death of one of the opera's leading characters is being set up here, Scribe treats the confrontation between Masaniello and his rival Piétro as a minor matter, so that the fourth of Stanton's structural features— "the counterpunch of peripeteia or upset followed by a *scène à faire* or obligatory scene, in which the hero is victorious because of the release to his opponent of the formerly withheld secrets"—is significantly modified. Piétro is not a victorious hero, and Masaniello's undertaking to Alphonse does not amount to a knowingly "withheld secret." Nevertheless, Scribe chooses to have a contemplative ensemble at this precise moment, to serve as a *scène à faire* in which all the major characters express their contrary feelings; furthermore the scene shows how he intensifies the conflict between Masaniello's efforts on behalf of moderation and the uncompromising demands of the radicals led by Piétro, which has already been indicated in the earlier ensemble "Mais on vient. C'est Piétro," but now reaches the point of no return.

One of the most surprising things to emerge from close reading of the libretto is the fact that Masaniello never learns that Alphonse is his sister's seducer. Fenella does no more than signify to him, in the fourth scene of Act II, that it was a Spaniard who had promised to marry her. It is the anger aroused by this revelation which, in the completed version of the opera, drives Masaniello to start the revolt against the rule of the Spanish Viceroy, but the motive for the revolution is vitiated by his saving the life of the very Spaniard who seduced Fenella. Masaniello recognizes that Alphonse is the Viceroy's son, and blames him (in Act IV, scene 8) for the wrongs that follow from the accident of his birth, but completely fails to realize that he has before him the individual responsible for dishonoring his sister. Even if this misapprehension is less glaring than Raoul's mistaken belief in Valentine's unfaithfulness in *Les Huguenots*, it is nonetheless a dramatic device which hitherto had been possible only in comedies, Stanton's number 5, "a central misunderstanding or *quiproquo*, made obvious to the spectator but withheld from the participants."

Finally, the sixth of those "structural features," the "reproduction in miniature of the overall delayed-action pattern in the individual acts," shows very clearly how much Scribe's first libretto for a serious opera owes to principles of dramatic structure that originated in the spoken theater and opéra comique. In the case of his second, those origins were reflected in its genesis: *Robert le diable*, set to music by Meyerbeer and performed at the Opéra in 1831, had at first been intended for the Opéra-Comique. But in *La Muette de Portici*, too—which, like *Robert le diable*, was expanded from three to five acts after much revision—the connections with opéra comique are not confined to dramaturgy, and similarly Auber's music, with its barcaroles and cavatinas, and its overall predilection for short-breathed forms, cannot deny its opéra-comique ancestry.[35] Even in his lifetime, people questioned whether Auber's musical language was really suitable for grand opéra. Bellini's friend Cottrau commented maliciously that all Auber's operas were opéras comiques in the last analysis.[36] Franz Liszt, in one of a number of articles he wrote in the 1850s about well-known contemporary operas, advised against overrating the musical quality of *La Muette de Portici*. Consciously (if tacitly) adopting a contrary view to the enthusiasm expressed by Wagner, which has influenced opinions of Auber to this day, Liszt recommends listeners not to close their eyes to the fact that in general the style of the opera is "short of breath and meanly cut . . . falls a long way short of Rossini."[37]

If the musical language does not bear out one much more recent writer's view that *La Muette de Portici* already fully represents a new "subgenre" of serious opera,[38] the dramaturgical elements it owed to opéra comique became standard features of works written for the Paris Opéra after Rossini's *Guillaume Tell*. While a barcarole in strophic form would have been perceived as a stylistic intrusion in one of Meyerbeer's grands opéras, the influence of the principle of dramatic concision is omnipresent in them. In the historical operas composed after 1830, to be sure, such traits were bound up with a new concept that was closer to *Guillaume Tell* than to *La Muette* in striving for the grandiose. But it took the successful combination of the two traditions, to which Scribe aspired in the texts of *Gustave III, ou Le Bal masqué* (1833) and *La Juive* (1835), but which was not realized musically until Meyerbeer composed *Les Huguenots* (1836), to lead French grand opéra to a culmination in

35. See Pendle, *Eugène Scribe*, 403.

36. See Bellini's letter to Francesco Florimo dated 10 October 1834, in Bellini, *Epistolario*, 459; see also Pendle, *Eugène Scribe*, 406.

37. "daß [der Gesammt-Charakter des Styls dieser Oper] kurzathmig und knappen Zuschnitts ist . . . weit hinter dem Rossinis zurückbleibt"; Liszt, *"Die Stumme von Portici von Auber,"* 28.

38. See Finscher, *"Aubers La Muette de Portici,"* 87.

which the few surviving conventions of tragédie lyrique and the structural principles of opéra comique melded in a new conception.[39]

The Mélodrame

While essential structural innovations in Auber's first serious opera went back to contemporary opéra comique, its visual spectacle, which makes a far more immediate impact on the audience, was very closely associated with a genre that dominated the Parisian boulevard theater in the early years of the nineteenth century. A new form of popular theater had evolved, known, from about 1800 onward, as *mélodrame*—a term that did not acquire pejorative overtones until later. The influence of the aesthetic theories of Diderot and Mercier bore fruit in dramas such as *Coelina, ou L'Enfant du mystère* ("Celina, or, The Child of Mystery") (1800) by François-René Guilbert de Pixérécourt (1773–1844), a successful playwright who was nicknamed "the Corneille of the boulevards." The successors of the middle-class comédie larmoyante, *Coelina* and the like depicted simple people embroiled in sentimental complications, garnished with high-sounding monologues and a sizeable pinch of horror. The essence of these pieces was "this mixture of the merry and the sad, of music, elocution, and ballet, in short, this confusion of genres,"[40] which conservatives of course deplored as contrary to the rules of literature, but which plainly revealed its historical origins. As late as 1841, in the introduction to a collection of Pixérécourt's plays, Charles Nodier asserted that mélodrame embodied "the morality of the revolution";[41] but in 1814, immediately after the return of the Bourbon monarchy, an opportunistic playwright demanded an end to "these scenes of impiety, murder, and folly" arguing that there was no longer any need for a genre born of "those terrible times when it was necessary to familiarize people with crime, to accustom their eyes to the most hideous scenes," for now France had seen the restoration of "religion, peace, and reason."[42]

In fact, however much mélodrame owed to Romantic-Gothick hor-

---

39. See Pendle, *Eugène Scribe*, 426.

40. "ce mélange du gai, du triste, de la musique, de la déclamation et des ballets, en un mot cette confusion des genres," Pixérécourt, *Guerre au mélodrame!!!*, 9.

41. "la moralité de la révolution," Nodier, introduction to Pixérécourt, *Théâtre choisi*, 1:viii (cited hereafter as Nodier, Introduction).

42. "ces tableaux d'impiété, de meurtres et de folies"; "ces temps affreux, où il fallait familiariser le peuple avec les crimes, où il fallait accoutumer ses yeux aux tableaux les plus hideux"; "la religion, la paix et la raison"; [Hapdé], *Plus de Mélodrames!*, 30–31, 1, 30.

ror, it never glorified crime or criminals. On the contrary, good and evil were clearly identified and unambivalent, and it was always certain that the former would triumph over the latter in the end. Stereotyped characters, like the wily tyrant, the innocent damsel in distress, the country bumpkin, and the gallant knight ever ready to draw his sword in defense of innocence[43] were fixtures of the new genre as immovable as the dramaturgical technique whereby the happy ending resulted from the amazing mutual recognition of two of the principal characters.

Although a small orchestra was on hand at performances of these mélodrames to accompany selected scenes of dialogue and passages of pantomime,[44] it is not easy to characterize the genre as one particular form of musical theater (unlike Rousseau's *Pygmalion* [1770], for which he adapted the name "mélodrame" from *melodramma*, the regular word for "opera" in Italian, or the works by Georg Benda in a similar form), for in the early years there was usually no written codification of the music played in them. Nevertheless, contemporary audiences could not miss the operatic affinities: if the English poet and librettist W. H. Auden decreed in the twentieth century that "a good libretto plot is a melodrama in both the strict and the conventional sense of the word,"[45] Pixérécourt had expressed the corollary as long ago as 1818: "A *mélodrame* is simply a *drame lyrique* in which the music is performed by the orchestra instead of being sung."[46]

There is no mistaking Pixérécourt's intention, in drawing that parallel, of appropriating on behalf of the despised mélodrame some part of the nimbus surrounding one of the highest-ranking art forms. The gulf that prevented mélodrame, with its poor reputation and its audiences drawn primarily from the middle and lower classes of the population of Paris, from being performed at the Opéra, with its aristocratic and hautbourgeois clientele, was as much social as aesthetic, and it was unbridgeable. All the same, the plentiful production of new melodramas in the many boulevard theaters was plainly followed with interest by all theater professionals: Rossini described the mélodrame on which his opera *La gazza ladra* (1817) was based as a "most beautiful subject,"[47] and Meyer-

---

43. See A!A!A!, *Traité du mélodrame*, 14–26.

44. See Sala, *L'opera senza canto*.

45. "Notes on music and opera," 471.

46. "Un mélodrame n'est autre chose qu'un Drame lyrique, dont la musique est exécutée par l'orchestre au lieu d'être chantée"; *Guerre au mélodrame!!!*, 14; see also Sala, "Dal *Mélodrame à grand spectacle*," 178.

47. "soggetto bellissimo"; Rossini's letter to his mother, dated 19 March 1817, in Roberti, "Da autografi di grandi musicisti," 626.

beer is said to have been able to recite the titles of all fifty-nine of Pixérécourt's melodramas from memory.[48] Victor Hugo actually wrote a
drame for performance in one of the theaters that specialized in mélodrame (the bloodthirsty *Lucrèce Borgia* [1833], which was also composed
in short order by Donizetti), and it takes only a quick look at the immense output of Eugène Scribe to realize just how much he owed to
the genre.

Besides technical innovations that will be considered below, Scribe's
most important stylistic borrowing from mélodrame in a libretto like
that of *La Muette de Portici* was its manner of distributing light and
shadow, good and evil, with a broad brush across characters that were
types rather than individuals. The kind of inner conflict that is an essential ingredient of classical drama is just about discernible in the indecisive hero, Alphonse, but it is completely alien to Masaniello and, above
all, Fenella. Scribe dispenses with the tradition of tragic conflict as the
essence of drama and depicts the mute girl from the first as the epitome
of victimized innocence. With her means of expression limited to
mime, she lacks the ability to acquaint the audience with her problems
in any detail and can only arouse a generalized feeling of compassion.
Already she displays the "polarization of the female character between
guilt and innocence"[49] that was to be typical of Italian Romantic opera
and, in grand opéra, in *Les Huguenots* for example, led to passages in
which the meek Valentine almost disappears from view altogether. The
characterization of Masaniello, too, has more in common with the stereotype of the knightly champion of virtue from mélodrame than with
the alternative models in French tragedy, who always brought political
considerations to the foreground in the admittedly exceptional instances
when leaders of popular rebellion were represented. Finally, Fenella's
hopeless love for Alphonse, which determines her actions right up to
her death, is not a conscious affect, and to that extent it is not amenable
to discursive explication in monologues or arias: it is only a blind—
not to say mute—"passion capable of generating large and rapid contrasts."[50]

An earlier chapter contained Grétry's reflections on the dramatic potential of violent contrast and showed Jouy beginning to exploit it in
his librettos; in *La Muette de Portici* Scribe systematically extended that
potential to the structure of an entire opera and its line-up of characters.

48. See J. Weber, *Meyerbeer*, 49–50; Véron, *Mémoires*, 1:258.
49. Accorsi, "Il melodramma melodrammatico," 118.
50. Ibid.

Like Pixérécourt in his mélodrames, Scribe organizes the order of events so that each new setting in turn is a striking contrast to the one before it,[51] and the same principle governs the ballets and the overwhelming final scene. For the ballet in Act III, Scribe did not even contrive an external reason in the plot to justify a pause in the action for celebratory dances, as Rossini and Jouy still took the trouble to do a year later for the ballets in the first and third acts of *Guillaume Tell*. The dance of the young people in the marketplace in Naples is, rather, an integral part of the action, in that the rapid movement of the dancers enables Fenella to hide among them from the soldiers who are pursuing her. This model of direct confrontation between innocent, harmless dancers and murderous soldiers (which Scribe used again in Act III of *Les Vêpres siciliennes*) owes more than the principle of contrast to contemporary mélodrame: there was a direct precursor for it in Pixérécourt's *Marguerite d'Anjou* (1810) where the ballet in Act II is set up in exactly the same way.[52] The spectacular eruption of Vesuvius with which *La Muette de Portici* ends also had direct predecessors in plays written for the popular Paris theaters: the Théâtre de l'Ambigu-Comique had thrilled its patrons with a volcanic eruption as long ago as 1788, Pixérécourt's *Le Belvéder, ou La Vallée d'Etna* (1818) repeated the effect thirty years later in the same theater, while he famously buried the action of his *La Tête de mort* (1827) under the lava of Vesuvius.[53]

Compared with an inferno of such proportions, the way Scribe and Auber's opera ends seems almost conciliatory, even if the melodramatically heightened contrasts and differences between the rebellious fishermen and the members of the Neapolitan viceregal court are finally unresolved. In the extreme confrontations between the "good" fisherfolk and their arrogant Spanish rulers, the "good" Masaniello and the "bad" Jacobins Piétro and Borella, and indeed sinful mankind and mighty nature, Scribe seems to have adopted the fundamental structural principle of mélodrame. But however melodramatic (in the pejorative sense) we find *La Muette de Portici* today, Scribe was still a long way from the conventions of the mélodrame of his day. Innocence is persecuted and virtue is unassailable in the fishing village of Portici, but no villain is depicted in the act of persecuting or attempting to assail them. Alphonse's father, the person really responsible for Fenella's imprisonment, remains unseen in the background, and both the indecisive

51. See Pendle, "The Boulevard theaters," 517.
52. Ibid., 515, 529.
53. Ibid., 517, 532; Sala, "'Que ses gestes parlants,'" 509–10.

10 This engraving by Nash, dating from the early 1830s, depicts the interior of the Paris Opéra during a performance of *La Muette de Portici*; Vesuvius can be seen at the back of the stage, while a comparison with figure 6 shows the result of the alterations to the auditorium

Alphonse and his courtiers are far removed from the part-cynical, part-sadistic exercise of power evinced by Gesler in *Guillaume Tell*. While authors like Pixérécourt offered their audiences a simple view of the world and uncomplicated characters with whom to identify, Scribe's characters, in this libretto for an operagoing public, are none of them free from human weaknesses or able to avoid making mistakes that have grave consequences: in depicting them thus, Scribe already adumbrated the apologia for the *juste milieu* which is an important feature of Meyerbeer's operas.

MIME

Even Fenella, the heroine of *La Muette de Portici*, is not completely unaffected by the cautious modification of the stock, black-and-white stereotypes of melodrama. For although Scribe keeps very close to the conventional figure of the innocent heroine hounded by vice in his depiction of her, and although she affirms her innocence repeatedly, careful reading of the libretto reveals that in her love affair with Alphonse she has undoubtedly lost what counted as the one essential criterion of feminine innocence according to the moral double standards of the nineteenth century. Admittedly, her share of guilt plays only a very subordinate part in the unhappy events that are seen taking place on the stage. Her muteness, necessarily restricting her to mime as a means of expression, becomes the dominant motive, and it is presented less as a physical defect and more as the proof of a moral integrity uncorrupted by speech's potential for deceit. To have one of the key roles played by a dancer-mime instead of a singer is an extraordinary experiment to undertake in an opera, and once again Scribe got the idea from Pixérécourt, several of whose mélodrames give a major role to a mime.[54] But something that aroused no special attention in a theatrical medium already inclined to sensationalism, in which crucial dramaturgical functions devolved not only to mutes but also to the deaf, the blind, and even animals, mystified critics even half a century after the première when they encountered it in opera where they were accustomed to greater dignity; thus Eduard Hanslick asserted more than once that Scribe and Auber had only designed the title role for a dancer because there was no suitable singer.[55]

54. See Brooks, *The Melodramatic Imagination*, 59–61.
55. *Die moderne Oper*, 130; idem, "Aubers *Stumme von Portici*" [1884], in *Musikalisches Skizzenbuch*, 130–37 (p. 134).

Hanslick was wrong, however. The role of Fenella was already conceived as mute in the draft treatment that Scribe submitted to the Opéra's literary jury in 1825, long before the question of actual performance arose. It is perfectly obvious, moreover, that the "aesthetics of muteness"[56] had a decisive function in the dramaturgy not only of melodrama but also of Scribe's first operatic libretto, making it very hard indeed to see how this aesthetic virtue could have been born of the necessity of a difficulty in casting. That the pantomime sequences have a central significance in Scribe's libretto and Auber's score becomes clear from study of Fenella's first entrance in Act I.

At the end of a short ballet, which—unlike the dancing integrated into the action of Act III—is a set piece, part of the festive prelude to Alphonse and Elvire's wedding, a lot of noise breaks out. Alarmed, Elvire asks the cause, and a lady-in-waiting tells her that a young woman has forced her way into the palace: a moment later Fenella is there, throwing herself at Elvire's feet. Elvire is prepared to hear the petitioner, but Fenella replies to her command to speak ("Que voulez-vous? parlez!") with gestures—she cannot speak. Only after Elvire has questioned the soldiers does a dialogue slowly develop between Elvire, singing her questions, and Fenella, miming her answers. The surprising thing about this dialogue is not so much the musical accompaniment to Fenella's gestures, which is modeled on the sort of thing that Alexandre Piccinni, for example, composed for Pixérécourt's mélodrames,[57] as rather the concision with which events that have not been seen onstage are summarized. In the space of at most eighty seconds, Fenella tells Elvire about her seducer, how he swore eternal love, and then disappeared never to be seen again; further, of how Selva, the Viceroy's officer, carried her off by force and locked her up, how she escaped with the help of a rope ladder fashioned from the bedclothes, how the guards raised the alarm, and how her only hope lies in Elvire's protection.

What the mime achieves is to recapitulate all these colorful events in a form that explains to the entire audience, quickly and with admirable clarity, all they need to know about the prehistory in order to follow the rest of the plot. In place of a lengthy narration, much of which would have remained inaudible and incomprehensible if delivered as recitative, Scribe uses a technique comparable to the cinematic flashback. As in a modern film, the music is intimately linked to the action, without being tied to a verbal abstract of it, and while it is always significant "it re-

---

56. See Brooks, *The Melodramatic Imagination*, 62.
57. See Sala, "'Que ses gestes parlants,'" 507–9.

mains discreet, serving the poetry like a sister, and honoring only the overall impression."[58]

A German contemporary of Scribe's wrote those words with reference to the mélodrame, but they also encapsulate one of the important traits of the dramaturgy of *La Muette de Portici*, even if the traditional image of a music that serves the poetry is scarcely adequate to describe the uncommon nature of a theatrical concept in which the poetry itself is so far subordinate to the "overall impression" as to opt for speechlessness. This logical relativization of the literary qualities of a dramatic text shows, however, how radically Pixérécourt, in his mélodrames, and Scribe, in his first serious opera libretto, had broken with classical aesthetic conventions.

While Jouy still supported the ideal of the operatic libretto as a potentially independent work of literature in its own right, it was obvious by now that the librettist's task was only to provide material that could be worked up into a dramatic event by means of its musical and theatrical realization. After the mélodrame, the libretto renounced its direct descent from French verse tragedy and applied itself instead to contributing to a new ideal of the union of diverse arts, as envisaged even by such a literature-oriented librettist as Jouy himself when—in direct contradiction to some of his other maxims—he decreed that an opera should be "the collective work of four different authors," that is, the librettist, the composer, the choreographer, and the designer.[59]

What was required now was close collaboration between different artists, and the intermeshing of different elements, aspiring toward a previously unknown synthesis of theatrical effects along the lines of what was later to be called *Gesamtkunstwerk*. There was still an order of precedence within the synthesis, however, with priority going to the visual elements, as in the definition of grand opéra given by Louis-Désiré Véron, looking back on his time as director of the Opéra: "An opera in five acts cannot exist without a highly dramatic action, bringing into play great passions of the human heart and powerful historical interests; at the same time this dramatic action must be capable of being comprehended by the eyes, like the action of a ballet."[60] In *La Muette de Portici*

58. "so bleibt [die Musik] doch discret, die dienende Schwester der Dichtung, um nur dem Gesammteindrucke zu huldigen"; Lewald, *Ein Menschenleben*, 4:302–3; see also Bergman, "Der Eintritt des Berufsregisseurs," 449.

59. "l'ouvrage collectif de quatre auteurs différents"; *Essai*, 231 (1987 ed., 65); see also Gerhard, "Incantesimo o specchio dei costumi," 59.

60. "Un opéra en cinq actes ne peut vivre qu'avec une action très dramatique, mettant en jeu les grandes passions du coeur humain et des puissants intérêts historiques; cette

Scribe had shown how to present a "highly dramatic action" in such a way that simply seeing the events on the stage sufficed for understanding. On top of that he had even demonstrated in a positive tour de force that even a great tragic opera could dispense with the verbal content of a literary dialogue. Even if his first libretto for a serious opera remained, to that extent, without a successor, yet most serious operas after 1830, and above all every grand opéra, observed the principle of pantomimic comprehensibility highlighted by Véron. In this fundamental change in the techniques of dramatic presentation, practical men of the theater like Scribe and Véron, and later Meyerbeer and Wagner, drew the obviously necessary consequence of a deep-seated change in the perceptual models of contemporary audiences.

Where serious opera at the beginning of the century reckoned on a well-read public able to follow well-known classical myths without needing to read the libretto immediately before, or during, the performance, three decades later it had to cater to audiences that had neither the literary culture nor the leisure to arrive at the theater already informed about the subject matter. Consequently the custom of buying the libretto and reading it in the theater as the performance went along fell into abeyance during the course of the nineteenth century, probably somewhat earlier in France than in more conservative Italy: there, as late as 1853, a Florentine critic expressed his amazement that the audience could follow the events of Meyerbeer's *Le Prophète* for themselves, instead of having to guess at them on the strength of "two verses of recitative, ill-understood or drowned by the double basses," and that therefore "the libretto is not necessary for understanding the dramatic situation."[61] At the same time the ground was prepared for another change: after the experiment was first made in Wagner's Festspielhaus in Bayreuth, opera-house auditoriums, which had blazed with light in the eighteenth century,[62] were plunged into almost total darkness before the beginning of the twentieth.[63]

There is yet another respect in which this trend toward the primacy

---

action dramatique doit cependant pouvoir être comprise par les yeux comme l'action d'un ballet." *Mémoires*, 3:252.

61. "due versi di recitativo mal capito o soffocato dai contrabbassi"; "non c'è bisogno del libro per capire l'importanza della situazione drammatica." Anonymous critic in *Il pirata*, 9 January 1853, pp. 221–22; quoted from Della Seta, "L'immagine di Meyerbeer," 176.

62. See Baumann, *Licht im Theater*, 48; on the festive character of the eighteenth-century opera-house auditorium, see ibid., 52.

63. Ibid., 128–31; on this change as it specifically affected the Paris Opéra, see Bernard, "L'Évolution du public d'Opéra," 36.

of the visual aspect reflected a rejection of conventions taken for granted under the ancien régime. Although grand opéra after 1830 made use of subject matter that was as a rule new and therefore not necessarily already known to the public, and although an accepted pattern of vocal types and role-characters had not yet established itself (as was the case with Italian opera seria), yet Scribe and Véron were evidently confident that dramatic interaction could be made comprehensible through the medium of mime. This confidence rested on a tacit and completely new conception of personality, connected with the conditions of life in the anonymous big city in a way pointed out by the American sociologist Richard Sennett. Writing of the stage of the 1830s in general, he observes "a passionate . . . attempt to have characters in plays wear costumes which were absolutely correct and accurate re-creations from the period in which the plays were set," and explains it in terms of the paradoxical needs of theatergoers:

> men and women dressed so that you couldn't "know" a person by casually looking at him or her. Yet these people believed intimate "knowledge" was contained in clothes. What these people tried to find in the theater was a world where you could indeed be absolutely sure that the people you saw were genuine. The actors really represented what they played. There was no possible deception, no act of deduction which might go wrong. In the theater, unlike the street, life was unshielded; it appeared as it was.
>
> Now this was a remarkable occurrence. Theater historians . . . speak of the mid-19th Century as the "age of illusion." But in the world of illusion there was certainty. The cosmopolitan city was a world in which physical appearance had no certainty. That is to say, under conditions of illusion, consciously worked at, there was more accessible truth about men and women than there was in the streets . . . for a play to be believable it had to establish a truth of time and place—a truth the players and the audience could not establish in their own lives.[64]

But a dramaturgical conception, as in the many operas of Scribe, which required not only the costumes[65] but all other details of the production to be such as to eliminate as far as possible any "acts of deduction which might go wrong" was also a form of reaction to a big-city audience's lack of orientation. The universal comprehensibility of mime, realized in French opera for the first time in *La Muette de Portici*, thus satisfied

64. Sennett, *The Fall of Public Man*, 174–76.
65. See Wild, "La Recherche de la précision historique."

the secret needs of spectators who had not come to terms with the uncomfortable anonymity of their daily life.

PANORAMA

Once again, essential characteristics of grand opéra seem to be very closely related to the silent cinema, and the very kinship feeds the suspicion that it was not by coincidence that grand opéra's exceptionally successful days were numbered at the very moment when silent films made their first appearance.[66] In all probability representational means directed at the sense of sight are more dependent than others on technology,[67] for—as was said of the diorama in 1826, when it was the latest thing—their aim is "to dupe [the spectator], to make him take a copy for the original."[68] A connection between the development of new technical resources and the sudden demise of grand opéra seems plausible to the extent that the emergence of grand opéra around 1830 itself coincided with the sudden collapse of interest in mélodrame, which had previously carried all before it. Whereas no fewer than thirty-one premières of works so designated took place in Paris in 1831, in the period 1836–41 the average annual number dropped to seven, there was just one in each of the years 1841 and 1842, and in 1843 and 1844 none at all.[69]

In terms of technology, the differences between the Opéra and the boulevard theaters where mélodrames were staged were only ones of degree, whereas the differences between opera and silent cinema, when the time came, fundamentally affected every aspect of production technique. But with the steady growth of interest in stage spectacle on the part of producers and audiences alike, financial resources became the critical factor, and it is not surprising that the heavily subsidized Opéra quickly left all other theaters far behind. The Opéra also had the largest stage in Paris, and even earlier than 1830 the management had secured the services of people such as the set-designer Cicéri: experienced professionals previously employed in the boulevard theaters, where they had become virtuosos of every kind of scenic effect imaginable.

Advances in other areas of visual spectacle were based on techniques that had earlier been developed at the Opéra: Louis Daguerre, for example, now thought of as the father of photography, began his career as

66. See below, 401–2.
67. See Koschorke, "Das Panorama," 169.
68. "de rendre dupe [le spectateur], de lui faire prendre une copie pour un original"; Vitet, "Diorama," 111.
69. See Matthes, *Vaudeville*, 219.

a set-designer, but in 1822, after two years spent working for the Opéra, he opened his own theater, where he developed further the idea of the panorama, which was already a big success. In his "diorama," as he called his premises, he showed large paintings of landscape or big churches, outdoing the effects of the panorama by alternating direct light and lighting from behind, and using colored filters, in order to create the illusion of time passing.[70] It had become as easy to alter light and shade as to represent natural scenery with deceptive realism, crowned by the effect of sunrise, sunset, or the romantic light of the full moon. And the calculated insertion of variably-lit transparencies enabled the previously immobile images of the panorama to be inhabited by people, who even appeared to be in motion. All these effects were combined in two of Daguerre's most successful dioramas, one depicting Holyrood Chapel, Edinburgh (1823), and the other the church of Saint-Étienne du Mont, Paris (1834). In the first Daguerre played with the effect of moonlight spilling over the ruins of the Gothic chapel at midnight and then introduced the figure of a woman in white, praying in this atmospheric setting.[71] In the second the public beheld the church interior lit as by light entering through stained-glass windows; this was succeeded by the onset of dusk and the lighting of candles, then the empty pews filled with worshippers, "quickly enough to surprise the spectators but slowly enough to appear natural"; after a celebration of midnight mass the candles were gradually extinguished, leaving the church dark and empty again until daylight returned as at the beginning of the show.[72]

But Cicéri had already created the effect of a slow sunrise on the stage of the Opéra, in the closing tableau of Rossini's *Guillaume Tell*, thereby launching a tradition in opera production that was taken up and developed further in similar scenes in Verdi's *Attila*, Wagner's *Rheingold*, and Meyerbeer's *Prophète*, while Scribe, in his second libretto for the Opéra, provided the opportunities for two big tableaux that clearly owed something to Daguerre's dioramas. Those midnight scenes, harmless though they were, nevertheless caused a certain shiver by a hint of blasphemy. At the end of Act III of *Robert le diable*, first performed in 1831, the devilish Bertram carries off his son Robert—and the audience—into a ruined convent for a midnight phantasmagoria. At first, under a clear, starry sky, a few rays of moonlight permit only the convent cemetery to be seen, with the statues of dead nuns. Gradually, however, these white

70. See Oettermann, *Das Panorama*, 63.
71. See Gernsheim, *L. J. M. Daguerre*, 25 and 176; Pendle, "The Boulevard theaters," 521.
72. See Oettermann, *Das Panorama*, 65.

marble shapes come to life, and the scene created by fiendish magic is filled not only with unexpected movement but also with new light: "During this, the flame in the lamps has also revived of its own accord. The darkness has ceased" *(Pendant ce temps le feu des lampes s'est aussi de lui-même rallumé. L'obscurité a cessé)*. The resurrected nuns—impersonated by the corps de ballet, of course—then adopt voluptuous postures and engage in some distinctly earthly pleasures, in the attempt to persuade the undecided Robert to commit sacrilege.

Robert succumbs, does the blasphemous deed, and falls so deeply into the toils of hell that he is only rescued by a final twist of fortune at the very end of Act V. Once again it is midnight, Bertrand's lease of influence runs out as the clock strikes, and Robert is released from his diabolical shadow-side. Once again the scene changes phantasmagorically: "the curtains at the rear have opened to reveal the interior of Palermo Cathedral, filled with worshippers at prayer" *(les rideaux du fond, qui se sont ouverts, laissent apercevoir l'intérieur de la cathédrale de Palerme remplie de fidèles qui sont en prière)*. Even Chopin, who was not alone in his reservations about grand opéra, could not deny the exhilaration he felt at such a spectacle, and wrote: "On the stage there's a diorama in which, towards the end, you see the inside of a church and the whole church itself at Christmas or Easter all lit up."[73]

Even though in scenes like this the Opéra took advantage of the technical and aesthetic achievements of the diorama, with its introduction of the appearance of movement, yet such imposing closing tableaux differed little from the older panorama in their dramatic content and their effect on the audience. The scene at the end of *Robert le diable* presents more than a detailed depiction of Palermo Cathedral. The sight of Princess Isabelle in the middle of the scene, with an empty chair at her side intended for Robert, sums up the happy outcome of the story for the spectator in a succinct and unambiguous image: nothing now stands in the way of Robert and Isabelle's marriage. The practice of arranging the characters in an easily interpretable group at the end of an act—assisted, if necessary, by clear gestures—so as to summarize the essence of the situation at that moment, recurs regularly in all Scribe's librettos. The stage direction at the end of Act IV of *La Muette de Portici* is a good example:

> *Masaniello est monté sur un cheval au milieu du peuple qui se presse autour de lui, et il est environné de danses. — Pendant ce temps, Piétro et les conjurés le*

73. Letter to Titus Woyciechowski, 12 December 1831, Chopin, *Selected Correspondence*, 100.

*menacent de leurs poignards. — Fenella, qui est près de Piétro, l'examine avec
crainte, et pendant que le cortège s'empresse autour de son frère, ses regards in-
quiets s'élèvent vers le ciel et semblent prier pour lui.*

   ꝑ   ꝑ   ꝑ

Masaniello has mounted a horse in the middle of the people pressing
about him, and he is surrounded by dances. Meanwhile, Piétro and the
conspirators make threatening gestures towards him with their daggers.
Fenella, who is near Piétro, studies him fearfully, and while the procession hastens to surround her brother she looks anxiously up to heaven
and seems to pray for him.

This fourth act has seen an especially large number of turns of fortune
before it culminates in this static tableau vivant, so providing us with
another example of grand opéra making use of a visual form that had
already been developed to its utmost perfection in another genre and
with close dependence on contemporary painting.[74] (The novel and the
print would later also milk the possibilities of the tableau vivant.)[75] If
the creators of panoramas—simply for technical reasons—had no other
choice than to present their chosen scene in the most impressive way
possible, with its elements in an immobile group, in the same era the
mélodrame used the technique because its distancing effect was, once
again, ideally suited to the perceptual requirements of contemporary
audiences. No mélodrame was complete without a carefully arranged
tableau at the end of an act, and the *Traité du mélodrame* of 1817, which
has already been cited in this chapter, makes no secret of what this practice owed to the comprehensibility achievable with mime.

> At the end of each act care must be taken to bring all the characters to-
> gether in a group, and to pose each of them in the attitude appropriate to
> his or her situation. For example: sorrow will place a hand to his brow,
> despair will tear his hair, and joy will have one leg raised. This general
> aspect is called a tableau. It will be clear how agreeable it is for the specta-
> tor thus to take in the moral state of each character at a glance.[76]

74. See Holmström, *Monodrama*, 209–42.
75. See Wechsler, *A Human Comedy*, 20.
76. "A la fin de chaque acte, il faut avoir soin de réunir en groupe tous les personnages,
et de les mettre chacun dans l'attitude qui convient à la situation de son âme. Par exemple:
la douleur placera une main sur son front; le désespoir s'arrachera ses cheveux, et la joie
aura une jambe en l'air. Cet aspect général est désigné sous le nom de Tableau. On sent
combien il est agréable au spectateur de ressaisir d'un coup-d'oeil l'état moral de chaque
personnage." A!A!A!, *Traité du mélodrame*, 47.

Not agreeable alone but also necessary for spectators experiencing the spread of the new, technicized forms of pictorial representation into all kinds of areas and the introduction of a development—"the graphic revolution" as Daniel Boorstin has called it[77]—which would eventually change not only the pleasures of spectacle as a pastime but even the shape in which information was transmitted in the field of politics. Discourse about a matter was replaced by looking at its image, and this shift in perceptual preferences—long before the age of television—from literary representation to panorama, from tragedy to melodrama, from opera of a literary orientation to the spectacle of grand opéra was noticed by a clear-sighted German journalist as early as 1833: "Just as music, since it became a fashionable art, has caused a decline in the importance of conversation in social intercourse, similarly in the theater *drama* has lost interest by comparison with opera."[78]

Grand opéra had to pay a high price for this orientation toward the perceptual requirements of a public thirsty for spectacle. As was already the case in contemporary panoramas and dioramas, regular display of overwhelming representational techniques led to escalation of the element of spectacle. A pass was reached where the only guarantee of success with the public, apparently, was for every new subject at the diorama, every new grand opéra, to surpass its predecessors in at least one respect. This development is illustrated very clearly in the two successful librettos Scribe wrote for the Opéra after *La Muette de Portici* and *Robert le diable*—*Gustave III, ou Le Bal masqué*, set by Auber and first performed in 1833, which will be discussed in a later chapter in connection with Verdi's 1859 treatment of the same subject to an Italian libretto; and *La Juive* (Halévy, 1835). In both of these texts, Scribe attempted to trump his earlier operas by systematically piling on decorative details in order to reproduce the splendor of the historical situations. Where the libretto of *La Muette de Portici* is notable for its brevity, in the case of *Gustave III* Scribe took such pains to legitimize every detail of the plot through its historical accuracy that he ended up with one of his wordiest librettos, alongside *Les Huguenots* and *Le Cheval de bronze*. In this attempt to create a historical opera on the subject of the assassination of the King of Sweden in 1791 that would rival the

77. Cited in Postman, *Amusing Ourselves to Death*, 75.
78. "Wie aber durch die Musik, seitdem sie eine Modekunst geworden, in der gesellschaftlichen Unterhaltung das Gespräch als Nebensache zurückgetreten, so hat auch seitdem in gleicher Weise auf der Bühne das *Drama* gegen die Oper an Interesse verloren." Mundt, "Ueber Oper, Drama und Melodrama," 82.

historical novels of Sir Walter Scott in point of corroborative detail and cogent argument,[79] Auber's distinctly limited dramaturgical talent was of little help, any more than Halévy, in *La Juive*, was up to the challenge of evoking by musical means an ambience as remote as that of the city of Constance during the Council of 1414. In spite of that, both operas were enormously successful, above all on account of their spectacular qualities. The Swedish ambassador in Paris, for example, declared that during a performance of *Gustave III* the uncommonly exact reproduction of the antechamber in the royal palace in Stockholm made him think for a moment that he was actually back in his homeland.[80] What impressed audiences above all in the case of *La Juive* was the extravagance of several hundred extras and a number of real horses crowding onto the stage during the entrance of the Holy Roman Emperor and his suite, accompanied by the college of cardinals arriving in Constance to take part in the Ecumenical Council, at the end of Act I. Once again, the eyes even of those more inclined to be critical opened a little wider at this scene. The Austrian dramatist Franz Grillparzer was profoundly reserved in the face of all else he saw during his visit to Paris, but was overwhelmed by the spectacle of *La Juive*. Although his summary comment on the work as a whole was that it was "without interest," he went on to write about the production at length in his diary.

> But what external trappings! The sets are the real things—no, paintings rather. The difference between French stage sets and those of other countries lies in the fact that the latter depict objects in accordance with truth, and then leave it to chance whether the fallacious lighting, and the grouping and costumes of the characters, will enhance, diminish, or destroy the effect. But here they paint the light into the sets at the outset, its strengthening and its dimming, its permanent and transient features alike. . . . This results in what are actual pictures, with an effect people in our country cannot begin to imagine. The curtain rises on the market-square of an Imperial City, a church left in shadow in the foreground, with groups of people standing and kneeling. Across the square, men sitting on barriers and guard-stones, swinging their feet, standing, recumbent, urchins. In the background, rising in perspective, armed men, with a grey sheen to their armor so as not to stand out too much. Add to this the sounds of the organ and the choir coming from the church. Women with page boys carrying their trains, going to mass. The cardinal appears

79. See Walter, "A la recherche de l'histoire perdue."
80. See *Le Temps*, 4 March 1833; cited in Crosten, *French Grand Opera*, 63–64.

on the steps. It has to be seen to be believed. I think I possess imagination. Here, for the first time in my life, I have seen a theatrical production.[81]

Even the most benevolent of the Parisian critics attending the first performance were unable to deny that the music was bound to be overshadowed by that kind of spectacle, which obviously owed so much to historical panoramas—certainly the not particularly innovative music of Halévy, which Bellini dismissed as utter rubbish.[82] Hector Berlioz was especially sarcastic in his review in a newspaper:

> Despite the efforts that were made to prevent the audience from hearing the score, despite the clanking of all those suits of armor, the stamping of the horses, the tumult of the crowd, the volleys of bells and cannon, the dances, the groaning tables, the fountains flowing with wine, despite all the antimusical fracas provided by the Royal Academy of Music, now and then one caught snatches of the composer's inspiration.[83]

However much the deployment of material magnificence and scenic superlatives on such a scale pandered to one section of the public in its

81. "Das Ganze ohne Interesse. Aber welche äußere Ausstattung! Die Dekorazionen Wirklichkeiten, oder nein: Bilder. Dadurch unterscheidet sich die französische Dekorazionsmalerei von der der übrigen Nazionen, daß letztere die Gegenstände der Wahrheit gemäß abbilden und nun dem Zufall überlassen, ob das unwahre Lampenlicht, die Gruppirung und Bekleidung der Figuren die Wirkung steigern, stören oder aufheben werde. Hier aber malt man das Licht, die Steigerung und Abschwächung, das Wesentliche und die Beiläufigkeit gleich von vorneher in die Dekorazion hinein . . . So entstehen eigentliche Bilder, von deren Wirkung man bei uns keine Vorstellung hat. Der Marktplatz einer Reichsstadt gleich beim Aufziehen des Vorhangs, eine Kirche im Vorgrunde dunkel gehalten, mit stehenden und knieenden Gruppen. Gegenüber Männer auf Barrieren, Ecksteinen sitzend, mit den Füßen schlenkernd, stehend, liegend, Straßenjungen. Im Hintergrunde, perspektivisch sich emporhebend, gewappnete Männer, die Harnische graulich glänzend, um nicht zu sehr vorzutreten. Dazu aus der Kirche Orgeltöne, Chorgesang. Frauen mit schlepptragenden Pagen, die in die Messe gehen. Der Kardinal erscheint auf den Stufen. Man muß das gesehen haben. Ich glaube Phantasie zu haben. Hier zum erstenmale in meinem Leben habe ich ein theatralisches Arrangement gesehen." Entry in Grillparzer's diary, 20 April 1836, Grillparzer, *Sämtliche Werke*, sec. 2, vol. 10 (*Tagebücher*, 4), 30.

82. "una vera porcheria"; letter to Francesco Florimo, 27 February 1835, in Bellini, *Epistolario*, 529.

83. "Malgré les efforts qu'on a faits pour empêcher d'entendre la partition, malgré le cliquetis de toutes ces armures, ce piétinement de chevaux, ce tumulte populaire, ces volées de cloches et de canons, ces danses, ces tables chargées, ces fontaines de vin, malgré tout le fracas anti-musical de l'Académie royale de Musique, on a pu saisir au vol quelquesunes des inspirations du compositeur." *Le Rénovateur/Courrier de l'Europe*, 1 March 1835; cited in *Fromental Halévy: La Juive*, 151.

hunger for sensation, nevertheless Scribe's intention (it was not his only aim) of filling his historical panoramas with dramatic life depended in the end on their world being translated fittingly into music, so that an integrated musico-dramatic event could be formed in the meld of libretto, composition, and staging.

~: 5 :~

MEYERBEER
AND THE
HAPPY MEDIUM

LES HUGUENOTS

TEXT
Eugène Scribe (1791–1861)

MUSIC
Giacomo Meyerbeer (1791–1864)

FIRST PERFORMANCE
Paris, Académie Royale de Musique, 29 February 1836

PLACE AND DATE OF THE ACTION
Touraine and Paris, August 1572

CHARACTERS
Marguerite de Valois, betrothed to Henry of Navarre (soprano);
Comte de Saint-Bris, Catholic nobleman and governor of the Louvre (bass);
Valentine, Saint-Bris's daughter (soprano); Comte de Nevers, Catholic noble-
man (bass); Cossé (tenor), Thoré (tenor), Tavannes (tenor), de Retz (bass),
Catholic noblemen; Raoul de Nangis, Protestant nobleman (tenor);
Marcel, Huguenot soldier and Raoul's servant (bass); Urbain,
Marguerite's page (soprano)

SYNOPSIS

ACT I
A large hall in the château of the Comte de Nevers, where Catholic nobles
have assembled for a banquet (No. 1b. *Ouverture et Introduction — Choeur,* "Des
beaux jours de la jeunesse"). They are astonished to learn that Nevers has invited a Protestant to join the feast, in the interests of reconciliation between the
hostile religious parties, but after some barbed comments they give Raoul a
friendly welcome (No. 1c. *Morceau d'ensemble et entrée de Raoul,* "De ces lieux

enchanteurs" / "Sous ce beau ciel de la Touraine"), and as they sit down to dine together (No. 1d, *Orgie*, "Bonheur de la table"), they invite him to tell them a tale of amorous adventure. Raoul tells them about a fleeting encounter with a young woman whom he rescued from the importunities of a mob of students, and now loves passionately, although he does not know her name (No. 2. *Scène et romance*, "Non loin des vieilles tours" / "Plus blanche que la blanche hermine"). His servant Marcel arrives, a strict Protestant who is horrified to find his master in the company of detested Catholics and fearfully starts to sing Luther's chorale "Ein' feste Burg" (No. 3. *Récitatif et choral*, "Quelle étrange figure" / "Seigneur! rempart et seul soutien"). Nevers's guests take this fanaticism as an exotic entertainment, however, and invite Marcel to sing for them. He responds with a bloodthirsty Huguenot war song (No. 4. *Scène et chanson huguenote*, "Eh! mais plus je le vois" / "Pour les couvents c'est fini"). When Nevers leaves the room, because a lady wishes to speak to him, his guests draw a curtain at a window giving on to the next room, in order to catch a glimpse of their host's latest inamorata; Raoul is appalled to see that it is the woman he loves (No. 5. *Morceau d'ensemble*, "L'aventure est singulière"). Nevers returns and reveals in an aside that he has unwillingly agreed to the wish of his fiancée, Valentine, who has Marguerite's support, to break off their engagement and cancel their wedding which was to have taken place the next day; his guests, in ignorance of this development, congratulate him on yet another conquest (No. 6a. *Final — Choeur*, "Honneur au conquérant"). Urbain brings a message for Raoul, requesting him to don a blindfold and go to a secret rendezvous (No. 6b. *Cavatine du page*, "En ce château que cherchez-vous, beau page?" / "Une dame noble et sage"). The other guests immediately recognize Marguerite's seal on the letter, and try to ingratiate themselves with her new favorite (No. 6c, *Suite du final*, "Trop de mérite"), before Raoul, who understands nothing of any of this, is led away by some masked figures (No. 6d. *Stretta*, "Les plaisirs, les honneurs, la puissance").

ACT II

The gardens of the riverside château of Chenonceaux. With her ladies-in-waiting, Marguerite enjoys the peace of the countryside (No. 7. *Entr'acte et air*, "O beau pays de la Touraine!"). She explains to Valentine that the plan to make her Raoul's wife will accomplish two things at once: fulfill the couple's own secret wishes and strengthen the fragile peace between the religious factions. The ladies are taking a refreshing dip in the river (No. 8. *Choeur des baigneuses, dansé*, "Jeunes beautés sous ce feuillage") when Urbain arrives with Raoul (No. 9. *Scène du bandeau*, "Le voici! du silence!"); Marguerite dismisses her attendants before allowing Raoul to take off the blindfold. Overwhelmed by her beauty, Raoul vows unconditional fidelity, while Marguerite expresses her regret that circumstances do not allow her an amorous adventure (No. 10. *Duo*, "Beauté divine"). It is not until Urbain announces the approach of Protestant and Catholic nobility that Raoul understands who Marguerite is, and he at once consents to her marriage plans for him (No. 11. *Récitatif et entrée de la cour*, "Madame!" / "Oui, d'un heureux hymen préparé par mes soins"), whereupon all present vow eternal friendship (No. 12a. *Final — Serment*, "Par l'honneur, par le nom"). When Valentine is led in, however, and Raoul sees the woman he believes to be Nevers's mistress, he is outraged and declares that he cannot marry her (No. 12b. *Scène*, "Et maintenant je dois offrir à votre vue"). No one understands his reaction and the Catholics swear to take revenge for the affront (No. 12c. *Stretta*, "Ô transport! ô démence").

ACT III

The Pré-aux-Clercs, a meadow on the left bank of the Seine in Paris, on a Sunday evening. A large crowd sings a song in praise of the day of rest (No. 13. *Entr'acte et choeur*, "C'est le jour du dimanche"). Some Huguenot soldiers strike up a battle-song (No. 14a. *Couplets militaires des soldats huguenots*, "Rataplan, rataplan"), Catholic bridesmaids conduct Valentine, who must now marry Nevers after all, to a chapel, singing an "Ave Maria" (No. 14b. *Litanies*, "Vierge Marie"), and Marcel, seeking the Comte de Saint-Bris, refuses to doff his hat to the procession (No. 14c. *Morceau d'ensemble*, "Rataplan" / "Vierge Marie"). This brings the latent hostility between the Huguenots and the Catholics to the point of erupting in violence, but that is prevented by the entrance of some gypsies, who divert the crowd with their singing and dancing (No. 15. *Ronde bohémienne*, "Vous qui voulez savoir d'avance"; No. 16. *Danse bohémienne*). Some men leave the chapel where Valentine remains to pray. Nevers goes toward the city while Saint-Bris ponders revenge on Raoul. After receiving Raoul's challenge to a duel, brought by Marcel, he plots with a confidant how to get Raoul out of the way before he can become a threat to Nevers. The nightwatchman calls the curfew and the crowd disperses (No. 17. *Couvre-feu*, "Rentrez, habitants de Paris"). Valentine, who has chanced to overhear the murder plot, leaves the chapel, wearing her veil, and warns Marcel of the danger threatening Raoul, whom she still loves (No. 18. *Scène et duo*, "Ô terreur!" / "Dans la nuit, où seul je veille"). Marcel goes to warn his master, but is prevented by the arrival of the duellists and their supporters (No. 19. *Septuor du duel*, "En mon bon droit j'ai confiance"), and has to summon other Huguenot soldiers hastily as Saint-Bris's thugs fall upon Raoul in the darkness (No. 20. *Choeur de la dispute*, "Nous voilà! félons, arrière!"). The brawl is halted by the arrival of Marguerite, who asks the reason for it. Marcel points out the veiled stranger, Saint-Bris, in a rage, tears off the woman's veil and discovers his daughter (No. 21. *Final*, "Ma fille!"). Marguerite explains the circumstances to the perplexed Raoul, Saint-Bris is triumphant, as he can tell the hated Protestants that his daughter is now married. The Huguenots swear revenge for the deception, as Nevers arrives with a large following to carry his bride away to his house by boat.

ACT IV

A room in the Comte de Nevers's house in Paris. Valentine is alone, lamenting her fate, when Raoul appears, hoping to see her once more (No. 22. *Entr'acte*, "Je suis seule chez moi!"). He hides when he hears Catholic noblemen approaching, and thus overhears them finalizing the plan to murder all Huguenots that very night; only Nevers refuses to take part in the massacre and Saint-Bris orders him to be put under guard. Monks bless the weapons and novices distribute white armbands as a means of identification, while the conspirators work themselves into a bloodthirsty frenzy (No. 23. *Conjuration et bénédiction des poignards*, "Des troubles renaissants" / "Pour cette cause sainte"). When they have all left, Raoul wants to hurry to warn his co-religionists, but Valentine tries to detain him, at last confessing that she loves him. Raoul falls into a reverie of love and happiness which is interrupted by the sound of church bells, the signal for the massacre. He rushes away, leaving Valentine in a swoon (No. 24. *Grand duo*. "Ô ciel! où courez-vous?" / "Le danger presse").

ACT V

First setting: the ballroom in the Hôtel de Nesle. The Protestant nobility are celebrating the wedding of Marguerite and Henry of Navarre (No. 25. *Entr'acte et ballet*) when Raoul bursts in, wounded, to announce the massacre raging outside and issue a call to arms (No. 26. *Récitatif et air*, "Aux armes, mes amis!" / "À la lueur de leurs torches funèbres").

Second setting: a churchyard. Raoul joins Marcel and other Huguenot men, who have erected barricades in the hope of protecting their women and children hiding in the church. Valentine rushes in with a white armband for Raoul, whose life will be spared if he renounces his faith; since Nevers has been killed by his own men for protecting Marcel, the couple can even look forward to a future together. Raoul is tempted, but Marcel forces him to reject the offer, whereupon Valentine declares her readiness to adopt his faith and die with him (No. 27. *Scène et grand trio*, "C'est toi, mon vieux Marcel"). Marcel hastily marries the couple (No. 27a. *Interrogatoire*, "Savez-vous qu'en joignant les mains") before the murderers burst into the church (No. 27b. *Choeur des meurtriers*, "Abjurez, huguenots, ou mourez!"); Marcel has a vision of Heaven opening to receive him as a martyr (No. 27c. *Vision*, "Ah! voyez, voyez!").

Third setting: beside the Seine. Severely wounded, Raoul is being helped along by Marcel and Valentine when Saint-Bris confronts him; with his last breath he cries "Huguenot!," and Saint-Bris has all three shot; too late he recognizes his dying daughter. Marguerite's attempts to halt the massacre, as she returns to the Louvre, also fail to have any visible effect: the murderers, wholly out of control, pursue their victims (No. 28. *Scène finale*, "Par le fer et par l'incendie").

EDITIONS: The full score published by Schlesinger in Paris in 1836 is available in many libraries as a reprint (*Early Romantic Opera* 20 [New York: Garland, 1980]); the piano-vocal score was frequently reprinted and is also widely available.

RECOMMENDED RECORDING: The recording issued in 1970, directed by Richard Bonynge, with Joan Sutherland (Marguerite), Gabriel Bacquier (Saint-Bris), Martina Arroyo (Valentine), Dominic Cossa (Nevers), Anastasios Vrenios (Raoul), Nicolai Ghiuselev (Marcel), and Huguette Tourangeau (Urbain), is not ideally cast in every role, and Bonynge's choice of tempos is not always wholly convincing. Overall, however, the performance conveys a good impression of an exceptionally problematic work.

COLOR

As an ever greater variety of special effects and ever more extreme dramatic contrasts were offered to opera audiences, so the question of aesthetic unity grew ever more urgent, exacerbated by the fact that the unifying power formerly exercised by "the marvelous" had gone for ever, mourned by Jouy and other classicists.[1] For this reason, French aesthetic theorists of the early nineteenth century turned increasingly to color, *la couleur*, in the hope that uniform coloration of a full-length play or opera could guarantee the cohesion that was now seriously threatened by the kaleidoscopic character of everything seen and done on stage. They said scarcely anything, however, about how such cohesion might be achieved, and librettists were only too ready to leave the question of the means to composers. Significantly, Jouy mentioned the subject in his *Essai* only in connection with the overture, saying of this purely instrumental number that it should reflect the "general color of a work."[2] Similar considerations led to a growing number of instances of composers writing a relatively brief *Introduction* rather than a full-scale overture, as the "color" of the drama that was to follow could more easily be established in a shorter piece of music lacking an elaborate formal structure. The procedure was tried out by Rossini in several of his operas for Naples, and in *Moïse et Pharaon*, and subsequently Meyerbeer adopted it for all his grands opéras.[3]

The development of compositional techniques to bind the several hours of music in a four- or five-act opera together convincingly was a gradual process, admittedly. The demand for color as a unifying element had been made in the 1820s, but it was the middle of the century before it was met at all successfully. Verdi's technique of repeating characteristic intervals and rhythms gave *Rigoletto*, and many of his later operas, the basic musical color to which he already referred as *tinta musicale* by 1850,[4] while Wagner, also during the 1850s, produced even more stringent results with the development of leitmotivic technique. But while Wagner was able to build on the advances in motivic working made by Liszt on the basis of his intimate knowledge of Beethoven, the compos-

---

1. On the relationship of "the marvelous" and *couleur locale* see also Dahlhaus, "Drammaturgia dell'opera italiana," 85.

2. "la couleur générale d'un ouvrage"; *Essai*, 268 (1987 ed., 84).

3. See Steinbeck, *Die Ouvertüre*, 117–18.

4. See the letter to Carlo Marzari, 24 August 1850, in Verdi, *I copialettere*, 106; see also de Van, "La notion de *tinta*."

ers who were writing operas for Paris in the 1830s had no such technical models to show them how formal phenomena that differed musically could be made to relate to each other logically.

On a less abstract level, therefore, the recourse to *couleur locale* was an obvious move. The category had been introduced into aesthetic discussions by a few theorists in the last third of the eighteenth century,[5] and had developed into an omnipresent, fashionable concept in the early years of the nineteenth. It was Chateaubriand who set the example of the proper use of local color in French literature, in his novel *Les Martyrs, ou Le Triomphe de la religion chrétienne* (1809),[6] and in the next few years the highly successful novels of Sir Walter Scott, in particular, became famous for the authenticity of their recreation of the "color of other times and places."[7] Critics, too, became increasingly prone to discuss the use of local color in productions of plays and operas, and although Victor Hugo's preface to his play *Cromwell* (1827) is always cited in this connection, Étienne Sauvo had uttered a word of warning against the unthinking use of local color as early as 1809, in a review of Le Sueur's opera *La Mort d'Adam et son apothéose*, given at the Académie Impériale de Musique: "Local color is a word easy to use and very easy to misuse."[8]

Sauvo's warning fell on deaf ears for the most part, however. The use and, inevitably, the misuse of local color for its purely external effects persisted until the early twentieth century, in French opera, in German opera, and later even in Italian opera, so that in 1882 Verdi, by then nearly seventy, had good reason to include "color locale" among the terms "which are used so much but serve more often than not only to conceal a lack of thought."[9] But in grand opéra too, where the earliest systematic attempts to apply local color were made, it scarcely penetrated beneath the surface. The set designer Cicéri went to Switzerland in 1828, for example, solely in order to look for inspiration for the

5. See above, 58.

6. See Tanguy-Baum, *Der historische Roman*, 18.

7. "la couleur des temps et des lieux"; Jean-Pons-Guillaume Viennet, "Choix de poésies de Byron, Walter Scott et Moore," *La Minerve littéraire* 1 (1820): 293–308, cited in Massmann, *Die Rezeption der historischen Romane Sir Walter Scotts*, 22.

8. "La couleur locale est un mot dont il est facile de se servir, et très facile d'abuser"; *Gazette nationale, ou Le Moniteur universel*, 1 April 1809, p. 4, cited in Charlton, *Grétry*, 232.

9. "di cui si fa tant'uso, e che il più delle volte non servono che a coprire la mancanza dei pensieri"; letter to Opprandino Arrivabene, 17 March 1882, cited in Alberti, *Verdi intimo*, 296.

forthcoming production of *Guillaume Tell*.[10] In the same spirit, over the following decades designers bent every effort toward making the scenery of any work reproduce as accurately as possible the historical period in which it was set, and contemporary critics went into ecstasies over the painstakingly exact sets of Auber's *Gustave III* and Halévy's *La Juive*. This fetish of authenticity (or what passed for it) led to some strange excesses, of which a good example is the specific mention, in the printed libretto of Félicien David's *Herculanum*, an epigonal grand opéra performed in 1859, of the fact that although the evidently extravagant geological configuration of the rocks might be taken for a caprice of the scene painter, it was nothing of the kind, but had been copied exactly from some actual rocks at Sorrento.

It was not only the set designers but the majority of composers, too, who confined themselves to externals in their efforts to achieve an accurate milieu in their musical scene-setting. In a textbook published in 1833, for example, Antoine Reicha, professor of composition at the Paris Conservatoire, recommended aspiring opera composers "to introduce a national air sometimes, or rather a song, because their airs are better known and have more melodic interest," and to employ instruments characteristic of the country in which the opera is set, such as mandolin, guitar, or bagpipes, or, failing that, to make their music more or less "as if destined for [the composer's] native country."[11] That sort of thinking lay behind the barcaroles and tarantella rhythms in Auber's *La Muette de Portici;* the tarantella soon became an obligatory element in operatic scenes depicting the "ordinary" people of Italy. Some who heard *La Muette de Portici* in Berlin took Auber's creations for genuine Neapolitan airs,[12] but Rossini actually did resort to original Swiss alphorn melodies in *Guillaume Tell*—the very ones that Grétry had incorporated into his opéra comique of the same title of 1791, after having conducted firsthand research, like the most advanced of avant-garde composers, among Swiss soldiers traveling through France.[13]

Following in Grétry's footsteps, when he came to compose *Robert le diable* Giacomo Meyerbeer drew on things he had learned while collect-

10. See Émile-Timothée Lubbert's letter to La Rochefoucauld, 11 June 1828; F-Pan, O³ 1680, I.

11. "d'introduire quelquefois un air national, ou plutôt une chanson, lorsque ces airs sont avantageusement connus et qu'ils ont un intérêt mélodique"; "comme si elle était destinée pour son propre pays"; *Art du compositeur dramatique*, 1:96.

12. See Eugène-Théodore Troupenas's letter to François-Joseph Fétis in *Revue musicale* 5 (1829): 231; see also Schneider, "Die Barkarole und Venedig," 27.

13. See H. Becker, "Die *Couleur locale* als Stilkategorie der Oper," 35.

ing Sicilian folk songs.[14] Similarly, in 1838 the veteran Spontini tried to persuade the Prussian court to pay for him to travel to England and Scotland in order to pursue field studies for his unfinished opera *Cromwell*.[15] Even Verdi had Sicilian folk melodies sent to him in Paris in 1855, to help him with the ballet in *Les Vêpres siciliennes*.[16] Forty years later he was sufficiently detached from this naive conception of color to laugh at such concerns. After having made several attempts, varying in their degree of non-success, to find some Venetian airs and dances and Greek melodies for the ballet he added to the 1894 Paris version of *Otello*, he finally sent the finished score off to his publisher with an accompanying letter:

> This very day I'm sending the registered package containing the *ballet* for *Otello* in Paris. Your doctors of music were unable to find me a thing . . . but I found a *Greek song* of 5 thousand years before the coming of Christ! . . . If the world had not existed then, so much the worse for the world! Then I found *a Muranese* composed 2000 years ago for a war between Venice and Murano, which the people of Murano won. Never mind if Venice did not exist then.[17]

Meyerbeer, like Verdi, did not take the exact origins of his "characteristic" melodies too seriously. He declared his readiness to study appropriate musical-historical material, in 1832, when preparing to go to work on *Les Huguenots*,[18] and may possibly have taken the opportunity at this time to acquaint himself with the style of old French court dances;[19] but when it came to the Huguenots in his opera, he used Luther's "Ein' feste Burg ist unser Gott" in preference to any of the "authentic" reformed psalm tunes that the historical Huguenots would actually have sung—no doubt because of the more distinct musical identity of the chorale that Heinrich Heine dubbed "the *Marseillaise* of the Reformation."[20] As for the chorale "Ad nos, ad salutarem undam," sung by the Anabaptists in *Le Prophète*, which is set in the year 1530, it

14. Ibid.

15. Ibid., 36; see also Meyerbeer, *Briefwechsel*, 3:677.

16. See Verdi's letter to Cesare de Sanctis, 10 April 1855, in Luzio, *Carteggi Verdiani*, 1:30–31; the matter is discussed in detail by Conati in "Ballabili nei *Vespri*."

17. Letter to Giulio Ricordi, 21 August 1894, *Carteggio Verdi–Boito*, 456; cited here in the translation in Busch, *Verdi's "Otello" and "Simon Boccanegra,"* 1:412.

18. See Meyerbeer's letter to his wife Minna, 1 September 1832, *Briefwechsel*, 2:635.

19. See H. Becker, "Die *couleur locale* als Stilkategorie der Oper," 35; however, some of Becker's theories are criticized as overhasty by Walter in *"Hugenotten"-Studien*, 110–11.

20. *Zur Geschichte der Religion und Philosophie in Deutschland* [1834], in *Sämtliche Schriften*, 3:505–641 (p. 547).

was composed by Meyerbeer himself, although it can be shown to contain reminiscences of the Protestant chorale "Wer nur den lieben Gott
läßt walten"—composed in 1641![21]

But Meyerbeer's idea of characteristic color was more abstract than
that held by naive champions of local color, and at the same time it was
directly related to his own present time. As his rejection of subjects from
ancient Greek literature[22] made perfectly clear, he knew very well that
the historical subjects of his successful operas had a strong bearing on
the Zeitgeist of his own day, for the historical actions underlying them
were those in which, as Jean F. Schucht put it in his biography of Meyerbeer, "the spiritual struggles and disputes of the modern era are reflected [and] the blood of our hearts, the life of our souls pulsate."[23] On
the other hand, as Meyerbeer told Schucht himself, "allowing people in
the mists of antiquity to speak and sing in our modern music" seemed
to him to be

> the greatest nonsense to be met with anywhere in art. When poets and
> composers have tried it, the people who stand before us are not Greeks
> and Romans, they are not Old Germanic or Norse heroes, they are wholly
> modern people just like ourselves. Old costumes and old weapons don't
> do it, characters of the ancient world don't grow from them.[24]

Meyerbeer's line of argument is surprising, for it can be applied to
the theatrical representation of any period in history, not merely the
mists of antiquity. It is clear that he based it tacitly on a conception of
modern times that reached from his (nineteenth-century) present as far
back as the sixteenth century, and so included events like the Saint Bartholomew's Day massacre and the setting-up of an Anabaptist kingdom
in Münster—a disconcerting premise from today's standpoint, yet a direct explanation for it can be found in musical decisions Meyerbeer had
to take. Plainly, ancient Greek and Roman as well as "Old Germanic or
Norse" melodies were irretrievably lost, and furthermore, for a com-

21. See Eymieu, *L'Oeuvre de Meyerbeer,* 72.
22. See above, 61.
23. "in welchen das geistige Ringen und Kämpfen der Neuzeit sich widerspiegelt . . .
unser Herzblut, unser Seelenleben pulsiert"; *Meyerbeer's Leben und Bildungsgang,* 342.
24. "Menschen der grauen Vorzeit in unsrer modernen Musik singen und sprechen
zu lassen . . . der größte Widersinn, dem man in der Kunst begegnen kann. Wo Dichter
und Komponisten es versucht haben, da sind es nicht Griechen und Römer, nicht altger-
manische oder nordische Helden, welche vor uns stehen, sondern ganz moderne Menschen wie wir selbst. Das alte Gewand und die alten Waffen tun es nicht, daraus entstehen
keine antiken Charaktere." Letter of 6 February 1857, cited ibid., 397; on the authenticity
of Schucht's quotations from letters by Meyerbeer, see above, chapter 2, n. 66.

poser with a sense of history, it was out of the question to apply the musical means at his disposal to any historical period separated from modern times, in musicological terms, by the evolution of European polyphony. On the other hand, he was able to weave the tune of Luther's chorale of 1528 and musical techniques dating from before 1789 into a nineteenth-century operatic score in such a way that, for all the chronological imprecision, the evocation of the past was sufficient to give contemporary audiences a "color of other times" more convincingly than "old costumes and old weapons" could.

Apart from his quotation of "Ein' feste Burg," Meyerbeer dispensed with concrete references to music or musical styles of the sixteenth century. This was certainly not due to a lack of interest or ability on his part, but to the realistic assessment that the music was too remote for his audiences to be able to connect it with the era in question. Instead, at certain critical points in his score, he imitated stylistic characteristics typical of early eighteenth-century music: thus the stepwise movement in rapid sixteenth-note motion in Marcel's Huguenot song derives from baroque conventions found, for example, in Handel's oratorios,[25] and there are several places—the music preceding Marcel's first entry, the entrance of the courtiers in Act II, and of the monks in the big scene in Act IV—where he composed grave, weighty melodies that draw on typical stylistic traits of the baroque French Overture: dotted eighth notes, massive instrumentation spotlighting the lower registers of the orchestra, and contrapuntal development. For the minuet at the beginning of Act V, Meyerbeer composed an uncommonly stiff music with, again, dotted rhythms, thereby creating a cipher which his contemporaries identified with the glories of the French court in the sixteenth century.[26] As later with Meyerbeer's *Prophète*, Wagner's *Meistersinger*, and even most of Massenet's operas, it only required "the aesthetic appearance of archaism to give the music a historical coloring, the authenticity of which is immaterial."[27]

In taking such stylistic traits as these out of their original context and preferring to use them rather than quote complete melodies, Meyerbeer also drew the consequences of his recognition that the isolated insertion of a few barcaroles as in Auber's *Muette de Portici*, a suggestion of Sicilian inspiration as in his own *Robert le diable*, or the inclusion of an old-sounding Te Deum as in Act I of Halévy's *Juive* did not produce con-

25. See Walter, *"Hugenotten"-Studien*, 113.
26. Ibid., pp 113–20.
27. Dahlhaus, "Gattungsgeschichte und Werkinterpretation," 23.

vincing coloration, still less aesthetic unity. He was thus the first composer to take to heart the warnings of the dangers of applying local color superficially. Although others had said it earlier, no one expressed the warning more trenchantly than Victor Hugo in his preface to *Cromwell* (1827):

> It will not do to "make local color," as people call it nowadays: to add, that is, a few garish spots of color here and there to a composition that is otherwise perfectly artificial and conventional. It is not on the surface of the drama that local color must lie but at its basis, in the very heart of the work, and from there it should spread to the surface of its own accord, naturally, evenly, and one might say to every corner of the drama, like sap rising from the roots to the last leaf on a tree. The drama should be radically impregnated with the color of its time, it should be in the very air in some sort, so that one is conscious of the change of century and atmosphere only at the moments of entering and leaving.[28]

Even if the unifying power of historical coloration as used by Meyerbeer in *Les Huguenots*—or by Hugo in his plays for that matter—scarcely stands up to the comparison with the techniques of musical-motivic integration developed by Verdi and Wagner, nevertheless the audiences of 1836 were obviously persuaded that Meyerbeer had succeeded in impregnating every corner of his score with characteristic color. A glance at the evolution of grand opéra up to that date is enough to show the qualitative leap he had made; the novelty of his achievement is especially well illustrated by the comparison with *Guillaume Tell*. In his last opera, Rossini had allowed reminiscences of the intervallic structure underlying his alphorn melody to recur in several other numbers that appeared on the surface to have nothing to do with the original melody. In doing this he was experimenting with a motivic procedure in a form that was ignored by all other composers until Verdi took it up. The musical incidents derived from this motive were so widely scattered across Rossini's immense score, however, that they could scarcely be

---

28. "Non qu'il convienne de *faire*, comme on dit aujourd'hui de la *couleur locale*. C'est-à-dire d'ajouter après coup quelques touches criardes çà et là sur un ensemble du reste parfaitement faux et conventionnel. Ce n'est point à la surface du drame que doit être la couleur locale, mais au fond, dans le coeur même de l'oeuvre, d'où elle se répand au dehors, d'elle-même, naturellement, également, et pour ainsi parler, dans tous les coins du drame, comme la sève qui monte de la racine à la dernière feuille de l'arbre. Le drame doit être radicalement impregné de cette couleur des temps; elle doit en quelque sorte y être dans l'air, de façon qu'on ne s'aperçoive qu'en y entrant et qu'en y sortant qu'on a changé de siècle et d'atmosphère." *Théâtre complet*, 1:437.

perceived as a dominant coloration: Rossini's prodigal melodic invention gave his listeners all too many opportunities to lose track of the "Swiss" motive.

The mixture of direct quotations of "authentic" tunes with motivic manipulation in *Guillaume Tell* on the one hand, and with reminiscences of baroque music in *Les Huguenots* on the other, together with Hugo's switch from "local color" to the "color of [the drama's] time," which is scarcely justified in the context, indicates how far aesthetic discussion and artistic experimentation of the period around 1830 were from achieving complete agreement or clarity about the category of color in drama. It also shows how inadequately the reduction of the concept to the term "local color," now usual in writing about opera of the period, expresses the multifarious reality. However prominent characteristic local color may be in isolated scenes in numerous nineteenth-century operas, the restriction of color to details that are in some way typical of a particular time or place was wholly inadequate for a genre that had raised a claim to be taken seriously as a manifestation of "absolute" art. Opera's adoption of the tragic ending hitherto reserved for spoken tragedy was only one step in making that claim: more was necessary if it was to be acknowledged.

The relative importance of color in grand opéra is explained by the need to give a coherent form to these very large-scale works, but another, complementary reason for it is to be found in the social upheavals of the early industrial era. It is obvious that the compartmentalized work available in a complex metropolis, where commerce was preeminent, was further removed from the realities of life and death than existence among the rural structures of an older environment; it is equally obvious that the transition from self-confident absolutism to a concept of "citizen kingship" anxious to ingratiate itself with the haute bourgeoisie led to the loss of all the color attendant upon the court ceremonial of the ancien régime. The gradual disappearance of color at the beginning of the nineteenth century manifested itself even in so mundane a realm as men's fashion:

> A few colours were still to be seen in the ballrooms—in embroidered satin coats—but by about 1825 even dresswear, the last stronghold of masculine elegance, was eventually overcome by the strength of neutrality—and the fine peacock that graced the ballrooms of the eighteenth century was replaced by the penguin of the nineteenth and twentieth.[29]

29. Brooke, *Western European Costume*, 142.

From that point of view, the determined search for the most characteristic colors possible, and for an overall coloration that would make as much impact on audiences as possible, can be regarded as, not least, an attempt to restore in the theater something that had already vanished from everyday life.

CHARACTER

The desire for color is inseparable from that for character and "the characteristic." Following the publication of Louis-Sebastien Mercier's *Du Théâtre* in 1773, which included a chapter on the need for "character" in drama,[30] it rapidly became one of the key terms in an avant-garde aesthetics propagated, for example, by Schiller and Körner in Germany in the 1790s. Characteristic details were essential if coloration was to have an individual and unmistakable color value, and precise coloring was essential to the depiction of the kind of complex, contradictory characters that became the rule in opera and in other genres during the nineteenth century. As with local color, in the search for the most comprehensive and precise characterization possible, with respect to both the persons and the situations of the drama, a qualitative leap separates Meyerbeer's operas for Paris from those by Rossini, Auber, and Halévy; it was no accident that the concept of the characteristic was "a catchword of Meyerbeer apologetics."[31] Meyerbeer was not content to follow the models already available around 1830, in which characteristic detail was confined to the mise-en-scène and elements superimposed on the essential musical fabric from outside. Instead he attempted to meet the challenge represented by the definition of character given by the contemporary writer on music Castil-Blaze, according to which a specific musical expression has "some particular thing which will seize the listener's ear and soul and make him believe that the emotion depicted here could not have been rendered in any other way."[32]

The reworking of existing models in accordance with a new aesthetic can be seen particularly clearly in Meyerbeer's manipulation of reminiscence motives, which will be examined in more detail in a later chapter in connection with *Le Prophète*. Half a century earlier, Grétry had made an epoch-making experiment with melodic recurrence in his *Richard*

30. "Du Caractère qu'il faut imprimer au Drame," 148–55.

31. Dahlhaus, "Die Kategorie des Charakteristischen," 19.

32. "quelque chose de particulier qui saisisse l'oreille et l'âme de l'auditeur, et lui fasse croire que le sentiment qu'on a voulu peindre, ne pouvait être rendu d'aucune autre façon"; *Dictionnaire de musique moderne*, 1:90.

Coeur-de-lion (1784), using the celebrated *romance* "Une fièvre brûlante" to evoke one specific dramatic situation.[33] No one before or since had gone beyond that: even Rossini, whose *La donna del lago* (1819) contains what was hailed, by French writers in particular,[34] as the first example of melodic recurrence in Italian opera, did not add anything qualitatively new to the process.

But Meyerbeer turned away from those examples of rather mechanical use of the process, and as early as 1831, in *Robert le diable*, he used two different melodies as reminiscence motives. It is true that the recurrences both of Raimbaut's ballade, which has revealed Robert's origins to the audience, and of the brief timpani motive announcing the chimerical Prince of Granada relate directly to the precise dramatic situations in which they were first heard, but that significance is overlaid by Meyerbeer's use of the motives to serve the musical characterization of certain people in the drama in *different* situations. Both melodies can also be understood as symbols of Bertram's influence, as manifested both in Robert's origins and in the deception involving the Prince of Granada.[35] In his next opera Meyerbeer finally took this development an important step further: the one recurring reminiscence motive in *Les Huguenots*, the chorale "Ein' feste Burg," serves only to characterize a particular group of people in the opera (like "Ad nos, ad salutarem undam" in *Le Prophète*) and is no longer associated with a particular dramatic situation.

Additionally, Meyerbeer made a fundamental move away from the use of fixed melodic formulas when he wanted to characterize individual members of the cast. Already in *Robert le diable*, for example, the timpani motive claims attention more by its unusual instrumentation than by its melodic structure, and it adumbrates the individual sonority that identifies the demonic sphere, and the devilish Bertram in particular.[36] Obviously Meyerbeer had come upon this process of extending the "identifying sonorities" of basic dramatic configurations throughout an entire opera in Weber's *Der Freischütz*,[37] and he put it to use again in *Les Huguenots*, where he consistently associates an unusual timbre with one particular person.

From the outset, the entrances of the fanatical Huguenot Marcel are

33. See Charlton, *Grétry*, 245–48.
34. See Lahalle, *Essai sur la musique*, 53.
35. See Döhring, "Giacomo Meyerbeer," 14.
36. Ibid.
37. "identifying sonority" is a translation of *Leitklang*, a term analogous with *Leitmotiv*, used by Jürgen Maehder (see "Verfremdete Instrumentation," 119).

announced by cellos and double basses, and in his recitatives, unlike any of the other characters, he is accompanied by divided low strings.[38] This singling-out of a character who plays no part in the private intrigue involving the lovers, and is introduced only as Raoul's servant to begin with, is of course disconcerting to an unprepared audience, but it shows how central Marcel's role is in the conception of the entire opera. As Heinz Becker has commented, Meyerbeer's music for *Les Huguenots* in general and for the role of Marcel in particular represented a notable breach with convention, but it was the means whereby the composer realized a completely new aesthetic concept, and in overstepping the bounds of an "aesthetic of the beautiful" in the interests of an "aesthetic of the characteristic" he was the first composer of French opera to make the radical break with tradition that Hugo and others were calling for.[39]

The full extent of Meyerbeer's achievement can only be appreciated when we bear in mind that the character of Marcel is largely his invention. The writing of the libretto of *Les Huguenots* was a long and complicated process, with Meyerbeer constantly intervening and urging Scribe to make alterations in order to ensure that this particular character corresponded to the composer's unconventional idea of him. Even when the work was at so early a stage as Scribe's first prose draft of September 1832, which did not provide for either Marcel's Huguenot song or "Ein' feste Burg," Meyerbeer commented in the margin:

> I would wish the character of the old servant to be treated in a wholly *patriarchal* manner, with a sublime naivete, and a religious piety that penetrates everything. A fanatical Protestant, detesting Catholics, whom he has scarcely ever seen, since he has always lived near La Rochelle in his master's castle. A fanatical love for his young master whom he has educated. He makes long speeches quoting the Bible (or religious maxims, if you like) at every instant; we must have them even in his recitatives. This role must be distinguished from all the other roles in the opera, even in the very form of its language, so that it can be painted musically in the same distinct manner. As he has only one important number (the duet in Act III), we must give him frequent speeches, four or six lines long, in the ensembles in which he takes part, so as to make him stand out.[40]

38. See Frederichs, "Das Rezitativ in den *Hugenotten*," 67.
39. See H. Becker, "'. . . der Marcel von Meyerbeer,'" 80.
40. "Je désirerais que le caractère du vieux domestique fût traité d'une manière tout à fait *patriarcale*, d'une naïveté sublime, d'une piété religieuse qui perce partout. Protestant exalté détestant les catholiques qu'il n'a presque pas encore vus puisque il a toujours vécu près de La Rochelle dans le château de son maître. Amour exalté pour son jeune maître qu'il a éduqué. Il cite des tirades de la Bible (ou des maximes religieuses, si l'on veut) à

As early as Act I, Meyerbeer wanted Marcel to be characterized by the contrast he presented to the revelers at Nevers's dinner. Although he had already stated the wish that "the first act should be brilliant and very gay, from start to finish,"[41] in the end the stylistic unity and brilliance of the opening scene mattered less than having this rough-hewn soldier vividly characterized.

All Meyerbeer's requests are satisfied in the definitive version of the libretto: Marcel ignores the polite conventions of the courtiers' speech, refers uninhibitedly to "papists" ("les gens du pape"), and imitates the sound of cannonballs: "piff, paff, piff." Marcel's role in the completed score is considerably more substantial than in any of the earlier drafts. He intervenes repeatedly in the action to decisive effect, repeatedly calls the youthful Raoul to order, and in the last act he becomes the mainspring of the action, "preserving" Raoul from converting to Catholicism, and pronouncing the blessing on his union with Valentine.

Marcel has nothing in common with servants of the classic type that lived on in French opera up to *La Muette de Portici*[42] and *Les Vêpres siciliennes*, and in Italian opera into the 1840s. He does not play the role of the confidant, listening to his master's intimate revelations, but rather has the authority to remind Raoul of something the young man has forgotten: the duty he owes to the faith of his fathers.

It would be an oversimplification, however, to take Marcel for the opera's principal character.[43] He exists only in relationship to Raoul, he never acts in his own interests but always does only what he believes is necessary for his master's spiritual good. His position in the dramatic configuration is inseparable from that of Raoul, and we might call him the personification of Raoul's upbringing in the Protestant faith, which throws the hotheaded young man into an unresolvable conflict when he falls in love with the Catholic Valentine. Meyerbeer had personified his protagonist's conflict of loyalties, thus making it theatrically effective, in a very similar way in *Robert le diable*: there, Alice embodies Robert's

---

tout instant; il en faut jusque dans son récitatif. Ce rôle doit trancher même par la forme de son langage avec tous les autres rôles de l'opéra pour qu'on puisse le peindre de même en musique. Comme il n'a qu'un seul morceau important (le duo du 3e acte) il faut lui donner souvent dans les morceaux d'ensemble où il entre des tirades de 4 ou 6 vers pour qu'on puisse le faire ressortir." F-Pn, n.a.f. 22502, fol. 65. See also Mongrédien, "Aux sources du livret," 161.

41. "que le premier acte fût brillant et très gai, d'un bout à l'autre"; ibid. fol. 62. See also Mongrédien, "Aux sources du livret," 158.

42. See Arvin, *Eugène Scribe and the French theatre*, 194.

43. Becker takes a contrary view: see "'. . . der Marcel von Meyerbeer,'" 98. See also Döhring, "Der andere Choral."

human traits and his potential for good, which enable him to thwart the devilish Bertram's evil plans in the end.

Robert and Raoul are alike, then, in being determined by external influences, in roles apparently dependent on the function assigned to them in a plot controlled by others, if not by an inscrutable fate. It is significant that the titles of all Meyerbeer's Paris operas use a form of words denoting a function, never merely a person's name, whereas the usual thing in the French theater at that date, including grand opéra, was for such explanation or description to appear—if at all—in the form of an alternative title, following the name of the protagonist(s) and prefaced by the word "or" *(ou)* (Scribe and Halévy's *Guido et Ginevra, ou La Peste de Florence* of 1838 is an example of this type of "double title").[44] It is certainly no accident that Meyerbeer's opera of 1836 was not called *Valentine*, even though the working title was *Léonore* for a time, when that was envisaged as the heroine's name, or that his later works for the Opéra were not entitled *Jean de Leyde* or *Sélica*—whereas Verdi, quite the reverse, did *not* call *Rigoletto* "*Il buffone del rè*" (or "*Il rè si diverte*," which would have been a direct translation of the original title of Hugo's play, *Le roi s'amuse*), or *Aida* "*La schiava dei Faraoni*," and Wagner did not give his *Lohengrin* a descriptive title—*Der Gralsritter* perhaps?

Even a purely external feature like that is indicative of the unique nature of Meyerbeer's oeuvre within the context of nineteenth-century opera. There are, it is true, a number of operas by other composers which have descriptive, functional terms in their titles, but in none of them does the fact express profound doubt about the autonomy of the individual in the way it does in Meyerbeer. We may interpret this as a sign of a modern, realist aspect of Meyerbeer's dramaturgy, but we cannot deny that it is also indicative of one of the problems that made it harder for Meyerbeer's operas to outlive their age: their heroes lack the greatness to which some of their contemporaries, such as Berlioz's Benvenuto Cellini and Wagner's Tannhäuser, aspire. Meyerbeer's protagonists are also caught up in tragic conflicts of course, but they are relatively passive figures and never embody a utopian dream reaching beyond the confines of the dramatic action.

The passivity of these irresolute characters is exemplified, not least, in the formal provisions of their roles. In none of his large-scale historical operas does Meyerbeer give his tenor protagonist an aria in the traditional four-part form, though its contrasts of mood would be an ideal expression of the conflict of loyalties in which these characters are

44. See Rothe, *Der Doppeltitel;* see also idem, *Der literarische Titel.*

caught as surely as Verdi's tenors are. The rule in this form of aria is for a recitative *scena* to be followed by an exposition of the conflict troubling the character in a section which is usually slow, and called the *adagio* for that reason. In the next section, called the *tempo di mezzo*, which is usually a looser structure somewhere between recitative and arioso, an intervention occurs that enables the protagonist to work himself up to a decision in the final section, a piece in a closed form, which became known in Italian theatrical jargon as a *cabaletta*[45] from about 1800 onward.[46] Once this model had gradually become standard in Italian opera in the early nineteenth century, its underlying structure was used stereotypically not only there but also in French grand opéra. In Act III of Rossini's *Guillaume Tell*, for example, we see Mathilde, first despairing over the hopelessness of her love for Arnold, then—shaken out of her reverie by the sound of distant music—finding the strength to persuade her lover of the need to bid each other a final farewell. Again, in Act IV of the same work, Arnold is seen giving way to sorrow and anger before the approach of the Swiss reminds him that he can realize his desire for revenge by taking arms.

The situation is similar in Act IV of Halévy's *La Juive* when Eléazar sings his celebrated aria, "Rachel, quand du Seigneur la grâce tutélaire": he could save Rachel's life by revealing that she is not really his daughter but was born a Christian. In the adagio he wavers between fidelity to Judaism and pity for his foster-daughter's life. But his pride stiffens when he hears the Christian mob outside howling for Jewish blood ("Au bûcher les juifs!"): he will demand of Rachel that she share his martyrdom. In itself the aria is highly conventional, and draws its dramatic effect from the fact that the penultimate act of the opera ends with it and not with the *grand tableau* expected by the audience—and as originally planned. A later example shows that Halévy was even prepared to weaken the usual effectiveness of the kind of "super-scene"[47] that allowed the focus to switch from the group to the single character, and was typical of grand opéra, in order to retain the traditional four-part aria. In the finale of Act IV of his opera *La Reine de Chypre* (1841), he allows an aria of that type, highlighting the tenor Gérard's emotional journey from insensate revenge to humble submission to the will of God, to interrupt the grandiose progress of the triumph of the Queen

45. See Rosen, "A musicological word study," 168.

46. See Powers, "'La solita forma,'" 106 (in *Acta musicologica*, 69; subsequent references to this work include page numbers for both of the sources listed in the bibliography); see also Balthazar, "Ritorni's *Ammaestramenti*," 287–90.

47. See above, chapter 3, 99.

of Cyprus, thus making it impossible for the audience to grasp the sequence as an integrated whole.

Meyerbeer, by contrast, refused to present his characters by means of large formal solos, even in very similar dramatic situations. With a rigor that can still seem surprising today, he denied an aria even to protagonists who provide the titles of their operas, like Robert and the Anabaptist prophet John. Raoul has one aria in *Les Huguenots*, in Act V, when he tells the people celebrating Marguerite's wedding of the torchlit approach of the Catholics, intent on murder ("A la lueur de leurs torches funèbres"); the call to arms in its last section ("Courons aux armes, à la vengeance") has certain cabaletta-like traits but also an agitato character that makes it more like a dramatic recitative. A soloist needs a moment of repose and release from immediate pressures in order to launch into an aria, and that Meyerbeer denies his tenor: as in his other solos, what Raoul has to express is not an emotional conflict drawn up from within himself for consideration but something he has to communicate to other people. His *romance* in Act I is sung in response to the Catholic noblemen's invitation to recount one of his amorous adventures, and his aria in Act V is an attempt to warn the Huguenots of the impending massacre.

Seen from this perspective, Meyerbeer's concern with "character" and "the characteristic" appears in a completely new light. If there were no more big solo scenes displaying the characters of the principal persons in the drama, who instead were revealed only through their relations with other people, in the shorter solo passages that remained to them, then there had to be something to compensate for that: virtually of necessity, that something was a heightened focus on the characters of minor actors in the drama and on smaller solo forms. "'Orchestral comment' came to take the place of physically"—or verbally—"objectified action," as Jürgen Maehder observes,[48] and it is not by chance that the entrance numbers of both Raoul and Marcel claim attention above all by their unusual orchestration. The combination of piccolo, four bassoons, double basses, bass drum, and cymbals that accompanies Marcel's *Chanson huguenote* was not only quite new to the first audiences but also created the desired character of grotesqueness;[49] the use of a solo viola as a typical troubadour instrument in Raoul's *romance* had precedents, to be sure, in Grétry and the *chanson gothique*, "Le roi de Thulé,"

---

48. "Verfremdete Instrumentation," 111.
49. See Walter, *"Hugenotten"-Studien*, 141–47.

in Berlioz's *Huit Scènes de Faust* (1829),[50] but it upset the expectations of audiences attuned to the orchestra of Rossini, Auber, and Boieldieu. Here, the aesthetic principle of the "emancipation of timbre" from the conditions of musical-structural contexts,[51] which informs Berlioz's treatise on instrumentation, published only a few years later, corresponds directly to the emancipation of individual small forms from the musico-dramaturgical context of an action spread out over five acts.

Like grand opéra's striving for comprehensibility through the medium of pantomime, its concretization of characteristic details, expressed in an extreme form in the examples cited above, can also be explained in terms of urbanized perceptions. When the actors in a drama on the stage revealed as little about their personalities through their constitution and actions as the anonymous passers-by in the streets of Paris did by their outward appearance, it became essential to exaggerate individual attributes, if the Opéra's audiences were not to suffer the same disorientation they experienced in their everyday lives. The concern for clarity on such terms set in train a development, however, which in later works of the grand opéra genre made it impossible for genuine character—whether in the depiction of individuals or in the overall conception—to exist side-by-side with the emphasis on "the characteristic." From the distance of a century and a half, and with the application of a pinch of critical irony, we can discern, behind the superabundance of "the characteristic," an attempt to disguise the lack of character that afflicts dramatis personae like Raoul, Robert the Devil, and John the Prophet.

THE OBEDIENT DAUGHTER

If a certain passivity is one of the distinguishing marks of the male heroes of grand opéra, it afflicts the women they love to a much greater degree. This, a reflection of the blinkered bourgeois idea of womanhood that reached serious opera only after manifesting itself in opera buffa and opéra comique, is yet another development of which Meyerbeer's *Huguenots* provides a first outstanding example, in the extreme case of Valentine. From the outset, the daughter of the aristocrat Saint-Bris is presented as entirely dependent on men, intent solely on living up to society's expectations of a "godly virgin" ("vierge divine"), "whiter than

---

50. See Charlton, *Grétry*, 236.
51. See Dahlhaus, *Die Musiktheorie im 18. und 19. Jahrhundert*, 91.

the white of ermine," as Raoul describes her in his Act I *romance* ("Plus blanche que la blanche hermine").

It is true that she allows Marguerite to persuade her to visit Nevers, whom she does not love, in order to ask him to break off their engagement, but when she is later "given" to him as wife anyway, she acquiesces without protest. She tries to forget her passionate love for Raoul, and resists his despairing protestations of love when she unexpectedly encounters him again. As will be shown in the next section of this chapter, when she does admit to her true feelings, in the big scene at the end of Act IV, it is only inadvertently.

She is finally united with her lover in the last act, after her husband has been killed, but once again she is ready immediately to deny herself and fulfill what men expect of her by adopting Raoul's religion:

> VALENTINE *hors d'elle-même*
> Eh bien! tu connaîtras tout l'amour d'une femme!
> Tu veux, quand tout nous joint, me fuir par le trépas!
> Non! non! non! non! je ne sais pas s'il faut risquer mon âme,
> Enfer ou Paradis, je ne te quitte plus!
> Oui, cette âme en tumulte, cette âme ne reconnaît plus rien!
> Toi! tu maudis mon culte! moi! . . . j'adopte le tien!
>   (*Les Huguenots*, Acte V, scène 3)

ꜟ   ꜟ   ꜟ

> VALENTINE *(beside herself):* Well then! You shall know a woman's entire love! Everything unites us, yet you wish to flee me through death! No! no! no! no! I do not know if I risk my soul, come hell or paradise, I will never leave you now! Yes, this soul in tumult, this soul knows only this one thing! You—you curse my faith! I—I adopt yours!

This image of a submissive woman had hovered before Meyerbeer, at least, when the opera was still at a very early stage. In the notes he made on Scribe's first prose draft in 1832 he saw fit to remind the librettist of this attribute of the principle female character, at that date called Gabrielle: "Let us not forget that Gabrielle should be very devout."[52] This reduction of the character, in the role that would have been assigned to the prima donna in an Italian opera, to a dependent being with no will of her own is even more flagrant in the score than in the libretto. Although it was intended for a time that her name (changed from Gabrielle to Léonore) should be the opera's title, the version Meyerbeer finally set to music does not give Valentine a single solo number.

52. "N'oublions pas que Gabrielle doit être très dévôte"; F-Pn, n.a.f. 22502, fol. 65v. See also Mongrédien, "Aux sources du livret," 161.

At one stage, to be sure, she was to have had two *romances:* in Act I she would have had the opportunity to express the wish to break off her engagement to Nevers and go to a convent ("Au sein d'un couvent"),[53] and at the beginning of Act IV, immediately before Raoul bursts in on her, she should have had another *romance* lamenting her inability to forget her beloved: this number, "Parmi les pleurs mon rêve se ranime," is to be found in some piano-vocal scores, but Meyerbeer cut it from the full score, along with the Act I *romance.*

In the end she has no musical presence in Act I at all, but is only seen making her way in silence across the garden of Nevers's castle. In Act II her role is confined to five lines of recitative in conversation with Marguerite before she is presented to Raoul, who refuses to marry her because she is Nevers's mistress. Even in the ensuing stretta as people react to this shock, her part is only one voice in the general ensemble, and it is not until the start of the concluding Allegro con spirito in C major that she is given her first short solo, a mere four bars long. At least she is permitted to speak up for herself, asking what she can have done to merit such an insult ("Et comment ai-je donc mérité tant d'outrage?"), but even that minimal self-expression is taken away from her immediately when the melody is appropriated by Raoul.

The first audible evidence that Valentine is more than a minor character does not come until Act III, when she reveals her father's plot to murder Raoul in her scene and duet with Marcel. Yet even here her musical existence is granted only in ensemble with a male character, and this continues to be the case in the rest of the opera, in the consecration of the swords and her subsequent duet with Raoul in Act IV, and in the trio in Act V. Only when dying is she given a melody that is not immediately taken over by someone else, but even here the text relates to an authoritarian male figure, as she assures her murderous father that she will pray for him in heaven:

> VALENTINE *se soulevant avec peine*
> Oui, c'est moi, moi qui vais prier pour vous!
> *(Elle expire.)*
>   (*Les Huguenots,* Acte V, scène 4)

        ♪   ♪   ♪

VALENTINE (*raising herself with difficulty*): Yes, it is I, I, who will pray for you! (*She expires.*)

---

53. See the autograph score of this number, F-Po, Rés. 177.

Thus the image of a passive, dependent woman is presented, fully developed, in *Les Huguenots*, for the first time in French serious opera. It is true that earlier French operas had frequently shown women involved in conflicts where they were required to conform to norms set by father and country. But Olimpie in Spontini's opera of that name, Pamyra in Rossini's *Siège de Corinthe*, and Anaï in his *Moïse et Pharaon*, as well as Halévy's "Jewess," Rachel, are depicted as women who, though capable of rebellion against their fathers, are not ready to surrender to their lovers unconditionally. In the end the heroic decisions that they take to conquer their feelings of love and do their filial duty are represented by them as their own, underlined musically by large-scale arias.

Additionally, as well as women of that order, the casts of earlier operas often included royal and aristocratic heroines. Another of the landmarks registered in *Les Huguenots* is the conclusion of the process discussed above in chapter 3 under the heading "The Retreat of the Princess," when Marguerite, in the last act, "is robbed . . . of the chance to sing." From then onward, in later grands opéras, and also in Italian opera after 1850, the pattern of the meek, self-denying maiden was the rule, even in those cases where the female protagonist is first depicted as an active heroine, or even a woman of doubtful virtue. Hélène in Verdi's *Vêpres siciliennes*, for instance, is depicted as one of the leaders of Sicilian resistance in Act I, when she makes a thinly disguised call for revolt, but in the decisive conflict which takes dramatic shape in the Act V trio she is presented as a woman who does her best to conform to what the men expect of her, and is no longer capable of making an independent, sovereign decision of her own. And Violetta, the courtesan presented in Act I of Verdi's *Traviata* as a woman used to getting her own way with men, falls in with the ruthless demands made of her by Alfredo's father in Act II so readily that she appears to have been positively waiting for the opportunity to sacrifice her happiness and her love for Alfredo on the altar of patriarchal authority.

With this image of the submissive woman a "bourgeois" conception of the respective roles of the sexes took shape in serious opera, and was not challenged until a new image, that of the femme fatale, took the stage in Bizet's *Carmen* (1875). Even then, the submissive type lived on, transfigured by Verdi in *Otello*, as he wrote to his publisher while working on the composition:

> To judge *terre à terre*, the character of Desdemona, who allows herself to be mistreated, slapped, even strangled, who forgives and commends herself [to God], seems a bit stupid! But Desdemona is not a woman, she is

a type! She is the type of goodness, of resignation, of sacrifice! Such beings are born for others, unconscious of their *own self*![54]

Perhaps it seems strange that audiences that continued to include a considerable proportion of aristocrats even after 1830, and pursued amorous affairs—or took a lively interest in those of others—even while in the opera house, were regaled with an almost unvarying succession of virtuous, passive women on the stage. Once again, it was a matter of the theatrical representation of a dream image inseparable from the moral double standards of the upwardly mobile classes. In real life, no one believed in love free of material considerations, and no one believed in marital fidelity. The *physiologies* that began to be published in huge numbers around 1840 underlined this aspect of everyday existence, describing concepts such as fidelity, constancy, honor, and self-sacrifice as at best desirable, and setting out a "physiological analysis" of love that invariably uncovered infidelity, inconstancy, or dishonesty;[55] the ideal of a sincerely loving and faithful wife, on the other hand, was dismissed as an unrealizable illusion.[56]

In the areas of life where legislation could be brought to bear, it had been possible to limit women to a passive, male-dependent role. Under a provision of the Napoleonic *Code civil* that was not revoked until after 1938, married women were deemed to be incapable in law.[57] But the Opéra itself was another institution where a woman was regarded as merely an appendage of a man: she was admitted free of charge if she was in the company of one,[58] while selling single seats to women was unheard of. Yet women never lost the power to play a decisive and active role in the sphere of the emotions: that last dignity was denied them only in theatrical fictions. Meyerbeer's operas are outstanding examples of this systematic suppression of feminine personality in fictive actions. The development was already apparent in *Les Huguenots*, and it was even more sharply etched by 1849, in *Le Prophète*, of which a contemporary critic remarked "the hero's betrothed is an insignificant character, the emotion which she inspires and shares is not in any way a determining cause of her lover's fate."[59]

54. Letter to Giulio Ricordi, 22 April 1887, cited in Abbiati, *Giuseppe Verdi*, 4:322; cited here from Busch, *Verdi's "Otello" and "Simon Boccanegra,"* 1:301.
55. See Biesbrock, *Die literarische Mode der Physiologien*, 211.
56. Ibid., 253.
57. See Tetu, "Remarques sur le statut juridique," 10.
58. See Castil-Blaze, *Mémorial du Grand Opéra*, 62.
59. "La fiancée du héros est un personnage insignifiant, le sentiment qu'elle inspire et qu'elle partage n'est point une cause déterminante dans la destinée de son amant"; Paul

The Fleeting Moment

Like many other operas of the late 1820s and early 1830s, *Les Huguenots*
starts with an impressive set piece, providing the opportunity for the
initial exposition of the private intrigue, in the context of an extended
choral scene: the friends of the Comte de Nevers are assembled at his
château in Touraine for a banquet. The act begins with a solo for the
host, urging his guests to enjoy themselves:

> NEVERS
> Des beaux jours de la jeunesse,
> Dans la plus riante ivresse
> Hâtons-nous, le temps nous presse,
> Hâtons-nous de jouir.
> (*Les Huguenots*, Acte I, scène 1)

NEVERS: The happy days of our youth, in the midst of laughing elation,
let us hasten—time is at our heels—let us hasten to enjoy them.

This linking of hedonism with the repeated exhortation to make haste
is disconcerting enough in itself, and becomes yet more so when one
reflects that it comes at the beginning of an act which is almost an hour
in length, and of an opera which is due to last a good five hours. The
restlessness the lines express is underlined by Meyerbeer's musical setting: Nevers begins each of the first three lines at a measured pace, in
quarter notes, then suddenly switches to triplet eighth notes, hastening
to the end of the line; the fourth line, in which the chorus joins, is in the
eighth-note-and-triplet rhythm from the first, with the words "hâtons-
nous" repeated three times.

The unusual rhythmic pattern is a further variation on the triple meters for which Meyerbeer had already revealed his liking in *Robert le
diable*,[60] and it proves to be characteristic of the entire act. Robert Schumann was enraged by the frequent recurrences of "that celebrated,
fatally throbbing, indecent rhythm."[61] The sequence of a measured
start and a hurried continuation in the context of a fully regular four-
or eight-bar metrical structure occurs again when Raoul enters ("Sous

---

Scudo in *Revue des deux mondes*, 22 April 1849, cited in Coudroy, *La Critique parisienne*, pt.
2, p. 74.

60. See Macdonald, "*Robert le diable*," 467.

61. "Fragmente aus Leipzig," 4 [1837], in *Gesammelte Schriften*, 2:220–25 (p. 225).
Cited here in the translation by Henry Pleasants, in Schumann, *The Musical World of Robert
Schumann*, 137–40 (p. 139).

le beau ciel de Touraine"), and in the chorus with which the other guests comment on the arrival of the veiled unknown woman ("L'aventure est singulière"). The tempos which Meyerbeer then prescribes for the fugato in the act-finale, during which the courtiers attempt to ingratiate themselves with Raoul ("Vous savez si je suis un ami sûr et tendre"), and for the chorus entitled *Orgie*, actually make it almost impossible for singers to articulate the words comprehensibly. Both these choruses make the impression of restless haste, which, in the case of the "orgy," was precisely what Meyerbeer had asked of Scribe before he made the first verse draft: "I would like a bacchanale as lively, irregular, and crazy as possible here. I would like lots of words, because I can see that we will have to make them talk fast and furious in this piece."[62]

But why was it necessary to make them talk so fast in this bacchanale? We can find a hint of the possible reason for it in the scene which comes directly after Nevers's opening solo. The Catholic nobleman Tavannes speaks up:

> TAVANNES, *s'addressant au comte de Nevers*
> De ces lieux enchanteurs châtelain respectable
> Pourquoi, cher Nevers, pourquoi ne pas nous mettre à table?
> (*Les Huguenots*, Acte I, scène 1)

TAVANNES (*addressing Nevers*): Worthy lord of this enchanting place, why, my dear Nevers, why do we not sit down at your table?

Once again, the rhythmic and melodic realization of these two lines betrays a certain restlessness in the eighth-note triplets at the end of the first half of the musical period, but for the time being the regular meter keeps the speaker within the bounds of good manners. In the second line, however, Tavannes's impatience proves stronger than etiquette. The question ends with hurried sixteenth notes, so that the period is finished in seven bars instead of the regular eight. It becomes clear that Tavannes's impatience reflects a general mood, for the chorus at once repeats the last line with the syllabic sixteenth notes.

Nevers is unable to satisfy the request, however, because he awaits a last guest: Raoul, the tenor protagonist, has yet to arrive. In delaying the entrance of this major character, Meyerbeer not only heightens the tension in an exposition already filled with expectancy, but he also

---

62. "J'y désirerais une bacchanale aussi vive, déréglée et aussi folle que possible. Je désirerais beaucoup de paroles parce que je vois qu'il faut faire parler vite et beaucoup dans ce morceau." F-Pn, n.a.f. 22502, fol. 62v. See also Mongrédien, "Aux sources du livret," 158.

allows the audience an opportunity to identify with Tavannes, for there is an obvious parallel between the culinary expectations of the characters in the opera and the no less culinary expectations of the audience. They too must wait for the opera's star to arrive before they can enjoy one of the evening's pleasures, namely a virtuoso tenor solo, or other kinds of pleasures in the intermission to follow. It may seem an odd parallel, but it provides a basis for understanding the wider significance of the phenomenon described. The reason why a group of dinner guests in Touraine in 1572 should feel the constant pressure of time may be obscure, but in the case of Parisian society in 1836 it is easier to pinpoint.

Since the end of the eighteenth century people's perception of time had been subjected to a fundamental change as a consequence of "the new historical experience of acceleration," a phenomenon that historians have identified only fairly recently.[63] George Steiner wrote of it as follows:

> No strings of quotations, no statistics, can recapture for us what must have been the inner excitement, the passionate adventure of spirit and emotion unleashed by the events of 1789 and sustained, at a fantastic tempo, until 1815. Far more than political revolution and war, on an unprecedented scale of geographical and social compass, is involved. The French Revolution and the Napoleonic wars—*la grande épopée*—literally quickened the pace of felt time. We lack histories of the internal time-sense, of the changing beat in men's experience of the rhythms of perception. But we do have reliable evidence that those who lived through the 1790s and the first decade and a half of the nineteenth century, and who could recall the tenor of life under the old dispensation, felt that time itself and the whole enterprise of consciousness had formidably accelerated. . . .
>
> Together with this *accelerando*, there occurred a "growing more dense" of human experience. The notion is difficult to set out abstractly. But it crowds on us, unmistakably, from contemporary literature and private record.[64]

Another historian of the "consciousness of time," Rudolf Wendorff, places less emphasis on the acceleration in "public" history and more

---

63. Koselleck, *Futures Past*, 149. On the recognition of the phenomenon, see also ibid., 252–53; Pichois, *Vitesse et vision du monde*; and Hoeges, *Alles veloziferisch*.
64. Steiner, *In Bluebeard's Castle*, 11–12.

on the changes to which the everyday perceptions of the inhabitants of modern cities were exposed, and which did not become noticeable in the arts until after 1815. Wendorff argues that the many processes of acceleration affecting modern civilization created an inner restlessness, which could be both an exhilarating stimulus and a cause of anxiety.[65] An indication of the anxiety caused by the acceleration on so many fronts is given by the fact that all at once doctors everywhere were diagnosing a condition called "over-excitement of the nervous system," which was also taken seriously in academic medicine. The author of an award-winning study completed in 1840, examining "the influence of physical and moral education on the production of over-excitement of the nervous system and the maladies that are a consequence of it," nevertheless avoided the question of civilization's role, and pontificated: "As for the problem of the influence of civilization on the production of over-excitement of the nervous system, we believe it to be insoluble."[66]

Not all writers of the period were so restrained, and depictions of restless and overexcited city life were produced in huge numbers in the middle decades of the nineteenth century. One example, published anonymously by a Polish immigrant in 1840, is particularly informative, for the absence of any kind of literary elegance provides an immediate insight into the particular difficulties of describing Paris, which the opportunistic writer mentioned in his preface: "So, the study not admitting any delay, it is the duty of him who wishes to illustrate Paris to explain it incessantly, never to stop."[67]

The author, who published little else besides these "physiological studies of western European cities," devoted a whole chapter to Paris in motion, beginning it with a plunge into the attempt to express in words what was so extraordinary about the movement in the city:

> It's fast, it's fiery, it foams. One would say it was the pool of a cataract! In the streets, in the alleys, in the gardens, in the squares, on the quays, on the bridges, under the bridges—men, beasts, vehicles, boats, walk, trot, rumble, glide, and the air vibrates, the air is riven by brief tones and long

65. *Zeit und Kultur,* 421.

66. "Quant au problème de l'influence de la civilisation sur la production de la surexcitation du système nerveux, nous le croyons insoluble." Cerise, *Déterminer l'influence de l'éducation,* 173.

67. "Or, l'étude n'admettant pas d'arrêt, il est du devoir de celui qui veut illustrer Paris, de l'expliquer sans cesse, de ne s'arrêter jamais." Niépovié, *Études physiologiques,* ii; cf. Citron, *La Poésie de Paris,* 2:114–15.

tones, and the air is wearied by buffets of bizarre sounds that are born and die suddenly.[68]

For all the differences of artistic pretension and quality of realization, a similarly frenetic movement, with rhythmic effects to the forefront, can be observed in the musical construction of Act I of *Les Huguenots*. It is all the more striking in the opera because it is curiously incongruous in the context. The act is uncommonly long and contains few of the events necessary to the understanding of the plot, yet in detail it presents a turbulent succession of numerous short scenes.

In the second and third acts, too, there is a similar tension between rapidly altering details and a slowly developing dramatic action. Almost every contemporary report comments on the "revue-like" and "undramatic" impression the work made.[69] Blaze de Bury grumbled: "The first two acts proceed at a slow walk, the piece labors at a snail's pace, it is only in the grace of the details that the composer gives you something of interest."[70] Franz Grillparzer criticized the "somewhat distracting effect" created before the music actually got going with a duet in the middle of the third act.[71] A Paris critic found the effect of the first three acts was "less alive, less electric, less general than that of the last two acts,"[72] and an Italian critic saw fit to recall in an obituary of Meyerbeer that "the first three acts are without interest, without action, inert, and cold."[73]

It did not occur to any of the critics that the supposed weaknesses, which they naturally ascribed to Scribe, might be the result of a fully conscious aesthetic standpoint—as Meyerbeer claimed privately[74]—that went far beyond an unconventional attitude toward the pseudo-

68. "C'est rapide, – c'est ardent, – c'est écumant. – On dirait le bassin d'une cataracte! Dans les rues, dans les passages, dans les jardins, sur les places, sur les quais, sur les ponts, sous les ponts, – hommes, bêtes, voitures, bâteaux, marchent, courent, roulent, glissent, et l'air vibre, et l'air est déchiré par des notes brèves, par des notes longues, et l'air est fatigué de bouffées de sons bizarres qui naissent et meurent soudain." From the chapter "Mouvement de Paris: ses faits et ses gestes dans les rues"; *Études physiologiques*, 108.

69. See Walter, *"Hugenotten"-Studien*, 107.

70. "Les deux premiers actes marchent lentement, la pièce va d'un train pénible, embarrassé, ce n'est que par la grâce des détails que le musicien vous intéresse"; *Meyerbeer et son temps*, 115.

71. "[eine] etwas zerstreuende Wirkung"; entry in Grillparzer's diary, 22 April 1836, *Sämtliche Werke*, sec. 2, vol. 10 (*Tagebücher*, 4), p. 35.

72. "moins vif, moins électrique, moins général que celui des deux derniers actes"; *Le Constitutionnel*, 2 March 1836, cited in Coudroy, *La Critique parisienne*, pt. 1, p. 151.

73. "I tre primi atti sono senza interesse, senza azione, inerti e freddi"; "Meyerbeer: Studii critico-biografici" [1864], in Filippi, *Musica e musicisti*, 140–181 (p. 170).

74. In a letter to his wife Minna, 6 March 1836, *Briefwechsel*, 2:511.

Aristotelian unities of place and action.[75] The continual "growing more dense" of the events and the concomitant acceleration of the action serve rather to point out how central the time motive is to the dramaturgical conception of this opera. The first two acts show the society of the French court doing its best to enjoy the present time, at the cost of ignoring the signs of the time. Things that would bring about an abrupt change of direction in the action of any other opera are integrated into the festive scene that makes up the first act: neither Marcel's undisguised hostility nor Raoul's astonished discovery of Valentine's supposed infidelity has enduring consequences for the musico-dramatic course of events. True, there is an everpresent sense of danger from the outset. When Nevers celebrates the reconciliation between Huguenots and Catholics as "an eternal peace" ("une éternelle paix"), Tavannes responds "ironically" (*ironiquement*): "Which won't last long" ("Qui durera bien peu!").

But that reminder of the disaster to come is revoked at once. Members of the audience will have been schooled by experience to expect some event that will disrupt the merriment of the banquet, but Meyerbeer continually disappoints that expectation.[76] By this means he heightens the tension awakened by the work's very title to a previously inconceivable degree. In the second act, too, despite the overpointed contrast, the tension is raised even higher during the first scene, for the "idyll of emotion free of repression"[77] has no foundation firmer than wilful ignorance:

> MARGUERITE
> Que Luther et Calvin ensanglantent la terre
> De leurs débats religieux;
> Des ministres du ciel que la morale austère
> Nous épouvante au nom des cieux!
> (*Les Huguenots*, Acte II, scène 1)

~ ~ ~

MARGUERITE: Let Luther and Calvin soak the earth in blood with their religious debates; let the austere morality of these ministers of heaven shock us in heaven's name!

This broad, panoramic depiction of the deceitful (and already disrupted) calm before the storm inevitably throws the coups de théâtre that follow each other so rapidly during the second half of the opera into even

75. See Walter, *"Hugenotten"-Studien*, 106–7.
76. Ibid., 156.
77. Döhring, "Giacomo Meyerbeer," 17.

higher relief. In this, Scribe demonstrated his skill at manipulating contemporary habits of perception, treating the spectator, as he did in most of his dramas, "as a confidant and a dupe at the same time," carelessly dropping

> a telltale but unnoticed word in a corner, which enters [the spectator's] ear without his paying any attention, and then, at the moment when the coup de théâtre breaks, forces from him that exclamation of pleasure, that "Ah!" which means, "It's true, he did tell us! How stupid of us not to have guessed!"[78]

What made the discreetly prepared surprises so overwhelmingly effective, however, was Meyerbeer's decision to apply the principle of contrast consistently across the entire structure of a five-act opera. Another of his notes in the margin of the first prose draft of September 1832 shows him, yet again, to have been one of the most innovative dramatists of his time:

> The first three acts have been so long that we must try to make the last two really short. I think therefore that there should not be any number at all in Valentine's scene, or in the one for Raoul and Valentine. All of that should take place in recitative.[79]

He kept to that resolve, right up to the final stage of preparing the score for publication, when he cut Valentine's *romance* in the first scene in Act IV, as already noted, as well as the first of the duets he had composed for her and Raoul, which survives in his autograph.[80]

The outcome is that Act IV is dominated by the rapid succession of events. Meyerbeer made the dangerous deterioration in the religio-political situation palpable by systematically reducing the musical self-sufficiency of individual scenes and limiting the opportunities for closed musical structures to unfold without disruption. This was in complete contrast to the leisurely procedures of the first three acts. *Les Huguenots* is the first opera in which even the smallest musical events are subordi-

---

78. "à la fois pour confident et pour dupe"; ". . . négligemment dans un coin de la pièce un mot révélateur, mais inaperçu, qui lui entre dans l'oreille sans qu'il y fasse attention, et qui, au moment où éclate le coup de théâtre, lui arrache cette exclamation de plaisir, ce ah! qui veut dire 'C'est vrai, il nous l'avait annoncé! Que nous sommes bêtes de ne pas l'avoir deviné!'" Legouvé, *Eugène Scribe*, 19–20.

79. "Les trois premiers actes ont été si longs qu'il faut tâcher de rendre bien courts les deux derniers. Je crois donc qu'il ne faudrait pas aucun morceau dans la scène de Valentine et de même dans celle entre Raoul et Valentine. Tout cela doit se passer en récitatif." F-Pn, n.a.f. 22502, fol. 71v. See also Mongrédien, "Aux sources du livret," 167.

80. See Döhring, "Die Autographen der vier Hauptopern Meyerbeers," 46–47.

nated to a dramaturgy that galvanizes the excitement as the end of the act approaches and makes the audience, quite involuntarily, perceive the events on the stage as following thick and fast. The result of this apparent acceleration of time, as it is perceived, is comparable to the effect of using time-lapse photography; however, very few contemporaries recognized it as a sovereign compositional achievement: all the critics cited above perceived only its precondition, the slowness of the first three acts.

An outsider with an interest in music but no training in it, the novelist Jules Verne, was the first to demonstrate that he had understood Meyerbeer's unusual dramaturgy of acceleration; he could, after all, regard it with some justification as a forerunner of his own ingenious games with the frontiers of perception of time and space. Verne's story *Une Fantaisie du Docteur Ox (Dr Ox's Experiment)*, published in 1872, is set in a small town in Flanders called Quiquendone, where the tempo of life for centuries has been so slow that people have formed the habit of allowing a good quarter of an hour to pass in silence before they answer a question, and where even the mayor regards a decision taken in an urgent matter of communal politics after ten years of discussion as overhasty. Opera, too, in this town "where people do not grow enthusiastic about anything,"[81] is governed by the same, unimaginable phlegm.

> As nothing was done in a hurry at Quiquendone, the dramatic pieces had to be performed in harmony with the peculiar temperament of the Quiquendonians. Though the doors of the theatre were regularly thrown open at four o'clock and closed again at ten, it had never been known that more than two acts were played during the six intervening hours. *Robert le Diable*, *Les Huguenots*, or *Guillaume Tell* usually took up three evenings, so slow was the execution of these masterpieces. The *vivaces*, at the theatre of Quiquendone, lagged like real *adagios*. The *allegros* were "long-drawn out" indeed. The demisemiquavers were scarcely equal to the ordinary semibreves of other countries. The most rapid runs, performed according to Quiquendonian taste, had the solemn march of a chant. The gayest shakes were languishing and measured, that they might not shock the ears of the *dilettanti*. To give an example, the rapid air sung by Figaro, on his entrance in the first act of *Le Barbier de Séville*, was performed at crotchet 33 and lasted fifty-eight minutes—when the actor was particularly enthusiastic.[82]

81. Verne, *Dr Ox's Experiment*, 25.
82. Ibid., 42.

In the course of this anarchic tale these immemorial habits suffer such a shock that nothing is ever the same again. The eponymous Dr. Ox, with his assistant Ygène ("oxygène," the French word for oxygen), has prepared a scientific experiment; his intention is to test the effect of pure oxygen on the dozy people of Quiquendone, and his first step is to persuade them to let him lay the pipes for what they believe is a new gas supply. "After having laid down his gas-pipes, he . . . saturated, first the public buildings, then the private dwellings, finally the streets of Quiquendone, with pure oxygen, without letting in the least atom of hydrogen."[83] He selects the opera house as the site for his first experiment, and pumps it full of oxygen on an evening when, as it happens, Act IV of *Les Huguenots* is due to be given. (Acts I–III have been spread out over the previous three weeks, each occupying an entire evening as usual.) Even before the curtain rises, a certain fidgetiness can be observed in the auditorium, but nevertheless the orchestral introduction begins in its usual style: "The *allegro appassionato* of the inter-act is played as usual, with a majestic deliberation which would have made Meyerbeer frantic, and all the majesty of which was appreciated by the Quiquendonian *dilettanti*."[84] Before long, however, the conductor can no longer hold the tempo back, and it increases perceptibly as the action proceeds:

> Saint Bris, Nevers, Tavannes, and the Catholic nobles have appeared, somewhat prematurely, perhaps, upon the scene. The composer has marked *allegro pomposo* on the score. The orchestra and the lords proceed *allegro* indeed, but not at all *pomposo*, and at the chorus, in the famous scene of the "benediction of the poniards," they no longer keep to the enjoined *allegro*. Singers and musicians break away impetuously. The leader does not even attempt to restrain them. Nor do the public protest; on the contrary, the people find themselves carried away, and see that they are involved in the movement, and that the movement responds to the impulses of their souls.[85]

Eventually the duet (andante amoroso) is performed vivace furioso, and the stretta, "which the composer marks *allegro con moto*, becomes a wild *prestissimo*. . . . The fourth act of the *Huguenots*, which formerly lasted six hours, began on this evening at half-past four, and ended at twelve minutes before five. It had lasted only eighteen minutes!"[86] It is striking that Verne directed his biting satire on uncritical faith in industrial

83. Ibid., p 101.
84. Ibid., 47.
85. Ibid., 48–49.
86. Ibid., 51–52.

progress not at some technological marvel, but—of all things—the fourth act of *Les Huguenots*, and it is also certainly no accident that he selected the "consecration of the swords" for the subject of the central chapter, entitled "In which the andantes become allegros, and allegros vivaces,"[87] for that is precisely the moment in Meyerbeer's opera when the apparent acceleration of the dramatic events becomes palpable.

That fact is itself anything but accidental, for it is in this sequence of scenes, which even Meyerbeer's enemies admired, that the historical events of the opera and the private intrigue at last come together. At the beginning of the act the curtain rises on Valentine's room in Nevers's house in Paris. Raoul enters, desiring to see his beloved just once more before he dies, but hides when he hears her father and a group of Catholic noblemen approaching. This puts him in the position to overhear the orders being given for the massacre of the Huguenots. When the conspirators go, he wants to hurry away to warn his co-religionists, but Valentine throws herself in his path and tries to stop him, fearing for both his life and her father's. Raoul insists on carrying out his intention, however, and the situation alters only when Valentine makes a last desperate appeal:

> VALENTINE
> Reste, Raoul, puisque tu me chéris, je t'implore enfin
> Pour moi-même, car si tu meurs, je meurs aussi!
> Reste! reste!
> (*Les Huguenots*, Acte IV, scène 6)

ꜱ   ꜱ   ꜱ

> VALENTINE: Stay Raoul, since you cherish me, I implore you lastly for my sake, for if you die I shall die too! Stay, stay!

The intensifying chromaticism with which Meyerbeer sets these highly dramatic lines suddenly ceases, and the weeping Valentine sings "I love you!" ("Je t'aime!") with the simplest, recitative-like intonation and in the "simplest" key, C major. In the rather conventional version of the text which Scribe sent to the printer, the wording of this confession of love is such as to make it appear a "conscious step, the last means of forcing Raoul to stay with her," as Michael Walter says;[88] but in the definitive version of the text in Meyerbeer's score, Valentine falls out of her role as Nevers's loyal wife, and exposes her inmost feelings against her will. The stage direction reads: "She hides her face in her hands, as

87. Ibid., 40.
88. *"Hugenotten"-Studien*, 81.

11 This watercolor, ascribed to François-Joseph-Aimé de Lemud (1816–87), captures the fleeting moment in Act IV of *Les Huguenots* in which Raoul's indecision, between his beloved Valentine and his solidarity with his co-religionists, is at its most concentrated. The artist, best-known in Lorraine, tried to match the intensity of Meyerbeer's representation of the hopeless situation by the vivid contrast between Valentine's dress and the darkness of the setting.

if devastated by what she has just said" *(Elle se cache le visage dans ses mains comme anéantie de ce qu'elle vient de dire)*.

It is only when Raoul repeats her words ecstatically that she realizes that she has revealed her feelings and asks in a state of dread *(avec terreur)*, if she really spoke the words aloud ("O terreur, l'ai-je dit?"), which Raoul confirms with the words that launch the Andante amoroso: "You did say it . . . yes, you love me" ("Tu l'as dit . . . oui, tu m'aimes"). Time has been racing by ("You would say an express train was whirling by," to quote Verne's story again),[89] but now it stops. For the first time in the entire opera, a calm melody unfolds, free of any kind of rhythmic trickiness. Yet the calm lacks perspectives: the melodic idea does not require continuation, and its accompanying harmonies remain stuck in G-flat major, an "extreme" key, as remote as it could possibly be from the C major of the recitative, making it all too clear that the lovers have completely lost touch with reality. Meyerbeer's formal organization of the cavatina reinforces this impression, letting all its parts do no more than circle around the one melodic idea. As Carl Dahlhaus wrote, "if the melodic idea expresses an isolated moment, its almost obsessive repetition and imitation convey an urge to cling against all odds to an instant destined to pass."[90]

Cling to it as the lovers may, the instant must pass, and time moves inexorably onward. The tocsin starts to toll, tearing them out of their dream. Meyerbeer expresses the tension between what is visible on the stage and what is happening offstage by musico-dramatic means. In this literally avant-garde scene Meyerbeer does something no composer had done before him, appropriating what Rudolf Wendorff called "an extraordinary achievement of the occidental consciousness of time in the nineteenth century," and converting "the tension between involvement in the historical process and active self-assertion in the given present moment" into the dynamic of his drama, while simultaneously heightening awareness of what distinguishes one particular moment from the whole of the past and of the future.[91] In this he also created a model for future operatic love duets: the marks of his influence are as clear in the duets in Wagner's *Lohengrin* and *Die Walküre*[92] as they are in *Les Troyens*, where Berlioz directly adopts the extreme tonalities and triple meters characteristic of the whole nineteenth century.[93]

89. *Dr Ox's Experiment*, 51.
90. *Nineteenth-Century Music*, 12.
91. *Zeit und Kultur*, 415.
92. See H. Becker, "Das Duett in der Oper," 93.
93. See Macdonald, "[Nine-eight time, G flat major]," 227–28.

The modernity of this scene, which the composer himself described as "the opera's culminating point,"[94] becomes even more apparent if it is compared with the treatment of a very similar situation in Act III of Scribe and Auber's *Gustave III, ou Le Bal masqué* (1833). There the heroine, Amélie, has no sooner admitted to the king that she loves him ("Eh bien, oui, Gustave, eh bien, je t'aime!") than she takes the confession back and begs him to be a gentleman and not take advantage of her ("Mais sois noble, sois généreux et défends-moi contre moi-même!"). The confession itself gains no special emphasis from its musical setting, and after a few bars of arioso it is subsumed into the duet's conventional cabaletta. Together, Gustave and Amélie run through a stereotyped list of synonyms for the pangs of love ("Ô délire, ô tourment, à peine je respire") that has no more direct relevance to what is unique about their particular situation than do the conventional thirds of Auber's setting.[95] It took Verdi, tackling the same material in 1859, to turn the dramatic event into a musical one by following the recipe that Donizetti had formulated for the Paris Opéra as early as 1839: "Then between each cabaletta you should always introduce a poetry which elevates the action without merely repeating lines as our poets usually do."[96] Thus in *Un ballo in maschera* the declaration of love is repeated between the two stanzas of the cabaletta, and enhanced on the repeat by a $^7_9$ chord played *ff* by the whole orchestra.[97]

At the same time, *Gustave III* shares with *Les Huguenots* a characteristic that separates them both irrevocably from operatic traditions prior to 1830. There is, of course, nothing new about the fact that the love of the young couple is threatened from the outside, and impossible for social reasons. But the circumstances were always clear from the start in earlier opera: even if consummation remained out of the question, the two lovers could be confident of their love, for either it had been declared before the curtain rose or it was revealed at the very start of the exposition (as in Rameau's *Hippolyte et Aricie* of 1733, for example). It was never the case that either lover could be seriously surprised by the declaration. And before Meyerbeer's epoch-making opera, in which

94. "Culminationspunkt der Oper"; in a letter to Wilhelm Speyer, 22 September 1837, *Briefwechsel*, 3:64.

95. Cited as a music example in D'Amico: "Il ballo in maschera prima di Verdi," 1273–74 (in the 1969–70 edition, pp. 524–25; subsequent references to this work include page numbers for both sources listed in the bibliography).

96. "Poi in tra l'una e l'altra cabaletta avvi sempre una poesia che innalza l'azione senza la solita ripetizione de' versi di cui i nostri poeti fanno uso"; in a letter to Giovanni Simone Mayr, 8 April 1839, cited in Zavadini, *Donizetti*, 494–95.

97. See Schnebel, "Die schwierige Wahrheit des Lebens," 56.

time itself becomes a dramaturgical motive, love was never threatened by the mere passage of time.

It was only when a threat of such a nature was presented on the stage that a modern, skeptical view of love and its possibility could be realized in a work of music theater. Raoul's "frenzied love"[98] for Valentine is not threatened by social rules alone, nor exclusively by the inexorable advance of history, but it is impossible in itself. Raoul, who has been blind to the fact that Valentine has always loved him alone, takes refuge, at the very moment of learning it from her own lips, in the unreality of the G-flat major melody, repeating the three syllables of "Je t'aime" like a charm, and stammering cries wholly innocent of syntactical rigor ("ever there, forgetting, forgotten"—"là toujours, oubliant, oublié"), for all the world like an anticipation of Wagner's Tristan. And Valentine, having suffered the trick played on her wifely virtue by her subconscious, tries in vain to draw herself and her lover back into the real world, when, in the middle of the cavatina, she exclaims in an aside "Such danger! The moment has come, oh my God! What have I done?" ("Quel danger! voici l'heure, ô mon Dieu! Qu'ai-je fait! quel danger . . .").

The total failure of the couple to understand each other is realized musically by Meyerbeer with the utmost urgency in the repetition of the first section of the cavatina, when Valentine sings her words marking the expiry of what time was left to them, and foretelling imminent death ("C'est la mort, voici l'heure! Il n'est plus d'avenir"), with performance directions like "fortissimo," "forte," and "despairingly" (avec désespoir), to the very same G-flat major melody to which, one bar behind her, Raoul is still invoking her avowal and dreaming of love ("Tu l'as dit . . . oui, tu m'aimes! Nuit d'amour, nuit d'amour!"), singing the while "piano," "pianissimo," and "intoxicatedly" (avec ivresse). Meyerbeer illustrates the unreality of an emotion governed, on Raoul's side, more by narcissism than by love through the unusual means of a canon in which the voices are melodically identical but dynamically contrasted, and this is given even greater emphasis at the end of the act. Valentine falls in a faint, and as Raoul asks heaven to bless her, his phrase breaks off on the leading note, as if he has suddenly realized the inescapable reality. In this negative variant on a traditional closing cadence, the vocal line is denied resolution onto the tonic, which is replaced, so to speak, by the soundless cry of Valentine as she recovers consciousness.[99]

98. "amour délirant"; Meyerbeer, in a letter to Scribe, 9 November 1834, Brief-wechsel, 2:414.

99. See Schläder, Das Opernduett, 40.

12 In this sketch by the stage designer Charles Polycarpe Séchan (1803–74) for the second setting of Act V of *Les Huguenots*, the Huguenot temple bears a strong resemblance to a Romanesque church, but its most important function was to separate the front area of the stage, where events were visible to the audience, from the rear area, where events were unseen and reported (see chapter 6, pp. 234–35).

The fact that in Act V the lovers are joined in marriage by Marcel, and experience the ecstasy of belonging to each other, might be regarded as detracting from the radical conclusion of Act IV. But in the opera's last scene Meyerbeer contrives a further forward-looking element that continues the unreality of this remarkable love relationship "for ever and ever." Raoul and Valentine meet death *together*. It is true that it is not a love-death in the sense adumbrated by E. T. A. Hoffmann in his opera *Undine* of 1816 and realized in all its implications by Wagner in *Tristan und Isolde*, for Raoul and Valentine are shot. Nevertheless, the idea of death as the concomitant of the apparent impossibility of real love was already inherent in the first intimate exchange between the two lovers, embodied by Meyerbeer in the dual text which he set to the G-flat major melody.

Shock

After the breathtaking excitement of Act IV of *Les Huguenots*, Act V proceeds on the understanding that the spectator knows that the St. Bartholomew's Day massacre is already in full swing, and is only waiting nervously for the opera's main characters to become involved in the slaughter. Already in the first scene, the distant sound of the tocsin disturbs the solemn ballet music during the wedding celebrations in the Hôtel de Nesle. When Raoul bursts into the room, with his clothes already bloodstained, it is clear that the killing has already begun. As yet, however, it is still outside in the streets, and offstage; it is not until the end of the scene in the churchyard, the second setting, and in the brief final tableau, on the banks of the Seine, that the gangs of murdering Catholics reach the front of the stage.

During the first part of the scene set in the churchyard, however, the area at the front of the stage is reserved for the lovers and Marcel, while unnamed Huguenots can be seen sheltering from their pursuers in the church (or "temple," the Huguenot term) at the rear. The music accompanies only the foreground action to begin with, but after Marcel's recitative, for the first time, the chorus of women inside the temple is "dubbed on," in Matthias Brzoska's term,[100] singing "Ein' feste Burg ist unser Gott" "as if from very far away" *(comme de très loin)*. This is the first time the chorale has been heard in a melodically and harmonically closed form since Marcel's entrance in Act I, but now it expresses something very far removed from the belligerent self-confidence the soldier

100. See "Historisches Bewußtsein," 60.

showed then. Where Marcel sang it in C major *ff*, now, as in the love
duet in Act IV, Meyerbeer has recourse to the "extreme" key of G-flat
major, and in so doing not only emphasizes the danger hanging over
the Huguenot women and the lovers alike but also points out a motivic
relationship between the two scenes, in that the melody of "Tu l'as dit"
uses exactly the same segment of the scale as the ending of the first line
of the chorale and the start of the second.

This is the last time Luther's chorale is heard "intact," and attention
switches back to the foreground. Marcel blesses Raoul and Valentine's
union, to the accompaniment of bass clarinets—the first time in the
instrument's history that it was introduced into the orchestra pit. At the
very end of the lovers' prayer, the women are heard singing the chorale
again—this time in unison, and with a minimal instrumental accompaniment, *p*. But the chorus suddenly breaks off in the middle of the second line, as the detailed stage direction explains: "Here the singing is
interrupted abruptly by the loud clash of arms and threatening cries
inside the temple. Torches and the glint of steel can be seen shining
through the windows. The murderers have just forced their way into the
church and broken its windows" (*Ici le chant est interrompu brusquement
par un grand bruit d'armes et des cris menaçants dans l'intérieur du Temple.
A travers les vitraux on voit briller les torches et le fer des lances. Les meurtriers
viennent de pénétrer dans l'église dont ils ont brisé les vitraux*). There is a
general pause, in which only the beat of a tam-tam is heard, apart from
the onstage noise, followed by the *Choeur des meurtriers*, Allegro feroce
for the male chorus only, ordering the Huguenots to submit to heaven's
will and recant ("Abjurez, Huguenots, le ciel l'ordonne!"). The women's
voices have not yet been silenced, however, the first line of the chorale
is heard again twice, until its final note, altered to a dissonance, is
drowned by a discharge of harquebuses inside the church. There is a
second volley, and now all the Huguenots can be presumed dead.

The chorale continues to be used fragmentarily, however, in the next
scene, in which, following Marcel's apocalyptic vision, the protagonists
confront their murderers. Once again the chorale melody, sung in unison, is interrupted in the second line by the noise of the barricade breaking under the onslaught, and then Meyerbeer three times "dissolves"
the end of the first line into a fortissimo dissonance symbolizing the
irresistible advance of the Catholics. This advance is not only visible to
the audience, but, as Matthias Brzoska set out in his paper on "historical
consciousness and musical shaping of time,"[101] Meyerbeer organizes the

101. Ibid., 60–63.

musical passage of time in such a way as to make it the "form-determining parameter" of this whole scene in the churchyard, by prescribing a faster tempo for each return of the increasingly fragmented chorale melody. The first time it is heard, sung by the women, "dubbed on" to the lovers' prayer, it is marked "poco andante" and "mouvement de choral," and given a precise metronome marking of 46. When it is repeated (before being interrupted by the general pause and the murderers' chorus) it is already slightly faster, at metronome 54, and the fragmented first line sung during the *Choeur des meurtiers* is markedly faster, at metronome 80. The trio for Valentine, Raoul, and Marcel at the end of the bass's "vision" has the metronome marking 84, and for a while Meyerbeer heightens tension not by increasing the tempo further but by "turning the screw" in pitch, as the quotations of the chorale rise stepwise from E-flat major, through F major and G major, to A major. At the same time, however, the "head" of the theme is gradually hived off and diminished in terms of tempo, resulting in its being doubled, to metronome 168. The sixth and last step, a basic pulse of 184, is reached at the end of the churchyard scene, when the chorus of murderers is drawn into the process and melodic fragments of the chorale are only to be heard dying away in the orchestral postlude.

As the screw tightens, the catastrophe takes place simultaneously in the murderers' advance, their physical contact with the protagonists, and the destruction of the musical foundation of the scene in the churchyard. Meyerbeer's treatment of the chorale, the symbol of the Huguenots' indestructible faith, reduces it to fragments, exactly as the martyrs' last physical refuge is destroyed visibly on the stage.[102] At the same time the spectator is drawn into the horrors depicted to a degree never before experienced in theatrical history. After the audience has seen the events of St. Bartholomew's Day advance steadily from the back of the stage toward the auditorium, as Matthias Brzoska points out,[103] it has no means of escape from the final scene, and the massacre is no mere theatrical illusion.

If Meyerbeer's montage-like use of the repetitions of fragments of "Ein' feste Burg" is suggestive of a technique that was not invented until the twentieth century, this ultimate heightening of the tension is more like the technique of the filmmaker Alfred Hitchcock than anything familiar from the theater of the eighteenth or nineteenth centuries. And Meyerbeer knew exactly how his unprecedented musical conception

102. See Gerhard, "Lieu et espace," 8.
103. "Historisches Bewußtsein," 62.

might be supported by the use of precisely calculated optical effects. When *Les Huguenots* was to be performed in Dresden, he gave instructions that the church should be shrouded in total darkness and lit up only twice,[104] and when it was revived in Paris in 1852 he recommended that the set for the churchyard scene should be designed as carefully as possible, so as to ensure "the horrifying effect of fear and terror."[105] In thus intensifying the expectation of "fear and terror" to the utmost by every scenic and musical means, Meyerbeer induced a feeling equivalent to what is meant by the word "suspense" in the discussion of twentieth-century cinema. Its importance for the success of grand opéra was already apparent to Meyerbeer's contemporaries: less than two decades after the première of *Les Huguenots*, the director of the Opéra, Roqueplan, spoke of the process "of keeping the spirit in suspense, of making a lively attack on the senses" as, allegedly, "the sole means of attracting the public to his theater."[106]

In Hitchcock's films, one of the outstanding features of the event in which the virtuosic build-up of suspense eventually culminates, having been drawn out as long as possible, is its hideous uniqueness. In the churchyard scene in *Les Huguenots* rather the reverse is the case, in that the initially striking effect of the progressive fragmentation of "Ein' feste Burg" is repeated several times, even though the effect the first time the tune is heard depends directly on its unexpectedness—in a manner that, again, has been compared to a cinematic technique, this time the change of scene given by the cut, and in the context of a discussion of Berlioz.[107] It is the same quality of unexpectedness, the *imprévu*, that Berlioz claimed, with good reason, as one of the predominant features of his own music,[108] and in his recourse to it Meyerbeer pushed the general dramaturgical principle of unmediated contrasts toward an extreme.

Meyerbeer, however, evidently shied away from the radicalism of Berlioz's "unexpectedness," a notable characteristic of which is the unrepeatable nature of the critical turning points at which Berlioz brings it into play. Nothing follows the moment in the cantata *La Mort de Cléo-*

104. See Meyerbeer's letter to Karl Winkler, 21 March 1838, *Briefwechsel*, 3:674.

105. "die schaudererregende Wirkung von Angst und Schrecken"; Meyerbeer's letter to Louis Gouin, 30 May 1852, cited in H. Becker, *Giacomo Meyerbeer: Ein Leben in Briefen*, 202.

106. "de tenir l'esprit en suspens, d'attaquer vivement les sens . . . le seul moyen qui existe pour attirer le public à son théâtre"; cited in Asselineau, "De l'État de la musique en France," 606.

107. See Danuser, "Symphonisches Subjekt und Form," 208.

108. See Berlioz, *Memoirs*, 478.

pâtre (1829) at which the Queen of Egypt's reflections suddenly break off except a few laconic, conventional, closing cadences, and the same is true when Juliette dies in the last instrumental movement of the dramatic symphony *Roméo et Juliette* (1839).[109] In *Les Huguenots*, on the other hand, the interruption of the chorale is made a repeatable event, and thus Meyerbeer domesticated a revolutionary musico-dramatic idea, for which he was mercilessly mocked by Offenbach in the closing tableau of *Ba-ta-clan* (1855).

Meyerbeer's attitude is easier to understand in the light of the psychoanalytical theory of traumatic neurosis and the development of protection against stimuli, which Walter Benjamin advanced as an explanation of what modern civilization causes to happen to human consciousness.[110] Against the background of the mass phenomenon of shell shock in the First World War,[111] Freud developed theses to explain "common traumatic neurosis as a consequence of an extensive breach being made in the protective shield against stimuli."[112] His premise was that a protective outer layer develops that is able to shield the consciousness against all but the very strongest stimuli emanating from

> an external world charged with the most powerful energies . . . *Protection* against stimuli is an almost more important function for the living organism than *reception* of stimuli. The protective shield is supplied with its own store of energy and must above all endeavour to preserve the special forms of conversion of energy operating in it against the effects threatened by the enormous energies at work in the external world.[113]

Walter Benjamin defines the threat from these energies as "shocks"— the word shock, incidentally, was used in the French press about dramatic works as early as 1835.[114] Freud cites the absence of preparedness for anxiety as a precondition of shock,[115] and as Benjamin explains, "the more readily the consciousness registers these shocks, the less likely are they to have a traumatic effect."[116]

The neurosis that Freud observed in those traumatized by an accident, whose dreams reproduce the shock over and over again, seems to

---

109. See Danuser, "Das imprévu in der Symphonik," 75–77.
110. *Charles Baudelaire,* 113–20.
111. See Schivelbusch, *The Railway Journey,* 150.
112. *Beyond the Pleasure Principle,* 38.
113. Ibid. 32.
114. See Wentzlaff-Eggebert, *Zwischen kosmischer Offenbarung und Wortoper,* 31.
115. *Beyond the Pleasure Principle,* 38.
116. *Charles Baudelaire,* 115.

take musical shape in Meyerbeer's opera: the shock of the massacre is represented in the sudden interruption of the chorale, and each time this musical formula is reiterated the consciousness becomes more accustomed to registering the shock, and the traumatic effect gradually diminishes. A bloodbath similar to the one sketched in a rapid, fresco-like style in the very much shorter final scene of Rossini's *Le Siège de Corinthe*, is here extended over an entire act.

Meyerbeer's dramatic representation of terror denotes precisely the transition from a traditional concept of shock to that diagnosed as typically modern by Walter Benjamin. The military origin of the perception of shock is obvious in *Les Huguenots*, in that the slaughter of the Huguenots is depicted as a military action on the part of a group equipped with firearms.[117] At the same time, the massacre does not take place on a battlefield during a war but is carried out by an anonymous mob in the middle of the city of Paris, the very home of the opera's first audience, so that, two decades before Baudelaire, Meyerbeer was drawing attention to the inner association "between the figure of shock and contact with the metropolitan masses," to cite Benjamin on Baudelaire yet again.[118] The representation of the crowd in *Les Huguenots* will be discussed in greater detail in the following chapter, but it can already be said that "fear, revulsion, and horror were the emotions which the big-city crowd aroused in those who first observed it"[119] in the middle of the nineteenth century.

Music in Space

The way the shocks in Act V of *Les Huguenots* are presented on the stage is directly linked to a musico-dramatic technique that is characteristic of grand opéra, though its origins go back to the 1780s. The "dubbing on" of a musical structure, initially heard as if at a distance, to a course of musical events determined by the visible, onstage action is yet another innovation that appears to have a direct association with the perceptual expectations of an age shaken by incessant wars, for in all the early examples of this modern *da lontano* effect the sound heard approaching is a military march. That is true of operás comiques by Grétry and Monsigny that are thought to be the very first examples, and of Simon Mayr's *Zamori, ossia L'eroe delle Indie* (1804), which was prob-

117. See Schivelbusch, "Excursus: The History of Shock," *The Railway Journey*, 150–58.

118. *Charles Baudelaire*, 119.

119. Ibid., 131; but see also Brüggemann, *"Aber schickt keinen Poeten nach London!,"* 89.

ably the first opera to employ a separate wind band on the stage *(banda
sul palco)*,[120] and it is also the case in Weber's use of this essentially theatrical effect in his Konzertstück in F minor for piano and orchestra
(1821).[121] The prime example in nineteenth-century French opera,
however, must be the finale of Spontini's *Fernand Cortez*, in the versions
of 1809 and 1824, in the course of which the gradual advance of the
besieging army is represented by several "dubbed on" reiterations of a
triumphal march.[122]

In the cases both of Spontini's opera (on a libretto by Jouy) and
of Act V of *Les Huguenots*, the musical material held up for contrast is
confined to fragmentary structures, and the disruption of a "one-
dimensional" musical course of events is justified by the chaos and destruction enacted on the stage. This is quite different—and not merely
because it involves much less artifice—from the process of deploying a
number of melodies in such a way that they can be wholly combined
with one another. Once again, early examples of this kind of "dissolve"
of two different musical structures in simultaneous contrast, as a means
of audibly representing the simultaneity of wholly separate actions, are
to be found in Grétry, and were mentioned in chapter 2, in connection
with the description in his memoirs of the drastic contrasts of the execution of Louis XVI. But—setting aside the one exceptional example in
the Act I finale of Mozart's *Don Giovanni* (1787)—this technique was
not used systematically until after 1830, when it was adopted by Berlioz,
in particular, in symphonic music, and by Meyerbeer in opera.

Where Mozart fitted together three different dances to such good
artistic effect in order to depict the different levels in a hierarchical society, in grand opéra the technique first appeared in direct imitation of
the simultaneity of sensual impressions experienced by city crowds.[123]
In the Mozart the aristocratic minuet is the dominant layer in the music,
and the other two dances are placed in relation to it; in Meyerbeer's
examples, in the "real dialogue, the contrast of voices and characters
which now oppose one another, and now act together in concert, and
yet preserve the distinctive features of their nature," even the choruses
achieve to some degree "the polyphonic power of music . . . in which
we see united the simultaneous representation (grouping) of sculpture
and the successive development of poetry"—which, to contemporaries
such as the musicologist Adolf Bernhard Marx, constituted the very idea

120. See Maehder, *"Banda sul palco,"* 294.
121. See Kirsch, "Carl Maria von Webers Konzertstück f-moll opus 79," 377.
122. See Gerhard, *"Fernand Cortez,"* 98–105.
123. Brüggemann, *"Aber schickt keinen Poeten nach London!,"* 71.

of opera.[124] (In Marx's view, however, "the idea of the opera has as yet been by no means completely realized; not even by Gluck"—and not by Meyerbeer, either.)[125] At the start of Act III of *Les Huguenots*, Meyerbeer has the Huguenot soldiers singing unaccompanied while imitating the action of drumming with their hands. Immediately following these rowdy *couplets militaires* from the men of the chorus, however, their female colleagues enter in the role of young Catholic girls singing a hymn to the Virgin Mary, in an example of "successive development." Alas, Huguenot provocateurs disrupt the pious procession, and the soldiers resume their "Rataplan" which is now heard simultaneously with the girls' "Vierge Marie." The confrontation thus expressed in musico-dramatic terms is in danger of taking the physical form of a fight between the two factions in the crowd but that is averted by the arrival of a troupe of dancing gypsies—a coup de théâtre that Meyerbeer again handles with the immediacy of a cinematic "cut."

The technique of bringing latent tensions to light by having contrasting choruses follow one another in quick succession was, admittedly, not new in grand opéra: Rossini began Act II of *Guillaume Tell* with a chorus of Austrian huntsmen, followed immediately by one of Swiss herdsmen, but he evidently shrank from the next step, that of having both choruses sung simultaneously; instead the scene ends with a reprise of the huntsmen's chorus while the Swiss fall silent.[126]

By the middle of the nineteenth century, however, the simultaneous presentation of contrasts had become one of the standard techniques of grand opéra. Meyerbeer himself took it to the limits of the musically possible in *Ein Feldlager in Schlesien*, an occasional piece written in 1844 to celebrate the reopening of the Prussian Court Opera after a fire. In the second finale of that work, the simultaneous approach of several separate military units culminates in an ensemble of four distinct musical strata: the famous Prussian infantry slow march *Der alte Dessauer*, a *pas redoublé* of the grenadiers, a fanfare of the cavalry, and an oath of loyalty to Frederick the Great sung by the chorus, stacked above each other.

Verdi adopted the pattern too, and had French revelers singing a barcarole at the same time as the Sicilians watching them express their anger, shame, and humiliation ("C'en est trop, je frémis et de honte et de rage") in the second finale in *Les Vêpres siciliennes* (1855). In later

124. *The Music of the Nineteenth Century*, 104.
125. Ibid., 103; for Marx's opinion of Meyerbeer, see also 64.
126. See Gerhard, "'Sortire dalle vie comuni,'" 206–9.

operas, he can be seen moving toward something more enterprising than the stereotypical pattern of exposition A – exposition B – ensemble AB. In the first finale of *Un ballo in maschera* (1859), it is true that the themes that are to be combined follow each other separately, but they are collected under a common tempo direction, and in the celebrated finale of Act II of *Aida* (1871) the melodies are combined in an overriding form of great complexity but undoubted unity.

This last example shows, in fact, how far Verdi had moved away from the original model. It is true that the chorus of the Egyptian people ("Gloria all'Egitto, ad Iside") is distinct from that of the priests ("Inni leviamo ad Iside"), but the decisive contrast is between these two choruses and the expression of dismay from Aida and Radames, singing in unison, although their words are different. Here the accent is no longer, as in *Les Vêpres siciliennes*, on the differences between two choral groups, but—as already in *Un ballo in maschera*—on the isolation of individuals from the crowd.

In this particular respect Verdi draws close to a procedure that Berlioz began to use in his symphonic music much earlier: in all four movements of *Harold en Italie* (1834) and in the Allegro depicting the ball in the Capulets' house in *Roméo et Juliette* (1839), a theme standing for the hero in each case—Harold and Romeo, respectively—is superimposed on the primary musical structures. However, although they are heard simultaneously the various themes are not incorporated in a common metrical structure, as they are in the Verdi and Meyerbeer instances cited above, but run together without interrelating.[127] In his depiction of the melancholy heroes' isolation, Berlioz created "a musical counterpart to the melancholic, tragic loneliness of the numerous artists and geniuses found in literature since the early nineteenth century,"[128] to which nineteenth-century opera can offer nothing comparable.

If the use of simultaneous contrast in Berlioz's symphonies evokes the melancholy heroes of the literature of his time, in grand opéra it is closer to the technique found in the history painting of a Géricault or a Delacroix, who also filled their canvases with huge crowd scenes.[129] In both these genres the artistic process suffered from the tendency to make grandiose effect an end in itself; some of the more hackneyed history paintings of the mid-nineteenth-century school owe more to the effect of accumulated mass than to the idea of dramatic contrast, and

127. See Dömling, "Szenerie im Imaginären," 196.
128. Dömling, *Hector Berlioz*, 73.
129. See Maehder, "Historienmalerei und Grand Opéra."

that is also true of the second finale of Meyerbeer's *Ein Feldlager in Schlesien* after transplantation to his opéra comique *L'Étoile du Nord* in 1854.

A new sensitivity toward time and place, which evolved as a response to what Rudolf Wendorff described as "synchronization of an ever greater number of processes,"[130] was thus absorbed into the attempt to gain technical mastery over place. In extreme cases this might lead to the breaching of what little remained of the theatrical convention of the unities of time, place, and action. In the finale of Berlioz's *Les Troyens*, there is a cinematic "cut" from Dido's suicide at the front of the stage to an apotheosis in which the audience beholds the Roman Capitol in a distant glory, with the word "Roma" in shining letters on its pediment, and a triumphal procession of a victorious Roman army. While this effect owes some of its inspiration to the arrival of an old-style deus ex machina at the end of a tragédie lyrique, the combination of two scenes separated by several hundred years in historical reality as well as several hundred miles in distance has a breathtaking modernity about it which it is almost impossible to overstate. Like the only recently invented electric telegraph, it transports the audience "into a world of simultaneity and instancy that went beyond human experience."[131] This most extreme reaction to the change that the new, electrical communications media caused in perceptual structures also highlights a problem common to all the simultaneous images discussed so far, for both here and in the, so to speak, industrial treatment of orchestral instruments the individual value of the separate elements is threatened by the superior mass of the ensemble. Seen in this light, it is hardly surprising that something so characteristic of Parisian grand opéra is only rarely encountered in Italian opera of the nineteenth century: Rossini's cast of mind remained obdurately preindustrial, and he kept his distance from any procedures of the kind (as we saw in chapter 3), while Verdi modified them in a way that restored the individual to the foreground.

THE HAPPY MEDIUM

Italian opera at this period in the nineteenth century was separated from Parisian grand opéra by rather more than a certain reserve in regard to the effects obtainable with simultaneous contrast. The dramaturgy of Italian opera was altogether more inclined to concentrate on protagonists as individuals. Meyerbeer might treat his principal characters as

130. *Zeit und Kultur,* 415.
131. Postman, *The Disappearance of Childhood,* 70.

one element among many in a complex dramaturgy dominated by the concern to recreate a historical event on the stage by all available musico-dramatic and theatrical means, but operagoers in nineteenth-century Italy were plainly not prepared to give up the pleasure of devoting their attention to a leading character. It is not surprising, therefore, that Carlo Ritorni, the author of one of the few nineteenth-century Italian treatises on opera, published in 1841, insisted on the tacit pact between an opera's composer and his audience. A fundamental principle of the pact was that listeners should be able to identify in imagination with the opera's hero, empathize with his excitements, and be rewarded with experience of the same sweet sensations.[132] Even if French critics never spoke up as unequivocally for the importance of characters with whom audiences can identify, nevertheless, no composer of French opera could pretend to be in any doubt that every member of a theater audience is ready to allow sympathy for the hero on the stage to lead him or her to share in his sensations.

Although it is commonly believed that the dramaturgy of grand opéra is inseparable from the predominant ideology of the July Monarchy, it is not easy to single out the characters with which the genre gave audiences their essential opportunities for identification. It is obvious, of course, that these operas did not depict the isolation of romantic heroes but the entanglement of passive characters in a fate they could not comprehend, and that makes it possible to suggest a connection between their indecisiveness and the contemporary ideology of "the happy medium": *le juste milieu*. Heinrich Heine was able to refer to this as early as 1832, in his comments on Meyerbeer's first opera for Paris; even at the time what he wrote was recognized as a "classic characterization of the *juste milieu*."[133]

> Everyone is still flocking to the Académie de Musique to see *Robert le Diable*, but enthusiastic Meyerbeerians will have to pardon me, for I believe that the attraction for some of them is not the music alone but also the opera's political significance! Robert le Diable, son of a devil who was as vilified as Philippe Égalité and a princess who was as pious as Penthièvre's daughter, is drawn toward evil and revolution by his father's spirit, and toward good and the old regime by his mother's. The two in-

132. "l'uditore s'immedesimi nella supposizione del canto per favella in quegl'eroi, [. . .] già [li] vede con suo grande commuovimento palpitare, e per premio del suo sforzo, e della fatta concessione ne riporta la dolcezza di particolari sensazioni." See Ritorni, *Ammaestramenti*, 12; see also Bianconi, introduction to *La drammaturgia musicale*, 18.

133. Wolfgang Menzel, in his review of *Französische Zustände*, *Literaturblatt*, 11 January 1833, cited in Heine, *Sämtliche Schriften*, 3:761.

herited natures are at war within his personality and he hovers somewhere in the middle between the two principles, he is the happy medium personified.[134]

Brilliantly as Heine expressed this, with an eye to making a political point,[135] it would nevertheless be overhasty to assume from his words that Meyerbeer's indecisive heroes were generally received as figures with whom the public identified. It is true that Raoul—like Robert before him and Jean in *Le Prophète* later—is represented as someone to whom things instigated by others happen.[136] He understands nothing of what is going on around him, nothing of the political background to Marguerite's marriage plans for him, and nothing of the conflict between Catholics and Protestants. His naivete does not help him to master the difficult situations in which he is placed: in Act I, Nevers's guests laugh at him because he tells them of his love with such unfeigned passion, in Act II he fails to recognize that he is confronting the princess—and so the misunderstandings continue.

Yet no one in the Paris of the 1830s could identify with Raoul. True, he is the handsome, young lover, true, his is the leading tenor role, but he is depicted in every situation as the rather simple country gentleman who has never moved in real society. This, however, as a quick glance at any novel by Balzac will show, was an irremediable failing in the eyes of nineteenth-century Parisian society.

The opera's title is not *Raoul*, in any case, or *Valentine*, but *Les Huguenots*. Were audiences expected, then, to identify with the persecuted Protestants? This question is not so easy to answer. It is true that Meyerbeer himself attempted a defense of this view, in a personal letter to the German critic Gottfried Weber, who had attacked the work:

> It is my belief that the Protestant religion is placed in the noblest, most dignified light throughout the entire drama. For the Catholics, the entire

134. "Noch immer strömt alles nach der Académie de Musique, um 'Robert le Diable' zu sehen; aber die enthusiastischen Meyerbeerianer mögen mir verzeihen, wenn ich glaube, daß mancher nicht bloß von der Musik angezogen wird, sondern auch von der politischen Bedeutung der Oper! Robert le Diable, der Sohn eines Teufels, der so verrucht war, wie Philipp Egalité, und einer Fürstin, die so fromm war, wie die Tochter Penthièvres, wird von dem Geiste seines Vaters zum Bösen, zur Revolution und von dem Geiste seiner Mutter zum Guten, zum alten Regime hingezogen, in seinem Gemüte kämpfen die beiden angeborenen Naturen, er schwebt in der Mitte zwischen den beiden Prinzipien, er ist Justemilieu." *Französische Zustände* [1832], *Sämtliche Schriften*, 3:89–279, esp. 150; but see also Rieger, "Eugène Scribe et l'anticipation," 109–10. "Philippe Égalité" and "Penthièvre's daughter" were the parents of Louis-Philippe.

135. See G. Müller, "Ein politischer Stellvertreterkrieg," 243.

136. See Herz, "Für einen lebendigen Meyerbeer," 215.

St. Bartholomew affair is simply a political fact in the drama, as it was historically. As to whether it is an unprecedented scandal to present religious disputes on the stage, and even to include a real chorale in an opera, that is a question which, in my view, was answered twenty-five years ago, for it is already that long since Werner's *Die Weihe der Kraft* [The Consecration of Strength] was given in Lutheran Berlin. In that work the hero was Martin Luther himself, and the subject of the drama his religious disputes with the Pope and the Emperor, and furthermore several of his chorales were sung in it. None of this caused scandal at the time—on the contrary, countless performances were given before audiences which were moved and elevated by it. I grant you, that if the chorale had been turned into an operatic aria . . . then that really would have been scandalous. But it is quite the contrary: the chorale is always treated in a severe and ecclesiastical style, as a contrast to the secular music; it is always heard as an emanation from a better world, as a symbol of faith and hope, and always as a rallying call at times of danger or in moments of the highest exaltation; and the individual reminiscences of it—threaded, I grant you, throughout the whole piece—are placed without exception in the mouth of the character (the servant Marcel) depicted as the representative of a simple but unshakable pious faith, and, indeed, a martyr. When a hymn is treated like that, it is my belief that it deserves to be called consecration rather than desecration.[137]

But the special pleading is suspiciously long-winded, and the strategy is too obvious to allow it be taken at face value. The anxiety to avoid doing

137. "Mich dünkt, die protestantische Religion wird durch das ganze Stück in das edelste, würdigste Licht gesetzt. Für die Katholiken, ist in dem Stücke, wie es auch geschichtlich war, die ganze St. Barthélemy nur ein politisches Faktum. Ob es aber überhaupt ein noch nicht dagewesener Skandal sei, religiöse Streitigkeiten auf die Bühne zu bringen und sogar einen wirklichen Choral in der Oper anzubringen, die Frage, dünkt mich, ist schon vor 25 Jahren beantwortet worden; denn so lange bereits ist es her, daß in dem lutherischen Berlin "Die Weihe der Kraft" von Werner gegeben ward, wo Luther selbst der Held des Stückes war und seine religiösen Streitigkeiten mit Papst und Kaiser den Stoff des Dramas bilden und wo auch mehrere seiner Choräle in dem Stücke gesungen werden. Alles dieses erregte damals keinen Skandal, ward im Gegenteil vom Publikum unzählige Male mit Rührung und Erhebung gesehen. Freilich wenn der Choral zur Opernarie gemacht würde [. . .], so wäre das wirklich ein Skandal. Allein wenn gerade im Gegenteil dieser Choral als Gegensatz der weltlichen Musik stets streng und kirchlich behandelt ist, wenn er als Anklang aus einer besseren Welt, als Symbol des Glaubens und Hoffens immer nur als Anrufung bei drohender Gefahr oder in den Momenten der höchsten Erhebung ertönt und sich in einzelnen Anklängen zwar durch das ganze Stück zieht, aber immer nur im Munde derjenigen Person (der Diener Marcel), welche als Repräsentant eines einfachen, aber unerschütterlichen frommen Glaubens, ja als Märtyrer gezeichnet ist, so ist, dünkt mich, eine solche Behandlung eher Heiligung als Entweihung eines

anything that could harm his works in any way is ever-present in all Meyerbeer's dealings with the world. In the case of *Les Huguenots*, one of his comments on Scribe's first prose draft, in 1832, had been: "Although I have already had occasion to say so face to face, I again finish my observations by praying Monsieur Scribe not to forget that this work is, after all, to be performed in a Catholic country."[138] And in 1837, when he wrote the letter to Gottfried Weber that is quoted above, he was consciously preparing the ground for the reception of *Les Huguenots* in Germany, where Protestant influence was responsible for a widespread belief that it was frivolous to represent religious conflicts on the stage.

While there can be no denying that Marcel is depicted as a martyr, the composer's claim that "the Protestant religion is placed in the noblest, most dignified light" is simply not true. Marcel—whose designation "Huguenot" in the cast list already distances him from the "Protestant" Raoul[139]—is shown to be as murderous and merciless from the start as the Catholic mob in the last two acts. In his song in Act I he sings:

> MARCEL *rudement*
> Pour les couvents, c'est fini!
> Les moines à terre!
> Guerre à tout cagot béni!
> Papistes, la guerre!
> Livrons à la flamme, au fer
> Leurs temples d'enfer
> Terrassons-les,
> Cernons-les
> Frappons-les,
> Perçons-les!
> Qu'ils pleurent!
> Qu'ils meurent!
> Mais grâce . . . jamais!
> (*Les Huguenots*, Acte I, scène 3)

↙ ↙ ↙

MARCEL *(brusquely):* An end to convents! Down with monks! War on every tonsured bigot! War on all papists! Let us put their hellish temples

---

Kirchengesangs zu nennen." Meyerbeer to Gottfried Weber, 20 October 1837, *Briefwechsel*, 3:72.

138. "Quoique j'aie déjà eu occasion de le dire de vive voix, je finis de nouveau mes observations en priant M. Scribe de ne pas oublier que cet ouvrage doit être représenté d'ailleurs dans un pays catholique." F-Pn, n.a.f. 22502, fol. 65v. See also Mongrédien, "Aux sources du livret," 161.

139. See Faure, "Opéra historique et problématique sociale," 95 and 100, n. 19.

to the torch and the sword, let us cut them down, encircle them, smite them, run them through! Let them weep! Let them die! But mercy— never!

In the face of such bloodthirstiness, it is hard to refute the German critic who blamed the librettist for the impression that the beliefs of Huguenots and Catholics alike consisted of "nothing but excess. Their actions are guided by no other principles than those of mutual hatred and mutual revenge. Religion is treated with such cavalier indifference that one imagines oneself transported to the year 1836."[140] A point in favor of Meyerbeer's protestations, on the other hand, is the fact that the dogmatism and belligerence completely fall away from Marcel in the last act.[141] The answer he gives to Raoul's demand for revenge for the Huguenot deaths is resigned: their murder, he says, allowed them to die like saints, and all that remains for Raoul, Valentine, and himself is to share that death ("Pour mourir saintement! Venez . . . pour tout effort, il ne nous reste qu'à partager leur mort!"), whereas in the version of the libretto which Scribe sent to the printer his last words are still filled with inveterate hatred:

> VALENTINE *tombant*
> Ciel! mon père!
>
> SAINT-BRIS *se précipitant vers elle*
> > Ah! qu'entends-je!
> Ma fille!
>
> MARCEL *se soulevant*
> > Oui, déjà Dieu nous venge!
> Devant son tribunal nous nous reverrons tous!
> Je vais t'y accuser! . . . *(Il retombe et meurt.)*
> > *(Les Huguenots,* Acte V, scène 4)

؎   ؎   ؎

> VALENTINE *(falling):* Heavens, my father!
> SAINT-BRIS *(rushing to her):* Ah, what do I hear? My daughter!
> MARCEL *(rising):* Yes, already God is revenging us! We shall all meet again at his judgment seat! I go there now to accuse you! . . . *(He falls again and dies.)*

140. ". . . aus nichts anderm als Ausschweifung. Sie handeln nach keinen anderen Grundsätzen als nach denen wechselseitigen Hasses und wechselseitiger Rache. Die Religion wird mit einer so chevaleresken Gleichgültigkeit behandelt, daß man sich ins Jahr 1836 versetzt glaubt." Joseph Mainzer, reviewing *Les Hugenots* in the *Neue Zeitschrift für Musik* 5 (1836), cited in Walter, "'Man überlege sich nur Alles,'" 130–31.

141. See Döhring, "Giacomo Meyerbeer," 16.

In the score, however, Marcel is no longer the fanatical Huguenot warrior of his Act I song, but a martyr, meekly entrusting himself, along with Raoul and Valentine, to the mercy of the Almighty. Sieghart Döhring argues from this alteration that the true concept of the work was actually "the settling of accounts between the two Christian confessions, in favor of a radical, transcendental 'religion of love,' with Jewish overtones,"[142] but that view is perhaps too one-dimensional and wilfully "positive." Tempting though it may be to associate the skeptical depiction of both kinds of Christian with Meyerbeer's experience (as an observant Jew) of Christian antisemitism, we must not lose sight of the fact that in the last act of *Les Huguenots* the word "love" is still reserved for the use of the two young lovers—it never crosses Marcel's lips even after his transformation.

The opera's long cast list includes one further character who plays a decisive part in the plot, without exhibiting either the primitive brutality of Marcel or the provincial naivete of Raoul. This is Nevers. It is true that he is presented in the first instance as a cynical libertine, interested only in ephemeral pleasures, yet he proves to be the only person in the whole cast who does not incur guilt of any kind. In Act I he magnanimously releases Valentine from their betrothal when she tells him that she loves another. In Act IV he is the only Catholic who refuses to take part in the murderous conspiracy of St. Bartholomew's night, and is imprisoned for that reason.[143] Consequently he is not seen on the stage in Act V at all, but although dialogue is kept to a minimum in that act, space is found to relate his further fate. The immediate reason for that lies in the complications of the plot: in order to be perceived as the desired culmination of the personal aspect of the drama, the union of Valentine and Raoul must be in accordance with conventional morality and its omnipresent restrictions, and that means that Valentine's husband must first be dead. He is therefore murdered by his co-religionists—an act which also fits in only too well with the image of the murderous Catholic mob. Yet, astonishingly, one last good deed is attributed to him. Without troubling themselves over the inconsistency of the fact that the Count was earlier made a prisoner, Scribe and Meyerbeer have Marcel report how he was saved from the Catholic butchers by Nevers, "that generous warrior," who then fell to their swords himself, "the victim of his zeal" ("Ce guerrier généreux, c'est lui qui m'a

142. Ibid., 18.
143. See Döhring, "Private Tragödie und politischer Akt," 116.

sauvé des bourreaux et, victime de son zèle, il est mort, assassiné par eux!").

Generosity on such a scale—underlined by the dual meaning of the French word *zèle* ("zeal," but also "impetuosity")—verges on excess. Clearly we are being invited to admire a character whose human weaknesses are combined with the ability to behave exemplarily. Nevers is intelligent, experienced, sociable, knows how to enjoy life, and distances himself from disputes that do not touch him personally. Only when there is a risk of his being drawn into taking an active part in a criminal conspiracy does he make a stand. He is a model of the attitude to life summed up in the expression *le juste milieu*, which Louis-Philippe had proclaimed as the watchword of his reign in January 1831.[144] At the time, admittedly, the King had to contrive to give this comfortable maxim some philosophical respectability by referring to its use in the tract on the duties of a prince which the quietist theologian Fénelon wrote for his pupil, Louis Duke of Burgundy, grandson of Louis XIV. The sentence in question ran: "The wisdom of every government whatever consists in finding the happy medium *[le juste milieu]* between . . . the tyrannical despotism of sovereigns [and] the despotism of the multitude."[145] (No one in the nineteenth century could know that the word "juste" is not to be found in Fénelon's manuscript, which he did not intend for publication when he wrote it in 1697, but was inserted by the editor when it was published posthumously in 1734.)[146] Only a few months before the première of *Les Huguenots*, however, one of Louis-Philippe's ministers made a speech which can have left nobody in any doubt as to how the government really interpreted the tag: the policy of the happy medium, he told the Chamber of Deputies, was "essentially the enemy of absolute principles, and of consequences driven too far."[147]

In this context, even the most idealized depiction of other characters in the drama would not have prevented what the authors may well have been content to allow to happen: Nevers, whom one modern commen-

144. See the King's speech at the audience of 29 January 1831, in Bourbon-Orléans, *Discours, allocutions et réponses*, 1:567–68.

145. "la sagesse de tout Gouvernement quel qu'il soit, consiste à trouver le juste milieu entre . . . le despotisme tyrannique des souverains [et] le despotisme de la multitude"; *Examen de conscience sur les devoirs de la royauté composé pour l'instruction de Louis de France, duc de Bourgogne*, in Fénelon, *Oeuvres complètes*, 7:85–102, 101–2.

146. See Fénelon, *Écrits et lettres politiques*, 93.

147. "essentiellement ennemie des principes absolus, des conséquences trop loin poussées"; François Guizot, speech of 28 August 1835; see [Guizot], *Chambre des Députés*, 10.

tator describes as "liberal," and another as "infinitely sympathetic,"[148] was inevitably the character with whom Parisian audiences of the 1830s identified most strongly. Like the heroes of Scott's novels, in his fundamental passivity Nevers is "committed to prudence and the superiority of civil society. . . . He represents the modern and conservative model of a member of civil society."[149] He was the means whereby operagoers were confirmed not only in their own hypocrisy and apathy but also in the belief that political conflicts were fundamentally destructive and that therefore the best course for the prudent citizen, like Nevers, was as far as possible to avoid situations in which conflict might arise.

Indeed, in view of the sad end to which Nevers comes in *Les Huguenots*, some of the original audience may have concluded that even his minimal moral integrity was a mortally dangerous departure from the happy medium.

148. Walter, *"Hugenotten"-Studien*, 60; Herz, "Unverantwortliche Gedanken," 241.
149. Welsh, *The Hero of the Waverley Novels*, 57.

VICTOR HUGO, THE ILLUSTRIOUS POET AS LIBRETTIST

LA ESMERALDA

TEXT
Victor Hugo (1802–85)

MUSIC
Louise-Angélique Bertin (1805–77)

FIRST PERFORMANCE
Paris, Académie Royale de Musique, 14 November 1836

PLACE AND DATE OF THE ACTION
Paris, 1482

CHARACTERS
La Esmeralda, a gypsy (soprano); Phoebus de Châteaupers (tenor);
Claude Frollo, archdeacon (bass); Quasimodo, bellringer of Notre-Dame
(tenor); Fleur-de-Lys (soprano); Dame Aloïse de Gondelaurier, her mother
(mezzo-soprano); Diane (mezzo-soprano); Bérangère (mezzo-soprano);
Vicomte de Gif (tenor); M. de Chevreuse (bass); M. de Morlaix (bass);
Clopin Trouillefou (tenor); Town-crier (baritone)

SYNOPSIS

ACT I
The Cour des Miracles, at night. The beggars of Paris are celebrating carnival, and sing in praise of their vocation (No. 1b. *Introduction — Choeur des
truands*, "Vive Clopin, roi de Thune!"). The corrupt priest Frollo, from a
hiding-place, watches Esmeralda dancing (No. 1c. *Choeur dansé*, "Danse, jeune
fille!"). This is interrupted by the entrance of Quasimodo, who has been
crowned Fools' Pope (No. 1d. *Choeur et marche du pape des fous*, "Saluez, clercs
de basoche!"). Frollo is outraged to see his subordinate in a place of such ill

repute, but the beggars attack him and Clopin has to come to his rescue (No. 1e. *Fin de l'introduction*, "Il nous menace"). His anger makes Frollo realize for the first time how madly he is in love with the gypsy girl (No. 2. *Récitatif et air*, "O ciel!" / "Eh bien, oui! qu'importe"). After the nightwatchman has passed, with Quasimodo's help he tries to abduct Esmeralda, but the attempt fails when Phoebus and his platoon of guards intervene and arrest Quasimodo, while Frollo escapes (No. 3a. *Final—Scène et choeur*, "La nuit est sombre"). Esmeralda and Phoebus engage in a flirtatious conversation, and he gives her a scarf; when he becomes too insistent, she runs away (No. 3b. *Duo*, "Daignez me dire").

ACT II

First setting: the Place de Grève. Quasimodo has been sentenced to the stocks and the crowd mocks him, but Esmeralda takes pity and gives him something to drink (No. 4. *Choeur*, "Il enlevait une fille!").

Second setting: a magnificent interior. As preparations are made for a large evening reception in the house of his betrothed, Fleur-de-Lys, Phoebus admits to himself that he has fallen in love with Esmeralda (No. 5. *Scène, récitatif, et air*, "Mon futur gendre, écoutez, je vous aime" / "Elle dit vrai; près d'elle encore"). The guests arrive (No. 6a. *Final—Sextuor*, "Salut, nobles châtelaines!"; No. 6b. *Choeur*, "Venez tous à la fête"). Some are drawn to the window, fascinated by Esmeralda's dancing in the street (No. 6c. *Scène*, "Oh! viens donc voir"), and she accepts the invitation to come inside the house (No. 6d. *Quintette et choeur*, "Oh! l'adorable créature!"). As she dances she pulls out the scarf Phoebus gave her, but Fleur-de-Lys recognizes it as one that she gave him, and with this proof of his infidelity all the guests turn against Esmeralda and Phoebus (No. 6e. *Scène et stretta*, "Allons, enfant" / "Est-il vrai? Phoebus l'aime!").

ACT III

First setting: outside a tavern. Phoebus's friends sing of the joys of their libertine lifestyle (No. 7. *Chanson avec choeur*, "Sois propice et salutaire"), and listen to his account of his latest conquest (No. 8. *Scène et air avec choeur*, "Cette Égyptienne si belle" / "Oh! l'amour, volupté suprême!"). Phoebus is to meet Esmeralda later this same evening and Frollo vainly tries to prevent it, by warning him of her magic arts (No. 9, *Scène et duo*, "Capitaine!" / "Il m'étonne").

Second setting: a room. Clopin shows Frollo a niche in the wall that will allow him to watch the lovers from the next room; eventually, wild with jealousy, the priest draws a sword and attacks Phoebus, who remains behind with Esmeralda, badly wounded (No. 10, *Scène et trio*, "D'ici vous pourrez voir" / "O fille adorée").

ACT IV

First setting: a prison. Esmeralda, who believes that Phoebus is dead, has been accused of his murder (No. 11. *Entr'acte, récitatif, et romance*, "Quoi! lui dans le sépulcre" / Phoebus, n'est-il sur terre"). Frollo promises to get her released, if she will yield to him, but she refuses indignantly (No. 12. *Récitatif et duo*, "Quel est cet homme?" / "Détresse extrême!").

Second setting: the square outside Notre-Dame. Quasimodo rings the bells joyfully (No. 13. *Air*, "Mon Dieu! j'aime"), although they sound to summon the people to Esmeralda's execution. Frollo plans once more to abduct her, with the help of Clopin (No. 14. *Récitatif et duo*, "Donc Phoebus est à Montfort?" / "Bientôt on va mener ici l'Égyptienne"), while the crowd is already streaming into the square (No. 15a. *Final — Choeur et marche*, "À Notre-Dame") and a dirge is sung inside the cathedral (No. 15b. *Choeur religieux*, "Omnes fluctus fluminis"). With Phoebus in her thoughts, Esmeralda prepares herself for death (No. 15c. *Trio avec choeur*, "C'est mon Phoebus qui m'appelle"), when Quasimodo snatches her up and rushes her into the sanctuary of the cathedral where the secular power cannot reach her. The attempt to get her out is interrupted by the arrival of Phoebus, whose testimony saves Esmeralda's life, but the long ride to Paris has made his wounds reopen, and he dies in her arms (No. 15d. *Scène et choeur*, "C'est lui!" / "Asile! asile! asile!").

EDITIONS: The autograph manuscript of the full score is in the Bibliothèque Nationale in Paris, and there is a copy in the Bibliothèque de l'Opéra, but it has never been published. Only a few copies survive of the piano-vocal score, published in Paris by Troupenas in 1838. The libretto can be found in full, however, in editions of the complete works of Victor Hugo.

PERFORMANCE HISTORY: The opera was withdrawn after six performances in 1836. Excerpts were performed at a concert in 1865. Since then the work has been ignored, and there is no recording.

TWO CONCEPTIONS OF DRAMATURGY

The preface that Victor Hugo wrote for his gigantic historical play *Cromwell* has already been cited several times in earlier chapters. Its demand for a fundamental renewal of French tragedy ensured its place in the history of literature as a preeminent manifesto of the theater of the Romantic period. Hugo named only Shakespeare in his polemic against the classicism of academic verse tragedy but in fact he also owed much to more recent models, such as Diderot and Mercier, and to the popular French theater of his own time. When Hugo asked for a verse that was "free, frank, and faithful, daring to say everything without prudery, and express everything without affectation,"[1] he was only asking for things that had long been the norm in the comédie dramatique and especially in the mélodrame à grand spectacle. These associations justify Arnold Hauser's sarcastic use of the term "mélodrame parvenu" to describe French Romantic drama.[2]

Opera too, in its own various ways, fulfilled the requirements of Hugo's manifesto, both in the Italian Romantic opera of Bellini and

1. "vers libre, franc, loyal, osant tout dire sans pruderie, tout exprimer sans recherche"; *Théâtre complet*, 1:441.
2. *The Social History of Art*, 693.

Donizetti[3] and in French grand opéra. All too often, however, music historians have represented this coincidence as if it involved a direct connection: one writer even went so far as to claim that the "insertion" of realistic scenes in Scribe's libretto for *La Muette de Portici* (begun in 1825) "probably derives from Victor Hugo's demand . . . for couleur locale."[4] Such an interpretation not only confuses tendencies typical of the age with Victor Hugo's personal aesthetic goals, but also underestimates the significance of melodrama's role in the development of grand opéra, which has already been discussed in a different context.

Yet it is tempting to pursue the possible parallels between Hugo's and Meyerbeer's conceptions of dramaturgy, and indeed one French literary scholar, Francis Claudon, published a comparison of the two. But even this study jumped too quickly to the conclusion that Meyerbeer was directly dependent on Hugo, speaking of "over-skilfully executed convergence" and "Meyerbeer's over-close fidelity to the aesthetics and philosophy of Hugo's drama."[5] The evidence Claudon advanced in support of these statements is not particularly convincing, however. The various features listed as common to Hugo's plays and Meyerbeer's grands opéras—the concern with local color, the bold mingling of political matter and private emotional conflicts, and "the sense of fate which . . . characterizes . . . the pairs of lovers"[6]—can be found in almost all French operas of the period, and are by no means peculiar to Meyerbeer's.

The one thing mentioned by Claudon that Meyerbeer's operas have and many others do not is "the idea of the mixture of tones,"[7] and that particular feature might be due to the direct influence of Hugo. In the *Préface de Cromwell*, Hugo proclaims a drama "that mingles in the same breath the grotesque and the sublime, the awesome and the farcical, tragedy and comedy,"[8] and this breach of stylistic unity does indeed become a dramaturgical principle in Meyerbeer's operas. The composer consciously turned away from the conventions of tragédie lyrique when he wrote numbers like the Nuns' Ballet in *Robert le diable*, Marcel's *Chanson huguenote* in *Les Huguenots*, or the *Trio bouffe* in Act III of *Le Prophète*, and in doing so he was the first to introduce the grotesque and the farci-

---

3. See Ringger, "'Che gelida manina. . . ,'" 125.
4. Walter, "Die Darstellung des Volkes," 387.
5. Claudon, "G. Meyerbeer et V. Hugo," 111.
6. Ibid., 106.
7. Ibid., 107.
8. "qui fond sous un même souffle le grotesque et le sublime, le terrible et le bouffon, la tragédie et la comédie"; *Théâtre complet*, 1:422.

cal into serious opera—a subject that will arise again in our discussion of *Un ballo in maschera.*

Meyerbeer's biographer Schucht cited the aria which Jean's mother, Fidès, sings in Act IV of *Le Prophète,* when she has sunk to beggary, as an example of the composer's skill in transforming a horrible subject into something sublime:

> Meyerbeer gives a practical proof in *Le Prophète* that an ugly subject, an ugly situation, can be transfigured and made aesthetically beautiful by means of poetry and music. Begging is hideous, low, unfortunate, and a great misery of life here on earth. But who has not admired the "begging" aria of Fidès!![9]

There are, as a matter of fact, instances of much closer association between Meyerbeer's dramaturgy and literary procedures used by Hugo; surprisingly, however, they are not found in any of Hugo's stage plays— the conceptual dependence of which on the theses he set out in the *Préface de Cromwell* is open to doubt[10]—but in the novel *Notre-Dame de Paris, 1482,* published in 1831. There, scenes are set in readiness before principal characters make their entrances, as if on a stage and as if the author did not have all the means of narrative at his disposal. "Wherever they appear for the first time, it is in the context of a crowd scene, and at first they stand out by virtue of just one aspect of their personality. . . . The individual heroes emerge from the crowd which observes them, in the same relationship as exists between soloists and chorus in opera."[11]

Given the theatrical qualities of this novel, it is not surprising that there is a direct connection between it, and its author, and the history of the Paris Opéra. Hugo himself was the first person to adapt his successful tale for the operatic stage, in the form of a libretto to be set by the daughter of his friend Louis-François Bertin. Louise-Angélique Bertin had already attracted attention as a composer, but it has to be admitted that it was due to her father's influence, as the powerful proprietor of the *Journal des débats,* that her first major opera was given its première at the Opéra. Not only was Hugo, after initial misgivings, prepared to collaborate in the enterprise, but the Opéra management lined

9. "Meyerbeer hat im 'Prophet' durch die Tat bewiesen, daß man auch ein häßliches Thema, eine Situation des Häßlichen 'durch Poesie und Musik' zur ästhetischen Schönheit verklären kann. Betteln ist häßlich, gemein, unglücklich und eine große Misere des Erdenlebens. Wer aber hat wohl nicht die Bettelarie der Fides bewundert!!" *Meyerbeer's Leben und Bildungsgang,* 300.

10. See Wentzlaff-Eggebert, *Zwischen kosmischer Offenbarung und Wortoper,* 8.

11. Klotz, *Die erzählte Stadt,* 113–14.

up a star cast with Hector Berlioz to take the rehearsals, and Franz Liszt made the piano reduction of the full score that was published later. In spite of these uniquely favorable conditions, *La Esmeralda* enjoyed only a succès d'estime before political opponents of the composer's liberal father and the literary opponents of Hugo discovered a welcome target for their hostility. The sixth performance, on 16 December 1836, had to be abandoned in the face of an unprecedented tumult, and the opera was never performed complete again.

Today the opera interests us less as a work in its own right than for the unusual circumstances of its genesis. Unlike Meyerbeer, the composer was unable to set her own dramaturgical seal on the work,[12] in spite of the fact that the librettist had even less experience of opera than she had. The balance of power was too unfairly distributed between the famous poet with a good conceit of himself and the gifted amateur who, besides suffering the normal social consequences of being a woman, was regarded first and foremost as an influential man's daughter and only secondarily as a composer.

Subject only to the musical necessities as he perceived them,[13] the most famous dramatist of the age was free to create his own personal idea of an opera libretto. Consequently, some tendencies of contemporary opera occur in an extreme form in *La Esmeralda*, and some of the essential aspects of grand opéra are illustrated with especial clarity in this unique work and in its relationship to its literary source.

The City in Opera

La Esmeralda, like the last three acts of *Les Huguenots*, takes place in Paris—essentially the same city as the one in which the people for whom both works were written still lived. Although both operas are set in relatively remote historical periods, respectively 354 and 264 years before 1836, the year in which both had their premières, the sight of their own city on stage was not as common an experience for the audience as we might suppose. Prior to these two works, Hérold's opéra comique *Le Pré-aux-Clercs* (1831—but also set in 1572) had been the only opera seen on the Paris stage to require scenery that approximately resembled the contemporary appearance of Paris familiar to every member of the audience. The city of 1482—or 1572—did not differ

12. See Bertin's undated letter to François-Joseph Fétis, cited in Tiersot, "*La Esmeralda*," 397.

13. See the preface to the libretto of *La Esmeralda*, in V. Hugo, *Oeuvres complètes*, 5:493–94.

very much in its physical appearance from that of 1836: fundamental change only came about after 1850, under the administration of Prefect Haussmann.

The identity of the Paris of *La Esmeralda* with their own city was brought home to the audience by the image of the cathedral, still one of the dominant buildings of the French capital in the late twentieth century. Like Hugo's novel *Notre-Dame de Paris*, the opera (which would have had the same title but for a ruling by the censor) is about more than a famous cathedral, it is also about the city surrounding it,[14] and to some extent *Les Huguenots*, too, is about Paris. In *La Esmeralda* there are reminders of the existence of the cathedral even in scenes set at some distance from it; for example the stage direction setting the scene at the start of Act III runs:

> *Le préau extérieur d'un cabaret. A droite la taverne. A gauche des arbres. Au fond une porte et un petit mur très bas qui clôt le préau. Au loin la croupe de Notre-Dame, avec ses deux tours et sa flèche, et une silhouette sombre du vieux Paris qui se détache sur le ciel rouge du couchant. La Seine au bas du tableau.*

⸎ ⸎ ⸎

> A tavern yard. To the right the inn, to the left some trees. To the rear, a gate and a very low wall enclosing the yard. In the distance the upper part of Notre-Dame, with its flèche and two towers, and the dark silhouette of old Paris against the red sky at sunset. The Seine at the foot of this tableau.

The atmosphere and "character" of this tableau, like an urban view-painting, was the quality audiences appreciated most about the opera's staging. In his article about *La Esmeralda* for a Parisian paper, Hector Berlioz singled out the central importance of the work's other, architectural heroine:

> It was a very fine idea, in my view, to show the church of Notre-Dame in all its aspects, from afar and from nearby, in almost every set; the great building becomes, so to speak, a character in the drama unfolding around it, and its somber majesty adds to the grandiose or picturesque atmosphere of the scenes over which it presides.[15]

14. See Klotz, *Die erzählte Stadt*, 92.

15. "C'est une idée fort belle, à mon sens, d'avoir montré l'église de Notre-Dame sous tous ses aspects, de loin et de près, dans presque toutes les décorations; le monument devient, pour ainsi dire, un personnage du drame qui se déroule autour de lui, et la majesté sombre de son aspect ajoute au grandiose ou au pittoresque des scènes auxquelles il préside." Berlioz, "*La Esmeralda*," 410.

The breach, in *La Esmeralda*, of the convention that had restricted the operatic stage to exotic, ancient Greek and Roman, or pastoral and idyllic locations, went beyond making much of a great building familiar to the audience from their everyday lives; in addition, most of the important events in the opera take place in the streets. *La Muette de Portici* is set in Naples, but only one scene takes place in a street in the city, whereas in Bertin's opera four out of the seven settings are in public places in Paris. This is not given legitimacy in terms of classicist aesthetics by any emphasis on public affairs—affairs of state or government— and it is obviously due first and foremost to Hugo's conviction that the continual presence of a chorus was indispensable in a French opera in the 1830s.[16]

The first act opens at night, in the Cour des Miracles, where a crowd of beggars and thieves cheer Quasimodo, whom they have elected "Fools' Pope" to preside over their carnival celebrations. This sets the scene for Frollo's attempted assault on Esmeralda. The arrival of the guard prevents him from carrying her off, however, and the act ends with the nightwatchmen's *ronde*. The first setting in Act III, the stage direction for which was cited a few lines above, is the yard of a tavern at sunset, where Phoebus de Châteaupers holds forth to his friends about his imminent rendezvous with Esmeralda and invites them to celebrate with him. It is only after the curfew that the tipsy crowd leave the lover alone, but for Frollo, as darkness falls. The other two street scenes take place by day: the first scene of Act II depicts the crowd jeering Quasimodo in the stocks on the place de Grève, and in the last act the same mob is seen milling about the pavement at the west end of Notre-Dame, looking forward to Esmeralda's execution for the alleged murder of Phoebus in a mood of bloodthirsty excitement.

Only two of the settings in *Les Huguenots* are open spaces (the gardens of Chenonceaux in Act II and the fenced churchyard which is the second setting of Act V are out of doors but confined). Of those two exterior scenes, one runs its course as the sun sets, and it is already the dead of night as the other begins. The setting for Act III is the Pré-aux-Clercs, a large meadow on the left bank of the Seine where the people of Paris go for recreation. At curtain-rise, it is six in the evening and a panoramic tableau fills the stage, made up of worthy citizens out for a stroll, Catholic students, Huguenot soldiers, and many others. It is not

16. On this and the discussion in the following paragraphs, see Gerhard, "Die Macht der Fatalität."

an ordinary working day, but Sunday, the day of rest, as the opening *Choeur des promeneurs* informs the audience: "C'est le jour du dimanche, c'est le jour de repos!" The walkers are enjoying their day off, like nineteenth-century Parisians whose lives were compartmentalized into work and leisure time, and like the characters in numerous nineteenth-century novels and stories, in which the "Sunday walk" is so regular and useful a means of scene-setting that it becomes a convenient literary convention, as Walter Bruno Berg pointed out in his study of the "literary Sunday": "the fact that it is Sunday, with its unique vacuum, signals that the action has reached a significant climax or is about to take a surprising turn."[17]

The only thing that prevents the growing tension between the religious factions from erupting in violence is the fortuitous arrival of a troupe of dancing gypsy girls. Night falls and the watchmen do their rounds, announcing the curfew and sending the people of Paris home. No one remains on the stage in the darkness until the parties arrive for the duel between Saint-Bris and Raoul. The duel is not what it seems, however: the criminally duplicitous Saint-Bris has arranged for a gang of assassins to take advantage of the darkness and murder Raoul, which Marcel prevents in the nick of time.

In the final scene of *Les Huguenots*, however, nothing gets in the way of the deaths of Valentine, Raoul, and Marcel at the hands of a band of Catholics. It is remarkable that there is a change of setting at this late stage in the work, for the scene of their deaths lasts only eighty seconds. The three have already been overtaken by their assailants in the previous scene, in which the Huguenots sheltering in the church are butchered, but the principals are spared for a moment: "The raging murderers fall upon them, separate them, and drag them away; they disappear past the crossroads to the right and at the same moment several shots are heard offstage on that side" (*Les meurtriers furieux se jettent sur eux, les séparent, les entraînent; ils disparaîssent par le carrefour à droite, et au même moment on entend en dehors et du même coté plusieurs coups de feu*). Still only the two men are mortally wounded, and they are dragged back on to the stage once more, together with Valentine who is evidently unhurt.

This contrivance entailed improbabilities in the structuring of the action as well as additional complications of a purely technical nature in the staging, and in 1841, in connection with a new production in London, Meyerbeer thought seriously about wholly rewriting the final

17. *Der literarische Sonntag,* 79, 81, 100.

scene and letting it end with a chorus of thanksgiving for all surviving characters.[18] In the end, however, he left the 1836 version as it was, with the leading characters in the private drama highlighted against the backdrop of the historical events for one last time. Unlike Pamyra in *Le Siège de Corinthe*, Valentine does not die with the anonymous crowd, and by the time the catastrophe arrives it does not come as a surprise—its multiple postponements have prepared the audience for the heroine's death ("heroine" in the sentimental sense at least). At the end, shock gives way to melodramatic transfiguration: Valentine forgives her murderers.

But all this could have been staged in the churchyard which is the last act's second setting. Why the change of set at this unusual juncture? It serves to underline the fact that the action takes place in Paris. The stage direction in the libretto actually reads: "The stage represents the sight of the quays of Paris in 1572. Starry night" *(Le théâtre représente la vue des quais de Paris en 1572. Nuit étoilée)*. A lithograph of the set designed for the 1836 production shows that it was conceived as if from the main gate of the Louvre (see fig. 13). The *quais* are in the foreground and the silhouette of the Île de la Cité can be seen in the background—a part of the city that, by the early nineteenth century, with its unsanitary, decaying buildings, depicted so vividly in Eugène Sue's documentary novel *Les Mystères de Paris*, had become a byword for crime.[19]

But it is not this scene alone: all the scenes on the open street, in both operas, are dominated by crime or criminal associations. Those that are also in darkness provide a background for violent crimes, from an attempted abduction, through a (thwarted) murder, to a wholesale massacre. The two in *La Esmeralda* that take place in daylight depict cruel punishments either already taking place or awaited, and are suffused with the aura of criminality. The perception of the city of Paris in these operas is inseparably mixed with a deep-seated fear of its disturbing manifestations, and the sight of hideous poverty is paraded with no more thought of highlighting social injustice than it is in French novels of the 1830s and '40s; its sole purpose is to attract a public hungry for sensation.[20] All at once, crimes were being enacted on the operatic stage which had previously only been reported: the violent uprising of Neapolitan fisherfolk in *La Muette de Portici* takes place offstage, and so too does the duel in Hérold's *Pré-aux-Clercs* that pits two honorable

18. See Meyerbeer's diary, 26 April 1841, in *Briefwechsel*, 3:348.
19. See Nathan, "Délinquance et réformisme dans les *Mystères de Paris*," 64.
20. See Brockmeier, "Die gefährliche arbeitende Klasse," 227.

13   This lithograph of 1837 by Gubian, of the third setting of Act V of *Les Huguenots*, shows that it was seen as if from the main gate of the Louvre, allowing the eye to pass across the quais to the Île de la Cité and its huddled, decaying housing, associated with criminals and crime in the minds of Meyerbeer's contemporaries.

men against each other on the selfsame spot selected for the murderous ambush in Act III of *Les Huguenots*.

All these onstage crimes take place at night. The reason for this is not just the wish to exploit the recent technical improvements in stage-lighting;[21] it was far more a matter of the diffuse fear of crime characteristic of the upper classes of Parisian society in the nineteenth century.[22] In earlier ages criminality was confined to a small number of professional criminals and particular places, but now it lurked everywhere, nurtured by the impoverishment of an ever-increasing range of social groups. The degree to which night was mixed up with the fear of crime[23] is illustrated in the German actor and theater director Eduard Devrient's account of a stay in Paris in 1839.

21. See H. Becker, "Die *Couleur locale* als Stilkategorie der Oper," 40.
22. See Chevalier, *Classes laborieuses et classes dangereuses*.
23. See also Amiard-Chevrel, "Aux sources d'une typologie," 18, 27.

It was after one o'clock when the company broke up, and for the first time I found the streets of Paris almost empty of humanity. I passed only isolated individuals on the boulevards, and I did not see a soul in the rue Vivienne and place de la Bourse, where one must elbow one's way by day. I heard nothing but my own footsteps and the murmur of a few fountains, whereas by day one is hard put to it to escape from the deafening roar. Near the Palais-Royal I met a patrol. The soldiers walked along both sides of the street, hugging the walls, singly, one behind the other, some five or six paces apart, so as not to be attacked all at the same time, and so as to be able to go to each other's aid. I was reminded that I had been advised, at the very start of my stay here, that that was the way to walk in Paris at night, if I was with others, but to take a fiacre at all costs, if I had to make my way home alone.[24]

In fact, the association between crime and opera is already implicit in Jouy's description of an execution on the place de Grève, cited in chapter 2. At a later date, in his *Essai sur l'Opéra français*, Jouy would categorically reject "the triumph of crime or, worse, fate in a theater where everything is addressed to the senses and the heart,"[25] but on that day in 1813 he marveled at the contrast between the deportment of Parisians when they were at the Opéra and when they were in the place de Grève, waiting for an execution. In his barely concealed disgust at the pleasure some of his contemporaries took in public executions Jouy doubtless reflected a common feeling. In 1832 the authorities drew the political consequences of sensibilities such as his and moved the place of execution from directly outside the Hôtel de Ville in the city center to the outskirts, and for the first time those with finer feelings could avoid the bloody spectacle.[26] The introduction of criminal acts and public execu-

24. "Nach ein Uhr trennte sich die Gesellschaft, ich fand zum ersten Male die Straßen von Paris fast menschenleer. Auf den Boulevards begegnete ich nur einzelnen Personen, in der rue Vivienne, auf dem Börsenplatze, wo man am Tage sich hindurchwinden muß, keiner Seele. Nichts vernahm ich als meine eigenen Tritte und das Rauschen einiger Brunnen, wo man am Tage vor dem betäubenden Geschwirre sich nicht zu retten weiß. In der Nähe des palais royal begegnete ich einer Patrouille. Die Soldaten gingen zu beiden Seiten der Straße dicht an den Häusern, einzeln, hintereinander, in Entfernung von fünf bis sechs Schritten, um nicht zu gleicher Zeit angegriffen zu werden, und sich gegenseitig beistehen zu können. Das erinnerte mich, daß man mir gleich am Anfang meines Aufenthaltes hier geraten hatte, auf diese Weise des Nachts in Paris zu gehen, wenn ich mit Mehreren sei, unbedingt aber einen Fiacre zu nehmen, wenn ich allein meinen Heimweg zu machen habe." Devrient, *Briefe aus Paris*, 248.

25. "le triomphe du crime ou même de la fatalité, sur un théâtre où tout parle aux sens et au coeur"; *Essai*, 245 (1987 ed., 72).

26. See Chevalier, *Classes laborieuses et classes dangereuses*, 156–59.

tions into serious opera only four years later meant that the two things in which Jouy had discovered a contradiction were brought together in one place—the Opéra.

Fear of the Mob

Jouy's observation that the crowd waiting to watch an execution was filled with a "savage curiosity"—a phenomenon later translated into operatic choruses in comparable situations in Halévy's *Juive* and Bertin's *Esmeralda*—is tinged with an element of fear, for the crowd is perceived as swayed by invariably uncontrollable emotions. The criminal masses, the "dangerous classes" as they were called, had become a popular subject of literature by around 1830, most notably in Victor Hugo's novel *Notre-Dame* itself, in which the Cour des Miracles, the hub of the life of the asocial elements who went to ground on the Île de la Cité, is depicted with unusual thoroughness.[27] In adapting his novel for the libretto of *La Esmeralda*, Hugo actually chose to start the action in this infamous den ("repaire infâme," as Clopin calls it in the first scene), among the vagabonds and beggars who are its normal habitués. "These ignoble vagabonds whom Monsieur Hugo has drawn up out of the mire that serves as their sepulcher, thank God!, in order to parade them in the light of a noble theater" (in the words of the critic Henri Blaze de Bury, writing about the opera when it was new)[28] naturally attracted the disapproval of established critics, but they stood also for a more widespread fear of the anonymous city crowd. There is no other explanation for the fact that only a few years after Rossini had introduced into French opera the image of the masses as a sublime manifestation of a nation's collective identity, it was possible to invert the image completely in this opera set in a big city. It is true that after 1830 there was an increasing tendency in opera throughout Europe to favor subject matter involving bandits and gypsies,[29] but *La Esmeralda* was the first opera to represent the criminal and asocial quarter of a large city.

The way had been prepared, to some extent, in *Les Huguenots*. Having already breached French operatic convention with a detailed depiction of dicers, cheating in various ways, in Act I of *Robert le diable*, Meyerbeer

27. See Klotz, *Die erzählte Stadt*, 112.

28. "Ces ignobles figures de truands que M. Hugo a tirées de la fange qui leur sert de sépulture, Dieu merci! pour les produire à la lumière d'une noble scène"; "De la Musique des femmes," 623.

29. See Abert, "Räuber und Räubermilieu," 123; Angermüller, "Zigeuner und Zigeunerisches"; Vaux de Foletier, "Les Bohémiens dans la littérature," 194.

and Scribe went a great deal further in their second joint enterprise, when they compiled the panoptic view of city crowds on the Pré-aux-Clercs in Act III. Gypsy girls dance for money there, as Bertin's Esmeralda does, and even though thieves and beggars are not involved in the hostility festering on that St. Bartholomew's Eve, the express listing of grisettes, workers, and students in the lengthy stage directions allows no denial that "the Parisian crowd of the nineteenth century is paraded before the audience" in this scene.[30] Grisettes, workers, and students are not mentioned in other nineteenth-century literary accounts of the St. Bartholmew's Day massacre, such as Mérimée's historical novel *Chronique du règne de Charles IX*,[31] but on the other hand, after the leading role they had played in the July Revolution, students, in particular, were associated with fears that the existing order might be violently overthrown once again and law-abiding citizens offended in ways that went far beyond harmless high spirits.[32]

This presentation of an underworld in *Les Huguenots*, even though less flagrant than in *La Esmeralda*, was evidently more than a conservative German public could tolerate. In an annihilating polemic of 1837, contrasting *Les Huguenots* with Mendelssohn Bartholdy's *St. Paul*, Robert Schumann fulminated: "What is left after *The Huguenots* but actually to execute criminals on the stage and make a public exhibition of whores? Just consider what happens, and where it all leads!"[33] It is true that the people whose executions were represented on stage in later operas were usually as innocent as Eléazar and Rachel in Halévy's *La Juive* (1835), and prostitutes remained rare: Verdi's *La traviata* (1853) is an exception. But from this time forward the operatic stage was filled to overflowing with gypsy girls, camp followers, and other social undesirables, and that not only in the context of scenes set in army camps, like the one in Verdi's *La forza del destino* (1861), but even in the chic surroundings of a Parisian salon, as in Act II of *La traviata*.

The context in which Meyerbeer and Scribe placed the scene depicting the aristocratic conspirators' preparations for the St. Bartholomew's massacre is scarcely less raffish. In the celebrated "benediction of the swords," however, Meyerbeer gave the criminal atmosphere a musi-

30. Walter, *"Hugenotten"-Studien*, 54.
31. See ibid., 55.
32. Ibid., 52–53.
33. "Fragmente aus Leipzig," 4. [1837], in *Gesammelte Schriften*, 2:220–25 (p. 222); cited from Schumann, *The Musical World of Robert Schumann*, 137–40 (p. 138). See also Walter, "'Man überlege sich nur Alles.'"

cal fashioning far more effective than anything conveyed merely by the visual representation, and in that respect this crucial scene went far beyond any offered in Bertin's *Esmeralda*. First, Saint-Bris asks the assembled Catholics to vow to destroy the enemies "of Heaven and our homeland" ("du ciel et de la patrie"). Only Nevers speaks out against this murderous intent, but because of his knowledge of it he is placed under guard by the others, who then repeat their martial oath. Up to this point the music has resembled the oath-taking on the Rütli in Act II of Rossini's *Guillaume Tell*, but now Meyerbeer strikes out on a completely new path. Saint-Bris has a lengthy recitative, in which he gives detailed strategic instructions for the coming night, and exhorts his listeners to kill without mercy. The tension rises, the emphatic dotted rhythm of the phrase "For this our sacred cause" ("Pour cette cause sainte") persists in Saint-Bris's arioso, but the tempo steadily quickens: Andantino gives way to Allegro and finally to Allegro vivace.

All of a sudden this process stops, however, as three monks appear in the doorways at the back of the room and bless the conspirators' weapons with a solemn hymn. Saint-Bris and the monks praise "avenging God" ("Dieu vengeur"), and the chorus join in. After a short time this Poco andante unexpectedly loses its majestic gravity. Saint-Bris and the monks enjoin the ruthless destruction of the enemy, and the rhythm switches abruptly to dotted fourth, sixteenth, and thirty-second notes, accompanied by chromatic scales on the piccolo. The chorus respond with one word "[we'll] smite" (*frappons*), repeated mechanically, while they modulate from the original A-flat major through F minor, to C-sharp minor, and then return to A-flat major in the concluding cries of "Anathema!" ("Anathème sur eux").

At this moment, highlighted by the return to the key from which the inconclusive modulations started, there is a complete change of mood. Trumpet fanfares in a dotted $\frac{6}{8}$ rhythm blare out in the final cadence to A-flat major, and the chorus, without any encouragement from the leaders for whose instructions they have waited until now, sing—no, they *yell*, Allegro furioso:

> (*Tous se précipitent avec fureur sur le devant de la scène brandissant leurs épées et leurs poignards.*)
>
> CHOEUR GÉNÉRAL
> Dieu le veut! Dieu l'ordonne!
> Non! non! grâce à personne!
> A ce prix il pardonne
> Au pécheur repentant.

Que le glaive étincelle!
Que le sang ruisselle,
Et la palme immortelle
Dans le ciel vous attend!
(*Les Huguenots*, Acte IV, scène 5)

⟨ ⟨ ⟨

(*All rush furiously to the front of the stage, brandishing their swords and daggers.*)
CHORUS: It is God's will! It is God's command! No! No! Mercy to none!
For this price He will pardon the repentant sinner. Let the blade flash! Let
blood flow, and an immortal palm await you in Heaven!

All at once the crowd has no need of leaders, it has been let off the
leash, and works itself unaided into a frenzy of blood-lust. There is good
reason for seeing here, in the carefully constructed theatrical representation of the mood of a pogrom, "the coded commentary of a believing
Jew [Meyerbeer] on one of the bloodiest chapters in the religious history of Europe,"[34] all the more so because the calculated blend of solemn consecration and screamed exhortations to murder hair-raisingly
anticipates the aesthetics of twentieth-century fascists. Parisian operagoers in 1836 would have made a completely different association,
however. The scene impressed them with its masterly evocation of "the
soul of the crowd," recalled in memoirs published over sixty years later.[35]
It not only confirmed contemporary conceptions of the irrationality of
crowd psychology,[36] but could be referred directly to French historiog-
raphy in the early nineteenth century, in which the Jacobin terror of
1792–93 was consistently compared to the horrors of the St. Bartholomew's Day massacre, after Madame de Staël had developed this bold
analogy in considerable detail in 1818.[37] In an age when this "collective
trauma"[38] was still far from having been assimilated, it became a common practice to explain the events of 1572, not in terms of their specific
political and religious causes, or the fact that they were set in train by
the highest authorities, but by ascribing them to the apparently incorri-
gibly destructive nature of the Parisian mob.

It was precisely in this tendentious falsification of historical truth
that Meyerbeer's representation of a mob went far beyond anything at-

34. Döhring, "Giacomo Meyerbeer," 17.
35. "[il] avait su . . . évoquer en maître l'âme des foules"; Bocher, *Mémoires*, 2:561.
36. See Le Bon, *Psychologie des foules*.
37. See Delon, "La Saint-Barthélemy et la Terreur chez Mme de Staël."
38. Gier, "Jakobiner-Austreibung," 233.

tempted by contemporary novelists like Scott, Manzoni, or Hugo,[39] and it speaks for the unique modernity of his denunciation of mass hysteria that the representation of bloodthirsty mobs in later operas fell short of the light and shade achieved in *Les Huguenots*. Meyerbeer's own later depiction of a raging mob, in the chorus demanding a traitor's blood in Act III of *Le Prophète* ("Du sang! que Judas succombe"), was as static as Halévy's in the chorus "Quel plaisir! quelle joie!" in Act V of *La Juive*. Admittedly, Halévy's mob consists of bystanders, merely expressing pleasure while others perform antisemitic acts, whereas Meyerbeer depicts his chorus taking an active part in the violence, but only Verdi, in the chorus of Egyptian priests and generals shouting for war ("Guerra! guerra!") in Act I of *Aida*, succeeded in recreating something of Meyerbeer's hair-raising representation of the gradual unfurling of criminal energies.

In the "benediction of the swords," Meyerbeer brought off a crucial scene in which the essence of the St. Bartholomew's Day massacre can be seen at the moment of crystallization, and it is no accident that even declared anti-Meyerbeerians call attention to its quality, to this day. A journalist whose column of "letters from Paris" was widely read cited the scene, in 1844, in a context that initially strikes us as inappropriate, since it appears to associate the nervous precautions taken by law-abiding citizens with the murderous frenzy of the Catholic fanatics; if we study it more carefully, however, it is yet further proof of how the sixteenth-century Paris represented in *Les Huguenots* reflected nineteenth-century fears:

> For a month all the talk has been of nocturnal attacks, of ambuscades, of audacious robberies . . . Paris is quite disturbed by these sinister adventures, and family reunions are being most disagreeably affected by the preoccupation with self-defense. Every intimate evening party ends, as the fourth act of *Les Huguenots* begins, with the blessing of weapons. Hosts do not allow relatives and friends to leave until their arms have been inspected, and there follows a terrifying display of daggers, swordsticks, knives, and stilettos; an elegant salon is metamorphosized at a stroke into an armorer's shop.[40]

39. See Hempel, *Manzoni und die Darstellung der Menschenmenge*, 86–87.

40. "On n'entend parler depuis un mois que d'attaques nocturnes, de guet-apens, de vols audacieux. . . . Paris est assez troublé par ces aventures sinistres, les réunions de famille se ressentent désagréablement de ces préoccupations défensives. Chaque soirée intime finit, comme le quatrième acte des Huguenots commence, par la bénédiction des poignards. On ne laisse sortir de chez soi ses parents, ses amis qu'après avoir visité leurs

VOYEURISM

A substantial section of the audiences at the Opéra went there to see the obligatory ballet rather than for any interest in music. There was undoubtedly an element of voyeurism in this. As in many other cities, the principal opera house in Paris had a monopoly on the performance of ballet, but its practice differed from what was usual in Germany and Italy, where double bills were made up of a complete ballet and a short opera. In Paris, every full evening's opera included scenes of ballet integrated more or less plausibly into the dramatic action. Spectators who set great store by their reputations could therefore satisfy their voyeuristic desires at the premières of serious operas, and still reassure themselves with the thought that they had attended an outstanding cultural event. All the same, everyone knew perfectly well what the ballets meant to most people in the audience. Grandville's illustration to his book *Un autre monde* (1844), of a theater audience turned into gigantic eyes, popping out of shirt-collars and waist-coats (fig. 14), says all that needs to be said about the character of the ogling lorgnette-bearers, and in another novel published in 1844 by a writer of vaudevilles, Albéric Second, a regular operagoer explains:

> The habitués of the accursed box have had lorgnettes made for them by the engineer Chevalier, which magnify objects 32 times, and bring them closer by the same amount. Thanks to these monster binoculars—which might equally well be termed binocular monsters—a pair of tights is a chimera. The legs do not exist, however well covered, that they do not decipher when petticoats part.[41]

This passage alludes to the refrain of a chorus in *Robert le diable* in which dead nuns rise from their graves and declare gold a chimera ("L'or est une chimère") while adopting seductive poses. It is true that the dancers remained clothed even in scenes like that, but nudity was one of the few taboos that remained inviolate throughout the nineteenth century. The

---

armes, et c'est alors une exhibition effrayante de poignards, de cannes à épées, de couteaux, de stylets; l'élégant salon se métamorphose aussitôt en une boutique d'armurier." Gay, *Le Vicomte de Launay*, 4:144–45 (article originally published 21 December 1844).

41. "Les familiers de la loge maudite se sont fait fabriquer par l'ingénieur Chevalier des lorgnettes qui grossissent trente-deux fois les objets et les rapprochent d'autant. Grâce à ses binocles-monstres qu'on pourrait tout aussi bien appeler des monstres de binocles, pour eux le maillot est une chimère. Il n'y a pas de jambes si bien cuirassées qu'ils ne déchiffrent à jupons ouverts." *Les petits mystères de l'Opéra*, 84–85.

14   The fantasy-novel *Un autre monde* (1844) includes the tale of a wooden doll that falls in love with the goddess Venus in the ancient world, then finds itself suddenly transposed to the Paris Opéra in the nineteenth century, where it recognizes the goddess in a box. The grotesque metamorphosis depicted in this illustration by the book's author, the caricaturist Grandville (1803–47), represents a sharp social criticism of the audience whom Grandville clearly regarded as voyeurs pure and simple.

July Revolution of 1830 saw the departure of La Rochefoucauld from his position as minister in charge of the Opéra, where he had insisted that the skirts worn by the ballerinas should not be excessively short.[42] In the years that followed, more and more ingenuity was devoted to satisfying operagoers' desire for erotic spectacle. Scenes in which ballerinas appeared as ghosts, as in *Robert le diable* Act III, or taking a dip in the river, as in *Les Huguenots* Act II, were pretexts for showing them in ever more "delicate" positions. The Venusberg ballet in the Paris production of Wagner's *Tannhäuser* in 1861 led this development to a new high point, but was not appreciated by a hostile public.

   The ballets were not the only scenes in which the Opéra opened inti-

42. See Gourret, *Ces Hommes qui ont fait l'Opéra*, 109–10.

mate encounters up to the gaze of those who had no business to be there. It is a common dramaturgical convention of the operas under discussion that crucial scenes are observed clandestinely by other characters from a neighboring room. In Act III of *La Esmeralda*, the second setting is clearly a *maison de passe*, and the scene begins with a shady character showing Frollo to an alcove from which he can watch the lovers alone before he attacks Phoebus. Little is done to disguise the nature of the place, which explains the complaints of conservative contemporaries about the opera's "immorality,"[43] and the insistence of the censor (who let Hugo off lightly on the whole) that the unambiguous words "From here you will be able to see the captain and the gypsy girl without being seen yourself" ("D'ici vous pourrez voir, sans être vu vous-même, le Capitaine et la bohème") should be given, not to an anonymous old woman, but to the ubiquitous Clopin.[44]

In *Les Huguenots*, Scribe and Meyerbeer denied both hot-blooded lovers and breathless voyeurs such blatant satisfaction of their desires; indeed, in his final revision of the love duet in Act IV, the composer yielded to the objections of the star tenor Nourrit and cut from the cabaletta Raoul's demand that Valentine should open the door of her nuptial chamber and allow him to slake his thirst for her ("Ouvrez la chambre nuptiale! C'est trop souffrir—j'ai soif de toi!").[45] Nevertheless, there are three decisive places in the opera where the dramaturgical motif of clandestine, passive watching is a feature. In the first-act finale Nevers's friends draw a curtain so as to be able to see his unidentified woman visitor; in Act IV Raoul witnesses the preparations for the massacre from the next room; and in Act V Valentine watches the massacre taking place in the Huguenot church:

VALENTINE
(*Elle regarde par les vitraux ce qui se passe dans l'église.*)
Ces enfants . . . ces femmes . . . arrêtez . . . infâmes! . . .
Quoi! . . . partout la mort! (*douleureusement*) Ils chantent encor!
(*regardant dans l'église*)
Ce viellard qui prie . . . ce moine en furie . . . Ciel! le-voilà mort!
(*douleureusement*) Ils chantent encor!
     (*Les Huguenots*, Acte V, scène 3)

     ِ   ِ   ِ

VALENTINE (*watching what happens in the church through the windows*): The children . . . the women . . . stop . . . wretches! . . . What! . . . death ev-

43. See La Rochefoucauld-Doudeauville, *Mémoires*, 13:418.
44. See Gerhard, "Die Macht der Fatalität."
45. See Huebner, "Italianate duets," 234.

erywhere! *(Sorrowfully)* Still they sing! *(Looking into the church)* That old man praying . . . that monk in rage . . . Heavens! he is dead! *(Sorrowfully)* Still they sing!

The necessity of this third example of a dramatic technique, *teichoscopy*, which has been used for thousands of years, is more apparent than real, for the massacre in the church takes place on the stage, even if in the background where the audience has difficulty in seeing it. But it resembles the other two examples in dividing the stage into two areas. This was the first time in tragic opera that the stage forfeited its ideal unity. Previously this "dissolution of architectural forms into functional structures"[46] had been confined to comic genres. As early as 1830, one of the most successful of nineteenth-century comic operas provided a particularly significant example of the development of voyeuristic situations: in Act II of Auber's *Fra Diavolo*—libretto, yet again, by Scribe—the eponymous hero and two other bandits are shown watching the innkeeper's daughter undressing and getting into bed through a hole in their own bedroom wall. They are as well aware as Frollo in *La Esmeralda* and the young noblemen in Act I of *Les Huguenots* that what they are doing is taboo. But the spectator, too, is seeing what they (and he) should not be seeing, so that the circumstances acknowledge the impropriety of presenting visible criminal or erotic acts on the stage.

The presence of a surrogate observer not only placed a protective layer between "shocking" scenes and the spectator in the auditorium, it also lent visual expression, for the last time, to what Richard Sennett terms "the eroding line between privacy and publicness."[47] Sensitivity toward distinctions between private and public spheres had gradually declined since the middle of the eighteenth century. Increasingly the experience of living in a large city like Paris or London was one of passive spectactorship. As Sennett observes, Balzac's highly detailed descriptive technique provides particularly good examples of the "instability in what [was] perceived" and the corresponding "passivity in the perceiver."[48] His novel *Le Père Goriot* is frequently cited in this context, but *La Maison Nucingen* (1837), a shorter fiction that is nonetheless central to his oeuvre as a whole, gives an especially extreme example of passive observation.

The first-person narrator of this tale is able, from the private room of an inn in Paris, to follow the conversation of four people in the next

46. Gabler, *Der Zuschauerraum des Theaters*, 103.
47. *The Fall of Public Man*, 126.
48. Ibid., 159.

room, whom he can hear but not see. The conversation presents a sketch of the world of Parisian banking, as Balzac viewed it (he originally planned to call the work *Une Vue du monde*). As narrator, however, he not only makes no use of his eyes, he also remains completely passive in the act of narration. After a short introduction he reproduces the conversation—lasting several hours—as he hears it, without a word of comment. Even at the end, the words exchanged between two of the unseen speakers remain in the foreground rather than he: "'Goodness, there was someone in the next room,' Finot said, hearing us leave. 'There's always someone in the next room,' replied Bixiou, who must have been drunk."[49]

But even in a work as diametrically different in character and conception from Balzac's panorama of the Paris of his own age as Victor Hugo's *Notre-Dame de Paris, 1482*, similar manifestations can be found of a wholly detached perception of events which ultimately even the protagonists confront passively. In this novel, too:

> There is a stereotyped grouping that occurs again and again: the individual doing something or, rather more often, suffering something, and, gathered around, or confronting the scene, the watching crowd which, whether enthusiastically or indignantly, cruelly or compassionately, always enjoys the spectacle, demands it, indeed, as tribute. Apart from the storming of the cathedral, it can be said that while the individuals live their lives, and suffer their fates, the many are there merely to watch. They bestir themselves only when there is something to look at.[50]

This pleasure in looking on is inseparable, however, from the passivity of the crowd, whose eyes are loaned to the reader:

> Hugo's definitive onlooker is almost always the collective, and insofar as it is only there, watching, it is passive and unproductive. Furthermore, what it is watching does not involve it in the work like a narrator.... Readers' reception of the thing observed is twofold: they receive both what it is and the way it is received by the listeners or watchers. In either case narrating and narratability, or seeing and visibility, are emphasized in their own right.[51]

49. "'Tiens, il y avait du monde à côté,' dit Finot en nous entendant sortir. 'Il y a toujours du monde à côté,' répondit Bixiou qui devait être aviné." *La Maison Nucingen* (1838), in *La Comédie humaine*, 6:329–92 (p. 392).

50. Klotz, *Die erzählte Stadt*, 114–15.

51. Ibid., 117–18.

This type of perception aesthetic is realized more fully in *Les Hugue-nots* even than it is in Hugo and Bertin's ill-starred operatic version of *Notre-Dame*. In Meyerbeer's opera—rather as in postrevolutionary painting and graphic art—an event is no longer sufficient in itself to deserve representation, but only if it is also experienced by observers.[52] The requisite observer is one who enjoys seeing everything without being able to intervene but has not yet absorbed this passivity into himself as an apparent given. This contradiction takes theatrical form in the interposition of the clandestine watcher. But the employment, as in *La Esmeralda* and *Les Huguenots*, of a passive observer to watch something represented on the stage was only a temporary solution in the history of musical dramaturgy. Once the management of the Opéra understood that presenting intimate scenes in the middle of a vast stage set only diminished their effect,[53] and once it was technically possible (from about 1830 onwards) to present a separate, enclosed room *(salon fermé)* at the front of the stage,[54] the dramatic device of indirect observation even of the most intimate encounters became superfluous: by 1849 Wagner was able to put a bridal bed on the stage, in Act III of *Lohengrin*, without needing to refract the audience's perception through a surrogate witness.

This reduction of the visible acting-area for a few intimate scenes went hand-in-hand with a tendency for spectacular scenes on a large scale to be a self-justifying necessity. Such set pieces were not intended for the voyeur seeking erotic delight, but for those who nevertheless took more pleasure in spectacle than in dramatic concision and coherence. The seeds of this development were already present in Hugo's historical novel and Meyerbeer's historical opera, but it culminated, in grand opéra, in large-scale scenes set in army camps, full of color and bustle but only loosely connected to the plot. The example in Act II of Meyerbeer's *Feldlager in Schlesien*, duplicated in the French version of that opera, *L'Étoile du Nord*, has already been mentioned, and there are others in the third acts of Meyerbeer's *Prophète* (1849) and Verdi's *Forza del destino* (1861). This type of scene gathered together in a kind of revue everything that might arouse the superficial interest of a passive spectator; like the flaneur strolling along the boulevard, the operagoer only had to decide on which details to focus his attention.

52. See Kemp, "Masse—Mensch," [12]; see also idem, "Das Bild der Menge."
53. See Véron, *Mémoires*, 3:226.
54. See Bosselt, *Das Zimmer auf der Bühne*, 29.

THE POWER OF FATE

In adapting his novel, with its superabundance of incidents and characters, to make a libretto, Hugo had to be rigorously selective and make many changes to what he did select. In the event, his alterations went much further than rejecting everything that was beyond the means of an opera to reproduce. Perhaps overeagerly, he subjected himself to many of the traditional operatic conventions that had recently been overridden in the new genre of grand opéra. In *La Muette de Portici*, Scribe and Auber had demonstrated that it was possible to construct an opera around a mute heroine, but Hugo never so much as considered the possibility of an equally bold experiment with deafness, and although the deaf hunchback Quasimodo is a fully developed and central character in the novel, in the opera he is reduced to the minor role of Frollo's accomplice. Hugo also greatly reduced the light and shade in the characterization of the two lovers. It is true that Esmeralda's love for Phoebus is already so naive in the novel that it hardly constitutes a complication, but it is only an episode beside more important incidents that give the gypsy girl human depth and character. In the libretto, however, Hugo made that love the object around which the entire plot revolves, and transformed Phoebus from a coldhearted opportunist into a wholehearted adorer of Esmeralda. In so doing he took all dramatic interest away from the central intrigue. But if Hugo seems to be bowing to the immutable laws of nineteenth-century libretto-writing in trivializing the ideal love of a tenor for a soprano, the appearance of conformity is deceptive, for in every other grand opéra this stereotyped relationship is developed against the backdrop of a historical ambience that not only justifies lavish architectural sets but also takes dramatic shape in the musical numbers.

Hugo was even more ruthless in his treatment of the ending. This is all the more surprising because the two surviving prose drafts of the last act of the libretto show that he first intended to use the events narrated in book 11, chapter 2, under the title "La creatura bella bianco vestita." The earlier draft reads like a much abbreviated summary of the ending of the novel:

Acte III, scène 4. Le haut des tours de Notre-Dame. Le jour se lève. Peu à peu on distingue Paris, le vieux Paris, qui se développe au loin autour de l'église. Au moment où le soleil se montre à l'horizon, toutes les cloches s'éveillent. Musique de tous les carillons de Paris. Claude paraît sur la plate-forme. Un dernier chant de désespoir et de vengeance satisfaite. Il va s'accouder à la balustrade qui donne

*sur la Grève. A son agitation on devine qu'il voit quelque chose de terrible. Quasi-
modo paraît et se place derrière lui. Tout à coup, à un rire de Claude, il le pousse
dans l'abîme. Alors il s'accoude à la balustrade, regarde tour à tour Claude et
l'égyptienne, morts tous deux, et dit: Oh! tout ce que j'ai aimé!*[55]

❧ ❧ ❧

Act III, scene 4. The summit of the towers of Notre-Dame. Day breaks.
Bit by bit Paris, old Paris, comes into view, spreading out into the distance
around the church. At the moment when the sun appears above the horizon, all the bells awake. Music of all the carillons in Paris. Claude [Frollo]
appears on the platform. A last song of despair and satisfied vengeance.
He goes and leans on the parapet overlooking the place de Grève. His
agitation reveals that he can see something dreadful. Quasimodo appears
and stands behind him. All at once, as Claude laughs, he pushes him over
into the abyss. Then he leans his elbows on the parapet, looks down at
Claude and the gypsy girl in turn, both dead, and says "Oh, everything
I loved!"

Having composed that sketch, Hugo must have realized that the decidedly undramatic idea of the music of numerous carillons, however picturesque, would hardly suffice to give the otherwise almost wordless
passage of this closing scene a convincing musical form. In the second
sketch he held onto the idea of a voyeur, a clandestine observer, but
added opportunities for a duet for Frollo and Quasimodo, and for the
specifically operatic medium of offstage choirs:

*Acte III, scène 3. Le haut de la plate-forme d'entre les tours. Cette plate-forme
est très élevée. On ne voit au loin que l'air et l'espace. Le jour commence à poindre.
Claude paraît. C'est l'heure où la Esmeralda doit mourir. Il va s'accouder à la
balustrade. Le jour se lève, et avec le jour s'éveillent l'un après l'autre tous les
carillons et toutes les cloches de Paris. Concert des cloches. Quasimodo survient. Il
sait que c'est Claude qui a livré la Esmeralda. Il a la rage de la vengeance au
coeur. Claude, absorbé, ne le voit pas. On entend des voix fraîches d'enfants de
choeur chanter matines dans l'église. Choeur lointain du peuple de Paris qui
s'éveille. Claude pousse un cri. La Esmeralda est entre les mains du bourreau. Il
la voit du point où il est placé. Elle est morte! Quasimodo prend Claude par le
bras, et lui déclare qu'il faut maintenant qu'il meure à son tour. Lutte et résis-
tance de Claude. Elle est inutile. Quasimodo le pousse dans l'abîme.*[56]

❧ ❧ ❧

55. *Oeuvres complètes,* 5:538.
56. Ibid., 539.

Act III, scene 3. On the platform between the two towers. It is very high. In the distance only air and empty space can be seen. Day begins to dawn. Claude appears. It is the hour at which Esmeralda is to die. He goes to lean on the parapet. Day breaks and with the day one after another all the carillons and all the bells in Paris awaken. Concert of bells. Quasimodo enters. He knows that it was Claude who informed on Esmeralda. Vengeance rages in his heart. Claude is too absorbed to see him. The fresh voices of choir boys are heard singing matins in the church. Distant chorus of the people of Paris awakening. Claude gives a cry, Esmeralda is in the executioner's hands. He can see her from his vantagepoint. She is dead! Quasimodo takes Claude by the arm, and tells him that now he must die in his turn. Claude's struggle and resistance. It is in vain. Quasimodo pushes him over into the abyss.

In the final version, however, he did without this scene altogether and decided to depict Esmeralda's walk to the scaffold as a tableau against the background of the cathedral, rather than refracted through the eyes of the observers on the tower, and to end the work not with Esmeralda's execution and Frollo's murder but with the arrival of Phoebus to rescue his beloved. As an Englishman who saw one of the few performances commented: "Thus the whole story was at once the slightest of the slight—the most melodramatic of melodrama."[57] The conclusion no longer focuses on the wretchedness of three totally different people, each destroyed in an individual way, but shows us two lovers' happiness blighted by fate.

As Hugo's wife later intimated,[58] the poet was persuaded to make this fundamental change by the arguments of theatrical professionals. Blaze de Bury found room in the review already cited in this chapter for some background information supporting this:

> Later, the dispositions of the piece, chopped up into five acts, having been restrained, Mademoiselle Bertin had no choice but to overthrow the ordinances of her music and hammer in the peripeteia of a new dénouement. This is the history of the fifth act: Monsieur Hugo had perched it upon the towers of Notre-Dame, to take place between the bellringer, the priest, and a few owls—the customary inhabitants. However, when the mise-en-scène came under serious discussion, Monsieur Hugo's idea was seen to be impractical, and the director, while professing the fifth act nothing short of sublime, took it upon himself to inform our great poet

---

57. Chorley, *Music and manners in France and Germany*, 1:15.
58. See [A. Hugo], *Victor Hugo raconté par un témoin de sa vie*, 2:439–40.

that the abyss is too simple an element to furnish an effective stage set. So Monsieur Hugo resigned himself to humbling his impertinent fifth act, which had lifted its head so high and sought comparison with the waves of the Latin poet. Its head went back into its shell, its blade into the scabbard, and Monsieur Hugo composed a few more decastichs which had the double advantage of explaining an inexplicable dénouement and of ruining the music from top to bottom.[59]

But even if Hugo was obliged to relinquish the scene he had imagined on the dizzy heights of the towers of Notre-Dame, he was not forced to bring Phoebus hurrying on to rescue Esmeralda. This change in the plot is not to be explained in terms of what can and cannot be done on a stage or the aesthetic premises of an experienced producer. Rather, it is symptomatic of a quality in the opera which is not present in the novel, and that is the insistence on the power of fate: *fatalité* became the libretto's key word. It lacks the cobweblike density of αναγκη, the Greek word for necessity or constraint which is the novel's epigraph; in the novel Esmeralda, Quasimodo, Frollo, and the mysterious recluse Paquette la Chantefleurie are bound intricately together by the thread of abduction in infancy, which is entirely absent from the opera.[60] Also, in the definitive version of the libretto, Hugo dispensed with the cursing of Esmeralda by the recluse, who is her unknown mother (in the first setting of Act II, in the first prose draft).[61] This change, too, is surprising at first glance, when we consider that the "malediction" of a father or a mother was one of the most effective—if already rather hack-

---

59. "Plus tard les dispositions de la pièce, coupée en cinq actes, ayant été restreintes, force a été à Mlle. Bertin d'intervertir l'ordonnance de sa musique, et d'y faire entrer à coups de marteau les peripéties d'un nouveau dénouement. Voici l'histoire de ce cinquième acte. M. Hugo l'avait perché sur les tours de Notre-Dame; il se passait là entre le sonneur, le prêtre et quelques hiboux, habitants ordinaires du logis. Cependant, lorsqu'on en vint à discuter sérieusement la mise en scène, l'idée de M. Hugo parut impraticable, et le directeur, tout en trouvant le cinquième acte fort sublime, s'efforça d'apprendre à notre grand poète que le vide est un element trop simple pour qu'on puisse en faire une décoration de theâtre. M. Hugo se résigna donc à renfermer dans sa coquille cet impertinent cinquième acte, qui levait si haut le bout de son nez, et prétendait imiter les vagues du poète latin. La tête rentra dans le corps, la lame dans le fourreau, et M. Hugo composa quelques dizains de plus, qui eurent le double avantage d'expliquer au public un dénouement inexplicable et de ruiner de fond en comble la musique." "De la Musique des femmes," 623.

60. See the chapter *"Arachne-Ananke:* La Mère terrible ou la fatalité," in Baudouin, *Psychanalyse de Victor Hugo,* 127–48 (pp. 157–81 in the new edition); see also Ubersfeld, *Le Roi et le bouffon,* 23–24.

61. *Oeuvres complètes,* 5:537.

neyed—tools of operatic dramaturgy, since its use by Rossini in *Otello* (1816), *Maometto II* (1820), and *Le Siège de Corinthe* (1826).

In the constricted context of the libretto, however, the curse would have acquired too much weight; it would have been difficult, if not impossible, to subordinate it to the *anonymous* fate that governs the opera. In the libretto Esmeralda regards herself as the victim of dark forces, and the entrance song given her by Hugo (but not set to music) ends with the quatrain:

> Je suis la colombe
> Qu'on blesse et qui tombe.
> La nuit de la tombe
> Couvre mon berceau.

ᕤ   ᕤ   ᕤ

I am the dove which is wounded and falls. The night of the tomb covers my cradle.

It is true that Bertin did not establish references to the final scene, in any leitmotivic sense, as Verdi did with the repeated reminiscences of Monterone's "Maledizione!" in his "Hugo" opera, *Rigoletto* (1851). But in the emphasis she gives to the cries of "Fatalité!" in the C major apotheosis of the final bars the composer underlines the word's central importance—the more so as she cut the text a little. Hugo's version, printed in his collected works, reads:

> PHOEBUS *chancelant*
> Je meurs.
> *(Elle le reçoit dans ses bras. Attente et anxiété dans la foule.)*
> Chaque pas que j'ai fait vers toi, ma bien-aimée,
> A rouvert ma blessure à peine encor fermée.
> J'ai pris pour moi la tombe et te laisse le jour.
> J'expire. Le sort te venge;
> Je vais voir, ô mon pauvre ange,
> Si le ciel vaut ton amour!
>
> CLAUDE FROLLO
> Fatalité!
>
> LE PEUPLE
> Fatalité!
> *(La Esmeralda, Acte IV, scène 4)*

ᕤ   ᕤ   ᕤ

PHOEBUS *(swaying)*: I am dying. *(She takes him in her arms. Anxious attention in the crowd.)* Each step I took toward you, my dearly beloved, re-

opened my wound which had scarcely closed. I chose the tomb for myself and life for you. I perish. Destiny avenges you; I go, o my poor
angel, to discover if heaven is worth your love!

FROLLO: Fate!

THE CROWD: Fate!

In his formulaic treatment of that last word, Hugo paid homage to a
conception which was even then in the process of assuming in opera the
significant role it had had in some types of spoken drama since about
1810. Fate determined the outcome in a number of mélodrames in the
French theater, but in the German theater a specific genre of "fate tragedies" *(Schicksalstragödien)* had come into existence, in which whole families were destroyed by some particular implement, or on some particular day, preordained as fateful to them, as a consequence of some past
event.[62] The virtuosity of playwrights like Hugo himself and the Austrian Franz Grillparzer enabled them to transform the schematic configurations of the German genre into something more subtle, in which
people were doomed by the workings of a fate beyond their comprehension. It was in 1836 that Giuseppe Mazzini developed his ideas of a
modern poetic drama, centered on the concept of "fate considered as
an element in the drama," and made a clear distinction between his idea
of a "drama of providence" and the currently popular convention
whereby

> human liberty is sacrificed ... to the irresistible influence of a sentence
> prescribed in heaven, which watches over man, determines his actions,
> burdens him with guilt and remorse, and casts him down into an abyss of
> perdition, with a final, fatal blow dealt by the striking of a clock, the toll-
> ing of a bell, at a destined hour.

Mazzini's conception of fate as a "means of reconsecrating the theater"[63] underlies *La Esmeralda*, and, like chance in the melodramas of
the 1830s and 1840s, Hugo's idea of fate is distinguished by its having
"set aside all traces of chance, arbitrariness, and banality" and become
"the manifestation of necessity."[64] The overall significance of the nu-

62. See Thiergard, *Schicksalstragödie als Schauerliteratur,* esp. 76–81; and Werner, *Die
Schicksalstragödie und das Theater der Romantik,* esp. 13.

63. "[la] fatalità considerata come elemento nel Dramma"; "Dramma della Prov-
videnza"; "la libertà umana è immolata ... alla influenza irresistibile d'una condanna
scritta in cielo, che veglia sull'uomo, ne determina gli atti, lo trascina fra la colpa e il
rimorso in un abisso di perdizione, e s'adempie fatalmente allo scoccare d'un oriuolo, al
tocco di una campana, in un'ora determinata"; "Destino ... riconsecratore delle scene."
Della Fatalità considerata come elemento nel Dramma, in *Scritti,* 8:167–200 (pp. 196; 173).

64. Strieder, *Melodramatik und Sozialkritik in Werken Eugène Sues,* 86–87.

merous coincidences is that they come to deny the random nature of chance: chances like that cannot be accidental.

In fact, Scribe's librettos, full of rationalizing and realistic detail as they are, also resolve their plots in a similar fashion, even if the word *fatalité* itself is never spoken there. Whether it is the lover killed by his mistress's jealous husband immediately after taking the decision to renounce her, as in Auber's *Gustave III*, or the daughter shot on her father's orders, as in *Les Huguenots*, or the Cardinal discovering too late that the heretic over whose execution he has just presided was his long-lost daughter, as in *La Juive*, or the Governor of Sicily unwittingly giving the signal for the start of a massacre by the act that he intends to be a symbol of reconciliation, as in *Les Vêpres siciliennes:* in all these cases well-meaning people are prevented from attaining the "happy end" that is almost within their grasp by the entanglements of a fate they cannot grasp.

These are extreme examples of a dramaturgical device which is used in most nineteenth-century operas—in Verdi's *Forza del destino* and in Massenet's *Manon* alike—and still colors our conception of a typical operatic plot. With irresolute protagonists who are ultimately incapable of guilt, an omnipresent fate takes the place of human responsibility and thus allows opera to preserve the semblance of tragedy, to the social standing of which it was to make an ever stronger claim as the century progressed. Simultaneously, it created opportunities of identification for a public which found itself robbed of every certain orientation in the face of rapid economic and social changes. As Richard Sennett has described, the ideas middle-class people involved in trade and industry in the nineteenth century formed of the mechanisms of economic developments were hazier than we can easily conceive today. In a situation in which preindustrial concepts lived on, in which rumors took the place of sure information, and in which the absence of independent control mechanisms left the doors of stock exchanges and other institutions wide open to all kinds of fraudulent manipulation, it was impossible for those who had to make investment decisions to do so according to rational criteria. It was not economic life alone that was a game of chance: Balzac described Paris itself as "the capital of risk."[65] Sennett says of the trading and administrative class that

> those who experienced this new system . . . did not understand it very well . . . But the way in which they tended to misunderstand the industrial

65. "la capitale du hasard"; *Les Illusions perdues* [1839], in *La Comédie humaine*, 5:123–732 (p. 626).

order is important, for it reveals a fundamental view of industrial life which conditioned all attitudes towards the public realm: this was that bourgeois respectability was founded on chance.[66]

"At the historical moment when the world was rid of the gods once and for all," in the words of Erich Köhler, chance—in opera, chance transfigured by music—erected "the bridge between the individual and the general."[67] As a result, the chance kindling of romantic love between two individuals was elevated to an imperative beyond the reach of rational reflection,[68] and in cases of doubt every twist in the plot could be explained by the power of fate. By 1864, the idea was hackneyed enough for Meilhac, Halévy, and Offenbach to mock it in *La belle Hélène:*

> HÉLÈNE
> Taisez-vous . . . taisez-vous! . . . car, si cela était . . .
>
> CALCHAS
> Eh bien! reine? . . .
>
> HÉLÈNE
> Elle! . . . toujours elle! . . .
>
> CALCHAS
> Qui, elle?
>
> HÉLÈNE
> La main de la fatalité, qui pèse sur moi!
> (*La belle Hélène*, Acte I, scène 5)

> HÉLÈNE: Be silent, be silent! For, if it was . . .
> CALCHAS: Well, what, Ma'am?
> HÉLÈNE: She! Always she!
> CALCHAS: She! Who?
> HÉLÈNE: Fate! The hand of Fate, weighing upon me!

With hindsight, it is hardly less absurd when Adèle Hugo, in her official biography of her husband, attributes the failure of *La Esmeralda* to the working of fate. She does not appear to intend to be ironic but rather provides an ultimate example of "popular-metaphysical"[69] faith in its power:

> The novel was founded on the word *ananké*, the opera finished with the word *fatalité*. The first stroke of fate was the annihilation of a work that

66. *The Fall of Public Man*, 138.
67. *Der literarische Zufall*, 19, 22.
68. Luhmann, *Liebe als Passion*, 181.
69. Jauß, *Das Ende der Kunstperiode*, 128.

had Monsieur Nourrit and Mademoiselle Falcon as singers, music by a woman of great talent, a libretto by Monsieur Victor Hugo, and Notre-Dame de Paris as its subject. Then fate laid its finger on the actors: Mademoiselle Falcon lost her voice; Monsieur Nourrit went to Italy and killed himself. A ship called Esmeralda, crossing from England to Ireland, went down with all hands. The Duke of Orléans called a valuable mare Esmeralda: she collided with another horse at the gallop during a steeplechase, and her skull was crushed.[70]

Perhaps it was all for the best that the illustrious poet never worked in the opera house again.

70. "Le roman est fait sur le mot ananké; l'opéra finit par le mot fatalité. Ce fut une première fatalité que cet écrasement d'un ouvrage qui avait pour chanteurs M. Nourrit et mademoiselle Falcon, pour musicienne une femme de grand talent, pour librettiste M. Victor Hugo et pour sujet Notre-Dame de Paris. La fatalité s'attacha aux acteurs. Mademoiselle Falcon perdit sa voix; M. Nourrit alla se tuer en Italie. – Un navire appelé Esmeralda, faisant la traversée d'Angleterre en Irlande, se perdit corps et biens. – Le duc d'Orléans avait nommé Esmeralda une jument de grand prix; dans une course au clocher, elle se rencontra avec un cheval au galop et eut la tête fracassée." *Victor Hugo raconté par un témoin de sa vie*, 2:440–41.

∽ 7 ∽

MEYERBEER
AND REACTION

LE PROPHÈTE

TEXT
Eugène Scribe (1791–1861)

MUSIC
Giacomo Meyerbeer (1791–1864)

FIRST PERFORMANCE
Paris, Opéra—Théâtre de la Nation, 16 April 1849

PLACE AND DATE OF THE ACTION
Holland and Westphalia, 1530

CHARACTERS
Jean de Leyde [John of Leyden] (tenor); Zacharie (bass); Jonas (tenor);
Mathisen (bass); Count Oberthal (bass); a sergeant (tenor); two peasants (tenor
and bass); a soldier (tenor); two citizens of Munster (tenor and bass); Fidès
(mezzo-soprano); Berthe (soprano); two choirboys (treble and alto)

SYNOPSIS

ACT I

A meadow beside the Meuse, near Dordrecht; in the background, Count
Oberthal's castle. Peasants and millhands prepare to eat in the open air (No. 1.
Prélude et choeur pastoral, "La brise est muette! . . ."). Berthe looks forward to
seeing her lover, Jean (No. 1bis. *Cavatine*, "Mon coeur s'élance et palpite").
Jean's mother, Fidès, has made the preparations for celebrating their engagement: the only thing outstanding is the permission of Berthe's feudal lord (No.
2. *Scène*, "Fidès, ma bonne mère"). Three Anabaptists, Jonas, Mathisen, and
Zacharie, appear in the background, preaching the overthrow of the feudal system, but when Oberthal shows himself, the peasants lose courage and the Anab-

aptists are driven off by the Count's soldiers (No. 3. *Le prêche anabaptiste*, "Ad nos, ad salutarem undam"). Although the two women tell the moving tale of how Jean saved Berthe from drowning (No. 4. *Romance à deux voix*, "Un jour, dans les flots de la Meuse"), Oberthal refuses to consent to the marriage and has the two women dragged off to his castle; helpless and angry, the peasants take flight, while the three Anabaptists reappear (No. 5. *Récitatif et final*, "Eh quoi! tant de candeur" / "O nouvelle infamie!").

ACT II

Inside Jean's inn in the suburbs of Leyden. While his customers make merry to the strains of a waltz, Jean waits longingly for Berthe; the three Anabaptists are startled by his resemblance to a painting of King David which is venerated in Westphalia (No. 6. *Valse villageoise*, "Valsons toujours"). They engage Jean in conversation, and he readily tells them of a dream in which he was honored as a messiah but then cursed by God (No. 7. *Le songe*, "Ami, quel nuage obscurcit ta pensée?" / "Sous les vastes arceaux"). This convinces the Anabaptists that they have found in Jean the charismatic leader they need for their mission, but he refuses their request, for he wants nothing more than to live in modest contentment with Berthe (No. 8. *Pastorale*, "Pour Bertha, moi, je soupire"). Then Berthe rushes in, having escaped, and hides from her pursuers; hot on her heels, Oberthal enters and threatens Jean that his mother will be killed if he does not hand Berthe over; furiously, Jean hurls his betrothed into the tyrant's arms (No. 9. *Scène et morceau d'ensemble*, "Ils partent, grâce au ciel!" / "Ah! d'effroi je tremble encore"). Fidès blesses her son for his decision (No. 10. *Arioso*, "Ah! mon fils, sois béni!"), but he wants to be alone. In his thirst for revenge he is ready to take up the offer of the Anabaptists who now return; they regard him as God's elect, but insist on the condition that he renounce all earthly ties and follow them without taking leave of his mother, to which Jean agrees only after long hesitation (No. 11. *Scène et quatuor*, "O fureur! le ciel ne tonne pas sur ces têtes impies!" / "Gémissant sous le joug et sous la tyrannie").

ACT III

The Anabaptist camp in Westphalia, with a frozen lake in the background. The Anabaptist army has won significant victories under Jean's leadership, and now the fanatical soldiers demand the blood of their prisoners (No. 12. *Entr'acte et choeur des anabaptistes*, "Du sang! que Judas succombe!"). They are pacified when Zacharie tells them of the victorious outcome of another expedition (No. 13. *Couplets de Zacharie*, "Aussi nombreux que les étoiles"). Country people arrive on skates with provisions for the hungry army (No. 14. *L'arrivée des patineurs*, "Voici les fermières") and entertain the troops with peasant dances (No. 15. *Ballet*). Mathisen and Zacharie are discussing the imminent attack on Münster when they notice a stranger prowling nearby. He claims to want to join their army and swears obedience to the Anabaptists, before Jonas recognizes him in the candlelight as Oberthal, their hated enemy (No. 16. *Trio bouffe*, "Sous votre bannière"). They are about to execute him when Jean, sickened by the incessant atrocities of his comrades-in-arms, reprieves the prisoner and abides by the decision even when he recognizes him. Oberthal tells him that Berthe escaped again and has been seen in Münster. On hearing this Jean, who a moment earlier was ready to lay down his leadership of the Anabaptists, is eager to take the city. Without his knowledge Mathisen has already led one attack which was repulsed; the disappointed soldiers mutiny against Mathisen (No. 17. *Choeur des soldats révoltés,* "Par toi, Munster nous fut promis"), but Jean brings them under control (No. 18. *Scène,* "Qui vous a, sans mon ordre, entraînés aux combats?"), prays for divine assistance (No. 19. *Prière,* "Éternel, Dieu sauveur"), and leads the troops into battle with a song of triumph (No. 20. *Hymne triomphal,* "Roi du ciel et des anges").

ACT IV

First setting: a square outside Münster city hall. The Anabaptists have taken the city and demand the citizens' money; the citizens sing the praises of the Anabaptist prophet, but only from fear, and in their hearts they curse him (No. 21. *Entr'acte et choeur des bourgeois,* "Courbons notre tête!"). Fidès has also come to Münster and begs for her bread (No. 22. *Complainte de la mendiante,* "Donnez pour une pauvre âme"). She is amazed to meet Berthe and tells her that Jean, too, has been killed by the prophet; Berthe decides to avenge her lover and starts to lay plans to free the land from the tyrant (No. 23. *Scène et duo,* "Un pauvre pélerin! . . ." / "Pour garder à ton fils").

Second setting: inside Münster cathedral. Jean is conducted to the altar in a grand procession (No. 24. *Marche du sacre*). The Anabaptists pray for their leader, while Fidès curses the false prophet (No. 25a. *Final—Prière et imprécation.* "Domine, salvum fac regem"). Jean has just been crowned king and the people are singing in his honor (No. 25b. *Choeur d'enfants et choeur général,* "Le voilà, le roi prophète!") when Fidès recognizes her son and cries out to him. In spite of her protestations, Jean professes not to know her while the Anabaptists threaten to kill her if he allows the myth of his divine birth to be destroyed (No. 25c. *Couplets et morceau d'ensemble,* "Qui je suis?" / "Qu'entends-je? ô ciel!"). The people begin to doubt Jean's mission, so he forces Fidès to take back her claim by commanding his companions to kill him if he has lied. The scene ends with a chorus of praise for his healing of a madwoman (No. 25d. *L'exorcisme,* "Tu chérissais ce fils").

ACT V

First setting: a vaulted underground chamber in Münster castle. The city is under siege by imperial troops and the three Anabaptists decide to accept the offer of buying their own freedom by betraying Jean (No. 26. *Entr'acte et scène,* "Ainsi vous l'attestez?"). Fidès, realizing now that Jean is the target of Berthe's plan to assassinate the prophet, has found a way to reach him and sways between anger at his treatment of herself and her unconditional, maternal love for him (No. 27. *Scène, cavatine et air,* "O prêtres de Baal" / "O toi qui m'abandonnes!" / "Comme un éclair précipité"). When Jean appears she forces him to kneel and ask her forgiveness, and promise to give up the power he has usurped (No. 28. *Scène et grand duo,* "Ma mère!" / "Mais toi, qu'on déteste, tyran"). Berthe, who plans to set fire to the castle in order to slay the prophet, finds them and all three dream of fleeing to start a new life; but the foe is at the gate, and when Jean is told of the betrayal Berthe at last understands that he is in fact the hated prophet; she curses him and, to punish herself for loving him still, kills herself (No. 29. *Scène et trio*, "Voici le souterrain!" / "Loin de la ville"). Seeing all his hopes dashed, Jean decides to stay and punish his betrayers; he tells his mother to save herself.

Second setting: the grand hall in the castle. While the Anabaptists celebrate Jean's coronation in a bacchanalian orgy and girls perform lascivious dances (No. 30a. *Final — Bacchanale, Choeur dansé*, "Hourra! hourra!"), Jean gives orders for an iron gate to be closed at a given moment and the castle to be blown up, so that his betrayers and the imperial army will all perish with him. He sings a song in praise of drunkenness, which is interrupted by the arrival of the conquering army, led by Oberthal, and by an immense explosion. Jean dies as the castle collapses around him, and Fidès manages to force her way through the ruins to die with her son (No. 30b. *Couplets bachiques*, "Versez! que tout respire").

EDITIONS: The full score published by Brandus in Paris in 1849 is available in many libraries in a reprint (*Early Romantic Opera* 21 [New York: Garland, 1978]); the piano-vocal score has been reprinted frequently and is also widely available.

RECOMMENDED RECORDING: The only complete recording is the 1977 studio performance under the direction of Henry Lewis, with James McCracken (Jean), Jerome Hines (Zacharie), Jean Dupouy (Jonas), Christian Du Plessis (Mathisen), Jules Bastin (Oberthal), Marilyn Horne (Fidès), and Renata Scotto (Berthe). Although the overall conception is less than ideally inspired, and the tenor sometimes audibly struggles with the title role, the performance takes a commendable first shot at a work presenting formidable vocal and technical demands.

A PAMPHLET

Complaints about the state of opera were rife throughout the 1840s. The sensational success of the first grands opéras of Rossini, Auber, and Meyerbeer was scarcely matched by any of the new productions that had followed them, and at the same time the standard repertory had shrunk to a few works which were performed repeatedly. As early as August 1840, the Opéra's business manager confessed to the banker Aguado, who had sunk a considerable amount of capital into the institution as the business partner of the then director, Duponchel, that there was no disguising the fact that the repertory was growing exceedingly old.[1] It was indeed the case that after *Les Huguenots* Donizetti's *Favorite*

---

1. "On ne peut se dissimuler cependant que le répertoire devient excessivement vieux"; letter from Gile La Baume to Alexandre-Marie Aguado, Marquis de la Marismas, 23 August 1840, cited in Montmorency, *Lettres sur l'Opéra*, 16.

(1840) was the only work to enter the charmed circle of operas that were revived year after year, like *La Muette de Portici, Guillaume Tell, Robert le diable*, and *La Juive*.

The other works that Donizetti composed for the Opéra, *Les Martyrs* (1840) and *Dom Sébastien, roi de Portugal* (1843), both disappeared from the repertory after one season, in spite of the fact that, with librettos by Scribe, they were much closer in spirit to grand opéra than *La Favorite*, which was originally conceived for the Théâtre de la Renaissance. Halévy's *Reine de Chypre* (1841) and *Charles VI* (1843), two historical costume dramas, were both reasonably successful, but there was no denying that, indebted as they were to the formal conventions of Italian opera and lacking a catastrophe to end with, they came nowhere near rivaling the spectacular popularity of *La Juive*, his first grand opéra.

After *La Muette*, Auber had concentrated his efforts exclusively on opéra comique, and enjoyed several successes in that genre during the 1840s. Berlioz, still hoping for a breakthrough in the opera house, worked on *La Nonne sanglante* but gave it up in the face of the Opéra management's delaying tactics: in the end the libretto—yet another by Scribe—was composed by Gounod and reached the stage in 1854. The hope that Rossini would ever compose for the theater again had been abandoned after ten years of silence, and the Opéra management turned to having his early Italian works adapted for Parisian circumstances. But the moderate success of *Otello* (1844) and the pasticcio *Robert Bruce*, pieced together from a number of different sources (1846), convinced even the greatest optimists that Parisian audiences in the 1840s were not to be fobbed off with musico-dramatic techniques of the 1820s.

No wonder, then, that the following caustic verdict was passed in 1844: "The Opéra was bashful under La Rochefoucauld, splendid under Véron, brilliant under Duponchel. . . .What is it today? Moribund."[2] The reason for this desperate situation, however, was the fact that no new opera by Meyerbeer had been presented since the overwhelming success of *Les Huguenots*. True, he and Scribe had thought about a new historical opera before his second opera for Paris had even been premièred: the earliest prose sketch for *Le Prophète* in Scribe's notebook can be dated to December 1835.[3] After some hesitation Meyerbeer decided

2. "L'Opéra fut pudique sous La Rochefoucauld, splendide sous Véron, brillant sous Duponchel. . . . Qu'est il aujourd'hui? Cadavéreux." Arago, *Mémoires d'un petit banc de l'Opéra*, 237.

3. See "Le Prophète, opéra en cinq actes. Plan," in Eugène Scribe, "Vademecum ou Brouillon et plans de pièces" [May 1833 to March 1836] (F-Pn, n.a.f. 22562), fols. 663–70;

in 1838 to concentrate on *Le Prophète* rather than *L'Africaine*, and he worked on it exclusively during 1839 and 1840. He had a provisional full score ready by March 1841, when he deposited it with a Paris lawyer in fulfillment of his contractual obligation to Scribe.[4] *Le Prophète* should then have taken its place in the schedule of works due for production, but Meyerbeer stubbornly refused to allow it to happen, because he wanted Pauline Viardot, and no one else, to sing the role of Fidès with its very low tessitura, whereas the new director of the Opéra, Léon Pillet, was determined that the role should go to his mistress, Rosine Stoltz. Stoltz had earlier sung Valentine in *Les Huguenots*, however, in which role, in Meyerbeer's opinion, she had been "beneath criticism."[5] Time passed, as Pillet tried to pressure Meyerbeer by means of contractual deadlines, while Meyerbeer gambled on Pillet's being forced to capitulate unconditionally, sooner or later, and probably regarded the delay as an opportunity to revise the opera thoroughly at his leisure.

Eventually any trust in the relationship between Meyerbeer, Scribe, and Pillet was completely destroyed, and it was clear that *Le Prophète* would not be put on until the Opéra had a new director. Only in August 1847, when the process enforcing Pillet's resignation was in train, was the way clear at last for the opera, eagerly awaited by all Paris, to go into production. But in the interval Meyerbeer had formed a habit of revising new works thoroughly, and that he now proceded to do. He also insisted on a prolonged period of rehearsals, and as a result the première of *Le Prophète* did not take place until 16 April 1849.

These exceptional delays had the fortuitous consequence of giving the opera's theme, the rise and fall of a social revolutionary movement, an immediately contemporary relevance that the authors could not have foreseen when they began planning it thirteen years earlier. It was true that the frequent hunger riots in Lyon and Paris in the early years of the July Monarchy had established that thenceforth the target of any new unrest would be the bourgeoisie, who would no longer have the opportunity to exploit insurrection for their own interests, as they had

---

this manuscript is very hard to read and there is a paraphrase version in Armstrong, "Meyerbeer's *Le Prophète*," 424–38. The date at which Meyerbeer and Scribe started to plan the opera is arrived at by correlating Scribe's "plan" with the note dated 15 October 1835 in the same manuscript (fol. 629) and the entry "Scribe. Market scene, opera plan" in Meyerbeer's pocket-diary for December 1835 (*Briefwechsel*, 2:491). Armstrong (5, n. 1) dates the conclusion of Scribe's prose sketch to March 1836.

4. See Meyerbeer's diary, 25 March 1841, *Briefwechsel*, 3:343.

5. "unter aller Kritik." See Meyerbeer's letters to his wife Minna, early January 1838 and 7 June 1838, ibid., 82, 130.

in July 1830. But nobody could have reckoned on the fact that *Le Prophète* would reach the stage in the uneasy situation following the fall of the Citizen King, Louis-Philippe, in February 1848, or that the fear of desperate action by the dispossessed, which had already left its mark on operatic subject matter, would cease to be an abstract premonition and become an illustration of the class differences between the poor and the rich that had erupted in the revolution of May 1848 and its bloody suppression. An anonymous critic who attended the first performance of *Le Prophète* expressed the surprise of many when he asked: "It is ten years since Scribe wrote the libretto: is he, too, a prophet?"[6]

The opera's depiction of the Anabaptists who set up a short-lived "kingdom" in sixteenth-century Münster may have been historically inauthentic, but it gave a very close likeness of the revolutionary bogymen who swarmed in the imaginations of well-to-do Parisians in the late 1840s: so much so that nearly all the critics reacted as if the work had actually been influenced by recent events. Many assumed, then and since, that Scribe and Meyerbeer adapted their conception to the altered circumstances following the events of 1848.[7] However, Alan Armstrong's study of the genesis of *Le Prophète* includes a survey of the numerous draft versions of the libretto, not all of which can be dated with certainty, and this indicates that the revisions concerned primarily the psychological nuances of the triangular relationship of Jean, Fidès, and Berthe, while the representation of the Anabaptists and the masses was scarcely altered at all.[8] Alexandre Dumas *père* was less certain of the assumption than some, but commented that "the subject of the libretto seems expressly chosen for the preoccupations of the present time. The hero is the king of these Anabaptists whose political doctrines offer so many resemblances to those of our own communists."[9] The general impression was summed up in a newspaper review by Théophile Gautier, who likened Meyerbeer's three French operas to the "three principal phases of the human spirit," associating the latest with visionary utopianism: "Each of these ideas has assumed the form necessary to make

6. "Il y a pourtant dix ans que Scribe a composé ce poème. Serait-il prophète, lui aussi?" *La Gazette de France*, 19 April 1849; cited in Coudroy, *La Critique parisienne*, pt. 2, p. 28.

7. See Coudroy for one, ibid., 31–32; and Asholt, "Ein Sonnenuntergang, der zum 'Vorschein' wird."

8. See Armstrong, "Meyerbeer's *Le Prophète*."

9. "Le sujet du livret . . . semble choisi exprès pour les préoccupations du moment. Le héros de la pièce est le roi de ces anabaptistes, dont les doctrines politiques offrent tant de ressemblance avec celles de nos communistes"; *Le Mois*, 1 May 1849, p. 160; cited in Coudroy, *La Critique parisienne*, pt. 2, p. 29.

itself visible: *Robert le diable* the fairy tale, *Les Huguenots* the chronicle, *Le Prophète* the pamphlet."

To Gautier, the pamphleteering was obvious: "The Anabaptists and the peasants have dialogue that one could well believe tailored in the prose of the communist papers."[10] The authors of this "pamphlet" made their meaning clear not only in the words of the libretto but also in the structure of the opera as a whole: the revolutionary leaders are brought on stage in Act I before the action has shown any reason for revolution; the curtain rises on a pastoral idyll and it is the entrance of the three Anabaptist fanatics, preaching hatred of the feudal lord, that disturbs it first, before Oberthal provides an example of willful tyranny in refusing Berthe leave to marry. In representing the Anabaptists in this way, the opera certainly fell in with the way the wind started to blow in 1848–49, as the Paris correspondent of a German newspaper concluded: "The activities of these sixteenth-century socialists, as people here like to call the Anabaptists, their burning and killing, their murdering and thieving, their polygamy and immorality, paint a timely picture of what we might expect from a victory of modern socialism."[11]

Meyerbeer would probably have protested against the impression that his opera acknowledged the tendentious desires of a frightened public. Privately he justified the opera's reactionary perspective a good decade before it was performed by referring to the difficulties that might arise with the censor:

> There are two pitfalls we must avoid. One is preaching revolution against all governmental and religious authority, followed by complete success up until the last scene. That could perhaps cause difficulties for a production of the piece in Paris, but it would certainly get it banned everywhere in Germany and northern Europe. We ought to counterbalance this revolutionary tendency in the piece by giving one of the characters (and I think it should be the old mother) a love of the existing order of things, of their legitimate princes, and above all of religion. She would spell out

10. "trois phases principales de l'esprit humain"; "Pour se rendre visible, chacune de ces idées a pris sa forme nécessaire: Robert le Diable, le conte bleu; les Huguenots, la chronique; le Prophète, le pamphlet"; "les anabaptistes et les paysans ont des dialogues qu'on pourrait croire taillés dans la prose des journaux communistes"; "Théâtre de la Nation, *Le Prophète*," *La Presse*, 23 April 1849; cited in Gautier, *Histoire de l'art dramatique en France*, 6:80–92 (p. 82).

11. "Das Thun und Treiben dieser Socialisten des 16ten Jahrhunderts, wie man hierzulande gern die Anabaptisten nennt, ihr Sengen und Brennen, Mord- und Raublust, Vielweiberei und Sittenschänderei gibt ein erwünschtes Bild von dem, was wir von einem Sieg des heutigen Socialismus zu erwarten haben dürften"; *Augsburger Allgemeine Zeitung*, 24 April 1849, p. 1735; cited in Meyerbeer, *Briefwechsel*, 4:633.

these maxims to her son Jean, whom she sees inclining to the Anabaptists' ideas, pointing out to him the danger of such ideas, which would subvert all order and morality.[12]

But the wording betrays that Meyerbeer's position is only neutral on the surface. He talks of "governmental and religious authority," not of the abuse of power; of "order and morality," not of tyranny, whereas the feudal lord Oberthal behaves like a cynical tyrant in the opening acts of the opera. The pusillanimous citizens of Münster, too, are depicted as shabby opportunists in their chorus in Act IV, so that the pamphleteering character of this apparently apolitical opera is not directed exclusively against the "communist" Anabaptists, but against all parties. Yet behind the "unpolitical spirit" from which Carl Dahlhaus claims that this opera was born,[13] it is only too easy to discern the perspective of the "happy medium" already found in *Les Huguenots*, the comforting illusion that a position opposed to politics is not a political position. As Meyerbeer's own comment reveals, his antipolitical stance amounts to no more than approving the status quo.

Meyerbeer's reactionary attitude was shared by most of his audiences. Only people who regard politics as a "grubby business" can sit back and enjoy it as a stage spectacle. And only people who think they live their lives outside politics can develop a passive form of receptiveness that might seem characteristic of late twentieth-century society, which receives so much via television screens, but is already foreshadowed in Meyerbeer's reaction to the first of the revolutions of 1848, that of February, as reflected in his diary. Having recorded the start of "serious unrest in Paris" on 22 February, the next day he occupied himself with the stretta of the *Prêche anabaptiste* in Act I, in which the agitators incite the peasants to join in the armed struggle.

Worked with fairly good results on the new stretta for the *Prêche* in Act I. Spent the rest of the day on the street, to observe the course of the

---

12. "Il y'a deux écueils qu'il faut tâcher d'éviter. L'un, c'est la prédication à la révolte contre toute autorité gouvernementale et religieuse, suivi d'un plein succès jusqu'à la dernière scène de la pièce. Ceci pourrait faire naître peut-être des difficultés pour la représentation de la pièce à Paris, mais à coup sûr elle serait défendue dans toute l'Allemagne et les pays du Nord. Il faudrait contrebalancer cette tendance révolutionnaire de la pièce, en donnant à un personnage de la pièce (et je crois que cela devrait être la vieille mère) l'amour de l'ordre existant des choses, de leurs princes légitimes et surtout de sa religion. Elle préciserait ces maximes à son fils Jean qu'elle voit enclin aux idées des anabaptistes, en lui montrant le danger de ces idées subversives de tout ordre et morale." F-Pn, n.a.f. 22504, fol. 37. Armstrong dates this manuscript to October 1838 ("Meyerbeer's *Le Prophète*," 24–25).

13. *Realism in Nineteenth-Century Music*, 83.

unrest. The National Guard declared itself in favor of electoral reform and prevented the regular troops from pitching into the people. Toward midday news spreads that the King has dismissed the Guizot administration and consents to electoral reform. Great rejoicing: all seems to have ended well. In the evening however the show starts up again. Outside the Foreign Ministry the military fire on the crowd and take many lives. As yet I haven't heard what the cause of it was. Dinner and soirée at Vatel's, the director of the Italian Opera. (23 February 1848)[14]

So much for the death of more than fifty demonstrators in a hail of bullets fired by troops loyal to the King: to the bystander who goes out to "observe" it, it is just a "show." (He will also spend "almost all day on the street" on the following day, 24 February, "to join others watching the course of the insurrection.") He shows no interest at all in the deeper causes of the uprising, and his curiosity as to the reason for the massacre gives way to a need to mention the dinner party at the house of a man who runs a theater. The difference between theatrical imagining and bloody reality is blurred in a way anticipating the attitude of present-day consumers who do not distinguish between television images of political reality and the fictional horrors of feature films, and are not put off their food, however dreadful the sights on the screen.

The ordinary people of Paris, already depicted as an easily led crowd in *Les Huguenots*, lose their remaining shreds of dignity and autonomy in the complacent cosmopolitan's perception of them. At least Scribe and Meyerbeer showed the crowd in *Les Huguenots* working themselves up into a murderous frenzy of their own accord, once their leaders had kindled their enthusiasm. In Act I of *Le Prophète*, on the other hand, they do not even have the courage to stand up to a handful of their feudal lord's soldiers: the stretta, which Meyerbeer wrote out in full after the February Revolution came to a successful conclusion on 27 February,[15] is followed by a stage direction: "Count Oberthal comes down

14. "Mit ziemlich gutem Erfolg an der neuen Stretta der Prêche im 1. Akt gearbeitet. Den übrigen Teil des Tages auf der Straße zugebracht, den Gang der Unruhen zu beobachten. Die Nationalgarde erklärt sich ebenfalls für die Wahlreform und verhindert die Linientruppen, auf das Volk einzuhauen. Gegen Mittag verbreitet sich die Nachricht, daß der König das Ministerium Guizot abgedankt habe und die Wahlreform bewillige. Großer Jubel: alles scheint glücklich beendiget. Abends aber geht das Spektakel wieder los. Vor dem Ministère des affaires étrangères feuert das Militär auf das Volk, und viele Opfer fallen. Was dazu Veranlassung gegeben hat, weiß ich bis jetzt nicht. Diner & Soirée bei Vatel, dem Direktor der italienischen Oper." This and other excerpts from Meyerbeer's diary, 22–27 February 1848, are to be found in Meyerbeer, *Briefwechsel*, 4:366–69.

15. On the relation that this stretta bears to earlier versions of the final scene of Act I, see Armstrong, "Meyerbeer's *Le Prophète*," 256–61.

from the castle followed by gentlemen and guards. At the sight of him the peasants draw back in fear" *(Le Comte d'Oberthal descend du château suivi de seigneurs et de gardes. A son aspect les paysans reculent effrayés).* Here, then, the insurrection is merely the work of a few criminal ringleaders, who unscrupulously exploit sheeplike crowds and the naive eponymous hero.

The insurrection they start will not be successful, however, unless the social wrongs are supplemented by motives that will have more effect on an "apolitical" observer than any of the things whose causes do not interest him. It takes until the end of Act II before the exposition has unrolled far enough for Jean's career as a revolutionary to begin. After one last return to his sentimental self, Jean lets the Anabaptists persuade him to assume the role of their prophet. The complexities of the private, sentimental intrigue receive far greater weight, therefore, than in any other grand opéra, and consequently Scribe and Meyerbeer spread their development over the first two acts, at the same time that they establish the historical circumstances. For an exposition to occupy two full acts in this way is most unusual. Meyerbeer acknowledged as much in making the final chorus of Act I very short, and in having the following stage direction inserted in the published full score: "The scene changes in full view, and the curtain does not fall" *(Le théâtre change à vue et la toile ne tombe pas).*

The reason for devoting two acts to the exposition is therefore "to expound both the historical social conditions of the Anabaptist movement and the personal relationships of the invented characters in terms specific to the opera," as Christhard Frese wrote in his study of Meyerbeer's dramaturgy.[16] Certainly the dashing of Berthe and Jean's hopes of happiness occupies far more space than the impossible love affair in *Les Huguenots*, the telling of which in Raoul's *romance* is, at the end of the first act, still no more than a highlight in the hubbub of the banquet. To say that is to grasp only one aspect of the unusual dramatic structure of *Le Prophète*, however, for the extraordinary fact that the title-hero, Jean, does not appear until the second act cannot be explained by the purely technical necessities imposed by the insertion of a private intrigue, without historical basis, into an outwardly political action.[17]

The exposition unfolded in these two acts concerns both the private relationships and the political action. Jean is spoken of from the first. At the start of the very first recitative Fidès refers to her son by name,

16. *Dramaturgie der großen Opern Giacomo Meyerbeers*, 172.
17. See Dahlhaus, *Realism in Nineteenth-Century Music*, 83.

declaring that he awaits his fiancée with more ardor than ever ("Et Jean, mon fils, attend plus ardemment encore sa fiancée"). He is not present but he is central to the private action in Act I. His mother has come to fetch Berthe to him, and the two women work together to try to persuade Count Oberthal to forgo his feudal rights over the younger. They tell him of how Jean pulled Berthe out of the river in the *Romance à deux voix*, "Un jour, dans les flots de la Meuse." Berthe's words in the refrain, however, do not take a form as straightforward as, perhaps, "Give me leave to marry him," but subtly focus on Jean: "Give me leave to be his wife" ("Ah! mon seigneur, mon doux seigneur, permettez-moi d'être sa femme!").

Tendencies already incipient in *Les Huguenots* are developed further within this remarkable dramaturgical structure: there the "characterless" Raoul was accompanied by an alter ego, Marcel, here Jean is contained and presented in a frame held up by the two women. The protracted delay before he appears on the stage in person also has to do, once again, with the "pamphlet" aspect of *Le Prophète*.

The central difference between the first two acts lies, for the analyst of the dramaturgy, in the absence and presence of Jean, but the audience can hardly fail to notice another, and that is the application of the principle of contrast, a foundation stone of the grand opéra tradition, to whole acts. The first act takes place in the open air, in fields, in an idyllic rural setting; the second in an interior, a room in Jean's inn on the outskirts of Leyden. Meyerbeer underlined the contrast in the music: a "curtain" of string-playing "rises" after 21 bars on a passage for two solo clarinets. The following *Choeur pastorale* (taken from the 1843 divertissement *Das Hoffest von Ferrara*)[18] observes a readily understood convention of setting rural scenes: it shares with the opening chorus of Rossini's *Guillaume Tell* not only the lilting $\frac{3}{8}$ meter and the G major key signature but also a generous measure of open fifths.

The chorus at the start of Act II is a drastic contrast: in spite of the open fifths in the third of its eight-bar segments, in spite of the superficially similar $\frac{3}{8}$ meter, this is no idyll. The whole orchestra, playing $f\!f$ and "heavily" (*lourdement*), launches the *Valse villageoise*. Harmonic disjointedness replaces the stable harmonies of the *Choeur pastoral*; two eight-bar segments in E major are followed abruptly by the third-related A-flat major, before a modulation, via C-sharp minor, back to the home key.

The message is clear: even if the feudal lord abuses his power, the

18. See Meyerbeer's diary, 28 June 1848, *Briefwechsel*, 4:405.

very structure of the rustic life depicted in Act I inclines it toward peace; the only elements to disturb the idyllic balance—the Anabaptist fanatics—can achieve nothing and have to leave at the end. The mere threat of military force is enough to nip the peasants' revolt in the bud. The urban environment, on the other hand, is one where the revolutionary movement can unfurl, and only there can a character like Jean, lacking his mother's "love of the existing order," be imagined to live. The title of the opening number in the act, *Valse villageoise*, seems to contradict this thesis but not very profoundly. The ambience of Jean's dingy tavern obviously has none of the civilization that would justify an adjective like "urban," but it is equally far from the pastoral idyll of Act I. There is one truly anachronistic detail by which Scribe and Meyerbeer reveal precisely where they believe the breeding ground of revolutionary agitation to be. Although this second act of *Le Prophète* is set in quite a small town in the first half of the sixteenth century, the stage direction specifies that the inn is "in the *suburbs* of Leyden" *(dans les faubourgs de la ville de Leyde)*. That word "faubourgs" invokes not only the area in which the "primitive" ways of people who had newly left their villages met and mixed with urban forms of living, but also every contemporary reader of the libretto was certain to associate it with the overpopulated suburbs of Paris, where poorly paid artisans lived in close proximity to those who had nothing.

Perhaps this interpretation seems to place too much emphasis on one detail in the stage directions. Act II is set, after all, in a tavern, and there is a strong case for interpreting the location, along with many other details of the setting, as being taken, first and foremost, from scenes typical of seventeenth-century Dutch genre-painting. But the tavern itself is actually more than just an element of Dutch local color. The historical John of Leyden on whom Jean is based was a tailor (his name was Jan Bockelsen), so Scribe and Meyerbeer knowingly changed his profession, and the change would certainly have helped their audience to relate the setting to actual conditions in Paris: in the big cities of the nineteenth century the tavern, the cafe, the "public house," the "Wirtshaus," was *the* proletarian meeting place,[19] a function that made it feared by the property-owning classes. How great that fear was is illustrated by the fact that "a system of spies was set up" in Paris in the 1840s, "to report on where the little molecules of laborers congregated, in which cafes, at which times."[20] By showing a revolutionary cell, so to speak, on

19. See Schivelbusch, *Das Paradies, der Geschmack und die Vernunft*, 177.
20. Sennett, *The Fall of Public Man*, 214.

the operatic stage, *Le Prophète* increased the tally of works about the fear
of social change that infected the operagoing public, in an age of reaction, and forced itself to the foreground in this startlingly up-to-date
"pamphlet," in defiance of operatic convention.

DREAMS AND VISIONS

Jean's first entrance, in Act II, somewhat resembles Arnold's in *Guillaume Tell*, in that he is singled out for a "close-up" against the background of the noisy crowd in the tavern. He expresses his longing for
Fidès's return in an aside:

> JEAN *remontant le théâtre et regardant vers la porte du fond*
> Le jour baisse et ma mère
> Bientôt sera de retour
> Avec ma fiancée . . . Ma Berthe! ô mon amour!
>   (*Le Prophète*, Acte II, scène 1)

> JEAN (*going upstage and looking toward the rear door*): Daylight is fading
> and my mother will soon be back with my fiancée . . . My Berthe! O my
> love!

Even though he can know nothing of the dramatic events of the first
act, his waiting is presented as distracted and uneasy. His naive A minor
melody above primitive open fifths is "disturbed" in several respects:
first by the Neapolitan sixth chord in the fifth bar, which is quite inappropriate to the simple harmonic language, then with the extreme pro-
longation of the last phrase, "Ma Berthe! ô mon amour!" Instead of filling four bars, as might be expected, added to the preceding twelve in
order to complete a regular period, it is extended to almost four times
the length: fifteen bars, and the stepwise shifts to B-flat major, B major,
and C major disrupt the conventional harmonies and regular metrical
pattern totally.

It is as if, in repeating Berthe's name three times in this extended
conclusion, Jean wants to obliterate the memory of the fact that he
thought of his mother first and only secondly of his allegedly so much
loved and longed-for bride—and to the same tune moreover. The most
important thing, however, is that the musical treatment establishes
Jean's dreamy, undisciplined, and intemperate character. This was something that Meyerbeer had emphasized to Scribe when their plans were
still at an early stage; after outlining the possible trouble the revolutionary theme might cause them with censors, in the comment cited earlier,
he went on to discuss another potential problem:

A second pitfall is the character of Jean, on which the entire success of the piece depends. If he's an impostor he will inspire only disgust; if he becomes an Anabaptist in order to have his revenge, because his beloved has been snatched from him, he will be pardoned but will cease to hold any interest. I think he will have to be an eccentric, prey to dreams and visions, exalted by the Anabaptist doctrines with which he is already acquainted. The peasants he serves with drink in the first scene of the second act will have to mock him, and call him Jean the visionary, dreamer, and so on.[21]

In the completed work, the peasants do not actually laugh at him, and are given only a short ritornello before their exit, while Jean's solo is followed immediately by the three Anabaptists' discussion of his looks. But even without the mockery Jean's "eccentricity" is quite adequately depicted by musical means. It is developed further in the following scene, when Jean is alone with the Anabaptists; the first thing the audience hears from his lips that adds something new to what it already knows from Act I is his narration of a visionary dream he had a few days previously.

The inclusion of visionary scenes in operatic dramaturgy is less revolutionary than one might at first suppose. Even before the Opéra itself was founded, the comédie-ballet *Les Amants magnifiques* by Molière and Lully, first performed in 1670, contained a dream scene,[22] and others occur not only in two of Lully's best-known works, *Atys* (1676) and *Armide* (1686), but also in Rameau's *Dardanus* (1739) and Gossec's *Sabinus* (1773), to name only two of many examples from the eighteenth century.[23] In the first decade of the nineteenth, Le Sueur took this manifestation of the "marvelous" to a new height when he represented the content of the dream itself, in Act IV of his opera *Ossian, ou les Bardes*, in a huge tableau entitled *Le Rêve d'Ossian*, for which the stage was divided into two areas. For the musical treatment of this spectacular scene,

21. "Un autre écueil c'est le personnage de Jean, duquel cependant dépend tout le succès de la pièce. Si c'est un imposteur il n'inspirera que de dégout; s'il se fait anabaptiste par vengeance parce qu'on lui a ravi son amante, on l'excusera mais il n'intéressera pas encore. Je crois qu'il faudrait que ce fût un personnage excentrique, en proie à des rêves, des visions, monté par les doctrines des anabaptistes qu'il connaît déjà. Il faut que les paysans auxquels il sert à boire dans la première scène du second tableau se moquent de lui, l'appellent Jean le visionnaire, l'homme aux rêves, etc." F-Pn, n.a.f. 22504, fol. 37v. On the date of this manuscript, see above, n. 12.

22. See Wood, "Orchestra and spectacle in the *tragédie en musique*," 34.

23. See Garlington, "The Concept of the Marvelous in French and German Opera," 150–51.

however, Le Sueur resorted to the traditional forms of recitative, aria, and chorus, just as Bellini and Donizetti did in the dream narrations of their Italian operas,[24] and as Meyerbeer himself did in the "phantasmagorical apparition" with which he ended *Ein Feldlager in Schlesien*.[25]

Convention continued to dominate the musical means employed to conjure up these visionary dreams until the middle of the nineteenth century, but their content, too, seldom ventured far beyond what could be seen on the operatic stage in other circumstances. Even though this was the very place for the supernatural apparitions sanctioned by the aesthetic concept of the "marvelous," the scenes were always unambiguous and logically constructed, and neither the audience nor the dreamer on the stage needed any further elucidation of their meaning.

Meyerbeer departs from that tradition totally in the representation of Jean's dream, juxtaposing disparate images disconnectedly, and dispensing with the comfortingly familiar convention of the dreamer lying asleep. In having the dreamer recall his dream later, instead of experiencing it directly on the stage, Meyerbeer allows the audience a certain critical detachment and prevents it from identifying, as it inevitably does, with a peaceful sleeper. Jean's vision of being hailed by the people as a messiah can thus be played out in all its hybrid contradictoriness, with the inclusion of an ominous cry warning of disaster ("Malheur à toi!"), leading up to the final stage in which the dreamer sees himself carried away in a torrent of blood to confront God and the Devil, while hearing voices, some cursing him and others pleading for mercy to be shown him. The confused content of the dream is completely incomprehensible both to the Leyden innkeeper, who asks the three Anabaptists to interpret it, and also to the audience, which does not yet know what is to happen later in the opera. In thus departing from every kind of realism, the scene is a milestone in the history of modern music theater, especially as it is the first time in the history of opera that the ego stands quite alone at the center of a dream scene; the perfect realization of the dream moreover demonstrates very similar tendencies to dreams and visions in literature of the same period.[26]

With the loose-jointed form of a dramatic recitative, the harmonic alienation of melodies that return in the corresponding scenes in Act IV, and the vivid contrasts in the orchestration, Meyerbeer achieved a de-

24. See Lippmann, *Vincenzo Bellini und die italienische opera seria*, 17.

25. "fantasmagorische Erscheinung"; Meyerbeer's diary, 19 February 1847, *Briefwechsel*, 4:197.

26. See Bousquet, *Les Thèmes du rêve dans la littérature romantique*, 341.

gree of perfection[27] that does justice both to the disturbing juxtaposition of prophecies of glory and terror, and to the neurotic character
of Jean, which Meyerbeer also underlined elsewhere by alterations to
Scribe's libretto.[28]

Admittedly, in the context of the second act, Meyeerbeer's avant-
garde conception of a psychological representation of the unconscious
loses some of its radical quality: Jean's unusual outpouring is followed
by a two-stanza *Pastorale*, which in several respects negates what has just
preceded it. At the end of the first couplet Jean sings the word "No!"
(Non!) no fewer than fifteen times, in vehement rejection of the Anabaptists' explanation that his dream foretells his coronation as a king.
Obviously, for himself, he wants to forget the disturbing visions, and
invokes his naive feelings for Berthe to help him do so, and the composer, too, seems to want to let the radical recitative of the dream narration be forgotten in the simple harmonies, formal regularity, and attrac-
tive melody of the *Pastorale*. The unprecedented overthrow of every
convention is followed by a strophic song, the musical form used in *Les
Huguenots* for the tenor's first solo.

But in spite of being negated in that way, Jean's dream remains at the
heart of the exposition. His visions not only anticipate the content of
the whole opera, but more importantly they also show us the first step
in the transformation of the naive innkeeper into the megalomaniac
prophet. At this stage, it is still a matter of the confused expression of
his unconscious, and both Scribe and Meyerbeer went to some trouble
to add "realistic" motives for Jean's change of mind during the rest of
Act II, but the effect of this rationalization on every member of the
audience must be that events are inevitably reinforcing a self-fulfilling
prophecy. This focusing of the whole two-act-long exposition on Jean's
dream reveals two tendencies new to grand opéra: the tenor protagonist's entrance solo is not embedded in a choral scene, like Raoul's, but
delivered for the benefit of just three other characters. The anxious interest in the crowd gives way to the nameless fear of unaccountable agitators, and so the individual returns once more to the center of the
dramatic structure. It was not by chance that Meyerbeer and Scribe
changed the original title, *Les Anabaptistes*, to *Le Prophète*. But individuals are no longer the easily read characters of melodrama: the new-style
protagonist breaks away from the norm, destroys all that audiences have

27. Ibid.
28. See Pendle, *Eugène Scribe*, 502–4.

come to expect, and leads them they know not where. The change does not make these characters any more credible human beings than their predecessors in the 1830s, but now the accent falls on their neurotic constitution and their consequent inability to establish mature relationships with other people.

Jean presents spectacular proof of that inability in the scene that comes directly after his *Pastorale*. No sooner have the Anabaptists left him than he hears mounted soldiers riding up to the inn. Even before he sees them, however, Berthe, who has escaped from Oberthal's clutches, throws herself into his arms. Jean hides her behind a curtain, Oberthal enters, commands Jean to hand her over, and threatens to kill his hostage, Fidès, if he does not. But only after the powerless terror of Jean and Berthe and the cold-blooded cynicism of Oberthal have been depicted side by side in a brief ensemble, does Fidès herself appear on the stage. What happens next is dispatched in some 30 seconds of pantomime:

> *(Oberthal remonte le théâtre, ouvre la porte et fait signe d'amener Fidès. Pendant ce temps Berthe, pâle et tremblante, entr'ouvre le rideau. Jean fait un pas vers elle, mais en ce moment on a traîné Fidès à la porte du fond. Elle tombe à genoux en étendant les bras vers son fils, des soldats lèvent la hache sur sa tête, Jean se retourne, l'aperçoit; il pousse un cri, s'élance vers Berthe et la fait passer devant lui, au moment où Oberthal redescend le théâtre.)*
> JEAN *avec fureur en jetant Berthe aux mains des soldats*
> Ah! va-t'en, va-t'en! tu le vois, il le faut! va-t'en!
> *(Les soldats entraînent Berthe; Jean tombe hors de lui sur une chaise, ne regardant pas sa mère et se cachant le visage dans ses mains.)*
> (*Le Prophète*, Acte II, scène 5)

       ℯ   ℯ   ℯ

> *(Oberthal walks upstage, opens the door, and signs for Fidès to be brought in. Meanwhile Berthe, pale and trembling, parts the curtain. Jean takes a step toward her but already Fidès has been dragged to the door upstage. She falls to her knees, holding out her arms to her son, soldiers raise an axe above her head, Jean turns and sees her; he lets out a cry, rushes to Berthe, and pushes her in front of him at the moment when Oberthal returns downstage.)*
> JEAN *(furiously thrusting Berthe into the soldiers' hands):* Ah! Go, go, you see, you must! Go! (*The soldiers drag Berthe away; Jean falls on a chair, beside himself, not looking at his mother and hiding his face in his hands.*)

Fidès blesses her son in an expressive arioso, but he remains silent. At the end of the mother's solo there is another stage direction: "Jean makes a gesture to show his mother that he is calm and inviting her to go to her room and rest. Fidès, worried, hesitates then obeys, withdrawing slowly" (*Jean par un geste indique à sa mère qu'il est calme, et l'invite à se retirer dans sa chambre pour se reposer. Fidès inquiète, hésite, puis obéit, en se retirant lentement*). Only then does Jean give utterance, but after a very short outburst of rage he hears the Anabaptists offstage singing their chorale. He calls out to them, and although the stage direction has specified that their singing was "far off" (*très loin*), they are back onstage in fifteen seconds. Jean gives no sign of the terrible thing that has just happened but asks them very coldly if he will really reign as a king, as he saw in his dream. When the Anabaptists assure him that there is no doubt of it, he is ready to agree even to the extreme conditions Zacharie dictates to him, bidding him consider that he must give up all his earthly ties and will never see his home or his mother again ("Mais, envoyé du ciel, songe bien désormais que tout lien terrestre est brisé pour jamais! Que tu ne verras plus ton foyer ni ta mère!") Then he silently walks out on his sleeping mother, whose life meant more to him than his fiancée such a short time ago, and goes off to fight with the Anabaptists.

It is more than a little difficult, if not impossible, to interpret this train of events, represented exclusively from Jean's point of view, as a consistent sequence of things that depend upon each other, or even connect with each other in a certain logical order. The persecution of innocent Swiss at the end of Act I of *Guillaume Tell* is the natural result of the aggravation of the political confrontation, and the outbreak of open hostility in the finale of Act II of *Les Huguenots* can be understood at least as the unavoidable consequence of unfortunate misunderstandings, once it is accepted that neither party can have any notion whatever of the other party's motives, but the disjointedness of this scene in *Le Prophète* raises a lot of questions. Why does Oberthal threaten to kill his hostage Fidès, but not bring her onto the stage for such a long time? Why does the following, highly dramatic episode take the form of pantomime? Why does Jean hand over his fiancée "furiously" if he really sees no alternative? Why is he then silent, "beside himself," and why does he not even try to get to the bottom of his violent emotions when the Anabaptists return? Why does he tell his mother to go into another room and rest—again in pantomime?

Christhard Frese examined these points in his study of Meyerbeer's dramaturgy. In his view, Meyerbeer's decisions provide additional evidence of the importance of pantomime in the dramaturgy of grand opéra, and the whole sequence can be put down to the primacy of the scenic aspect over the sung text. Jean's silence during Fidès's arioso is a necessary consequence of a situation "which leaves the two characters remaining on stage in similar emotional states, which—rendered in a

duet—would not have been able to avoid the impression of inappropriate talkativeness," and Frese argues that that difficulty was the reason for
postponing the articulation of one character's emotional outburst, while
taking the opportunity in the meantime to portray the personality of
the other, the mother Fidès, in a solo. According to this interpretation,
therefore, Meyerbeer was left with no alternative but to find a theatrically convincing way to delay the "playing-out of the situation," and he
was assisted in that by "the 'melodramatic trick' of exaggerating one
character's state of being beside himself until it is a distraughtness that
leaves him incapable of 'playing' at all."[29]

But even if we accept that a duet in which Jean and Fidès expressed
their similar but not identical emotions, at the musico-dramatic level of
the one in *Les Huguenots*, would necessarily have left "the impression of
inappropriate talkativeness," Meyerbeer could still have given the solo
to Jean—the central character, after all—as an opportunity to reveal his
feelings, with Fidès's reaction limited to a few words in the concluding
bars or as she leaves the stage. And even if he decided to let Fidès express
her feelings at this point, following the precedent he set himself in *Les
Huguenots* of transferring something of his tenor's inner conflicts to
someone close to him, he was still not obliged to leave Jean sitting there
in total silence: a far more obvious course would have been to follow
the version preserved by Scribe in the printed libretto, which provided
for an extended dialogue between the pair. For in the full-score version
Jean's emotional outburst is not postponed until later, as Frese implies:
it is never articulated at all. Meyerbeer cut the invocation of the Furies,
which survives in the printed libretto, to a single line of recitative: "O
rage! heaven does not thunder on these impious heads!" ("Ô fureur! le
ciel ne tonne pas sur ces têtes impies!"). That is not an emotional outburst but a terse bottom line drawn under emotions already experienced.

Precisely the palpable differences between Meyerbeer's score and
Scribe's printed libretto betray that Jean's silence at this critical moment
must have causes going beyond considerations of dramaturgical economy. The absence of any escape from the dreadful situation seems to be
the thing that has struck Jean dumb, but study of the score—and once
again it reveals Meyerbeer diverging from Scribe's libretto—establishes
that this is not the first time he has reacted to something appalling in
silence: "Mute . . . dumbfounded . . . by dread and horror" ("Muet . . .
anéanti . . . d'épouvante et horreur") is how he describes his reaction to

29. Frese, *Dramaturgie der großen Opern Giacomo Meyerbeers*, 167–68.

the visions of his dream. This parallel between his behavior in the real confrontation with Oberthal and in his dream suggests a completely different way of interpreting the pantomime. Jean's speechlessness is not just a new extreme reached in a dramaturgy which represents its heroes as passive but bears all the marks of a nightmare just experienced.

It may at first seem surprising to describe Fidès's solo arioso—a point of repose awkwardly inserted when the logic of the situation calls for an outburst of emotion—as another "vision," but analysis of the music supports it. The swift repetition of chords, *ppp*, and the remote tonality, F-sharp major, already lend it a dream-like quality, far removed from reality. But the F-sharp major, together with the reduction of the ac-companiment to woodwinds at this point, is a direct reminiscence of the point in Jean's dream narration when he tells of a very soft voice praying for mercy for him. In the context of the opera as a whole, it makes sense to recognize that voice as his mother's.

Above all, the extraordinary construction of the preceding scene is best understood from a "dream" perspective. There, too, normal behav-ioral logic has been suspended. It is more than improbable that a despot of Oberthal's type would waste his time bargaining with an underling, when he could achieve his purpose far more quickly by having the house searched. Furthermore his threat to have Fidès killed remains wholly hypothetical so long as she is concealed from the sight of both Jean and the audience. Yet far from demanding proof, Jean is convinced by the mere mention of his mother. And when he actually sees the axe blade poised above Fidès, he is not content to point resignedly to where Berthe is hidden: no, he thrusts her at the soldiers "furiously."

All behavioral logic is subordinated in this scene to the end of render-ing the conflicts raging within Jean, between his close ties to his mother and his love of Berthe, between prophecy and damnation, visible in a brief moment of pantomime. But again, in this nightmarish pantomime, the musical detail can be related to the dream narration: the drumroll and Jean's "Ah! va-t-en!" refer back to the diminished-seventh shape that accompanies the warning cry ("Malheur à toi!") in that. Meyerbeer makes it clear, in these parallels between the two central scenes in Act II, that the second, the "nightmare," simply dramatizes the first inevita-ble step on Jean's path toward carrying out his "divine" mission: if he is to be a false messiah, a "son of God," he must free himself of all earthly ties, and so he first betrays Berthe, then abandons respect for the politi-cal order, and finally denies his mother.

True, in his conscious decisions, Jean still appears to be dependent on others, the plaything of powers outside himself. The dialogues go to some trouble to represent him as someone even less capable of making up his own mind than Raoul. He seems to follow the Anabaptists in Act II only because they promise that he will be able to take revenge on Oberthal if he does. In Act III he seems to give up the idea of leaving his comrades-in-arms only because he learns that Berthe is in the city they are about to storm, and in Act IV he seems to force Fidès to deny that he is her son only because the Anabaptists threaten her life. But if a reading of the libretto could well give the impression that he becomes entangled more or less guiltlessly in a fate beyond his comprehension, at the same time the dream narration in Act II predetermines his actions in a quite different sense. In so conducting himself that one by one all the prophecies of the vision are fulfilled, he carries out to the letter the script already imprinted on his subconscious when he embarks on his first solo. This is the version of Jean's doubly predetermined course that impresses the listener in the opera house: the pedantic details of the rationalizing dialogue never stand out clearly in the flow of simple recitative, and vanish from sight altogether beside the impressive musical realization of the dream narration. Thus the revolutionary quality of what Meyerbeer himself called "the best score I've done in my life"[30] lies not least in drawing attention so spectacularly to the determining power of the unconscious.

MEMORY

The power of the unconscious in *Le Prophète* can also be viewed from the contrary point of view: if Jean's future journey toward disaster is already presaged in his dream, so too the moments at which the prophecies are fulfilled must be able to be referred back to the dream. Meyerbeer points up this indissoluble connection by including two melodies in Jean's dream that represent the events of Act IV. Admittedly the idea of doing so did not occur to him until he was working on the final revision, as the entry in his diary for 14 July 1848 reveals: "I had a good idea in the bath, of using the theme of the *Choeur d'enfants* (in the Act IV coronation) for the dream in Act II, and I revised a large part of the dream accordingly, after it had been lying finished for years."[31] There

---

30. "la meilleure partition que j'ai fait de ma vie"; letter to Louis Gouin, 23 May 1842, *Briefwechsel*, 3:399.

31. "Im Bade hatte ich den glücklichen Einfall, für den Traum im 2. Akt das Thema des Choeur d'enfants (in der Krönung des 4. Aktes) zu verwenden und arbeitete demgemäß einen großen Teil des schon jahrelang fertigen Traumes wieder um"; ibid., 4:410. See also Armstrong, "Meyerbeer's *Le Prophète*," 239, 749–50.

was nothing new as such about the procedure of citing two easily mem-
orable melodies—the children's chorus and the opening of the coronation march, also not composed until 1848—in order to create a musical
cross-reference between the two scenes, and to that extent it is perhaps
even surprising that it took Meyerbeer seven years from the date when
he had completed the score provisionally to come up with the idea of
using motivic recall to add to the musical characterization of Jean—the
more so as he was already using the technique in the opera with the
chorale "Ad nos, ad salutarem undam."

On taking a closer look at the dramaturgical function of the melodies
that are recalled in *Le Prophète*, we find, admittedly, that the terms "reminiscence motive" and "motivic recall" are not really appropriate to Meyerbeer's procedures. Even though the first attempts at terminological
systematization were made relatively early,[32] they failed to prevent some
very different phenomena being collected together under one heading—from the technique of strengthening the musical unity of an entire
opera with one or two recurring motives, developed in French operas of
the 1780s and '90s like Lemoyne's *Electre* (1782)[33] and Méhul's *Ariodant*
(1799),[34] through the recall of complete melodies, to examples in German Romantic operas, such as those by Schubert, Weber, and Marschner, of procedures which already point the way forward to Wagner's
weaving of the fabric of an entire opera by the use of *Leitmotive*. Discussion of motivic recall to date has scarcely distinguished between the
constant musical alteration of brief motives and the deployment of
much more elaborate themes. Compositional procedures involving the
reintroduction of musical structures already heard "in association with
the repetition . . . of earlier utterances or the return of previous situations"[35] are repeatedly discussed, without differentiation, alongside
techniques of using musical configurations to symbolize individual
characters, their character traits, or even wholly abstract ideas or emotions.[36]

Meyerbeer, too, had experimented with a good number of these techniques—less systematically than most composers of German operas
working in the middle decades of the century, and less often than French
composers around the year 1800, but more often than his contemporaries at the Opéra, such as Rossini, Auber, or Halévy. Unlike almost all

32. See Wörner, "Beiträge zur Geschichte des Leitmotivs."
33. See Rushton, "An early essay in *leitmotiv*."
34. See Grace, "Méhul's *Ariodant* and the early leitmotif."
35. Wörner, "Beiträge zur Geschichte des Leitmotivs," 151.
36. Ibid., 159.

the available models, however, he had restricted the use of such techniques to the "characterful" secondary figures in his operas. While Bertram in *Robert le diable* and Marcel in *Les Huguenots* are profiled by "identifying sonorities," and while chorale melodies, through repetition, become associated with the Huguenots and the Anabaptists, it evidently did not occur to Meyerbeer to apply similar procedures to the "characterless" protagonists such as Robert, Raoul, Valentine—or Jean. That statement is not really contradicted by the use he made of the two melodies in Jean's dream narration, for on closer inspection it becomes clear that they serve the process of reminiscence but they do not add anything to Jean's characterization. The *Choeur d'enfants* melody is not a "Savior" motive appearing every time Jean is uplifted by a messianic vision, and the *Marche du sacre*, too, is associated solely with the one event, the coronation, and its prevision, and has nothing to say about Jean's psychology. Neither tune stands for a trait of Jean's character but only for his future status; they have no transcendent symbolic value beyond that. Their inclusion in the crucial scene in Act II is, rather, a promise that these improbable visions, which appear far beyond anything the Leyden tavernkeeper could hope for at the moment when he tells of them, will be fulfilled.

By this means Meyerbeer was able, once again, to achieve something radically new. In all the examples of motivic recall prior to *Le Prophète*, the recurring motives stood for concrete circumstances in the characters' lives or for emotions that they could consciously experience and express. And it went without saying that the composer did not introduce the motives in musically altered shapes until after the definitive version had been stated; even Berlioz did not distort the *idée fixe* in his *Symphonie fantastique* before it had been expounded in its "regular" form in the first movement. Meyerbeer's procedure in *Le Prophète*, introducing the derivatives before the themes occur in their rightful place, therefore marks a radical innovation. It makes their function one of premonition or presage, not reminiscence, of events which only become accessible to the memory later. They emerge, in the dream narration, out of the protagonist's unconscious, as their strange—unearthly, it might be said—instrumentation underlines: just two clarinets for the *Marche du sacre* and a flute for the *Choeur d'enfants* melody. Where circumstances already known to the characters and the audience are newly illuminated by memory in other operas, in this one there is a premonitory flash from events that are yet to happen. And where motivic recall serves in most cases to clarify circumstances at the moment of reminding the audience of them, here memory and its antithetical complement premonition—whether conscious or unconscious—have a decisive effect on the protagonists. The recurrence of the melodies not only reveals their meaning to the audience but also determines the future actions of the characters in the opera.

In taking account of the psychological and problematic aspects of the function of memory in this way, Meyerbeer drew on a musico-dramatic tradition that may be said to have developed in the shadow of motivic recall. In some operas of the late eighteenth century, composers reintroduced melodies without any intention of shaping character or structure—although of course the recurrences aided the audience in orientation and strengthened the formal integration of longer scores. The recurrence arose simply and straightforwardly out of the drama, as the melodies acquired an immediate significance in the action visible on the stage. One of the earliest and most outstanding examples of the process, which is quite distinct from contemporary and later experiments with reminiscence motives, is Grétry's use of the *romance* "Une fièvre brûlante," heard nine times altogether in his *Richard Coeur-de-lion* (1784), deliberately introduced by the characters themselves in order to make themselves known to others during the course of a complicated plot. Alfred Hitchcock, incidentally, used much the same technique in the dénouement of the 1955 version of *The Man Who Knew Too Much*. Although Grétry's *romance* is arguably best described, therefore, as a melody of recognition or identification, it is a reminiscence theme as well, of course, for it reminds both Richard Lion-heart and his beloved, Countess Marguerite of Flanders, when they hear it, of the now remote circumstances in which he composed it for her.

So Richard's troubadour, Blondel, before singing the *romance* for the first time, in order to attract Marguerite's attention, says to himself: "Let's see if it's really her. If it is Marguerite, her soul will be unable to resist the sweet impressions of an air her lover composed for her in happier days" ("Voyons si vraiment c'est elle. Si c'est Marguerite, son âme ne pourra se refuser aux douces impressions d'un air, qu'en des temps plus heureux, son amant a fait pour elle"). And in fact Marguerite is astonished by the unexpected sound of the song: she "stops, listens, approaches" (s'arrête, écoute, s'approche). But although this episode and a number of similar ones elsewhere in the opera's three acts illustrate the process leading from initial puzzlement to the making of the correct association between present and past aural impressions, Grétry's work does nothing to elucidate the problems all too often connected with reminiscence in its effect on strata of the memory that are not, or are no longer, accessible to the conscious mind. In composing the first work of music theater in which the power of memory is a dramatic theme, Grétry confined himself to its simplest, most naive aspects. Within a couple of years, however, the less obvious aspects were tackled by another French composer. "Memory, . . . the phenomena of its operation and breakdown, was one of the central themes of . . . *Nina, ou la folle par amour* (1786)"[37] by Nicolas-Marie Dalayrac, which enjoyed one of the longest-lasting successes in the history of opera in its original French version as well as in Paisiello's setting of an Italian version of the text (1789). The heroine of this comédie larmoyante has lost all grasp of reality since being told (falsely) of her fiancé's death in a duel. Poor Nina, believing that he will return to her, sings her *romance* "Quand le bien-aimé reviendra" every day, it appears. The air, widely known in the nineteenth century,[38] stands for the disturbed state of her memory and for her inability to assimilate the traumatic experience. Nina recovers her memory and her wits in the end, when her father realizes that his opposition to her marrying the man of her choice was vain; his stratagem having failed, he is forced to seek the young man's help in order to prevent his daughter's derangement becoming permanent.

In *Nina*, the repair of the damage done to the heroine's memory and the restoration of her reason are represented only by the words and the action, not by the music as such, but in a later opera Dalayrac developed the means of expressing the gradual return of a memory buried in the unconscious mind in musical language. In Act II of his *Camille, ou Le Souterrain* (1791), a Gothic horror story, one of the characters, Fabio, starts to hum in his sleep the tune of a folk song that has been heard earlier. At the end of the first four-bar phrase he tries to remember the next line but gives up after two failures, and a long note on "hmm" represents his snoring. But while he snores, Dalayrac has the orchestral violins play the third four-bar phrase and then Fabio continues with the last phrase in a convincingly natural process of remembering.[39] There is a plausible connection between that kind of sensitive depiction of the gradual return of a memory, like an operatic scene when one character's reverie is interrupted by another's arrival on stage, and contemporary techniques of hypnosis, especially as practiced by the touring "magnetist" Mesmer and his adepts, and it is certainly no accident that Da-

37. Charlton, "Motif and recollection in four operas of Dalayrac," 39.
38. See, for example, Berlioz, *Memoirs*, 32, 48.
39. See Charlton, "Motif and recollection in four operas of Dalayrac," 40–41.

layrac began his experiments in the mid-1780s, when interest in mesmerism was at its peak in Paris.[40]

Fascination with mesmerism ebbed in the following years, but faith in the supernatural abilities of gifted hypnotists and the effort to explain these remarkable phenomena with models of animal magnetism and other now somewhat bizarre-sounding theories remained undimmed into the 1860s. Neither the fantastic tales of E. T. A. Hoffmann nor many of the poems of Victor Hugo or Théophile Gautier can be fully understood without reference to this development, yet it escaped historians' attention until recently. Perhaps the first opera to spring to mind in this connection is Bellini's *La sonnambula* (1831), in which the heroine's sleep-walking causes apparently insoluble problems,[41] but another deserving to be looked at is Boieldieu's *La Dame blanche* (1825), one of the most successful opéras comiques ever written, with, at first glance, no elements of Hoffmannish "fantasy."

The plot, pieced together by the librettist, Scribe, from elements taken from several novels by Sir Walter Scott, culminates in one of the recognition scenes that were the stock-in-trade of contemporary melodrama. The son of a wealthy nobleman, abducted in infancy, has survived all the caprices of fate and returned to his family's castle purely by chance, his true identity unknown either to himself or to the majority of the other people involved. Most authors of melodrama fall back on birthmarks, or some similar physical sign, as the means of identifying the long-lost heir in such situations,[42] but Scribe and Boieldieu had a brilliant idea that allowed music to play the decisive role. The hero (a young officer in the English army) proves he is the legitimate heir to the estate because he recognizes a folk song the Scottish clansmen are singing, interrupts the chorus after a few lines, and goes on to sing the refrain from memory. The idea appears to have originated with Boieldieu,[43] but Scribe, not content with placing this demonstration of the power of memory at the center of the last act, constructed the scene in such a way as to demonstrate the problems connected with the gradual remembering of events that have long disappeared from the conscious mind. Even before the first note of the song is sung the young man, entering the castle for the first time, has been asking himself in some bewilderment where he can have seen these chandeliers and old suits of armor before, and after the chorus's exit he remains on the stage alone,

---

40. See Darnton, *Mesmerism and the End of the Enlightenment in France*, 3–43.
41. On mesmerism in Italian tradition see Gallini, *La sonnambula meravigliosa*.
42. See Brooks, "Il corpo melodrammatico."
43. See Adam, *Derniers Souvenirs*, 287–88; see also Pendle, *Eugène Scribe*, 553, n. 104.

absorbed in reverie and humming the refrain once more, yet cannot answer his own disturbing question: "Where did I hear this tune before?" ("Où donc ai-je entendu cet air?").

Thus memory is a theme of *La Dame blanche*, but Boieldieu did not resort to motivic recall in order to make it so. Although the Scottish folk song has all the traits of a recurring reminiscence motive, and fulfills one of the many dramatic functions of one, it is not heard before the decisive scene in Act III. The paradox that a reminiscence motive appears to be used here when it is not a reminiscence motive can be resolved, however, for it is a musical reminiscence, and one that recurs, but it originates somewhere beyond the limits of the onstage action. The same can be said of the trio in Act I of Meyerbeer's last Italian opera, *Il crociato in Egitto* (1824), in which four temporal strata are layered above each other by the end of its three stanzas. It can also be said of the melodies used in Jean's dream in *Le Prophète*, although this last instance differs fundamentally from all precedents, admittedly, in that when the tunes in question are first heard they are audible to the audience yet do not belong to the visible onstage action, being the subjective vision of a confused protagonist. Nevertheless, this survey of earlier operas in which contemporary interest in memory and its operations becomes increasingly evident has helped to show that Meyerbeer's dream narration and its initially obscure glance into the unconscious dovetailed with an existing tradition of French opera. It has not been possible to do more than gesture toward the changing relationship between memory as a dramatic motive and the use of musical motives to prompt and arouse memories and associations, which became increasingly formalized during the eighteenth and nineteenth centuries and culminated in the complex fabric of leitmotivic technique. More detailed discussion of that topic will have to wait until sharper conceptual and terminological distinctions have been drawn between the manifold dramaturgical functions of reminiscence motives. We must also hope that future writing about operatic mad scenes, which almost always rely heavily on reminscence motives,[44] will find a way to distinguish between those in which characters have irretrievably lost all grasp of reality (such as Donizetti's Lucia, Halévy's Charles VI, or Verdi's Lady Macbeth) and those depicting characters not only in a state of distraction but also returning, suddenly or gradually, to themselves (such as those in the instances mentioned in the previous few paragraphs).

The issues raised in dramatic shape in mad scenes, and above all in

44. See Döhring, "Die Wahnsinnsszene."

Jean's dream scene in *Le Prophète* with its illustration of premonitions welling up from the subconscious, were also simultaneously a focus of scientific attention, as the development of academic psychology shows: to cite the title of a modern study of the subject, the middle of the nineteenth century witnessed "the discovery of the unconscious."[45] *Le Prophète* is only one of several works of music theater to reflect the changing perception of the inner working of the human mind: Wagner's *Lohengrin*, contemporary with *Le Prophète* but written wholly independently of it, has Elsa's narration of a dream that is realized almost immediately afterward, but there is another opera by Meyerbeer, first performed a decade later, which throws new light on the earlier work by its much fuller development of the interaction of premonition and memory that is only suggested in Jean's dream narration. Meyerbeer's late opéra comique *Le Pardon de Ploërmel* (1859), which might be described as a mannerist variation on Dalayrac's *Nina*, contains a key scene in which the mad Dinorah imagines she is once again in the procession preceding what should have been her wedding, which was interrupted by a thunderstorm and her bridegroom's disappearance. As in *Le Prophète*, two easily assimilable tunes (a march and a hymn—both very similar in gesture to the corresponding motives in Jean's dream scene) represent a seemingly unattainable event, related simultaneously to both the past and the future in this instance. The experience that so shocked and traumatized Dinorah took place before the opera begins, but Meyerbeer integrates it into the action by setting out and fragmenting the two tunes in the overture, adding an unseen chorus to the orchestra. However, the two tunes stand not only for that past unhappiness but also for the happy ending that inexorably arrives, for the procession takes place again at the end, under better auspices, and Meyerbeer uses the music to subtle dramatic effect to show how Dinorah recovers her sanity as the memory of the hymn gradually returns to her.[46]

Jean too, very like Dinorah, seems troubled by the memory of the images fixed in his subconscious, although there is the difference that the images belong to his visions, not to actual past experience; another difference is that the possibility of a happy end is barred to him. It was clearly important to Meyerbeer to depict his volatile protagonist as someone whose failure to integrate his memories into his personality is a permanent character trait, not just a feature of the dream scene. In an undated entry in his diary, perhaps from the end of 1844, he asked him-

45. Ellenberger, *The Discovery of the Unconscious.*
46. For a more detailed consideration, see Gerhard, "Religiöse Aura."

self: "Might it be possible to let Jean's Act II *romance* snake through the whole opera?" and made a note of places where it might put in an appearance:

> It could come back in Act III in the recitative before the rondo, "Berthe, ah tu n'es plus" ["Berthe, thou art no more"]. Also in the recitatives with Jonas . . . he could always be thinking of Berthe whenever he speaks of his mother; and again in the same act when he asks Oberthal for news of Berthe. In Act IV, during the coronation, when he says to himself "Jean, tu regneras" ["Jean, thou shalt reign"], he could add "Mais . . . O souvenir . . . hélas" ["But . . . memory . . . alas!"], while the orchestra plays the ritornello of the *romance*. Lastly a moment for an allusion to it must surely be found somewhere in the final scene of Act V.[47]

In the end Meyerbeer decided against recalling this motive throughout the work, and referred to the *romance* and its catchy tune just once, at one of the points he mentioned in Act III. It is not really possible, at the present state of our knowledge of Meyerbeer, to reconstruct his reasons for not using the technique of motivic recall to relate Jean's later actions to the *romance* as well as to the dream narration, for their occurrence so close together in Jean's first scene and the marked contrast between them establish the extremes in the character. Perhaps he foresaw the danger of overdetermination in this respect, if he used reminiscence motives with too great a degree of consistency. Perhaps he did not see a role in the polyperspective dramaturgy of his historical opera for lining up reminiscence motives one after the other as he did in his incidental music for a dream scene in *Struensee*, a tragedy by his brother, Michael Beer, first performed in 1846; the original plan in that instance had been to "amalgamate the principal thematic material of all the musical numbers as a mirror-image of the dream."[48] Another reason, and perhaps the

47. "Könnte man nicht die Romanze Jeans im 2. Akt durch die Oper schlängeln lassen?" "Im 3. Akt könnte sie bei der Stelle wiederkommen des Rezitatives vor dem Rondo 'Bertha, ah n'es plus'. Auch in den Rezitativen mit Jonas . . . könnte er sich immer Berthas erinnern, wenn er von der Mutter spräche; ferner wenn er in demselben Akt sich bei Oberthal nach Bertha erkundiget. Im 4. Akt bei der Krönung, wenn er sich selbst sagt: 'Jean tu regneras', da könnte er hinzufügen 'Mais . . . O souvenir . . . hélas' und dabei das Orchester das Ritornell der Romanze spielen. Endlich müßte man in der Schlußszene des 5. Aktes noch einen Moment für einen Anklang daran finden." *Briefwechsel*, 3:539. For various musical drafts of the number "Berthe, ah, tu n'es plus" (eventually cut) see Armstrong, "Meyerbeer's *Le Prophète*," 944–49, 953–61; however, neither here nor in other paralipomena published by Armstrong is there any indication that Meyerbeer ever realized the intention outlined here.

48. "als Spiegelbild des Traumes die Hauptthemata sämtlicher Musikstücke zusammen [zu] verschmelzen"; entry in Meyerbeer's diary, 19 August 1846, *Briefwechsel*, 4:104.

strongest, for not recalling the *romance* may have been connected with the gradual diminution of Berthe's significance during the opera's lengthy gestation, particularly with respect to Jean's motivation.[49]

But even if we do not know the reasons for Meyerbeer's change of mind, there is much to be learned from a closer reading of the ideas he rejected. The word "snake" *(schlängeln)* in the 1844 diary entry is not an everyday one, and its symbolic connotations show once again the place the unconscious had achieved in Meyerbeer's dramatic thinking, after this alarming quality had already manifested itself so flagrantly in Valentine's involuntary declaration of love in Act IV of *Les Huguenots*. Significantly, long after the composer had abandoned the idea of allowing Jean's *Pastorale* to "snake" through *Le Prophète*, he clung to the snake symbolism and had the other recurring melody, the chorale "Ad nos, ad salutarem undam," encircled by "flickering," serpentine string triplets on its last appearance in Act V, so that there can be no mistaking its negative connotation.[50] Another thing that strikes the reader is Meyerbeer's idea that the *romance*, associated with Berthe, might be recalled whenever Jean mentions his mother. It can hardly be a mistake in the diary, because the final version of the opera contains a very precise example of that very thing. At the only place in the score where the *romance* is recalled, in Act III, Scene 7, Jean sings "softly" and "with feeling" *(doux . . . avec émotion)*, "How much I want to see my mother, my beloved mother" ("Que je veux voir ma mère, ma mère chérie!") while the accompaniment quotes the *Pastorale*. If we require any further proof that the operation of memory in *Le Prophète* has lost all touch with the unquestioning, unproblematic nature of reminiscence motives as used by Grétry, it is provided by this "mistake" of Jean's, remembering his beloved at the moment when he speaks of his mother.

MOTHER AND SON

It is not in the dream narration alone but also in his reactions to other people that Meyerbeer represented his protagonist in a way that cries out for psychoanalytical interpretation. Jean's complete inability to loosen the ties binding him to his mother is illustrated on more than one occasion, although he is introduced in the recitatives of the first two acts as Berthe's lover before all else. Yet at the moment of critical decision in Act II this young lover is ready to sacrifice his fiancée to save his

49. See Armstrong, "Meyerbeer's *Le Prophète*," 55, 222, 306–8.
50. See Döhring, "Meyerbeers Konzeption der historischen Oper," 97.

mother, and, having found his mother again at the end of the convoluted plot, he is happy to meet death with her. It is true that he is also capable of leaving her, apparently for ever, without a word of farewell, and of killing her with words in publicly denying her and compelling her to deny him, but she is always in the forefront of his mind: when Berthe takes her own life, his reaction is to tell his men to look after his mother, but he has nothing to say about the lover he has just lost. And so in his confrontation with Zacharie and Jonas in Act III it is his mother's image that is in his mind's eye as he tries to extricate himself from further responsibility for the atrocities of the Anabaptist army. As is demonstrated in the previous paragraph, Meyerbeer accompanies Jean's expression of the wish to see his mother in this scene with a quotation of the Act II *Pastorale*, but the unexpected association with Fidès is underlined by the tonality: when the *romance* is cited by the orchestra alone at the start of this scene it is in B-flat major, as it is originally in Act II, and that is also the key of Berthe's cavatina in Act I (composed in the last months before the première),[51] but at the point when Jean thinks of Fidès the tune is recalled in A-flat major, the key of the decisive encounters that are yet to come between Jean and his mother in Acts IV and V. Jean's *romance*, however, is dedicated to Berthe and the happiness of the "humble empire" he looks forward to when she alone will be all his loves ("mes seuls amours"), and the text does not contain a single reference to his mother. Whether or not Meyerbeer was wholly aware of the significance of this remarkable confusion must remain an open question, but he certainly acted in full awareness, having conceived that Jean "could always be thinking of Berthe whenever he speaks of his mother." The confusion is no less intriguing in his diary than in the score of the opera, but it leaves no doubt that it is his mother that Jean loves. It is only logical, in the circumstances, that Meyerbeer transferred material composed for a duet originally planned for Jean and Berthe to the duet for Jean and Fidès in Act V, making scarcely any changes in doing so.[52]

Conversely, the mother, with her loaded name ("Faith"), is filled with an almost unconditional love for her son and remains faithful to him in spite of the humiliations she experiences. The final version of the libretto leaves no doubt of that, yet it is shown even more clearly in a prose draft of Fidès's scene at the beginning of Act V, which Meyerbeer

51. See J. Weber, *Meyerbeer*, 79; see also Armstrong, "Meyerbeer's *Le Prophète*," 318–23.

52. See Armstrong, "Gilbert-Louis Duprez and Gustave Roger," 161, n. 47.

wrote for Scribe to work up during the final revision (probably 7 February 1848):

> Very impassioned recitative. Terror that Jean will be assassinated unless she can warn him of his danger. Anger with Jean for having denied her and had her arrested. Anxiety, anger render her almost deranged, she is on the point of cursing . . . Ah no! she cries to herself, God, do not hear that sacrilegious word . . . I? Curse my beloved, adored child, for whom I would shed every drop of blood? Cavatina, very gentle. Return of tenderness: she recalls Jean's childhood, his innocence, his love for his mother, their happiness in that simple cottage. (This piece could have an almost pastoral character.)[53]

And before despatching this Meyerbeer added: "Refrain: 'Mon bien-aimé, sois pardonné' ['My beloved, I forgive you']."

This depiction of a mother's passionate love for her son is a little short on artistic detachment, and the reader may well start to wonder about the light such an intense view of an oedipal situation sheds on Meyerbeer's psychology. He revered his own mother, and remained deeply attached to her until her death. Reading the family letters published to date confirms the impression that his troubled relationship with his wife never had the quality of his obviously vital link with his mother. For example, he asked her for a written blessing before the première of each of his operas, in a form corresponding to the Jewish ritual observed in the family. And he wrote to her in Berlin, the day after the first performance of *Le Prophète:* "I read the maternal blessing in your letter to me with reverence and emotion at the prescribed moment, kissed your dear name fervently, and carried your letter next to my heart up until the end of the performance."[54]

53. "Récitatif très passioné. Terreur de ce que l'on assassinera Jean sans qu'elle puisse l'avertir du danger qui le menace. Colère contre Jean qui l'a reniée, qui l'a faite arrêter. L'angoisse, la colère la rendent presque insensée, elle est sur le point de maudire . . . Ah non! s'écrie-t-elle, Dieu, n'entendez point ce mot sacrilège . . . moi, maudire l'enfant chéri, adoré, pour lequel je donnerais tout mon sang? Cavatine très douce. Retour de tendresse; elle se rappelle l'enfance de Jean, son innocence, son amour pour sa mère, quel bonheur dans cette simple chaumière. (Ce morceau pourrait avoir un caractère presque pastoral.)" F-Pn, n.a.f. 22504, fol. 31. On the dating, see entries in Meyerbeer's diary, 7, 25, and 26 February 1848 (*Briefwechsel*, 4:361, 369) and Meyerbeer's undated autograph letter to Scribe [26 February 1848], F-Pn, n.a.f. 22504, fols. 27–28 (cited in part in Huebner, "Italianate duets," 257, n. 69); see also Armstrong, "Meyerbeer's *Le Prophète*," 187–89.

54. "Ich habe den mütterlichen Segen, den Du mir in Deinem Brief geschickt hast, mit Andacht und Rührung in dem vorgeschriebenen Moment gelesen, habe Deinen teuren Namen mit Inbrunst geküßt, und habe Deinen Brief auf der Brust bis zur Ende der Vorstellung getragen"; letter to Amalia Beer, 17 April 1849, *Briefwechsel*, 4:486.

Even without access to documents like that, Meyerbeer's earliest biographers recognized the critical importance that the theme of maternal
love had for his life as well as his work. Eymieu, for example, remarked
in 1910: "Maternal and filial affection is expressed in almost all Meyerbeer's works."[55] In fact, this categorical statement is scarcely applicable
to *Les Huguenots* or *L'Africaine*, but the really surprising thing about it
is that neither here, nor in four pages devoted exclusively to the character of Fidès, does Eymieu betray the slightest wonder at the very strange
representation of "maternal and filial affection" in *Le Prophète*. Like the
many critics at the first performance of the work in 1849, Eymieu, sixty
years later, treated the extraordinarily close ties binding Jean and Fidès
together as the most natural thing in the world. To us, in the late twentieth century, the relationship seems psychopathic in the extreme. Did
our great-grandparents really accept it as normal?

They may have done, insofar as it was an ideological constant in almost all nineteenth-century operatic librettos that close family relationships appeared in a transfigured form, although in a majority of them
the spotlight fell on a father. We can be sure that contemporary observers were aware that real life bore less and less resemblance to the ideal
underlying the fiction. In *Le Prophète*, however, the relationship goes
beyond a mother's naive love and her son's dutiful obedience: in two
instances, the coronation scene in Act IV and the reconciliation scene
in Act V, Jean and Fidès meet in confrontations undeniably infused with
sado-masochism.

After denying his mother in the fourth-act finale, Jean commands
her to kneel before him, to which Fidès responds with a "gesture of
indignation" (*geste d'indignation*). But the undutiful son succeeds in forcing this ultimate humiliation on her by a look, as described in the score
in a stage-direction not found in the published libretto: "During this
ritornello Jean approaches Fidès, places his hands on her head and fixes
on her a look so fascinating that she falls involuntarily to her knees"
(*Pendant cette ritournelle Jean s'approche de Fidès, étend les mains sur sa tête
et la fascine tellement de son regard qu'involontairement elle tombe à genoux*).
Even Berlioz, who found little else to admire in Meyerbeer's latest opera, could not deny the power of this moment, the expressive climax
of the visual side of the drama, and described this "pantomime" in his
newspaper column as "one of those things one cannot describe. One
trembles with excitement, watching [the tenor], following the mute elo-

55. *L'Oeuvre de Meyerbeer*, 109.

quence of his face and eyes."[56] The mute, even hypnotic, expressive force in Jean's "exorcism"—*exorcisme* is the movement title in the published editions of the score—casts such a spell over Fidès, however, that she finally declares that he is not her son.

Admittedly, she exacts her revenge for the humiliation the next time she encounters Jean, in Act V. Although she is already wholly intent on being reconciled with him, and he is begging her forgiveness, she insists on his kneeling:

> FIDÈS *d'un ton sévère et solennel*
> Et maintenant que Dieu seul nous contemple,
> A genoux!
>
> JEAN *tombant malgré lui à ses pieds*
> Ah! pardon pour un fils égaré!
> (*Le Prophète*, Acte V, scène 4)

>   ◡   ◡   ◡

> FIDÈS *(in severe and solemn tones):* And now that God alone sees us, kneel!
> JEAN *(falling at her feet in spite of himself):* Ah! pardon for a straying son!

The concentration of the ambivalent relationship between Jean and Fidès into two key scenes, the pantomime in which appears to express how little the two people involved have reflected on their motives, is a further stage in the psychological penetration that has already been seen at work in the treatment of Jean's visions and the operation of memory. Unlike other motifs in this variegated tapestry, however, the idea of depicting the Anabaptist prophet declaring himself the son of God in the presence of his earthly mother did not necessarily originate with Meyerbeer and Scribe. The following account of one Anabaptist, whose acts were reported in Groningen around 1530, occurs in a seventeenth-century history of the Anabaptists, the French translation of which, published in 1695 and frequently reissued, may have been used as a source for the libretto:[57]

> Thereupon he who had entered the Assembly last . . . spoke and said that he was the Son of God and the true Mediator for mankind, and other similar nonsense. Following this, he asked his mother, who was present . . . , if she did not believe that she had indeed borne the Son of God. To

---

56. "une de ces choses qu'on ne décrit point. On palpite à voir [l'acteur de Jean], à suivre l'éloquence muette de son visage et de ses yeux." *Journal des débats*, 20 April 1849; cited in Meyerbeer, *Briefwechsel*, 4:629.

57. See Haudek, *Scribes Operntexte für Meyerbeer*, 75–76.

15 This sketch by Charles Polycarpe Séchan for the first set of Act V of Meyerbeer's *Prophète* impresses even the modern spectator by the exaggerated monumentalism of the structure and its vaulted ceiling, which must have enhanced the moment when the false prophet, deified by all his followers, is cut down to size as a humble sinner by his mother. At the same time its perspective, disappearing toward an imaginary infinity, stands as a metaphor for an overpowering historical principle to which all the characters are subject. One might even go as far as to relate the highly stylized effect of a tunnel to the widespread nineteenth-century fear of the railways, before the seemingly uncontrollable speed of which people of the time were equally helpless.

which at first she did not dare answer positively, because the thing seemed too exorbitant to her; but at last, seeing that the eyes of all were upon her, and fearing that if she hesitated longer it would give rise to disorder in the Assembly, she finally said yes, in some kind of fear withal, and in a low voice.[58]

Admittedly, this account lacks a number of the details that make Meyerbeer's coronation scene so exceptional psychologically. Meyerbeer's prophet is not content with claiming to be the son of God, he also wants to deny having an earthly being as mother—a highly idiosyncratic element and actually contrary to the myth of Christ's birth. In the opera, moreover, Fidès yields only to a hypnotic command, delivered in a way that places her and her son at the center of the action, while the mother of the Groningen prophet makes herself as inconspicuous as she can. In spite of this adaptation of earlier motives, neither the contemporary reviews of the early performances nor twentieth-century studies of Meyerbeer make any comment on the exceptional nature of the mother–son relationship in Meyerbeer's opera, and the only explanation for this fact must be that already by 1849 ideas of the identity of the isolated subject had reached a crisis in which neurotic reactions were deemed natural, while on the other hand the mother was—and still is— expected to conform to the "ideology of devotion and self-sacrifice."[59] When writing of "Woman" in 1860, Jules Michelet, though inclined to careful and balanced analysis in his historical work, ascribed ecstatic emotions to young mothers, culminating in the "innocent surprise of having given birth to a god."[60]

The consignment of the chorus to the background in order to focus more intensely on the complex personal relations of the characters at the heart of the private intrigue is an important difference between *Le Prophète* and *Les Huguenots*,[61] and it also showed the way for opera com-

58. "La dessus celui qui étoit entré le dernier en l'Assemblée . . . , se mit à dire qu'il étoit le Fils de Dieu & le véritable Mediateur du genre humain, avec plusieurs autres fadaises semblables. En suite de cela, il demanda à sa mere, qui étoit la présente . . . , si elle ne croyait pas bien avoir enfanté le Fils de Dieu. A quoi elle n'osa pas d'abord repondre positivement, parce que la chose lui semblait trop exorbitante; mais enfin comme elle vit que tout le monde avoit les yeux sur elle, craignant que si elle hesitoit encore davantage, cela ne causât quelque desordre en cette Assemblée, elle dit finalement qu'oüi, quoi que toutefois avec quelque espece de crainte, & de voix basse." Hortensius, *Histoire des anabaptistes*, 114.

59. Badinter, *The Myth of Motherhood*, 232.

60. "innocente surprise d'avoir enfanté un Dieu"; *La Femme*, 8.

61. See the detailed statistical comparison in Frese, *Dramaturgie der großen Opern Giacomo Meyerbeers*, 163.

posers with an innovative bent to bring troubled human relationships onto the stage with a previously unknown range of nuances. In the event it was not French composers who followed in Meyerbeer's footsteps so much as Giuseppe Verdi. The most successful Italian opera composer of his day called the coronation scene in *Le Prophète* a "miracle,"[62] and some years later, with *Il trovatore*, created one of the few other nineteenth-century operas to make an important theme of a highly ambivalent mother–son relationship.

DEMAGOGUERY

The treatment of family ties is not the only thing for which *Le Prophète* finds previously unknown means of expression: the political subject matter is also presented with an astonishing degree of psychological insight. The "pamphlet," as Gautier called the opera, does not merely summon up the means of demagoguery, it lays bare its very mechanisms. Jean exploits the aura of his messianic status without restraint in the last three acts to bend the crowds to his will, but Meyerbeer and Scribe augment such traditional techniques of the demagogue with specifically modern ones, the future potential of which can scarcely have been foreseen in 1849.

Jean does not become the leader of the Anabaptist rebellion through his own ambition, he is put forward by men who pull the wires in a political campaign, and they do not choose him for any political qualities or experience of authority but for a purely physical coincidence: the astonishing resemblance he bears to a portrait of King David, venerated—according to the libretto, at least—in Münster and throughout Westphalia. The three Anabaptists make up their minds that he is the "apostle" they seek the moment they set eyes on him (Zacharie: "Chers amis! n'est-ce pas là l'apôtre qu'il nous faut?"). He will be the charismatic "prophet" who will draw the credulous masses to join the rebellion they want to foment. There are lines in Scribe's libretto that reveal Zacharie's cynicism quite uncompromisingly: "A popular idol! . . . useful for our plans, and after our success our hands will overturn it!" ("Idole populaire! . . . utile à nos desseins, et qu'après le succès renverseront nos mains!"). (Although the passage appears in the printed libretto, in Act III, scene 5, Meyerbeer cut it when rehearsals were at an advanced stage.)[63]

62. See below, 336.
63. See Meyerbeer's diary entry for 11 April 1849, *Briefwechsel*, 4:482; see also Armstrong, "Meyerbeer's *Le Prophète*," 285, n. 37, and 914–15 for an edition of the cut passage.

To begin with, the Anabaptists have every reason to be pleased with the way Jean carries out the role they have assigned him. True, he is not kept informed about his forces' military actions, and early in Act III he is found wandering around the camp "with a pensive air" (d'un air pensif). But the mere sight of him is enough to recall the mutinous troops to order, and he whips them up into the mood for more fighting in the *Hymne triomphal*, combining ruthless brutality and ecstatic religiosity in equal parts—underlined in the scoring by the alternation between piano arpeggios on four harps, and fortissimo, staccato blasts from the brass section.

The mixture of naked force and sacral aura is taken to a new height in Act IV when the unscrupulous demagogue—"frankly an impostor," in Meyerbeer's words[64]—has himself crowned king in a pompous ceremony. The *Marche du sacre*—the one number from *Le Prophète* that is still widely known today—contains an extreme contrast between the cantabile melody of the middle section, marked *con molto portamento* (and echoed in the triumphal march in Verdi's *Aida*), and the downright bombastic beginning. The steady motion in quarter notes, with a rhythmic quickening (dotted eighth and sixteenth notes) on the fifth beat refers back quite clearly to the *Hymne triomphal*, both in tempo (metronome 104 as against metronome 108) and in the underlying ductus. But Meyerbeer uses various devices to disrupt the continuing steady flow that appears prescribed: a repetition in the first four-bar phrase, extending it to five bars, breaks up the metrical regularity; modulation to C minor in the second four-bar phrase destroys the expected regularity in the harmonic structure; and eighth-note triplets on the strongest beats, the first in the first and third bars of each four-bar group, impede the inexorable forward movement. These triplets, however, taking up a full beat which is by no means consistent with march-time conventions, are not there to decorate the melody: rather, Meyerbeer changes the harmony on each of the three notes, and involves the entire orchestra in the change, from piccolo down to bassoons, trombones, and ophicleide, and the effect, from the first bar onward, is indescribably bombastic.

The rhythmic flurry with which the march begins can be regarded as a further development of Meyerbeer's preference for triple meters and triplets, discussed earlier in connection with *Les Huguenots*.[65] The rhythmic figure has particular dramatic connotations as well, however,

---

64. "franchement imposteur"; F-Pn, n.a.f. 22504, fol. 78.
65. See above, 182–83.

in the context of the 1849 score: Zacharie's *Couplets* in Act III also begin with a triplet figure, very similar in structure and also filling a whole beat, and as in the coronation march Meyerbeer underlines his intentions with the directions *molto maestoso* and *pesante*. In the dramatic situation in that scene, however, the remarkable rhythmic pattern stands for the Anabaptists' brute vitality; the orchestral introduction plays while Zacharie enters, straight from combat, "joyfully brandishing his axe as a sign of victory" *(Zacharie revient du combat [et] brandit sa hache joyeusement en signe de victoire)*. An echo of this triplet, distant but confirmed by the agreement of the tonality, E major, and the joining of the third note, is heard in the duet in Act V, serving as a reminder of the Anabaptists' power precisely at the moment when Fidès exhorts her son to renounce his kingship and those who gave it to him ("Renonce à ton pouvoir, à ceux qui t'ont fait roi!").

Thus Meyerbeer denounced the Anabaptists' force in the very scene where it unfurls in its full panoply. It is certainly one of the ironic aspects of the work's reception history that the coronation march (which "droned in the ears of the rest of the century [and] seems to have anticipated the whole pernicious grandeur of Napoleon III," in the opinion of an Austrian theater-historian, published, admittedly, in 1941)[66] was played for years to come in honor of legitimate monarchs. To ears that did not catch the intentional rule-breaking in the march in *Le Prophète*, there was nothing to distinguish it from the march played at the coronation of William II (later the first German Emperor) as King of Prussia in October 1861: the conventional melodic elements Meyerbeer used in the latter are confusingly similar to those found in the opera march, but for the real coronation he arrayed them in a regular harmonic and metrical framework. William II was crowned, not in his capital, Berlin, but in the East Prussian city of Königsberg, in accordance with tradition, and another irony of Meyerbeer's remarkable success as a march composer is that scenes of the Red Army's conquest of Königsberg, shown in a Soviet Russian newsreel in the spring of 1945, were accompanied by the better-known of Meyerbeer's coronation marches: the one from *Le Prophète*, not the one he wrote for performance in Königsberg in 1861.[67]

Jean's power rests, admittedly, not only on brute force and triumphalist gestures but also on his ability to overcome doubt and compel

66. Gregor, *Kulturgeschichte der Oper*, 320–21.
67. This was revealed in a television program about Königsberg (Kaliningrad) shown on Zweites Deutsches Fernsehen, 13 March 1988.

a crowd's admiration, time and time again. In the scene following the coronation march, he is on the verge of losing everything by spontaneously falling into his mother's arms when she cries out in recognition of him. But he sees the danger in time, and saves himself by throwing his personal credit into the balance. He risks his life in the knowledge that there is no real risk, because he knows his mother's love for him is unconditional:

> JEAN *au peuple*
> Et vous qui m'écoutez, peuple, tirez la glaive!
> *(Tous tirent leurs épées et leurs poignards.)*
>
> FIDÈS
> Ah! je frémis!
>
> JEAN *en montrant Fidès*
>   Eh bien! eh bien!
> Si je suis son enfant, si je vous ai trompés,
> Punissez l'imposteur! . . . voici mon sein . . . frappez!
> *(Sur un signe de Jean plusieurs anabaptistes mettent la
> pointe de leurs poignards sur sa poitrine.)*
> JEAN *s'adressant à haute voix à Fidès*
> Suis-je ton fils?
>   *(Le Prophète*, Acte IV, scène 3)

    ع ع ع

> JEAN *(to the people):* And you who hear me, people, draw your swords!
> *(All draw their swords and daggers.)*
> FIDÈS: Ah! I tremble!
> JEAN *(pointing to Fidès):* Well, then! If I am her child, if I have deceived you, punish the impostor! Here is my breast . . . Strike!
> *(At a sign from Jean several Anabaptists place their dagger-points against his breast.)*
> JEAN *(addressing Fidès in a loud voice):* Am I your son?

Of course she denies it, to save his life. And the prophet has not merely recovered his position but enhances it by showing that, like Christ, he can restore a mad woman's reason. His "providence" has saved him, and the people praise the "miracle."

Meyerbeer's opera is prophetic, not only because it prefigured, already in the late 1830s, a revolutionary mood that was later identified with the spirit of 1848, but also because of its characterization of a charismatic leader who has no inhibitions about mixing his private life into his political existence and impresses the masses by skilful image-management. In the crowd scenes in *Le Prophète*, Meyerbeer uses the resources of music theater to express the convictions behind Gustave

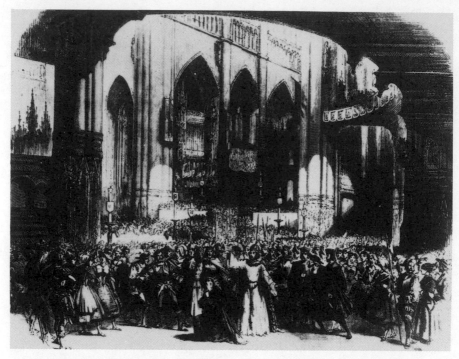

16 An engraving distributed with the illustrated weekly paper, *L'Illustration*, issue of 28 April 1849, showing the key scene of Act IV of Meyerbeer's *Prophète*. Jean's "exorcism" of his mother takes one of the crucial elements of grand opéra, the tension between an intimate exchange between two people and a colossally large crowd scene, to its ultimate extreme.

Le Bon's theory of crowd psychology, formulated at the end of the nineteenth century.[68] The nineteenth century's muddled belief in the power of hypnosis is reflected in Jean's confused visions, but a scene like Jean's confrontation with Fidès, called "the exorcism," and Jean's manipulation of mass emotions in general could only have been imagined by someone who had attended public exhibitions of hypnotic experiments. Serge Moscovici has argued that the conjunction between waves of revolution and schools of hypnosis was the reason why crowd psychology, as a science, was born in France rather than in Italy or Germany.[69] The idea is relevant to *Le Prophète*, for the coronation scene is one of those ceremo-

68. Le Bon, *Psychologie des foules*. For a study of the correlation between Le Bon's theory and the depiction of the crowd in *Le Prophète*, see Moeller, "'Peuple à genoux,'" 244–45, 247–50.

69. See *L'Age des foules*, 116–17.

nies which could be described as masses or eucharists, led by one who is simultaneously officiant and god, and conceived on hypnotic, rather than religious, principles.[70]

So Jean's role anticipates the modern dictator who calculates his appearances in public and the demagogic means appropriate to such occasions very precisely. The première of *Le Prophète* was attended by Louis-Napoleon Bonaparte, nephew of the great Napoleon, who had been elected president of the Second French Republic four months earlier, on 10 December 1848. He had achieved a huge majority, which he owed above all to the skillful propaganda use he made of the Napoleon myth. As a member of the Bonaparte family, and employing every means of demagoguery available at the time, he presented himself to the people of France as a guarantor of France's imperial standing in the world, and it was a logical further step when he arranged a coup d'état three years later to make himself emperor.

There is yet another aspect of twentieth-century political developments anticipated in *Le Prophète*, and it is one which flourishes even in parliamentary democracies. The key scene shows an essentially weak character who knows how to present his private credibility as a political quality, in a carefully stage-managed event that gives him the charismatic power to hold the crowd in thrall.[71] Viewed in this light, the fact that the private and political spheres of the action amalgamate at the opera's climax is anything but a "retrogression into an antiquated mode of thought, dating from the age of absolutism"—the phrase Carl Dahlhaus used to describe the musical structures of this scene.[72] Rather, it foreshadows a political culture in which, for politicians and electorate alike, the boundaries between private life and public office have been virtually obliterated.[73]

SUICIDE

The mingling of the private intrigue and the historical action framing it, which interact with each other to a far greater degree than in all earlier grands opéras, persists to the very end of *Le Prophète*. All three of those involved in the private drama take their own lives, in one way or another, in the last act. Berthe, having managed to get into the castle undetected with the intention of killing the tyrannical prophet she be-

70. Ibid., 193–94.
71. See Sennett, *The Fall of Public Man*, 236–37.
72. *Realism in Nineteenth-century Music*, 83.
73. See Sennett, *The Fall of Public Man*, 271–77.

lieves responsible for the death of her fiancé, abandons the plan when, to her great amazement, she comes upon Jean still alive. Unaware of Jean's true identity, she is overjoyed at finding him again and joins with him and Fidès in painting a picture of the joys of a new life, far from the city with its terrors. Meyerbeer underlines the unreality of this longing for the serene idyll of the opera's opening, by using for this *Allegretto pastorale ben moderato* a melody which turns out to be an inversion of the start of Jean's *Pastorale* in Act II, with the same rocking rhythm, and wrapped in triadic harmonies.[74]

This last glimmer of hope is extinguished by a new twist in the action: the entrance of someone with a message for Jean betrays to Berthe that the man responsible for the Anabaptist terror is he who stands before her. Instead of reverting to her original plan of ridding the population of the tyrant by killing him, she turns her anger against herself. She cannot bear the knowledge that she has loved a man who turns out to be the abhorred prophet:

BERTHE
Je t'aimais, toi que je maudis.
Je t'aime encor peut-être . . . et m'en punis.
(Elle se frappe d'un poignard, et tombe dans les bras de Fidès.)
(Le Prophète, Acte V, scène 6)

BERTHE: I loved you, you whom I curse. I love you still perhaps . . . and punish myself for that. *(She plunges a dagger into her breast and falls into Fidès's arms.)*

This surprise turn of events goes back to alterations that Meyerbeer undertook only in the very last phase of the opera's protracted genesis, and his indecisiveness about the contradictions in Berthe's role is symptomatic of how far the final version had moved away from operatic conventions. A trio for Berthe, Fidès, and Jean in the last act was not envisaged in the version provisionally completed in 1841,[75] and the surviving drafts in Scribe's literary estate show that originally Jean should have stayed alone in the castle after Fidès had persuaded Berthe to abandon her plan of assassination. One draft of the complete libretto, datable to 1839, contains a version of Act V in which Berthe persuades Jean to repent, whereupon he takes all the guilt upon himself and dies alone in

74. See Brzoska, "Historisches Bewußtsein," 64–65, n. 24.
75. See Meyerbeer's diary entry for 17 February 1841, *Briefwechsel,* 3:330.

the ruins of his castle, having had Berthe and Fidès escorted to safety.[76] Another fragment has Jean and Berthe dying together.[77] The idea that Berthe cannot live with her shame appears for the first time in a prose sketch by Meyerbeer, from March 1848:

> Stretta in the manner of the anathema in the trio in *La Juive*, and a coda for Berthe alone: "to lose what one loves is terrible, but to have to despise it is even worse; I feel I shall not survive this dreadful blow; my eyes grow dim; my strength leaves me; adieu, poor Fidès. Jean, I forgive you, repent so that we may meet again in heaven; adieu." (she swoons).[78]

To this he added: "We'll leave the audience unsure whether she has died or fainted." It was not long before he began composing the music for this scene of his own devising: he made the first reference to his work on the trio in Act V in his diary on 12 May 1848, and on 31 May he recorded that he had worked on the death scene in the trio for the first time.[79] He devoted a lot of attention to this scene, composing an arioso for Berthe to sing the words "Déjà mon oeil s'éteint, hélas, mon sang glacé s'arrête" ("My sight fails, alas, my freezing blood grows still"), accompanied only by cellos, timpani tremolos, and a few wind chords; "the extreme audacities of articulation and expressive mannerisms" of this passage were unparalleled.[80] He obviously thought a lot of it, and months later, on 16 March 1849, at the urging of the instrument-maker Adolphe Sax, decided to replace the cellos with the new alto saxo-

76. F-Pn, n.a.f. 22504, fols. 101–59v (on the dating of this manuscript, see Armstrong, "Meyerbeer's *Le Prophète*," 416); for two similar fragments, see ibid., fols. 52–59 and fols. 60–67; see also Armstrong, 415).

77. F-Pn, n.a.f. 22504, fols. 68–72; see Armstrong, "Meyerbeer's *Le Prophète*," 138–40, where this manuscript is dated to January 1843.

78. "Stretta dans le genre de l'anathème du Trio de la Juive, et une Coda que Berthe aurait seule, 'perdre ce que l'on aime est terrible, mais devoir le mépriser c'est plus affreux; je sens que je ne survivrai pas à ce coup affreux; ma vue se trouble; mes forces m'abandonnent; Adieu, pauvre Fidès. Jean, je te pardonne, repens-toi pour que nous nous revoyons dans les cieux; adieu.' (elle tombe évanouie.)"; "on laissera le public dans l'incertitude si elle est morte ou évanouie." F-Pn, n.a.f. 22504, fol. 30. This manuscript can probably be dated to soon after 5 March 1848, as it seems to correspond to the composer's comments on a new section of libretto versified by Scribe, which in turn corresponded to the changes Meyerbeer asked for on (probably) 26 February 1848 (see above, n. 53); see Meyerbeer's diary, 5 March 1848, *Briefwechsel*, 4:370. See also Armstrong, "Meyerbeer's *Le Prophète*," 194–96, 210–11.

79. *Briefwechsel*, 4:387, 395.

80. See Döhring, "Die Autographen der vier Hauptopern Meyerbeers," 56–57. The text Döhring gives there (music example no. 22) needs to be corrected in the light of one of the complete libretto drafts: see fol. 215 in F-Pn, n.a.f. 22504, fols. 160–218v, and see also the edition of the cut passage in Armstrong, "Meyerbeer's *Le Prophète*," 1367–74.

phone.[81] Yet a very short time later, probably early in April 1849,[82] he decided on a radical cut, as his private secretary recalled: "At last, one morning he told me the scene was deleted. Berthe stabs herself, falls into the wings, and that's that."[83]

By making this cut Meyerbeer sacrificed one of the expressive high points of his score and also one of the few opportunities to add a little shading to Berthe's character, but on the other hand it improved the overall coherence of the work. His ruthless surgery reduced Berthe to a musically secondary character once and for all, and diverted attention away from an unresolved dichotomy that he had noticed as long ago as 1838:

> To have a contrast with all these rough, impassioned, or savage charac-
> ters, such as Jean, Jonas, or the chorus of Anabaptists, we need a very
> pious character, one of angelic sweetness. Shall we draw the girl on those
> lines? But I'm afraid that it won't square with her Charlotte Corday act.[84]

Thereafter Meyerbeer and Scribe had proceeded to heap most of the "piety" they considered necessary onto Fidès, but they did nothing to alter the introduction of Berthe in the first act as a naive and gentle country girl—which of course did not square with her eventual resolution to assassinate a revolutionary-turned-tyrant, as Charlotte Corday had murdered Marat in 1793. A public regularly regaled with new versions of Corday's story, in painting as well as in the popular theater,[85] was bound to notice the parallel, and indeed it was obviously indispensable to Meyerbeer and Scribe, for it allowed them to create a connection

81. Meyerbeer's diary, 16 March 1849, *Briefwechsel*, 4:479.

82. See his pocket-diary, 7 April 1849, ibid., 482.

83. "Enfin, un matin il m'annonça que la scène était supprimée. Bertha se donne un coup de poignard, tombe dans la coulisse, et tout est dit"; J. Weber, *Meyerbeer*, 86. See also Armstrong, "Meyerbeer's *Le Prophète*," 331–32.

84. "Pour avoir un contraste entre tous ces caractères rudes, passionés ou féroces de Jean, Jonas & les Choeurs anabaptistes, il faudrait un caractère très pieux, & de la douceur d'ange. Faut-il dessiner de cette façon la jeune fille? Mais j'ai peur que cela ne cadre pas avec son action de Charlotte Corday." F-Pn, n.a.f. 22504, fol. 49v; see also Armstrong, "Meyerbeer's *Le Prophète*," 42. This comment of the composer's can probably be dated 16 September 1838: see (1) Meyerbeer's note "at the same time send M. Scribe the acknowledgment of Act I" ("envoyez en même temps à M. Scribe le reçu du 1er acte," fol. 44 of the same manuscript); (2) the entry in Meyerbeer's pocket-diary, 16 September 1838, *Briefwechsel*, 3:160; (3) Meyerbeer's letter to Minna Meyerbeer, 23 September 1838, ibid., 163.

85. See Marrinan, "Images and ideas of Charlotte Corday."

with recent French history much as they had in *Les Huguenots*, with its parallels with the Terror. By making the would-be assassin turn her murderous feelings against herself in the final version of 1849, they mixed one more element into the opera, that of the woman who kills herself for disappointed love: a motive that has been described as a "cultural obsession" of the nineteenth century.[86] Berthe's suicide has nothing of the heroic self-denial with which Pamyra in *Le Siège de Corinthe*, or Cassandra and her companions in *Les Troyens*, take their leave of life, while it joins the death of Valentine in *Les Huguenots* as a reinforcement of the "familiar assumption that woman lives for love, man for himself."[87] The fact that she remains fixated on Jean even as she dies also focuses the audience's attention on his fate, and enhances the climactic effect of the final catastrophe.

For after Berthe's death has put an end to any hope of personal happiness Jean may have had, he too decides to end his life. It is for this purpose that he stages a bacchanalian orgy, because he decides to take all those he believes to have betrayed him with him. Faced with a hopeless military situation and the imminent capture of the castle by the imperial army he gives orders for the castle to be blown up, after the gate has been closed so that no one can escape. For the last time he allows his followers to celebrate him as their prophet. After lascivious dances by young girls, he starts to sing his *Couplets bachiques:*

> JEAN *avec force et une gaîté sauvage*
> Versez! que tout respire
> L'ivresse et le délire!
> Que tout cède à l'empire
> De ce nectar brûlant!
> Ah! la céleste fête,
> Ô triomphe si brillant!
>> (*Le Prophète* Acte V, scène 6)

JEAN *(with vehemence and a wild gaiety):* Pour the wine! Let all respire intoxication and delight! Let everything surrender to the power of this fiery nectar! Ah, heavenly banquet, brilliant triumph!

But his second stanza is interrupted by the traitors bursting into the hall to capture him with the intention of buying their own safety from the imperial forces by handing him over to them.

86. Higonnet, "Suicide: Representations of the feminine," 103.
87. Ibid., 108.

JEAN
Versez! que tout respire
L'ivresse et le délire,
Que résonne la lyre et . . .
(Dans ce moment les portes s'ouvrent avec fracas. Oberthal
à la tête des troupes impériales, s'élance dans la salle.)
JONAS, MATHISEN, ZACHARIE, CHOEUR
La mort, la mort au faux prophète!
    (Acte V, scène 6)

        ~   ~   ~

JEAN: Pour the wine! Let all respire intoxication and delight, let the lyre resound and . . . (At this moment the doors burst open. Oberthal rushes into the room, at the head of imperial troops.) JONAS, MATHISEN, ZACHARIE, CHORUS: Death, death to the false prophet!

The point at which the interruption comes is itself indicative of Jean's destructive temper: he calls for the sound of the lyre and his next wish is for death—only the word emerges from the mouths of others. Just before the castle finally collapses, Fidès, who Jean believes is already somewhere safe, makes her way to her son through the ruins, in order to die with him. The two sing together a last "bacchic couplet," ecstatically welcoming death as a divine fire that will carry them to God ("Ah! viens, divine flamme, vers Dieu qui nous réclame"). The castle walls tumble down in the blazing inferno, burying all, suicides, Anabaptist traitors, and imperial soldiers, beneath the ruins.

For this extravagant suicide, Meyerbeer drew on the legend of Sardanapalus, made part of the general fund of cultural knowledge by Byron's play of 1821 and above all by Delacroix's famous painting of 1827, which, interestingly enough, was influenced by Cicéri's stage settings for Le Siège de Corinthe.[88] Like the legendary Assyrian king of the seventh century B.C., the false prophet stages his death as a hybrid spectacle. But this appropriation of a myth that appealed to the Romantic imagination also gives yet another illustration of how closely Meyerbeer's depiction of the Anabaptists paralleled recent French history; the ode Les Révolutions written in 1831 by the aristocrat Lamartine, inspired by the hunger riots in Lyon, also invokes the example of Sardanapalus as a warning of the possible perversion of revolutionary violence, and ends with an exhortation:

88. See Piot, Les Palettes de Delacroix, 75; Spector, Delacroix: The Death of Sardanapalus, 119, n. 2.

Mais ne ressemblons pas à ces rois d'Assyrie
Qui traînaient au tombeau femmes, enfants, patrie,
    Et ne savaient pas mourir seuls;
Qui jetaient au bûcher, avant que d'y descendre,
Famille, amis, coursiers, trésors réduits en cendre,
Espoir ou souvenirs de leurs jours plus heureux,
Et, livrant leur empire et leurs dieux à la flamme,
Auraient voulu qu'aussi l'univers n'eût qu'une âme,
    Pour que tout mourût avec eux![89]

       ⸎   ⸎   ⸎

Let us not resemble those kings of Assyria who dragged their wives, children, fatherland down into the tomb, and could not die alone; who, before descending into the grave, cast into the flames family, friends,
steeds, treasures reduced to ashes, hopes and memories of their happiest
days, and, putting their empires and their gods to the torch, would have
wished the universe itself to have but one soul, so that all might die with
them!

Meyerbeer's depiction of the prophet Jean as one who, as a critic remarked after the première, "began like Masaniello and ends like Sardanapalus,"[90] is not simply a reference to a Romantic analogy and a political interpretation: there is also, as there is in Lamartine's poem, a moral
aspect. Jean's macabre death provides a striking example of the way the
negation of existing values necessarily leads to chaos, if not apocalypse.
The composer cannot explain revolution to himself or his public as the
ultimate resort of bitter distress or political determination, only as the
aberration of neurotics and eccentrics. The logical consequence is that
Jean (whom Meyerbeer considered making an epileptic at an early
stage)[91] and those closest to him die by suicide. Self-destructiveness is
an inherent trait of revolution.

In being so constructed as to culminate in a triple suicide, the opera
appropriates a commonly accepted theory of its day, according to which
suicide was a direct expression of the moral crisis of postrevolutionary
French society. Yet again, Scribe and Meyerbeer permitted themselves
massive deviations from historical fact in order to focus directly on the

89. Lamartine, *Oeuvres poétiques complètes*, 519.

90. "[il] a commencé comme Mazaniello et finit comme Sardanapale"; Jérôme Sol-
dièze in *Le Tintamarre*, 22–28 April 1849, cited in Coudroy, *La Critique parisienne*, pt. 2,
p. 56.

91. See Meyerbeer's note on the manuscript, F-Pn, n.a.f. 22504, fol. 36.

fears and obsessions of the contemporary urban public. Suicide was the topic of an impassioned debate in the "capital city of the nineteenth century," fueled primarily by conservative publicists, and reaching a new height in the 1840s with a flood of publications. The forerunners of modern sociology had begun to apply statistical methods to suicide figures in the early years of the Bourbon restoration, and diagnosed a steady increase in the worrying phenomenon. It may well be that it was not the figures that led to the conclusion that there was a crisis in society, but the conviction that a crisis existed that created a disposition to seek out the figures.[92] There is some evidence that the increase in the suicide statistics is connected both with greater efficiency in collecting data as the century advanced and with a simultaneous waning of people's tendency to conceal the fact that a relative had chosen a way of death that was still stigmatized.[93] Nevertheless, the comparison of the figures for 1818 and 1847 is arresting even today: three years after the restoration, the figure of suicides registered in Paris was 46 per 100,000 of the population, but in 1847 it was 87 per 100,000; the figure fell in 1848 but only to 66.[94] The common assumption at the time, that the figure would continue to rise as urbanization and industrialization spread, proved false, however; at the end of the nineteenth century the suicide rate stagnated in almost every European country, while the figure, published in 1985, of 26 per 100,000 per year in what was then West Berlin, where the pressures on the population were regarded as aggravated by the city's isolation, can be seen to be decidedly low.

The fact remains that in the mid-nineteenth century the French ruling classes and the average Parisian operagoer were agreed that suicide was one of the greatest ills of city life in an age of anxiety and instability, and that responsibility for its increase lay with all those who called for change in a social order distinguished by blatant inequality and injustice. A professor of philosophy, writing in 1840, made no bones about equating "the mania of suicide" with "the spirit of revolt":

> It is impossible not to be struck by two moral phenomena which are like the expression of an evil now working in a particular manner on the limbs and the body of society: we refer to Suicide and Revolt. Impatient with all laws, dissatisfied with every position, men rebel equally against human nature and against mankind, against themselves and against society. Thus

92. See Baechler, *Les Suicides*, 16–17.
93. Ibid. 32–34.
94. See Chevalier, *Classes laborieuses et classes dangereuses*; the figures are extrapolated from tables on 470 and 539.

suicide and revolt are nothing other than a dual effect of a single cause, two symptoms of one moral malady, namely: a burning unrest, the consequence of a void in heart and spirit alike.[95]

While *Le Prophète* can be regarded as an extremely suggestive realization of such ideas (in 1854 a desperate man chose to end his life at a performance of it in the Paris Opéra: according to a newspaper report, "because his life was empty and because he hadn't a sou, [he] blew his brains out on the last couplet of *Le Prophète*"),[96] the closing scene of the opera is open to other, quite different interpretations. Given the prominence in Jean's role of the charismatic traits of a political demagogue, the all-embracing catastrophe at the end might be regarded as a foreshadowing of the developments that enabled unscrupulous dictators like Napoleon III to involve whole nations in their own downfalls. One element supporting such a view of the last scene is the music itself, which has nothing of any "spirit of revolt" about it; rather, its brilliant dance rhythms in $\frac{6}{8}$ meters are closer to the spirit of pleasure characteristic of the Second Empire. It is true that in the final version of the score two elements illustrating contemporary French society's lubricious tastes rather too well disappear in the background. Meyerbeer dispensed with the idea he formed some years before the première of introducing "grotesque dances," inspired by opium, in the *Bacchanale*,[97] and he also watered down substantially the original plan of presenting the corps de ballet in sexually explicit postures,[98] partly because cuts in Act IV had already eliminated a scene before the coronation in which the Anabaptists would have chosen twelve daughters of Münster citizens as their king's harem.[99] All the same, the collage of erotic displays, "bacchic" dance

---

95. "Il est impossible de ne pas être frappé de deux phénomènes moraux qui sont comme l'expression d'un mal qui travaille maintenant d'une manière particulière les membres et le corps de la société: nous voulons parler du Suicide et de la Révolte. Impatient de toute loi, mécontent de toute position, on se soulève également contre la nature humaine et contre l'homme, contre soi-même et contre la société. Ainsi le suicide et la révolte ne sont qu'un double effet d'une même cause, deux symptômes d'une seule maladie morale, savoir: une inquiétude brûlante, conséquence d'un vide commun au coeur et à l'esprit." Tissot, *De la Manie du suicide et de l'esprit de révolte*, v.

96. "parce que la vie l'ennuyait, et parce qu'il n'avait plus le sou, [il] s'est fait sauter la cervelle au dernier couplet du *Prophète*"; J[oseph]-H[enri de] Collet, "Chronique parisienne: Revue de la semaine," *Figaro: Journal non politique*, 4 June 1854, p. 1.

97. See an undated entry in Meyerbeer's diary, probably late 1844, *Briefwechsel*, 3:539.

98. See Frese, *Dramaturgie der großen Opern Giacomo Meyerbeers*, 200.

99. See Meyerbeer's prose sketch in F-Pn, n.a.f. 22504, fols. 41v–42. See also Armstrong, "Meyerbeer's *Le Prophète*," 358–62 and the edition of the passage in question on 1133–49.

music, and the deafening noise of the collapsing castle walls with which this unusual opera ends, seems to anticipate the fears of a society that found fulfillment in luxurious pleasures but was also conscious that the dance was being performed on the rim of a volcano. Wholesale cataclysm as the ending of an opera went a stage further in Wagner's *Götterdämmerung* (1876),[100] but it was hardly by chance that this earlier example dates from the years when the upper classes began to have serious fears for the continuing existence of capitalist society.

Magic Fire

The decision, taken only ten days before the première of *Le Prophète*, to have Berthe die by her own hand, enhanced the dramatic unity of the last act but left Meyeerbeer without the time to revise his score yet again in the light of that new unity and find musical means with which to delineate the three characters' shared propensity to suicide. Berthe's death scene represented an opportunity for something spectacular, but it could make little musico-dramatic impact once Meyerbeer found himself forced to cut the arioso he had composed for it. It emerged at the general rehearsal that the score was far too long, in any case, so the composer had to be glad of every bar saved, and too little time remained before the première for him to insert a new musical development at this point in the drama. Necessarily, therefore, the fifth act lacked some of the dramaturgical stringency and architectural logic of the fourth, as Meyerbeer himself recognized. He admitted to his mother that "the musical effect declines" in the scenes following the duet between Jean and Fidès; luckily Berthe's entrance and death did not claim the audience's attention to the same full extent as did the duet with its "quite extraordinary tragic effect" and the overwhelming finale: "A wonderful fire, with which the opera ends, came to my aid in sustaining enthusiasm to the very end."[101]

It may raise a smile, at this distance, to find Meyerbeer attributing the effectiveness of the final scene to the "wonderful fire" alone, that is, to its staging, not to his conception which embraced all the resources available to the musical theater. But his emphasis on the spectacular element in this finale can also be taken seriously as an indication of the

---

100. See Döhring, "Meyerbeers Konzeption der historischen Oper," 99.

101. "die musikalische Wirkung in den folgenden Scenen sinkt"; "ganz außerordentlichen tragischen Wirkung"; "ein wundervoller Brand, womit das Stück endiget, kam mir zu Hülfe, um den Enthusiasmus bis zu letzt wach zu halten"; letter to Amalia Beer, 17 April 1849, *Briefwechsel*, 4:487.

significance of fire in the motivic repertory of mid-nineteenth-century opera. *Le Prophète* was by no means the first operatic tragedy to end in a conflagration: to give one obvious example, the numerous eighteenth- and early nineteenth-century settings of Metastasio's libretto *Didone abbandonata* had all called for a similar climax. That type of scene had remained an exception in Parisian grand opéra, however, after Rossini's *Siège de Corinthe* had drawn attention to the dramaturgical problems created by an uncompromisingly tragic ending. Yet there was a succession of operas, in the second half of the nineteenth century, in which the mysterious and destructive power of fire engulfed the stage at a climactic moment. The "Magic Fire" in Wagner's *Die Walküre* (first performed 1870) and the final catastrophe in his *Götterdämmerung* spring to mind immediately, and the same composer's *Rienzi* (1842), conceived in the grand opéra tradition, ends similarly; other instances are the mass burning of heretics at the stake in Act III of Verdi's *Don Carlos* (1867) and the destruction of the Libyan camp in Reyer's *Salammbo* (1890).

The sun, the strongest imaginable source of illumination, provided other opportunities for opera to exploit the most recent technical advances in breathtaking lighting effects. The prologue of Verdi's *Attila*, first performed in Venice in 1846, depicts a slow sunrise, for example; admittedly the tone-painting in that is scarcely an advance on what Haydn achieved in his symphony *Le Matin* (1761) or his oratorio *The Creation* (1798), or, indeed, on the effects in the ode-symphonie *Le Désert* by Félicien David, first performed in a concert hall, not a theater, in Paris in 1844; *Le Désert* was a phenomenal success and may have served Verdi as a model.[102] Inevitably the stage-realization of the effect was doomed to remain inadequate for as long as gaslight and candles were the only forms of lighting in the theater. It is significant that the sunrise in the first of Verdi's operas to reach Paris, his rewritten *Jérusalem* (1847), did not greatly excite audiences long accustomed to the effect, whereas it made a great impression on the critics at the Milan première in December 1850.[103]

Theatrical sunrises were transformed by the advent of electricity, and the fact that electric light was used for the first time in operatic history in the third act of *Le Prophète* was not the least of the reasons for its huge success. Electric arc lamps gave a far greater intensity than gas lamps could, and, even better, the light was evenly distributed, steady, and un-

102. See Basevi, *Studio sulle opere di Giuseppe Verdi*, 93.
103. See the review in the *Gazzetta musicale di Milano*, January 1851, cited in *Gerusalemme*, ed. Mario Medici (*Quaderni dell'Istituto di Studi Verdiani*, 2; Parma: Istituto di Studi Verdiani, 1963), 106.

flickering. A Parisian optician invented a carbon arc lamp, long regarded as the first of its kind, specially for the production of Meyerbeer's opera, although it has recently been discovered that a precursor
was installed in a London theater in December 1848. The English version attracted little notice, however, while the Parisian one spread to all
the leading theaters in Europe, in step with the opera itself.[104] Subsequently, electricity revitalized the theatrical rainbow, already familiar
from the finale of Rossini's *Guillaume Tell*, but now able to glow with
unprecedentedly lifelike splendor; this was seen for the first time at the
Paris Opéra in 1860, for a new production of Rossini's *Moïse et
Pharaon*.[105]

In contrast to David, Verdi, or Wagner in *Das Rheingold*, Meyerbeer
did not underpin the visual stage-effect with his music, which is more
of an advantage than a disadvantage in the context of the finale of Act
III of *Le Prophète*. It means that, like the Anabaptist troops, the audience
is quite unprepared for the sunrise and is therefore astonished by it,
while the music runs on as if oblivious to it, with the postlude to Jean's
Hymne triomphal. Instead of the cliché of major chords rising up the
scale in a slow crescendo to depict the sunrise, Meyerbeer envisaged a
juxtaposition of initially separate levels of perception, and it is only
when this is realized with all the musical and stage resources of the theater that its allegorical significance is perceived, lending the ecstatic
"hymn" with its messianic charge a splendor that music alone could
scarcely achieve. In the words of Sieghart Döhring:

> The sunrise . . . acts as a visual symbol of the victory charismatically pre-
> dicted by Jean . . . The great musical build toward a climax in this act-
> finale thus receives its crowning touch from an optical effect, and in fact
> any additional musical interpretation at this point would interrupt the rise
> in tension and decisively diminish the overall effect. That Meyerbeer the
> composer yielded to Meyerbeer the dramatist in this way is a testimony
> to his theatrical genius.[106]

The overwhelming success proved Meyerbeer's theatrical instinct
right. His fellow-composer Adolphe Adam could hardly contain
himself:

> The effect of the sunrise is one of the most novel and beautiful effects
> ever seen in the theater: thanks to the electric light we saw a real sun

104. For a description of how the effect was achieved, see Rees, *Theatre Lighting in
the Age of Gas*, 65–78; see also Baumann, *Licht im Theater*, 139–40.
105. See Bergman, *Lighting in the Theatre*, 279.
106. "Multimediale Tendenzen," 498.

that we could not look at steadily without being dazzled, and whose light projected itself to the very back of the boxes furthest from the stage.[107]

Adam's enthusiasm for being "dazzled" gives a hint, admittedly, that there was more to the popularity of such effects than the fact that they relied on completely new technical resources, never before available for use on the stage. The illumination of large spaces by artificial light was now part of the experience of city life, but still far from taken for granted: we can perhaps surmise that both the artists who worked in a city like Paris and the public who lived there were sensitized to light and perceived it as something extraordinary. Since the start of the nineteenth century people had experienced the gradual transition of street lighting, for example, from small circles of weak light shed by isolated lamps to large areas flooded with light.[108] Naturally, writers, too, had reacted to the illumination every night of the kind of spaces—city squares or streets—which, in the eighteenth century, would have been brilliantly lit only exceptionally, when a festival or some court ceremony was being celebrated. The brightness of the lights is a recurring motif in descriptions of city life in these years, and significantly, as late as the 1860s, it is still represented as something extraordinary, retaining the festive associations of the past, while "the effects of a technological innovation, artificial light, [were] enfolded in the aura of a natural process or a ritual."[109]

The operatic uses for dazzling sunlight or the destructive glow of fire were not confined to religious associations as in *Le Prophète*. More and more frequently, fire acquired a symbolic significance with the power to affect characters' actions. In the case of Verdi's *Trovatore*, for example, the highly involved plot gains its dramatic unity from the dominating effect on the gypsy, Azucena, of a traumatic event which took place long ago and is presented in the opera itself only in the form of narrative. The gruesome image of her mother dying in flames at the stake is an *idée fixe* that pursues Azucena throughout the opera. The "troubadour" of the title, too, is obsessed by the thought of "that fire, and its dreadful flames," as he reveals in his celebrated cabaletta, "Di quella pira, l'or-

---

107. "L'effet du lever du soleil est une des choses les plus neuves et les plus belles que l'on ait vues au théâtre: grâce à la lumière électrique, nous avons vu un vrai soleil, qu'on ne pouvait regarder fixement sans être ébloui, et dont la lumière se projetait jusqu'au fond des loges les plus reculées de la scène"; review in *Le Constitutionnel*, 18 April 1849, cited in Meyerbeer, *Briefwechsel*, 4:619.

108. See Schivelbusch, *Disenchanted Night*, 115.

109. See Brüggemann, *"Aber schickt keinen Poeten nach London!,"* 51, n. 19.

rendo foco."[110] *Il trovatore* and *Don Carlos* were not the first operas to feature this manner of execution: it had already been used by Halévy and Scribe in *La Juive*, which actually had the title *Rachel, ou L'Auto-da-fé* during the planning stage.[111] In fact Rachel and her father Éléazer are thrown into a boiling cauldron suspended above the fire, but it burns onstage and the text of this final scene frequently mentions the flames. As in *Il trovatore*, indeed, the symbolism of flames has already played an important part in the opera's prehistory: once Éléazar rescued the daughter of his enemy Brogni from the burning ruins of Rome, and the grisly irony toward which this skillfully worked plot makes its inexorable way is that Rachel, the supposed Jewess thrown to the flames on Brogni's orders, is that same daughter. Originally Scribe and Halévy thought of contriving a happy ending, but changed their minds.[112]

The increasing use of fire to shock and horrify audiences was not restricted to the opera house, but was at least equally characteristic of popular forms of theater in the nineteenth century as well as cinema in the twentieth. This specific manifestation of an "aesthetic of horror" is only to be understood, admittedly, against the background of the fact that the elemental power of fire was far more of a threat to the life of the theatergoing city-dweller in the nineteenth century than it is in an age when almost every conceivable contact with flammable materials is subject to stringent safety precautions. Fire had been harnessed by technology ever since the beginning of the so-called industrial revolution, not only in the machinery used to drive factories and locomotives but even in the theater itself, where big fires had grown more frequent since the introduction of gas lighting (in 1822, in the case of the Paris Opéra). In Paris alone, at least nine theaters were destroyed by fire between 1826 and 1849, and a theater-historian of the time recorded at least fifty theaters in Europe suffering the same fate in the twenty-year period 1861–81.[113]

As well as transfiguring an only too real fear, the representation of fatal fires on the operatic stage also permitted the frequent catastrophes to be interpreted as a symptom of a society that had lost the stability of the ancien régime. Viewed thus, the use of fiery imagery (infernos, volcanoes, etc.) borrowed from Romantic painting by not only Meyerbeer but also Balzac before him to enhance their representation of social

110. See Gerhard, "Dalla fatalità all'ossessione," 63.

111. See Scribe's prose sketch, F-Pn, n.a.f. 22502, fols. 8–19.

112. See the copy of Act IV and V, ibid., fols. 28–50, and the copy of Act V, ibid., fols. 51–58.

113. See Pougin, *Dictionnaire historique et pittoresque du théâtre*, 368, 371.

conditions is yet another manifestation of the nineteenth century's fondness for phantasmagoria.[114] The inexorable build toward total destruction by the power of explosion and fire entails what Walter Benjamin identified as an aspiration to allegory,[115] and that aspiration, in its context, raises the conclusion of *Le Prophète* far "above the traditional catastrophic endings of earlier operas," as Sieghart Döhring has written: "the flames in which reactionaries and revolutionaries perish together signal the end of history, in the Last Judgment."[116]

The flames also reveal how much there is in Meyerbeer's opera of the nineteenth century's fascination with apocalyptic visions. Several French composers were obsessed with the idea of depicting the Last Judgment in music. Berlioz once planned an opera about "the last day of the world," and Félicien David projected an oratorio to be entitled "The Last Love," into which he wanted to integrate music he had composed for a never-performed mélodrame on the same subject (*La Fin du monde, ou Le Jugement dernier*, 1849). Though neither of these plans was realized, both composers brought off apocalyptic scenes, at least: Berlioz in his *Grande Messe des Morts*, and David in his Pompeian opera *Herculanum*, produced at the Paris Opéra in 1859 with considerable success. Verdi, too, in the Dies Irae of his *Requiem*, extended the resources of his musico-theatrical language to extraordinary heights, and Halévy's opera *Le Juif errant* (1852), another work with a libretto by Scribe, also culminates in a vision of the end of the world.[117]

MOSAIC

The visual dominance of the "wonderful fire" in Act V of *Le Prophète* was reinforced by Meyerbeer's rigorous pruning of the music he had composed for the finale. The first general rehearsal of the complete work had forced him to recognize that, although he had already cut several numbers, at four hours and ten minutes it was still too long. Since he acknowledged the legitimacy of the audience's preferences, he had no choice but to undertake more cuts, as he noted in his diary: "I must

114. See Brüggemann, *"Aber schickt keinen Poeten nach London!,"* 171.
115. See *Das Passagen-Werk. Aufzeichnungen und Materialien*, in *Gesammelte Schriften*, 5:468.
116. "Meyerbeers Konzeption der historischen Oper," 99.
117. See Besnier, "Musique pour la fin du monde," 171–82; on Berlioz's plans see also Holoman, *Catalogue of the Works of Hector Berlioz*, 128; on those of David see Locke, *Music, Musicians and Saint-Simonians*, 216–17.

therefore cut at least forty minutes: a hard and difficult task."[118] This renewed work on a score which at that date could boast the longest gestation in operatic history made it even more obvious that its different musical sections, ranged side by side more or less unmediated, were not conceived at the same time but in some cases as much as ten years apart.

This gave some support to Verdi's comment, made two decades later, that in the end a grand opéra was "not a work in one piece but a mosaic. That may be fine if you like it, but it's still a mosaic."[119] There was nothing very original about this opinion: the very words clearly allude to the demand in August Wilhelm Schlegel's *Lectures on Dramatic Art and Literature* (1809–11) that a drama "must in the first place be a connected whole, and complete within itself."[120] Verdi's term "in one piece"—"di un solo getto," in Italian—is a direct quotation of Schlegel's words as they appear in the very free Italian translation published in 1817 and frequently reprinted.[121] Nor was Verdi the first person to use Schlegel's criterion as a stick with which to beat grand opéra, for a French critic had already done so when reviewing the first performance of *Les Huguenots*,[122] before another Italian, the critic Nicola Marselli, gave the diagnosis that the analytical character native to the Germans had "transfused" Meyerbeer's music, "already a synthesis of the various genres and elements poured into its large-scale form," so that "the Mother Idea, the Generatrix Unity" vanished, as it almost inevitably must.[123] And after all, Meyerbeer himself, in 1841, had deplored "the mosaic-work, pieced together from infinitely tiny scraps" of an opéra comique by his colleague Halévy.[124] Unlike Verdi, however, it is clear that neither Marselli nor Meyerbeer saw that the fault lay, not in a congenitally German fogginess, nor in the fallibility of an individual composer, but, to a very great extent, in the conditions that prevailed at the Paris Opéra. When a new work was in rehearsal, the singers, the producer, the management,

118. "Ich muß also 40 Minuten Musik wenigstens schneiden: eine harte und schwierige Aufgabe"; entry for 1 April 1849, *Briefwechsel*, 4:483.

119. Letter to Camille Du Locle, 8 December 1869, *I copialettere*, 220; cited from *Letters of Giuseppe Verdi*, 152.

120. *A Course of Lectures on Dramatic Art and Literature*, 1:30.

121. See Della Seta, "Verdi: La tradizione italiana," 140.

122. See G[ustave] Planche, *Chronique de Paris*, 3 March 1836, pp. 250–53 (p. 252).

123. "sintetica per i vari generi o elementi che getta nella grande forma, è poi analitica di soverchio pel modo con cui li maneggia"; "l'Idea madre, l'Unità generatrice"; Marselli, *La ragione della musica moderna*, 65–66; see also Della Seta, "L'immagine di Meyerbeer," 166.

124. "die aus unendlich kleinen Teilchen . . . zusammengefügte Mosaikarbeit"; see Meyerbeer's diary, 19 October 1841, in *Briefwechsel*, 3:375 (my thanks to Karl Leich-Galland, of Saarbrücken, for drawing this to my attention).

and the set designer all repeatedly exerted influence on the final version of the score, in the interests of theatrical success in every department. An additional problem for Meyerbeer was that he always found it extremely hard to choose between alternatives. The fact that the material eventually cut from the definitive score of each of his four grands opéras amounts to several hours of playing time makes his an extreme case, but even second-rate composers like Niedermeyer or Mermet, who were not troubled by uncertainty like his, and were allowed scarcely more than a few months in which to write any of their operas, left behind bulky autograph scores, such as those of *Stradella* (1837) and *Roland à Roncevaux* (1864), in which numerous sections are to be found that were cut even before their premières.

It is true that Marselli's opinion of Meyerbeer was based solely on knowledge of *Robert le diable*,[125] and the only concrete example Verdi gave in support of his opinion was *Guillaume Tell*, so there would be some justification in arguing that as both were among the very earliest of grands opéras they suffered from teething troubles attributable to the genre's heterogenous origins and overcome in the first mature examples, such as *Les Huguenots*. But for all his diplomatic restraint, Verdi directed his diatribe at Parisian grand opéra as a whole, and even if *Les Huguenots* has always been acknowledged as the best integrated of Meyerbeer's large-scale historical operas, it is not altogether innocent of the fault of being a "mosaic." It is not surprising if modern-day audiences, schooled by a totally different repertory, necessarily receive Meyerbeer's works as a mosaic of pieces which they refer, albeit anachronistically, to more familiar music by the next generation of composers, such as Offenbach, Verdi, or Wagner;[126] but the audiences of 1836 must have registered the kaleidoscopic variety of "characteristic" detail filling the stage in Act III of *Les Huguenots* as a breach of classicist norms of artistic unity. All the same, the term "mosaic" is more justified in the case of *Le Prophète*, that is, an opera whose third act is made up of a series of events in an army camp.

This act, like the army-camp scene in Meyerbeer's 1844 opera for Berlin, *Ein Feldlager in Schlesien*, is based on a wholly undramatic situation, a period of calm before military action, so that the revue-like traits of the composer's dramaturgy are more conspicuous than they would be in any other context. Even before the arrival of peasant women skating

125. See *La ragione della musica moderna*, 46; Della Seta, "L'immagine di Meyerbeer," 167, n. 53.

126. See Pospíšil, "Der positive Beitrag der französischen *Grand Opéra*," 78.

across the ice with supplies, in an action scene providing the occasion for a spectacular ballet, the mosaic effect is already present in the *Entr'acte*, at the end of which a C major dominant-seventh chord and a fortissimo chord of F-sharp major are played side by side with no mediation between them. The chorus which follows the *Entr'acte* is even more of a heterogenous montage, with a disjointed series of bloodthirsty shouts ("Du sang!"), a march-time injunction to be vigilant for spies ("Frappez l'épi quand il se lève"), and an unaccompanied Te Deum. The purpose of this, obviously, is to depict the hysterical volatility of the Anabaptist masses, and can surprise us nowadays by its anticipation of cinematic techniques, but it has its moments of weakness, when Meyerbeer adds elements that contribute no sense of "characteristic" color and are musically highly conventional. An example of this is the recitative between the opening chorus, composed in 1841, and Zacharie's *Couplets*, conceived in 1839,[127] for the bald parlando style of these four bars necessarily disrupts the musico-dramatic flow.

More than any other type of scene, the "army-camp scene," in spite of the inherent problems revealed by this example, met the needs of audiences that enjoyed spectacle, for it enabled the kaleidoscopic variety of contemporary panorama shows to be transferred to the opera house. Striking evidence of the exceptional attraction of such scenes is found, surprisingly, in the works of Verdi. Although the Italian's constant goal was the greatest possible concision, he set a long sequence of scenes in Act III of *Il trovatore* in a camp, and when planning *La forza del destino* he required his librettist to write him a whole extra act that had no connection with the Spanish sources of the rest of the opera. This satisfied his wish to compose motifs from Schiller's play *Wallensteins Lager* (a one-set, one-act work which is the army-camp scene par excellence), including a vivid hellfire sermon; the latter had also been one of Meyerbeer's ideas for *Le Prophète* two decades earlier, and at one stage he asked Scribe to write some text for the Anabaptist Jonas "in the style of the sermons of Abraham à Santa Clara or the Capuchin in Wallenstein's Camp."[128] Surprisingly, given his declared disapproval of "mosaic," Verdi did not make his military scene strictly relevant to the personal intrigue of *La forza del destino*, so that, to an even greater extent than the scenes in Act III of *Il trovatore*, it comes over as a purely decorative

127. See Meyerbeer's diary entries for 17 February 1841 and 8 June 1839, *Briefwechsel*, 3:330, 186.

128. "dans le genre des prêches du père Abraham à Santa Clara, ou comme le Capucin dans le camp de Wallenstein"; Meyerbeer's note on the manuscript, F-Pn, n.a.f. 22504, fol. 36.

interlude. Meyerbeer, on the other hand, in both *Ein Feldlager in Schle-sien* and *Le Prophète*, cemented his mosaic of large and small scenes of life in an army camp firmly into the historical dramaturgy of the opera. In both cases, the army commander is also the male protagonist of the private intrigue and the imminent battle will decide his future; in the context of a dramatic structure of several acts, the revue-like army-camp scenes, like the third act of *Les Huguenots*, draw their specific character and their musico-dramatic legitimation from the tense quiet before the violence to come.

Le Prophète differs from *Les Huguenots*, however, in that the last two acts also have some revue-like traits rendering them open, in the last analysis, to the "mosaic" charge. In his version of the St. Bartholomew's Day massacre, Meyerbeer concentrates on the encounters and relation-ships between individual characters, and even if he unfolds these against the ever-present background of the historico-political events, he delays the moment at which the two strands must eventually combine at the forefront of the action until the penultimate scene. In *Le Prophète*, on the other hand, he brings the historical events and the climax of the personal intrigue together earlier, in the coronation scene in Act IV. The manner in which he does it is breathtakingly modern, directly jux-taposing expressions of Fidès's maternal feelings and the religiously mo-tivated hysteria of the Anabaptist masses in both the preamble and the closing bars of this great act-finale: in the opening ensemble, *Prière et imprécation*, Fidès's prayer is heard against the hymn "Domine, salvum fac regem," sung offstage, while in the closing stretta the contrasting musics of the Anabaptist hymn, the people's chorus, and Fidès's solos create an effect like a series of rapid cinematic dissolves, "synthetically" constructing the overall scene.[129]

Meyerbeer's synthetic compositional process reveals itself at its best in scenes like this with their "cinematic" tendencies, and gains addi-tional dramatic impact from the assembly of heterogenous elements in a common frame. In the conception of other sections of this finale, on the other hand, he was obviously not ready to jettison all the conven-tions of lyric opera (he was, after all, born in the eighteenth century). There are several places where he might have shaped the transitions between the presentation of the overall scene and the concentration on one character's emotions with the uncompromising radicality that per-meates so much of *Le Prophète*, but did not. On the one hand he linked

129. The cinematic simile is Sieghart Döhring's: see his "Multimediale Tendenzen," 500.

the children's chorus to Jean's expression of satisfaction that his vision of a kingdom has now been fulfilled by keeping the organ accompaniment going and binding Jean's parlando into the concluding cadence on to the tonic; on the other hand he followed Fidès's indignant cry "Mon fils!" with four bars that at once dissipate the skillfully accumulated atmosphere of the coronation scene by introducing, for the first time in the scene, a simple recitativo intonation. Of course there were good dramatic reasons for this: Fidès's exclamation destroys Jean's presumption to be the son of God in an instant, and it would be nonsense if this peripeteia employed the same musical means with which Jean's castle of lies has just been built up. Instead Meyerbeer turns once again to pantomime. Fidès's cry follows a general pause in the music, supplemented by a lengthy stage direction, just as Jean's hypocritical question "What woman is this?" ("Quelle est cette femme?") is followed by another general pause (marked *Silence*): the son's effrontery silences the mother and the orchestra alike.

Sieghart Döhring's comment on Meyerbeer's treatment of the sunrise in Act III, cited earlier, is apt here too: "That Meyerbeer the composer yielded to Meyerbeer the dramatist . . . is a testimony to his theatrical genius." There, the opportunity for the scenic resources to make the required effect on their own occurs at the very end of the act, after all the musical trumps have been played; here in Act IV, the musical resources are put on hold at a point at which yet more musical highpoints can, and do, follow. It is likely that when listeners hear the *Couplets* in which Fidès begins to answer Jean's question ("Je suis, hélas, je suis la pauvre femme"), they will feel confirmed in their expectations that opera is primarily a matter of solo singing, but when they come to look back at the whole they will regard the complete absence of any music to bridge the gap between Jean's and Fidès's solos as a deficiency. The melodramatic interruption of the large-scale, set-piece finale breaks up its musical structure into lyrical segments placed unconnectedly side by side. The mosaic character of the finale becomes yet more obvious in the ten bars Meyerbeer places betweeen the ensemble that follows Fidès's *Couplets* and the ironic male chorus praising the powers of the prophet-king ("Tout est possible au roi prophète"). The brief exchange of words between Jean and his mother is set, once again, as simple recitative, accompanied by a few string chords, but in this case the disruption of the musical tension is not justified by dramatic considerations. In missing the opportunity to support the dialogue at this point with a musically significant orchestral commentary, Meyerbeer betrays himself as the adherent of an outmoded aesthetic convention that such points of repose were indispensable in an opera, in order to avoid tiring the audience with "the incessant flow of the orchestra."[130] Antoine Reicha, in his 1833 treatise on opera, had already censured the most recent Italian operas for their lack of simple recitatives, "which would allow the ear to rest when it is made weary by hearing the mass of the orchestra playing away unceasingly for two or three hours at a time."[131] Meyerbeer himself felt "deafened by a senseless superabundance of orchestration"[132] after attending a performance of Wagner's *Rienzi* in 1844, and nearly twenty years later he was still incapable of concentrating on more than one act of *Lohengrin*, a contemporary of *Le Prophète*, "on account of the spiritual weariness and strain" listening to it imposed on him.[133]

Meyerbeer's conception of listeners well able to continue concentrating at length is far removed from what Adorno represented as Wagner's cavalier assessment of the limited receptive capabilities of an audience "unable to concentrate—something not unconnected with the fatigue of the citizen in his leisure time," yet Meyerbeer, too, was not wholly innocent of allowing his music to "hammer its message home" on the assumption that a large proportion of the audience would be "listening less attentively" to works that are every bit as long as Wagner's.[134] Having decided that he had to include still, recitative-like passages in order to manage the extreme contrasts of the coronation scene, he could not avoid the risk that this juxtaposition of traditional elements and the most recent developments would strike less tradition-loving members of the audience as nervous indecisiveness, especially as he had long ago abandoned the formal foundations of an obsolete aesthetic. In accommodating both Fidès's strophic couplets and the great *Exorcisme*, the finale of Act IV uniquely modifies the conventional form of the multipartite finale found in Italian opera until the 1860s, and thus it robs the audience of any chance of simply orienting itself by the stereotyped formal sections and perceiving simple recitative as a natural instance of a still-valid convention. Freely as he treated conventions, Meyerbeer could never steel himself to break the rules altogether, and nowhere else

130. See H. Becker, "Zwischen Oper und Drama," 86–88.

131. "qui feraient reposer l'oreille actuellement fatiguée d'entendre sans cesse les masses d'orchestra en permanence deux ou trois heures de suite"; *Art du compositeur dramatique*, 1:20.

132. "[von] einer unsinnigen Überfülle der Instrumentation betäubt"; diary, 20 September 1844, *Briefwechsel*, 3:527.

133. "wegen der geistigen Ermüdung und Anspannung"; diary, 23 October 1862; unpublished to date, cited in H. Becker, "Zwischen Oper und Drama," 94.

134. Adorno, *In Search of Wagner*, 32.

in his oeuvre is the antithesis between breathtakingly modern elements and remains of older conventions so plainly exposed as in the coronation scene in *Le Prophète*.

A quick look at the dramaturgy of the finale is enough to reveal where the dividing line between the two elements lies. Meyerbeer invents completely new formal means in the scenes in which he develops the historico-political aspects of his drama, depicts the hysteria of the Anabaptist crowds, and presents the neurotic relationship of Jean and Fidès as a public spectacle in the *Exorcisme*. When he focuses on the emotions of the individual, as in Fidès's *Couplets*, he resorts to more conventional structures, with a soloist accompanied by the chorus. This discrepancy between a highly original representation of the crowd and rather traditional characterization of the principal characters is particularly evident in the concluding montage, where there is a harsh contrast between the B-flat major homophony of the Anabaptist hymn, accompanied only by the organ, and the G major of Fidès's agonized comment on what she has just experienced. It exemplifies a problem affecting most grands opéras, especially those with historical settings and librettos by Scribe, but *Le Prophète* is the most extreme case. As Carl Dahlhaus wrote in a passage comparing Scribe and Meyerbeer's treatment of history with the more Shakespearean approach of Pushkin and Musorgsky in *Boris Godunov*:

> The conflicting claims of might and right, the mechanisms of expedience and *force majeure* which drive the wheels of the struggle for power in Shakespeare's histories, are depicted in *Le Prophète* as the outcome of emotional conflicts in which politics originally had no part at all. . . . Politics merely reflects the private affairs of those who think they are the makers of history.[135]

As was already shown in connection with Jean's dream scene in Act II, Meyerbeer and Scribe considered it necessary to give every single one of Jean's actions a concrete personal motive, however nugatory it might appear when set beside the historical and political events. This was in spite of the fact that, as experienced men of the theater, they must have known that these contrived and sometimes highly convoluted motives could be understood only by those who read the libretto. Thus it is Berthe's abduction by Oberthal and his men that finally makes Jean decide to throw in his lot with the Anabaptists; then, at the end of Act III, his

135. *Realism in Nineteenth-century Music*, 83, 87.

decision to lead the assault on Münster is based on the information that Berthe has been seen in the city; in the imposing final tableau of Act IV, it is once again the absent Berthe to whom the last words sung by a soloist refer: Fidès knows of her intention to assassinate the prophet, and now that she herself knows his true identity undertakes to prevent it. Close reading of the libretto in this light makes even Jean's suicide appear the necessary consequence of the fact that, following Berthe's recoil from him, all his hopes as a lover have been finally dashed.

Behind this unfolding of easily comprehensible, personal motives, seemingly so very disproportionate both to the historical setting and overwhelming dramaturgical structure of the opera, and to its psychological subtlety, lies the widespread nineteenth-century belief that large-scale effects in the course of history were due to tiny causes. Franz Liszt cited Voltaire as chief witness for this notion, claiming that he had coined the dictum "little causes—big effects" with respect to historical events.[136] In fact, what Voltaire said, in the course of a general discussion of the philosophical concepts of cause and effect, was: "There are thus immediate effects produced by final causes, and a very large number of effects that are remote products of these causes."[137] It is likely that the true originator of the idea cited by Liszt was an obscure historian who struck gold with two little volumes originally published in French in the 1750s and frequently reprinted, translated into German and English, and even into modern Greek in 1819. In them, a wide variety of historical events were retold in such a manner as to make them all appear to have been the effects of very insignificant causes, from Adam's "fatal apple," through the fate of Queen Semiramis, to the career of William Tell, summarized as follows in the chapter heading: "The folly of a Governor, who wishes the people under his governance to bow to his hat, gives birth to a new Republic."[138]

Such an ultradeterministic view of the world was a gift to artists, one of whose functions is to entertain the public, after all, especially as the

136. "Petites causes—grands effets"; Liszt, "*Die Stumme von Portici* von Auber"; see also the editors' commentary on p. 220 of the edition of Liszt's criticism cited in the bibliography.

137. "Il y a donc des effets immédiats produits par les causes finales, et des effets en très grand nombre qui sont des produits éloignées de ces causes"; article "Causes finales," in *Dictionnaire philosophique*, Voltaire, *Oeuvres complètes*, 53:112–27 (p. 123).

138. "La folie d'un Gouverneur, qui veut que les Peuples de son Gouvernement saluent son bonnet, donne naissance à une nouvelle République"; Richer, *Essai sur les grands événements*, 2:64. (The English translation of Richer's *Essai* [London, 1767] does not include this chapter.)

author had modestly stressed that his aim was "to amuse, not to teach history."[139] So it is hardly surprising that Scribe embraced this philosophy of history with even more enthusiasm than Liszt; in any case, what had begun as anecdotal entertainment literature in the eighteenth century became the basis of convictions held by leading philosophers of history during the nineteenth. The most successful of all Scribe's plays was the comedy *Le Verre d'eau* (1840) which was performed 345 times in Paris alone by 1870,[140] and was filmed twice in the twentieth century. The play's subtitle, significantly, is "Effects and Causes" *(Les Effets et les causes)*, and it represents historical events at the English court in the early eighteenth century solely as consequences of personal intrigues and wholly trivial causes. Scribe used all his virtuosity to push this structural principle as far as it would go, making misinterpretation of the Queen's asking a courtier for the glass of water of the title the cause of complications that have a farreaching effect on both internal politics and world history, and placing the following wisdom in the mouth of one of the leading characters:

BOLINGBROKE
Vous croyez peut-être, comme tout le monde, que les catastrophes politiques, les révolutions, les chutes d'empire, viennent de causes graves, profondes, importantes. . . Erreur! Les états sont subjugués ou conduits par des héros, par des grands hommes; mais ces grands hommes sont menés eux-mêmes par leurs passions, leurs caprices, leurs vanités; c'est-à-dire par ce qu'il y a de plus petit et de plus misérable au monde.
(*Le Verre d'eau*, Acte I, scène 4)

ᷰ ᷰ ᷰ

BOLINGBROKE: Perhaps you suppose, like everyone else, that political catastrophes, revolutions, the falls of empires, have grave, profound, important causes . . . You are wrong! States are subjugated or led by great men, but these great men are themselves governed by their passions, their whims, their vanities, that is, by the slightest and meanest things in the world.

As in his plays, so too in his librettos for Meyerbeer, Scribe rated precision-engineering of the plot more important than characterization.[141] True, he could not go as far under the formal restraints of a genre that gave a high priority to the expression of intimate emotions as he did in a prose play (at the end of *Le Verre d'eau*, a character sums

139. "Mon but est d'amuser, non d'apprendre l'histoire"; ibid., 1:x.
140. See Descotes, *Le Public de théâtre et son histoire*, 290.
141. See Gillespie, "Plays: Well-constructed and well-made," 320.

up the plot with the line: "And all that thanks to a glass of water!," but it can be said of *Le Prophète*, as much as of any of his plays, that

> the qualities and traits [of the agents in the drama] are not often included for their own sake, either for what they might contribute to the central issue of the play or for their worth in terms of sheer comic [or tragic] potentiality; they are assigned instead to accord with the rigorous demands of the many and complicated lines of action.[142]

But such elements rest on an unshakable belief in the significance of court intrigue and arbitrary misunderstandings, and are drastically at odds with a musical dramaturgy that presents historical events in a framework in which the crowd regularly presses into the foreground, visibly and vocally.[143] However, the outcome is that most of the principal characters' actions in *Le Prophète* are motivated doubly—in the interpersonal relationships and in the paramount force of the anonymous historical processes (which make themselves very clearly felt in the powerful musical realization even if they are not very precisely delineated)—so it must be admitted that the opera's dramaturgy is overdetermined from beginning to end.

This tendency to overdetermination, typical of Scribe's librettos, is reinforced by Meyerbeer's interest in the psychological shading of his characters, which led him to adapt the most up-to-date changes in contemporary perception to operatic ends, not only specifically in dream scenes but in many other scenes as well. So it can have been only the abundance of motivation already fueling the rush toward the catastrophe and the final tableau—the self-destructive urge of the socially unstable, the mechanisms and effects of charismatically projected demagoguery, and an oedipal relationship to crown it all—that dissuaded him from adding the two extra motives of opiate intoxication and sexual license, both of which would have directly engaged nightmares and real problems of contemporary Paris.

The accumulation of all kinds of "effects" remains discernible everywhere in *Le Prophète*, even after the cuts affecting the last scene in particular, and it rendered Meyerbeer almost defenseless against a criticism supported by aesthetic premises in the light of which such a polyperspective dramaturgy could not help but appear overloaded. And although even the "effects" that Meyerbeer finally dispensed with had a precise "cause" in the detailed historical dramaturgy of his work, Wagner's po-

142. Ibid.
143. See Dahlhaus, *Realism in Nineteenth-century Music*, 82.

lemical jibe "effects without causes" hit a vulnerable point in Meyerbeer's "mosaic"-like compositional technique. There is an element of
antisemitism in Wagner's comments on Meyerbeer, but Meyerbeer's
apologists could not simply dismiss this particular point. However,
Wagner impeded the kind of serious discussion it deserved, partly because it was so obvious that he was motivated by his own interests and
partly because he used terms and concepts which have completely different emphases in German and French. From E. T. A. Hoffmann onward, the concept of "effect" ("Effekt" or "Wirkung," the latter being
the word Wagner used) in German discussion of musical aesthetics had
had a decidedly pejorative connotation, while for the French the word
"effet" remained aesthetically neutral, capable of being used positively
or negatively.[144] Consequently the "effect on the public" only became
an aesthetic problem for Meyerbeer (and for Berlioz)[145] when it was
sought at any price and without regard to its appropriateness, whereas
Verdi used "effetto" when he wanted to distinguish between dramatic
and abstract poetic qualities, as when he had been particularly severe
with the librettist of Aida: "Let me say once and for all, that I never
mean to criticize your verses, which are always good, but merely to tell
you my opinion as regards the theatrical effect."[146]

Yet "theatrical effect" had to be borne in mind by every composer
who wrote for the theater, and only a public distracted by a national
inferiority complex could subscribe to the nonsense that there was a line
to be drawn between ideal works in which the effects had a metaphysical
foundation and welled up from the creator's inmost being, unbidden, as
the only kind of emanations with any artistic legitimacy, and profane
productions which exposed the audience to calculated effects in the
cold-blooded desire for financial gain. Anyone composing a work of
music theater due to last several hours had to give some thought to how
best to create the effects he wanted, whether his name was Verdi, Meyerbeer, or even Richard Wagner, and while it is undeniable that there
are operas which have no effect because there is no dramaturgical basis
for one, nevertheless, in the theater as in the real world, there are no
"effects without causes."

In appropriating precisely the concepts that Scribe had used to express the essence of his historical dramaturgy in a different context,
Wagner, who had been living in Paris at the time of the première of Le

144. See Reckow, "'Wirkung' und 'Effekt,'" 6.
145. Ibid., 31.
146. From Verdi's letter to Antonio Ghislanzoni, 8 October 1870, I copialettere, 651;
cited here as translated by Julian Budden in The Operas of Verdi, 3:172.

Verre d'eau, took advantage of widespread prejudices against the librettos of Meyerbeer's operas in order to denigrate not only the mechanisms of their plots but also, and without making any distinction between the two, the works as a whole. As a result, impartial assessment of the strengths and the weaknesses, the problems and the unique achievements of Meyerbeer's dramaturgy was rendered impossible for the next hundred years, for the tone of the diatribe uttered by the theorizing creator of mythological music-dramas compelled each and every onlooker to take one side or the other. It is only too understandable, therefore, that the prejudices against grand opéra that have prevailed since Schumann and Wagner have simply been disregarded in Meyerbeer studies. Yet the criticism of the very precise, uncommonly elaborate, and inordinately lengthy calculations Meyerbeer made before deploying the artistic resources available to him, and the impression of eclecticism left by the mosaic-like construction of his works, will not be stilled by being ignored.

Even if we can accept "Meyerbeer's claim to be measured by his own yardstick, rather than by other people's aesthetic-cum-historical standards,"[147] the disturbing idiosyncrasies of his way of working are clear enough. No composer before him was so afflicted by anxiety about the success of his operas, even the most successful, to the extent that he thought it necessary to conform to the Parisian custom of assuring himself of favorable reviews by making payments to well-disposed journalists.[148] Although the charge of an excessively commercial relationship with the public and the press could be leveled with equal justice against Massenet or Puccini,[149] this anxious regard for the reactions of others is a blot on Meyerbeer's reputation to this day, and has been ever since Heine, recalling the early 1830s, remarked that "he lacked a victor's faith in himself, he showed his fear of public opinion, the slightest adverse comment frightened him."[150] And no composer before Meyerbeer was ever found to have taken such meticulous forethought, or subjected every spontaneous inspiration to such critical, intellectual scrutiny, and to have compulsively sought a highly worked synthesis rather than trust himself to make a single throw and so produce the "work in one piece"

147. Dahlhaus, "Motive der Meyerbeerkritik," 41.

148. See Fétis's letter to his wife, 6 March 1836, cited in Bloom, "François-Joseph Fétis," 272.

149. See Lindenberger, *Opera: The Extravagant Art*, 233.

150. "Es mangelte ihm der siegreiche Glaube an sich selbst, er zeigte Furcht vor der öffentlichen Meinung, der kleinste Tadel erschreckte ihn"; *Über die französische Bühne: Vertraute Briefe an August Lewald* [1837], in *Sämtliche Schriften*, 3:339.

esteemed by Verdi. Once again, it was Heine who described this aspect of Meyerbeer with unique empathy:

> The predominance of harmony in Meyerbeer's works is perhaps an inevitable consequence of his broad cultivation, embracing the realm of ideas and of phenomena. A king's ransom was spent on his education, and his mind was receptive. . . . What he learnt he took as nature, and he developed to the fullest in the world's school; he is one of the small number of Germans whom even France must acknowledge as models of urbanity. . . . Yet we may fairly ask whether or not the breadth of comprehension and clarity of overall vision was gained at the cost of other attributes. Cultivation destroys that sharp emphasis in the artist, that unexpected coloring, that originality of ideas, that emotional immediacy, that we admire so much in rough-hewn, uncultivated natures.[151]

Without making any reference to the prevailing aesthetic theory of genius, Heine outlines the charge made against every intellectually developed artist. His portrait of the scion of the richest family in early nineteenth-century Berlin could also have been written of Felix Mendelssohn Bartholdy, and, with a few modifications, of himself. But the passage also indicates the social circumstances that could not be evaded by any of those who took advantage of Jewish emancipation to exchange the security of a well-to-do family home for the exposed position of an artist with international aspirations. Meyerbeer's neurotic anxiety struck even his contemporaries as excessive, yet the rampant antisemitism he encountered everywhere goes a long way to explain it. And however faithfully he expressed the overt and secret desires, the social problems, the fantasies, and the expectations of the cosmopolitan and urban society of Paris, his very "urbanity" and his tendency to ironic detachment, both characteristics discernible in his dramaturgy, were bound to arouse the dislike of those who regarded Paris in the years between 1830 and 1850 as the quintessence either of a modernity they experienced nega-

151. "Die Vorherrschaft der Harmonie in den Meyerbeerschen Schöpfungen ist vielleicht eine notwendige Folge seiner weiten, das Reich des Gedankens und der Erscheinungen umfassenden Bildung. Zu seiner Erziehung wurden Schätze verwendet und sein Geist war empfänglich . . . das Gelernte war ihm Natur und die Schule der Welt gab ihm die höchste Entwicklung; er gehört zu jener geringen Zahl Deutscher, die selbst Frankreich als Muster der Urbanität anerkennen mußte. . . . Aber ob nicht was an Weite der Auffassung und Klarheit des Überblicks gewonnen ward, an anderen Eigenschaften verloren ging, das ist eine Frage. Die Bildung vernichtet bei dem Künstler jene scharfe Akzentuation, jene schroffe Färbung, jene Ursprünglichkeit der Gedanken, jene Unmittelbarkeit der Gefühle, die wir bei rohbegrenzten, ungebildeten Naturen so sehr bewundern." Ibid., 345.

tively or of a time of transition they considered passé. So each generation must decide for itself whether Meyerbeer's synthetic procedures anticipate an illusionless modernity, or whether the consistency of an aesthetic that used "the quasi-industrial technology"[152] of a new age to take an artistic genre nourished by its historical aura to unprecedented heights is a topic still needing to be debated.

152. See Rienäcker, "Wirkung ohne Ursache," 237.

·: 8 :~

THE COMPOSER
AS LIBRETTIST

The Librettist's Martyrdom

Praising the composer to the detriment of the librettist has been a commonplace of operatic criticism since the early nineteenth century. Everything good about an opera is attributed to the composer's mastery of his craft, everything that seems less successful, or incomprehensible on first acquaintance, is the librettist's fault. This underlying assumption is still popular in the secondary musico-historical literature of our own day, and the basis for it, obviously, is the fact that the text of an opera is by no means an equal partner in a Gesamtkunstwerk but at best what Mozart, in a phrase invariably cited in this context, called "the obedient daughter of the music."[1] And indeed the history of opera is also a catalogue of instances of librettists subordinating their poetic imagination to composers' dictates, time and time again, sometimes to the extent of doing no more than providing suitable texts to go with preexisting music. This was required of them in the case of what is known as "parody" opera—the adaptation of numbers from earlier works, with new texts, which was especially popular with eighteenth-century composers such as Gluck; but Meyerbeer, too, used the technique on occasion. It was also by no means uncommon for a composer to make a start on a number before its textual form was settled, and therefore present the librettist with a fait accompli. For example, when Mozart was writing *Die Entführung aus dem Serail*, he told his father that he had explained to the librettist, Gottlieb Stephanie, exactly what words he wanted in Osmin's

1. Mozart's letter to his father, Leopold Mozart, 13 October 1781; cited from *The Letters of Mozart and His Family*, trans. and ed. Emily Anderson, 773.

Act I aria: "Indeed I had finished composing most of the music for it before Stephanie knew anything whatever about it."[2] Meyerbeer, too, did not stint on his instructions to Scribe, regularly sending him "monsters": detailed rhythmical and metrical schemata of numbers which the librettist then had "only" to fill in with text that made some kind of sense.[3]

Of course there are countless examples of the opposite extreme: operas where a composer had nothing more to do than set a libretto exactly as he received it from his employer or patron; but this too is by no means the rule. An unprejudiced look at the history of opera leads, rather, to a recognition that the concrete possibilities for composers or librettists to influence the dramaturgical construction of their works depended far less than is generally supposed on the libretto's status under the institutional conventions and aesthetic beliefs prevalent at the date of composition, and were just as likely to be an expression of the relative status of the persons involved in the individual case. Hasse, for example, composed *Attilio Regolo* without altering a word of Metastasio's text, and indeed he followed the detailed suggestions for an ideal setting sent to him by Metastasio. Hasse was undoubtedly the most successful opera composer of the day, but even for him it was a very special honor to be commissioned to write the first setting of an unpublished libretto by the imperial court poet. Yet in spite of the towering position of Metastasio in the world of eighteenth-century opera, and the universal estimation of his librettos as models of the genre, other, lesser composers had no scruples about having them altered to suit their own requirements when it was a matter of "only" a new setting of a well-known text.

Composers like Gluck and Mozart in the eighteenth century, and Verdi in the nineteenth, now famous for their self-confident, even dictatorial dealings with subservient librettists, readily accepted the librettos they were given at the beginning of their careers, knowing full well that as unknown newcomers they were lucky to have the chance of having their first tragic opera staged at, in all three cases, so prestigious a house as the leading theater in Milan. In eighteenth-century France, where the foremost aesthetic theorists regarded the text and the musical realization of the tragédie en musique as equal in artistic importance, composers regularly took all kinds of liberties with the librettists' work, once they realized that they held the stronger position. While Gluck was working on the Paris version of his *Alceste* (1776), for example, he re-

2. Letter of 26 September 1781; ibid., 768–69.
3. See Huebner, "Italianate duets," 207.

jected one of the few new ideas the librettist had introduced into the translation of Calzabigi's original libretto, and made him adhere to his own conception of the final scene in every detail. And for his last French opera, *Iphigénie en Tauride* (1779), Gluck's standing was such that he could convince the librettist, Guillard, not only to make all the changes he wanted but also to condense the original five acts to four.

Less is known about relations between the most successful Parisian opera composers and their librettists in the decades between the French Revolution and the Bourbon restoration. As Cherubini, Méhul, and Spontini, and the librettists too, generally lived in Paris, there was no need for them to exchange letters, and as yet no one has compared versions of the librettos at different stages of their genesis. But when we look at the dramaturgy of these operas, which is always tailored precisely to the composers' musical preferences, it is hard not to conclude that here again the composers were able to overrule any literary scruples on the part of the librettists.

Such was certainly the case for Rossini and his Parisian operas, especially *Guillaume Tell*, as is shown by the substantial changes the composer demanded in Jouy's libretto. Although the attempt has been made in our own time to present Rossini as the victim of his librettists,[4] his contemporaries were well aware that he acted from a conscious position of strength. Berlioz came out in the librettists' defense in his review of *Guillaume Tell*, attributing responsibility for its dramaturgical weaknesses to the composer alone: "I say 'the composer,' for a man like Rossini always gets whatever he wants from his poet."[5] All this applies, if anything, even more strongly in the case of Scribe's texts for the Paris operas of Meyerbeer and Verdi. I have already given many examples of how the composer–librettist collaboration worked in practice in discussing *Les Huguenots* and *Le Prophète*, and this chapter contains more. The spectacular success of his first opera for Paris, *Robert le diable*, gave Meyerbeer a renown that not only allowed him later to keep the Parisian public waiting thirteen years for a new opera from him, but also gave him the upper hand in his dealings with his librettist, although Scribe was no less successful in his own profession than Meyerbeer in his.

Meyerbeer's strong position rested on his success and the fact that he was the best-paid composer of his day, but it gained additional support

---

4. See Gerhard, "'Sortire dalle vie comuni,'" 186.

5. Hector Berlioz, "*Guillaume Tell*, de Rossini," 337 (in Radiciotti, 141); cited from Strunk, *Source Readings*, 5:73–74.

from the aesthetic premises of grand opéra. In a theatrical genre that concerned itself, first and foremost, with overwhelming its audiences by every conceivable means, the text lost all pretension to literary merit on its own account. Already in the eighteenth century, with the exception of Metastasio's model texts, very few librettos indeed had really measured up to their authors' claim that they led a separate existence as dramatic poems in their own right, even without their musical settings, and now that fiction was exploded. Admittedly, that did not stop librettists from clinging to the belief that they produced autonomous texts of imperishable value. Scribe and almost every other nineteenth-century librettist observed the practice—set aside allegedly for the first time in the case of Rossini's *Guillaume Tell*[6]—of publishing their texts separately. These versions, which could be bought at the opera house before performances, differed to varying degrees from the text actually sung on the stage. However, in Scribe's case at least, original manuscript drafts also survive, and comparisons show that the printed versions preserved only a fraction of the "literary" qualities that had had to be sacrificed to the composer's dictates. Some librettists—not just Jouy, who had a rather good conceit of himself, but Scribe too, and even Italians, like Luigi Romanelli who wrote texts for composers like Simon Mayr, Rossini, and Mercadante during the first three decades of the nineteenth century—published complete editions of their works, including the opera librettos. That word, a diminutive of the Italian *libro*, relates primarily to the small format in which texts were sold to audiences in the theater, but it also betrays something of the estimation in which they were held.

Nothing could prevent the literary standing of the libretto declining even further during the course of the nineteenth century. Though the Italian writer Ugo Foscolo dreamed, in 1821, of authoritarian measures to force music "to regard poetry as a little sister, not a servant, a slave, or a vile prostitute,"[7] the position only got worse in an age in which not only Wagner's music dramas but all operas of any quality approached the utopian ideal of the Gesamtkunstwerk. The libretto had to change accordingly. Where once librettists had been expected to cast the expressive content of each successive scene as artistically as possible in a form corresponding to the conventions of musical dramaturgy as well as to the established repertory of classical verse meters, now they were

---

6. See Gerhard, "'Sortire dalle vie comuni,'" 187.

7. "a riguardar la poesia come sorella, e non come una serva, una schiava ed una vile prostituta"; "Dell'impresa d'un teatro per musica," 387.

asked to provide easily understandable words and even use expressions and idioms from everyday speech. Traditional literary art was no longer a high priority for scenes in which only a thin disguise veiled sights and situations familiar to contemporary urban audiences from their own lives, or for musical realizations that were increasingly concerned with putting over the inexorable dynamic of the historical events on the stage without regard to any conventions. Composers played their part in a development which gradually eradicated all literary and formal qualities from librettos. Meyerbeer's ruthless treatment of the verses Scribe wrote for the love duet in Act IV of *Les Huguenots* is only one particularly flagrant example among many of the way in which composers pulled apart skillfully crafted verses and ordered metrical forms and reduced them to the prose-like fragments of dialogue that they needed to enhance the dramatic excitement of their setting. And few of Verdi's letters provide a better illustration of the way he treated "his" librettists than the one he wrote to Piave after receiving some revisions of the text for *La forza del destino.*

> I have received your verses and, if I may say so, I don't like them. You talk to me about 100 syllables!! And it's obvious that 100 syllables aren't enough when it takes you 25 to say the sun is setting!!! The line "Duopo è sia l'opra truce compita" is too hard, and even worse is "Un Requiem, un Pater . . . . . . e tutto ha fin" . . . For the love of God, don't end lines with "che," "più" and "ancor."[8]

Thus by the middle of the century things had reached the stage where most librettos for through-composed operas had more in common with the journalism of a prosaic age than with the arcadian ideal of a poetically polished drama nurtured in the age of Metastasio. The provision of the text for an opera had finally sunk to the level of hack work, as remote from the artistic products of well-regarded dramatists as most of the serials published in magazines were from serious novels. Librettists of the generation after Scribe no longer even considered publishing their versions of texts as independent literary works, or of creating a printed record of textual variants. Printed librettos continued to go on sale, it is true, but as time went by the librettist's name on the title page grew smaller and the composer's larger.

There was no retreating from the fact that the libretto had become a mere adjunct to a work exclusively associated with the composer, who

---

8. Letter to Piave, 20 December 1864, *I copialettere*, 614; cited from *Letters of Giuseppe Verdi*, trans. and ed. Charles Osborne, 135.

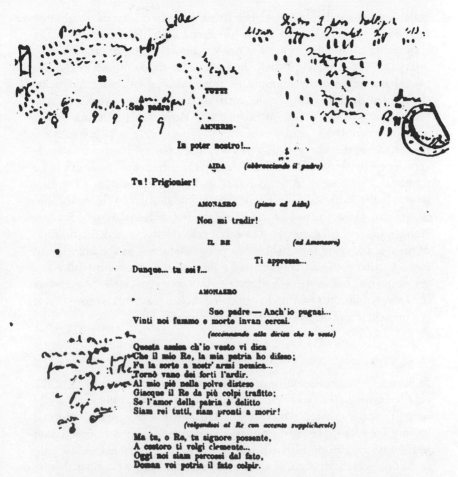

AMNERIS.

In poter nostro!...

AIDA   (abbracciando il padre)

Tu! Prigionier!

AMONASRO   (piano ad Aida)

Non mi tradir!

IL RE   (ad Amonasro)

Ti appressa...

Dunque... tu sei?...

AMONASRO

Suo padre — Anch'io pugnai...
Vinti noi fummo e morte invan cercai.

(accennando alla divisa che lo veste)

Questa assisa ch'io vesto vi dica
Che il mio Re, la mia patria ho difeso;
Fu la sorte a nostr' armi nemica...
Tornò vano dei forti l'ardir.
Al mio piè nella polve disteso
Giacque il Re da più colpi trafitto;
Se l'amor della patria è delitto
Siam rei tutti, siam pronti a morir!

(volgendosi al Re con accento supplichevole)

Ma tu, o Re, tu signore possente,
A costoro ti volgi clemente...
Oggi noi siam percossi dal fato,
Doman voi potria il fato colpir.

17   A copy of the printed libretto of Verdi's *Aida* survives (in the Pierpont Morgan Library, New York) marked with the composer's own annotations. This page from the triumph scene in Act II gives a striking impression of the influence Verdi exerted on the staging, as well as the text, of "his" librettos.

in many cases, to all intents and purposes, was the author of a good part of the text. As Eduard Hanslick stated, with good reason, in 1875, it was "an irreversible advance and an axiom of modern aesthetic awareness that the composer of an opera is responsible for the text he has chosen."[9] Musical dramatists with the self-confidence of a Verdi extended active

9. "ein unverlierbarer Fortschritt und ein Axiom des heutigen ästhetischen Bewußtseins, daß der Opern-Componist für die von ihm gewählte Dichtung verantwortlich sei"; *Die moderne Oper*, 163.

collaboration in shaping the libretto to an extreme far beyond what Gluck and Meyerbeer had done, not contenting themselves with the conception of isolated scenes but prescribing the structure of an entire opera in a prose sketch, which then needed only to be versified. *Aida* (1871) is a noteworthy example of this development, with Verdi insisting that the librettist, Ghislanzoni, should not begin work until the scenario was fully worked out in prose.[10] More than ten years earlier Verdi had adopted a similar procedure with *Un ballo in maschera*, with the difference that there the libretto was based on one written a quarter-century earlier by Scribe. In fact, *Aida* is the only work in Verdi's large output that originated in a prose sketch devised especially for the purpose: all the others derive from preexisting dramas. While Antonio Somma, to whom the task of versifying the Italian translation of Scribe's *Gustave III, ou Le Bal masqué* was entrusted, showed a realistic opinion of his role in trying to insist on not being identified as the librettist of *Ballo*, Ghislanzoni was content to be named in connection with *Aida*, yet eloquently bemoaned the librettist's lot some years later: "Nowadays the *métier* of libretto writing has become such a cruel martyrdom that it is a miracle if any intelligent man dares undertake it."[11]

"La Parola Scenica"

In his resigned assessment of the librettist's lot in the second half of the century, Ghislanzoni was quite candid in admitting that the work could now attract only writers who had failed to gain any success with original literary creations. His own literary experience was broadly based, and in the case of writing librettos was by no means restricted to working up Verdi's sketch for *Aida*. He had every right to regard the texts that he had written for Petrella, Ponchielli, and Gomes as his own independent works. But he repeatedly found himself in situations where the librettist's and the composer's interests were hard to reconcile. Music dramatists like Verdi, who, like their compeers in other art forms, had to work constantly to produce new things to satisfy the unprecedented visual and perceptual expectations of an urban population in changing times, had no patience with the self-regarding aspirations of librettists to fashion the text as elegantly and eloquently as they could. Their differences

10. See Verdi's letter to Giulio Ricordi, 2 June 1870, cited in Abbiati, *Giuseppe Verdi*, 3:367.

11. "Oggimai il *mestiere* di scriver libretti è divenuto un sì crudele martirio, che è da far meraviglia se qualche uomo d'ingegno osi ancora affrontarlo"; "Del Libretto per musica," 18.

came into the open especially often in connection with those scenes, not confined to French opera alone, where the pantomimic techniques of the *mélodrame à grand spectacle* were expected to predominate, feeding the audience's eyes first of all, and then its ears, with its sensitivity to poetic nuance coming a very poor third. In one such instance, when Ghislanzoni was working on Act II of *Aida*, Verdi wrote him a letter which has been often quoted:

> The verses are fine until "A te in cor destò." But then, when the action warms up, I feel it lacks "the theatrical word." I don't know if I can explain what I mean by "theatrical word," but I think I mean the word that most clearly and neatly brings the stage situation to life. . . .
>
> I realize that you will say to me, "But what about the verse, the rhyme, the stanzas?" I don't know what to say, except that, if the action calls for it, I would immediately abandon rhythm, rhyme and stanza. I would use blank verse in order to be able to say clearly and distinctly what the action requires. Unfortunately it is sometimes necessary in the theatre for poets and composers to have the talent not to write either poetry or music.[12]

All that his vigorous defense of the primacy of theatrical effect proves is that Verdi had taken to heart the lesson offered to every ambitious composer of the younger generation by French grand opéra, with its exceptional highlighting of dramatic climaxes. It is true that neither Meyerbeer nor Scribe ever took the trouble to theorize about this aesthetic convention of their librettos, and Verdi himself only hit on the expression for it after he had written his Paris operas. In 1857, when working on *Un ballo in maschera*, he complained to his librettist, Somma, of language that did not serve his turn in this respect.[13] But examples of "the theatrical word" (*la parola scenica* in Italian), the arresting phrase that takes no account of the metrical structure of the neighboring lines but etches a moment of tension before a set-piece ensemble,[14] can be found in operas written before 1850. Verdi's *Nabucco* contains some, to be sure, but there are others in operas composed for Paris by Meyerbeer: Valentine's "Je t'aime" in Act IV of *Les Huguenots*; and several in *Le Prophète*:

12. Verdi's letter to Ghislanzoni, 17 August 1870, *I copialettere*, 641; in *Letters of Giuseppe Verdi*, 159–60.

13. On this occasion he wrote: "la parola non scolpisce bene"; letter to Antonio Somma, 6 November 1857, cited in Pascolato, *"Re Lear" e "Ballo in maschera,"* 80; see also Ross, "Amelias Auftrittsarie im *Maskenball*," 134, n. 18. [Budden translates this phrase as "the words don't strike home" (*The Operas of Verdi*, 2:366). Verdi's verb, *scolpire*, has the double meaning of "carve" or "sculpt," and "enunciate clearly."—Trans.]

14. See appendix 3, "The *parola scenica*," in Powers, "*Simon Boccanegra* I.10–12," 128; Della Seta, "'Parola scenica' in Verdi," 276–86.

Jean's "Ah! va-t'en!" when he surrenders Berthe to Oberthal in Act II,
Fidès's cry "Mon fils!" in Act IV, and Berthe's scream "Prophète, prophète!" in the last act.

Only those who discounted the importance of sustaining the dramatic interest of an opera over several hours could find fault with the
renunciation of poetic elegance represented by the use of everyday expressions like "Va-t'en." Verdi thought of himself as a man of the theater
rather than a musician,[15] and although he inveighed against grand opéra
he spoke out in defense of the much-criticized libretto of *Les Huguenots*,
as late as 1896: "Some say the libretto is badly written. But what do I
care! The libretto is true theatre."[16] Verdi's idea of "true theater" stems
from a development referred to in an earlier chapter as a "graphic revolution."[17] That this reached Italian opera was due above all to Verdi, and
its effect was that in Italy, too, the primary aim of operatic dramaturgy
now was to please an audience that experienced an abundance of stimuli
in daily life and therefore gave its attention solely to visual spectacles
that it could accept as realistic. These were the changes in public expectations that Ghislanzoni had in mind when, in the essay on libretto writing already quoted earlier in this chapter, he wrote "The interest of an
opera, in my opinion, ought to result almost exclusively from its events,
and these events, taking place on the stage, ought to be *comprehensible to
the eye*."[18] This is remarkably similar to Véron's attempted definition of
grand opéra, published twenty years earlier (cited in chapter 4).

It was virtually inevitable that the librettos for operas conceived on
such a basis would have less and less in common with other dramatic
texts, and that their function would grow closer to that of the film scripts
of our own day. While stage directions and the descriptions of sets became more and more detailed as the century wore on, the words intended for singing actually became fewer. In the end, published librettos
appeared to be meant primarily for directors and designers rather than
for the general public. Although they continued to be on sale to audiences, they were no longer essential reading, for the aesthetic premise
of grand opéra, like director's theater today, is that the visual and pantomimic presentation of the most important stages in the drama will give

15. See Pizzetti, "Giuseppe Verdi maestro di teatro," 23 (reprint, 761).

16. Pizzi, *Ricordi verdiani inediti*, 42 (reprint, 334); cited here in the translation by
Richard Stokes, in Conati, *Interviews and Encounters*, 337–57 (p. 344).

17. See above, 154.

18. "L'interesse di un melodramma deve, a parere mio, risultare quasi esclusivamente
dai fatti, e questi fatti che si svolgono sulla scena debbono in certo modo essere *comprensi-
bili all'occhio*"; "Del Libretto per musica," 22.

even unprepared members of the audience sufficient understanding of what is going on. At all events the habit, universal in the first half of the nineteenth century, of following the libretto during a performance gradually died out, even before it was made completely impossible by the new practice of extinguishing the lights in the auditorium, which was established by the end of the century. As an aid to reception, the libretto was replaced by the synopsis, printed in theater programs for the benefit of the theatergoer in the minutes before curtain-rise, and in opera guides for those with a little more time to prepare themselves. This became the general rule only in the twentieth century, but by the 1850s in France, in individual cases, it was already possible to buy a four-page leaflet with a brief plot summary as an alternative to the complete libretto. Thus we have yet more evidence that someone raised in the eighteenth century, like Jouy, was fighting a hopeless rearguard action with his demand that the librettist must be the first and most important originator of an opera. Stronger influence than he possessed would still not have been enough to halt the literary decline and fall of the opera libretto.

THE IDEAL COLLABORATOR

With composers taking a more and more decisive part in the writing of the texts they set, it was inevitable that some would start to think of doing away altogether with the division of labor between composer and librettist. Wouldn't the ideal solution be for composers to write their librettos without any outside help? There are indeed isolated examples of this going back to earlier ages, but the number of composers who decided to write their own texts began to multiply around the middle of the nineteenth century. Richard Wagner is the most famous, but French opera can offer Berlioz with *Les Troyens* (1863), and Auguste Mermet with *Roland à Roncevaux* (1864) and *Jeanne d'Arc* (1876). These remained exceptions, in which originally, at least, the practical difficulty of finding anyone else willing to collaborate in seemingly utopian projects played as significant a role as aesthetic conviction, but Wagner's theoretical writings brought about a shift of opinion, persuading many that librettos by the composer must have a higher aesthetic worth. Writing both text and music seemed to be the only way to preserve composers from the bad habits of notoriously unsympathetic librettists, and in a bird's-eye view of opera the outstanding example of Wagner is confronted by only a very small number of ideal collaborations between pairs: Da Ponte and Mozart, Boito and Verdi, Hofmannsthal and Strauss.

Admittedly, the structural weaknesses of a collaboration that was always prey to conflict and other problems were recognized even by someone like Salvadore Cammarano, a prolific, professional librettist, working out of Naples (Wagnerians would no doubt cite him as a dreadful example of the mass-production methods of Italian opera in the first half of the nineteenth century). Donizetti's *Lucia di Lammermoor* (1835) is one of Cammarano's many librettos, and Verdi's *Luisa Miller* (1849) is another. While working on the latter, he wrote to Verdi: "If I were not afraid of being thought Utopian I would be tempted to say that to achieve the peak of perfection in an opera the same mind should be responsible for both words and music."[19]

While there could be no disputing the fact that bringing "the same mind" to bear on the different tasks had advantages for an opera's unity, on the other hand it was, and remains, debatable that this "utopian" procedure was really the way to achieve "the peak of perfection." Artists with the dual gifts of a Berlioz, who was not only an outstandingly innovative composer but also a brilliant literary stylist, were rare, and most composers had good reason to shrink from venturing into a realm where they would need skills and experience that they were conscious of lacking. In making a realistic assessment of the difficulties of working with equal professionalism in two different arts, it was, and remains, possible to arrive at the conclusion that sharing the labor, when the co-workers are in close agreement, promises better results than a monomaniac procedure. Certainly, the latter has positive advantages, in the form of united, integrated purpose and ideas, but they may be negated by a too obsessive insistence on certain poetic formulas, such as old German Stabreim in Wagner's case. To that extent, we should not necessarily convict Meyerbeer of being too timid to abandon convention, when we find him writing, as early as 1820, that "I have decided to write operas for Germany again only if I find a like-minded poetical friend who thinks as I do about the necessity of amalgamating southern, Italian form with German individuality and strength."[20] We might interpret it instead as the wise self-limitation of a man who doubted composers' literary competence and preferred to trust to the established métier

19. Salvadore Cammarano's letter to Giuseppe Verdi, 11 June 1849, *I copialettere*, 473; cited after Budden, *The Operas of Verdi*, 1:422–23.

20. "Ich habe mich jedoch entschlossen nur auf den Fall wieder in Deutschland Opern zu schreiben, wenn ich den gleichgesinnten poetischen Freund fände, der wie ich über die vorzunehmende Verschmelzung der südlichen italienischen Form und deutsche Eigenthümlichkeit und Kraft denkt"; letter to Franz Sales Kandler, 31 March 1820, *Briefwechsel*, 1:420.

rather than to dilettantism, even if that might be "monumentalized by a supreme effort of the will and intelligence—a dilettantism raised to the level of genius," as Thomas Mann described Wagner's art.[21]

Meyerbeer found the "like-minded friend" he sought in Paris, not Germany, and although Scribe has always been the scapegoat for the dramaturgical inconsistencies in Meyerbeer's operas, recent research reveals that Scribe not only placed all his immense experience at the composer's disposal but also showed a readiness to meet his precise wishes that was unprecedented in the history of opera to that date.[22] The drafts and discarded versions of librettos among Scribe's papers in the Bibliothèque Nationale have already been referred to several times;[23] scholars have scarcely touched this Nachlass, which also includes a lot of his correspondence, but even a cursory look at it shows that, as a general rule, when Scribe was working on a libretto he was ready to make changes in accordance with composers' wishes, but also that composers accepted the subject matter and fundamental conception in the form prescribed by Scribe. This was true of Donizetti, in particular, of whom Scribe was reported by Eduard Hanslick to have said: "He is the most agreeable of all my musical collaborators; satisfied with everything, he accepts everything, and never asks for anything."[24] But Auber and Halévy, who worked almost exclusively with Scribe, as well as many less well-known composers like Marliani, Ambroise Thomas, and Clapisson, also made few demands of Scribe, confining them to alterations he could carry out with ease.

Meyerbeer was different from all Scribe's other musical partners. He would have the librettist work out a first draft, often, as in the case of *Les Huguenots*, before signing a contract;[25] he would then send that draft back to Scribe with detailed comments and indications of alterations he wanted.[26] Scribe found himself obliged to produce one new draft after

21. "The Sorrows and Grandeur of Richard Wagner," in *Pro and contra Wagner*, 103.

22. See Döhring, "Giacomo Meyerbeer: Grand opéra als Ideendrama," 12.

23. See also Gerhard, "Die französische 'Grand Opéra' in der Forschung," 237–40.

24. "Er ist der angenehmste von allen meinen musikalischen Mitarbeitern; mit allem zufrieden, fügt er sich allem und verlangt niemals etwas"; Hanslick, *"Die Ballnacht (Le Bal masqué): Oper von Auber"* [1877], in Hanslick, *Aus dem Opernleben der Gegenwart*, 178–86 (p. 183).

25. See Meyerbeer's letter to Minna Meyerbeer, 18 September 1832, *Briefwechsel*, 2:222. The assertion made by Michael Walter in *"Hugenotten"-Studien*, 4–5, that Meyerbeer had thought of *Les Huguenots* as early as July or August 1832 goes back to the erroneous dating, in *Briefwechsel*, 2:205, of Scribe's letter to Meyerbeer of 7 July 1834. (See Adolphe Crémieux's letter, also of 7 July 1834, which was delivered to Meyerbeer at the same time; ibid., 378–79.)

26. See F-Pn, n.a.f. 22502, fols. 62–74.

another for scenes where Meyerbeer wanted changes, and to follow Meyerbeer's precise instructions in the versification as well. The composer's comments leave no room for doubt as to his conception of the librettist's role; this, for example, dates from an early stage of the work on *Les Huguenots:*

> My dear friend! Although we agreed that I would not convey my observations on your work until you had finished it, I must permit myself the two following remarks, because they will affect what still remains to be done. The first relates to the role of Marcel. In creating for an artist of Levasseur's distinction a role in which he has only one number (the duet in Act III), we agreed that you would set up sorties for him in the ensembles, lightning-flashes 3 or 4 lines long in which he would stand out. You have not done so. . . . I hope you will see to that when the rest is finished, but meanwhile, my dear friend, do not neglect it in the third act.[27]

But he also continued to ask for more changes from Scribe even after a libretto had been finished. When we consider that each of Meyerbeer's operas after 1830 took several years to complete, it is scarcely surprising that Scribe, accustomed as he was to finish projects quickly, finally lost patience. Meyerbeer decided, accordingly, that it would be prudent to get a third person to carry out further modifications, and recruited the Italian librettist Gaetano Rossi to do some work on *Les Huguenots* in the autumn of 1833. Having already set some of these lines written by Rossi to music, he then handed them over to Scribe for translation, pretending that he had written them himself, in Italian "and not in German, although it would have been easier for me . . . because you understand this language."[28] Evidently Scribe expressed some reluctance to perform such a menial task, whereupon Meyerbeer turned to Émile Deschamps, then best known as a translator, and asked him to undertake this part of the task.

27. "Mon cher ami! Quoique nous étions convenus que je ne présenterai mes observations sur ce qui est fait jusqu'après la fin de votre travail, pourtant je ne puis à moins que de me permettre les deux observations suivantes parce qu'elles influeront sur le reste à faire. La première est relative au rôle de Marcel. En faisant pour un artiste aussi distingué que Levasseur un rôle dans lequel il n'a qu'un seul morceau (le Duo du 3e acte) nous étions convenus que vous lui ménageriez dans les morceaux d'ensemble des sorties, dès éclairs de 3 ou 4 vers dans lesquels on pourrait le détacher. Vous ne l'avez pas fait. . . . J'espère que vous retoucherez cela quand tout sera fini; mais en attendant, mon cher ami, ne le negligez pas au troisième acte." Unpublished letter from Meyerbeer to Scribe, mid-October 1832 (ibid., fol. 75).

28. "et pas en allemand quoique cela m'eut été plus facile . . . parce que vous comprenez cette langue"; letter to Scribe, 2 July 1834, *Briefwechsel*, 2:377; see also H. Becker, "Giacomo Meyerbeers Mitarbeit an den Libretti seiner Opern," 159.

Meyerbeer must have been pleased with Deschamps's work, because he went straight to him for help with many further modifications, without approaching Scribe at all. Deschamps had already agreed that he should not be named, and waived any copyrights.[29] Years later, after both Meyerbeer and Scribe were dead, the seventy-five-year-old Deschamps made all this very clear in an open letter, provoked by claims that his part in the libretto of *Les Huguenots* had amounted to no more than routine revision.[30] It is not inconceivable that Deschamps might have wanted to claim more credit than was his due, but now that the sources are available, they reveal nothing to contradict his claim not only to have written substantial parts of the love duet at the end of Act IV but also to have been responsible for Marcel's *Chanson huguenote* and Urbain's entrance cavatina in Act I, the duet for Marcel and Valentine in Act III, Valentine's *romance* at the beginning of Act IV (later cut), and many more minor alterations.[31] *Les Huguenots* was not the only work of Meyerbeer's in which Deschamps had a similarly clandestine hand. Fourteen years later, in March 1848, he undertook to help with the final revision of *Le Prophète*, for a lump-sum payment of 1,000 francs, in return for which he promised "to observe the most profound silence on the subject of this agreement."[32] On this occasion it appears that, in addition to many minor alterations in matters of poetic detail, his only original contribution was the text of Berthe's cavatina in Act I.[33]

We can look forward to much more information about the complexities of the genesis of Meyerbeer's opera librettos emerging from closer study of the numerous documents left behind by both Scribe and Deschamps; even a preliminary survey leaves no doubt that Meyerbeer, not Scribe, was the originator of the new conception of the dramaturgy of the historical opera,[34] although publicly, and with good reason, Meyerbeer did not stint his praise of Scribe's specific qualities. At lunch in his house in Berlin, in May 1844, for instance, he exclaimed to his guests:

> Oh, why have I not got a Scribe or a Romani here? . . . the things I could do with them, but we would have to be together, work together, think

29. See the commentary in Meyerbeer, *Briefwechsel*, 2:669–70.

30. See Anne, "Le Temps passé," 165.

31. See Deschamps, "Le Duo du 4e acte des *Huguenots*," 171–72.

32. "d'observer le plus profond silence sur l'objet de cette convention"; Deschamps's letter to Meyerbeer, 17 March 1848, in Meyerbeer, *Briefwechsel*, 4:372–73.

33. See entries in Meyerbeer's diary, 5 October and 27 December 1848, ibid., 447, 465; and 12 and 17 January 1849, ibid., 467ff.

34. See Döhring, "Giacomo Meyerbeer: Grand opéra als Ideendrama," 12; see also Zimmermann, "Komponist extremer Wirkungen," 229.

and create as one, like Beaumarchais and Salieri. Scribe is so wide-awake, so versatile, so fertile, he enables every composer to display a thousand skills, unfolds the most varied aspects of a talent.[35]

Although in many cases Scribe had only lent his name to the work of others, he incurred the blame of German critics for the "weaknesses" of Meyerbeer's works, already in the 1830s,[36] but the French critic Henri Blaze de Bury, in a book produced to mark Meyerbeer's death, made a much more realistic assessment of the working relationship between the composer and the librettist:

> As much of a poet as it is possible to be, Meyerbeer needed only a skilled contractor to find a convincing situation for the idea he provided. Scribe did not always understand Meyerbeer's idea at first, he stripped it of its originality, gave it bourgeois coloring, and then it was Meyerbeer's turn to take it back and restore to it its original essence.[37]

This passage, colored by an intimate knowledge of both men as well as by adherence to the Romantic aesthetics of genius, reveals circumstances that would not have been known to the wider public, but in addition it displays the well-nigh mythical valuation set on "originality" by Meyerbeer himself, the first opera composer to do so. Auber, Rossini, Verdi, and their librettists were little troubled by the thought that they were not the first to dramatize the revolt of Neapolitan fishermen in 1647, or the birth of the Swiss nation in the thirteenth century, or the assassination of King Gustav III of Sweden, but it was obviously of the greatest importance to Meyerbeer that his historical operas were the first to be written about their subjects. He emphasized the originality of *Les Huguenots* in a letter to his wife:

> I haven't told you anything about the subject matter, as it's not easy to describe. The story is almost entirely invented, only the period and the actual ending of the piece are historical. It's "La St. Barthélemy" (the mas-

---

35. This conversation, which Meyerbeer held with Alexey Fyodorovich L'vov and his secretary Wiktor Każyński, 21 March 1844, was recorded in Polish in Każyński, *Notatki*, 57, but they probably spoke French or German. On the precise dating of the occasion, see Meyerbeer's diary, 21 May 1844, *Briefwechsel*, 3:508.

36. See Kirchmeyer, "Die deutsche Librettokritik," 372.

37. "Poète autant qu'on peut l'être, Meyerbeer n'avait besoin que d'un metteur en oeuvre habile à donner force de situation à l'idée qu'il apportait. Cette idée, Scribe ne la comprenait pas toujours du premier coup; il la *désoriginalisait*, lui donnait la couleur bourgeoise, et c'était au tour de Meyerbeer, la reprenant de ses mains, de lui rendre sa virtualité première." *Meyerbeer et son temps*, 331–32.

sacre of the Protestants in the reign of Charles IX) (1572). But there are
a lot of gay and pleasing scenes in the first three acts. Please, my sweet
lily, say nothing about it to anyone *without exception*, for this event has
never been put on the stage before.[38]

In his pleasure at the innovation, the composer exaggerated somewhat,
for the St. Bartholomew's massacre was new only to the operatic stage.
At least five plays about it were produced in various theaters in Paris
between 1826 and 1834.[39] It was only natural that the spectacular religious strife of sixteenth-century France was among the subjects to attract attention, given the general surge of interest in history, whether
on the printed page or on the stage. The best-known evidence of this
interest is one of the most successful historical novels published in
France in the period around 1830, Prosper Mérimée's *Chronique du
règne de Charles IX* (1829). The question of the influence this novel may
have had on the genesis of *Les Huguenots* has yet to be settled. Although
it is regularly referred to as a model or a source in the literature on
Meyerbeer,[40] there is no documentary evidence to support the hypothesis that it was either, and comparing it with the libretto does not produce
any conclusive results. It has been shown that there are no significant
correspondences between Mérimée's version and Scribe's, and furthermore that many essential details in the libretto actually come from book
6 of Théodore-Agrippine d'Aubigné's *Histoire Universelle*, published in
1619[41]—nevertheless, that does not fully rule out the possibility that
the novel, which Scribe certainly read, was what initially ignited his and
Meyerbeer's interest in the subject.

That possibility must be mentioned, because there is no overt trace
in the definitive text of *Le Prophète* of a historical novel about the Anabaptists, Carl Franz van der Velde's *Die Wiedertäufer*, published originally
in German in 1821, and in French translation in 1826, which is known
to have been a source for the opera, and was the work to which Meyer-

---

38. "Ich habe Dir nichts von dem Sujet geschrieben, da es schwer zu beschreiben
ist; die Fabel ist fast ganz erfunden, und nur die Epoche und der eigentliche Schluß des
Stückes historisch. Es ist nämlich 'La St. Barthélemy' (das Massacre der Protestanten
unter Karl IX.) (1572). Doch sind in den ersten 3 Akten sehr viele heitere und anmutige
Szenen drin. Ich bitte Dich, süße Lilie, niemandem o h n e A u s n a h m e etwas davon
zu sagen, da dieses Ereignis bis jetzt noch nicht auf der Bühne behandelt worden ist."
Letter to Minna Meyerbeer, 10 October 1832, *Briefwechsel*, 2:232.

39. See Duchet, "La Saint-Barthélemy"; Frese, *Dramaturgie der großen Opern Giacomo
Meyerbeers*, 291, n. 115.

40. See Pendle, *Eugène Scribe*, 472–75.

41. See Walter, *"Hugenotten"-Studien*, 32–35, 43–46.

beer referred as "the novel" when writing to Scribe: "I should like the character of Jonas to be a little like Tuiskoschirer in the novel."[42] On the other hand, another possibility, put forward only recently,[43] is that the interest of either the composer or the librettist was first aroused in the subject, not by the novel, but by the historian Michelet's *Mémoires de Luther*, which, in the section about the Münster Anabaptists, goes into considerable detail about their king's dreams and visions. Meyerbeer and Scribe would have had good reason to pay attention to Michelet's book, which attracted enormous interest.[44] It was published on 18 September 1835, while they were working on the final revision of *Les Huguenots*—and just a few weeks before they started work on *Le Prophète*. However, there can be no doubt that the novel, written under the influence of Scott, was a better model for a text intended to appeal to audiences' emotions than Michelet's historical treatise.

In any event, the fact that in librettos like those of *Les Huguenots* and *Le Prophète* numerous heterogeneous sources and the many original ideas of Meyerbeer and Scribe are woven together to produce something completely new is yet one more confirmation of the uniqueness of these historical operas. Furthermore, until we know who was originally responsible for the choice of subject matter, we should not rule out the possibility that it was Meyerbeer, in which case his exaggerated insistence on the novelty of the subject of *Les Huguenots* would be an expression of satisfaction with his own idea. Yet there is an anxious note in his harping on the originality of his operas, betraying something of the contradiction in his own experience; living in the age when the Romantic aesthetic of genius reigned, he never even thought of pursuing the utopian ideal of being responsible for both words and music, but placed himself in the hands of a dramatist who wrote librettos for financial rather than artistic rewards. In the account book in which he summed up his activities for 1841, Scribe wrote down an estimation of his librettos which seems to confirm all the prejudices of hostile critics:

> The Grand Opéra, where I have earned so much money, finds, with reason perhaps, that my creations are too dear—I want to be paid for them in accordance with what they bring in, that is: a lot. The current director only wants to pay what they are worth, that is: precious little.[45]

42. "Je voudrais que le caractère du rôle de Jonas fût un peu comme le Tuiskoschirer du roman"; F-Pn, n.a.f. 22504, fol. 36.
43. See Asholt, "Ein Sonnenuntergang, der zum 'Vorschein' wird."
44. See Viallaneix, introduction to *Mémoires de Luther*, 232.
45. "Le grand opéra où j'ai gagné tant d'argent, trouve avec raison peut-être, que mes ouvrages sont trop chers—je veux les faire payer d'après ce qu'ils rapportent, c'est à dire:

In employing not one but several librettists, however, Meyerbeer was able to make the most of all the advantages that a highly complicated, synthetic procedure could bring to the precisely detailed execution of works to which, at a later stage, other specialists—set designers, costumiers, choreographers, and many others—would also make their contributions. At the same time, however, he exposed himself to critics who deplored the introduction of techniques based on the principle of the division of labor, and planned with military precision, into the process of realizing works of art in the theater. To those who held this view such practices were an unartistic manifestation of an industrial age whose innovations they feared and distrusted.

LIBRETTOS FROM STOCK

Verdi's approach to the most successful French librettist of the nineteenth century was quite different from Meyerbeer's. In Italy, by 1852, he had already won the battle to make librettists accept his right, as composer, to have the last word in all decisions at every stage of a work's genesis, by dint of strenuous efforts and ruthless disregard for their hurt feelings, but, having chosen Scribe as the librettist for the new opera he was commissioned to write for Paris, he treated him with profound respect. The only explanation for this highly uncharacteristic behavior is that he thought Scribe was entitled to a restraint that otherwise he exercised only toward the eminent Salvadore Cammarano when they worked together for the first time, on *Alzira* (1845), and the aristocratic man of letters Andrea Maffei, the librettist of *I masnadieri* (1847). Not only was Scribe much the elder, but by that date he had already completed the great majority of his total of 116 published librettos, and even if most had been written for the Opéra-Comique, no fewer than twenty-seven had been performed at the Paris Opéra itself; he was indisputably the most highly regarded librettist of nineteenth-century Europe.

Of course he was able to produce so much only by adopting a craftsmanlike attitude to the work, integrating fundamentally similar patterns into new contexts, and arranging reliable dramatic situations in new sequences; Karin Pendle actually drew up a list of just nineteen stock situations in her book on Scribe.[46] It was a working method employed by many other librettists, though none took it to quite the extreme that

---

beaucoup. Le directeur actuel ne veut les payer que d'après ce qu'ils valent, c'est à dire: fort peu." F-Pn, n.a.f. 22573, fol. 121v.

46. See *Eugène Scribe*, 390–93.

Scribe did, and for all its drawbacks it had the advantage that composers could survey his stock-in-trade and select the models that best suited them.

This aspect comes to the fore with especial clarity in Verdi's correspondence with Scribe, when he was looking for a suitable subject for the first new opera he was to compose for Paris. He turned down the first two scenarios Scribe sent him, which Scribe then consigned to his store of several dozen such that he never worked up into librettos. In order to explain to Scribe what it was he hoped for, Verdi referred to the libretto of an opera that had seen the light of day.

> Before writing especially for the Opéra . . . I should like, I need, a grandiose, impassioned, original subject, calling for an impressive, overwhelming production. Ever before my eyes I have the many, many magnificent scenes to be found in your librettos: among others, the Coronation Scene of *Le Prophète*! No other composer could have done better with that scene than Meyerbeer did: nevertheless, with that spectacle, and above all with that situation so original, grandiose, and at the same time so impassioned, no composer, however little feeling he had, would have failed to produce a great effect. Indeed! those scenes are miracles! But you work them so regularly that I hope that you will be good enough to work one for me, too.[47]

Of course Verdi could not have known that the libretto of *Le Prophète* owed a good part of its dramaturgical strengths to the active intervention of Meyerbeer, which makes his hopes for an equally effective text for himself look a little naive. But Scribe made a suggestion that Verdi accepted, apparently without long hesitation. *Le Duc d'Albe* was a libretto originally written in 1836 for Halévy, then taken over by Donizetti, but it was refused by the then director of the Opéra, Pillet. Refurbishing it for Verdi had two attractions for Scribe: he would get a return at last on the work he had put into it, and he would not have to stir himself to invent something new. Verdi agreed to this rather unusual arrangement, because the text provided one of the "magnificent scenes" he hungered for, and it seemed safe to assume that, once the action had been transferred from its original setting in the Spanish Netherlands in the sixteenth century, the public would not be aware that the libretto was not really "original" at all.[48] Verdi could not have known that Don-

---

47. Letter to Scribe, 26 July 1852. The original text and this translation are reproduced in Porter, "*Les Vêpres Siciliennes*," 96.

48. In fact, rumors about the origins of *Les Vêpres siciliennes* began to circulate in Paris as early as 1855; see Gartioux, *Giuseppe Verdi: Les Vêpres Siciliennes*, 39, 102.

izetti had actually set a substantial amount of the text, nor foreseen that some three decades later musical archaeologists would have the bright idea of putting Donizetti's score on the stage in Rome, in a version completed by Matteo Salvi, and with the text translated into Italian, as *Il duca d'Alba* (1882). This made the whole world aware that *Les Vêpres siciliennes* had begun life as *Le Duc d'Albe*, whereupon Verdi declared that he had known nothing of it, and that Scribe had deceived him. As Julian Budden comments: "Verdi in later life had a way of forgetting what he did not wish to remember."[49]

But in 1853, after coming to his arrangement with Verdi, Scribe had written to Charles Duveyrier, who had had a hand in planning the original *Le Duc d'Albe*—one of no fewer than 130 collaborators employed by Scribe over the years. Scribe's letter is very revealing of his attitude to the historical and geographical settings of the librettos he wrote, looking on them as backgrounds that could easily be changed, and always placing the emotional intrigue in the forefront.

> As usual, I had in my head many subjects of my own invention, but then I had the happy idea of resuscitating that poor *Duc d'Albe* whom everyone believed dead. . . . I suggested this to Verdi, making no secret of the adventures of the deceased. Many of the situations were to his liking, but some things weren't. First, the fact that the piece was origially intended for Donizetti, so that we might seem to be treating a subject that had been cast aside, deflowered, that had been around too long, in a word shop-worn.
>
> "We'd have to change the title." I made no difficulty. "Change the principal character." Not so easy, almost impossible. But I think I have the solution. We'd have to change the scene of the action, set it somewhere less chilly than the Netherlands; in a climate full of warmth and music, like Naples or Sicily. Not so difficult: I did it.
>
> But then we had to change the whole of the second act since there are no beer halls in that country; likewise the fourth act representing the embarkation and departure of the Duke of Alba had to be changed and a fifth act added since he wants a fine, grand work in five acts on the same vast scale as *Les Huguenots* or *Le Prophète*.[50]

49. *The Operas of Verdi*, 2:174–75.

50. From Scribe's letter to Charles Duveyrier, 3 December 1853 (F-Pn, n.a.f. 22546, fols. 441–42), cited in Bonnefon, "Les Métamorphoses d'un opéra," 888. This letter and an undated one that Scribe wrote to Duveyrier a few weeks later are discussed, with English translations of substantial quotations, in Budden, ibid., 173–74, and in Porter, "Don't blame Scribe!" Translations from the letters here and in chapter 9 draw on those versions.

18 The caricaturist Benjamin (Benjamin Roubaud, 1811–47) drew this impression of Scribe at work, at a clerk's desk. His stock-in-trade ("dramas," "vaudevilles," "operas," and "comedies") is arranged round his desk in stacks, with money bags labeled "rights" leaning against them, while the drawers behind him contain the ingredients of his works, ready for use: "wit, no. 1," "wit, no. 2," "common situations," "bons mots," "puns," etc. (Reproduced from the lithograph by Marcelin, [Émile Planat, 1825–77] *Panthéon charivarique*.)

It is obvious that at this first, decisive stage of planning, Verdi accepted all Scribe's suggestions. It was not until much later that he began to have doubts about the quality of the libretto, and tried to get Scribe to accommodate his precise musico-dramatic intentions. The librettist had predicted this, in his letter to Duveyrier: "I shall consent to everything: not only to rewriting some of the text, which is nothing, but also to working with Verdi day by day, making the changes he will ask for, that's the real bore, as I'm finding every day with Meyerbeer."[51]

As the following chapter will show, Scribe was prepared to make concessions, but could not be persuaded to rethink the entire dramatic structure of individual acts. This may partly have been because Verdi had weakened his position at the start of their collaboration by his respectful attitude, but it is also clear that his wearing experiences with Meyerbeer had tired Scribe and he was apparently less ready, in his sixties, to let finicky composers have as much say as they wanted in the conception of his librettos. Meyerbeer seems to have sensed this. They worked together on *Le Prophète* and *L'Africaine* from their conception in the 1830s until both were finished in the 1840s; and again it was Scribe, the author of the original scenario, to whom Meyerbeer turned in the mid-1850s, when he wanted *Ein Feldlager in Schlesien* adapted as a French opéra comique (*L'Étoile du Nord*). But he did not undertake any further new projects with his most important Parisian librettist.

It is true that he signed a contract with Scribe and his collaborator Saint-Georges in January 1846, concerning a three-act opera with an Old Testament subject, provisionally entitled *Noëma, ou Le Repentir*.[52] But before long he was overcome by doubts about the effectiveness of Scribe's dramaturgical ideas,[53] and so he turned to his friend Germain Delavigne, whose advice he often sought, ever since Delavigne had worked on *Robert le diable* with Scribe.[54] Delavigne had also collaborated with Scribe on the librettos of *La Muette de Portici* and *La Nonne sanglante*, and with his own brother Casimir on that of Halévy's *Charles VI*. More recently he had had a hand in the final revisions of *Le Prophète*,[55] but he drew the line at rescuing *Noëma*, and Meyerbeer abandoned the project forthwith.[56] He had shown the great respect he had for the opin-

---

51. Ibid.; Bonnefon, "Les Métamorphoses d'un opéra," 889.
52. The contract, dated 15 January 1846, is included in Meyerbeer, *Briefwechsel*, 4:509–11.
53. See Meyerbeer's letter to Scribe, 21 April 1846, ibid., 49–51.
54. Ibid., 50, see also Meyerbeer's letter to Louis Gouin, 16 May 1846, ibid., 62–63.
55. See the entry in Meyerbeer's diary, 31 December 1847, ibid., 350.
56. See entries in Meyerbeer's diary, 5 and 7 November 1847, ibid., 333ff.

ion of this "grey eminence" nearly ten years earlier, when Delavigne's advice led him to put aside *L'Africaine* in favor of *Le Prophète*.[57]

Apart from *L'Étoile du Nord*, Meyerbeer composed one more opera for Paris in the 1850s, and for this he ignored Scribe and called on the services of two librettists at the start of their careers. Jules Barbier and Michel Carré, who wrote the libretto of Meyerbeer's second opéra comique, *Le Pardon de Ploërmel* (1859), became France's leading librettists during the 1860s and '70s and are best known for Gounod's *Faust* (1859) and Offenbach's *Les Contes d'Hoffmann* (1881). The advantages of working with relative novices were twofold for Meyerbeer: not only did they have fresh ideas, so that he did not have to make do with Scribe's somewhat moth-eaten stock, but also he was able to insist on incorporating his own, evidently highly idiosyncratic, ideas in the opera. Having begun as an idea for a one-acter, it ended up with three lengthy acts. Barbier still revealed signs of shock at the way Meyerbeer had gone to work when he was interviewed about his career over thirty years later. He had experienced real pleasure, he said, only when working with Victor Massé, Ambroise Thomas, and, above all, Charles Gounod. With Gounod, "all that one had to do was write the libretto as one felt it should be, after having come to an agreement with him, and he always declared himself satisfied." These three composers

at least did not seek to absorb the librettist but rather to enter into perfect communication with him. . . . That was not how Meyerbeer or Fromental Halévy, for example, understood collaboration, they turned your libretto upside down, transforming one act into a four-act opera and vice versa. That was what happened to us, to Carré and me, with *Le Pardon de Ploër-mel*, which we wrote as a modest little work, and which Meyerbeer returned to us chewed to bits, tortured, stretched on the rack. We didn't recognize it as ours! It was impossible to work in such conditions.[58]

57. See Meyerbeer's letters to Minna Meyerbeer. 10 and 15 (?) July 1838, ibid., 3:142, 145f.

58. "il n'y avait qu'à écrire le poème comme on le sentait, après s'être concerté avec lui, et il se déclarait toujours satisfait"; "Eux du moins ne cherchaient pas à absorber le poète, mais plutôt à entrer en communication parfaite avec lui. . . . Ce n'est pas ainsi que Meyerbeer ou Fromental Halévy, par exemple, entendaient la collaboration: ils bouleversaient votre poème de fond en comble, si bien qu'un livret en un acte était transformé en un opéra en quatre actes et réciproquement. C'est ce qui nous arriva, à Carré et à moi, pour le Pardon de Ploërmel dont nous avions fait un tout petit ouvrage, et que Meyerbeer nous a présenté trituré, torturé, allongé. Nous ne nous y reconnûmes plus du tout! Le travail était impossible dans ces conditions." Lapauze, "La Reprise de *Faust* à l'Opéra."

If Meyerbeer's last completed opera turned into a bad memory for Bar-bier, it also offended Scribe. Meyerbeer had not only turned his back on Scribe's huge store of ideas for dramas, where he would have found several subjects suitable for an opéra comique that had not been com-posed already, but he had also spurned Scribe's practical theatrical expe-rience. That might have prevented some quite extraordinary dramatur-gical notions from persisting in the final version of a work that has never been a success. Much as Meyerbeer was attracted to the idea, which took off in his lifetime, that an opera's essential author was its composer, he actually lacked both the self-confidence and the hardheadedness that made it possible for Verdi to conceive entire operas on his own. At all events, Scribe, who must have been more conscious of the faults of *Le Pardon de Ploërmel* than anyone else, allowed himself the private luxury, in his diary, of a verse epigram:

> Si Meyerbeer demande, au public, comme au ciel
> Pardon! . . . c'est d'avoir fait celui de Ploërmel.[59]

⁊   ⁊   ⁊

If Meyerbeer asks the public's pardon, and Heaven's as well / it must be for writing *The Pardon of Ploërmel.*

59. Eugène Scribe, "Distique sur le Ploërmel" (F-Pn, n.a.f. 22569, fol. 441).

·: 9 :·

VERDI AND AN INSTITUTIONAL CRISIS

LES VÊPRES SICILIENNES

TEXT

Eugène Scribe (1791–1861) and Charles Duveyrier (1803–66)

MUSIC

Giuseppe Verdi (1813–1901)

FIRST PERFORMANCE

Paris, Académie Impériale de Musique, 13 June 1855

PLACE AND DATE OF THE ACTION

Palermo and the vicinity, March 1282

CHARACTERS

Guy de Montfort, Governor of Sicily under Charles d'Anjou, King of Naples (baritone); the Sire de Béthune (bass) and the Count de Vaudemont (bass), French officers; Henri, a young Sicilian (tenor); Jean Procida, Sicilian doctor (bass); Duchess Hélène, sister of Duke Frédéric of Austria (soprano); Ninetta, her maid (contralto); Daniéli, a Sicilian (tenor); Thibault (tenor) and Robert (bass), French soldiers; Mainfroid, a Sicilian (tenor)

SYNOPSIS

ACT I

The marketplace in Palermo. Sicily is under French rule. French soldiers drink to their homeland while Sicilians curse the occupation (No. 1. *Introduction*, "Beau pays de France"). The soldiers force Hélène, whose brother was executed by the French, to sing to the crowd. She responds with a song about a ship in distress, maintaining that trust in God, courage, and vigor will vanquish every danger—an unmistakable reference to Sicily's situation (No. 1b. *Scène, air et choeur,* "Quelle est cette beauté . . ." / "Au sein des mers et battu par l'orage" /

342

"Quels accents! quel langage!"). The Sicilians are on the point of attacking the French when Montfort, the Governor, appears on the palace steps, and the crowd take to their heels. Montfort, Hélène, and the servants who remain with her, are astonished at their cowardice (No. 2. *Quatuor,* "Quelle horreur m'environne"). Henri, a young man raised by his mother to hate the French, joins the group and, not recognizing the Governor, gives vent to his hostility. Montfort reveals himself and forces Henri to answer his questions (No. 3. *Duo final,* "Quel est ton nom?" / "Punis mon audace!"). Henri's provocative stance invites punishment, but Montfort is impressed by his courage. Henri refuses to join the French army, and the Governor lets him go, but, having seen that the two young people are in love, forbids him to see Hélène.

ACT II

A valley near Palermo, with the sea in the background. Procida has returned from a secret mission and is welcomed by Henri, Hélène, and other conspirators (No. 4. *Entr'acte, air et choeur,* "Palerme, ô mon pays!" / "Et toi, Palerme, ô beauté qu'on outrage"). Procida reports that other states will only support the Sicilians if they themselves begin an uprising, in which Henri is expected to play a leading role. Hélène promises her love to Henri, if he will do so and thus avenge her brother's death (No. 5. *Récit, scène et duo,* "Fidèles à ma voix!" / "Comment, dans ma reconnaissance"). Some soldiers arrive, bringing an invitation to Henri to go to the Governor's palace; when he refuses they carry him off by force (No. 6. *Récit et final,* "A vous, et de la part de notre gouverneur!" / "Voilà, par saint Denis! de belles fiancées!"). Meanwhile, six young couples arrive, intending to celebrate their betrothals. The French soldiers force the young women to dance with them, and show respect only to Hélène. Sicilian anger is raised to the boiling point. A ship sails into sight, carrying French nobles to Palermo for the ball that the Governor is giving that evening. Procida will mingle with the guests and assassinate him.

ACT III

First setting: Montfort's study. The Governor is reading a letter from a Sicilian woman he ravished many years ago. She begs him at least to protect their son, should he ever fall into his hands: his name is Henri (No. 7. *Entr'acte et air,* "Oui, je fus bien coupable" / "Au sein de la puissance"). Henri is brought in, and Montfort tells him he can move freely within the palace (No. 8. *Scène et duo,* "Je n'en puis revenir!" / "Quand ma bonté toujours nouvelle"). Montfort shows the letter to Henri, who thus, for the first time, learns the identity of his father. Montfort tries to embrace him, but Henri rushes away in horror.

Second setting: a ballroom in the Governor's palace. The guests assemble for the ball, wearing masks (No. 9. *Marche*), and watch a lavish ballet representing the four seasons (No. 10. *Ballet*). As the guests begin to dance, Hélène and Procida reveal themselves to Henri (No. 11. *Final,* "Ô fête brillante"). Henri cannot bring Procida to abandon the planned assassination, or persuade Montfort to leave the ball. Hélène is about to stab Montfort when Henri throws himself in the way. All the conspirators are arrested and curse the traitor, Henri, who bewails his fate.

ACT IV

The courtyard of a prison. Thanks to Montfort's magnanimity, Henri has free access to the prison. He cannot bear the thought of being hated by Hélène as a traitor (No. 12. *Entr'acte, récit et air,* "C'est Guy de Montfort!" / "Ô jour de deuil et de souffrance!"). Hélène is brought into the courtyard and repulses Henri. When he tells her that Montfort is his father, however, she forgives him—for she still loves him (No. 13. *Duo,* "De courroux et d'effroi" / "Jamais de pitié pour le traître"). Montfort orders the execution of Hélène and Procida; the latter laments that he will not live to see Sicily gain its freedom (No. 14. *Récit,* "Par une main amie"). When Procida learns that Henri is Montfort's son, he shows no compassion and weeps for Sicily (No. 15. *Quatuor,* "Adieu, mon pays"). Montfort promises Henri that he will pardon the two conspirators if Henri will only call him "mon père" (No. 16. *Final,* "De profundis!"). Hélène forbids her lover to make the concession, but when the executioner lays hands on her Henri cries the words aloud. Montfort stops the execution and orders the immediate marriage of Henri and Hélène as a guarantee of Franco-Sicilian reconciliation.

ACT V

The gardens of the Governor's palace. Sicilian women and French men celebrate the new friendship of their peoples (No. 17. *Entr'acte et choeur,* "Célébrons ensemble"). Girls strew flowers before Hélène, who thanks them (No. 18 *Boléro,* "Merci, jeunes amies"). Henri comes and dreams of his future happiness (No. 19. *Mélodie,* "La brise souffle"). Procida confides to Hélène that when the bells ring out during her wedding it will be the signal for the uprising against the unsuspecting French (No. 20. *Récit et scène,* "A ton dévouement généreux"). Hélène does not dare betray Procida's plot but wants to save Henri's life, at least. She tells him, therefore, that she cannot marry him; he believes himself betrayed (No. 21. *Trio,* "Sort fatal"), and tells his father of Hélène's decision. Montfort is convinced that Hélène still loves Henri in her heart, and gives the command for the wedding to proceed. The bells peal out and general massacre ensues (No. 22. *Scène et choeur final,* "Ah! venez compatir" / "Oui, vengeance!").

EDITIONS: The full score is only available for hire from the publisher, Ricordi; the commentary in this chapter is based on the composer's original manuscript in the Bibliothèque Nationale in Paris. Copies of the piano-vocal score based on the original French version (Paris: Escudier 1855) are rare, while the usual piano-vocal edition published by Ricordi, and reprinted by Kalmus, gives the text only in an Italian translation that not only distorts the meaning of the French but also exhibits remarkable incompetence in fitting the words to the music.

RECOMMENDED RECORDING: The only complete studio recording, issued in 1973, uses the old Italian translation, but at least it is uncut. It has Martina Arroyo (Elena), Placido Domingo (Arrigo [Henri]), Sherill Milnes (Monforte), and Ruggiero Raimondi (Procida), and is conducted by James Levine. The performance accentuates the dramatic impetus of the score and gives the listener an introduction to the opera, in an—in every sense—Italianized version.

Regular Miracles

When the directors of the Paris Opéra at last, in 1852, managed to persuade Verdi to undertake a completely new work for them, he insisted on a libretto by Scribe.[1] He had been under no illusion that Alphonse Royer and Gustave Vaëz, who were recommended to him for the French version of his *I Lombardi alla prima crociata*, originally written for Milan and given in Paris in 1847 under the title of *Jérusalem*, were anything other than second best; now, the huge international success of *Rigoletto* put him in the position to dictate the best terms for his work in Paris. Yet it is surprising to find Verdi so eager to work with Scribe, by then over sixty and set in his ways. Innovative music-dramatist and critical observer that Verdi was, he should have had opportunity enough to realize that it was becoming increasingly difficult for Scribe to find new material to pour into the form of the five-act grand opéra that he himself had established. His most recent librettos—*Le Juif errant* (1852), set by Halévy and with its first performance imminent, *Jeanne la folle* (1848), set by Clapisson, and *L'Enfant prodigue* (1850), set by Auber—all betrayed it. But the spectacular Coronation scene in Act IV of *Le Prophète* had obviously dazzled Verdi, as he declared in the letter to Scribe of 26 July 1852, quoted in chapter 8.[2] In citing as his example of the "magnificent scenes to be found in your librettos" one from Meyerbeer's latest opera, however, he also revealed the crucial motive for his interest in working with Scribe. He himself was the most successful Italian composer active at the time and, with his true debut in Paris in prospect, he clearly intended to challenge the most successful opera composer in Europe, Giacomo Meyerbeer, on his own ground, with one of the great five-act, historical operas for which Meyerbeer, too, had always got his librettos from Scribe.

Verdi was not famous for generosity in the making of compliments, and we could be forgiven for suspecting that sound commercial motives were what drove him to flatter Scribe so extravagantly for the "miracles" which he worked "so regularly." But Verdi's admiration for the dramaturgical conception of *Le Prophète* was wholly unfeigned and survived all

1. See Budden, *The Operas of Verdi*, 2:170–71.
2. See above, 336.

the changes of the second half of the nineteenth century; in 1896, he once again singled out the Coronation scene in *Le Prophète*, in a conversation reported by Italo Pizzi:

> In *Le Prophète* he acknowledged the unusual dramatic power, greater perhaps than in *Robert*, or *Les Huguenots*, particularly in the fourth act at the marvellously dramatic moment when the mother of John of Leyden, who has been made King and prophet, is forced by her son's magnetic power to deny him.[3]

Yet in referring to the regularity with which Scribe worked such "miracles" as this, in his letter of July 1852, Verdi intuitively put his finger on grand opéra's problem. The concentration on spectacle inevitably meant that every single work had to offer something new, and something that would overshadow all predecessors whenever possible. The formal framework in which this was to be accomplished had not changed, however, since the mid-1830s.

In fact the libretto Scribe finally sent Verdi, by dint of transforming *Le Duc d'Albe*, the nonseller of 1836, into *Les Vêpres siciliennes*, did contain a magnificent scene worthy of comparison with the climax of *Le Prophète*. Just as, in Meyerbeer's opera, within the highly public context of his coronation, Jean forces Fidès to deny that she is his mother in order to save his life, so here, in the context of an imminent execution, Montfort forces his son to acknowledge him publicly as his father, in order to save the life of the woman he loves. Verdi, in whose work difficult relationships with severe fathers form a well-nigh obsessively recurring theme, was delighted with it, as Scribe told Duveyrier: "In the fourth act, the best moment in the work, according to Verdi: the conspirators are led to the scaffold: Henri, who has refused up to this moment to call Montfort his father, throws himself at his feet: 'Ah! so you *did* love her!'"[4]

No wonder Verdi was moved to put his pleasure on record when he took delivery of Scribe's completed libretto at the very end of 1853. Wholly abandoning his usual habits, he wrote a personal opinion on the receipt, though it was required for purely legal reasons: "I acknowledge having received from M. Scribe, in accordance with the terms of his

---

3. Conati, *Interviews and Encounters*, 344.
4. "Au quatrième acte, la plus belle situation de l'ouvrage, suivant Verdi: on mène les conjurés au supplice: Henri, qui jusque-là a refusé d'appeler Montfort son père, se précipite à ses genoux: *Ah! tu l'aimais donc bien!*" Scribe's letter to Charles Duveyrier, undated (late December 1853/early January 1854; F-Pn, n.a.f. 22546, fols. 446–47), text in Bonnefon, "Les Métamorphoses d'un opéra," 889–93. See also above, chapter 8, n. 50.

contract with M. Roqueplan, the complete five acts of *Les Vêpres sicilien-nes*, with which I am very satisfied."[5] But in spite of the splendid finale to Act IV, which we will look at more closely below, and notwithstand-ing Verdi's enthusiastic reaction, Scribe's adaptation of a libretto he had conceived originally for Halévy and then for Donizetti is dominated by his usual habits. One of the leading opera critics of the time, discussing this libretto, had good reason to comment on the "small number of dra-matic contrivances, which he [Scribe] reproduces so readily and without varying them very much."[6]

The most blatant example of Scribe's recycling comes in the finale of Act III, which itself adds a completely new element to the plot. Once it had been decided to link the private intrigue that had been the subject of *Le Duc d'Albe* with the legend of the Sicilian Vespers of 1282, the failed attempt to assassinate the Governor—the Duke in *Le Duc d'Albe*, Montfort in *Les Vêpres siciliennes*—could no longer be left until the end of the work.[7] Scribe transferred the incident to a new context, a masked ball at the Governor's palace, but with that the situation became nearly identical to the last-act finale in Scribe and Auber's *Gustave III, ou Le Bal masqué*. However, if representing a masked ball on the stage of the Opéra was a revolutionary novelty in 1833[8]—the more so because an-other three years were to pass before guests at the public balls held in the building were allowed to wear masks and fancy dress[9]—two decades later such a scene was bound to be received as the repetition of an all too familiar model.[10]

There are many other details in Scribe's libretto for Verdi of which much the same can be said. Once again the subject is a historical one, concerning the enmity between two parties, depicted as equals in ruth-lessness and cruelty. On this occasion, admittedly, Scribe thought it nec-essary to publish a wordy preface in the libretto, explaining that the

5. "Je reconnais avoir reçu de M. Scribe en termes de son traité avec M. Roqueplan les cinq actes complets des Vêpres Siciliennes dont je suis très content" The French text of this receipt, dated 31 December 1853, is quoted in Porter, "*Les Vêpres siciliennes*: New letters," 101.

6. "[Le] petit nombre de combinaisons dramatiques qu'il reproduit si volontiers et sans les varier beaucoup." Paul Scudo in *Revue des deux mondes* 11 (July–September 1855): 218; see also Gartioux, *Giuseppe Verdi: Les Vêpres Siciliennes*, 106.

7. Cf. the text of Scribe's libretto for *Le Duc d'Albe*, published complete by Lo Presti ("*Le Duc d'Albe*"). This is from a copy preserved in Siena, but it clearly corresponds to the fair copy in Scribe's literary estate (F-Pn, n.a.f. 22506, fols. 125–71). There is a useful synopsis of *Le Duc d'Albe* in Budden, *The Operas of Verdi*, 2:172.

8. See Join-Dieterle, "La Monarchie source d'inspiration de l'Opéra," 439.

9. See Boigne, *Petits Mémoires de l'Opéra*, 180.

10. On the ballet numbers, see Jürgensen, *The Verdi ballets*, 32–56.

deviations from historical truth in his fictionalized version were not due to ignorance on his part: on the contrary, he had made a careful study of the historical literature. He summarized his case as follows:

> We hasten to inform those who will, as usual, reproach us with historical ignorance, that the wholesale massacre known by the name of the "Sicilian Vespers" never happened. Once that historical point is recognized, each and every person should be permitted, more or less, to interpret the subject as he thinks fit.[11]

The confusing halfheartedness of Scribe's self-defense, asserting his artistic freedom only to qualify it immediately with the formula "more or less," gives rise to the suspicion that even he had come to recognize that the days of treating historical subject matter in the style of the grand opéra of the 1830s were over. Nevertheless, he clung to exactly the same dramaturgical techniques that had already proved themselves in earlier librettos. As in *Les Huguenots*, the mutually hostile groups of the population confront each other in direct contrast—although here it happens not merely at the end of the second act but as soon as the curtain rises on the first, thus giving the exposition a substantially more dramatic character than Meyerbeer thought appropriate to his style of dramaturgy. As in Act III of *Guillaume Tell*, soldiers of the army of occupation provoke the anger of the resident population by forcing young women—here, brides—to dance with them. Like the crowd in *Le Prophète*, however, the Sicilians are depicted as impotent and cowardly: the mere appearance of Montfort in Act I quenches their rebellious mood, even though he is "alone and without guards."

As in *Guillaume Tell*, a leader of the occupying power tries to persuade the tenor protagonist to join the "right" side. Henri in *Les Vêpres siciliennes* differs from his Swiss counterpart, Arnold, in demonstrating strength of purpose from the first, and yet he is burdened with all the known attributes of the indecisive hero, for he cannot make up his mind between loyalty to his father and his patriotic duty. Like Raoul in *Les Huguenots*, he suffers disaster in love, for at first the two lovers are not prepared to have the conversation that would explain everything, and

---

11. "A ceux qui nous reprocheront, comme de coutume, d'ignorer l'histoire, nous nous empresserons d'apprendre que le massacre général connu sous le nom de Vêpres Siciliennes n'a jamais existé. Ce point historique une fois reconnu, il doit être à peu près permis à chacun de traîter ce sujet comme il l'entend." On the relationship Scribe's libretto bears to the historical facts, see also Maehder, "L'opera storica dell'Ottocento e *I vespri siciliani*," 99–101.

then later, when their union seems to be possible after all, the violence of the mob destroys everything.

There is only one important departure from the typical grand opéra model in the libretto as delivered by Scribe in December 1853, and that is in the conception of the principal female character, Hélène. Anything but the "dutiful daughter," she is the first to incite the Sicilians to rebellion with her hymn to martial courage, in which the evocation of Delacroix's painting *Liberty leading the people* is almost certainly intentional. On the other hand, like other women in grand opéra, she does not act on her own convictions but only out of loyalty to the all-powerful family: she is obsessed by the thought of avenging her brother's death. Even so, the brother occupies the place in her emotional life that a venerable father holds for other women of her type, and a comparison with the text of *Le Duc d'Albe* uncovers that originally the murder victim crying out for vengeance was indeed the heroine's father, and that it was only the need to accommodate the characters' circumstances to the known facts about their historical counterparts that made Scribe forgo the opportunity to make Hélène's inner conflict resemble Henri's even more closely than it does.

Other characteristics of grand opéra, such as lovingly detailed depiction of local color or of urban atmosphere, are already less pronounced in Scribe's libretto, and recede even further from the foreground in Verdi's music, although the Sicilian setting, and the streets and squares of Palermo in particular, would have supported a decision to abide by the familiar model. The most significant departures in *Les Vêpres siciliennes* from the pattern of the large-scale, five-act, historical opera came about, however, because Verdi decided to have the libretto altered after Scribe delivered it or to modify its structures by the way he set them to music.

Tête-à-Tête

The first act provides particularly clear evidence of the ways in which Verdi turned away from the characteristic models of French operatic tradition while he was working on *Les Vêpres siciliennes*. It is true that in the first part of the act the events necessary for the exposition of the plot are placed within the framework of a big scene with the chorus; to that extent, Hélène makes her first entrance within a tableau-like, setpiece, big scene in accordance with the dramaturgical example set by Meyerbeer in the first act of *Les Huguenots* (the kind of scene Michael

Walter would call a Großszene).[12] But Montfort's entrance heralds a
radical change from precedent. The crowd of ordinary people who, up
to this point, have been allowed a generous share in the succession of
musical forms flee from the scene in fright and leave the Governor
alone with Hélène and her confidante Ninetta. The stretta of the big
choral scene is followed by an ensemble for soloists, accompanied only
by a few drumrolls, "Quelle horreur m'environne"; Verdi's decision to
include the Sicilian Daniéli and so make this number a quartet may have
been taken with an eye to avoiding too close a resemblance to the *trio
sans accompagnement* "Fatal moment, cruel mystère" in Act III of Meyerbeer's *Robert le diable*. Henri enters when the quartet is finished, but after
a brief exchange of words he is left alone on the stage with Montfort.

The idea that the climax of the first act should be the meeting of
father and son went back to *Le Duc d'Albe*. But just as in that text Scribe
ensured that a Spanish captain and some soldiers were constantly in
view at the back of the stage throughout the scene, so in the version of
the libretto that he delivered to Verdi in December 1853 he took care
that this extensive first act should not end with a purely private encounter, and provided for a cinematic "dissolve" at the end of the duet, "Quel
est ton nom," by bringing a unit of French troops on to the stage for
a parade.

> (*A la fin de ce duo De Béthune et Vaudemont à la tête d'un corps de soldats et sur
> un air de marche sortent de la caserne à gauche; sur un signe de Guy de Montfort
> ils s'arrêtent rangés en bataille, devant le perron du palais. De Béthune et Vaude-
> mont s'approchent de Montfort et restent à quelques pas derrière lui.*)
> MONTFORT *à Henri qui pendant ce temps s'est dirigé vers la porte du palais*
> [d'Hélène] *à droite*
> Je saurai briser ton orgeuil!
> De ce logis ne franchis pas le seuil,
> Car je te le défends . . .
>
> HENRI
> Vous!
>
> MONTFORT
> Moi! Guy de Montfort!
> (*Henri lève le marteau de la porte qui s'ouvre et s'élance dans le palais.*)
>
> DE BÉTHUNE *voulant le suivre*
> Ah! c'est trop d'insolence . . . et il faut mettre un terme!
>
> MONTFORT *lui faisant signe d'arrèter*
> Arrêtez! c'est à moi d'ordonner de son sort!

12. See above, chapter 3, 99.

DE BÉTHUNE
Qu'ordonnes-tu?

MONTFORT *à part, avec satisfaction*
C'est le seul dans Palerme
Qui m'ait osé braver! *(haut)* . . . l'on devine aisément
Et rien qu'à sa fierté qu'il soit d'un noble sang!

DE BÉTHUNE
Qu'ordonnes-tu? . . .

MONTFORT *lentement*
                    Que tout s'apprête . . .

DE BÉTHUNE
Pour sa mort . . .

MONTFORT *gaîment*
                    Pour la fête
Qu'en mon palais je donne à tous mes compagnons
Demain . . . je vous invite *(à part)* ainsi que lui . . . *(haut)* marchons!
(L'air de marche qui pendant la scène précédente s'était fait entendre en sour-
dine reprend ici avec force. Les troupes rangées en bataille agitent leurs épées et
commencent à défiler devant Guy de Montfort qui les regarde. La toile tombe.)
Fin du premier acte[13]

ح ح ح

(At the end of this duet De Béthune and Vaudemont emerge from the barracks,
left, at the head of a troop of soldiers and to a march-tune; at a sign from Guy
de Montfort they halt in battle order at the foot of the palace steps. De Béthune
and Vaudemont approach Montfort and stop a few paces behind him.)
MONTFORT *(to Henri who, meanwhile, has moved towards the door of* [Hé-
lène's] *palace, right):* I shall break your pride! Do not cross the threshold
of that house, for I forbid you!
HENRI: You!
MONTFORT: I! Guy de Montfort!
(Henri lifts the knocker on the door which opens, and he dashes inside the
palace).
DE BÉTHUNE *(making to follow):* Ah! Such insolence . . . it must be
stopped!
MONTFORT *(stopping him with a gesture):* Stop! it is for me to command
his fate!
DE BÉTHUNE: What is your command?
MONTFORT *(aside, with satisfaction):* He is the only one in Palermo who
has dared defy me! *(aloud)* It's easily guessed, if only by his pride, that
he's of noble blood!
DE BÉTHUNE: What is your command?

13. F-Pn, n.a.f. 22506, fol. 59v.

MONTFORT *(slowly):* Let everything be made ready . . .
DE BÉTHUNE: For his death . . .
MONTFORT *(gaily):* For the feast I shall give in my palace for all my com-
rades tomorrow . . . I invite you *(aside)* and him . . . *(aloud)* March!
*(The march-tune which was heard muted throughout the preceding scene re-
turns at full strength. The soldiers, in battle order, flourish their swords and
begin to file past Guy de Montfort, who watches them. The curtain falls.)*
End of Act I

Although Scribe conceived this passage with a clear idea of how it might
be set, Verdi composed none of it. Concision was always important to
him, so it is not very surprising that he regarded the somewhat wordy
dialogue as dispensable. But at the same time he dispensed with the idea
of the march as a pantomimic means of conveying Montfort's military
power, and in doing that he altered radically the balance in the blend of
private intrigue and public-cum-historical setting which was a fundamental feature of grand opéra. In the final version of the scene, as Verdi
set it, Henri and Montfort remain alone on the stage at the end of the
act. Neither the Sicilian people nor the French soldiers are seen: only
the presence of the third person involved in the private drama, Hélène,
is indicated by the fact that Henri takes refuge in her house. All the
emphasis falls on the personal aspect of the conflict which brings father
and son face to face.

This concentration of the drama to a tête-à-tête is characteristic of
the structure of the whole opera. The climactic "Sicilian Vespers" come
about as the conclusion of a series of encounters between just two
people at a time. Henri takes part in a duet in each of the four acts, with
his father on two occasions, and with Hélène on the other two, all of
them constructed in several sections. But in discarding the passage from
the first version of the libretto quoted above, Verdi was only taking still
further a principle already represented in Scribe's text, and which he
himself, without any assistance from Scribe, had already made the dominant characteristic of his most recent Italian operas. He was fully justified in claiming, in 1852, that he had "conceived *Rigoletto* almost without arias, without finales but only an unending string of duets,"[14] and
when he decided to compose *Les Vêpres siciliennes* a year later, the "unending string of duets" may not have been the least of the positive aspects that attracted him to the subject when Scribe suggested it.

The almost symmetrical layout of the four large-scale duets was yet
another survival from the abortive *Duc d'Albe*. All the numbers affected

14. From a letter to Carlo Antonio Borsi, 8 September 1852, quoted in Italian in
Abbiati, *Verdi,* 2:175–76; cited from Budden, *The Operas of Verdi,* 1:483.

were already to be found in the rhymed version of that libretto, which dated from 1838, and Scribe may very well have had the concept in mind when he first sketched the work in 1836. It was, however, the first time that he had adopted on a large scale a formal convention of recent Italian opera that Meyerbeer had had to explain to him only a few years earlier. Commenting on Scribe's first draft for *Les Huguenots*, Meyerbeer had asked expressly for duets "of Italian cut," and had explained that these differed from duets "of French cut" in that the concluding ensemble did not reprise the text (and music) of the middle ensemble, in the manner of a rondo, but expounded new material.[15]

In requesting duets "of Italian cut" Meyerbeer invoked a convention that had become the norm in Italy over the course of the first two decades of the nineteenth century, from early examples in works by Simon Mayr dating from around 1800 to the point when it was consolidated in Rossini's late opere serie.[16] It had become the manner in which composers such as Bellini, Donizetti, and Mercadante, and the young Meyerbeer too, fashioned nearly all their duets—and most of their other ensembles and arias for good measure. Within a structure consisting of the succession of several sections, the forms of the individual sections were very different in themselves, but the alternation of now open, now static forms was largely standardized according to a model which modern scholars have only recently recognized. A *scena* in recitative style was succeeded by a *tempo d'attacco*, a section with a lively tempo and a musically very loose structure in which the dramatic situation was made clear. Then followed a movement in a closed form and a slow tempo *(adagio)*, which gave both soloists the chance for lyrical contemplation or meditative asides. A *tempo di mezzo* usually revived the short-breathed dialogue of the *tempo d'attacco*, but sometimes it served for longer excursions or even for interpolations from the chorus or minor characters, before the climax of both rhythmical and dramatic intensity was reached in the concluding fast movement, the *cabaletta*.[17]

Beyond doubt such a stereotype met the need of Italian audiences for easily understood conventions and musical patterns that did not distract attention from the succession of vocal high points that the operagoing public valued above all else. Connoisseurs of French opera, with its stronger emphasis on dramatic traits, were on the other hand inclined

15. "coupés à *l'Italienne*"; "coupés à la française." F-Pn, n.a.f. 22502, fol. 65; see also Huebner, "Italianate duets," 208 and 251, n. 20.

16. See Balthazar, "Mayr, Rossini," 385–95.

17. See Powers, "'La solita forma,'" 79–80 (in *Acta musicologica*, 68–70), and Balthazar, "Ritorni's *Ammaestramenti*," 290–91.

to look somewhat askance at the convention, for which the Italian critic Basevi coined the term *solita forma*.[18] Fétis, for example, after a performance of Rossini's *Semiramide*, asked himself "why as a whole it is so tiresome," and speculated that the fault lay "in the similarity of forms," especially the duets: "There are four duets in *Semiramide* . . . all four appear to be cast in the same mold."[19]

Since then, however, operas like *Robert le diable* had shown that where a work's aesthetic premises were based on the spectacular melodramas of the post-Revolutionary Parisian theater (unlike *Semiramide*, which went back to one of Voltaire's plays of the 1740s), the succession of several similarly constructed duets did not necessarily cause fatigue in the audience. Scribe's *Le Duc d'Albe*, exhibiting the very succession of four similar duets that Fétis deplored, is only one example of the versatility of which the Italian model was capable. No composer of grand opéra was willing to dismiss it out of hand, for it permitted the display of spectacular contrasts within a framework in which static and kinetic elements were perfectly balanced. In France, admittedly, it was only among composers of the second rank that the stereotype acquired the status of a convention needing no justification, which it continued to enjoy in Italy into the 1860s. Nevertheless, the model was also resorted to regularly by composers like Halévy, who had considerably more success at depicting intimate emotions in the smallest possible ensembles than at constructing the large-scale, set-piece scenes most typical of grand opéra. Halévy was the composer for whom *Le Duc d'Albe* had originally been written, and Scribe, hack that he was, cut the cloth of a libretto to suit the composer for whom it was intended: it will not have escaped him that *La Juive* (1835) owed its success not least to the duets, which were constructed with positively textbook fidelity to the Italian model.

All the same, when we look back now at the whole course of the development of French opera in the nineteenth century, Halévy and Scribe's loyalty to the form can only be called conservative. Rossini, in *Guillaume Tell*, had already tried to reduce the frequency of the stereotype which he himself had established in Italy; Meyerbeer, after having used the form six times in *Robert le diable*, had drastically cut its role in *Les Huguenots* (premièred at the time when Scribe was writing *Le Duc d'Albe*). Other French composers persisted in including a duet in every act, even in the 1840s, but Meyerbeer had only three in the whole of *Les*

18. *Studio sulle opere di Giuseppe Verdi*, 191.

19. *Revue musicale* 6 (1829): 181; cited here in Huebner's translation in "Italianate duets," 211 and see also 253, n. 28.

Huguenots, and it is clear that he had decided to restrict the tête-à-tête to the most important climactic moments in the drama. He would certainly have regarded a "duet opera" in the manner of *Le Duc d'Albe* as the acme of monotony, and in his next opera, *Le Prophète*, he reserved the conventional type of duet scene—not counting the brief *Romance à deux voix* in Act I, which originates in a different formal tradition—for the electrifying encounters between Berthe and Fidès in Act IV, and between Fidès and Jean in the last act.[20]

Meyerbeer, however, was concerned less with limiting the use of a by-then outmoded formal type than with subordinating what he had already in 1831 called a "mechanical procedure"[21] to the purposes of his musical dramaturgy. Thus although he kept essentially to the Italian model in the two duets in *Le Prophète*, the way he developed it in the love duet in Act IV of *Les Huguenots*, with the text cut up into short pieces of prose and the totally irregular cabaletta, burst the bounds of every generic tradition. By that date, admittedly, the more advanced Italian composers had also tried to make the mechanical formal model more interesting by introducing individual modifications, as Meyerbeer had noticed, praising Donizetti's *L'esule di Roma* (1828) with good reason for the "interesting treatment of the forms and departure from the *procédé fixe*, from stereotyped forms."[22] But while Meyerbeer was not afraid of breaking either with formal models or with a convention that no one had ever violated before him, namely that of using only texts in regular poetic meters in closed numbers, composers such as Bellini, Donizetti, and Verdi continued to accept the external conditions of Rossini's stereotype and confined themselves to making alterations within the framework thus imposed. Those conditions had dramaturgical strengths of their own, which should not be underestimated.[23]

Italian composers were fully inventive enough to go on extracting new kinds of nuance from the "customary forms" even as late as the 1850s and '60s. To that extent it was convenient for Scribe that his formal conception, clumsy as it was by French standards in the 1830s, and apparently intended to enhance the strengths and disguise the weaknesses of the Italian-oriented Halévy, was just what Verdi wanted twenty

20. See Huebner, "Italianate duets," 209.

21. "procédé mécanique": a comment on the technique of Rossini's followers; Meyerbeer's diary, 14 February 1831, in *Briefwechsel*, 2:134.

22. "[die] interessante Behandlung der Formen & Abweichen von dem procédé fixe, von den stereotypen Formen"; Meyerbeer's diary, 20 April 1832, ibid., 169.

23. See Balthazar, "The *Primo Ottocento* duet," 496, and idem, "Analytic contexts," 1–33.

years later. True, the dramatic situations for which Scribe proposed duets fell a long way short of the sensational context which Verdi, humorously considering the possibility of adding a scene to *Rigoletto* in 1852, postulated as ideal for a truly dramatic duet: "We would have to show the Duke and Gilda in the bedroom!! You see what I mean?! In any case it would be a duet—a magnificent duet!!"[24] No Italian censor would have permitted that, of course. But in spite of all the limitations, the duets in *Les Vêpres siciliennes* allowed the composer to concentrate the musical dramaturgy of his opera wholly upon isolated characters, as they expressed their most intimate feelings.

Verdi went beyond the relatively schematic conditions created by Scribe in undertaking substantial modifications in two of the four duets, which allowed him to be innovative within the established formal pattern. He was content to accept Scribe's suggestion in the duet in Act I, following a *tempo d'attacco* with a first lyrical episode marked "Cantabile," in which Henri's courage moves Montfort to admiration ("Punis mon audace"), then, after a *tempo di mezzo*, composing the obligatory cabaletta, marked "Prestissimo," in which Montfort tries to dampen that same courage ("Téméraire! téméraire!"). When Verdi came to the duet in Act II, however, in which Henri and Hélène acknowledge their love in the consciousness that their politically inspired actions may lead to their deaths, he cut everything that Scribe had intended to follow the first slow movement ("Près du tombeau peut-être où nous allons descendre"). The result, shorn of Scribe's *tempo di mezzo* section and cabaletta, was what might be described as an "incomplete" succession of just two movements, a *tempo d'attacco* and an adagio, which was actually far better suited to the dramatic situation—the first private encounter between the two lovers. In Scribe's cabaletta, designated *Strette du Duo*, Henri and Hélène would have spent some of this time together addressing the spirit of Frédéric: "Martyr for our homeland, beloved shade, our vows and our hearts will be united to bring down tyranny" ("Ô martyr de la patrie, pour briser la tyrannie nos serments, ombre chérie, et nos coeurs seront unis"),[25] but Verdi preferred to postpone the patriotic avowals to the third-act finale.

Thus, in Act II, Verdi pursued the possibilities of abbreviated duet form that he had explored already in operas such as *I due Foscari* (1844), *Giovanna d'Arco* (1845), *I masnadieri* (1847), and *Il corsaro* (1848),[26] but

24. From the letter to Carlo Antonio Borsi, 8 September 1852, cited here in Budden's translation (see above, note 14).

25. F-Pn, n.a.f. 22506, fol. 62v.

26. See Balthazar, "The *Primo Ottocento* duet," 492 and n. 33.

he did the opposite in the Act III duet, greatly enlarging it by the insertion of a further ensemble in two places during the *tempo di mezzo*.
Scribe's libretto for *Le Duc d'Albe* had anticipated this to some extent,
but where Scribe would have had the same text in both places, thus introducing a refrain-like element from French tradition into the Italian
formal model, Verdi used that text ("Comble de misère!," Allegro assai)
only for the first insert, in which father and son both give vent to their
extreme unhappiness, and for the second he composed a further slow
movement ("Quoi, ma tendresse, ma prière"), which provides an additional opportunity for Montfort to express his newly awakened paternal
feelings before the concluding cabaletta. In the cabaletta, Verdi again
departed from Scribe's original conception, which had Henri invoking
his dead mother ("Oui, c'est elle qui m'appelle") and Montfort making
a last appeal to his rebellious son ("Fils rebelle que j'appelle"),[27] because
the meter did not suit Verdi's purpose. The short-breathed lines with
their four stressed syllables served well enough to express angry, turbulent emotions, but in this context Verdi wanted to underline in tender
lyrical phrases how much Montfort, Henri, and Hélène depend on each
other. Already in Act I he had drawn the net of the family drama closer
than Scribe had prefigured, in making the music emphasize the mysterious bond between Montfort and Henri even on their first meeting.

It is true that at that point Henri is still free to ignore Montfort's
command to have nothing to do with Hélène. But Montfort's reaction
makes him appear not a tyrant conscious of the power he wields but an
old man prevented from reacting as he really wishes by a mysterious
power of which he himself is unconscious. True, his response to Henri's
bold defiance is a threat: "Malheur à toi"; but Verdi did not set this as
an explosion of uncontrolled anger, like Monterone's curse in *Rigoletto*,
for example. Rather, the words form an aside, a scarcely audible accompaniment to Henri's more extrovert cadenza-like music. Thus the closing bars of their first duet show father and son united, although they are
as yet unaware of their relationship. And it is precisely in order to give
the audience equally powerful visual evidence of Montfort's dependence
on Henri that the stage direction ordains, in the best traditions of melodrama: "Henri disappears, while Montfort watches him with emotion
but without anger. The curtain falls" *(Henri disparaît, pendant que Montfort le regarde avec émotion, mais sans colère. La toile tombe).*

Let us return to the cabaletta of their second duet, in Act III. Before
the duet begins, Montfort has discovered that Henri is his son, and dur-

27. F-Pn, n.a.f. 22506, fols. 70v–71; see also Lo Presti, *"Le Duc d'Albe,"* 294–95.

ing it he reveals this to Henri. In this situation, Verdi needed a text for the cabaletta with a different metrical structure from the words Scribe had originally provided, in order to give vivid musical expression to the fact that the dependence has become mutual. After numerous revisions,[28] he used a new text which Scribe did not even insert into the printed libretto. The new words Henri addresses to his mother's spirit, "Ombre sainte que je révère," enabled Verdi to give the tenor the same melody (in a different key and tempo) as the one previously used for the confession of unknown happiness with which Montfort begins the duet's adagio ("Pour moi, quelle ivresse inconnue"). And as Henri has stammered his astonishment in the slow movement, so Montfort now does in the cabaletta.

Verdi used the same technique in Henri and Hélène's second duet, in Act IV, which again follows Scribe's original draft by and large: in asserting his innocence of the treachery of which Hélène has accused him ("Malheureux et non coupable") Henri unfolds an expansive melody which Hélène takes up in a later section, after she has at last found out that Montfort is her lover's father. This method of drawing the musical material itself into the exchange of ideas between the characters is unique, even in Verdi's output, and it goes far beyond the procedure, beloved of Scribe but already hackneyed by the early 1850s, of conceiving the two opening solos in the first section of a duet in such a form that their metrically identical, rhymed lines could be sung one immediately after the other to the same melody.[29] Thus, at a stroke, Verdi not only put his own individual stamp on the formal schemata described above in some detail, but also underlined the principal characters' difficulty in asserting themselves as defined and independent individuals in a work that, like the later operas *Don Carlos* (1867), with no fewer than seven duets, and *Aida* (1871), with five, depended for its dramatic structures on direct encounters between two people at a time.[30] The characters in *Les Vêpres siciliennes* have a far greater capacity for intimate emotions than any created by Meyerbeer, but in the last analysis they are just as unfree and subject to external forces as his, even if capricious fate has been replaced by inescapable duties of which they are wholly conscious, and which are imposed on them by family ties.

28. See Bates, "Verdi's *Les Vêpres Siciliennes* (1855) and *Simon Boccanegra* (1857)," 1:326–27.

29. See Huebner, "Italianate duets," 220.

30. See Gossett, "Verdi, Ghislanzoni, and *Aida*," 300.

INVOCATION

When the principal characters of *Les Vêpres siciliennes* discover their mutual dependency, one of the direct consequences is that their political allegiances are painfully disturbed. As in most of his dramatic texts, so here too Scribe seems intent on expressing the conviction that political involvement inevitably deals a death-blow to all personal happiness. In its musico-dramatic realization of these ideas, Verdi's opera distances itself markedly from the schematicism of the great historical operas in the French tradition considered in earlier chapters in this book. The political position of someone like Raoul in *Les Huguenots* is a given and never questioned, but Verdi's characters in *Les Vêpres siciliennes* suffer personal anguish as a result of the dilemma forced upon them by their mutually irreconcilable personal and political preferences. For them, their political position is more than the inevitable consequence of their birth: they have chosen their causes and actually *want* to fight for them, with all their hearts, and thus they come to discover that, however strongly they desire them, their personal and political choices are in direct conflict.

So they seek refuge in invoking what they cannot achieve by mere wishing. In the third-act finale, when their attempt to assassinate Montfort has failed and they must fear the worst, Hélène, Daniéli, and Procida strike up a hymn to their homeland, in unison of course, and with the decidedly rare direction *cantabile grandioso*. But this is no solid unison with a powerful accompaniment, like the one in the finale of Act II of Rossini's *Guillaume Tell*, for example; instead of being merely doubled at the octave, like a traditional unison passage, this melody is sung across three octaves and so conveys the impression of a strange emptiness. The impression is strengthened by the pianissimo accompaniment of clarinets, bassoons, and pizzicato violas and cellos, also straddling two different octave registers; there is the suggestion of an inner part in its hinted thirds and sixths in eighth-note motion and it reaches the tonic B flat in a rhythmically stable position only at the end of the line. The unison melody lacks the foundation of a bass voice, and an ensemble of soloists is no longer an adequate basis for a patriotic invocation. Only later, when the melody is reprised by the masses, who have no individual will, can the monumental dimension bestowed by the choral tutti disguise the irreconcilability of individual emotions and communal ideals.

Even today the listener is disconcerted by the unexpected conversion of a patriotic hymn into a hollow gesture—it must have had an even more startling effect on audiences whose ears had rung with the immensely popular hymns from Verdi's *Nabucco* and *Ernani*. Verdi admittedly had good reasons for not going back to the tone of the chorus from *Nabucco*, "Va, pensiero, sull'ali dorate," sung by Hebrew captives in exile in Babylon, or the comparable "Si ridesti il Leon di Castiglia" from *Ernani*, for he had to take into account not only the particular political context in which the première of the new opera would take place but also the alteration in the atmosphere generally. In this depiction of oppressed Sicilians confronting French oppressors, any motive that might be referred to the struggle for Italian unity going on at that very time, or any musical language reminiscent of those choruses which came to be explicitly associated with the Risorgimento,[31] would inevitably have been received as an affront to the first audiences. The oppressors in *Les Vêpres siciliennes* were, when all was said and done, not the citizens of some remote empire in the far distant past, but the French—the very people whose leading opera house had commissioned the work, and whose government was lending military support to the Italian struggle for unification.

Quite apart from such essentially diplomatic considerations, which some critics raised at the time,[32] the historical moment for appeals to the revolutionary and patriotic sentiments of the 1840s was past. It is true that Verdi had composed a chorus for his opera *La battaglia di Legnano* (1849) that showed the impact of the revolutionary events of 1848–49 and succeeded more powerfully than any earlier examples in recapturing the spirit of the ancestor of them all, the scene on the Rütli in *Guillaume Tell*.[33] But significantly, after the failure of revolutionary action all over Europe in 1848–49, Verdi wrote no more such choruses. Even in the first version of *Simon Boccanegra* (1857), when the chorus sings "Viva Simon" at the end of the prologue and again at the end of the first act, he did not turn again to the successful model, apt though it might have seemed, especially given the nature of the plot and its Genoan setting; instead he set these ceremonial salutations—exactly as in *Macbeth* (1847)—to music which is less characteristic and almost perfunctory.

Verdi was not the only composer writing French grand opéra after 1849 to renounce powerful unison melodies in the manner of the *Marseillaise*. The Second Empire, established after the coup d'état engi-

31. See Pauls, *Giuseppe Verdi und das Risorgimento*, esp. 209–15.
32. See Gartioux, *Giuseppe Verdi: Les Vêpres Siciliennes*, 39, 46, 91, 106.
33. See Gossett, "Becoming a citizen," 59–60.

neered by Napoleon's nephew, lived out its term in the vacuum between the revolutionary enthusiasm which it shamelessly exploited and chauvinistic nationalism. The latter is still with us today but, despite scattered early signs of it, its hour did not really come until the French defeat by Prussia in 1870–71. Everything we know about people in the dominant social class in Paris, which of course included the audience at the Opéra, indicates that they valued a cosmopolitan openness and tolerance and, in a crisis, put commercial success and assured pleasures above almost nonexistent patriotic emotions. True, as early as 1826, Jouy had impressed upon future librettists the importance of celebrating "the great themes of our national history" in a section of his *Essai sur l'Opéra français* entirely devoted to "national subjects"; and his advocacy of the idea looked back to experiments in the 1790s.[34] Nevertheless, operas heeding his recommendation, such as Halévy's *Charles VI* (1843), which has a recurrent, even leitmotivic, chorus demanding "War on the English!" ("Guerre aux anglais"), were far less successful with the public than a work like *Les Huguenots*, which centered on one of the darkest hours in French history. The relative success of even an epigonal work like *Roland à Roncevaux* (1864), for which the composer, Auguste Mermet, wrote his own libretto glorifying the heroic deeds of Charlemagne and his paladins, paled into insignificance when set alongside that of Offenbach's cynical mockery of all militaristic and nationalistic symbols in *La Grande-Duchesse de Gérolstein* (1867). Against this background, not only is the uncharacteristic melody to which Verdi set "O noble patrie" appropriate to the situation of the failed assassins on the stage, but also *Les Vêpres siciliennes* as a whole seems to mirror with great accuracy the difficulties that kind of noble, patriotic sentiment presented to Parisian society in 1855.

THE POWERLESS FATHER

In his study of public life in the nineteenth century, Richard Sennett pinpoints the year of revolutions, 1848, as "the first moment at which the codes of ethology, silence, and isolation—the codes of bourgeois public culture—were sufficiently developed to affect the experience people had of a revolution"[35]—and, indeed, to influence the experiences

---

34. See above, chapter 2, and Jouy, *Essai* 250 (1987 ed., 75); see also Bartlet, "The new repertory at the Opéra," 109–11.

35. *The Fall of Public Man*, 224.

of individuals in every sphere of life. As people became aware that there was no personal meaning to be found in the objective conditions of social life, it was not only the bourgeoisie who tried to "find in the private realms of life, especially in the family, some principle of order in the perception of personality"; there was "a hidden desire for stability in the overt desire for closeness between human beings."[36]

The unique dramaturgy of *Les Vêpres siciliennes* can only be understood in the light of this change of focus in the perception of personality. In depicting the dislocation between public identity and private emotions, this work differs fundamentally from all earlier examples of grand opéra, in which characters are so consistent in the face of all vicissitudes that they remain an open book to the audience, even when their subconscious natures play tricks on them—as happens to Valentine in *Les Huguenots* or Jean in *Le Prophète*. The way Montfort and Henri are presented in Verdi's opera is very different, especially in the fine shading of their relationship to each other, which differs spectacularly from the rational mechanisms characteristic of almost every other plot contrived by Scribe. Reading the libretto of *Les Vêpres siciliennes* while keeping one's eyes open in particular for consistency and probability of the kind attentive readers can recreate for themselves uncovers more than one point of confusion.

A rebel falls into the hands of the feared Governor of Palermo, yet his hatred for the French occupying army is so great that he incessantly provokes him. The Governor does not punish him for these insults but is deeply impressed by his courage and lets him go free. A sudden access of humanity is one of the traditional attributes of authoritarian figures in opera, but Montfort's magnanimity goes a stage further than usual: having categorically forbidden the young stranger to do a particular thing (see Hélène again), he uses none of the power at his disposal to enforce his ban when Henri obdurately refuses to obey. Montfort is left alone on the stage at the end of Act I, and is not seen again until the beginning of Act III, in his study. He draws out a letter "from his breast" *(de son sein)*, which he describes as a "new affront" ("ce nouvel affront"). The letter is from the Sicilian woman who gave birth to Henri after Montfort ravished her. (It is perfectly clear that Montfort raped her: Scribe did not have the courage to say so in the libretto in so many words, but in one of his letters to Duveyrier about the changes he had made to *Le Duc d'Albe* he unequivocally uses the term "femme

36. Ibid., 259–60.

violée.")[37] On her deathbed she wrote to the Governor asking him to show mercy to their son. But, as we have already learned in Act I, Henri's mother has been dead for over a year. It would be more realistic to assume that Montfort received this letter some time ago, and therefore already knew during his first meeting with Henri that he confronted his son, and indeed two critics made that assumption in their reviews of the first performance.[38] But if that is the case, why does Montfort speak of a "new affront"? And why has he waited until this moment to surrender to the belief that he has found his long-lost son? Scribe and Verdi do nothing to explain these ambiguous anomalies, but rather seem to play on their ambivalence: if the father treats his son paternally, even without knowing he is his father, does it not illustrate the unshakable stability of family ties?

The peculiarities of the plot go further: Montfort wants his son to acknowledge him as his father at any price, and simply cannot bear to be rejected as a cruel tyrant. Although Henri saves his life by intervening at the last minute to prevent the assassination attempt during the masked ball, Montfort still insists on Henri's actually addressing him as "Father" ("Mon père"). The obsessive character of this wish struck another of the first-night critics, Gustave Héquet, who made a joke of it in his review: "Will Henri consent to say 'Papa'? After what he has done, it is hard to understand why he still hesitates, or why Montfort makes so much of dragging from him a word which will not prove his filial affection as conclusively as the service he has already rendered him."[39] Clearly, by this stage it is no longer a matter of a logical train of reactions but of heightening the dramatic representation of a disturbed father–son relationship that drives the people concerned to neurotic, if not actually regressive behavior. Héquet focused on this in a second piece that he wrote about the opera:

> "Call me your father or I'll chop off your mistress's head. Do you see the executioner, in his red costume? Do you see the axe in his hands? Do you hear the friars chanting *De profundis*? Look at her kneeling there, that

37. Scribe's letter to Charles Duveyrier, late December 1853/early January 1854; see above, n. 4.

38. E. Viel in *Le Ménéstrel*, 17 June 1855; Paul de Saint-Victor in *La France musicale*, 19 (1855): 193. See also Gartioux, *Giuseppe Verdi. Les Vêpres Siciliennes*, 125.

39. "Henri consentira-t-il à dire Papa? Après ce qu'il a fait, on ne comprend guère qu'il hésite, ni que Montfort tienne tant à lui arracher un mot qui ne prouvera pas son amour filial aussi nettement que le service qu'il lui a rendu." *L'Illustration* 25 (January–June 1855): 398.

beautiful girl you love so much. Call me 'Papa' or her head will roll." . . .
It is gruesome and puerile, all at the same time.[40]

A father's power was evidently no longer taken for granted. It is true
that his position in law was still paramount: in the second half of the
nineteenth century the French Civil Code still required paternal consent to the marriage even of people who had reached their majority. If
that was refused, it was still possible for men above the age of twenty-
five and women above twenty-one to marry, but only after enduring
elaborate procedures and a lengthy waiting period, which ensured that
marriage under such conditions remained an exception.[41] In everyday
life, however, patriarchal authority was threatened at its very foundations. As life under capitalism became increasingly complex, the family
unit lost more and more of its traditional economic function, and was
already affected by a process still at work a century later, as Alexander
Mitscherlich described it:

> The progressive fragmentation of labour, combined with mass produc-
> tion and complicated administration, the separation of home from place
> of work, the transition from independent producer to paid employee who
> uses consumer goods, has led to a progressive loss of substance of the
> father's authority and the diminution of his power in the family and over
> the family.[42]

From such a perspective it appears that the erosion of paternal authority,
which is illustrated in Les Vêpres siciliennes and continues to the present
day, was the inevitable consequence of what Jürgen Habermas has called
the "objectification"[43] of family relationships.

The gathering momentum toward a "fatherless" society is already
reflected in Verdi's early Italian operas. The patriarchal father was one
of the stock operatic roles, of course, sharing the attributes of the all-
powerful ruler, and even in the middle-class settings of the opere semis-
erie of Bellini and Donizetti the character still had a king-like status
inherited from the monarchs of eighteenth-century opera.[44] The young

40. "Appelle-moi ton père, ou je fais couper le cou à ta maîtresse. Vois-tu le bourreau
habillé de rouge? Vois-tu la hache dans ses mains? Entends-tu le De profundis que chantent les frères prêcheurs? La-voilà agenouillée, cette belle fille que tu aimes tant. Dis-
moi papa, ou sa tête tombe . . . Cela est tout à la fois horrible et puéril." L'Illustration 42
(July–December 1863): 69.

41. See Glasson, Le Mariage civil et le divorce, 268, 271.

42. Society without the Father, 147.

43. "Versachlichung"; see Habermas, Strukturwandel der Öffentlichkeit, 189.

44. Baldacci, Libretti d'opera, 164–65.

Verdi, however, had begun systematically to strip away those attributes, and although the figure of the stern father appears in the early operas with positively obsessive regularity, "the family is depicted . . . at the moment when its main support is crumbling, and paternal authority is waging the last desperate struggle against the contradictions undermining its legitimacy."[45]

In French opera, on the other hand, this view of the contradictions in the structure of the contemporary family was still a complete novelty even in the 1850s. Parental authority remained essentially intact in earlier grand opéras: Arnold, in *Guillaume Tell*, submits to the wishes of his dead father as meekly as Raoul, in *Les Huguenots*, does to the commands of his father-substitute, Marcel, and even Jean, in *Le Prophète*, bows to his mother's authority at the bitter end. Henri, however, defies his father. Even when, finally, he is driven to the despairing exclamation "Mon père! mon père!," in the context of the sadistic trial of strength arranged by his father, it is only the expression of his love for Hélène, not the proof Montfort so ardently desires of love for himself—as the father too appears to acknowledge in his ambiguous reaction, saying to the son prostrate at his feet: "Oh, cruel! oh, so you really did love her!" ("Ah! cruel! ah! tu l'aimais donc bien!")

This paradox can be resolved on a second level of comprehension: at first Henri refuses to speak the words that will save Hélène because she has forbidden him to do so, promising that she forgives him ("Ne le dis pas! et je pardonne . . . moi!"), and he dares not disobey a command she has expressed so forcefully (*avec force*, in the stage direction). Seen from that angle, Montfort forces Henri to follow his emotions, against his political convictions and against Hélène's and his own will. Yet he only achieves this victory of emotion over political loyalty by exercising his political power—the emptiness of which causes him so much suffering. Even more baffling, after having forbidden Henri to have any further contact with Hélène in Act I, in Act V Montfort orders them to marry: in the last analysis it is beyond belief that someone so successful at using his political power can imagine that the marriage will achieve reconciliation between the French and the Sicilians at a stroke. But in this very isolation of the personal element from reality Montfort's reaction resembles that of members of the upwardly aspiring classes of nineteenth-century society, who refused to recognize that their lives were totally

45. "la famiglia viene raffigurata . . . nel momento in cui crolla la sua colonna portante, in cui l'autorità paterna combatte per l'ultima volta disperatamente contro le contraddizioni che ne minano la legittimità"; Baroni, *Il declino del patriarca*, 102.

dependent on economic and political conditions outside their control. As Jürgen Habermas has written, within the intimacy of the immediate family circle, private people distance themselves from even the private sphere of their economic activity:[46] for economic, read political.

The difficulty of harmonizing public office with private desires is a recurring theme in several of Verdi's operas, notably those written after 1855. Simon Boccanegra, Riccardo in *Un ballo in maschera*, Philippe in *Don Carlos*, and Radames in *Aida* all share the problem. Gert Ueding has noted that the separation of daily life into professional and family spheres, leading to the relaxation of social controls over the latter so that it became the refuge for those needs left unsatisfied by professional life, had repercussions for every artistic utterance of so-called bourgeois society.[47] Even if the observation as such is beyond doubt, the fact remains that the paradox in this opera of 1855, whereby Montfort must use his public power in order to create a space for his private feelings, presents the irreparable breach between the two spheres in a form so extreme that it would be hard to point to another example anywhere else in nineteenth-century art to equal it. While fate, located somewhere outside the experience of the individual, is still responsible for the tragic outcome of most other operas of the period, in *Les Vêpres siciliennes* the cause is that irreconcilable breach, just as it is in the case of *Un ballo in maschera*, first performed four years later.

SPLEEN

It is only when those who hold power perceive this irreparable dislocation of the private and public spheres that they become aware of their isolation. Indeed, the loneliness power brings to the powerful is another theme that plays an important part not only in *Les Vêpres siciliennes* but in Verdi's oeuvre as a whole. As with the disruption of the father–son relationship, admittedly, it is another element introduced by Scribe quite independently of Verdi's predilections: the text of the aria in which Montfort, after reading the letter from Henri's mother, laments the "immense, horrifying void" ("vide affreux, immense") at the core of his greatness, was taken from *Le Duc d'Albe* with only minor changes.[48] Scribe contrasted these bitter feelings quite conventionally with the new hope the despondent father draws from merely saying the words

46. *Strukturwandel der Öffentlichkeit*, 66.
47. See *Glanzvolles Elend*, 27.
48. See Lo Presti, "*Le Duc d'Albe*," pp, 286–87.

"my son!" ("mon fils!"), and Verdi strengthened the contrast by changing the line of text introducing the new mood from "But a new existence
presents itself" ("Mais s'offre un nouvel être"—which Scribe retained
in the published libretto) to the emphatic declaration "Heaven opens!"
("Le ciel vient apparaître"). Merely by adding a metaphysical dimension
in this way to the hope Scribe expressed in simpler words, Verdi demonstrated the importance he attached to the second quatrain of the aria
text. In his setting of the first four lines ("Au sein de la puissance") the
use of dotted, triplet rhythms which were almost a cliché in French
grand opéra results in a melody which, in Julian Budden's view, "is
clearly indebted to Meyerbeer for its rhythmic cut (compare 'Pour cette
cause sainte' from Les Huguenots),"[49] but Verdi took a completely different path for the second four lines.

The first eighteen bars of the aria have been determined by the harmonic span from the tonic, F-sharp minor, to the dominant, C-sharp,
but now Verdi counters that with sustained chords in F-sharp major;
lying at the furthest remove from C major in the cycle of fifths, F-sharp
major has an esoteric quality which Verdi exploits here to symbolize a
character's utopian dreams, as Rossini and Meyerbeer had done before
him (in the G-flat major passage in the duet for Arnold and Tell in Guillaume Tell, Act I, and in the love duet in Les Huguenots, Act IV). Verdi
further intensifies the mood of the vocal transports by a subtle accompaniment in the form of chords devoid of any dynamic impetus, played
by strings and woodwinds—instrumental means whose full potential he
would realize only in Don Carlos and Aida. Additionally, he modified
Scribe's formal layout for the aria in such a way that this F-sharp major
section became its turning point. Where Scribe had provided for the
repetition of the first two quatrains after a contrasting middle section,
Verdi expanded the concluding repeat of the second of those two quatrains to make it twice the length of all the other sections, and thus
depicted Montfort as completely overwhelmed by his dream. The process completely destroyed the symmetry underpinning the A–B–A form
taken from French tradition, but at the same time it added considerable
dynamism to what was in itself a static structure: the cry "Mon fils!," in
which the agonized loneliness of the father's earlier feelings seems to be
overcome, becomes the goal of the dramatic situation and not merely a
conventional phrase, used like a refrain.

But even while he concentrated on the ending of this short aria, Verdi
did not lose sight of a motive that dominates the entire opera: the pre-

49. The Operas of Verdi, 2:209; see also Budden, "Verdi and Meyerbeer," 11.

monition of the terrible way it will all end. He ensured that a trace of disquiet remains audible, by letting the orchestral accompaniment, as its motion intensifies from quarter notes to eighths to thirty-seconds, question the calm of the vocal line dying away in repeated whole notes. In this way the last fifth of the aria is dominated by a rhythmic figure that is almost omnipresent in the score of *Les Vêpres siciliennes*, consisting of an eighth note (or quarter note) preceded by two thirty-seconds, like an upbeat, on the same pitch. The overture begins with this figure, played no fewer than thirty-nine times on timpani and drums large and small, in a form pointing to the figure's historical origin. It was positively late in the day when Meyerbeer used it—also on timpani—in the overture to *Les Huguenots:* long before him, Lully had employed this anapestic rhythm precisely in places where the subject was murder or death, and eventually, at the latest by the time when it or related rhythms became the norm in music played at the funerals of military or political leaders of the French Revolution, the symbolic association was so fixed that it is fully justified to call it, with Frits Noske, a musical "figure of death."[50] Verdi made extensive use of it in most of his operas, but nowhere as persistently as in *Les Vêpres siciliennes;* in Act I alone, it is heard in the *tempo di mezzo* and the cabaletta of Hélène's entrance aria, in the quartet following that, and in Henri and Montfort's duet, several times in each case, and always at moments when the murderous tensions between the hostile groups are at least latent or actually overt.

Associating the figures in that particular rhythmic shape, played by the high strings in the coda of Montfort's aria, with the figure of death, which is usually assigned to low registers, may attract a charge of over-interpretation. This coda has a magical sound quality so far removed from the fury of the ensemble "Interdits, accablés" sung by the Sicilians in the Act II finale, for instance, that its anapestic rhythm may well not make any special impression amid the "delicate filigree" of the accompaniment,[51] at least if the music is performed without the rhythmic intensity that is a primary requirement for the successful performance of Verdi. Yet this rhythmic figure, which is so unmistakably part of the *tinta* of the work, is heard each time Henri and Montfort meet face to face, so that it is hard to believe that Verdi picked on it to accompany Montfort's imagined encounter with his son purely by chance. Be that as it may, at the very least the incessant repetition of this figure in the

50. See Noske, "Verdi and the musical figure of death."
51. See Budden, *The Operas of Verdi*, 2:210–11.

aria's coda seems to epitomize the almost manic fixation of the character upon an emotion outside his experience. The more Montfort repeats the words "Mon fils!," as if determined to accustom himself to them, the more insistently Verdi reminds his listeners of the inflexible rhythm which, without regard to any "unambiguous" symbolism of death, spotlights the emotional world of the lonely autocrat, as he oscillates between profound melancholy and obsessive desire. The composer has used the subtlest musical means here to represent his character as the victim of a psychological state which is almost ubiquitous in French literature of the mid-nineteenth century: the ennui, with its spectrum of meaning reaching from apathetic boredom to vague melancholy, that was regularly referred to from 1833 onward as "the sickness of the century"—*le mal du siècle.*

Montfort's aria comes midway between two other outstanding expressions of ennui in Verdi's dramatic oeuvre, the similarly constructed scenes in an early work, *Ernani*, and in *Don Carlos*, first performed twelve years after *Les Vêpres siciliennes* (and, like it, in Paris). A comparison of the three scenes sheds light on some of their defining traits. *Ernani*, based on Victor Hugo's play *Hernani*, was still regarded by Meyerbeer four years after its première as Verdi's best opera.[52] The situation at the start of Act III already resembles that of Montfort's soliloquy in several respects. Don Carlo (King Charles of Spain, soon to be the Habsburg Emperor Charles V) is alone with his melancholy thoughts, and laments, in a cavatina, the passing of his salad days ("verd' anni miei"). Necessity forced the librettist to reduce one of Hugo's longest monologues to a sliver of itself,[53] but far more impressive are the compositional means used by Verdi to portray the king's impassive self-centeredness, as he broods, sunk in melancholy. Carlo's cantilena is accompanied by an incessant ostinato figure made up of four sixteenth notes and an eighth, played on a solo cello; the rigorous restriction of the rest of the accompaniment to three further cellos and a double-bass, with the same registral compass as the singer, added to the stage setting in a subterranean vault in Aachen Cathedral, reinforces the atmosphere of gloomy ("cupo," in Verdi's word) depression which has dominated the act so far, beginning with its purely instrumental prelude, a solo for bass clarinet.

All of a sudden, however, Don Carlo succeeds in breaking out of his melancholy mood: if he is called to ascend the throne of Charlemagne

52. "Verdis beste Oper"; Meyerbeer's diary, 29 March 1848, in *Briefwechsel*, 4:375.
53. See Gerhartz, *Die Auseinandersetzungen*, 42–43, 50.

he will make his name the most renowned in history ("vincitor de' secoli il nome mio farò") and the mere prospect of additional power makes him forget his resigned farewell to his youth. The cello ceases its insistent ostinato figure, Verdi breaks one of the elementary rules of harmonic theory by modulating up a third by means of parallel octaves in the voice and the bass,[54] and finally the entire orchestra joins in with the now triumphant vocal line; only in the orchestral postlude, in the melody gradually ebbing away in the bass register of bassoon and solo cello, does something remain of the atmosphere which Verdi had painted so vividly with the ostinato figure.

Very much the same mood prevails at the beginning of Act IV of *Don Carlos*. Another Spanish king, the aging Philip II, is forced to admit to himself that his young wife has never loved him, and even his dream that his royal power might enable him to read what lies in others' hearts ("de lire au fond des coeurs") is not enough to lift him out of the "deep meditation" to which the stage direction refers. Once again, Verdi employs all his genius to express the king's despondency with means that are as effective as they are simple, drawing over the entire cantabile a network made up of two interdependent motives that can clearly be interpreted as emblems of a lament:[55] one, heard more than fifty times, consists of an appoggiatura preceding a sustained note one semitone higher, the other—also chromatic but traveling in the opposite direction—is a descending motion from which very nearly all the musical material of this unconventional number is derived.

Of course the three scenes also contain essential differences: while Don Carlo overcomes his ennui by his own resolution, Montfort's means of escape is the deceptive hope of happiness with his newfound son, and King Philip is left with no illusions intact—all that faces him is the bitter reality of a marriage that failed before it even started. In the original French libretto he expresses his recognition of the unalterable fact that "she does not love me" in the very simplest, everyday language: "Elle ne m'aime pas." This directness is completely lost in the Italian version, "Ella giammai m'amò," made pompous by an artificial vocabulary.

What all three scenes have in common, however, is the fact that in the end the setting of the text, however good, makes less of an impression on the musico-dramatic realization of the scene than the orchestral accompaniment's fixation on an inflexible musical figure, which Verdi

54. See Della Seta, "L'atto di Carlo Quinto," 173.
55. See Beghelli, "Per un nuovo approccio," 634–37.

has made the most cogent musical event by increasingly reductionist means. The time is ripe to introduce the word "spleen," another key term in nineteenth-century French literature, where it has precisely this meaning of an isolated individual's brooding on his hopeless situation, whether his despair of ever escaping from it is objectively justified or exists solely in his subjective view of it. This obsession was given classic poetic expression, unrivaled in the sharpness of its contrasts and precision of its abundant imagery, in Charles Baudelaire's *Fleurs du Mal* (The Flowers of Evil), published six years after the première of *Les Vêpres siciliennes.* This contains a group of four successive poems all entitled *Spleen.* The third of them develops the motive of the powerless king, found in several of Victor Hugo's plays, not only in *Hernani:* "I'm like the king of some damp, rainy clime, grown impotent and old before my time" ("Je suis comme le roi d'un pays pluvieux, / Riche, mais impuissant, jeune et pourtant très vieux"), but the second identifies overburdened memory as that which unleashes the lonely ruler's torments:

> J'ai plus de souvenirs que si j'avais mille ans.
> Un gros meuble à tiroirs encombré de bilans,
> De vers, de billets doux, de procès, de romances,
> Avec de lourds cheveux roulés dans des quittances,
> Cache moins de secrets que mon triste cerveau.
> C'est une pyramide, un immense caveau,
> Qui contient plus de morts que la fosse commune.

> ~ ~ ~

> I have more memories than had I seen
> Ten centuries. A huge chest that has been
> Stuffed full of writs, bills, verses, balance-sheets
> With golden curls wrapt up in old receipts
> And love-letters—hides less than my sad brain,
> A pyramid, a vault that must contain
> More corpses than the public charnel stores.[56]

To turn from these lines to the first scene in Act III of *Les Vêpres siciliennes* is to see the stage direction describing the set in a new light. Montfort is discovered sitting "near a table" in his private study, and even if the idea that it is a large writing-table can only be inferred here—only in the comparable stage direction in *Don Carlos*, Act IV,

---

56. *Les Fleurs du mal* [1861], poems numbered respectively 77 and 76, in Baudelaire, *Oeuvres complètes*, 1:74, 73. The translations cited here are by Roy Campbell, in *Poems of Baudelaire*, 100–101.

scene 1 is King Philip expressly stated to be leaning "upon a table strewn with papers"—nevertheless the Governor of Palermo draws out a letter, and immerses himself in spleen (and the reproach, in the letter from Henri's mother, that his "bloody axe" ["hache sanglante"] spares none is not a thousand miles from Baudelaire's image of the vault full of corpses). The choice of a private study as the only proper place for persons in authority to commune with themselves was a well-established convention in both spoken and sung drama of the eighteenth century, so that stage directions like these do not appear at first to add anything to the tradition. What is new, in the middle of the nineteenth century, is the overflowing desk, a metaphor for the burden which bears down on these authoritarian characters, a past converted into paper, preventing them from making important decisions with their old confidence. The way the depiction of the characters in these three soliloquys—Don Carlo in *Ernani*, Montfort in *Les Vêpres siciliennes*, as well as King Philip in *Don Carlos*—is limited exclusively to subjective states of weakened self-esteem is at least as far removed from any "classical" precedents (and even from the wholly political reflections of Hugo's Don Carlos in the corresponding scene in *Hernani*) as the spleen expressed by Verdi is from the melancholy Delacroix associated with the overwhelming natural spectacle in the closing tableau of Rossini's *Guillaume Tell*.

This is yet another instance showing how the composer of *Les Vêpres siciliennes* concentrated ever more rigorously on the emotions of isolated characters, while steadily diminishing the role of the historical paraphernalia of kaleidoscopic subject matter and the political implications of ingeniously contrived plots. A glance at comparable scenes in works by Meyerbeer and Halévy reveals just how far Verdi was moving away from the conventions of French grand opéra. In *Le Prophète* the rulers representing the ancien régime are virtually invisible, while in *Les Huguenots* Marguerite does flirt with the possibility of renouncing her position, in Act II, but the ironic tone of her brilliant solos shows clearly enough that she takes the exercise of power so much for granted that she immediately dismisses the thought of any contradictions between private feelings and official duties. At first sight the case of Tsar Peter, lamenting the loss of his happiness in love at the beginning of Act III of Meyerbeer's opéra comique *L'Étoile du Nord* (1854), appears different. He has a *romance* in two stanzas, in the first of which he sings that the sight of his beloved made him a king among men, and losing her makes him nothing, king though he is ("En la voyant j'étais roi sur terre, en la perdant, hélas! roi, je ne suis plus rien!"); at the end of the second he even swears that he will give up his rank and scepter if she will only come back to him ("Ah! reviens et j'abandonne le sceptre et la grandeur"). But in complete contrast to Verdi's princes the emptiness of power does not affect him in the slightest, the woman he loves is all he needs to make him completely happy, and the dénouement gives the lie to the old cliché of the blessings that result from the renunciation of power, for in the end it is only by exercising his imperial power and expending huge material resources that Peter recovers his beloved and restores her sanity in a finale even more spectacular than that of Meyerbeer's *Pardon de Ploërmel*.

Only in Halévy's *Charles VI* is there a scene that in any way resembles the Verdian examples cited above in its pointed representation of deep despondency. In the second act, in a *romance*, the French king, Charles VI, who has become the victim of a villainous plot while deprived of his wits, sings of his sorrows, but the deep depression suffered by a monarch in his loneliness is presented as a clinical exception in this context, and not, as in Verdi, as the inevitable consequence of the breach between political and private identities in a changing world.

FAREWELL

With Henri's last-minute intervention to stop the execution of the conspirators in Act IV of the refurbished libretto, Scribe provided Verdi with a scene that came close in its employment of "suspense" to the kind of "miracle" he had been asked for, but the self-willed composer made a number of substantial conceptual changes to the act before he set it. In Scribe's version—much as in the corresponding scene in Act III of *Le Duc d'Albe*—Henri would have remained alone on the stage with his father and the Governor's confidant, De Béthune, while Hélène and Procida would have been unseen. Only when the sound of *De profundis* sung offstage reached his ears would Henri have learned that his fellow-conspirators were about to be executed, and only the words of De Béthune, standing at the window and describing the preparations in the courtyard below, would have given him any details. Scribe designed the scene to focus attention yet again on the emotions of the suffering father and the rebellious son, who would have been singing simultaneously with De Béthune's commentary; the audience would not have seen Hélène and Procida until they were brought back onto the stage after their unexpected reprieve.

For his part, Verdi was little impressed by Scribe's plan to repeat what he had done in the last act of *Les Huguenots* and present the gruesome events to the audience indirectly, through the filter of a passive observer. Meyerbeer's facility for giving spatial dimensions to musical structures[57] had no place in the philosophy of an Italian composer who would still have subscribed at this date to Bellini's succinct (but to French ears somewhat simplistic) principle that "opera must make one weep, shudder, die, through singing."[58] Not surprisingly, therefore, when already at work on the composition, Verdi asked Scribe for a regular quartet, to unite the four main characters in a "traditional" ensemble in this decisive scene. In early June 1854 he sent Scribe a reminder: "Have you thought about the quartet you said you wanted to write for Act IV?" and underlined the musical advantages, if the right situation could be found for it, of bringing together "the fine voices" of the four singers who were expected to be cast in the roles.[59] Scribe was ready to do what he was asked and so it was decided that Hélène and Procida should remain on the stage and the preparations for their execution should proceed in full view of the audience. The only thing remaining of the earlier conception of the scene was the division of the stage into two areas, permitting the rear part to be revealed only just before the climax. The stage direction reads:

> *La grille qui est à droite du théâtre vient de s'ouvrir; on aperçoit une grande salle, à laquelle on arrive par plusieurs marches, et dans laquelle sont groupés des Moines en prières et des soldats tenant des torches. Sur le premier degré de l'escalier se tient le bourreau, appuyé sur sa hache.*

ᵔ   ᵔ   ᵔ

> The iron grill, stage left, has just opened to bring into view a large chamber approached by a flight of steps, in which are groups of monks at prayer and soldiers holding torches. On the first step stands the executioner, leaning on his axe.

With this—in the truest sense of the word—gradual revealing of the grim scene, however, interest was no longer centered exclusively on the father–son relationship but equally on the bearing of Hélène and Procida as they confront death, and death is the primary subject of the text of the quartet: two lines which Scribe wrote for the Sicilian patriots end in the rhymes "tombe" and "succombe" ("tomb" and "perish"). It was characteristic of Verdi's approach to this changed dramatic situation,

57. See above, chapter 5, 202–6.
58. Letter to Carlo Pepoli, spring 1834, in Bellini, *Epistolario*, 243.
59. See Verdi's letter to Scribe, dated 7 June 1854, in Porter, "*Les Vêpres siciliennes*: New letters," 102.

however, that he still made a minor alteration to the text he had had Scribe write specially, changing the line at the beginning of the quartet from "O my sweet country, I perish" ("Ô mon doux pays, je succombe")[60] to "Farewell, my country, I perish" ("Adieu, mon pays, je succombe"). Admittedly, this modification might be seen as nothing more than a whim of Verdi's, who displayed a particular fondness for the word "addio" all his life, and frequently signed his personal letters with a redoubled "addio addio."

But we have only to look at his Italian operas to discover that in them the use of the word "addio" always has more than superficial significance. From *Rigoletto* (1851) onward, it occurs in each of Verdi's operas several times, always in a musically prominent position, and not simply at times when characters literally take leave of each other—at the end of a duet, for example. On the contrary, in *Rigoletto*, Verdi made "addio" the constantly reiterated, key word of an entire cabaletta (in the duet for Gilda and the Duke in Act I), and in *La traviata* (1853) it is actually the first word in the aria in Act III in which the dying Violetta bids farewell to her past dreams of happiness, "Addio del passato, bei sogni ridenti." There the idea of farewell goes far beyond that of taking leave of any one individual person, and refers to much more than the immediate situation.

The same is true of the scene under discussion, in *Les Vêpres siciliennes*. As long as it seems that, at Hélène's insistence, Henri will continue to refuse to acknowledge his father, all the characters are involved in bidding farewell: Hélène and Procida to life, Henri to his beloved, and Montfort, finally, to the hope of ever being reconciled with his son. In this highly fraught situation, however, instead of focusing the audience's attention on the expression of these emotions "through singing" yet again, Verdi gives them the form of broken cries and entrusts the only more expansive musical structure to the orchestra. A melody of rare beauty is begun by the violins, muted and pianissimo, it is true, but reinforced by an accompaniment which lends the cantilena unusual stability by means both of a regular quarter-note motion and also of an exclusive use of harmonies unambiguously related to the tonic, D-flat major. This melody has been heard before, first of all in the overture, but there played tremolo by the high strings, so that it seems on the point of dissolving, like a hazy memory, and that, together with the lack of a harmonically stable accompaniment, makes it appear divested of a physical form. It recurs in Hélène's part in the quartet, "Adieu, mon

60. F-Pn, n.a.f. 22568, fol. 455.

pays, je succombe," before appearing once more in the orchestra, after the first "De profundis." In this third manifestation, fragments of a melody similar to the one in question, but not the same, are again woven into the string tremolo, as if in a fruitless attempt to recall the melody, but it is only remembered successfully after the second entry of the choral "De profundis," when the moment of farewell is imminent.

This time the ends of the two- and four-bar phrases which make up the melody are marked each time by drumbeats; these follow a rhythmic pattern of an eighth note with three appoggiatura-like thirty-second notes, thus presenting a further variant of the anapestic figure of death. This direct allusion to death, the crucial element ever present in the background of *Les Vêpres siciliennes*, confirms the violin cantilena as an instrumental lament with an emotional complexity far greater than that of comparable examples elswhere in Verdi's work, such as the concluding *unisono* of Elvira and Ernani's "Fino al sospiro estremo" in *Ernani* or the "bacio" theme in *Otello*,[61] but it also makes something much more of it: the fact that this melody is entrusted exclusively to instruments makes it clear that it refers to more than the various, if associated, emotions of the individual characters. Behind the theme of farewell, so characteristic of Verdi, looms lamentation as a general characteristic, a universal human feeling outweighing individuality. And even if the "metaphysical" dimension of lament is not yet as distinctly highlighted as it is in the finale of Act III of *Don Carlos*, where a melody performing a directly comparable dramatic function is given exclusively to the Voice from Heaven, accompanied by harp and harmonium,[62] the stepwise, gradual introduction of the "celestially" scored melody puts listeners in mind of lamentation in a sense divorced from any concrete association: lamentation for the eternally lost happiness of a better world, the image of which can only just, with difficulty, be remembered.

This apprehension, more than anything else, is what distinguishes Verdi's grand opéra of 1855 from all previous grands opéras. Even though the characters of *Les Vêpres siciliennes* are shown to be powerless victims of a political conflict that overwhelms them in the end, they are not blind to what is happening around them. They do not numbly recognize their fate, they measure their misfortune against their unfulfilled desires. Verdi ascribed to his characters a trait which is not to be found in the works of Meyerbeer or the other representatives of the generation influenced by Parisian mélodrame, and that is the ability to lament.

61. See Gossett, "The composition of *Ernani*," 53.
62. See Döhring, "Meyerbeers *Le Prophète* und Verdis *Don Carlos*," 731.

DECLINE

Although the situation at the end of Act IV, primed for catastrophe, could have served for a dramatic final scene in the manner of *Il trovatore*, Scribe and Verdi did not allow the execution to run its lurid course and bring the work to a grisly end like that of Halévy's *La Juive*. From the first Scribe had conceived of this tableau, with its pantomimic elements derived from the aesthetic of mélodrame, as a first climax in a plot unusually rich in peripeteias. He had originally intended it for the end of Act III of *Le Duc d'Albe*, where the real catastrophe would have come at the end of Act IV (the last), with Henri preventing his father's assassination by impetuously interposing his own body and thus receiving the fatal blow himself (a scene transferred with some retouching to Act III of *Les Vêpres siciliennes*). Thus far, Scribe was remarkably successful in integrating the two climactic scenes from *Le Duc d'Albe* into *Les Vêpres siciliennes*, but he needed more than a cunning rearrangement of the order of events to bring an opera set in a completely different historical environment to a satisfactory conclusion. He was obliged to fit the traditional narrative of the event known as the Sicilian Vespers into the progress of the sentimental intrigue which he could not alter, and as Verdi had insisted from the time of his first approach to the librettist that he wanted "a fine, grand work in five acts on the same vast scale as *Les Huguenots* or *Le Prophète*"[63] the obvious solution was to make the massacre the consequence of the execution scene. Scribe's task, therefore, in addition to all the necessary adaptation in matters of detail, was to modify the conventional but carefully balanced structure of his old libretto in such a way as to make it possible to expand it from four acts to five.

Inventing a new finale to accommodate the final slaughter was no problem, but it was far harder to fill the rest of the new act with meaningful material. Scribe's first idea was to begin the act with a duet for Hélène and Procida,[64] but he discarded it, evidently before even versifying the draft. Perhaps he and Verdi thought it too risky to emphasize the formal uniformity by a fifth duet, or perhaps the unconventionality of beginning an act with a duet rang alarm bells: we just don't know. Whatever the reason, Scribe provided for the last act to consist of two solo numbers preceded by a brief introductory chorus and followed by a second chorus and a concluding scene laid out on a grand scale.

---

63. See above, 337.
64. See Scribe's letter to Charles Duveyrier, late December 1853/early January 1854 (above, n. 4).

The two solos were destined for the characters enjoying the lead positions in the vocal hierarchy: the soprano and the tenor. In the dramatic situation as now constituted Hélène and Henri had scarcely anything new to say, for the personal strand in the plot had been brought to its conclusion with the general reconciliation of the fourth act. It is above all because of this lack of dramatic tension that Scribe's first version of Act V can scarcely be termed a success: after a chorus conveying nothing at all he proposed a big aria for Hélène which was as conventional as could be imagined, both in its traditional construction in several movements and in the ternary, A–B–A structure of the two closed sections, which he labeled "cantabile" and "cavatina." Henri would then have sung a two-stanza *romance*, after which a second chorus would have led into the finale.[65]

Verdi, too, despite his initial claim to be "very satisfied" with Scribe's text, began to have his doubts about this conception when he reached the stage of composing the last two acts. Nevertheless, in the first of the letters he wrote in the late summer of 1854, requesting alterations, he mentioned details only briefly, suggesting making the opening chorus more important and asking Scribe "to amplify and make more interesting the recitative for Hélène which follows this chorus."[66] Two more weeks passed before he dropped a hint of further misgivings about Hélène's aria: "I would have something to say about the aria but we have time to discuss it [later]."[67] In a later, undated letter, finally, he gave more exact instructions as to the structure of Hélène's aria, which by then was in only one movement, and asked whether it might not be better to cut the big quartet in the act finale.[68] (In the end, he did not compose it.) Scribe's replies, and his successive drafts of the libretto, which remain unpublished in the Verdi archives at Sant' Agata, reveal more about the composer's and librettist's discussions of the fifth act. In sum, Scribe "fashioned and refashioned [the libretto] to suit Verdi's requirements, and often enough to his precise instructions."[69]

Nevertheless, early in January 1855 Verdi wrote a letter to the director of the Paris Opéra—one which all his biographers love to cite— grumbling about "the fifth act, which everyone agrees in finding with-

65. For a complete text of this version see Gerhard, "Ce cinquième acte sans intérêt," 79–86.
66. Letter to Scribe dated 29 August 1854, in Porter, "*Les Vêpres siciliennes:* New letters," 102–3.
67. Letter to Scribe dated 13 September 1854, ibid., 104.
68. Ibid., 106.
69. Comment by Andrew Porter, ibid., 107.

out interest,"[70] and accusing Scribe of not having carried out the modifications he had asked for. It is quite clear that Verdi's purpose in making these complaints was to strengthen his position in the impending negotiations with the Opéra management, and for that reason alone this letter should not be taken as literally as it is by many of the composer's admirers, who mistakenly regard even his business letters as revelations of intimate personal feelings.

All the same, Verdi's criticisms of Act V of *Les Vêpres siciliennes* spotlight a genuine problem. Both as originally drafted by Scribe and as Verdi eventually set it, the text lacks climactic moments with a dramatic interest equal to the great finale of Act IV or the duet for Hélène and Henri which precedes that. In both those scenes, as well as the thrilling music unleashed by the sovereign disposition of conflicting emotions and moments of fear, the pantomimic expressions of those aspects strengthen the theatrical effectiveness of a last-minute change of fortune which is certainly not one of Scribe's best. The librettist fell back on methods whose reliability had been proven in the *mélodrame à grand spectacle* to compensate for the fact that, unlike the emotional volte-face experienced by Henri and Hélène, the reconciliation of the hostile parties merely at Montfort's command was scarcely to be rendered credible by say-so alone. The French and the Sicilians, having confronted each other with bitter hatred throughout Acts I and II, were supposed to unite in a colorful tableau on terms pushed to the limit already in *Le Prophète*, where the crowd's fickleness and lack of willpower is fundamental to the work. Scribe's original version contained the following final chorus:

> (*On a apporté du corps de garde des brocs et des verres. Les soldats français et siciliens trinquent ensemble et s'embrassent.*)
> CHOEUR GÉNÉRAL
> Buvons, trinquons . . . qu'entre nous désormais
> Règnent toujours le bonheur et la paix!
> (*Tableau final. La toile tombe.*)[71]

> *(Jugs and glasses have been brought from the guard-room. The French soldiers and the Sicilians clink glasses and embrace.)*
> WHOLE CHORUS: Let's drink, let's clink . . . to the hope that henceforth happiness and peace will reign among us! (*Final tableau. The curtain falls*)

70. See Verdi's letter to François Crosnier, dated 3 January 1855, in *I copialettere*, 157–59; cited here in the translation by William Weaver, in *Verdi: A Documentary Study*, 193–94.

71. F-Pn, n.a.f. 22506, fol. 84v.

Verdi cut that chorus. The stage-direction remains in the printed libretto, but it is decisively played down in its final effect by the visible reminder that behind the spectacle of the fraternizing masses the conflict is unresolved: Procida, the only one of the four principal characters who has not been involved in any of the various earlier tête-à-têtes, and who has reacted to the announcement of the marriage of Henri and Hélène with the categorical exclamation "Never!," stands aside from the rejoicing:

> *Montfort tient d'une main celle d'Hélène, de l'autre celle de son fils, et sort marchant entre eux deux. Procida reste, sur le devant du théâtre, à droite, retient près de lui ses amis, et semble leur expliquer, à voix basse, ses projets.*

> Montfort takes Hélène's hand in one of his and his son's in the other, and exits, walking between them. Procida remains, downstage left, with his friends grouped around him, and appears to be explaining his plans to them in a low voice.

It would not have come as any surprise had the fifth act pursued the implications of this ominous bit of mime and started with Procida unburdening himself. He is the only principal who might yet have been shown adapting to new circumstances. Would not a big scene and aria for the leader of the Sicilian resistance movement have been an answer to the problem of this act? So far as we know, neither Verdi nor Scribe ever entertained such an idea, and presumably had their reasons. Procida, who in any case has already been adequately catered for with an extensive aria in Act II, is the one completely new character, not one transferred from *Le Duc d'Albe,* and he presents problems within the dramatic structures of *Les Vêpres siciliennes.* Verdi seems to have recognized this himself, for another of his complaints in the letter to the Opéra management cited above was that the libretto offended Italians because, "altering the historical character of Procida, M. Scribe (in his favorite system) has made him a common conspirator, putting the inevitable dagger in his hand."[72]

Even Basevi, one of the most farsighted of Verdi's contemporary critics, was puzzled by Procida's role, which provoked unusually harsh criticism from him as early as the character's scene and aria in Act II: "The cabaletta does not correspond too well to the largo, however; furthermore, it does not have the virtue of novelty, being a slavish imitation, in

---

72. Letter to François Crosnier, dated 3 January 1855 (see above, n. 70.)

19   The Sicilian patriot Procida is a less fully rounded character than the other major roles in *Les Vêpres siciliennes*, as Verdi himself later admitted when he called him "a common conspirator." Contemporary caricaturists seized on the fact, too, as in this vignette (left) by Marcelin, published in *L'Illustration*, 12 January 1856, over the caption "The traitor Procida. An ugly bird!" Right: the singer Louis-Henri Obin in the role, as depicted in an engraving by Pierre-François Godard, fils (1797–1864).

form, of the aria in Act II of *Il trovatore*."[73] It is perfectly true that at the start of Procida's cabaletta, setting out his plans for stealthy vengeance ("Dans l'ombre et le silence, préparons la vengeance"), Verdi uses musical formulas commonplace in the representation of villains, such as pianissimo, staccato eighth notes, and the pronounced tritone leap, so that

73. "La *cabaletta* però non corrisponde troppo al *largo;* ed oltre ciò non ha il pregio della novità, essendo una servile imitazione, per la forma, dell'aria nel secondo atto del *Trovatore.*" *Studio sulle opere di Giuseppe Verdi*, 250.

there would be some justification for the charge that he shares in the guilt of making Procida "a common conspirator."

On the other hand, Verdi provides a contrast to the cabaletta in the aria's slow movement ("Et toi, Palerme"), giving the baritone a cantabile apostrophizing his home city in the rapturous key of G-flat major, thus allowing the man of violence to be seen as a warmhearted character inspired by love of country. Such striking contrasts in his musical characterization only serve in the end, however, to highlight the fundamental anomaly of placing this politically motivated character in a drama dominated by personal and familial sentiments. The story of a love affair doomed to end unhappily had become a stereotype in French and Italian opera since 1830, and it had no place for characters who were simultaneously "good" and politically active. Procida could not, therefore, be represented as a glorious champion of liberty, like William Tell in Rossini's opera, because there was no room for any doubt that *Les Vêpres siciliennes* would end in tragedy for everyone involved. Procida's responsibility for the concluding mass slaughter made it necessary to depict him as one who ruthlessly places his political mission above all humane considerations.

But neither Scribe, loyal to an aesthetic that had seen better days, nor the Verdi of the 1850s commanded the means to represent such an attitude in anything more than a purely negative light. Even if, with that intention, they had conceived a scene for Act V which, say, depicted Procida torn between compassion for the victims of an act of violence and the exigencies of the patriotic struggle, the net effect would have been to make him seem even more inhuman, for he would have been obliged to decide in favor of his abstract convictions. To that extent, therefore, it is hardly surprising that they dispensed with any finer shading in the characterization of Procida, and even abandoned the original plan of weaving him into the network of emotional relationships by making him Hélène's father or the wronged husband of Henri's mother.[74] The price for this decision was a high one: Procida's cardboard role seems colorless when set beside the highly developed light and shade of the contradictoriness molding the protagonists of the sentimental drama. When three characters are torn by inner conflicts, the presence of a fourth who is at one with his political goal and knows no conflict between personal inclination and official duty only confuses the issues. Integrity of this kind might be understood as a strength in a dif-

74. See Scribe's letter to Charles Duveyrier, late December 1853/early January 1854 (above, n. 4).

ferent context, but in a drama of the emotions underpinned by conceptions of the irreconcilability of the personal and the public spheres, such
as had manifested themselves in society by the middle decades of the
nineteenth century, it could only be seen as a signal deficiency: Procida
made the impression of "a common conspirator."

This division of the four main characters into three who represent a
"modern" level of consciousness and one who seems out of date is not
the only thing to be revealed by the pantomime at the end of Act IV of
Les Vêpres siciliennes. It is also a visual statement of the decisive problem
in the conception of the three "sentimental" characters: they leave the
stage together, hand in hand, signifying the resolution of the private
intrigue. It is true that Hélène and Henri have not actually taken their
leave of the drama, but there are hardly any new nuances to be drawn
from them at the beginning of Act V, after the detail in which they have
been depicted already. Everything that motivated the two lovers in the
conflict between private inclination and external duty has been set aside
by the startling peripeteia at the end of Act IV. Of course the potential
for further conflict has not been neutralized: Procida's announcement
that he will use the wedding as the signal for the massacre will inevitably
throw Hélène into an even worse conflict. From the viewpoint of the
late twentieth century, it might seem obvious to start Act V with this
new escalation, but there were good reasons for not doing so. To raise
the curtain on the resumption of the violent disputes that had stamped
the finale of Act IV, as if nothing much had changed, would disrupt the
principle of contrast which was essential to the dramaturgy of grand
opéra: like so much else in the genre, a new act had to contrast with the
one before it. Furthermore, starting at such a high pitch would have
made it impossible to build up the tension slowly to the point where it
is discharged in the ultimate climax during the last scene of the opera.

It was for this reason, therefore, that Scribe clung to the idea of depicting in as much detail as possible the condition of Hélène and Henri
torn between "festive airs" and gloomy forebodings. The dichotomy
was at the heart both of the way he constructed Hélène's big aria, in
which only invocation of her "patron saint" would have enabled her to
dismiss her previous expression of "fearful doubt," and of the *romance*
for Henri following the aria. The sequence would have depicted the
contrast between Hélène's fearful expectations, newly fueled by a brief
exchange of words with Procida, and Henri's happiness. Once again
Scribe recruited pantomime to underline the contrast, in that he wanted
Hélène to sing "I love you" ("Je t'aime!") at the end of Henri's verses,
then turn her gaze on Procida, who is still on the stage, and add "and I

am afraid!" ("et j'ai peur!"). But clearly Verdi was not to be persuaded of the dramatic efficacy of such constructions. The sudden switch from open conflicts to secret forebodings, from insoluble and objectively based oppositions of interests to terrors existing only in the imagination of sensitive individuals, inevitably struck him, the champion of the greatest possible dramaturgical concision, as weak and unmotivated, all the more so because of the complete absence of any drama in the two choruses which, in Scribe's original conception, would have framed the solos. The crowd was required to do nothing more than salute the bride with "joyous songs" ("chants joyeux") at the beginning of the sequence of scenes and celebrate "the happy day" ("cette heureuse journée") at the end. The word "heureuse" also occurs in the first of these choruses, too, describing Hélène, who then takes it up at the start of her response: Scribe's use of this device is surprisingly close to the original idea for the start of the second scene in Act I of *Guillaume Tell*, which Rossini had rejected in 1829.[75]

At the same time, Verdi could not simply proceed by setting aside this outmoded treatment of the chorus as a mere backdrop and beginning the last act immediately with the final tableau, in which the crowd would reveal itself in all its destructiveness as an active element. The composer was the prisoner of his own desire to write a fifth act to rival Meyerbeer. He evidently decided that his only option was to take Scribe's colorless basic idea and modify it. It must have been on his initiative that Scribe eventually eliminated every allusion to real or imaginary conflicts in Hélène's and Henri's solo numbers and provided completely new texts in which an atmosphere of unclouded happiness builds up, in striking contrast to the passions of Act IV and the problems still festering in the background.

The lovers are depicted in dreamlike genre scenes, transported away from the continuing drama. This has the advantage at least of enabling Verdi to hide the lack of color in the actual dramatic situation and characterization beneath the musical detail appropriate to such miniatures. Local color, which Verdi normally uses very sparingly, is applied with a broad brush in all three of the movements that launch Act V. In the chorus "L'amitié fidèle," by entrusting the accompaniment to harp alone for long stretches at a time, he reinforces the serenade-like character bestowed by its waltz tempo, while castanets provide mediterranean coloration. The bolero rhythm of Hélène's single-movement solo (mystifyingly entitled *Sicilienne* in the piano-vocal score) refers to yet an-

75. See above, 95–96.

other dance with obvious southern European associations. Finally the high string tremolos and the decorative woodwind in the accompaniment of Henri's *romance*, "La brise souffle au loin," create a shimmering atmosphere evocative of heat and sunlight by instrumental means that other composers besides Verdi have also used. This miniature has a *dolcissimo* character in striking contrast to the highly charged dramatic tone of other sections of the opera, as Basevi commented disapprovingly:

> The tenor's *mélodie* is a very sweet song, but recherché in some degree. Its character is that of a *canzonetta per camera*. As a result, this piece, like some of the others, disrupts the stylistic uniformity desirable in an opera if it is to make a lasting impression on the listener.[76]

Basevi's complaint that the stylistic uniformity he advocated is disrupted was not provoked by the chamber-music quality of this number alone but also, and to a greater degree, by a highly uncommon formal characteristic peculiar to the whole first half of this fifth act. Unlike every other part of the opera, and in contrast to Scribe's original version, these three numbers are not placed within a framework of recitative dialogue. Instead, Verdi has the chorus, Hélène's solo, and Henri's *romance* follow each other without a word of recitative to link them. The impression this creates of disparate, unlinked elements is strengthened by the composer's recourse to purely strophic forms for all three, which might have been acceptable in an opéra comique, but seems wholly out of place in the context of the formal musical vocabulary underlying all serious French and Italian opera of the 1850s. The two stanzas in the chorus take a regular *A–B–A* form, while both solo numbers consist of two stanzas in *A–A'* form.

Verdi dispensed altogether with individually characterized forms of expression here, both musically and dramaturgically. The dramatic motivation for each of the three numbers amounts to nothing more than following the steps in a prescribed ceremony. The chorus accompanies the bridesmaids' presentation of flowers to the bride, and Hélène's solo is merely an expression of thanks to them, instead of the self-communing envisaged by Scribe in his extended aria-text. Henri's *romance*, finally, with its artificial vocabulary, is less an outpouring of emotion than a metaphorical love poem, and it is not for nothing that in the

76. "La *melodia* del tenore è un canto assai dolce: ma ricercato in qualche punto. Il suo carattere è quello di una canzonetta per camera. Onde che questo pezzo, come altri notati ancora, si oppone ancora a quella ugualianza di stile che si vorrebbe conservata in un'Opera, affinchè potesse fare impressione durabile nell'animo dell'ascoltante." *Studio sulle opere di Giuseppe Verdi*, 256.

printed piano-vocal score this depersonalized, undramatic number is entitled *Mélodie*.

And although Scribe had already taken steps to rid the two solos of gloomy forebodings, Verdi systematically cut from the revised text every single remaining expression capable of being interpreted as a reference to the catastrophe brewing in the background. In the printed version of the libretto, Hélène's *boléro* still retains the line "my heart trembles at your words" ("mon coeur frissonne à vos accents"), but Verdi changed the verb to the unexceptionable but also weaker "smiles" ("sourit"); similarly, one line in Henri's *mélodie*, as set by Verdi, goes "Hélène . . . my heart is yours" ("Hélène . . . à toi mon coeur se livre"), but the published libretto shows that Scribe had seen no harm in giving him the words "What am I saying? . . . What danger remains to threaten us?" ("Que dis-je . . . quel danger peut encor nous poursuivre?").

So much insouciance is disquieting. Precisely because of the changes Verdi made, the text as set creates the impression that no one really believes in a happy ending. The characters are incapable of indulging any emotion at all, and merely go through the motions of a ritual laid down by convention. This "conventionality" in Act V of *Les Vêpres siciliennes* is not just a negative feature, however, a return to a position that operatic composition had already advanced beyond in the 1850s, it is also an eloquent example of the problems besetting the dramaturgy of the great five-act, historical opera, grounded in its origins in the 1830s, but surviving into a new era. Scribe's reworking of his *Duc d'Albe* is only one example of the crisis of traditional grand opéra, and of the fact that the precarious balance between the historical setting and the private intrigue, crucial to almost all the great operas of the age, had been disturbed.

The traditional model of grand opéra could not accommodate Verdi's generation's sensitivity to the intimate psychology of characters swayed by contradiction. In allowing his characters, torn between nostalgic longing for intimacy and their public roles, to express their difficulties as emphatically as they do in the successive tête-à-têtes between mutually dependent people, Verdi demonstrated how impossibly wide the breach between private and public became when the intimate emotions of the characters as individuals were taken more seriously than they had usually been in the dramaturgy of traditional French grand opéra (already undermined by the "mosaic" effect in works like *Le Prophète*). It is a testimony to Verdi's artistic sensitivity that he did not draw a perfunctory veil over this final decline of grand opéra in the fifth act of his first work in the genre but instead, by means of this disparate sequence of

20   This anonymous pencil drawing, made in connection with the Milan première of *Les Vêpres siciliennes* in 1864, does not represent the destructive fury of
the mob with anything like the power of the musical representation of the massacre, as the soloists fall silent before the overwhelming force of the chorus.

isolated numbers, gave an object lesson in how fragile the dramaturgy
of grand opéra had become in its interlocking of historical and personal motivation.

It is not surprising, therefore, that he brought this problematic opera
to an end with a lapidary chorus that in many respects resembles the
reductionist finale of Rossini's *Le Siège de Corinthe:* in both cases the
chorus is in A minor and $\frac{3}{4}$ time, and even if Verdi did not go as far as
Rossini, and allow the human voice to fall silent altogether, he once
again rejected Scribe's proposed version and let the historical framework occupy the limelight on its own.[77] The individual main characters
are robbed of utterance and play no role at all in the noisy fortissimo
chorus, which is over in a mere twenty seconds. This drastic solution
sent yet another signal that the relationship between the sphere of individual emotion and historical subject matter, between soloists and
chorus, needed to be redefined.

77. See Budden, "Varianti nei *Vespri siciliani*," 166–70.

∽ 10 ∽

THE
INTERNATIONAL
VIEW

Nationalism and Cosmopolitanism

The first performance of Verdi's *Les Vêpres siciliennes* took place exactly four weeks after Napoleon III presided at the opening ceremony of the Paris Universal Exposition on the Champs Élysées. This was the first event of its kind to be held in France, and only the second in the world, following the hugely successful Great Exhibition of 1851 in London. It was, admittedly, purely by accident that Verdi's dramatic representation of the isolation of the individual coincided with the gigantic, theatrical self-representation of a society that believed works of art were products to be bought and sold like machinery, exotic idols, and gemstones.[1] Although the impression persists, even in recent publications, that both *Les Vêpres*, in 1855, and *Don Carlos*, the première of which coincided with a later international exhibition in Paris, in 1867, were officially commissioned for these occasions, the dates of the two premières fell when they did solely because of the unpredictable delays that accompanied both operas' lengthy gestations. Both were commissioned by the Paris Opéra in expectation of much earlier completion: the contract for *Les Vêpres siciliennes*, signed in February 1852, specifies November or December 1854 as the date of the première,[2] and that for *Don Carlos*, signed in December 1865 after prolonged negotiations, December 1866.[3]

---

1. See Hofmann, *Das irdische Paradies*, 86.

2. See the draft version of the contract between Verdi and Nestor Roqueplan, dated 28 February 1852, in Verdi, *I copialettere*, 139.

3. See the draft version of the contract between Verdi and Émile Perrin, December 1865, in Günther, "La Genèse de *Don Carlos*," 33–34.

21   The brilliantly staged Universal Exposition of 1855 undoubtedly represents the highpoint of Paris's development as the "capital city of the nineteenth
century." The disposition of figures and groups at the opening ceremony in this
anonymous lithograph shows a disconcerting affinity with the principles of the
dramaturgy of grand opéra.

Yet even if it was not intentional, the coincidence in the dates provides a striking demonstration of the fact that the cosmopolitan spirit
that inspired the international exhibitions was also still a dominant factor at the Opéra in the 1850s and '60s. Neither the management nor
audiences regarded it as any stranger than Verdi himself did that a non-
French composer, not resident in Paris, should be commissioned to
write an opera in the French language. Whereas in Berlin, as early as
the 1820s, public opinion took exception to the performance of operas
on German librettos by the Italian-born Spontini, general music director at the Prussian court, a majority in Paris under the Second Empire
believed that the "capital city of the nineteenth century" gave the lead
to European culture as a whole, as well as to that of France. This confidence held good in all the arts to some degree or another, but it was
especially strong at the Opéra. Musicians of French origin had made a
rather small showing at the Opéra, in fact, since 1646, when the first
outstanding figure in its history, Giovanni Battista Lulli—universally
known today by the French form of his name—arrived from Florence.

It is no exaggeration to say that, with the single exception of the works of Rameau in the mid-eighteenth century, more successful and enduring works entered the repertory of the Paris Opéra at times when it was dominated by composers from outside France: Gluck and Piccinni in the last decades of the ancien régime, Spontini under the first Napoleon, Rossini, Donizetti, Meyerbeer, and Verdi in the era of grand opéra. Periods when the tone was set by native composers—the first decades of the eighteenth century, with Campra, Destouches, and Montéclair, the turn of the century, with Catel, Le Sueur, and Méhul, and the years from about 1860 onward, with Gounod, Thomas, and Reyer—seem dim by comparison, at least in retrospect.

There were, of course, always some musicians of French origin who distinguished themselves in those periods when "imported" artists were in the ascendant: Auber's *Muette de Portici* and Halévy's *Juive* did not achieve the same spectacular success as the contemporary works by Meyerbeer, but they are undoubtedly among the most frequently performed of all the grand opéra repertory. However, no fundamental dramaturgical differences exist between these operas and those by their German and Italian compeers: on the contrary, Halévy and Auber, in particular, stand out for their notable readiness to adopt Italian formal conventions, modified in Halévy's works only by an unadventurous melodic style, largely innocent of coloratura, and tending to place harmonically "sensitive" scale degrees like thirds and leading-notes in the foreground. And even if during the 1830s certain critics hoped to appeal to the chauvinism of their readers by declaring *La Juive* the product of a "French School," it was a figment of their imagination.[4] Opera, in particular, provides no justification at all for the strenuous efforts to abstract from the history of music in nineteenth-century France "the 'idea' of a French music distinguished by its clarity, sensitivity and fine shading, wariness of expressive overemphasis, and a tendency towards literary programs."[5] On the contrary, the open-minded historian cannot avoid the conclusion that "there was no such thing as a discrete, specifically French music in the nineteenth century, only a music of Paris."[6] Moreover, the cosmopolitan character of that music was continually revived and refreshed by the city's status in the eyes of musicians like Rossini and Meyerbeer, Chopin and Liszt, and even Verdi and Wagner too,

4. See Leich-Galland, "Pariser Pressestimmen."
5. Dahlhaus, "Französische Musik und Musik in Paris," 6.
6. Ibid., 5.

22 Although the Paris Opéra did not have the Universal Exposition of 1855 in view when it commissioned *Les Vêpres siciliennes* from Verdi, in the end the timing of the première fell in very conveniently with Napoleon III's policy of making Paris the cosmoplitan center of Europe. To Italian nationalists and adherents of Verdi, on the other hand, it looked like homage paid to the most successful contemporary Italian opera composer, as the gushing servility of Napoleon's stance expresses in this caricature by Melchiorre De Filippi dei Conti di Langano (1825–95), reproduced from an engraving by Perrotta. The caricaturist was an aristocrat resident in Naples who also composed operas but was best known for the drawings he published under the pen name of Delfico.

who looked on Paris as an essential station on their progress toward truly international fame.

The impression that music theater at the Paris Opéra transcended national frontiers was not confined to those who shared in its glory. In 1856 Meyerbeer was rumored to be composing an opera for Italy, and the leading music critic in Florence, Abramo Basevi, told his readers what they could expect from such a work, assuming that it built on its Parisian predecessors; it would be, he imagined, nothing less than "a beacon allowing Italians to return to the path from which they are steadily moving away in order to career blindly toward a place where art will encounter only abysses."[7] Even ten years later, his counterpart in Milan firmly refuted the view that the Opéra was an exclusively French theater, and called it "a temple . . . of universal music, cosmopolitan art."[8] The unprejudiced historian of the way music in Paris developed during the last thirty-five years of the nineteenth century cannot help observing that the temple's foundations were already under threat by the time that stirring assertion was made. It is true that industrial-based capitalism, promoting international trade and apparently in excellent condition, continued to prosper on a scale that seemed to confirm a cosmopolitanism which, Parisian society prided itself, was above selfish national interests. Yet in France, as in other countries, a development was already under way that made nationalism the dominant mode of thought of the last years of the century. When we consider, furthermore, that the style of musical theater presented at the Opéra-Comique and other houses frequented by the so-called bourgeois middle classes was distinguished already in the 1830s by its specifically French tone and reliance on librettos spiced with xenophobic jokes, the internationalism of the Opéra ceases to look quite so characteristic of the age, and rather more like an attitude surviving from the ancien régime among the privileged social classes who could afford the luxury.[9]

In countries like Germany and Italy, on the other hand, which only achieved national identity at the cost of some struggle during the course of the nineteenth century, there was a far greater readiness to consider all artistic questions from a standpoint where more importance adhered

7. "un lume, che permetterebbe agli Italiani di ritrovare quel sentiero da cui vanno sempre più allantonandosi per correre ciecamente là dove l'arte non può incontrare che precipizj"; Basevi, "Se Meyerbeer scrivesse oggi un'opera italiana," 23.

8. "il tempio . . . della musica universale, dell'arte cosmopolitica"; Filippo Filippi, "I detrattori della musica italiana," *Gazzetta musicale di Milano*, 1 April 1866, 5; cited in Della Seta, "L'immagine di Meyerbeer," 149, n. 4.

9. See Mayer, *The Persistence of the Old Regime*.

to the differences between nations than to what they had in common. Thus German critics, as early as the 1830s, subjected even the outstanding works that originated at the Paris Opéra to a system of values in which the concept of originality was mingled with ideas of what was deemed to be national.[10] The conscious amalgamation of different musical traditions, which distinguishes the work of Meyerbeer as much as it does that of Handel, Mozart, and Gluck, and which was approved in the eighteenth century as a successful synthesis of different national styles, was now looked upon, and not by Robert Schumann alone, as "want of originality and lack of style."[11] In the short and medium term, admittedly, the polemics of an artistic and journalistic élite had little effect on the widespread success which operas composed for Paris achieved in the German-speaking countries. In 1885 Meyerbeer's works still held their own against the music-dramas of Richard Wagner in theaters of the new German Empire: only *Tannhäuser* and *Lohengrin* were given more often than *Les Huguenots*, while performances of *Tristan und Isolde* were far fewer than those even of *Robert le diable*, the least frequently performed of Meyerbeer's operas.[12]

But it was not only questions of style criticism on which a nationalist, if not chauvinist, gaze was increasingly brought to bear as the nineteenth century wore on: the subject matter of operas, too, came to be referred to patterns of thought molded by contemporary political attitudes. It clearly did not even occur to the aristocratic potentates who suggested *La Muette de Portici* as a suitable opera for celebrating that royal birthday in Brussels in 1830 that its subject could be related to the contemporary Belgian struggle against Dutch rule. A quarter of a century later, no one at the Opéra, apparently, had thought anything of the fact that with *Les Vêpres siciliennes* the bloody confrontations of French and Italians were about to be presented on the stage of the first theater in France in a dramatic version from the pen of an Italian, until it occurred to Verdi himself to point out shortly before the première, in his letter to the Opéra management, dated 3 January 1855 and cited in the previous chapter, that Scribe's libretto was wounding to the French "because they are massacred," as well as the Italians for making their representative, Procida, "a common conspirator." The observation would have made perfectly good sense to the composer's compatriots, who had never failed to discover references to the Risorgimento in his

10. See Dahlhaus, "Motive der Meyerbeerkritik," 37.
11. *The Musical World of Robert Schumann*, 139.
12. See Kirchmeyer, "Psychologie des Meyerbeer-Erfolges," 472.

early works, but it must have surprised Crosnier when he read this reproach from Verdi of all people. It had been the composer, after all, who
had suggested Naples as a possible location for the action, and thus
taken the initiative for moving it to Italy from its original setting in the
Spanish Netherlands, and then, when Scribe had suggested the so-called
Sicilian Vespers of 1282 as the event on which to center the intrigue,
Verdi had promptly accepted the idea, without reflection.[13]

In fact, Verdi probably raised the point as part of a negotiating tactic
to put his Parisian clients in the wrong, but he nevertheless put his finger on the fact that the fundamental alteration of dramaturgical premises was not the only serious obstacle to the composition of any more
large-scale historical operas in the style of Meyerbeer. If audiences had
no better guide to the political conflicts of their own time than a blind
partisanship orientated wholly by nationality, they were not going to
enjoy dramatic works in which historical conflicts were represented
from a detached, moderate, "happy medium" viewpoint.

Thus the cosmopolitan character of the Paris Opéra, and grand opéra
as a genre, was already threatened in the 1850s and '60s; then, with
Prussia's defeat of France in 1871, all universalist trends in Parisian cultural life came to an abrupt halt, and the "capital city of the nineteenth
century" began its slow decline toward a poorly disguised provincialism.
Together with his close contemporary Jacques Offenbach, Verdi was the
last composer of foreign origin to write original works for Paris, setting
texts in the French language. Wagner made his debut at the Opéra in
1861 with the translated version of an opera—*Tannhäuser*—first performed fifteen years earlier, although he revised it for Paris. In the last
three decades of the century, virtually nothing remained of the Opéra's
unique status as the house which had set the lead followed by the rest of
Europe; the musical world looked to Milan and Turin, or to Munich
and Dresden, when it sought the novelties likely to score resounding
international successes. Verdi's operas for Paris, *Les Vêpres siciliennes* and
Don Carlos, received far less acclaim on the wider European stage than
Meyerbeer's had—in Germany they were heard frequently only at
houses such as the Darmstadt Court Theater that made a speciality of
taking works from Paris.[14] Thereafter, the Opéra was forced to accept
his later works, such as *Aida* and *Otello*, at second hand, in translation,

13. See Scribe's undated letter to Duveyrier, late December 1853/early January 1854
(cited above, chap. 9, n. 4). See also Budden, *The Operas of Verdi*, 2:173–74, and Porter,
"Don't Blame Scribe!"

14. See Hortschansky, "Die Herausbildung eines deutschsprachigen Verdi-
Repertoires," 151.

in order to have any share at all in the success of the composer who succeeded Meyerbeer as Europe's leading composer of opera—and pursued his career outside Paris.

MYTHOLOGY

In accepting operas by Verdi that had already been acclaimed in Italy, the Opéra management was following a policy that had come into being during the 1850s. The production of Rossini's *Otello*—or rather, *Othello*—in 1844 had represented the first breach of the longstanding principle of not performing works of which nothing was new except the translation of the libretto. Verdi's *Louise Miller* had followed in 1853, and *Le Trouvère* in 1857, though Verdi added a ballet to the latter. In taking this step, the Opéra entered into direct competition with the Théâtre Italien, which had won back some of its old prestige with its regular presentations of Verdi's works. The farsighted could already see in such developments the signs of the gradual decline of the unique character and status of the Paris Opéra. One omen was the serious crisis at this same period in sales of operatic music in the form of piano transcriptions, potpourris, and so on. Maurice Schlesinger, who had published most of the operas produced in Paris from 1830 onwards, was forced to sell his business in 1846 after suffering prolonged commercial difficulties.[15] The purchaser, Gemmy Brandus, was unable to overcome the problems, in spite of turning the concern into a joint-stock company. After 1860 Brandus relied less and less on the sales he could make from grand opéra, once so successful, and turned instead, above all, to the newly popular genre of opéra bouffe.[16]

It is also likely that, in addition to the dramaturgical and political factors already mentioned, this decline in the public's interest in grand opéra at the time of the transition from the July Monarchy to the Second Empire was also affected by problems familiar to us from the cultural industry of the twentieth century but already encountered in connection with the early nineteenth-century entertainment of the panorama: in brief, the desire for novelty at any price. For twenty years, the Opéra's composers had tried to outdo their rivals, and their own previous work, with ever greater visual spectacle and striking musicodramatic ideas, and it was only a question of time before they reached the limits of what could be realized within contemporary aesthetic

15. See Devriès, "Un Éditeur de musique 'à la tête ardente,'" 131.
16. See Devriès, "La Maison Brandus," 52, 80–81.

frameworks. Meyerbeer had good reason to make an opéra comique his next project once *Le Prophète* was staged: after spending thirteen years on an opera that was undoubtedly, of all his operas, the one "that he wrote with the greatest liberty,"[17] he must have been aware that even he would find it hard to set down a yet more extreme benchmark within the grand opéra genre, especially as the "liberties" he had taken in *Le Prophète* already seriously threatened its dramaturgical coherence. To that extent, it is more than a biographical accident that he did not complete another grand opéra after 1849, and left unfinished at his death only *L'Africaine*, a work of many contradictions and less advanced in some individual respects than *Les Huguenots* (in Verdi's opinion, it was "not . . . assuredly Meyerbeer's best opera").[18]

More than any other composer except perhaps Spontini, Meyerbeer had striven in each new opera to advance beyond the stage in musical dramaturgy that he had reached in the previous one, and he had tried all his life to surmount the formal obstacles to his unceasing concern with dramatic expression. He obviously detested uncritical adoption of traditional formal conventions, witness the unusual vehemence of an outburst in one of his letters to Jean Schucht, written at the age of sixty-five:

> What you said about the lack of good dramatic librettos was nothing less than the truth, and took the words out of my mouth. That's exactly how it was in those days! Nothing but trite verses in the usual conventional operatic forms. Librettists were incapable of higher dramatic aspirations, they thought music incapable of shaping great dramatic actions, they had no idea whatever of the through-composed opera of today. I conferred with many librettists and drew up my own scenarios, but always got the old forms in return.[19]

Meyerbeer's criticism of the "old forms" was not confined to the circumstances prevailing at the start of his career; he did not except even

17. "qu'il a écrit avec le plus de liberté"; J. Weber, *Meyerbeer*, 77.

18. "non . . . certo la miglior opera di Meyerbeer"; letter to Opprandino Arrivabene, 31 December 1865, in Alberti, *Verdi intimo*, 61.

19. "Hinsichtlich des Mangels guter dramatischer Operntexte haben Sie reine Wahrheit gesagt und mir die Worte aus der Seele geschrieben. Ja, so war es damals! Nichts anderes als die faden Reimereien in den gewöhnlichen hergebrachten Opernformen. Ein höherer dramatischer Aufflug war ihnen, den Dichtern nicht möglich; sie hielten die Musik nicht fähig, sich zum großen handelnden Drama zu gestalten, hatten überhaupt keine Idee von unserer heutigen durchkomponierten Oper. Ich habe mit vielen Dichtern konferiert und Entwürfe gemacht, aber stets kamen die alten Formen wieder zum Vorschein." Letter to Jean F. Schucht, 15 December 1856, cited in Schucht, *Meyerbeer's Leben und Bildungsgang*, 392.

the five-act opera on which he was still working, *L'Africaine*, when he admitted to one of his librettists in the early 1860s that "the old forms are wearing out, the five-act opera is no longer possible."[20] Although Meyerbeer in his old age was obviously not in the position to renovate his musical dramaturgy fundamentally, he was nevertheless reluctant simply to abandon the plan of his fourth grand opéra after all the years he had lived with it. With characteristic scrupulousness, he delayed finishing the work until literally the last minute, and died shortly after rehearsals had begun. Younger composers, however, were content to go on working with the five-act form which had served grand opéra well enough, and sought novelty in new fields of subject matter instead, turning from modern history to either myth and prehistory or stories in which the supernatural loomed large.

There are plenty of examples: Gounod took the subject of his early opera *Sapho* (1851) from the literary legends of ancient Greece, and transported the audience back to the reign of King Solomon for his later grand opéra *La Reine de Saba* (1862); Félicien David's *Herculanum* (1859) is set in Pompeii at the time of its volcanic destruction, and does not shrink from including Satan himself in the cast, while closely following the formal models of Meyerbeer and Halévy; and the success of Ambroise Thomas's *Hamlet* (1868) owed not a little to the effective depiction of the Ghost's several appearances. Such elements freed actions from the obsessively detailed realism of Scribe's librettos and helped them to transcend historical time. They were all united, finally, with uncommon conceptional rigor, in Berlioz's *Les Troyens*, completed in 1860. Based on myths from the ancient classical world, the opera includes Dido and Aeneas among its many mortal characters, but additionally there are the spirits of fallen Trojan heroes, as well as the god Mercury. Berlioz wrote his own libretto and turned not to history but to literature for his source: the *Aeneid* of Virgil. In the composer's eyes, this Latin verse epic, written in the first century of the Christian era, was *the* classical text. Virgil's narration of the foundation-myth of the city of Rome, presenting the heroic protagonists as the direct ancestors of his patron, the Emperor Augustus, was moreover for Berlioz, an ardent Bonapartist, the ideal subject for a French national opera under the somewhat different political conditions of the Second Empire. The leap from Aeneas via Augustus to Napoleon III was not as great as might appear: a sixteenth-century precedent for linking the legendary Trojans

20. "les vieilles formes s'usent, l'opéra en cinq actes n'est plus possible"; cited in Blaze de Bury, *Meyerbeer et son temps*, 297.

and the French state existed in Ronsard's verse epic *La Franciade*, modeled on the *Aeneid*. Three centuries on, Virgil's poem was still one of the undisputed foundations of education beyond the most elementary level, and the imperial claims of the nephew of the great Napoleon had given new encouragement to those who liked to think of France as a "Roman" nation and the modern successor to the imperium romanum.

Berlioz was an uncritical admirer of Napoleon III, and did not hesitate to lend his opera's support to such notions. True, he devoted a lot of space to the impossible love of Dido and Aeneas, but, unlike Metastasio's *Didone abbandonata* and all other earlier operatic treatments, his version relativizes the significance of the love story by including the prophetic visions of Cassandra and Dido to show that the human actions are predestined by the gods, and by leaving no room for any doubt that the work's overriding theme was the Trojans' journey from Troy, after its fall, to their ordained destiny, the foundation of Rome. The first two acts of this monumental opera are set in Troy, and Dido's suicide in the last act is only one element in a grandiose phantasmagoria in which the triumph of the Roman imperium already dawns. True, Berlioz changed his mind about his original idea of bringing the finale right up to the present, confessing that "it seemed to me in the end that the dying Dido's allusion to French dominion in Africa was pure chauvinist puerility,"[21] but it is clear that he abandoned it regretfully and only because all the hearers at a private reading of the libretto advised him to do so: "They found the idea of having Dido predict French dominion in Africa absurd, whereas they universally approved her prediction of the brief avenging glory of Hannibal. One must yield to . . . the majority."[22]

Though he modified the libretto to that extent, Berlioz was hopeful of creating nothing less than a French national opera in the most up-to-date sense in composing this "grand dramatic machine";[23] the musical means he uses to characterize the Trojans and the Carthaginians leave no doubt on that score. The *Marche troyenne* for example, heard so often in quasi-thematic recall that it takes on the function of "Ein' feste Burg"

21. "il m'a semblé dernièrement que l'allusion de Didon mourante à la domination française en Afrique était une pure puérilité chauvinique"; letter to Princess Carolyne Sayn-Wittgenstein, 25 or 26 December 1856, in Berlioz, *Correspondance générale*, 5:401.

22. "On a trouvé absurde l'idée de faire prédire par Didon la domination française en Afrique, et sa prédiction de la courte gloire vengeresse d'Annibal a été au contraire unanimement approuvée. Il faut se rendre à la raison . . . du plus fort." Letter to Princess Carolyne Sayn-Wittgenstein, 18 March 1857, ibid., 442.

23. "grande machine dramatique"; letter to Liszt, 12 April 1856, ibid., 286.

in *Les Huguenots* or "Ad nos, ad salutarem undam" in *Le Prophète*, plainly adopts the tone of the triumphal marches composed in honor of the first Napoleon, and the *Chant national* with which the Carthaginians pay homage to their Queen is not significantly different from any of the national anthems widely adopted in the second half of the nineteenth century. Above all, however, Dido's dying vision of immortal Rome's victory over her Carthaginian home in the closing scene, with its separate but simultaneous layers of action,[24] presents an image of a triumphant nation-state that would have been unthinkable before 1850. The theatrical convention of a concluding apotheosis came from the old *tragédie lyrique*, but what appears at the back of the stage, ringed with light and glory, is not a classical god or a monarch raised above the common run of humanity, but the abstract idea of the nation, mythically transfigured in a secularized world.

Compared with this appropriation of myth from the spirit of ascendant imperialism, the mysterious appearance of the Habsburg Emperor Charles V in the last act of Verdi's *Don Carlos* is much less spectacular. In flight from the all-powerful Inquisition, Carlos takes refuge at his grandfather's tomb in the monastery of Saint-Just, and there something happens that amazes his pursuers. In the words of the stage-direction, "the grille opens, the Monk appears, gathers Carlos in his arms, and wraps his cloak about him" *(La grille s'ouvre, le Moine paraît, attire Carlos dans ses bras et le couvre de son manteau)*. The "monk," however, is none other than he who purportedly lies buried there. The aged, blind Cardinal-Grand Inquisitor recognizes his voice with horror ("la voix de l'Empereur"), and the chorus cries his name in astonishment ("C'est Charles-Quint!"). Protected by this mysterious apparition, Carlos enters the monastery, while an offstage chorus, chanting that the mighty emperor is now dust and ashes ("Charles-Quint, l'auguste Empereur, n'est plus que cendre et que poussière"), laments the doom of the Spanish royal family and the curtain slowly falls. What is more surprising than any of the details of this brief concluding scene, however, is the simplicity of the theatrical and musical means Verdi uses to raise his "historical" drama onto a mythological plane. Berlioz deployed several choruses, an onstage orchestra, and a complete Roman triumph passing across the stage in the finale of *Les Troyens*, and another contemporary French composer, Auguste Mermet, whose name is virtually unknown today, similarly massed all available resources to achieve a spectacular end in his opera *Roland à Roncevaux* (1864: incidentally, it was received

24. See above, 206.

far more warmly than either *Don Carlos*, two-and-a-half years later, or *Les Troyens*). In his final scene, he too brings onto the stage a Holy Roman Emperor, Charlemagne himself, at the moment of the hero's eclipse. Roland is already slain, as a result of treachery. "The sun illuminates the valley. In the distance, on the heights, Charlemagne appears, surrounded by his captains. As Roland, borne by his companions, passes before him, he halts and stretches out his hand in sorrow toward his nephew's body. The warriors raise and brandish their swords and lances, making their pennants flutter" (*Le soleil éclaire la vallée. Au fond, sur la hauteur, apparaît Charlemagne entouré de ses capitaines. Au moment où Roland, porté par ses compagnons, passe devant lui, il s'arrête et tend avec douleur la main vers le corps inanimé de son neveu. Les guerriers élèvent et brandissent les épées et les lances et font flotter les étendards*). Mermet uses the appearance of the near-mythical ruler, bathed in sunlight, and guarding the retreat of his remaining warriors, in order to assert the historical continuum from the Frankish empire to modern France, and thus legitimize national pride. Verdi, on the other hand, radically distances himself from the French tradition of an apotheosis in the somber last scene of *Don Carlos*. In the original version composed for Paris the orchestra falls silent and the tuneless chant of the final chorus seems to die away in the distance of the monastery buildings. Verdi did not want to deny himself the mythic strand in the last opera he was to write for Paris, but by this means he emphasizes myth's uncanny, mysterious aspects.

The idea of replacing the often all too prosaic realism of earlier grand opéra with mysterious and/or mythological matter was by no means restricted to the composers mentioned so far. Eugène Scribe, too, had his ear to the ground and was ready to follow a trend which, while it reached its high point in Wagner's music-dramas, affected all opera composers except Meyerbeer and, for a time at least, the Italians. With the best will in the world, it cannot be claimed that Scribe's texts for Halévy's *Le Juif errant* (1852) and *La Nonne sanglante*, intended for Berlioz but finally composed by Gounod (1854), possess the qualities of his most successful librettos, but that makes it all the more remarkable that this highly experienced practitioner of his craft regarded it as important, even at the end of his career, to transform his subject matter with fantastic elements, ghosts, hauntings, and lurid coloration, rather than continue on the path that had served him so well of unfolding rationally posited plots through a precisely constructed sequence of unexpected complications. In the event, the librettos of both *La Nonne sanglante*, based on an episode in the archetypal Gothic horror novel, *The Monk* by M. G. Lewis, and *Le Juif errant*, based on a bestseller by Eugène Sue, draw on the popular literature of the day instead of the classical and historical myths invoked in other operas, but nevertheless Scribe made his contribution to the "transcendence" of historical grand opéra when, for example, in the finale of *La Nonne sanglante*, the clouds are seen on which the "bleeding nun" of the title (a ghost) and a mortally wounded murderer ascend to heaven, while the chorus falls to its knees and prays for those who remain as survivors of a deadly feud.

In comparison with Wagner's music-dramas, in which the epic qualities are inherent in the musical structures themselves, the legendary elements in the French operas mentioned so far, with the exception of *Les Troyens*, are no more than incidental splashes of color with no real consequences for the dramaturgy. Only in Berlioz's epic opera is the unconventional dramaturgy tailored to the needs of the mythical subject matter, but the audiences at the first performances in 1863 of *Les Troyens à Carthage*, the bleeding rump made up of the three acts set in Carthage, were not given the chance to appreciate that. Evidently France was not ready for an opera molded from the spirit of myth until Debussy's *Pelléas et Mélisande* (1902), and for that a generation spent assimilating the influence of Wagner was necessary. Such a fundamental renovation of French opera was out of the question forty years earlier, and so most composers, having made their halfhearted experiments with mythology, abandoned the five-act grand opéra and turned to the new *drame lyrique*.

Like *grand opéra*, drame lyrique is a term rarely used by the composers and librettists themselves to designate a genre, while it has been useful to later commentators to denote a specific type of French opera of the second half of the nineteenth century and the early years of the twentieth. Vague as the expression is, the characteristics allowing us to speak in this way of a "specific type" of opera can be listed relatively precisely. The recourse to literary subjects, often predetermined in plot and treatment by the novels from which they came, constituted a radical break with the dramaturgy of grand opéra, with its reliance on politico-historical matter. Subjects were overtly matters of private emotions and personal affairs; primarily psychological conflicts were worked out in intimate and atmospheric settings; and eventually the graphically depicted milieus in which the characters found themselves became important players in the drama.[25] "Beginning as a sort of hybrid, half way between grand opera and *opéra comique*," as represented in early examples like Ambroise Thomas's *Mignon* (1866) or Gounod's *Mireille*

25. H.-J. Wagner, "Lyrisches Drama und Drame lyrique," 78. For a recent survey of the history of the term, see Schneider, "Drame lyrique."

(1864), drame lyrique "soon acquired so firm a footing that it became the representative of French composition."[26] Opera in Paris had at last become specifically and definitively French opera, and even before Massenet's *Manon* (1884) and *Thaïs* (1894), or Charpentier's "novel in music" *Louise* (1900), *Mireille* was already representative of those operas in which works of French literature were quite deliberately used as the basis for atmospheric genre pictures. The cosmopolitan traditions which were once so distinctive a feature of the Opéra survived only in the "lowbrow" genre of opéra bouffe, and disappeared from there, too, by about 1880. The outstanding composer of opéra bouffe was Offenbach, and it is true that a text by his collaborators Henri Meilhac and Ludovic Halévy was the original source of the libretto of Johann Strauss the younger's *Die Fledermaus* (1874), but already characteristic elements of opéra bouffe were lost in the act of adapting it to Viennese circumstances.

With the loss of its European standing—which the wholesale recourse to mythology could not prevent—the terms on which the Opéra had enjoyed its past splendors also vanished. The ultimate index of the theater's decline is the fact that, of the operas first heard in Paris during the last forty or so years of the nineteenth century, the few that achieved enduring international success were premièred in other houses: Gounod's *Faust* (1859) at the Théâtre Lyrique, and Bizet's *Carmen* (1875) and Offenbach's *Les Contes d'Hoffmann* (1881) at the Opéra-Comique. And it is one of the special ironies of French musical history that in the end the Opéra was obliged to take all three into its repertory in order to retain its claim to be France's premier opera house: *Faust* in 1869; *Carmen* (after a single gala performance in 1907) not until 1959; *Les Contes d'Hoffmann* in 1974.

THE LEGACY OF GRAND OPÉRA

Grand opéra took a relatively short time to lose its influence on the development of French opera. By the turn of the century it was already a sign of good taste among Parisian composers to mock the "classics" of yesteryear like Meyerbeer and Halévy. Reviewing a revival of *Les Huguenots* in a weekly column in 1903, Debussy moaned that it was one of "the crosses we have to bear, together with such things as epidemics, the three percent devaluation, and the excavations for the Métro."[27] Before

26. Bekker, *The Changing Opera*, 216.
27. *Debussy on Music*, 153.

long the general public, too, lost its interest in works that had formerly been the staples of the operatic repertory. Meyerbeer's four major operas and Halévy's *La Juive* held their own in Germany as late as the 1920s, against the competition of a Verdi revival and the much-performed, recent works of Franz Schreker and Richard Strauss. It was the rise of National Socialism that finally swept them from the German stage, but in Paris this repertory had vanished before the First World War, relatively rapidly and with a few exceptions: *Les Huguenots* was given regularly until 1936, reaching a total of 1,120 performances, and *Guillaume Tell* stayed in the repertory until its 911th performance in June 1932, while *La Juive*, having not been heard since its 544th performance in 1893, was revived for another eighteen in the 1933–34 season. Other operas which had long enjoyed incredible success lost their drawing power by or soon after the turn of the century: *Robert le diable* had had 751 performances at the Opéra when it was dropped in 1893, not to be seen there again until 1985, but did better than *La Muette de Portici*, which vanished from the repertory in 1882 after 489 performances; and neither *L'Africaine*, since its 484th performance in 1902, nor *Le Prophète*, since its 573d in 1912, has been seen at the Opéra again to date (1997). These performance statistics are still exceptional—among other operas, only Donizetti's *La Favorite* (692 performances by 1918) comes anywhere near them,[28] and only Gounod's *Faust* (approximately 880 by 1900, and now approaching 3,000) exceeds them—and they make the suddenness with which these operas vanished from the canon of the Paris Opéra all the more remarkable. It suggests that the wish of a younger generation to shed the inheritance of the past was not the only factor at work and that another was grand opéra's unique modernity, for its time. It had always exploited the very latest technical advances in the theater, and was therefore peculiarly vulnerable to technical advances in other forms of spectacle. Perhaps grand opéra was the first victim of the cinema, but that hypothesis will only be confirmed (or otherwise) by research into cinema's early history from a novel perspective.

In any event, grand opéra's influence was unbroken until the start of the twentieth century, both inside and outside France. It is no exaggeration to say that even those composers who expressed their contempt for the aesthetics of the genre in the most outspoken terms, like Wagner and Richard Strauss, owed an incalculable amount to this first modern form of music theater. So too did the Italian Amilcare Ponchielli, com-

28. For this, and the figures given immediately above, see Wolff, *L'Opéra au Palais Garnier*, 117, 106, 130, 185, 152, 26, 178, 90.

poser of *La Gioconda* with its Hugo-based libretto (1876), and the Brazilian-born Carlos Gomes whose opera *Il Guarany* (1870) was much performed in its day—and so too did Giuseppe Verdi. Verdi's immediate reaction to *Robert le diable* was revealed in the comparable scenes in *Giovanna d'Arco* (1845).[29] There the influence was, admittedly, a matter of superficial detail, but we cannot begin to understand the profound change in Verdi's musico-dramatic vocabulary in the 1860s without considering the effect on him of decisive dramaturgical achievements of grand opéra. The debt is obvious, especially in *Don Carlos* and *Aida*, yet to this day ill-informed critics persist in referring it to Wagner.[30] (For what it's worth, Wagner, too, was influenced by the Parisian models he loathed.) But grand opéra's influence went even deeper in the work of those composers who had no national tradition of their own to look back to, and although the rise of Czech national opera is the only one to have been studied from this angle,[31] it is surely safe to assume that the operas of the Pole Moniuszko, the Hungarian Erkel, and even the Russians Tchaikovsky and Rimsky-Korsakov owe countless traits to the example of grand opéra.

Grand opéra's central significance for the whole of European opera in the nineteenth century was by no means confined to music and dramaturgy. The gradual transformation of works for the lyric theater from ephemera, produced by humble craftsmen for immediate consumption, to inviolable works of art would have been inconceivable without the example given in Paris. The process was begun by Spontini, who, with the monumental stage works he wrote for Paris, often occupying him for many years, raised on behalf of opera the absolute claims that Beethoven made good for the symphony in the same years. Meyerbeer arrived in Paris just as the conditions that permitted a composer to dispose of his operas as he wished were settling into place. He was already experienced, having worked in Italy, where, in the 1830s and '40s, it was still the normal practice to adapt operas at each performance to the current circumstances, now cutting numbers, now inserting ones from other works by the same composer, or composed specially by another person altogether. To say that most operas by Rossini and Donizetti exist in as many versions as there were contemporary productions is scarcely an exaggeration. Composers had no alternative but to abandon

29. See Conati, "Verdi et la culture parisienne," 223.

30. See H. Becker, *Giacomo Meyerbeer in Selbstzeugnissen*, 135.

31. See Ottlová, "Die französische Grand Opéra"; Ottlová and Pospíšil, "Zur Problematik der tschechischen historischen Oper"; Pospíšil, "Dramatická úloha Meyerbeerovy harmonie"; Ottlová and Pospíšil, "Oper und Spektakel im 19. Jahrhundert."

their works to their fate: only if they happened to be present at a later performance could they intervene and do the adapting themselves—but still in accordance with the local circumstances. Copyright law was still a frail craft in most countries, but in France in the 1830s it helped in the establishment of conditions such as those, for example, which enabled Meyerbeer to supervise productions of his work in other theaters besides the Opéra, or to refuse individual theaters the right to perform his work at all, if he did not think them capable of doing his demanding scores justice. Cuts and changes to the musical structure were also, in general, only permitted with the composer's approval.

Although this development represented the decisive step toward the modern conception of an opera as an autonomous work of art, until about 1860 it remained impossible for any composer of grand opéra to produce definitive versions of these large-scale works comparable, say, to the versions of his instrumental works that Beethoven sent to the printer. The conditions under which works were staged at the Paris Opéra combined with the "mosaic" tendency in the aesthetics of the genre to prevent it. It is true that almost all the works in question were published in full score, so that versions authorized by the composers can be said to exist, but a look at the cuts made during the rehearsal period suffices to show that the musical material discarded was often equal in conceptional significance to that which was eventually used. What composers were forced to accept by the limits on how long a performance could be expected to last, without getting the chance to restore the formal balance of an act by a new evaluation of the separate elements, could be illustrated by reference to Act V of *Le Prophète*, already discussed in some detail in an earlier chapter, but every other grand opéra might equally well be cited, up to Verdi's *Don Carlos*, from which the opening chorus—of woodcutters in the forest of Fontainebleau—was cut without anything to replace it. Over and above that, many members of the public regarded it as their right, sanctioned by custom, to influence the final form of an opera by making their reactions known at the first performance: many composers agreed to further cuts after the première, and jettisoned numbers that had not been applauded with as much enthusiasm as expected. Gounod was the first to attempt to forestall this practice by sending the piano-vocal score of *La Reine de Saba* (1862) to the engraver before the first night, but several critics castigated this as an act of unimaginable arrogance.[32]

It remains a remarkable paradox that these works, composed for the

32. See Huebner, *The Operas of Charles Gounod*, 64.

stage of the Paris Opéra, were among the first to embody the modern concept of the inviolacy of the work of art yet at the same time could not overcome the problem of the existence of plural versions with a bewildering stock of variants. This last stage in the progress of opera toward full aesthetic autonomy remained unattainable in France even in the 1860s and '70s; on the contrary, in the case of Gounod's *Faust* and Bizet's *Carmen*, new extremes were reached of "unfinished" works left behind in several versions that continue to cause musicological headaches to this day. Wagner and Verdi, in completely different circumstances, were the first to succeed in marrying the concept of the autonomous work of art to the concrete fact of a text set down in an inviolable form which proved essentially immune to the enthusiasm of managements and interpreters for cutting and adapting. While the nineteenth century lasted, that kind of fidelity to the text could only be achieved if the composer was as adamant and uncompromising as Verdi's countless letters to his publisher, Ricordi, show him to have been. His determination is summed up in a manifesto-like letter to a conductor who was also a friend:

> ... in selling my works to the publisher, I impose the condition of producing them in their entirety, as they were composed, without any concessions whatsoever. This is not affectation on my part, it is my firm conviction. I believe that a musical work, good, bad, or indifferent, should be left alone, as it was conceived.[33]

It had already become the established practice to leave librettos alone, and not make new settings of them, at least if the original setting was a success. This, too, started with Parisian grand opéra. For as long as operas could reckon with a performance career of at most a few years, it was the recognized practice for texts to be revised and reused. Meyerbeer, for instance, in his Italian opera *Semiramide riconosciuta* (1819), was only the latest in a long line of composers to set a libretto that went back to Metastasio. The young Verdi, too, was not surprised to be given a libretto that was nearly thirty years old and had been set several times before, which he set once more as *Un giorno di regno* (1840). As soon as

---

33. "... che io col vendere la proprietà delle mie opere all'Editore, impongo la condizione di farle eseguire integralmente, come furono composte, senza concessione di sorta. – Non è una pretesa la mia, è una convinzione. – Io credo, che un lavoro musicale buono, mediocre, o cattivo, bisogna lasciarlo tal quale è stato ideato." Verdi to Luigi Mancinelli; the letter survives in an undated draft of ca. 1890, published in Petrobelli, "La fedeltà al testo," 234.

a standard, permanent repertory began to be built up, however, such "remakes" became virtually impossible. Rossini had caused an uproar as early as 1816 among some aficionados of opera buffa when he directly challenged the still-popular *Il barbiere di Siviglia* by Paisiello (1782) with his own setting of a libretto based on the play by Beaumarchais—even though he prudently entitled it *Almaviva, ossia L'inutile precauzione*. But while other versions of Victor Hugo's *Hernani* besides the one by Verdi and Piave reached Italian opera houses in the 1830s and '40s,[34] the great majority of works in the grand opéra genre stand alone. Auber's *Muette de Portici* and Rossini's *Guillaume Tell* were both preceded by earlier operas on the same subjects, but there was no question of further ones after the success of these first two historical grands opéras, any more than anyone would have dreamt of composing a second *Huguenots* or *Prophète*. As Eduard Hanslick wrote in 1875: "Two settings of the same libretto cannot survive side by side in today's theater."[35]

The elaborate apparatus of grand opéra meant that each individual composition had an exemplary standing that made any attempt to reuse the libretto simply impractical. There were a very few exceptions: on the one hand Vernoy de Saint-Georges's libretto for Halévy's *Reine de Chypre* (1841), which was subsequently set by several composers in England, Germany, and Italy, although only Donizetti's *Caterina Cornaro* (1844) made any kind of showing, and on the other hand Scribe's libretto for Auber's *Gustave III, ou Le Bal masqué*. But while none of the new settings of *La Reine de Chypre* were really successful, and the earlier Italian settings of the Scribe were quickly forgotten, Verdi's version of the latter, originally planned with the title *Una vendetta in domino*, but eventually executed as simply *Un ballo in maschera* (1859), gradually succeeded in driving Auber's Parisian "original" from the stage.

What made this possible was the creative appropriation of essential attributes of grand opéra which allowed Verdi to exploit the musicodramatic potential of Scribe's text to the full, whereas Auber realized very little of it. However, another equally important factor in the enduring success of this grand opéra in Italian dress was that Verdi learned the lessons of the relative lack of success of *Les Vêpres siciliennes* and radically redirected the characteristics of the grand opéra genre, which were responsible for the crisis of French opera after 1850 in general and for

34. See Engelhardt, "Versioni operistiche dell' *Hernani.*"
35. "[daß] neben einander auf unseren heutigen Bühnen zwei Compositionen desselben Opernbuchs nicht bestehen können"; *Die moderne Oper* (1875), 241.

the dramaturgical inconsistencies of his 1855 opera in particular. In the process, many essential aspects were retained, some having been reevaluated, and in this form, as will be shown in the final chapter of this book, Parisian grand opéra served as a model and exemplar for Italian opera to the end of the century, up until Verdi's own *Aida* and *Otello* and some of the works of Puccini.

❧ 11 ❧

VERDI AND
INTERIOR SPACE

UN BALLO IN MASCHERA

TEXT
Antonio Somma (1809–65)

MUSIC
Giuseppe Verdi (1813–1901)

FIRST PERFORMANCE
Rome, Teatro Apollo, 17 February 1859

PLACE AND DATE OF THE ACTION
Boston, Massachusetts, at the end of the seventeenth century

CHARACTERS
Riccardo, Conte di Warwich, Governor of Boston (tenor); Renato,
a Creole, Riccardo's secretary and Amelia's husband (baritone); Amelia (soprano); Ulrica, a black fortune-teller (contralto); Oscar, a page (soprano);
Silvano, a sailor (bass); Samuel and Tom, Riccardo's enemies (basses)

NOTE
The action of Verdi's opera does not differ substantially
from that of *Gustave III, ou Le Bal masqué*, first performed at the
Académie Royal de Musique in Paris on 27 February 1833, which will be
referred to frequently throughout this chapter. *Gustave III*, with music by
Daniel-François-Esprit Auber and a libretto by Eugène Scribe, takes place in
Stockholm on 15–16 March 1792. One difference between the two operas is
that the action of *Gustave III* is spread over five acts, with Acts I and II corresponding to the two settings of Verdi's Act I, Act III to Verdi's Act II, and
Acts IV and V to the two settings of Verdi's Act III. Another difference is
the cast list. In Auber's opera the principal characters appear as: Gustave
[Gustavus III], King of Sweden; Ankastrom, a Swedish nobleman;

Amélie, Countess Ankastrom; Arvedson, fortune-teller; Oscar, the King's page; Christian, a sailor; Counts de Horn and Warting, conspirators.

SYNOPSIS

ACT I

First setting: a room in the governor's residence, during an audience. The people praise Riccardo, but Samuel, Tom, and their followers whisper together, plotting against him (No. 1a. *Introduzione*, "Posa in pace"). Riccardo is distracted from his official duties by thoughts of Amelia; his love for her is unknown to anyone and he longs to see her again (No. 1b. *[Scena e sortita]*, "S'avanza il Conte!" / "La rivedrà nell'estasi"). Renato tries to warn him of the danger of a conspiracy, but he will hear nothing of it and basks in Renato's assurance of unstinting loyalty (No. 1c. *[Scena e cantabile]*, "Deh come trist appar!" / "Alla vita che t'arride"). The Chief Justice raises the case of a fortune-teller, whom he wishes to have banished, but Oscar mounts a spirited defence of her (No. 1d. *[Scena e ballata]*, "Il primo Giudice" / "Volta la terrea"). On a sudden whim, Riccardo decides to judge the matter for himself and commands everyone present to accompany him to her lodgings, which is greeted as a welcome diversion (No. 1e *[Stretta dell'introduzione]*, "Signori, oggi d'Ulrica").

Second setting: Ulrica's gloomy dwelling. Surrounded by astonished onlookers, the fortune-teller conjures spirits (No. 2. *Invocazione*, "Zitti . . . l'incanto non dèssi turbare . . ."). Riccardo enters, disguised as a fisherman, and hears Ulrica tell Silvano's fortune. She promises him riches, whereupon Riccardo signs an order promoting the sailor to officer and slips it into his pocket with a roll of money. Everyone present is amazed by this instantaneous fulfillment of the prophecy. Amelia's manservant asks for a private consultation for his mistress, and Ulrica sends everyone away, but Riccardo manages to conceal himself. In great despair, Amelia asks for a means of ridding herself of her adulterous feelings for Riccardo; he is overjoyed to learn that she loves him and decides to be there when Amelia goes to pluck a magic herb as Ulrica advises (No. 3. *Scena e terzetto*, "Che v'agita così?" / "Della città all'occaso"). Amelia leaves, all the other visitors return, and now Riccardo introduces himself as a fisherman (No. 4. *Scena e canzone*, "Su, profetessa"). He gives Ulrica his palm to read, and she reacts with horror. She foretells his death by violence, and on his insistence tells him it will be at the hand of a friend. The governor complacently mocks his subjects' superstition and laughs at their consternation (No. 5. *Scena e quintetto*, "Chi voi siate"). He refuses to be disturbed by her further prediction that the assassin will be the next person to take his hand (No. 6. *Scena ed inno—Finale primo*, "Finisci il vaticinio"). Renato enters unexpectedly and quite spontaneously shakes Riccardo by the hand; unwittingly, he also reveals his master's real identity and the people strike up a song in praise of their beloved governor.

ACT II

A lonely place outside Boston. Amelia arrives shortly before midnight, following Ulrica's instructions, but the dreadful place terrifies her (it is the field of executions) and she does not know what to do (No. 7. *Preludio, scena ed aria*, "Ecco l'orrido campo"). Riccardo joins her, declares his undying love, and wins a reciprocal confession from her (No. 8. *Duetto*, "Teco io sto"). The lovers are not alone for long, however: Renato has followed Riccardo, to warn him of an ambush. Amelia veils herself and watches as the two men exchange cloaks and Riccardo commissions her husband to accompany his fair companion back to the city without saying a word to her (No. 9. *Scena e terzetto*, "Ahime! s'appressa alcun"). Riccardo makes himself scarce, Renato confronts his enemies, and a scuffle breaks out, during which Amelia's veil is removed. All the conspirators mock the wife's confusion and the husband's fury. Renato tells Samuel and Tom to come to his house in the morning (No. 10. *Scena, coro e quartetto — Finale secondo*, "Seguitemi").

ACT III

First setting: a study in Renato's house. Only Amelia's plea to be allowed to see their son once more prevents her husband from killing her there and then (No. 11. *Scena ed aria*, "A tal colpa"). Renato's gaze falls on a portrait of Riccardo, and in his hatred of his rival he decides to kill him, instead of his wife (No. 12. *Scena ed aria*, "Alzati"). When Samuel and Tom enter he asks to join their conspiracy, then sends for Amelia and makes her draw the lot that will determine which of them will kill her lover (No. 13. *Congiura, terzetto e quartetto*, "Siam soli"). His own name is drawn, and he exults as Oscar enters with an invitation from Riccardo to attend a masked ball that same evening, thus providing the conspirators with the ideal occasion for the assassination (No. 14. *Scena e quintetto*, "Il messaggio entri").

Second setting: Riccardo's study. After hesitating long, Riccardo makes up his mind to renounce Amelia completely and signs an order sending her and Renato back to England (No. 15a. *Finale terzo — Scena e romanza*, "Forse la soglia attinse"). Ignoring an anonymous warning he goes into the ballroom where the masked ball has already started (No. 15b. *Festa da ballo e coro*, "Ah! dessa è là . . ."). Renato tries to find out from Oscar how Riccardo is dressed but the page refuses to tell him (No. 15c. *Canzone*, "Saper vorreste"). Renato resorts to a lie, and Oscar gives the secret away (No. 15d. *Coro e scena*, "Fervono amori e danze"), while Amelia looks for Riccardo to warn him of the plot. The governor seizes the opportunity to bid her a lengthy farewell, however, and is thus unprotected when Renato strikes him down with his dagger (No. 15e. *Scena e duettino*, "Ah! perché qui"). A clamor for revenge arises, but Riccardo calls his murderer to him, tries to convince him of Amelia's innocence and his own forgiveness, then dies surrounded by the horrified onlookers (No. 15f. *Scena finale*, "Ella è pura").

EDITIONS: The full score published by Ricordi in Milan and the piano-vocal score have been regularly reprinted and are widely available.

RECOMMENDED RECORDING: There are numerous complete recordings of this work. The performance directed by Claudio Abbado, issued in 1981, with Katia Ricciarelli (Amelia), Placido Domingo (Riccardo), Renato Bruson (Renato), Edita Gruberová (Oscar), and Elena Obraztsova (Ulrica), falls short of the ideal in the representation of the lovers, but nevertheless is more successful than other recordings in its satisfactory balance of the multifarious facets and many contrasts of the score.

"Profound Observations"

Verdi regarded his duty to the public as done when he had composed his operas and seen them through rehearsals to their first performances. He left the authorship of aesthetic treatises to those nineteenth-century composers—Schumann, Liszt, Wagner—who felt called upon to write them, yet he was perfectly capable of expressing his aesthetic beliefs with the greatest decisiveness, even if he only did it privately in conversations or correspondence with his friends. Many of the letters and records of conversations have been published since his death, including one letter to which all his biographers grant the status of an artistic confession of faith. He wrote to the aristocratic art-lover Clara Maffei in 1876 about a stage play he had seen in Genoa, a long-forgotten comedy called, interestingly, *Colore del tempo*. Its realistic dramaturgy, aspiring to a precise study of the milieu it depicted, struck him as overexplicitly indebted to French models and, worse, lacking in substance. He summed up his opinion in a general maxim: "To copy truth may be a good thing, but *to invent Truth* is better, much better."[1]

The trenchant opposition of two different aesthetic concepts seems so immediately comprehensible that hardly any Verdi scholar has taken the trouble to look closer at exactly what he meant. Any art-lover would agree with Verdi's objection to overly literal realism, and accept the principle that truth, beauty, and goodness are preferable to the kind of artistic facility that Verdi, for one, compared to photography. It did not escape the composer, admittedly, that truth has as many different meanings as invention, and so he illustrated his apparently paradoxical juxtaposition of contradictory concepts by reference to Shakespeare, whom he called the "Papa" of all dramatists: "It may be that Papa found Falstaff just as he was, but it would have been difficult for him to find a villain as villainous as Iago, and never, never such angels as Cordelia, Imogen, Desdemona, etc. etc. and yet they are so true!"[2] The examples make it perfectly plain what it was that fascinated Verdi about plays that were by then nearly three hundred years old, but the letter itself does not explain what the practical consequences of such a love of Shakespeare might be in the aesthetic circumstances of Verdi's own time, and espe-

1. Letter to Clara Maffei, 20 October 1876; in *Letters of Giuseppe Verdi*, 201.
2. Ibid.

cially in the field of opera—Verdi's late, Shakespearean operas *Otello* and *Falstaff* were still "music of the future" in the most literal sense.

But even if Verdi refrained from explaining how truth could be invented in the circumstances of the late nineteenth century, he had more to say on the subject to Italo Pizzi, fifteen or twenty years later. Once again, he spoke of Shakespeare and described his reactions to reading him: "When one reads Shakespeare's works, he said, with their sharp thoughts and profound observations that spring up so suddenly, one has to cry out: 'But that could well be true! But it is true! It is like that!'"[3] On this occasion, therefore, he explained truth in terms not of Shakespeare's exemplary characterization of individuals but of much more general traits: "sharp thoughts and profound observations" were the essential foundations of successful drama. Compared with such fundamentals, the accumulation of detail in the name of historical precision and the bare bones of verisimilitude in the plot, typical of French grand opéra and likewise of Scribe's libretto for *Les Vêpres siciliennes*, could not fail to seem trivial. But however much he distanced himself from it, Verdi did not discard the aesthetics of French opera of the 1830s in every single point. His manifesto-like pronouncements should not be interpreted as expressions of a subjective aesthetic; rather, with the key concept of "observation" he pinpoints a quality which Jouy, too, in 1826, had identified as central. The difference is that, by the 1890s, the critical spirit of observation is no longer enough, and Verdi wants profundity as well.

Verdi went on to explain to Pizzi what he meant by profundity of observation: "Shakespeare . . . analyses the human mind so acutely and penetrates it so profoundly, that the words he puts into his characters' mouths are essentially human, essentially true, as they should be."[4] That is, the important thing is psychological understanding, rather than philosophy in any narrower sense. But this requirement, too, is related to aesthetic maxims familiar in Paris in the 1830s, as we find in opera and also in the novels of a Stendhal or a Balzac. It is not without a certain surprise that we discover Verdi's paradox about inventing truth in virtually the same words in the work of a novelist regarded as the supreme artistic realist. Balzac wrote in the preface of his novel *La Peau de chagrin* (1831): "Something moral, inexplicable, unheard-of happens with poets, or essentially philosophical writers, which science has difficulty in explaining. . . . They invent what is true, by analogy, or they see the

3. Conati, *Interviews and Encounters*, 341.
4. Ibid.

object that they must describe, whether the object comes to them or they go toward it.["](5)

In view of the startling affinity between Verdi's thinking and the literature produced under the July Monarchy, it becomes easier to understand why the composer's eye fell on texts produced in that same allegedly prosaic atmosphere when he was looking for a suitable subject for an opera commissioned for Naples in 1858, even though his requirements regarding the quality of an opera libretto had grown steadily higher since the beginning of his career. He had complained to Antonio Somma some three years earlier of the monotony of most librettos—including ones he himself had set. He would, he wrote, have refused *Nabucco* or *I due Foscari* if they had been offered to him "nowadays" (1853): "They present some very exciting theatrical moments, but they lack variety."[6] But while a good libretto needed variety, as the foundation for dramatic contrast, it also had to be effective: on that point Verdi was as frank as every other nineteenth-century operatic composer, except Wagner and his adherents, and he used the word "effetto" repeatedly in this letter to Somma, to denote dramatic quality as he understood it. Most grand opéra librettos combine these qualities, and so it seems only logical that, in spite of his ambivalent experience with *Les Vêpres siciliennes*, Verdi eventually chose another text by Scribe, the libretto originally written for Auber's *Gustave III, ou Le Bal masqué* (1833), as the source for his new opera.

It remains hard to understand how a man who was later to identify his central aesthetic requirement as the invention of truth could find anything to attract him in this mechanically constructed intrigue set in a royal court. But as Balzac's reflection of 1831 indicates, Parisian literature of that period was not really so remote from Verdi's conception of a truthfulness that went beyond "photographic" realism. Even if the observations in Scribe's libretto left something to be desired in the way of profundity, the structures of this historical grand opéra were not so closely tied up with the details of circumstance and characterization as to make it impossible to convert the libretto into something that would serve for a work of music theater in which the analysis of human states of mind and emotions was the primary concern. Furthermore, Verdi's

5. "Il se passe, chez les poètes ou chez les écrivains réellement philosophes, un phénomène moral, inexplicable, inouï, dont la science peut difficilement rendre compte . . . Il s'invente le vrai, par analogie, ou voient l'objet à décrire, soit que l'objet vienne à eux, soit qu'ils aillent eux-mêmes vers l'objet." In *La Comédie humaine*, 10:52.

6. Letter to Antonio Somma, 22 April 1853, cited from Budden, *The Operas of Verdi*, 2:361.

commission had come from an Italian opera house: he was on his home ground, and under no obligation to respect any mere librettist, as he had been with *Les Vêpres siciliennes*. He set to work to refashion the libretto of *Gustave III* to suit himself. He wrote to the secretary of the management of the Naples opera house on 19 September 1857: "At present I'm scaling down a French drama, *Gustavo III di Svezia*, libretto by Scribe, performed at the Opéra twenty years ago. It's vast and grandiose; it's beautiful; but it too has conventional things in it like all operas—something I've always disliked and now find intolerable."[7] A month later he sent Naples a draft which he regarded as sufficient foundation for the librettist to go to work on, even before he had consulted the latter.

> Here is the *Gustavo* libretto to show the censors. It's not in verse, but it's more than a sketch: the drama is there in full, with all the scenes, dialogue, speeches, everything, everything, except the rhymes. I had to do this to gain time. The poet is writing, and in a few days I shall be able to start. The libretto is very effective: there are new and powerful situations in it: all the spectacle you could want. It has come out better than I hoped.[8]

Verdi certainly scaled down Scribe's wordy libretto drastically. The prose version he sent to Naples appears not to have survived, but we have the versification by Antonio Somma, every detail of which was scrutinized by the composer, and its brevity is the first thing one notices. Although none of the dramatic situations were omitted, Somma does in less than 900 lines what took Scribe almost 1500 in the printed version. Admittedly Scribe put in a great deal of historical detail: he gave his work the subtitle "opéra historique," and his object was to put on stage the infatuation with detail that characterized the historical novels of the day.[9] In the second and third scenes of the first act King Gustavus is shown as, successively, kindly citizen-king benevolently accepting petitions from his subjects, patron of the arts conversing with a sculptor and a painter, statesman consulted by the ministers of war and justice, eager

---

7. Letter to Vincenzo Torelli, 19 September 1857; ibid., 363.

8. "Ecco il libretto del Gustavo da presentarsi alla censura, non è in poesia, ma non è degli schizzi ordinari: il dramma è disteso completamente con tutte le scene, dialoghi, parlate, tutto, tutto, salvo la rima—Ho dovuto far questo per guadagnar tempo—Il poeta scrive, e da quì a qualche giorno, io pure incomincierò—Il libretto è di grande effetto: vi sono situazioni nuove, e potenti: spettacolo finchè vorrete. È riuscito migliore di quanto io speravo." Letter to Vincenzo Torelli, 20 October 1857, cited in [Arpino], *Difesa del Maestro*, 46–47.

9. See Walter, "'A la recherche de l'histoire perdue.'"

host looking over the list brought by his page Oscar of the guests at the next day's masked ball, and finally author of an opera-ballet. The climax of this lengthy exposition is the opulently staged rehearsal of this royal creation, the first of the work's ballets, for which Auber wrote no less than twelve minutes of music, and Scribe an exhaustive specification of its pantomimic content. The libretto's documentary footnotes are nowhere more numerous than here.

Verdi's version retains only two of these elements: immediately after the opening chorus, taken almost word for word from the French original, the popular ruler receives a few petitions then turns his attention to the only thing that engages his interest, the preparations for the ball. All Scribe's other details were cut, by Verdi or by Somma, who wrote on his own initiative: "The war minister seemed to me quite pointless, so I've taken him out."[10] But the Naples censor, to whom the opera—like all stage-works—was submitted, did even more to rid the libretto of all elements that did not impinge directly on the private intrigue at the heart of the work. Attempts on the life of a monarch "by the Grace of God" ranked with criticism of the Christian religion itself as dramatic themes on which every censor frowned. Scribe had got away with it in Paris in 1833 simply because theatrical censorship was abolished for a time in the wake of the July Revolution, but he would have had to make substantial modifications only a few years later. There had been two earlier Italian versions of the opera, Gabussi's *Clemenza di Valois* (1841) and Mercadante's *Il reggente* (1843), in which the precaution was taken of transferring the action to medieval France and sixteenth-century Scotland respectively, in addition to other alterations.[11] Against this background, Verdi was guilty of a certain naivete if he really believed that such a subject would pass the censor unscathed, especially in the most reactionary of the Italian states, the Kingdom of the Two Sicilies.

The officials charged with protecting His Majesty's subjects against the representation of moral turpitude in the kingdom's theaters took exception not only to the assassination of a crowned head but also to the adulterous relationship between the king and his friend's wife, and much else besides. It was only a matter of time before Verdi realized that he would never get his work staged in Naples unless he changed not merely a few external details but the entire work to suit the requirements of the diligent censors. Some aspects of the affair had to be ar-

10. Letter to Verdi, 28 October 1857; cited from Budden, *The Operas of Verdi*, 2:366.

11. See D'Amico, "Il ballo in maschera prima di Verdi," 1297–98 (1969–70 ed., 549–51).

gued in a court of law, when Verdi and the theater management sued each other, and there are detailed records illustrating the difficulties composers and librettists had to struggle with in nineteenth-century Italy, if they were not prepared to exercise self-censorship from the start.[12] At all events, Verdi drew the consequences, and in the spring of 1858 took soundings as to the possibility of a production in Rome instead. The Pope still ruled Rome, and the censors there were in general scarcely more liberal than their colleagues in Naples; on the other hand they had allowed a version of Scribe's text by the then successful playwright Gherardi del Testa to be performed as a play only a few months previously. Verdi had to abandon his hopes of retaining the original setting at the Swedish court, but at the cost of making substantial concessions on the matter of the place he managed to preserve unchanged all the motives of the drama and above all the temporal location in modern history. He was able to inform Somma on 8 July 1858 that the Roman censors "will permit the subject and the situations, etc., etc., but would like the scene removed from Europe. What would you say to North America at the time of the English domination? If not America, somewhere else; the Caucasus perhaps?"[13]

To the present-day spectator, the idea of transferring the entire action from Stockholm to Boston seems rather farfetched, but not to Verdi, who was au courant with the Parisian theater of his day. One of Scribe's most successful plays was *La Bohémienne, ou L'Amérique en 1775* (1829) which was also set in the state capital of Massachusetts, and although there is no firm evidence that Verdi knew this play, by then nearly thirty years old, it seems very likely that he did, especially as his alternative suggestion alludes to something else by Scribe, a scenario offered him for his first Paris opera in 1852, with the title *Les Circassiens, ou Le Prisonnier du Caucase*.[14] Somma, and later the papal censors, consented to Verdi's solution to the problem, and so the Swedish King Gustavus became Riccardo conte di Warwich (or Richard, Earl of Warwick), British colonial governor in Boston, while the Swedish aristocrats of Scribe's original, most of whom derived from real historical figures, were transformed into fictional characters known only by first names. At least Boston is a port, like Stockholm, so Verdi was able to retain the "maritime" coloration of some scenes, and even if he respected the Italian censors' sensibilities by setting the action back from a date as recent

12. See Luzio, *Carteggi Verdiani*, 1:469–86; Budden, *The Operas of Verdi*, 2:367–72.

13. Letter to Antonio Somma, 8 July 1858, cited from Budden, *The Operas of Verdi*, 2:372.

14. See Porter, *"Les Vêpres Siciliennes:* New letters," 97.

as 1792 to a century earlier, he was left with an ambience in which a drama as modern in its feeling as this was not altogether incongruous. An actual advantage of the North American location was that the fortune-teller Ulrica could be presented as black, underlining her position as a social outsider.

The outcome of all these adjustments was that the libretto was purged of everything locating the action in a particular place at a particular moment in history. Scribe and Auber's opera had been praised in 1833, more than anything else, for the authentic reconstruction on the stage of actual places in Stockholm,[15] but in this new version time and place were at best secondary. Furthermore, even though the composer and his librettist had at first undertaken this process of generalizing a very specific story with great reluctance, in the end it created precisely the conditions that allowed Verdi to remodel Scribe's purportedly historically exact characters in such a way that any traits contingent on the time or the place completely disappeared behind the vivid depiction of their universal human properties. Only the abandoning of lavish local color made it possible for the composer to develop psychological nuances of a kind that were close, at least, to the profound observation of human behavior he later advocated.

Thus the two characters described as "conspirators" in Scribe's cast list are simply called "enemies of the count" in Verdi's, but no effort is made to explain the causes or history of this enmity. Samuel and Tom fall a long way short of the absolute evil of an Iago, admittedly, but they represent an ideal type of villain such as is scarcely ever encountered in real life. Precisely because his text provides virtually no motivation for their conspiracy, Verdi can express a far profounder level of human cunning and malice through these characters than Scribe could in his equivalents. The case is similar with regard to Riccardo, torn between duty and passion—reiterating one of the themes of *Les Vêpres siciliennes*, and to Renato, turning from blind loyalty toward his superior to furious jealousy. It was no accident that from the first Verdi contemplated giving the work a title beginning with an indefinite article. After discarding his original choice, *Una vendetta in domino*, in favor of something closer to Scribe's secondary title with its definite article, *Le bal masqué*, he and Somma still held to the form *Un ballo in maschera*, and so the unique masked ball of Auber's opera—unique in both its splendor and its gory end—became a masked ball that could have taken place anywhere, not necessarily in a particular large city such as Stockholm or Paris.

15. See above, chapter 4.

This makes it all the harder to understand why, in recent years, more and more productions "restore" the opera to its supposed "original" Swedish setting and date, with alterations to the libretto and elaborate sets[16]—in spite of the fact that it has become possible in the twentieth century, as never before, to stage operas and plays in Any Place, at Any Time. In this particular instance, however, the late twentieth century has actually gone back to a step before the original Italian audiences, who appreciated very well the general, "bourgeois" aspects of a story which, in the words of Filippo Filippi, reviewing the première in 1859, "could take place quite as well in the family of an ordinary citizen as in a royal palace, and at any latitude whatsoever."[17] Such conservational undertakings certainly have nothing to do with Verdi's dramaturgy and its foundations in "profound observations," for in this work, to cite the definitive judgment of Julian Budden, he "contrived through a variety of nuances unimaginable to Auber . . . to turn an ingenious but mechanical plot into a gripping parable of the human condition."[18]

CONCISION

It was this transformation that enabled Verdi to overcome the crisis confronting grand opéra in its last years of life. In the circumstances of the late 1850s, it was essential to strip off the great weight of detail for detail's sake characteristic of grand opéra, so that even a work whose subject had already been treated in a grand opéra could be conceived "in one piece," and not assembled like mosaic: the feature Verdi deplored in most French historical operas, as was discussed in chapter 7. Nothing could demonstrate more emphatically the necessity for Verdi's radical treatment of Scribe's historical libretto than the fact that *Un ballo in maschera* is the only opera conceived in the wake of grand opéra to have held the international stage from its first performances up to the present day. It owes its survival not only to the shedding of all the inessential historical details but also to the complementary striving for concision that was a mark of Verdi's dramaturgy from the very start of his career. His correspondence shows that he was fanatical in his pursuit of the utmost verbal economy his librettists could achieve. As early as 1846, when Piave was working on *Macbeth*, Verdi hammered his message home in capital letters: "ALWAYS BEAR IT IN MIND TO USE FEW

16. See also Roncaglia, "Riccardo o Gustavo III?"

17. "può stare tanto nella famiglia del cittadino, come nella reggia, in qualsivoglia latitudine"; "*Un ballo in maschera* . . . di Verdi," 131 (1862, p. ii).

18. *The Operas of Verdi,* 2:376.

WORDS . . . FEW WORDS . . . FEW FEW BUT SIGNIFICANT,"
repeating it a few lines later, and again toward the end of the letter,
lest Piave should forget: "CONCISE STYLE! . . . FEW WORDS . . .
understood?"[19] And he returned to the theme when Piave was writing
Rigoletto: "Lines in the theater are always long-winded if they are dispensable: a concept expressed in two lines is long-winded whenever it
can be expressed in just one."[20]

He was equally uncompromising in his determination to achieve the
utmost concision in *Un ballo in maschera.* This of course had nothing to
do with the short-breathed musical forms favored by Auber in *La Muette
de Portici,* which were obviously indebted to the opéra comique; Verdi
wanted brevity while keeping the creative benefits of the differentiated
dramatic forms of Meyerbeerian grand opéra. Thus where Scribe and
Auber give Gustave a ternary aria for his first entrance, Verdi and
Somma retain only the content of its contrasting middle section, in an
aside in which Riccardo dreams of his beloved Amelia. The conventional closed number becomes an unusually brief arioso, eight lines long
with no textual repetition, before opening out into a scene with chorus,
and Verdi takes less than two minutes altogether for both this first
"close-up" of Riccardo and the chorus accompanying the exit of the assembled court. The second tenor solo, at the beginning of the scene in
Riccardo's study in the last act, undergoes similar treatment. Scribe and
Auber provide a conventional Italian aria in several sections: an introductory *scena,* followed by a slow movement, then the sound of music
from the ballroom triggering Gustave's decision to renounce Amélie in
a cabaletta. Verdi reduces this to an *adagio romanza* in which Riccardo
contemplates the loss of Amelia ("Ma se m'è forza perderti"), and although the audience, familiar with the conventions of Italian opera,
must interpret the dance music played by the offstage banda as the *tempo
di mezzo* preceding a concluding cabaletta, the composer disappoints the
expectation:[21] Riccardo's further musings are expressed in a parlante
passage accompanied by the banda alone and a very brief reminiscence

19. "ABBIA SEMPRE IN MENTE DI DIR POCHE PAROLE . . . POCHE PA-
ROLE . . . POCHE POCHE MA SIGNIFICANTI"; "STILE CONCISO! . . . POCHE
PAROLE . . . hai capito?" Letter to Piave, 22 September 1846, cited in Abbiati, *Giuseppe
Verdi,* 1:644–45.

20. "Sono sempre lunghi quei versi in teatro che si potevano risparmiare: un concetto
espresso in due versi è lungo qualora si poteva esprimere con uno solo"; letter to Piave,
22 October 1850, ibid., 2:71.

21. See Kerman, "Verdi's use of recurring themes," 502, n. 9.

of his first solo in Act I, and thus they lead directly into the final scene, the masked ball.

In condensing conventional aria forms in this way, Verdi was following his own personal dramaturgical convictions, developed over two decades of experience in the opera house, but he was also following in detail the innovative techniques introduced into French opera by Meyerbeer twenty years earlier. Like Raoul in *Les Huguenots* and Jean in *Le Prophète*, Verdi's Riccardo is allowed only very brief solos that highlight his irresolute character. And just as Meyerbeer does, Verdi gives his protagonist something to sing in his first scene that at once sets him apart: where the melodic style and instrumentation of Raoul's *romance* draw on the means whereby troubadours are conventionally presented in French opera, and where Jean's *pastorale* emphasizes his rustic naivete, Verdi chooses the remote key of F-sharp major, which we have already seen used by both Rossini and Meyerbeer in its enharmonic equivalent G-flat major to characterize lovers intoxicated by their passion,[22] to enclose Riccardo's ecstatic vision within a frame so that it seems like an image from a dream.

It is the same with all the other characters in *Un ballo in maschera:* for the first time, Verdi rigorously denies himself arias in the conventional Italian forms. Renato's two arias—which have no direct precedents in Auber's opera, incidentally—are single-movement structures: that in Act I an *andante* attempting to warn Riccardo of a plot against his life ("Alla vita che t'arride"), which is only one element in the very long *Introduzione*, and that in Act III a lyrical *andante sostenuto* brooding on the destruction of his marriage ("Eri tu che macchiavi quell'anima"), which again functions as a slow movement not followed by a *tempo di mezzo* and cabaletta. In this respect "Eri tu" is similar to Amelia's second solo, her one-movement aria in Act III, pleading to see her son before she dies ("Morrò – ma prima in grazia"); the text draws on the corresponding cavatina in *Gustave III*, but that forms part of quite a long duet.

Verdi went a step further with Amelia's first aria, at the beginning of Act II. After repeated demands for changes to the text he eventually arrived at a multilayered form of exceptional modernity which has as little in common with the corresponding number in Auber's opera as with the abbreviation of Italian forms he practises elsewhere. Once again, Scribe and Auber give their prima donna an aria in the customary

22. See above, 102, 195.

Italian form: a very short slow movement springing from the realization that her hands are trembling ("Et lorsque d'une main tremblante") is followed by a generously proportioned *tempo di mezzo* of agitato character, before a cabaletta in which Amélie controls her fear and the call of honor overrides her forbidden passion ("Eh quoi! ma main balance"). Verdi determined from the first that he would have none of this affirmation of marital fidelity, so that Amelia is still undecided when Riccardo arrives—greatly enhancing the dramatic tension in their meeting. In addition, Verdi made Somma organize the text in stanzas, and would not be satisfied until he had three that he could set in such a way that the listener is scarcely aware of the stanzaic character of this highly individualized aria.[23] It begins with an Andante, setting two six-line stanzas in which Amelia mourns the necessity of suppressing her love, and adhering closely to Scribe's slow movement. The third stanza is as regular in its form—six rhymed, decasyllabic lines—as the first two, but embodies exactly the dramatic intensification that Verdi failed to find in one of Somma's earlier versions of which he complained: "There's no fire, there's no agitation, there's no confusion (and it should be extreme in this respect). . . . You must . . . find something different . . . something with the devil riding it: the situation demands it."[24]

The extreme confusion Verdi wanted is in generous supply in the version he finally set. The third stanza begins with scraps of unfinished sentences expressing Amelia's agitation and fear:

> AMELIA
> Mezzanotte! . . . Ah! che veggio? una testa
> Di sotterra si leva . . . e sospira!
> (*Un ballo in maschera*, Atto II, scena 1)

꒓ ꒓ ꒓

AMELIA: Midnight! . . . Ah! What's that? A head rising out of the ground . . . and breathing!

To match the text, Verdi composed these scraps as ultradramatic recitative, making plentiful use of the anapestic "figure of death" from *Les Vêpres siciliennes*, and returning to the musical structure of the first two stanzas, with solo English horn accompaniment, only for the last two lines, in which Amelia prays to God to have mercy on her. As a result, in

---

23. See Ross, "Amelias Auftrittsarie im *Maskenball*," especially pp. 130–34.

24. "Non c'è foco, non c'è agitazione, non c'è disordine (e dovrebbe essere estremo in questo punto) . . . Bisognerebbe . . . trovare qualche cosa di diverso, . . . qualche cosa che avesse il diavolo addosso: la situazione lo vuole." Letter to Somma, 26 November 1857, cited in Pascolato, *"Re Lear" e "Ballo in maschera,"* 84–85.

treating an extremely simple verse form with musical resources directly comparable to the dramatic recitative in the love duet in Act IV of *Les Huguenots*, he created a propulsive dynamism that all earlier Italian opera had achieved only by recourse to the much more expansive and elaborate procedure of gradual intensification from *scena*, through slow movement and *tempo di mezzo*, to cabaletta. It was his uncompromising insistence on concision alone that enabled him to individualize this aria as much as he does, not only in the fragmentation working against the closed form but also in the unique structure targeted on the specific situation on the stage.[25] This is the "absolutely new and original craftsmanship" that the Milan critic Filippo Filippi praised in this "masterpiece of musical expression."[26]

The breach with Italian operatic conventions was definitive, but the astonishing thing is that it was based on recourse to the convention of strophic form characteristic of so many arias in French opera. There, admittedly, the verse was normally treated by composers as a succession of wholly identical couplets without any attempt at musico-dramatic intensification. Auber's *Gustave III* contains examples of the form, which was obviously influenced by opéra comique, and it says much for Verdi's superior skill in exploiting various traditions that he set the couplets provided by Scribe for the fortune-teller's entrance aria in a very free variation form. As a result, although the first stanza, in C minor, and the second, in C major, have features in common, an uncanny atmosphere unfolds gradually as the *Invocazione* proceeds, creating a sense that something unique and irreversible is afoot. Elsewhere, Verdi observes the regular succession of largely identical couplets only when the characters involved radiate—or at least reflect—an unmistakably French elegance and lightness: that is, in Oscar's two solos (derived almost word for word from Scribe's text), "Volta la terrea" in the Act I *Introduzione*, and the canzone "Saper vorreste" in the Act III finale, and in the canzone "Di' tu se fedele" sung by Riccardo when disguised as a fisherman in the second setting of Act I.

Even these "closed" forms, however, given their rhythmically "fugitive" configuration and the fact that they are integrated into longer scenes, serve to create deceptive moments of repose in the inexorable, urgent, forward drive of the dramaturgy. All three of them end in ways that demand a quickening of the underlying pulse, reinforced by direc-

25. See Ross, "Amelias Auftrittsarie im *Maskenball*," 145.
26. "originalità assolutamente nuova nella fattura"; "capolavoro di espressione musicale"; "*Un ballo in maschera* . . . di Verdi," 140 (1862, p. iv).

tions such as *con slancio* or *poco più mosso*, so that the dynamic forward propulsion of the passage of time which informs the entire opera is apparent in the musical detail as well as in the idiosyncratic melding of Italian and French formal traditions. This is especially clear in Riccardo's first solo, in the Act I *Introduzione*. The unusual brevity of this number has already been discussed, but that is only one instance of the lack of every single element that might convey to the listener the sense of security usual in a traditional entrance aria. The wide-ranging vocal melody singles out, in the first bar, the harmonically least stable notes in the chosen tonality—the third and the seventh, while the restless pizzicato chords and complementary eighth-note motion of the string-quartet accompaniment set the whole in constant movement. In fact, although Riccardo's situation has a superficial similarity to the nervous tension of Act I of *Les Huguenots*, he entirely lacks the emotional certainty felt by Raoul in his entrance aria: Raoul tells of an encounter with his beloved that he has already experienced; Riccardo can only dream of one that may, possibly, come to pass.

Riccardo is so unsure of realizing his dream that he even speaks of himself in the third person, standing for his anima, but what, above all else, makes it absolutely clear that he is projecting his yearning into an uncertain future is the musical execution and especially the harmonic organization of the entire opening scene. The F-sharp major of Riccardo's solo refers back to the first notes of the opera's orchestral prelude, although there, like the dominant beginning of the opening chorus, they only made sense in the light of a B major that was yet to be established. The prelude, the opening chorus as the court waits for the governor to wake ("Posa in pace, a' bei sogni ristora"), and the driving staccato as the conspirators sing "the time for action is yet to come" ("l'ora d'oprar non è") all anticipate some future moment. The tension thus built up is released—partly, at least—only at the ecstatic climax of Act II when Amelia repeats her declaration that she loves Riccardo, "t'amo." (Filippo Filippi declared that it was one of those moments in opera "that contain a whole love story.")[27] The first time she utters this "theatrical word" it is accompanied by the heartfelt melody of the cellos and the tremolando of the other strings, like the love duet in Act IV of *Les Huguenots* or the love scene in the second part of Berlioz's *Roméo et Juliette*; but the second time the whole orchestra comes in, *tutta forza*, with chords relating to B major and E major, above a pedal B, prolonged over seven bars. This injection of a propulsive dynamism into the musi-

---

27. "di quei canti che contengono tutta una storia d'amore"; ibid., 141 (1862, p. iv).

cal drama radically altered the physiognomy of vocal solos and the construction of the entire opera alike, and it justified the critic who compared Verdi's principle of dramaturgical concision directly to the
breathtaking contemporary advances in engineering and communications: "Verdi . . . has divined the need of the moment: he has imported
steam and the *telegraph* into music. Speed and concision: behold the
grand formula of Verdi's impetuous genius."[28]

"Speed and concision" were also the properties enabling Verdi to accommodate the most extreme contrasts into a dramaturgy which nonetheless fully warranted Filippi's praise of its unity.[29] The prelude and
entire opening scene are governed by the extreme contrast between Riccardo's absorption in amorous reverie and the sinister plotting of his
enemies: a direct application of one of the defining characteristics of
grand opéra, and advocated by Jouy. However, Verdi subordinates the
successive stages of the exposition and the simultaneous "dissolve" of
the chorus of homage, Samuel and Tom's staccato figuration, and Riccardo's legato melody to the relentless dynamism of a tension that he
intends to sustain to the end of the third act. By this means he avoids
the risk of disintegration into individual elements that obliged Auber
to desist from introducing musico-dramatic contrast right at the start,
for fear of endangering the stability of his uncommonly cautious opening chorus.[30] It is the overriding desire for concision, too, that makes
Verdi dispense with authentic (colonial North American?) local color
throughout this series of scenes; a more sophisticated use of this often
overused term is justified, however, because the colors he does apply are
so characterful in themselves. Thus a critic attending the first performance in Venice, in 1861, wrote: "The most beautiful thing about the
Introduzione, the whole opera indeed, is the so-called local color, the
perfect appropriateness of modes and styles, which gives the idea and
situation of the drama the greatest possible degree of relief and informs
its character."[31] If the metaphor of local color originated in painting,

28. "Verdi . . . ha indovinato il bisogno del momento: egli ha portato il *vapore*, ed il
telegrafo nella musica. Sollecitudine, e concisione; ecco la gran formula del genio impe-
tuoso di Verdi." Basevi, "Le riforme," 1. I would like to express my warm thanks to Marco
Capra of the Centro Internazionale di Ricerca sui Periodici Musicali (Parma) for drawing
my attention to this article, and for his willing assistance in my research into other contemporary reports and reviews in the Italian press.

29. "la più completa unità di getto"; "*Un ballo in maschera* . . . di Verdi," 117 (1862,
p. ii).

30. See Walter, "A la recherche de l'histoire perdue."

31. "Il più bello della introduzione, come pure di tutta l'opera, è quella tinta, come la
chiaman, locale, quella perfetta convenienza di modi e di stile, che dà all'idea ed alla situa-

that of relief comes from sculpture, the art of three dimensions. Once again, the mixture of aesthetic categories shows how much Verdi's dramaturgical concision, in the balanced organization of color and contrast, owes to a new sensibility for changing perceptions of time and space.

MASQUERADE

Scribe's plot provided *Un Ballo in maschera* with lurid coloration, and plentiful chiaroscuro as Filippi noted,[32] but Verdi's treatment of them, as of other aspects of the libretto, differs from the compliance evinced by many Italian and some French scores of the nineteenth century. For although he applies very precise colors in painting numerous shorter numbers and the strophic structures discussed above, yet every time he evokes a specific sphere something quotation-like and alien hovers about it, in contrast to Auber's naive score. This is least in evidence in Ulrica's invocation of the devil ("Re dell'abbisso, affrettati"), where the tutti's fortissimo dissonant chords, the sustained, tritonal tension between the cellos' pedal C and the trumpets' ultra-low F sharp, and the repeated variants of the "figure of death" in the timpani establish vividly the fortune-teller's macabre aura. But even in this context Verdi left the underlying ambivalence of this outcast untouched. Scribe, a rationalist, did not clear up the matter of whether his Arvedson simply stages grandiose deceptions in her atmospheric premises and claims the credit for the self-fulfilling prophecies of her oracular pronouncements, or genuinely sees visions revealing the power of fate to which the other characters are helplessly subject. Here, as in *Le Prophète*, a distinctive feature of Scribe's plot construction is the fact that most of the characters' actions are doubly motivated and thus overdetermined. Arvedson's prediction that the common sailor Christian will be promoted to officer, and its immediate fulfillment, can be interpeted as breathtaking evidence of the fortune-teller's supernatural powers, but a skeptic might well say that Arvedson recognizes the King—a prominent public figure— among her visitors and gambles on his vanity and complicity; it is her prophecy, and nothing else, that inspires him to promote the sailor. For Gustave the incident is only a frivolous game with his subjects' superstitions, and the words of the aside in which he justifies his interven-

---

zione del dramma tutto il possibil risalto e la caratterizza"; Tommaso Locatelli, in *La gazzetta di Venezia*, 27 December 1861; cited in Della Corte, "Saggio bibliografico," 1184.
    32. "tutti gli effetti di chiaroscuro"; "*Un ballo in maschera* . . . di Verdi," 92 (1862, p. i).

tion were deliberately chosen to express his belief that he alone is in command of the situation: in Scribe's French text he says "I want her to have spoken the truth" ("Je veux qu'elle ait dit vrai"); in the Italian version this becomes Riccardo's succinct "She must not lie" ("Mentire non de'").

Verdi cannot have had the slightest reason to resolve this ambivalence inherited from the French opera, for the absence of clear-cut distinctions between the grotesque and the sublime, between laughable superstition and deadly earnest fate, gave him another opportunity to tackle a problem that had been with him since *Macbeth* (1847), making him ask one librettist, in 1849, for "this mixture of comedy and terror, in the manner of Shakespeare."[33] After the gradual decline of the eighteenth-century tradition of comedy, and under the influence of Victor Hugo's anticlassical theory of drama, the rigorous distinction between comic and tragic opera was no more than an arbitrary relic by about 1850. The circumstances positively demanded innovations, and Verdi, Berlioz, and Meyerbeer were all looking for new ways to overcome the old demarcations; even grand opéra experimented with "comic" elements, despite its descent from tragédie lyrique. One of the most striking examples is Meyerbeer's first work for Paris, *Robert le diable*, originally planned as an opéra comique before circumstances led to its staging at the Grand Opéra.

Le Prophète, too, has ensembles that are expressly termed "bouffe" in the score, but although they originate in situations viewed from a comedic perspective, Meyerbeer's idiosyncratic idea of the bouffonesque is remote from the stereotyped situation comedy of older musical theater—as remote as the attitude of a "modern" society, having lost the ability to think of itself, in everyday life, as an actor in constantly changing role play, was from the quite differently founded understanding of public life under the ancien régime.[34] In grand opéra "comic" figures are no longer fixed, unalterable stereotypes but "characters" endowed with highly individualized traits that determine their roles in the drama. For that reason the primary aim of numbers like the caricaturized *Duo bouffe* for the yokelish Raimbaud and the satanic Bertram in Act III of *Robert le diable*, or the *Trio bouffe* in Act III of *Le Prophète*, is to present grotesque or detestable figures to whom the audience feels comfortably superior, rather than hold up a mirror to the public in depicting all-too-

33. "questo misto di comico e di terribile (a uso Shakespeare)"; letter to Cammarano, 24 March 1849, cited in Abbiati, *Giuseppe Verdi*, 2:4.
34. See Sennett, *The Fall of Public Man*, passim.

human properties. In the latter instance, Oberthal's opportunistic denial of his beliefs, since it is the only way he can think of to save his neck, and the Anabaptists' sadistic pleasure in their prisoner's stammering helplessness can only be enjoyed, like Wagner's merciless mockery of Alberich and Beckmesser, by an audience possessing the appropriate measure of Schadenfreude. Such scenes crystallize the isolated audience-member's ill-will toward all those whom he is inclined to regard as social inferiors and who have not learned, as he has, to suppress their emotions in daily life.[35] Ready as the nineteenth century's passive operagoers were to be touched by the distress of members of the "weaker" sex, even to empathize with frailty betrayed in a context of passionate intimacy, they had nothing but contempt for men who could not manage to conceal their fears and feelings in the discussion of "business."

Verdi expressed a very similar idea of the bouffonesque in the character of Melitone in *La forza del destino* and some scenes in *Falstaff*, but at the same time he also pursued totally different ways of combining comic and tragic elements. The "fusion of genres" in *Rigoletto* (1851),[36] which cost him immense effort, is already fundamentally different from the hardhearted comedy of Meyerbeer and Wagner. It is true that he situates the court jester in the buffo realm (while promoting him to title-hero over the head of the Duke of Mantua, in this transposition of Victor Hugo's *Le Roi s'amuse* from the French court), but in the musico-dramatic realization he goes further even than Hugo in delineating the personal feelings and fears of a highly individualized character, whose professional routines and private happiness diverge beyond any hope of reconciliation. Rigoletto's mask of foolery has nothing in common with the stereotyped roles played by the characters in commedia dell'arte and its successors, but has become vitally necessary to him in his role in society. Being a loving, caring father is the only identity he values, but to preserve it he must conceal it from a hostile world. The cruel irony of the opera, which begins in the brilliant tone of an opera buffa after a foreboding prelude, develops from Rigoletto's failure to understand that no one can successfully split his identity into wholly separate public and private realms without any overlapping or frayed edges. He refuses to recognize that with his merciless mockery he has long since turned from perpetrator to victim, and in the end, when the tragedy has run its

---

35. Ibid., 206.
36. See Weiss, "Verdi and the fusion of genres," 151–56.

course, he is left unable to live a life without the mask, for no one will take him seriously in so unaccustomed a role.

The ironic mixture of the "comic" tone of a brilliant divertissement with the dreadful certainty that all honest human feelings are doomed to be destroyed in such an ambience is taken even further in *Un ballo in maschera* than in *Rigoletto*, for now masks are worn not only by the characters who have a professional familiarity with the art of disguise—the jester in *Rigoletto*, the page in *Ballo*—but by everyone else as well, in order to be able to communicate among themselves at all. The attitude is not confined to the particular circumstances of a masked ball (at which Verdi had already tried his hand in Act III of *Les Vêpres siciliennes*); rather the whole opera is a masquerade, and neither the fortune-teller nor the amorous governor, neither his friend Renato nor the conspirators provide an exception to this style of alienated personal communication. Only Amelia, when talking to one other person—the fortune-teller, Riccardo at their midnight meeting—finds a way of expressing her innermost feelings, yet gratefully hides behind her veil as soon as another person approaches.

The characters' predilection for wearing masks reaches a first high point in Act I, in the sequence in Ulrica's dwelling. In the corresponding episode in *Gustave III*, only the King appears in disguise, but Verdi's stage direction calls for the entire court—page, gentlemen, officials, Samuel, Tom, and the other conspirators—to accompany him, "wearing whimsical disguises" *(travestiti bizzarramente)*. Though it might appear a purely superficial detail, the composer insisted on it against all opposition. The Neapolitan censors wanted only Riccardo to be disguised, and as a hunter, but he refused to give in: "This change from fisherman to huntsman ruins a piece which was perhaps one of the most important in the opera. Why should he alone be disguised and not the others? All of them should be: it's necessary to the action."[37] Necessary it was, but primarily to Verdi's purpose of displaying the feigned indifference of blasé characters with a cutting irony. Anyone who constantly wears a mask to disguise his own feelings from himself and to prevent the words of others touching him, is no longer capable of recognizing threats against his own life, and it is expressly this suicidal ignorance that Verdi illustrates in the ensemble following Ulrica's prophecy that Riccardo will die at a murderer's hand.

37. "Questo cambiamento di *pescator* in *cacciator* ruina un pezzo che forse era dei più importanti nell'opera. Perché egli solo doveva essere travestito e gli altri no? Tutti devono

Once again, the tense dramatic situation and the extreme contrast contained in it were first conceived by Scribe, but here too Verdi went a decisive step farther than the French original. Auber composed a highly conventional ensemble, in G minor, for Oscar and the chorus to express their instantaneous shock and horror at the dread thought, which chills their individual souls ("O funeste pensée dont mon âme est glacée!"). The overriding mood is set by the word "funeste," to which Gustave's insouciant amusement ("Quelle plaisanterie! Oh! la bonne folie!") is at best a textual contrast. In Verdi's version, however, the first reaction of Oscar and the chorus is disbelief, as they whisper questioningly together ("E tal fia dunque il fato? Ch'ei cade assassinato?"), but it is the governor himself, with his mocking question "Is this a jest, or madness?" ("È scherzo od è follia?"), who starts the ensemble off with a graceful, elegant, dance tune. Only a few steps from the abyss, Riccardo exhibits an attitude reminiscent of the orgy in the finale of *Le Prophète*, except that there the dancers on the volcano's rim, heedless of the reality of their situation, are psychologically unstable, lost souls in the last hours of a failed social revolution, whereas Verdi represents the entirely "normal" behavior of a modern society too sophisticated to take any human utterance at face value. In fact, members of the audience without foreknowledge are no more able than the chorus to decide whether what they are witnessing should be interpreted as a joke, or madness, or even the alarming truth. And it is as if Verdi wanted to underline the fundamental ambiguity of this most precisely balanced drama when he returned to the question in his second-act finale, where, in the opinion of the French critic Gustave Héquet, "a master's hand has contrived the most gripping effects from the blend of tragic and comic styles."[38] Singing once again in B-flat major and $\frac{4}{4}$ time, at a point in the act which corresponds formally to the first-act chorus, the conspirators sum up the situation with cynical amusement in lines that Somma rhymed in accordance with Verdi's express wish.[39] These lines not only contain vastly more ambivalence and irony than Scribe's sarcasm at the same point ("La rencontre est jolie!") but also embody Verdi's determination

---

esserlo: ciò è necessario all'azione." Verdi's note in the synoptic copies of the two versions of the libretto, cited in Abbiati, *Giuseppe Verdi*, 2:479.

38. "une main magistrale a su tirer de la combinaison du style tragique et du style bouffe les effets les plus saisissants"; *L'Illustration*, 19 January 1861; cited in Gara, "Il cammino dell'opera," 711.

39. See Verdi's letter to Somma, 31(?) December 1857, cited in Pascolato, *"Re Lear" e "Ballo in maschera,"* 88–89; and Somma's answer of early January 1858, cited in Abbiati, *Giuseppe Verdi*, 2:464–65.

to mix the musical genres: "Look, the tragedy has turned into comedy" ("Ve', la tragedia mutò in commedia").

An action swaying on the narrow line between comedy and tragedy can tip over into tragedy with equal ease, however: at the end of the sequence in Renato's study in Act III, when Amelia expresses her utter despair in an aside ("Ed io medesma, io misera"), she takes up the buffa-like melody with which Oscar has already established this quintet's tone of sparkling pleasure ("Di che fulgor, che musiche")—only the minor third of her B-flat minor contrasts with Oscar's B-flat major to reveal something of her true feelings. The masking of all emotions would thus seem to have become a normal feature of interpersonal communications, but additionally people in the governor of Boston's circle are as strongly affected by ennui as those close to his colleague in Palermo in *Les Vêpres siciliennes,* leaving them no other means of assuaging their unsatisfied sensual desires but playing a frivolous game with their own identities.

This is yet another instance where the governor gives the lead, in presenting himself to the fortune-teller disguised as a fisherman. Once again it took Verdi's sure instinct for the musico-dramatic possibilities in Scribe's text to make this situation one of the high points of the score. Where Auber was satisfied to use a quadrille-like $\frac{2}{4}$ rhythm in his setting of Scribe's "sailor's song," without any musical allusion to maritime atmosphere, Verdi's swaying $\frac{6}{8}$ immediately establishes a tone which every member of the audience would associate with the familiar, traditional barcarole, and thus recognize as a symbol for the rocking of a boat. This particular coloration could be interpreted, indeed, as an example of local color in the narrower sense, given the fact that the opera was originally to have been performed in Naples: a critic at the first performance in Rome saw a resemblance to Bari sailors' songs, while Filippi in Milan discerned the stamp of popular Neapolitan songs;[40] but Verdi is playing with the convention, alienating the barcarole tone in the very act of invoking it.

Unlike the couplets with which Auber and Scribe's king presents himself in a new pose, Riccardo's canzone in Ulrica's hut is actually the tenor's first substantial solo in a closed form—his entrance "number" having been so drastically reduced—and it is significant that he is in disguise when he sings it. The principal character's falsification of his

40. "una certa somiglianza con i canti dei marinari baresi": Nicola Cecchi, in *Il filodrammatico. Giornale scientifico, letterario, artistico, teatrale,* 10 March 1859; cited in Gara, "Il cammino dell'opera," 125. "l'impronta dei canti popolari napoletani": Filippi, *"Un ballo in maschera . . .* di Verdi," 134 (1862, p. iii).

own identity is matched in the musical execution by the way Verdi gives the vocal line unmistakable similarities with real sailors' songs, yet also begins it in a melancholy A-flat minor, and has the melody repeatedly fade to *ppp*, so that it comes over as a nostalgic reminiscence of a long-lost world—as Filippi commented.[41]

There are further aspects to the song which are puzzlingly inconsistent with its naive barcarole rhythm. Before two bars are completed, the vocal line abandons the key in which it opened for the remote harmony of B-double-flat major; in terms of the tonal organization of the entire scene in Ulrica's house, B-double-flat major might be referred to its enharmonic equivalent, A major, which is selected by the common people for their song of homage in the act finale, after they have seen through the governor's disguise. But Riccardo departs from the simple harmonies appropriate to a humble fisherman at many other points. At the beginning of his second six-line stanza, by means of a dissonant minor ninth above a dominant-seventh chord, he creates six times in succession a variant of the chord which is heard so often in the course of the whole work that there is a case for regarding it as an element of the opera's characteristic *tinta*. The same interval has already been heard, in the form of a major ninth, in the scene in the governor's residence: it provides the melodic climax of Riccardo's cavatina, "La rivedrà nell'estasi," and recurs in Oscar's canzone "Volta la terrea" on the words "*È con Lu*cifero," and again in the ensemble directly following: first on Oscar's "*L'indovina ne dice di belle*," the sparkling character of which is underlined by the shrill octave-doubling on the piccolo, then above all on Riccardo's exclamation "alle *tre*." The major ninth also features in Riccardo's canzone, again repeated several times, as a means of modulating to the fourfold "no" in the first stanza, and the words "non entra terror" in the second. Finally, we do not have to wait until Amelia and Riccardo make their first mutual confession of love in the second act, when the music bursting in fortissimo on a dominant $^7_9$ chord marks the climax of the sentimental intrigue,[42] for proof of the overriding musico-dramatic significance of this harmonic motif. It is proved already in the first act, in Oscar's "E *tal* fia dunque il fato?" in the ensemble following Ulrica's prophecy—yet it entirely escaped notice in two wide-ranging theoretical studies of the harmonic and motivic structures of Verdi's opera.[43]

41. "Al primo udirla sembra una lontana reminiscenza"; Filippi (see note 40).
42. Already discussed with reference to the love duet in *Les Huguenots;* see above, 194.
43. See Levarie, "A pitch cell in Verdi's *Un ballo in maschera*"; Parker and Brown, "Motivic and tonal interaction."

That Riccardo is not wholly at ease in his disguise is suggested not only by such alienating features in the harmonies but also by the rhythms of this unusual canzone. True, the orchestra keeps up a perfectly steady pulse in the first stanza, with staccato articulation of just the first, third, fourth, and sixth eighth-notes of each line, but Riccardo soon diverges from the rocking, barcarole accompaniment with the dotted notes on the words "Con lacere vele." The accompaniment adopts the repetitions of the vocal line, which are unusually insistent and introduce the ninth chord mentioned above; the cellos' syncopation, in particular, emphasizes that such heavy rhythms inflict damage on conventional forms. The barcarole rhythm is abandoned altogether in the third six-line group, "Sollecita esplora," as the staccato falls equally on all six eighth notes. Now Riccardo's hectic parlando reveals him to belong to the brilliant sphere of the court, otherwise embodied by Oscar, even before the acceleration (*con slancio*) mentioned earlier in connection with Oscar's couplets hurries the music toward the concluding cadence. The dynamic propulsion of the passage of time, revealed even in the rhythmic details of Riccardo's canzone, is an indication that behind his affectation of serenity, the world-weary governor is prey to the same breathless unease that also pervades the banquet in Act I of *Les Huguenots*, where the rhythmic structures are again highly unusual.

In the end, in this ambience of disguise, hedonism, and nervous tension, where even Riccardo's mask slips, no one knows the truth about his own feelings any more. Only Oscar, a "beardless page, lively, feather-brained, who, being only a boy, takes the liberty to joke and gibe at everyone"—as the character is described in the written submission presented in Verdi's case against the Naples censors[44]—feels free to express emotions in a manner that is not infected by the general air of frenzy, simply because his boyish disinterest sets him outside the intrigue, so that he can be said to be above the drama. Although most of the time he attracts attention by his pert comments and brilliant staccato melodies, like his predecessors in *Gustave III* and, especially, *Les Huguenots*, he is the only character to whom Verdi gives a lyrical cantilena in the ensemble following Riccardo's canzone. Here, where even Ulrica succumbs to the outbreak of short-breathed, fragmented melodic scraps affecting everyone else on stage, it is the youngest character, evidently not yet wholly blunted in his sensibilities, for all the frivolity that goes with his job, who dominates the ensemble musically.

44. "paggio imberbe, di carattere vivo, spensierato, che nella sua qualità di ragazzo si permette di scherzare e lanciare frizzi a tutti"; [Arpino], *Difesa del Maestro*, 19.

But the occasions in *Un ballo in maschera* when Verdi drops his game with his characters' disguises remain rare exceptions. Even the gruesome scene in which the conspirators decide to draw lots to determine who shall assassinate Riccardo—described in Verdi's legal submission as "the most powerful, original, and culminating situation in the drama"[45]—is not altogether devoid of the spirit of masquerade pervading the whole opera. The lot is drawn in almost wordless pantomime, in a passage that takes the musical art of transforming melodramatic qualities to the ultimate height, framed within a trio in which the three conspirators vow to be revenged. But rather as Renato never questions that it is his duty to conform to social convention and repair his honor in the manner expected of a wronged husband, so too the music of this oath lacks the elemental force of the comparable scenes in *Guillaume Tell* and *Les Huguenots*, and comes over as dutiful and conventional. True, Verdi lends warlike resolution to the plotters' singing by means of a dotted rhythm that seems to be inspired by those two models, and even more by the duet "Suoni la tromba, intrepido" in Bellini's *Puritani*, while the doubling of the vocal parts by a solo trumpet and other winds is another reliable technique borrowed from earlier opera composers. But the oaths taken by Rossini's and Bellini's conspirators form the crowning conclusions to grandiose act finales, and the martial melody "Pour cette cause sainte" in Act IV of Meyerbeer's opera provides an expansive opening and closure to the "benediction of the swords," whereas the climax to which Verdi builds with repeated dominant chords played by the entire orchestra is realized in an oath of disconcerting brevity: as an eight-bar period presented twice, the music of the oath is just twice the length of the series of dominant chords ushering it in. Even though the sixteen bars end with a fortissimo, after which every listener familiar with this type of regularly constructed melody will be awaiting a continuation, the expectation is confounded, both here and in the repeat at the end of the scene, when it is actually reduced to merely thirteen bars.

But that is not all. Verdi "heaps up the expressive resources and superficial effects unrestrainedly," in the view of Eduard Hanslick, who dismissed the trio as "perhaps the worst number in the opera."[46] Verdi gives the singers an accompaniment of spread chords on double-basses and harp, with the harp arpeggios, expressly required to be "dry and

45. "la più potente, originale e culminante situazione del dramma"; ibid., 22.
46. "[Verdi] häuft maßlos die Ausdrucksmittel und äußerliche Effecte"; "vielleicht die schlechteste Nummer der Oper"; *Die moderne Oper*, 240.

loud" *(secche e forti)*, lending the whole an ostentatiously declamatory character. It did not occur to Hanslick that this underlining of externals is exactly what the dramatic situation requires. As comparison with Scribe's original libretto reminds us, Verdi's three characters entirely lack the political ideals invoked by virtually all other operatic conspirators: that is, they are common murderers, who cannot sustain the pose they adopt in these different circumstances. Blind hatred is what fuels Renato and his accomplices as they rush headlong toward their goal, and correspondingly Verdi does not make the slightest effort to remind the audience of the unbelievable confirmation of Ulrica's prophecy when Renato's name is drawn to be Riccardo's killer; the power of fate, introduced into opera only thirty years earlier, is now so well assimilated and taken so much for granted that the events of this third act only serve to prolong the suspense before the expected, inevitable blow falls.

In rigorously drawing every action in the opera into his dramaturgy of masquerade, Verdi drew the consequences of the fact that his characters' identities break down into political convictions and sentimental desires, as was already apparent in the irreconcilable contradictions of *Les Vêpres siciliennes*. There was only one recourse for characters in opera, as there was for people in the world outside who had assimilated the conventions of polite society in the 1840s and '50s, and that was to assume a mask, as a rough and ready means of hiding the gulf yawning between incompatible emotions. The ironic epigraph, purporting to come from the Proverbs of Solomon, with which the satirist Taxile Delord prefaced a contribution to Grandville's *Un autre monde* (1844), would transfer easily to Verdi's opera: "Put on your mask and I will tell you who you are."[47]

Verdi, however, took his ironic game with disguises a lot farther than Delord, or his fellow satirist Grandville (both wrote for the knowing readership of *Le Charivari*), when he integrated the catastrophe itself into the masquerade. Insofar as Riccardo's murder can be said to develop as a consequence of the masked ball, it was the first time anyone had fully exploited the possibilities offered by the plot-motive of a conspiracy played out against the background of a festive social occasion, although Jouy had discovered the idea in Schiller's *Die Verschwörung des Fiesko* (1783), and had recommended it to composers of opera as long ago as 1826.[48] In fact, Scribe's *Gustave III* libretto clearly owed much to

47. "Mets ton masque et je te dirai qui tu es"; Delord, "Caractères travestis et travestissements de caractère," in Grandville, *Un autre Monde*, 41 (see above, p. 232 and the caption to fig. 14).

48. *Essai*, 279 (1987 ed., 89).

Schiller's play, which was highly regarded in Paris in the early nine-teenth century,[49] but Scribe went a step further than Schiller in the corresponding scene, or Casimir Delavigne's adaptation of it in *Marino Faliero* (1829),[50] in that the conversations between characters take place in the ballroom, during dances, rather than in an anteroom. Verdi, in turn, took this idea to its logical conclusion and made the music heard from—and later in—the ballroom underlie the structure of the whole of his third act, whereas Auber gave so much independent life to the purely orchestral ballroom music that it lasts for over twenty minutes, after which the final scene, the climax of the drama, appears tacked on and weakly motivated. The almost photographic reproduction of contemporary Parisian costume balls in Auber's immense ball scene amounted to the "normality of everyday occurrence" for his audience.[51] Verdi far surpasses that, integrating the sentimental intrigue into the masked ball so successfully that the masquerade stands for the state of the society itself. It is a masterpiece of romantic irony, and "that certain je ne sais quoi of the strange and the bizarre which is always produced on the stage by *dominos* and *masks*," as Verdi believed,[52] is an essential in-gredient.

THE CHORUS AS SCENERY

In deciding to make the masquerading of un-self-confident principals the dramaturgical foundation of his opera, Verdi brought to a head an unsolved problem endemic to grand opéra in its later years: the relation-ship of chorus and soloists. For while individuals could stalk the stage in various disguises very effectively, it was difficult, if not impossible, to bring off the same trick in choral movements. Verdi himself had learned by experience that a choral number attempting to depict an entire group all wearing the same disguise has an inbuilt tendency toward the ludi-crous. The Chorus of Cutthroats (*Coro di sicari*) in Act II of his *Macbeth*, replacing the two murderers of Shakespeare's Act III, scene 3, was very successful when the opera was first produced in Italy, but began to at-tract ever more stringent criticism as the conventions of Italian opera of the 1830s and '40s began to be forgotten. Hanslick found that it

49. See Eggli, *Schiller et le romantisme français*, 1:449.
50. Ibid., 641.
51. Chabot, "Ballet in the operas of Eugène Scribe," 10.
52. "quel certo non so che di strano e di bizzarro che va sempre prodotto sulla scena dal *dominò* e dalla *maschera*"; Verdi's annotation in the synoptic copy of the two versions of the libretto, cited in Abbiati, *Giuseppe Verdi*, 2:482.

"makes an exceedingly hilarious impression with its mysterious pianissimos and staccatos."[53] The convention of secret asides, dear to Parisian
mélodrame, received its death-blow from Offenbach, in the parody in
Act II of his opéra bouffe *Les Brigands* (1869), when the titular brigands,
disguised as waiters and cooks, intone in unison, over and over again,
"let us dissimulate" ("dissimulons").

It is hardly surprising therefore that, although the chorus comes on
stage in four of the five settings in *Un ballo in maschera*, its significance,
both musical and dramatic, is reduced to an extent inconceivable to anyone accustomed to French grand opéra. The chorus does not even have
a closed musical number to itself until the last sequence in the opera,
the masked ball, and then the *Coro generale* "Fervono amori e danze"
only serves as part of the scene setting for the peripeteia of the private
drama of the principals. In every other scene the chorus's role is confined to commenting on events, doubling the utterances of individual
principals, or raising hearty cheers in their support—in other words, it
retreats to the subordinate status from which Rossini's French operas
had emancipated it thirty years earlier.

The change is already outlined in Scribe's text, in fact, which is not
constructed around large-scale choral scenes in the way that most of his
other grand opéra librettos are, but Auber nevertheless gave the choral
ensembles plenty of space: his first-act finale, for example, at the point
in the action when the king has decided to see the fortune-teller for
himself, turns the spotlight on the chorus in an expansive movement
giving the signal for general pleasure at the prospect of a diverting ex-
cursion. The corresponding scene in Verdi's opera, on the other hand,
opens with a solo for Riccardo, dismissing his official duties at the prospect of pleasure ("Ogni cura si doni al diletto"), and there are another
49 bars for soloists before the chorus is allowed to enter, and then only
to acclaim the governor.

The historical setting, nurtured by Scribe with such loving detail, is
not a central feature in *Un ballo in maschera*: human passions are, and
date and place could be changed without affecting their treatment. The
chorus, however, had acquired its special status in grand opéra as an
active participant in historical and political events, and even a composer
less concerned with concision than Verdi would have been obliged to
diminish it. The crisis in historical opera on the grand scale, already
looming in *Le Prophète* and growing more acute in *Les Vêpres siciliennes*,

53. "[es] macht mit seinen geheimnißvollen Pianissimos und Staccatos einen überaus
erheiternden Eindruck"; *Die moderne Oper*, 224.

forced Meyerbeer and Verdi to drastically rethink the nature of the historico-political aspects of their subjects. The outcome was that the crowd scenes, dominated by large choruses, which had been one of the defining characteristics of grand opéra in the 1830s, were already less central to *Le Prophète*, retreated further in *L'Africaine*, and finally lost any reason for existing.

This did not prevent Verdi, in *Un ballo in maschera*, from using the technique of simultaneous contrast that Meyerbeer had developed precisely in big choral crowd scenes. The discussion of this topic in chapter 5, with particular reference to *Les Huguenots*, also mentioned the first-act finale of *Ballo*.[54] The song there in homage to Riccardo ("O figlio d'Inghilterra") was praised by the Italian critics for having "all the attributes of solemn music, all the character of patriotic hymns,"[55] yet it seems to owe more to countless French models than to those Italian choruses by Verdi himself which his contemporaries associated with the Risorgimento. In some respects it obviously anticipates "hymns" in *Aida*: the A major tonality and stately melodic style resemble the battle hymn led by the king of Egypt in Act I ("Su! del Nilo al sacro lido"), while the verse meter and rhythm relate to those of the triumphal chorus "Gloria all'Egitto, ad Iside" in Act II. Verdi's later comment on them—that "they both sound a little like the Marseillaise"[56]—could equally well apply to "O figlio d'Inghilterra," with the proviso that by the time he said it (1883) he was thinking of the French national anthem's solemn dignity rather than the martial, revolutionary élan of what was written as the War Song of the Army of the Rhine—the association it still had for Auber in *La Muette de Portici*.

Patriotic anthems of this kind had long ceased to express any specific political sentiments, or to prepare for any action: they were part of the scenery, a foil for the private, emotional intrigue. Consequently their musical language and structure were no longer such as to demonstrate any united group's enormous potential for action but only to illustrate its prescribed function. Viewed thus, it makes sense that Verdi did not involve the chorus in the conspirators' martial song in the first setting of Act III of *Un ballo in maschera*—not even in the reprise. It would have happened as a matter of course in earlier operatic scenes of that nature, and Verdi's music even seems to have been tailored for it, but in fact the resolution expressed by the trio (even if the singers are only striking

54. See above, 203–6.
55. "tutti gli andamenti della musica solenne, tutto il carattere dei canti patriottici"; Filippi, "*Un ballo in maschera . . . di Verdi*," 135 (1862, p. iv).
56. Letter to Ghislanzoni, 22 August 1870, in *Letters of Giuseppe Verdi*, 160.

poses) refers to future action too directly for the chorus, now a wholly passive body, to have any plausible reason to join in.

In the patriotic choruses in *Aida* and "O figlio d'Inghilterra," by contrast, Verdi maintained the balance between hymnlike foundations and expressive cantilena. It was only in the special conditions of writing one more opera for Paris that he was ready for a radical further adjustment of the chorus's role, which was not palpably manifested in *Ballo* although it was already adumbrated in Scribe's "masked ball" libretto. In the first act of *Don Carlos* (1867), the news that Elisabeth is to be the bride of King Philip is greeted by a chorus of rejoicing at the prospect of peace ("O chants de fête"), while the princess and Carlos, who have only just met, fallen in love, and declared it to each other, react with horror to the realization that their moment of ecstasy will have no future. The content and music of the chorus has a function comparable to scenery, like all other songs of homage, but Verdi gives back to it a mobility that had seemingly disappeared. The crowd is off stage to begin with, singing from the wings, and draws closer gradually, with the menace of a mob in a different context, until it emerges onto the stage in a procession of loyal well-wishers, giving Elisabeth no alternative but to enter the carriage that will carry her away to her unloved bridegroom. Years later Verdi still recalled this effect of "far away, far away, far away" and how well it was done at the Opéra.[57] He did not end the scene with the C-major choral fortissimo, however, as the conventions of grand opéra would have indicated (and as an edition published in Germany in the 1940s, and quite frequently performed, directed),[58] but had the crowd and their sound withdraw again into the wings. The end of the act, therefore, does not represent visually the contrast between a large, colorfully rejoicing crowd, and silently despairing lovers—as seen in countless works of the grand opéra genre—but concentrates on the anguish and isolation of Carlos, lamenting the destiny that has destroyed his dreams as the last choral pianissimo steals from the wings.

There could hardly be a more convincing demonstration of the fact that it was absolutely necessary for the chorus to retire to the wings— literally into the scenery—when the dramaturgical conception placed the isolation of despairing individuals centerstage. They despair because although they nurture dreams of the sheltered privacy of an interior space they are involved in the public sphere and are torn by the conflict

57. "quell'effetto di *lontano lontano lontano* (che si fa così bene all'Opéra)"; letter to Ricordi, 21 October 1883, cited in Cella and Petrobelli, *Giuseppe Verdi–Giulio Ricordi*, 60.

58. I refer to the edition of the five-act version of *Don Carlos* prepared by Julius Kapp and Kurt Soldan, with text in German, published by Peters in Leipzig in 1944.

of duty and desire. The scene is therefore equally convincing as a demonstration that a public role and fear of the sheer numbers of an anonymous crowd are still as merciless in destroying hopes and dreams as they were in causing the victims' deaths in earlier works like *Les Huguenots* or *La Juive*.

THE LONGING FOR INTERIOR SPACE

The wholesale withdrawal from Meyerbeerian historical tragedy into the interior world of private, personal tragedies is a decisive event in French operatic history in the second half of the nineteenth century. The only five-act historical operas written in this period were epigonal. The characteristics of the new form of French opera, *drame lyrique*, as it came to be called later, were listed in chapter 10.[59] Anonymous big-city crowds and spectacular political events ceased to hold the stage, and were replaced by private individuals in quieter milieus. Novels rather than plays became far more common as sources of subject matter, especially those of a sentimental cast: it was not pure coincidence that two of the most successful examples of the new musical theater, Ambroise Thomas's *Mignon* (1866) and Massenet's *Werther* (1892), derive from novels by Goethe in which the influence of Empfindsamkeit is especially strong.

The retreat into the sheltered, intimate sphere of private life was not confined to the external development of French opera, but was also manifested in some of the later works in the grand opéra genre—the first-act finale of Verdi's *Don Carlos* is one example. This was a response by librettists and composers to the fact that the mosaic-like dramaturgy of grand opéra, constantly accommodating new effects and technical innovations, had become almost unmanageable, but it was also a reaction observable in all areas of life at this period. Just as grand opéra became ever more complicated, so breathtaking technological progress and other phenomena (not all rationally explicable) that accompanied the uncontrolled expansion of the capitalist economic order contributed to a general sense of vulnerability in a dangerous world. Thirty years earlier, in comparable circumstances, dramatists and novelists had invoked the power of fate to explain the inexplicable, but that was worn out by over-use and had lost the power to dispel such fears. The logical next step was to banish thoughts of what one was powerless to explain from one's conscious mind. The wage-earner confined his participation

59. See above, 401; see also Dahlhaus, *Nineteenth-Century Music*, 276ff.

in public life to the absolute minimum necessary, left political decisions to "professional" deputies elected for that purpose, and concentrated his efforts on defending his own private space against harmful outside influences, for it seemed to be the only sphere where he could do as he wanted. The authoritarian paterfamilias, concerned for the moral and material well-being of his children, became a stereotype character of novels and plays, short stories and full-length operas.

Verdi thus presented a highly contemporary social issue when he placed authoritarian father-figures centerstage with positively obsessive frequency, but he never included all the other dramatic motives and interpersonal confrontations in the same framework of family relationships. The younger composers who wrote drames lyriques, the next generation who composed verismo opera, and above all most authors of successful, popular novels did just that. It became one of the fundamental premises of popular fiction that the more opaque the external world, the clearer and simpler the inner world must be, and that all problems and social conflicts became accessible and amenable when they were reduced to the scale of that inner world.[60] Verdi, however, underlined the unreality of belief in the "safe" or "wholesome" nuclear family by his merciless depiction of fathers like Rigoletto, the older Germont in *La traviata*, and Montfort in *Les Vêpres siciliennes*, their complete failure in the role of protector, and their responsibility for destroying the lives of others. But if Verdi's theme in these operas was the characters' gradual disintegration as they failed to cope with the irreconcilable contradictions of their private and public roles, in the closing scenes of *Un ballo in maschera*—one of his few operas not to focus on a father's role— he turned his searchlight onto a character's unreal longing for a sheltered, interior space, and depicted the utter futility of such longing in a dramatic and musical image of rare penetration.

For the second setting of Act III, the curtain rises on Riccardo's study where he is alone, struggling to bring himself to a state of readiness to renounce Amelia. Eventually he signs an order sending her husband Renato back to England, as the means to put an ocean between her and himself. No sooner has he resolved on separation without bidding farewell ("senza un addio"), however, than the slow movement of his aria finds him dreaming of seeing her again for one last time, and as the sound of music reaches him from the ballroom, where the masked ball is beginning, he realizes just how easy it would be. Moral duty still has the upper hand, however, and he resolutely dismisses the possibility.

60. See Ueding, *Glanzvolles Elend*, 33.

Then Oscar enters, bearing an anonymous letter in which the governor is warned not to attend the ball, because an attempt will be made to assassinate him there. This alarming news makes the self-regarding Riccardo change his mind instantly. What determines his reaction is not concern for his safety—which would be reasonable—but for his reputation. Nobody shall say of him that fear for his own life stopped him performing a public duty. Thrusting aside all precautions, he decides to ignore a danger which has been obvious for a long time.

Up until this moment the libretto has followed the fifth act of Scribe's text, with minor exceptions, of which Riccardo's vow, "senza un addio," is especially characteristic of Verdi's dramatic vocabulary. But whereas Scribe leaves the explanation for Gustave's reckless behavior at that, and sends him and Oscar off to the ballroom together, in Verdi's version the page withdraws but Riccardo, "left alone, exclaims ardently 'Yes, I shall see you again, Amelia'" (*rimasto solo, vivamente prorompe* "Sì, rivederti, Amelia"). The decision of Verdi's protagonist to abide by the prescribed forms of behavior has been short-lived; he states his true reason for attending the ball after all in a few bars of parlando against the unchanging background of the dance music, and he can scarcely control his feelings. Doubling the tempo, he "enthusiastically" (*con entusiasmo*) takes up the soaring melody with which he was introduced in his short solo in Act I when, as now, the prospect of seeing Amelia dominated his thoughts. This unexpected "cut" inserted in the musical structure of the ball scene simultaneously relativizes the reason Riccardo has given for his change of mind. His reference to what people might say about him is shown to be merely an excuse masking his real concern, and the ardent outburst that follows reveals his true motives quite plainly.

With this divergence from Scribe's text, the audience's attention has been focused once again both on Riccardo's subconscious emotions and on the last meeting between the two lovers, to which everything has been leading. Now the scene changes: Riccardo's study is replaced by a splendidly decorated and brilliantly lit ballroom, and the hitherto off-stage dance music is brought on stage as the pit orchestra joins in fortissimo with the wind-players in the upstage banda who have been playing outside the study. A chorus of anonymous guests sing of their pleasure at being there before Verdi lets certain individuals identify themselves. While the unvarying $\frac{2}{4}$ dance music continues as background, various snapshots show first the three conspirators talking together and then Renato attempting to find out from Oscar which of the masked figures is his intended victim. The page gives him an ironic non-answer in the canzone "Saper vorreste" before the movement of the crowd separates them. The chorus resumes its singing, until the dance brings Renato and Oscar face to face again, and this time the page incautiously lifts his master's incognito.

Only then does Verdi single the two really central characters out from the crowd of masked dancers. Riccardo comes down to the front of the stage, "thoughtfully," as the detailed production book specifies (see fig. 23).[61] The composer enhances this close-up by changing the orchestration, the key, and the volume of the music. All operatic conventions go by the board as Riccardo's move is accompanied neither by the banda nor the pit orchestra but by a third ensemble, a twelve-man string orchestra placed on- and downstage, which softly plays a melody in $\frac{3}{4}$ time. While all the other people attending the ball were introduced against the background of the "galop"[62] played by the banda, this unusual and exquisite layer of sound is reserved for Riccardo. It is only after he recognizes Amelia, who follows him disguised in a white domino, that the pit orchestra adds its voice to the repetitive rhythms of the onstage ensemble—but represented by only five string soloists, as if the dotted accompanimental figures of the twelve players onstage were still not fragile enough. Verdi sustains this reduction of the orchestral apparatus to the softest possible sound—unprecedented in itself—throughout almost the whole of the duettino: only at its climax, when Riccardo interprets Amelia's insistent warnings of assassination as renewed declarations of love, do first a solo bassoon and a flute, then oboe, clarinet, and all the strings, enter from the pit. But even this relative augmentation of orchestral expression remains restrained, the dynamic marking, written more than once, is **ppp**, and in the last part of this scene, which lasts almost four minutes, the accompaniment is handed back to the five solo strings in the pit and the twelve on the stage. This unreal aural texture is brought to an abrupt end when Renato stabs Riccardo, and at that moment Verdi interrupts the musical flow by such radical means that the violins do not even reach the tonic from the leading note.

Verdi's decision to add a second onstage ensemble to the traditional banda might be interpreted simply as a means of enhancing the variety and splendor of the great ball scene. That is how most exegetes read it, not forgetting to refer to the similar cases in *Rigoletto* and Mozart's *Don*

61. "Riccardo discende pensieroso la scena fin quasi a bocca d'opera"; Cencetti, *Disposizione scenica*, 35.

62. Verdi's note in the synoptic copy of the two versions of the libretto, cited in Abbiati, *Giuseppe Verdi*, 2:482.

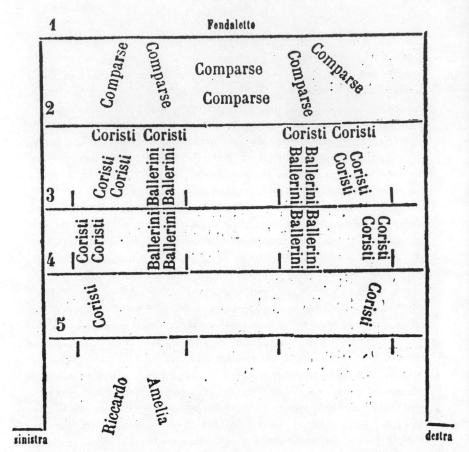

23 Verdi's *Ballo in maschera* is the first Italian opera for which a *disposizione scenica*, or production book, was printed as a record of the essential details of the first production, to provide a model for future stage directors. As with the French *livrets de la mise-en-scène* produced since the 1830s in connection with works first performed at the Paris Opéra, the *Ballo* production book, by Giuseppe Cencetti, contains a succession of diagrams of the stage illustrating the positions of the performers. This example, from page 35, shows clearly how Riccardo and Amelia come downstage to separate themselves from the throng of dancers, chorus, and supers during the masked ball in the last act.

Giovanni. It is true that the second ensemble also plays a stereotypical accompaniment of dance music, repeating over and over again a rhythmic pattern that some recent commentaries call a mazurka, but which Verdi himself, leaving no room for misunderstanding, called a "Valtz."[63] A crucial detail suggests that there is more to the stage orchestra than this, in any case. When all the ball guests have gathered round the dying Riccardo, exclaiming in shock and outrage at the treacherous attack ("Ah! morte, infamia sul traditor!"), the string ensemble strikes up once more with its waltz—clearly not as an invitation to dance, this time, but as introduction to Riccardo's last monologue, as he calls Renato, his rival and murderer, to his side.

This is the stroke that reveals the meaning of Verdi's musical disposition. Riccardo has tried from the first to ignore both the political realities and the limitations his official position places on his personal freedom of movement, and even now, with death staring him in the face, he wants to reduce all hostility to a matter of private, intimate relationships, and to gloss over the conspiracy's many causes with a personal exchange of words. With his last breath, he persists in regarding himself as a lover and a private individual, not a prominent public person whose life might well be threatened by conspiracy. The only appropriate setting for him to indulge such an attitude is the private room where he actually resolves to renounce Amelia: a "sumptuous cabinet," where "a table with writing materials" provides all he needs to sign the order for Renato's transfer. But once Riccardo decides to go to the ball, this sheltered den is swept away and replaced by a magnificent public space, the ballroom. In Scribe's libretto, the change of scene is expected to occupy some time, during which the king is to be imagined leaving the room in the court opera house where he delivers his monologue in this version, and traversing an adjoining gallery to reach the ballroom. The libretto of *Un ballo in maschera* has a surprise at this point, however. Riccardo's cabinet is not enclosed by walls but by huge curtains, which now are simply drawn aside, revealing "a vast and richly appointed ballroom splendidly illuminated and set out for a celebration" *(S'aprono i cortinaggi. Vasta e ricca sala da ballo, splendidamente illuminata e parata a festa).*

Thus it is not the agile protagonist but the apparently stable set that moves. Of course Verdi's decision to have the set changed in this way was partly a consequence of his decision to through-compose the transi-

---

63. See on the one hand Budden, *The Operas of Verdi*, 2:418, and on the other Verdi's note in the synoptic copy of the two versions of the libretto, cited in Abbiati, *Giuseppe Verdi*, 2:482.

tion from Riccardo's solo to the ball without a break in the music. But there must be more than this essentially technical consideration to the particular form taken by this instant change of scene, for many alternative ways of changing the set in the audience's sight existed, and if the way it was done in the first production had been of no particular consequence, Verdi would not have had any reason to prescribe it in the *Disposizione scenica*. It takes a closer scrutiny of Riccardo's behavior to reveal the wider implications of this striking set change. The discovery that the apparently intimate, secluded study is simultaneously, as it were, part of the huge ballroom shows every member of the audience the illusory nature of Riccardo's obsessive belief that he can be a public figure, the governor of a colony, yet enjoy a private life sheltered from the outside world.

Riccardo will not be moved. He clings to his fiction, and even after such a set change tries to reserve a space for his private feelings, aside from the bustle of the ball going on all around him. All his scenes in this sequence take place downstage, as if to represent his attempt to withdraw into the private space of his solo—which has gone. This is rendered not only visually, but also musically, in the accompaniment of the second onstage orchestra, whereby Verdi expresses Riccardo's vain endeavor to escape from the official sphere. The small string ensemble invokes the intimacy of the string quartet, as a symbol of the contemporary city-dweller's longing for a sheltered interior. Such longings are doomed to be denied, as the end of the opera reveals, and as the massacre unloosed by Montfort's efforts to ensure his family's happiness in *Les Vêpres siciliennes* reveals. Before Riccardo's *scena finale* begins, the string ensemble's melody dissolves in open fifths, descending from the first violins to the second, then to the violas, after the steady accompanimental rhythm has already ceased. The interior space for which Riccardo longed has proved a chimera.

HORROR

Yet even after the shattering of all his dreams, Riccardo, master of all forms of masquerade, is still very far from recognizing his plight and taking his mortal wound seriously. Even in the face of the profound despair into which the outcome of his earlier recklessness has cast those around him, he does not give a thought to his imminent death. It is quite different in Scribe's libretto, which has the king drawing a disillusioned line below his life:

GUSTAVE
Oui, quand je vois vos pleurs, je regrette la vie.
Adieu, Suède! adieu, gloire et patrie!
J'espérais mieux mourir! Mes amis, mes soldats,
Entourez-moi! Qu'au moins j'expire dans vos bras!
 (*Gustave III*, Acte V, scène 5)

      ‿   ‿   ‿

GUSTAVE: Yes, when I see your tears, I regret losing my life. Farewell,
Sweden! Farewell, glory and my country! I hoped for a better death! My
friends, my soldiers, gather round me! Let me at least die in your arms!

Auber added some typically operatic sentimentality to this unusually
sober text, letting Gustave take his leave of Amélie with the assurance
that she was his reason for living ("et toi par qui j'aimais la vie"). But
Verdi's protagonist does not fully comprehend, even now, that the game
is over and that all his closest friends can do for him is help him die. He
still relies on the irresistible charm that he obviously attributes to himself, and, having failed to obtain the privacy he longs for, reveals his
most intimate feelings to an entire ballroomful of people. He appears
to believe in all seriousness that by declaring Amelia's honor intact he
will save the marriage that he has played so active a part in wrecking.
Not content with asseverating the purity of his intentions in that particular respect, the apparently childless governor of Boston proceeds to
adopt the typical, mid-nineteenth-century pose of the concerned and
caring paterfamilias, although he leaves behind him any number of unresolved problems. While Amelia, Oscar, and Renato beat their breasts
in remorse, and a gloomy B-flat minor, he has nothing better to do than
bless everyone present: "Grace to each one: as your lord, my pardon
absolves you all" ("Grazia a ognun: signor qui sono: Tutti assolve il mio
perdono . . .").

The language is revealing. In the face of death, Riccardo preens himself as "signor," the benevolent father of a grateful country, although he
has spent the last three acts exercising the right to behave like an ordinary citizen, free to do as he likes and go wherever he pleases, and not
like someone set apart by his rank. His goodwill wipes the slate clean,
he believes. But his presumption goes further: in the same breath he
ascribes to himself the power to absolve everyone from their sins, and
thus assumes a role normally reserved for—not a mere "lord"—but *the*
Lord of the Christian faith. The chorus is devoted enough to fall in with
his sacral tone and group themselves into a genre picture. According to
the production book, "chorus, supers, dancers kneel, the soloists bow

their heads," while only "the guards remain motionless at their posts."[64] The chorus praises Riccardo's "great and generous heart" ("cor sì grande e generoso") in what may be termed a "chorale," in G-flat major, with a repeated emphasis on the subdominant and *ppp* harp arpeggios making almost too much of the religioso tone. For twelve bars, Verdi's opera draws close to the works of Gounod and other drames lyriques that "used religion as an ingredient in private affairs."[65] The tendency in these operas for doomed love affairs to be represented as martyr-tragedies reached what was perhaps its climax only in 1892, when Massenet's *Werther* was performed in Vienna (before its Paris première, incidentally), with Charlotte's sober final words "It's all over" ("Tout est fini") rendered in German with Christ's last words on the cross: "It is finished" ("Es ist vollbracht"). The translator, as Carl Dahlhaus points out, was not blaspheming, but simply acknowledging the existence of an element of some significance in the history of drame lyrique[66]—and also in Verdi's idiosyncratic adaptation of a work that began its existence as a grand opéra in 1833. The text certainly invites the question (put in 1979 in a satirical essay entitled: "The thirteenth 'Addio' was mortal") as to whether Riccardo perhaps finds it rather hard to deny himself the line "I am the Resurrection and the Life."[67]

This General Absolution is still not Riccardo's last word. For that, Verdi reserves the gesture of farewell he had used often before. But if the word "addio" in earlier works, and not least the "adieu" in Act IV of *Les Vêpres siciliennes*, suggests an infinite sorrow that reaches out far beyond the actual dramatic situation, it is hard to ascribe the same melancholy qualities to the radiant tenor cantilena with which Riccardo bids farewell to his "children" ("Addio per sempre, miei figli"). Rather, even the farewell seems to have rigidified into a pose, a mask, and it can scarcely be by chance that Verdi sets Riccardo's last ten bars in the very same key, B-flat major, which has accompanied disguises and role-playing throughout the opera: in Oscar's first canzone, "Volta la terrea," Riccardo's solo in the Act I finale, "È scherzo od è follia?," the cynical mockery of the conspirators in the second-act finale, the ballroom music in the third. Another striking thing is that although three of the characteristic features of Riccardo's Act I canzone, "Di' tu se fedele," are recalled in the first four bars of his last farewell—the rocking $\frac{6}{8}$ tempo, the

64. "coristi, comparse, ballerini s'inginocchiano, gli artisti [solisti] s'inchinano"; "le guardie rimangono ferme al loro posto"; Cencetti, *Disposizione scenica*, 37.

65. Dahlhaus, *Nineteenth-Century Music*, 278.

66. Ibid.

67. See Henscheid, "Das dreizehnte *Addio* war tödlich," 36.

airy staccato string accompaniment, and the cellos' syncopation—the
composer does not bring Riccardo's love motive, "La rivedrà nell'e-
stasi," back for a last time, nor permit him any special farewell from his
Amelia.[68] At this critical moment Verdi does not make the least reference to Riccardo's characterization, in his first brief solo, as ardent lover,
but only to his first substantial number: what is recalled, with his dying
breath, is the scene in which he disguised himself as a fisherman in the
pursuit of pleasure, and the process leading to his fate began to unreel.

The chorus, it is true, can be said to do its best to make the tenor
drop his pose and bring him back to earth in that it twice counters his
radiant B-flat major with the statement, in B-flat minor, that he is dying
("Ei muore!"), but he takes no notice of that and, with his strength audibly ebbing, sets off toward a high B flat which, however, he does not
reach, just as he does not reach the last syllable of "forev. . ." ("per
sem. . ."). "His voice fails" (la voce gli manca), as the stage direction states,
and Riccardo dies after this last effort, for which Verdi's direction, "he
shrieks" (grida), does for once justify modern tenors' widespread tendency to an ugly forcing of their vocal capabilities. The drama is over,
and musically, too, Verdi achieves an exceptional degree of the sense of
an ending in these few bars by the use of the notes G and G flat, at
Riccardo's "miei figli" and "diletta America" on the one hand and the
chorus's "Ei muore!" on the other, to form those two variants of the major and minor ninth above a dominant seventh chord which have already
been heard so often in the work, evoking its characteristic tinta, in the
places mentioned earlier in the chapter and at several more decisive
points in the third act as well. These motivic connections appear to have
some tinge of dramatic irony, even here: in the scene in Riccardo's study,
the characteristic ninth, after a more than unmotivated modulation
from B-flat major to E-flat major during the recitative preceding the
romanza, serves to recall his noble resolve to part from Amelia without
a farewell ("senza un addio"); then it recurs in the middle section of the
romanza itself ("Ed or qual reo presagio"), during the lovers' duettino
in the ballroom, when Amelia affirms her love for the last time ("T'amo,
sì, t'amo e in lagrime a' piedi tuoi m'atterro"), and finally at the moment
of her deepest humiliation ("Dunque vedermi vuoi d'affannno morta e
di vergogna").

Such details serve to reinforce the opera's balanced formal construction by harmonic means, although we may not (pace Siegmund Levarie)
"safely stipulate B flat, major or minor, as the tonic key of Un ballo in

68. Ibid.

maschera."[69] Nevertheless, the *scena finale*, up to Riccardo's last "addio," contributes a surprising amount to the dramatic and musical integration of this full-length work as a whole, and it is therefore all the more surprising that Verdi does not sustain the atmosphere so skillfully built up in the chorus "Cor sì grande e generoso," and allow the work to end in the same religioso tone, with a few more lines from the chorus or an orchestral postlude. As a skeptical observer of his contemporaries, however, he could not overlook the fact that in real life the reconciliation solemnized by Riccardo would not last five seconds after his death. Other solutions are conceivable, but he chose the radical break-up of the group formed around the dead governor. The death releases the chorus from its duty to maintain that pose, and Verdi gives it the last word of the opera, a summary expression of naked feeling in which something of the cold mercilessness of the final chorus in *Les Vêpres siciliennes* can also be detected: in a sudden allegro accompanied by a fortissimo of the full orchestra, all those grouped around the body of the murdered masquerader exclaim "Night of horror! ("Notte d'orror!").

Verdi's decision to ratchet the opera up to the pitch of an aesthetic of horror, as Rossini attempted in *Le Siège de Corinthe* thirty years before, also offers an explanation of why Riccardo is unmasked as a deluded monomaniac in such elaborate detail, although doing so meant moving a long way away from Scribe's original version and discarding a dramatic idea that may be termed the theatrical climax of the French libretto. Scribe wanted the opera to culminate in a simultaneous contrast extending the juxtaposition of carefree festivity and gruesome murder beyond the final chord. His libretto ends with an unusually long stage direction:

> *Les grenadiers qui portent Gustave sur leur fusils croisés se mettent lentement en marche et se dirigent vers l'escalier de granit, précédés de domestiques qui tiennent des torches. – A droite Ankastrom et les conjurés, sur lesquels les soldats ont dirigé la pointe de leurs baïonnettes. Gustave se soulève à peine, et de la main semble leur dire: Arrêtez! – A gauche, Amélie, Oscar, les seigneurs de la cour, en habits de fête, et qui ont ôté leurs masques; ils sont pâles, et la terreur est peinte sur leurs visages. – Au fond, les autres personnes du bal, différemment groupées et cherchant à apercevoir les traits du roi. – Partout le désordre, la confusion; et,*

69. See Levarie, "Key relations in Verdi's *Un ballo in maschera*," esp. 144; for the contrary view see Kerman, "Viewpoint," and Parker and Brown, "Motivic and tonal interaction," 262.

24   The title page of the first edition of the piano-vocal score of Verdi's *Ballo in maschera* is adorned with this lithograph by Tersaghi, depicting the moment of Riccardo's assassination by Renato. The tension in Amelia's attitude already suggests something of the horror that is not translated into musical terms until the very last bars of the long finale.

dans les salles où la nouvelle n'est pas encore parvenue, retentit toujours le son lointain et joyeux des instruments, tandis que sur le devant l'orchestre fait entendre un roulement lugubre.
   (*Gustave III*, Acte V, scène 5)

The grenadiers bearing Gustave on their crossed rifles move off slowly in the direction of the granite staircase, preceded by servants holding torches. Right, Ankastrom and the conspirators, on whom the soldiers have turned the points of their bayonets. Gustave raises himself slightly and seems to gesture to them "Stop!" with his hand. Left, Amélie, Oscar, the gentlemen of the court, in their festive garments, having removed their masks; they are pale, and their faces display terror. Upstage, the other ball-guests, grouped variously, and trying to see the King's face. Everywhere disorder, confusion; and from the rooms where the news has not yet arrived the distant and joyous sound of music, while a mournful drum-roll sounds from the orchestra pit.

Scribe's idea, which anticipates the use of stereophony in the cinema, was ignored even by Auber, who was evidently not up to the demands this extraordinary visual and musical montage made on him, and *Gustave III* ends with a sostenuto chorus observing all the conventions of an operatic lament. Such a contrast in Verdi's opera, on the other hand—where we can assume that the composer had the technique to effect it—would only have distracted attention from the dying protagonist's bleak isolation. Only a few years after Meyerbeer had taken the collage-like technique of accentuated contrasts to virtuosic heights in *Le Prophète* and *L'Étoile du Nord*, Verdi reacted to the obvious crisis in grand opéra and its leaning toward historicizing monumental tableaux by radically reducing the spectacular element and thereby simultaneously redistributing the relative importance of chorus and soloists. Precisely because his opera shows the governor of Boston turning his private affairs into matters of public concern, he did not need political subject matter in order to bring out the contrast between the private and the public that was the theme of so many operas. *Un ballo in maschera* is not only an illustration of how, "once our conception of public matters comes to include the social problems that manifest themselves in everyday domestic life, the centers of high political power no longer have exclusive dominance over what we take to be the public world," as Herbert Lindenberger comments of nineteenth-century historical drama in general;[70] it is also made plain, in this reworking of a libretto written in the heyday of French grand opéra, that the "common basis of the individual fate and society," taken for granted in the original, was now finally destroyed.[71]

The chorus, confined to a subordinate role for most of the action, has its moment in the last bars of *Un ballo in maschera*, when it advances from the scenery and for a few seconds asserts an independent identity with the cry "Notte d'orror!" Superficially this has a formal resemblance to the *sentenza morale* of earlier opera buffa, but its summary of the drama of passions just played out has nothing of the conciliatory abstraction of that tradition; rather, it expresses the bewilderment of uninvolved bystanders faced with so dreadful an outcome to something so apparently harmless. The horror decked with lavish historical tableaux in Rossini and Meyerbeer penetrates contemporary, urban, everyday life in Verdi. He had already shocked audiences with the contemporary subject matter of *La traviata* in 1853, and now in *Un ballo in*

70. *Historical drama*, 126.
71. Kunze, "Fest und Ball in Verdis Opern," 277.

maschera the horror is not confined to the remote principal actors in a stage drama but spreads to onlookers who, like the chorus in Hugo's *Esmeralda* or in Act I of Meyerbeer's *Huguenots*, have assumed the attitude of the voyeuristic bystander typical of nineteenth-century Paris, and thus it almost directly touches the audience itself. Verdi does not attempt to illustrate the destructive potential of social processes by filling the stage with impassioned crowds, let alone a violent mob, yet his cool representation of events at a viceregal court in a musically anonymous city has all the horror achieved in earlier works in the grand opéra genre, after the possibilities of depicting faceless mobs in music were exhausted. In *Un ballo in maschera* the responsibility for the destruction of human lives and dreams of a better existence does not lie with the frightening and unfathomable otherness of the crowd, but with all individuals, because they can no longer resist being absorbed by the all-embracing mass of a society that has become anonymous. To that extent, the lapidary reaction of the onstage onlookers, so brief that it resists every kind of comment, also finally matches that of the onlookers in the audience, who can feel hardly less bewilderment than Riccardo himself at the fact that the implacable, unconsoling ending of the drama reveals an absolute indifference to the longing for interior space.

Past and Future

In spite of this radical departure from a dramaturgical conception central to all grands opéras composed prior to 1859, we should not forget that the dramatization of the moment of bewilderment at the end of *Un ballo in maschera* was only possible because Verdi used musical means unmistakably derived from grand opéra itself. The concise expression of unbridled and destructive force in a concluding choral outburst that annihilates the pretended intimacy of Riccardo's death scene would be almost inconceivable without the models for it found in the finales of *Le Siège de Corinthe*, *Les Huguenots*, and indeed Verdi's own *Vêpres siciliennes*, and the stratification of the final tableau into several spatial and musical planes is further evidence that Verdi was always most receptive toward the dramaturgical achievements of grand opéra. But it is not only the pessimistic ending and the lightfootedness of some brilliant pages of the score, which to modern ears might have come from the pen of Offenbach or Delibes,[72] that show that *Un ballo in maschera* is rooted in French opera of the middle decades of the nineteenth century; the

72. See Budden, *The Operas of Verdi*, 2:376.

work's free-and-easy treatment of formal and stylistic conventions also has more in common with the individualized aesthetics of musical theater in Paris than with the tradition-ridden Italian opera of the period.

Nevertheless, after his ambivalent experiences with *Les Vêpres siciliennes*, Verdi was far from taking the dramaturgy of grand opéra, however successful it had proved to be in the past, as the basis for all his compositional decisions, as Filippo Filippi pointed out in his review of the first performance of the 1859 work:

> If [Verdi] has retraced the procedures of a foreign maestro and celebrated opera-maker, he has done it without a shadow of that feeble and servile imitation that obscures originality of conception and impairs the Italian quality of the music: let us agree that it can be said of Verdi that he proceeds from Meyerbeer in the sense that Rossini proceeded from Mozart![73]

Unlike the older Meyerbeer, Verdi recoiled from what Roger Parker has termed the "abyss of freedom" yawning before him (as it must have yawned before every composer who recognized the possibilities of grand opéra), and in the last four decades of his creative career confined himself with wise self-limitation to subjects like those of *Aida*, *Otello*, and *Falstaff*, where the danger he himself perceived lurking in "mosaic" was held at bay by the rigorous exclusion of subplots.[74] It is true that he wrote further works on a grand scale during the 1860s, like *La forza del destino* and *Don Carlos*, which exploited the panoramic variety of grand opéra, but the very fact that he felt compelled to make fundamental alterations to both works for later performances proves that, for all their other qualities, they fell short of *Un ballo in maschera* in the matter of stylistic unity. It was precisely in stylistic unity that *Ballo* set standards scarcely conceivable in Italian opera before it, as the enthusiastic judgment of a Turin critic, writing in 1861, demonstrates: "*Un ballo in maschera* is no longer simply an amalgam of more or less well coordinated numbers, but precisely a true music drama, with all the characters, all the twists of fortune, all the passions, all the effects that drama requires."[75]

73. "Se [Verdi] ha ricalcati i procedimenti di un maestro straniero, famoso costruttore di drammi musicali, egli lo ha fatto senza ombra di quella imitazione stentata e servile, che offusca l'originalità della concezione ed altera l'italianità della musica: accettiamo dunque che si possa asserire di Verdi che procede da Meyerbeer, come Rossini ha proceduto da Mozart!": Filippi, "*Un ballo in maschera* . . . di Verdi," 117 (1862, p. ii).

74. See Parker, "On reading nineteenth-century opera," 300–303.

75. "Il *Ballo in maschera* non è più soltanto un amalgama di pezzi più o meno ben coordinati, ma è precisamente un vero dramma musicale, con tutti i caratteri, con tutte le

There was much talk of "true music drama" at that time, and with this step toward it *Un ballo in maschera* positioned itself at the crossroads between earlier Italian opera on the one hand, and the first manifestations of modern music theater on the other. Older Italian opera was inextricably tied up in powerful conventions which mean that today it speaks essentially only to those familiar with the oeuvre of Donizetti, Mercadante, or Pacini, though it survives in the general repertory in the form of some of Verdi's middle-period operas; the new opera built on the spirit of Parisian grand opéra to establish an international success that endures undiminished to this day. So Verdi's radical reworking of a Parisian libretto of 1833 is Janus-headed, as Filippo Filippi, whose review of the Rome première has been quoted so often in this chapter, recognized and stated clearly in association with the Milan première three years later:

> In *Un ballo in maschera*, having rejected convention and formula, having assigned to each character his own particular language and having rendered the dramatic situation with evident effectiveness, in fact having moulded the drama, Verdi can take his seat between the past and the future and turning round to each of the two sides can say to one party: "Do you want tunes, ideas, proportions, a beginning, a middle, a continuation and an end? Do you want rhythm, phrasing, pure music? You have it and to spare. And you others, gentlemen of the future, do you want general colouring of the drama, faithful interpretation of the words, freedom from hackneyed and conventional forms? Do you want ideals, gracefulness, distinction of character? Do you want banality banished and in its place the new and the elegant? Do you want the orchestra and the stage to be like a single statue, and a kind of aesthetic pantheism to prevail everywhere? Help yourselves; there is plenty for all your needs."[76]

This opera stands between the past and the future in terms of Verdi's career as well, where it constitutes a turning point whose significance can scarcely be overstated. *Un ballo in maschera* was the last work he composed in response to a *scrittura*, the type of contract from an impresario usual in Italian opera in the eighteenth and nineteenth centuries. Verdi was now forty-six, and in the course of just two decades of incessant work he had brought no fewer than twenty-three operas from con-

vicende, con tutte le passioni, con tutti gli effetti che l'arte richiede"; anonymous review, *Il diritto: Foglio politico quotidiano della Democrazia Italiana*, January 1861; cited in Gara, "Il cammino dell'opera," 709.

76. "*Un Ballo in maschera*," *La Perseveranza*, 12 January 1862; in Della Corte, *Saggio bibliografico*, 1179. Cited here in Budden's translation, *The Operas of Verdi*, 2:423.

ception to their first performances. In view of the way his musico-dramatic standards had been transformed, while the deadlines he had to meet remained constant, it is not surprising that during his work on *Un ballo in maschera* he emitted a groan that has been quoted regularly ever since. Although most biographers relate it to the earlier works, which seem to deserve the dismissive comment, it actually takes in everything he had written up to 1858, thus including *Rigoletto, La traviata, Il trovatore,* and *Simon Boccanegra:* "I haven't had an hour's peace since *Nabucco:* sixteen years in the galleys!"[77] The irritations attending the genesis of *Ballo* itself, first intended for Naples, but premièred in Rome, certainly gave no reason to exclude it from this judgment, and indeed, after finishing the score, the weary composer appears seriously to have considered following Rossini's example and giving up further composition of works for the theater. A few weeks before the Rome première, his second wife, Giuseppina Strepponi, wrote to a friend: "Verdi is so tired, battered, disgusted by the stage that there is every probability that he will say regarding the theater what Rabelais said on his deathbed regarding life: 'Lower the curtain, the farce is over.'"[78]

In spite of this profound depression, Verdi was not content to rest on his laurels, but from then onward he kept the greatest possible distance between himself and the frenzy of the opera trade. It took a lucrative foreign commission to persuade him to compose something new for the stage—*La forza del destino* was written for St. Petersburg, *Don Carlos* for Paris, *Aida* for Cairo—unless he had complete control over the date, conditions, and cast of the first performance, as with *Otello* and *Falstaff.* On these terms, he proceeded steadfastly toward his own idea of musical drama on a route that bypassed Wagner and his theories—as hotly debated then as they are today. Rather, Verdi set off on this unexpected second career from an opera which he began with a libretto produced by Scribe in 1833 and rearranged to suit his own needs. What the audience saw and heard in 1859, at the first performance of *Un ballo in maschera,* was therefore only the settling of Verdi's account with grand opéra, long past the zenith it reached in the 1830s, not what he had yet to say to European opera from a platform based on the aesthetic achievements of an urbanized music theater.

77. "Dal Nabucco in poi non ho avuto, si può dire, un'ora di quiete. Sedici anni di galera!" Verdi's letter to Clarina Maffei, 12 May 1858, *I copialettere,* 572.

78. "Verdi è così stanco, abboiato, schifato di palcoscenico, che v'è tutta probabilità ch'ei dica riguardo al teatro quanto Rabelais disse ne' suoi ultimi momenti riguardo alla vita: 'Baissez le rideau, la farce est jouée.'" Letter to Mauro Corticelli, 15 January 1859; cited in Gara, "Il cammino dell'opera," 112.

BIBLIOGRAPHY

Manuscript Sources

F-Pan (Paris, Archives Nationales de France)

AJ^{13} 1050. [Rapport final de la censure concernant *La Muette de Portici*].

F^{21} 969. [Rapports de Laya et de Chazet concernant *La Muette de Portici*].

O^3 1680 (I). [Lettre d'Emile-Timothée Lubbert au Vicomte de La Rochefoucauld du 11 juin 1828].

o^3 1724 (II). [Lettre de Louis-Simon Auger au Vicomte de La Rochefoucauld du 24 octobre 1825].

F-Pn, n.a.f. (Paris, Bibliothèque nationale, Département des manuscripts, Nouvelles acquisitions françaises)

22502, fols. 62–219v. [Papiers manuscrits ayant appartenu à Eugène Scribe et concernant *Les Huguenots*].

22504, fols. 5–307. [Papiers manuscrits ayant appartenu à Eugène Scribe et concernant *Le Prophète*].

22506, fols. 53–95. [Papiers manuscrits ayant appartenu à Eugène Scribe et concernant *Les Vêpres Siciliennes*].

22506, fols. 96–227. [Papiers manuscrits ayant appartenu à Eugène Scribe et concernant *Le Duc d'Albe*].

22546, fols. 143–56. [Correspondance d'Eugène Scribe avec Casimir Delavigne].

22562. Eugène Scribe, *Vademecum, ou Brouillons et plans de pièces* [May 1833–March 1836].

22568. Eugène Scribe, *Pêlemêle dramatique commencé à Séricourt le 1er juillet 1851 et fini à Paris le 1er juillet 1855*.

22569. Eugène Scribe, [*Vademecum ou Brouillons et plans de pièces, 1855–1859*.]

22573. Eugène Scribe, *Fortune d'un homme de lettres ou Registre de ce que j'ai gagné par ma plume et par mon travail depuis le 25 août 1810, jour de ma sortie du collège Sainte-Barbe jusqu'au .. .. 18.., jour de ma mort.*

22574. Eugène Scribe, *Livre de dépenses particulières d'Eugène Scribe, depuis son entrée au collège Ste.-Barbe, l'an VIII 10 floréal* [30 avril 1802] *jusqu'à sa sortie l'an* [1810].

22575. Eugène Scribe, *Livre de dépenses* [1840–1850].

22576. Eugène Scribe, *Livre de dépenses pour les années 1850–1859* [continue en fait jusqu'en 1861].

F-Po (Paris, Bibliothèque de l'Opéra)

Archives de l'Opéra, AD 23. [Procés-verbaux des] *Séances du Jury d'examen des Poëmes* [1ᵉʳ décembre 1803 – 12 décembre 1821].

Archives de l'Opéra, AD 24. [Registre des pièces examinés par le Jury d'examen, entrées du 16 mai 1816 au 28 avril 1825 et du septembre 1828 au 1ᵉʳ avril 1830].

Archives de l'Opéra, AD 25. [Procés-verbaux des séances du Jury d'examen des Poëmes, 16 janvier 1822 – 15 décembre 1824].

C. 4895. *Mise en Sène / Mahomet II / ou / Le Siège de Corinthe.*

Mat. 19 [239: Goachino Rossini, *Le Siège de Corinthe*, parties d'orchestre].

Rés. 177. Giacomo Meyerbeer, [Romance de Valentine dans le quatrième acte des *Huguenots*, partition autographe].

References

A!A!A! [Abel Hugo, Armand Malitourne, and Jean Joseph Ader]. *Traité du mélodrame.* Paris: Delaunay/Pélicier/Plancher, 1817.

Abbiati, Franco. *Giuseppe Verdi.* 4 vols. Milan: Ricordi, 1959.

Abert, Anna Amalie. "Räuber und Räubermilieu in der Oper des 19. Jahrhunderts." In *Die "Couleur locale" in der Oper des 19. Jahrhunderts,* ed. Heinz Becker, 121–29. Studien zur Musikgeschichte des 19. Jahrhunderts, no. 42. Regensburg: Bosse, 1976.

Accorsi, Maria Grazia. "Il melodramma melodrammatico." *Sigma,* n.s., 13 (1980): 109–27.

Adam, Adolphe. *Derniers Souvenirs d'un musicien.* Paris: Lévy, 1859.

Adorno, Theodor Wiesengrund. *Gesammelte Schriften,* ed. Gretel Adorno and Rolf Tiedemann. 20 vols. Frankfurt am Main: Suhrkamp, 1970–86.

———. *In Search of Wagner,* trans. Rodney Livingstone. [N.p.]: NLB 1981.

Alberti, Annibale, ed. *Verdi intimo: Carteggio di Giuseppe Verdi con il Conte Opprandino Arrivabene.* Milan: Mondadori, 1931.

[Aldeguier, J.-B.-Auguste d']. *Le Flâneur. Galerie pittoresque, philosophique et morale de tout ce que Paris offre de curieux et de remarquable dans tous le genres [. . .] par un habitué du Boulevard de Gand.* Paris: Chez tous les Marchands de nouveautés, 1826.

Allemagne, Henry-René d'. *Histoire des jouets.* Paris: Hachette, 1902.

Amandry, Angélique. "Le Philhellénisme en France: Partitions de musique." *O eranistis* 17 (1981): 25–45.

Ambert, Joachim. *Portraits républicains: Armand Carrel, Godefroy Cavaignac, Armand Marrast, Le colonel Charras.* Paris: Librairie internationale, 1870.

Ambrose, Mary. "*La donna del lago:* The first Italian translations of Scott." *Modern Language Review* 67 (1972): 74–82.

———. "Walter Scott, Italian opera and romantic stage-setting." *Italian Studies* 36 (1981): 58–78.

Amiard-Chevrel, Claudine. "Aux sources d'une typologie: Représentations de Paris du romantisme au naturalisme." In *Images de la ville sur la scène aux XIXe et XXe siècle*, ed. Élie Konigson, 13–60. Paris: Presses du CNRS, 1991.

Angermüller, Rudolph. "Reformideen von Du Roullet und Beaumarchais als Opernlibrettisten." *Acta musicologica* 48 (1976): 227–53.

———. "Zigeuner und Zigeunerisches in der Oper des 19. Jahrhunderts." In *Die "Couleur locale" in der Oper des 19. Jahrhunderts*, ed. Heinz Becker, 131–59. Studien zur Musikgeschichte des 19. Jahrhunderts, no. 42. Regensburg: Bosse, 1976.

Anne, Théodore. "Le Temps passé. Souvenirs de théâtre: Le Duo du 4e acte des *Huguenots*." *Le Ménéstrel* 33 (1866): 164–65.

Anz, Heinrich. "Erwartungshorizont. Ein Diskussionsbeitrag zu H[ans] R[ob-ert] Jauß' Begründung einer Rezeptionsästhetik der Literatur." *Euphorion* 70 (1976): 398–408.

Arago, Jacques. *Mémoires d'un petit banc de l'Opéra.* Paris: Ébrard 1844.

Arlt, Wulf. "Einleitung: Aspekte des Gattungsbegriffs in der Musikgeschichts-schreibung." In *Gattungen der Musik in Einzeldarstellungen: Gedenkschrift Leo Schrade*, vol. 1, ed. Wulf Arlt, Ernst Lichtenhahn, and Hans Oesch, 11–93. Bern: Francke, 1973.

Armstrong, Alan. "Gilbert-Louis Duprez and Gustave Roger in the composi-tion of Meyerbeer's *Le Prophète*." *Cambridge Opera Journal* 8 (1996): 147–65.

———. "Meyerbeer's *Le Prophète*: A History of Its Composition and Early Per-formances." Ph.D. diss., Ohio State University, 1990.

[Arpino, Ferdinando]. *Difesa del Maestro Cavalier Giuseppe Verdi: Nel tribunale di Commercio di Napoli.* [Naples]: Tipografia del Vesuvio, 1858.

Arvin, Neil Cole. *Eugène Scribe and the French Theatre (1815–1860).* Cambridge, Mass.: Harvard University Press, 1924.

Asholt, Wolfgang. "Ein Sonnenuntergang, der zum 'Vorschein' wird: *Le Pro-phète* und 1848." In *Zwischen tragédie lyrique und Grand Opéra. Französische Oper im 18. und 19. Jahrhundert*, ed. Albert Gier and Jürgen Maehder. Per-spektiven der Opernforschung, no. 3. Frankfurt am Main: Lang, forth-coming.

Asselineau, Charles. "De l'État de la musique en France et du répertoire de l'Opéra." *Revue de Paris* 20 (1854): 599–610.

Auden, W. H. "Notes on music and opera." In *The Dyer's Hand and Other Essays*, 465–74. London: Faber and Faber, 1963.

Azevedo, Alexis. *G[ioachino] Rossini: Sa vie et ses oeuvres.* Paris: Heugel, 1864.

Bab, Julius. *Das Theater im Lichte der Soziologie.* Leipzig: Hirschfeld, 1931; re-printed, Stuttgart: Enke, 1974.

Babinger, Franz. *Mehmed der Eroberer und seine Zeit: Weltenstürmer einer Zeiten-wende.* Munich: Bruckmann, 1953.

Badinter, Elisabeth. *The Myth of Motherhood,* trans. Roger DeGaris. London: Souvenir Press, 1981.

Baechler, Jean. *Les Suicides.* Paris: Calmann-Lévy, 1975.

Baldacci, Luigi. *Libretti d'opera e altri saggi.* Florence: Valecchi, 1974.

Balthazar, Scott L. "Analytic contexts and mediated influences: The Rossinian *convenienze* and Verdi's middle and late duets." *Journal of Musicological Research* 10 (1990–91): 19–45.

———. "Mayr, Rossini, and the development of the opera seria duet: Some preliminary conclusions." In *I vicini di Mozart*, ed. Maria Teresa Muraro, vol. 1: *Il teatro musicale tra Sette e Ottocento*, 377–98. Studi di musica veneta, no. 15. Florence: Olschki 1989.

———. "Ritorni's *Ammaestramenti* and the conventions of Rossinian melodrama." *Journal of Musicological Research* 8 (1988–89): 281–311.

———. "The *Primo Ottocento* duet and the transformation of the Rossinian code." *Journal of Musicology* 7 (1989): 471–97.

Balzac, Honoré de. *La Comédie humaine*, ed. Pierre-Georges Castex. 12 vols. Paris: Gallimard, 1976–81.

Baroni, Mario. *Il declino del patriarca: Verdi e le contraddizioni della famiglia borghese.* Bologna: Università degli Studi, 1979.

Barouillet [Marie-Joseph Désiré Martin]. *Fabius: Tragédie lyrique en trois actes.* Paris: Imprimerie de l'Académie de Musique, 1792.

Bartlet, M. Elizabeth C. "The new repertory at the Opéra during the reign of terror: Revolutionary rhetoric and operatic consequences." In *Music and the French Revolution*, ed. Malcolm Boyd, 107–56. Cambridge: Cambridge University Press, 1992.

———. Preface to Gioachino Rossini, *Guillaume Tell*, ed. M. Elizabeth C. Bartlet. Edizione critica delle opere di Gioachino Rossini, sec. 1: Opere, vol. 39. Pesaro: Fondazione Rossini, 1992.

———. "Rossini e l'Académie Royale de Musique a Parigi." In *Rossini 1792–1992: Mostra storica-documentaria*, ed. Mauro Bucarelli, 245–66. Perugia: Electa, 1992.

———. "Staging French *Grand opéra*: Rossini's *Guillaume Tell* (1829)." In *Gioachino Rossini 1792–1992: Il testo e la scena. Convegno internazionale di studi, Pesaro, 25–28 giugno 1992*, ed. Paolo Fabbri, 623–48. Pesaro: Fondazione Rossini, 1994.

Basevi, Abramo. "Le riforme" [*signed* A.B.]. *L'armonia* 1 (1856): 1–2.

———. "Se Meyerbeer scrivesse oggi un'opera italiana." *L'armonia* 1 (1856): 22–23.

———. *Studio sulle opere di Giuseppe Verdi.* Florence: Tipografia Tofani, 1859; reprinted, Bologna: AMIS, 1978.

Bates, Carol Neuls. "Verdi's *Les Vêpres Siciliennes* (1855) and *Simon Boccanegra* (1857)." Ph.D. diss., Yale University, 1970.

Baudelaire, Charles. *Les Fleurs du Mal.* Vol. 1 in *Oeuvres complètes*, ed. Claude Pichois. 4 vols. Paris: Gallimard 1973–76.

Baudouin, Charles. *Psychanalyse de Victor Hugo*, Geneva: Édition du Mont-Blanc, 1943; new edition, Paris: Colin, 1972.

Baumann, Carl-Friedrich. *Licht im Theater: Von der Argand-Lampe bis zum Glühlampen-Scheinwerfer.* Die Schaubühne, no. 72. Stuttgart: Steiner, 1988.

Becker, Heinz. "Das Duett in der Oper." In *Musik—Edition—Interpretation: Gedenkschrift Günter Henle*, ed. Martin Bente, 82–99. Munich: Henle, 1980.

———. "'... der Marcel von Meyerbeer': Anmerkungen zur Entstehungsgeschichte der *Hugenotten*." *Jahrbuch des Staatlichen Instituts für Musikforschung Preußischer Kulturbesitz, 1979/80*, pp. 79–100. Berlin: Merseburger, 1981.

———. "Die *Couleur locale* als Stilkategorie der Oper." In *Die "Couleur locale" in der Oper des 19. Jahrhunderts*, ed. Heinz Becker, 23–45. Studien zur Musikgeschichte des 19. Jahrhunderts, no. 42. Regensburg: Bosse, 1976.

———. "Die historische Bedeutung der Grand Opéra." In *Beiträge zur Geschichte der Musikanschauung im 19. Jahrhundert*, ed. Walter Salmen, 151–59. Studien zur Musikgeschichte des 19. Jahrhunderts, no. 1. Regensburg: Bosse, 1965.

———. "Französische Grand Opéra und französische Gesellschaft." In *Der schöne Abglanz: Stationen der Operngeschichte: Oper als Spiegel gesellschaftlicher Veränderung*, ed. Udo Bermbach and Wulf Konold, 153–80. Hamburger Beiträge zur Öffentlichen Wissenschaft, no. 91. Berlin: Reimer, 1991.

———. *Giacomo Meyerbeer in Selbstzeugnissen und Bilddokumenten dargestellt.* Reinbek bei Hamburg: Rowohlt, 1980.

———. "Giacomo Meyerbeers Mitarbeit an den Libretti seiner Opern." In *Bericht über den Internationalen Musikwissenschaftlichen Kongreß Bonn 1970*, ed. Carl Dahlhaus, Hans-Joachim Marx, Magda Marx-Weber, and Günther Massenkeil, 155–62. Kassel: Bärenreiter, 1971.

———. Introduction to Giacomo Meyerbeer, *Briefwechsel und Tagebücher*, ed. Heinz Becker, 1:23–54. Berlin: de Gruyter, 1960.

———. "Zur Frage des Stilverfalls, dargestellt an der französischen Oper." In *Studien zur Trivialmusik des 19. Jahrhunderts*, ed. Carl Dahlhaus, 111–20. Studien zur Musikgeschichte des 19. Jahrhunderts, no. 8. Regensburg: Bosse, 1967.

———. "Zwischen Oper und Drama. Zu Meyerbeers Konzeption der dramatischen Szene." In *Wagnerliteratur—Wagnerforschung. Bericht über das Wagner-Symposium Munich 1983*, ed. Carl Dahlhaus and Egon Voss, 86–94. Mainz: Schott, 1985.

Becker, Heinz, and Gudrun Becker. *Giacomo Meyerbeer: Ein Leben in Briefen.* Taschenbücher zur Musikwissenschaft, no. 85. Wilhelmshaven: Heinrichshofen, 1983.

———. *Giacomo Meyerbeer—Weltbürger der Musik: Eine Ausstellung der Musikabteilung der Staatsbibliothek Preußischer Kulturbesitz Berlin zum 200. Geburtstag des Komponisten vom 31. Oktober 1991 bis zum 5. Januar 1992.* Ausstellungskataloge der Staatsbibliothek Preußischer Kulturbesitz, no. 38. Wiesbaden: Reichert, 1991.

Beghelli, Marco. "Per un nuovo approccio al teatro musicale: l'atto performativo come luogo dell'imitazione gestuale nella drammaturgia verdiana." *Italica* 64 (1987): 632–53.

Bekker, Paul. *The Changing Opera*, trans. Arthur Mendel. London: J. M. Dent, 1936.

Bellini, Vincenzo. *Epistolario*, ed. Luisa Cambi. Verona: Mondadori, 1943.

Benjamin, Walter. *Charles Baudelaire: A Lyric Poet in the Era of High Capitalism*, trans. Harry Zohn. [Contains: "The Paris of the Second Empire in Baude-laire"; "Some Motifs in Baudelaire"; "Paris—the Capital of the Nineteenth Century" (the last translated by Quintin Hoare)]. London: Verso Editions 1983.

———. *Gesammelte Schriften.* 5 vols. Frankfurt am Main: Suhrkamp, 1974–82.

Berg, Walter Bruno. *Der literarische Sonntag: Ein Beitrag zur Kritik der bürger-lichen Ideologie.* Studia romanica, no. 25. Heidelberg: Winter, 1976.

Bergman, Gösta Mauritz. "Der Eintritt des Berufsregisseurs in das französische Theater." *Maske und Kothurn* 10 (1964): 431–54.

———. *Lighting in the Theatre.* Acta universitatis stockholmiensis; Stockholm Studies in Theatrical History, no. 2. Stockholm: Almqvist and Wiksell; To-towa, N.J.: Rowman and Littlefield, 1977.

Berlioz, Hector. *Correspondance générale*, ed. Pierre Citron. Paris: Flammarion, 1971–.

———. *"Guillaume Tell*, de Rossini." *Gazette musicale de Paris* 1 (1834): 326–27, 336–39, 341–43, 349–51; reprinted in Giuseppe Radiciotti, *Gioacchino Ros-sini*, vol. 2 (1928), pp. 134–58.

———. *"La Esmeralda." Revue et gazette musicale* 3 (1836): 409–11.

———. *The Memoirs of Hector Berlioz*, trans. and ed. David Cairns. London: Victor Gollancz, 1969.

Bernard, Elisabeth. "L'évolution du public d'Opéra de 1860 à 1880." In *Regards sur l'Opéra: Du Ballet Comique de la Reine à l'Opéra de Pékin*, 33–46. Paris: Presses Universitaires de France, 1976.

Besnier, Patrick. "Musique pour la fin du monde: Les musiciens et l'apocalypse au XIXe siècle." In *Missions et démarches de la critique: Mélanges offerts au profes-seur Jacques Albert Vier*, 171–82. Paris: Klincksieck, 1973.

Beyer, Barbara. "Selbstverständigung und Verselbständigung: Eine Analyse von Giuseppe Verdis *Don Carlos*." Diss. phil., Technische Universität Berlin, 1986.

Bianconi, Lorenzo. Introduction to *La drammaturgia musicale*, ed. Lorenzo Bi-anconi, 7–49. Bologna: Il Mulino, 1986.

———. *Music in the Seventeenth Century.* Cambridge: Cambridge Univerity Press, 1987.

———. "Perché la storia dell'opera italiana?" *Musica/realtà* 17 (August 1985): 29–48.

Biesbrock, Hans-Rüdiger von. *Die literarische Mode der Physiologien in Frankreich (1840–1842).* Studien und Dokumente zur Geschichte der Romanischen Literaturen, no. 3. Frankfurt am Main: Lang, 1978.

Blaze de Bury, Henri. "De la Musique des femmes. Mlle. Louise Bertin" [*signed* H. W.]. *Revue des deux mondes*, 4th ser., 8 (October–December 1836): 611–25.

———. *Meyerbeer et son temps.* Paris: Lévy, 1865.

Bloom, Peter. "A review of Fétis's *Revue musicale*." In *Music in Paris in the Eighteen-Thirties/La Musique à Paris dans les années mil huit cent trente*, ed.

Peter Bloom, 55–79. Musical Life in 19th-century-France/La Vie musicale en France au XIXe siècle, vol. 4. Stuyvesant, N.Y.: Pendragon, 1987.

———. "François-Joseph Fétis and the *Revue musicale* (1827–1835)." Ph.D. diss., University of Pennsylvania, 1972.

Bocher, Charles. *Mémoires, précédés des souvenirs de famille (1760–1816).* 2 vols. Paris: Flammarion, 1907–9.

Bockholdt, Rudolf. *Berlioz-Studien.* Münchner Veröffentlichungen zur Musikgeschichte, no. 29. Tutzing: Schneider, 1979.

Bohrer, Karl Heinz. *Die Ästhetik des Schreckens: Die pessimistische Romantik und Ernst Jüngers Frühwerk.* Munich: Hanser, 1978.

Boigne, Charles de. *Petits Mémoires de l'Opéra.* Paris: Librairie nouvelle, 1857.

Bollème, Geneviève. *La Bibliothèque bleue: Littérature populaire en France du XVIIe au XIXe siècle.* Paris: Julliard, 1971.

Bonald, Louis-Gabriel-Ambroise de. *Mélanges littéraires et philosophiques.* 2 vols. *Oeuvres de M. de Bonald,* vols. 10–11. Paris: Le Clerc, 1819.

Bonnefon, Paul. "Les Métamorphoses d'un opéra: Lettres inédites d'Eugène Scribe." *Revue des deux mondes* 41 (September–October 1917): 877–99.

———. "Scribe sous l'Empire et sous la Restauration: D'après des documents inédits." *Revue d'histoire littéraire de la France* 26 (1920): 321–70.

Borchmeyer, Dieter. *Die Götter tanzen Cancan: Richard Wagners Liebesrevolten.* Heidelberg: Manutius, 1992.

———. "Wagner-Literatur—Eine deutsche Misere. Neue Ansichten zum *Fall Wagner.*" In *Forschungsreferate,* 2d ser., ed. Wolfgang Frühwald, Georg Jäger, Dieter Langewiesche, and Albert Martino, 1–62. *Internationales Archiv für Sozialgeschichte der deutschen Literatur* (special issue no. 3). Tübingen: Niemeyer, 1993.

Bosselt, Arno. "Das Zimmer auf der Bühne: Die Gestaltung des Innenraums von der Kulissenbühne der klassischen Zeit bis zum Naturalismus." Diss. phil., University of Kiel, 1935.

Bourbon-Orléans, Louis-Philippe de. *Discours, allocutions et réponses de S[a] M[ajesté] Louis-Philippe, roi des Français, avec un sommaire des circonstances qui s'y rapportent, extraits du "Moniteur."* 17 vols. Paris: Agasse, 1833–47.

Bousquet, Jacques. *Les thèmes du rêve dans la littérature romantique (France, Angleterre, Allemagne): Essai sur la naissance et l'évolution des images.* Paris: Didier, 1964.

Branca, Emilia. *Felice Romani ed i più riputati maestri di musica del suo tempo: Cenni biografici ed aneddotici raccolti e pubblicati da sua moglie.* Turin: Loescher, 1882.

Bréan de Fontenay, Adolphe, and Étienne de Champeaux. *Annuaire dramatique: Histoire des théâtres [. . .] Première année 1844–45.* Paris: rue Notre-Dame-des-Victoires, 64 [1845].

Brewster, David. *A Treatise on the Kaleidoscope.* Edinburgh: Constable, 1819.

Brockmeier, Peter. "Die gefährliche arbeitende Klasse: Zur Darstellung des Volkes in der französischen Literatur des 18. und 19. Jahrhunderts." *Romanistische Zeitschrift für Literaturgeschichte* 1 (1977): 204–28.

Brooke, Iris. *Western European Costume, Seventeenth to Mid-Nineteenth Century, and Its Relation to the Theatre.* London: Harrap, 1940.

Brooks, Peter. "Il corpo melodrammatico." In *Forme del melodrammatico: Parole e musica (1700–1800): Contributi per la storia di un genere*, ed. Bruno Gallo, 177–95. Milan: Guerini, 1988.

———. *The Melodramatic Imagination: Balzac, Henry James, Melodrama, and the Mode of Excess.* New Haven, Conn.: Yale University Press, 1976.

Brüggemann, Heinz. *"Aber schickt keinen Poeten nach London!" Großstadt und literarische Wahrnehmung im 18. und 19. Jahrhundert: Texte und Interpretationen.* Reinbek bei Hamburg: Rowohlt, 1985.

Brzoska, Matthias. *Die Idee des Gesamtkunstwerks in der Musiknovellistik der Julimonarchie.* Thurnauer Schriften zum Musiktheater, no. 14. Laaber: Laaber, 1995.

———. "Historisches Bewußtsein und musikalische Zeitgestaltung." *Archiv für Musikwissenschaft* 45 (1988): 50–66.

Budden, Julian. *The Operas of Verdi.* 3 vols. London: Cassell, 1973–81.

———. "Varianti nei *Vespri Siciliani.*" *Nuova Rivista Musicale Italiana* 6 (1972): 155–81.

———. "Verdi and Meyerbeer in relation to *Les Vêpres siciliennes.*" *Studi verdiani* 1 (1982): 11–20.

Busch, Hans. *Verdi's "Otello" and "Simon Boccanegra" (revised version) in letters and documents.* Oxford: Clarendon Press, 1988.

Cagli, Bruno. "L'edizione critica dell'opera lirica: lo specifico storico-letterario." In *Per la tutela del lavoro musicologico: Atti del Convegno Internazionale di Studi, Venezia, 9–10 settembre 1986*, 23–28. Milan: Ricordi, 1986.

Campbell, Roy. *Poems of Baudelaire: A Translation of "Les Fleurs du Mal."* London: The Harvill Press, 1952.

Carteggio Verdi–Boito, ed. Mario Medici and Marcello Conati in collaboration with Marisa Casati. 2 vols. Parma: Istituto di Studi Verdiani, 1978. [English translation in 1 volume: *The Verdi–Boito Correspondence*, ed. Marcello Conati and Mario Medici, with a new introduction by Marcello Conati; edition prepared by William Weaver. Chicago: University of Chicago Press, 1994.]

Castil-Blaze [François Henri Joseph Blaze]. *Dictionnaire de musique moderne.* 2 vols. Paris: Magasin de musique de la lyre moderne, 1821; reprinted, Geneva: Minkoff, forthcoming.

———. *Mémorial du Grand Opéra: Épilogue de l'Académie royale de musique, histoire littéraire, musicale, chorégraphique, pittoresque, morale, critique, facétieuse, politique et galante de ce théâtre, de 1645 à 1847.* Paris: Castil-Blaze, 1847.

Cella, Franca, and Pierluigi Petrobelli, eds. *Giuseppe Verdi–Giulio Ricordi: Corrispondenza e immagini 1881/1890: Catalogo della mostra.* Milan: Edizioni del Teatro alla Scala, 1981.

Cencetti, Giuseppe. *Disposizione scenica per l'opera "Un ballo in maschera" compilata e regolata sulla messa in scena del Teatro Apollo in Roma il carnevale del 1859.* Milan: Ricordi, [1859].

Cerise, L[aurent-Alexis-Philibert]. *Déterminer l'influence de l'éducation physique et morale sur la production de la sur-excitation du système nerveux et des maladies qui sont un effet consécutif de cette sur-excitation (Extrait du IXe volume des Mémoires de l'Académie royale de médecine).* Paris: Baillière, 1841.

Chabot, Carole. "Ballet in the operas of Eugène Scribe: An apology for the presence of dance in opera." *Studies in Music from the University of Western Ontario* 5 (1980): 7–14.

Charlton, David. *Grétry and the Growth of Opéra-Comique.* Cambridge: Cambridge University Press, 1986.

———. "Motif and recollection in four operas of Dalayrac." *Soundings: A Music Journal* 7 (1978): 38–61.

———. "Orchestration and Orchestral Practice in Paris, 1789–1810." Ph.D. diss., Cambridge University, 1973.

Chasles, Philarète. *Resumé de l'histoire de Suisse.* Paris: Lecointe et Durey, 1825.

Chevalier, Louis. *Classes laborieuses et classes dangereuses à Paris pendant la première moitié du XIXe siècle.* Paris: Librairie générale française, 1958. [English edition: *Labouring Classes and Dangerous Classes,* trans. Frank Jellinek. London: Routledge and Kegan Paul, 1973.]

Chopin, Fryderyk. *Selected Correspondence of Fryderyk Chopin,* abridged from *Fryderyk Chopin's Correspondence,* collected and annotated by Bronislaw Edward Sydow [1955], trans. and ed. with additional material and a commentary by Arthur Hedley. London: Heinemann, 1962.

Chorley, Henry F[othergill]. *Music and Manners in France and Germany: A Series of Travelling Sketches of Art and Society* [1841]. 3 vols. 2d ed. London: Longmans, 1844.

Citron, Pierre. *La Poésie de Paris dans la littérature française de Rousseau à Baudelaire.* 2 vols. Paris: Éditions de Minuit, 1961.

Claudon, Francis. "G. Meyerbeer et V. Hugo: Dramaturgies comparées." In *Regards sur l'Opéra: Du Ballet Comique de la Reine à l'Opéra de Pékin,* 101–11. Paris: Presses Universitaires de France, 1976.

Colenbrander, H. T. *De afscheiding van België.* Amsterdam: Meulenhoff, 1936.

Comeau, Paul Theodore. "Etienne Jouy: His Life and His Paris Essays." Ph.D. diss., Princeton University, 1968.

Conati, Marcello. "Ballabili nei *Vespri* con alcune osservazioni su Verdi e la musica popolare." *Studi Verdiani* 1 (1982): 21–46.

———. *La bottega della musica: Verdi e La Fenice.* Milan: Il saggiatore, 1983.

———. "Verdi et la culture parisienne des années 1830." In *Music in Paris in the Eighteen-Thirties/La Musique à Paris dans les années mil huit cent trente,* ed. Peter Bloom, 209–25. Musical Life in 19th-century France/La Vie musicale en France au XIXe siècle, vol. 4. Stuyvesant, N.Y.: Pendragon, 1987.

Marcello Conati, ed. *Interviews and Encounters with Verdi,* trans. Richard Stokes, with a foreword by Julian Budden. London: Victor Gollancz, 1984. [A translation of *Interviste ed incontri con Verdi.* Milan: Edizioni il Formichiere 1980.]

Correspondance littéraire, philosophique et critique de [Friedrich Melchior] Grimm et [Denis] Diderot, depuis 1753 jusqu'en 1790. Nouvelle édition. 15 vols. Paris: Furne, 1829–31.

Coudroy, Marie-Hélène. *La critique parisienne des "grands opéras" de Meyerbeer: Robert le diable — Les Huguenots — Le Prophète — L'Africaine.* Studien zur französischen Oper des 19. Jahrhunderts, no. 2. Saarbrücken: Galland, 1988.

Crosten, William L. *French Grand Opera: An Art and a Business.* New York: King's Crown Press, 1948; reprinted, New York: Da Capo, 1973.

Dahlhaus, Carl. "Die Kategorie des Charakteristischen in der Ästhetik des 19. Jahrhunderts." In *Die "Couleur locale" in der Oper des 19. Jahrhunderts,* ed. Heinz Becker, 9–21. Studien zur Musikgeschichte des 19. Jahrhunderts, no. 42. Regensburg: Bosse 1976.

———. *Die Musiktheorie im 18. und 19. Jahrhundert.* Part 1: *Grundzüge einer Systematik.* Geschichte der Musiktheorie, no. 10. Darmstadt: Wissenschaftliche Buchgesellschaft, 1984.

———. "Drammaturgia dell'opera italiana." In *Teorie e tecniche, immagini e fantasmi,* ed. Lorenzo Bianconi and Giorgio Pestelli, 77–162. *Storia dell'opera italiana,* vol. 6. Turin: EDT, 1988.

———. "Französische Musik und Musik in Paris." *Lendemains* 31/32 (1983): 5–10.

———. "Gattungsgeschichte und Werkinterpretation: Die Historie als Oper." In *Gattung und Werk in der Musikgeschichte Norddeutschlands und Skandinaviens: Referate der Kieler Tagung 1980,* ed. Friedhelm Krummacher and Heinrich W. Schwab, 20–29. Kieler Schriften zur Musikwissenschaft, no. 26. Kassel: Bärenreiter, 1982.

———. "Motive der Meyerbeerkritik." In *Jahrbuch des Staatlichen Instituts für Musikforschung Preußischer Kulturbesitz 1978,* 35–42. Berlin: Merseburger, 1979.

———. *Nineteenth-Century Music,* trans. J. Bradford Robinson. Berkeley and Los Angeles: University of California Press, 1989.

———. *Realism in Nineteenth-Century Music,* trans. Mary Whittall. Cambridge: Cambridge University Press, 1985.

D'Amico, Fedele. "Il ballo in maschera prima di Verdi." *Verdi: Bollettino quadrimestrale dell'Istituto di Studi Verdiani* 1 (1960): 1253–1328; reprinted in *Chigiana* 26/27 (1969–70): 501–83.

Danuser, Hermann. "Das imprévu in der Symphonik. Aspekte einer musikalischen Formkategorie in der Zeit von Carl Philipp Emanuel Bach bis Hector Berlioz." *Musiktheorie* 1 (1986): 61–81.

———. "Symphonisches Subjekt und Form in Berlioz' *Harold en Italie.*" *Melos/ Neue Zeitschrift für Musik* 3 (1977): 203–14.

Darnton, Robert. *Mesmerism and the End of the Enlightenment in France.* Cambridge, Mass.: Harvard University Press, 1968.

Daumard, Adeline. *Les Bourgeois de Paris au XIXe siècle.* Paris: Flammarion, 1970.

Dauriac, Lionel. *Rossini: Biographie critique.* Paris: Laurens, 1906.

Davin, Félix. Introduction [1834]. In *L'Oeuvre de Balzac publiée dans un ordre nouveau, sous la direction d' Albert Béguin et de Jean A. Ducourneau,* vol. 15, pp. 103–26. Paris: Club français du livre, 1964.

Debussy, Claude. *Debussy on Music,* trans. and ed. Richard Langham Smith. London: Secker and Warburg, 1977.

Delacroix, Eugène. *The Journal of Eugène Delacroix,* a selection ed. Herbert Wellington, trans. Lucy Norton. Oxford: Phaidon Press, 1980.

Della Corte, Andrea. "Saggio bibliografico delle critiche al *Ballo in maschera*." *Verdi: Bollettino quadrimestrale dell'Istituto di Studi Verdiani* 1 (1960): 1165–97.

Della Seta, Fabrizio. "Il tempo della festa: Su due scene della *Traviata* e su altri luoghi verdiani." *Studi Verdiani* 2 (1983): 108–46.

———. "L'atto di Carlo Quinto." In *Ernani ieri e oggi: Atti del convegno internazionale di studi, Modena, Teatro San Carlo, 9–10 dicembre 1984*, 161–75. *Verdi: Bollettino dell'Istituto di Studi Verdiani* 10. Parma: Istituto di Studi Verdiani, 1987.

———. "L'immagine di Meyerbeer nella critica italiana dell'Ottocento e l'idea di 'dramma musicale.'" In *L'opera tra Venezia e Parigi*, vol. 1, ed. Maria Teresa Muraro, 147–76. Studi di musica veneta, no. 14. Florence: Olschki, 1988.

———. "'Parola scenica' in Verdi e nella critica verdiana." In *Studi sulla lingua della letteratura musicale in onore di Gianfranco Folena*, ed. Fiamma Nicolidi and Paolo Trovato, 259–86. Le parole della musica, no. 1. Florence: Olschki, 1994.

———. "Verdi: la tradizione italiana e l'esperienza europea." *Musica/realtá* 32 (August 1990): 135–58.

Delon, Michel. "La Saint-Barthélemy et la Terreur chez Mme de Staël et les historiens de la Révolution au XIXe siècle." *Romantisme* 31 (1981): 49–62.

Dent, Edward J. *The Rise of Romantic Opera (Lectures originally delivered at Cornell University, 1937–8)*, ed. Winton Dean. Cambridge: Cambridge University Press, 1976.

Derré, Jean-René. "Les Théâtres parisiens en 1835 vus de Vienne." In *Littérature et politique dans l'Europe du XIXe siècle*, 331–57. Lyon: Presses Universitaires de Lyon, 1986.

Deschamps, Émile. "Le Duo du 4e acte des *Huguenots*" [letter]. *Le Ménéstrel* 33 (1866): 171–72.

Descotes, Maurice. *Le Public de théâtre et son histoire*. Paris: Presses Universitaires de France, 1964.

Deshayes, [André-Jean-Jacques]. *Idées générales sur l'Académie Royale de Musique, et plus spécialement sur la danse*. Paris: Mongie, 1822.

Desnoyers, Louis. *De l'Opéra en 1847: A propos de "Robert Bruce," des directions passées, de la direction présente et de quelques-unes des cinq cents directions futures*. Paris: Delanchy, 1847.

Deux amis des beaux-arts. *Académie royale de musique: A Messieurs les députés*. Paris: Imprimerie Proux, 1843.

Devrient, Eduard. *Briefe aus Paris*. Berlin: Jonas, 1840.

Devriès, Anik. "La Maison Brandus: Heurs et malheurs d'un commerce d'éditions musicales au XIXe siècle." *Revue de musicologie* 70 (1984): 51–82.

———. "Un Éditeur 'à la tête ardente': Maurice Schlesinger." *Fontes artis musicae* 27 (1980): 125–36.

Diderot, Denis. *De la Poésie dramatique* [1758]. In *Oeuvres complètes revues* [. . .] par J[ules] Assézat et [from vol. 18:] Maurice Tourneux, 6:299–394. 20 vols. Paris: Garnier, 1875–77; reprinted, Nendeln: Kraus, 1966.

Dieren, Bernard van. "Meyerbeer." In *Down among the Dead Men, and Other Es-*

says, 142–74. London: Oxford University Press, 1935; reprinted, Freeport, N.Y.: Books for Libraries, 1967.

Dimopoulos, Aristide G. *L'Opinion publique française et la révolution grecque (1821–1827)*. Nancy: Idoux, 1962.

Döhring, Sieghart. "Der andere Choral: Zur Dramaturgie von Marcels Monolog aus *Les Huguenots*." In *Giacomo Meyerbeer — Musik als Welterfahrung: Heinz Becker zum 70. Geburtstag*, ed. Sieghart Döhring and Jürgen Schläder, 39–61. Munich: Ricordi, 1995.

———. "Die Autographen der vier Hauptopern Meyerbeers: Ein erster Quellenbericht." *Archiv für Musikwissenschaft* 39 (1982): 32–63.

———. "Die Wahnsinnsszene." In *Die "Couleur locale" in der Oper des 19. Jahrhunderts*, ed. Heinz Becker, 79–314. Studien zur Musikgeschichte des 19. Jahrhunderts, no. 42. Regensburg: Bosse, 1976.

———. "Formgeschichte der Opernarie vom Ausgang des achtzehnten bis zur Mitte des neunzehnten Jahrhunderts." Diss. phil., University of Marburg 1969; (printed Itzehoe: George, 1975).

———. "Giacomo Meyerbeer: Grand opéra als Ideendrama." *lendemains* 31–32 (1983): 11–22.

———. "Meyerbeers Konzeption der historischen Oper und Wagners Musikdrama." In *Wagnerliteratur — Wagnerforschung: Bericht über das Wagner-Symposium Munich 1983*, ed. Carl Dahlhaus and Egon Voss, 95–100. Mainz: Schott, 1985.

———. "Meyerbeers *Le Prophète* und Verdis *Don Carlos*." In *Transmissione e recezione delle forme di cultura musicale: Atti del XIV° congresso della società internazionale di musicologia, Bologna, 27 agosto–10 settembre 1987, Ferrara-Parma, 30 agosto 1987*, ed. Angelo Pompilio, Donatella Restani, Lorenzo Bianconi, and F. Alberto Gallo, vol. 1, pp. 727–33. Turin: EDT, 1990.

———. "Multimediale Tendenzen in der französischen Oper des 19. Jahrhunderts." In *International Musicological Society: Report of the Twelfth Congress, Berkeley 1977*, ed. Daniel Heartz and Rachel Wade, 497–500. Kassel: Bärenreiter, 1981.

———. "Private Tragödie und politischer Akt: Zum Kompositionsprozeß der *Bénédiction des poignards* aus Meyerbeers *Les Huguenots*." In *Opernkomposition als Prozeß: Referate des Symposiums Bochum 1995*, ed. Werner Breig, pp. 113–25. Musikwissenschaftliche Arbeiten, no. 29. Kassel: Bärenreiter, 1996.

Dömling, Wolfgang. *Hector Berlioz: Die symphonisch-dramatischen Werke*. Stuttgart: Reclam, 1979.

———. "Szenerie im Imaginären: Über dramatisch-symphonische Werke von Hector Berlioz." *Melos/Neue Zeitschrift für Musik* 3 (1977): 195–203.

Duchet, Claude. "La Saint-Barthélemy: De la 'scène historique' au drame romantique." *Revue d'histoire littéraire de la France* 73 (1973): 845–52.

Dumas, Alexandre [père]. "Un Dîner chez Rossini." In *Les mille et un Fantômes*, 2:79–93. Brussels: Meline, Cans, 1849.

[Duvergier de Hauranne, Prosper-Léon]. "Du Mélange du comique et du tragique" [*signed* O.]. *Le Globe* 3 (January–August 1826): 308–10, 385–7.

Eckermann, Johann Peter. *Conversations with Goethe*, trans. John Oxenford. New York: Dutton, 1971.

Edler, Arnfried. "'Glanzspiel und Seelenlandschaft': Naturdarstellung in der Oper bei Weber und Rossini." In *Weber — Jenseits des "Freischütz": Referate des Eutiner Symposions 1986 anläßlich des 200. Geburtstages von Carl Maria von Weber*, ed. Friedhelm Krummacher and Heinrich W. Schwab, 71–83. Kieler Schriften zur Musikwissenschaft, no. 32. Kassel: Bärenreiter, 1989.

Eggli, Edmond. *Schiller et le romantisme français*. 2 vols. Paris: Gamber 1927; reprinted, Geneva: Slatkine, 1970.

Eichberg, Henning. *Leistung, Spannung, Geschwindigkeit: Sport und Tanz im gesellschaftlichen Wandel des 18./19. Jahrhunderts*. Stuttgarter Beiträge zur Geschichte und Politik, no. 12. Stuttgart: Klett-Cotta, 1978.

Ellenberger, Henry F. *The Discovery of the Unconscious: The History and Evolution of Dynamic Psychiatry*. New York: Basic Books, 1970.

Ellis, Katherine. *Music Criticism in Nineteenth-Century France: La Revue et Gazette Musicale de Paris, 1834–80*. Cambridge: Cambridge University Press, 1995.

Engelhardt, Markus. "Versioni operistiche dell' *Hernani*." In *Ernani ieri e oggi: Atti del convegno internazionale di studi, Modena, Teatro San Carlo, 9–10 dicembre 1984*, 104–22. *Verdi: Bollettino dell'Istituto di Studi Verdiani* 10. Parma: Istituto di Studi Verdiani, 1987.

Ernst, Fritz. *Vom Heimweh*. Zurich: Fretz and Wasmuth, 1949.

Escudier, Léon, and Marie Escudier. *Rossini: Sa vie et ses oeuvres*. Paris: Dentu, 1854.

Everist, Mark. "Meyerbeer's *Il crociato in Egitto*: 'Mélodrame,' opera, orientalism." *Cambridge Opera Journal* 8 (1996): 215–50.

———. "The name of the rose: Meyerbeer's 'opéra comique,' *Robert le Diable*." *Revue de musicologie* 80 (1994): 211–50.

Explication des ouvrages de peinture, sculpture, architecture et gravure des artistes vivans, exposés au Musée Royal des arts, le 25 août 1824. Paris: Ballard, 1824.

Eymieu, Henri. *L'Oeuvre de Meyerbeer*. Paris: Fischbacher, 1910.

Faure, Michel. "Opéra historique et problématique sociale en France, du premier au second Empire." In *La Musique et le pouvoir*, ed. Hugues Dufourt and Joël-Marie Fauquet, 87–101. Paris: Aux amateurs de livres, 1987.

Fénelon, François de Salignac de La Mothe. *Écrits et lettres politiques publiés sur les manuscrits autographes* par Ch[arles] Urbain. Paris: Bossard, 1920; reprinted, Geneva: Slatkine, 1981.

———. *Oeuvres complètes précédées de son histoire littéraire* par M. [Jean-Edme-Auguste Gosselin]. 10 vols. Paris: Méquignon, Leroux et Jouby, 1848–52; reprinted, Geneva: Slatkine, 1971.

Fétis, François-Joseph. "Académie royale de musique: Première représentation de *Guillaume Tell*." *Revue musicale* 6 (1829–30): 34–46.

———. Review of Castil-Blaze's *De l'Opéra en France*, 2d ed. *Revue musicale* 1 (February–July 1827): 472–78.

Filippi, Filippo. "*Un ballo in maschera*: Melodramma in tre atti, musica di Giuseppe Verdi." *Gazzetta musicale di Milano* 17 (1859): 91–4, 115–17, 131–5,

139–142, 147–150; reprinted, *Gazzetta musicale di Milano* 20, no. 2 (12 January 1862): supplement, i–vi.

———. *Musica e musicisti: Critiche, biografie ed escursioni: Haydn, Beethoven, Weber, Meyerbeer, Rossini, Schumann, Wagner, Verdi*. Milan: Brigola, 1876.

Finscher, Ludwig. "Aubers *La muette de Portici* und die Anfänge der Grand-opéra." In *Festschrift Heinz Becker zum 60. Geburtstag am 26. Juni 1982*, ed. Jürgen Schlöder and Reinhold Quandt, 87–105. Laaber: Laaber, 1982.

Foscolo, Ugo. "Dell'impresa d'un teatro per musica" [1821]. In *Opere edite e postume: Prose letterarie*, 4:378–412. Florence: Le Monnier. 1939.

Foucault, Michel. *The Order of Things: An archaeology of the human sciences*. London: Tavistock, 1970.

Franceschetti, Giancarlo. *La fortuna di Hugo nel melodramma italiano dell'Ottocento*. In *Pubblicazioni dell'Università del Sacro Cuore* [Milan], 3d ser. (*Scienze filologiche e letteratura*), 2 (1961): 168–251.

Frederichs, Henning. "Das Rezitativ in den *Hugenotten* G. Meyerbeers." In *Beiträge zur Geschichte der Oper*, ed. Heinz Becker, 55–76. Studien zur Musikgeschichte des 19. Jahrhunderts, no. 15. Regensburg: Bosse, 1969.

Frese, Christhard. *Dramaturgie der großen Opern Giacomo Meyerbeers*. Berlin-Lichterfelde: Lienau, 1970.

Freud, Sigmund. *Beyond the Pleasure Principle*, a new translation by James Strachey. London: The Hogarth Press and The Institute of Psycho-Analysis, 1950.

———. *Mourning and Melancholia*. In *The Standard Edition of the Complete Psychological Works of Sigmund Freud*, trans. from the German under the general editorship of James Strachey. Vol. 14 [works of 1914–1916], 237–60.

Frigessi Castelnuovo, Delia, and Michele Risso. *A mezza parete: Emigrazione, nostalgia, malattia mentale*. Turin: Einaudi, 1982.

Fromental Halévy: La Juive: Dossier de presse parisienne (1835), ed. Karl Leich-Galland. Saarbrücken: Galland, 1987.

Fulcher, Jane. *The Nation's Image: French Grand Opera as Politics and Politicized Art*. Cambridge: Cambridge University Press, 1987.

Gabler, Werner. *Der Zuschauerraum des Theaters*. Theatergeschichtliche Forschungen, no. 44. Leipzig: Voss, 1935; reprinted, Nendeln, Lichtenstein: Kraus, 1977.

Gail, Jean François. *Réflexions sur le goût musical en France*. Paris: Paulin, 1832.

Gallini, Clara. *La sonnambula meravigliosa: Magnetismo e ipnotismo nell'Ottocento italiano*. Milan: Feltrinelli, 1983.

Gara, Eugenio. "Il cammino dell'opera in un secolo d'interpretazioni." *Verdi: Bollettino quadrimestrale dell'Istituto di Studi Verdiani* 1 (1960): 112–33, 704–19, 1155–64.

Garlington, Aubrey Sam. "The Concept of the Marvelous in French and German opera, 1770–1840: A Chapter in the History of Opera Esthetics." Ph.D. diss., University of Illinois, 1965.

Gartioux, Hervé. *Giuseppe Verdi: Les Vêpres Siciliennes: Dossier de presse parisienne (1855)*. Critiques de l'opéra français du XIXème siècle, no. 6. [Bietigheim]: Galland, 1995.

Gautier, Théophile. *Histoire de l'art dramatique en France depuis vingt-cinq ans.* 6 vols. Paris: Hetzel, 1858–9.

Gay, Delphine [Mme Émile de Girardin]. *Le Vicomte de Launay, lettres parisiennes.* 4 vols. Paris: Lévy, 1857.

Gerbod, Paul. "La Scène parisienne et sa représentation de l'histoire nationale dans la première moitié du XIXe siècle." *La Revue historique* 266 (1981): 3–30.

Gerhard, Anselm. "'Ce cinquième acte sans intérêt': Preoccupazioni di Scribe e di Verdi per la drammaturgia de *Les Vêpres Siciliennes.*" *Studi Verdiani* 4 (1986–87): 65–86.

———. "Dalla fatalità all'ossessione: *Il trovatore* fra 'mélodrame' parigino e opera moderna." *Studi Verdiani* 10 (1994–95): 61–66.

———. "Die französische 'Grand Opéra' in der Forschung seit 1945." *Acta musicologica* 59 (1987): 220–70.

———. "Die Macht der Fatalität: Victor Hugo als Librettist." In *Zwischen tragédie lyrique und Grand Opéra. Französische Oper im 18. und 19. Jahrhundert,* ed. Albert Gier and Jürgen Maehder. Perspektiven der Opernforschung, no. 3. Frankfurt am Main: Lang, forthcoming.

———. "*Fernand Cortez* und *Le Siège de Corinthe:* Spontini und die Anfänge der 'Grand Opéra.'" In *Atti del terzo Congresso Internazionale di studi spontiniani, Maiolati Spontini/Jesi 1983,* 93–111. Maiolati Spontini: Comitato comunale permanente di studi spontiniani, 1985.

———. "Incantesimo o specchio dei costumi: Un'estetica dell'opera del librettista di *Guillaume Tell.*" *Bollettino del Centro Rossiniano di Studi* 1–3 (1987): 45–60.

———. "La 'Liberté'—inadmissible à l'Opéra." In *Rossini, Le Siège de Corinthe,* 69–71. L'Avant-Scène Opéra, no. 75. Paris: Loft, 1985.

———. "'La prière qui nous paraît être d'un pittoresque achevé': Ein Plädoyer für Hedwiges Solo im vierten Akt von Rossinis *Guillaume Tell.*" in *D'un Opéra à l'autre: Hommage à Jean Mongrédien,* ed. Jean Gribenski, Marie-Claire Mussat, and Herbert Schneider, 287–94. Paris: Presses de l'Université de Paris-Sorbonne, 1996.

———. "L'eroe titubante e il finale aperto: Un dilemma insolubile nel *Guillaume Tell* di Rossini." *Rivista italiana di musicologia* 19 (1984): 113–30.

———. "Lieu et espace comme éléments de la dramaturgie musicale." *Associação Portuguesa de educação musical: Boletim* 62 (July–September 1989): 5–11.

———. "Meyerbeer, Giacomo." In *Metzler Komponisten Lexikon: 340 werkgeschichtliche Porträts,* ed. Horst Weber, 490–93. Stuttgart: Metzler, 1992.

———. "Religiöse Aura und militärisches Gepränge: Meyerbeers Ouvertüren und das Problem der rein instrumentalen Form." In *Giacomo Meyerbeer 1791–1991: Bericht von den Symposien Schloß Thurnau, 25.–29. September 1991 und 20.–24. September 1995,* ed. Heinz Becker, Sieghart Döhring, and Gunhild Oberzaucher-Schüller. Munich: Ricordi, forthcoming.

———. "Republikanische Zustände: Der *tragico fine* in den Dramen Metastasios." In *Zwischen Opera buffa und Melodramma: Italienische Oper im 18. und 19. Jahrhundert,* ed. Jürgen Maehder and Jürg Stenzl, 27–65. Perspektiven der Opernforschung, no. 1. Frankfurt am Main: Lang, 1994.

————. "'Sortire dalle vie comuni': Wie Rossini einem Akademiker das Libretto verdarb." In *Der Text im Musiktheater: Romanistische Beiträge zur Libretto-Forschung*, ed. Albert Gier, 185–219. Studia romanica, no. 63. Heidelberg: Winter, 1986.

————. "'Une véritable Révolution opérée à l'Opéra français.'" In *Rossini, "Le Siège de Corinthe,"* 21–23. L'Avant-Scène Opéra, no. 75. Paris: Loft, 1985.

Gerhartz, Leo Karl. *Die Auseinandersetzungen des jungen Giuseppe Verdi mit dem literarischen Drama: Ein Beitrag zur szenischen Strukturbestimmung der Oper.* Berlin: Merseburger, 1968.

Gernsheim, Helmut, and Alison Gernsheim. *L. J. M. Daguerre: A History of the Diorama and the Daguerrotype.* London: Secker and Warburg, 1956.

Geyer-Kiefl, Helen. *Die heroisch-komische Oper, ca. 1770–1820.* Würzburger musikhistorische Beiträge, no. 9. Tutzing: Schneider, 1987.

Ghislanzoni, Antonio. "Del Libretto per musica." In *Giornale Capriccio* 15 (August 1877): 18–29; and 19 (October 1877): 9–19.

Gier, Albert. "Jakobiner-Austreibung: Das Volk in den grands opéras von Eugène Scribe." In *"Weine, weine, du armes Volk": Das verführte und betrogene Volk auf der Bühne: Gesammelte Vorträge des Salzburger Symposiums 1994*, ed. Peter Csobádi, Gernot Gruber, Jürgen Kühnel, Ulrich Müller, Oswald Panagl, and Franz Viktor Spechtler, vol. 1, pp. 233–42. Wort und Musik: Salzburger akademische Beiträge, no. 28. Anif/Salzburg: Müller-Speiser, 1995.

Gillespie, Patti P. "Plays: Well-constructed and well-made." *Quarterly Journal of Speech* 58 (1972): 313–21.

————. "Plays: Well-complicated." *Speech Monographs* 42 (March 1975): 20–28.

Glasson, Ernest. *Le Mariage civil et le divorce dans l'antiquité et dans les principales législations modernes de l'Europe: Étude de législation comparée précédée d'un aperçu sur les origines du droit civil moderne* [1879]. 2d ed. Paris: Durand et Pédone-Lauriel, 1880.

Godlewski, Guy. "L'étonnante carrière du Docteur Véron." *Souvenir napoléonien* 43 (1980): 34–40.

Gordon, Margaret Maria. *The Home Life of Sir David Brewster, by his daughter.* Edinburgh: Edmonston and Douglas, 1869.

Gossett, Philip. "Becoming a citizen: The chorus in *Risorgimento* opera." *Cambridge Opera Journal* 2 (1990): 41–64.

————. "Rossini e i suoi *Péchés de Vieillesse*." *Nuova rivista musicale italiana* 14 (1980): 7–26.

————. "The composition of *Ernani*." In *Analyzing Opera: Verdi and Wagner*, ed. Carolyn Abbate and Roger Parker, 27–55. California Studies in 19th-century Music, no. 6. Berkeley and Los Angeles: University of California Press, 1989.

————. "Verdi, Ghislanzoni and *Aida:* The uses of convention." *Critical Inquiry* 1 (1974): 291–334.

Gourret, Jean. *Ces Hommes qui ont fait l'Opéra, 1669–1984.* Paris: Albatros, 1984.

————. *Histoire des salles de l'Opéra de Paris.* Paris: Trédaniel, 1985.

Grace, Michael D. "Méhul's *Ariodant* and the early leitmotif." In *A Festschrift for*

Albert Seay: Essays by His Friends and Colleagues, ed. Michael D. Grace, 173–93. Colorado Springs: Colorado College, 1982.

Graevenitz, Gerhart von. *Mythos: Zur Geschichte einer Denkgewohnheit.* Stuttgart: Metzler, 1987.

Grandville [Jean-Ignace-Isidore Gérard]. *Un autre Monde: Transformations, visions, incarnations, ascensions, locomotions, explorations, pérégrinations, excursions, stations; Cosmogories, fantasmagories, rêveries, folâtreries, facéties, lubies; Métamorphoses, zoomorphoses, lithomorphoses, métempsycoses, apothéoses et autres choses.* Paris: Fournier, 1844.

Gregor, Joseph. *Kulturgeschichte der Oper: Ihre Verbindung mit dem Leben, den Werken des Geistes und der Politik.* Vienna: Gallus, 1941.

Grétry, André-Ernest-Modeste. *Mémoires, ou Essais sur la musique.* 3 vols. Paris: Imprimerie de la République, an V [1797].

Griepenkerl, Wolfgang Robert. *Die Oper der Gegenwart: Vortrag zur ersten Tonkünstler-Versammlung im Saale des Gewandhauses am 14. August 1847.* Leipzig: Hinrichs 1847; also published in *Neue Zeitschrift für Musik* 17 (July–December 1847): 97–104.

Grillparzer, Franz. *Sämtliche Werke: Historisch-kritische Gesamtausgabe*, ed. August Sauer. 3 sections: 23, 13, and 6 vols. Vienna: Schroll 1909–48.

Grimm, Gunter. *Rezeptionsgeschichte: Grundlegung einer Theorie: Mit Analysen und Bibliographie.* Uni-Taschenbücher, no. 691. Munich: Fink, 1977.

Grobert, [Jacques-François-Louis]. *De l'Exécution dramatique, considérée dans ses rapports avec le matériel de la salle et de la scène.* Paris: Schoell, 1809.

Groeber, Karl. *Kinderspielzeug aus alter Zeit.* 2d ed., rev. Juliane Metzger. Hamburg: Schröder, 1965.

[Guizot, François]. *Chambre des Députés, Session de 1835: Discours prononcé par M. Guizot, Ministre de l'instruction publique, dans la discussion du projet de loi sur la presse* (Extrait du *Moniteur* du 29 août 1835). Paris: Agasse, 1835.

Günther, Ursula. "La Genèse de *Don Carlos*, opéra en cinq actes de Giuseppe Verdi, représenté pour la première fois à Paris le 11 mars 1867." *Revue de musicologie* 58 (1972): 16–64; and 60 (1974): 87–158.

Habermas, Jürgen. *Strukturwandel der Öffentlichkeit: Untersuchungen zu einer Kategorie der bürgerlichen Gesellschaft.* Darmstadt: Luchterhand, 1962.

Hallays-Dabot, Victor. *Histoire de la censure théâtrale en France.* Paris: Dentu, 1862; reprinted, Geneva: Slatkine, 1970.

Hanslick, Eduard. *Die moderne Oper: Kritiken und Studien.* Berlin: Hofmann, 1875.

———. *Aus dem Opernleben der Gegenwart.* (*Die moderne Oper* 3) *Neue Kritiken und Studien.* Berlin: Hofmann, 1884.

———. *Musikalisches Skizzenbuch.* (*Die moderne Oper* 4) *Neue Kritiken und Schilderungen.* Berlin: Allgemeiner Verein für Deutsche Literatur, 1888.

[Hapdé, Jean-Baptiste Augustin]. *Plus de Mélodrames! Leurs dangers, considérés sous le rapport de la religion, des moeurs, de l'instruction publique et de l'art dramatique.* Paris: Dentu, 1814.

Haudek, Rosa. "Scribes Operntexte für Meyerbeer: Eine Quellenuntersuchung." Diss. phil., University of Vienna, 1928.

Hauser, Arnold. *The Social History of Art*, trans. in collaboration with the author by Stanley Godman. 2 vols. London: Routledge and Kegan Paul, 1951.

Heine, Heinrich. *Sämtliche Schriften*, ed. Klaus Briegleb. 6 vols. Munich: Hanser, 1968–76.

Heitmann, Klaus. *Der Immoralismus-Prozeß gegen die französische Literatur im 19. Jahrhundert.* Ars poetica: Texte und Studien zur Dichtungslehre und Dichtkunst, Studien, no. 9. Bad Homburg: Gehlen, 1970.

Hempel, Wido. *Manzoni und die Darstellung der Menschenmenge als erzähltechnisches Problem in den "Promessi Sposi," bei Scott und in den historischen Romanen der französischen Romantik.* Schriften und Vorträge des Petrarca-Instituts Köln, no. 26. Krefeld: Scherpe, 1974.

Henscheid, Eckhard. "Das dreizehnte *Addio* war tödlich: Der ewige Abschiednehmer Riccardo aus *Maskenball.*" In Eckhard Henscheid and Chlodwig Poth, *Verdi ist der Mozart Wagners: Ein Opernführer für Versierte und Versehrte*, 32–43. Lucerne: Bucher, 1979.

Henze-Döhring, Sabine. "'Combinammo l'ossatura . . .': Voltaire und die Librettistik des frühen Ottocento." *Die Musikforschung* 36 (1983): 113–27.

Herz, Joachim. "Für einen lebendigen Meyerbeer." In Giacomo Meyerbeer, *Die Hugenotten*, 212–17. Peters-Textbücher, no. 15. Leipzig: Edition Peters, 1979.

———. "Unverantwortliche Gedanken und zu verantwortende Erfahrungen mit Giacomo Meyerbeer." *Musik und Gesellschaft* 39 (1989): 238–41.

Heuvel, Gerd van den. "Terreur, terroriste, terrorisme." In *Handbuch politisch-sozialer Grundbegriffe in Frankreich 1680–1820*, ed. Rolf Reichardt and Eberhard Schmitt, with Gerd van den Heuvel and Anette Höfer, vol. 3, 89–132. Munich: Oldenbourg, 1985.

Higonnet, Margaret. "Suicide: Representations of the feminine in the nineteenth century." *Poetics Today* 6 (1985): 103–18.

Hiller, Ferdinand. *Aus dem Tonleben unserer Zeit: Gelegentliches.* 2 vols. Leipzig: Mendelssohn, 1868.

Hoeges, Dirk. *Alles veloziferisch: Die Eisenbahn—vom schönen Ungeheuer zur Ästhetik der Geschwindigkeit.* Literaturwissenschaftliche Monographien, no. 1. Rheinbach-Merzbach: CMZ, 1985.

Hofmann, Werner. *Das irdische Paradies: Motive und Ideen des 19. Jahrhunderts* [1960]. 2d ed. Munich: Prestel, 1974.

Holmström, Kirsten Gram. *Monodrama, attitudes, tableaux vivants: studies on some trends of theatrical fashion 1770–1815.* Acta universitatis Stockholmiensis; Stockholm Studies in Theatrical History, no. 1. Stockholm: Almquist and Wiksell; Totowa, N.J.: J. Boonin, 1967.

Holoman, D. Kern. *Catalogue of the works of Hector Berlioz.* Hector Berlioz, New Edition of the Complete Works, 25. Kassel: Bärenreiter, 1987.

Hortensius, Lambertus [trans. François Catrou]. *[Tumultuum Anabaptistarum] Histoire des anabaptistes ou Relation curieuse de leur doctrine, Regne & Revolutions, tant en Allemagne, Hollande, qu'Angleterre, ou il êt traité de plusieurs sectes de Mennonites, Kouakres, & autres qui en sont provenus.* Paris: Clouzier, 1695.

Hortschansky, Klaus. "Die Herausbildung eines deutschsprachigen Verdi-

Repertoires im 19. Jahrhundert und die zeitgenössische Kritik." In *Colloquium "Verdi-Wagner," Rom 1969: Bericht*, ed. Friedrich Lippmann, 140–82. Analecta musicologica, no. 11. Cologne: Böhlau, 1972.

Huebner, Steven. "Italianate duets in Meyerbeer's Grand Operas." *Journal of Musicological Research* 8 (1988–89): 203–58.

———. "Opera audiences in Paris 1830–1870." *Music and Letters* 70 (1989): 206–25.

———. *The Operas of Charles Gounod*. Oxford: Clarendon Press, 1990.

[Hugo, Adèle]. *Victor Hugo raconté par un témoin de sa vie*. 2 vols. Paris: Librairie internationale, 1863.

Hugo, Victor. *Oeuvres complètes*, ed. Jean Massin. 18 vols. Paris: Le Club français du livre, 1967–70.

———. *Théâtre complet*, ed. J.-J. Thierry and Josette Mélèze. 2 vols. Paris: Gallimard, 1963–64.

[Hus, Auguste]. *Le Kaléidoscope philosophique et littéraire, ou, l'Encyclopédie en miniature* 1 (1818).

Iknayan, Marguerite. *The Concave Mirror: From imitation to expression in French esthetic theory 1800–1830*. Stanford French and Italian studies, no. 30. Saratoga, Calif.: Anima Libri, 1983.

Jahrmärker, Manuela. *Ossian: Eine Figur und eine Idee des europäischen Musiktheaters um 1800*. Berliner Musik Studien, no. 2. Cologne: Studio, 1993.

Jardin, André, and André-Jean Tudesq. *La France des notables*. 2 vols. Nouvelle histoire de la France contemporaine, vols. 6–7. Paris: Éditions du Seuil, 1973.

Jauß, Hans Robert. "Das Ende der Kunstperiode—Aspekte der literarischen Revolution bei Heine, Hugo und Stendhal." In *Literaturgeschichte als Provokation*, 107–43. Frankfurt am Main: Suhrkamp, 1970.

Johnson, James H. *Listening in Paris: A Cultural History*. Studies on the History of Society and Culture, no. 21. Berkeley and Los Angeles: University of California Press, 1995.

Johnson, Janet. "Rossini e le sue opere al Théâtre Italien a Parigi." In *Rossini 1792–1992: Mostra storica-documentaria*, ed. Mauro Bucarelli, 221–44. Perugia: Electa, 1992.

———. "Rossini in Bologna and Paris during the early 1830s: New letters." *Revue de musicologie* 79 (1993): 69–81.

Join-Dieterle, Catherine. "La Monarchie source d'inspiration de l'Opéra à l'époque romantique." *Revue d'histoire du théâtre* 35 (1983): 430–41.

———. *Les Décors de scène de l'Opéra de Paris à l'époque romantique*. Paris: Picard, 1988.

———. "L'Opéra et son public à l'époque romantique." *L'Oeil* 288–89 (July–August 1979): 30–37.

Joly, Jacques. "Les Ambiguités de la guerre napoléonienne dans *Fernand Cortez* de Spontini." In *La Bataille, l'armée, la gloire, Actes du colloque Clermont-Ferrand 1983*, 239–55. Clermont-Ferrand: Association des publications de Clermont II, 1985.

———. "Gli elementi spettacolari nel *Fernand Cortez*." In *Atti del terzo Congresso*

Internazionale di studi spontiniani, Maiolati Spontini/Jesi 1983, 69–91. Maiolati Spontini: Comitato comunale permanente di studi spontiniani, 1985.

Jouy, Victor-Joseph Étienne de. *Essai sur l'Opéra français.* In *Oeuvres complètes*, vol. 22, pp. 225–82; modern edition, ed. Anselm Gerhard, *Bollettino del Centro Rossiniano di Studi*, no. 1–3 (1987), pp. 61–91.

———. *Oeuvres complètes.* 27 vols. Paris: Didot, 1823–8.

Jürgensen, Knud-Arne. *The Verdi Ballets.* Premio internazionale Rotary Club di Parma "Giuseppe Verdi," no. 4. Parma: Istituto Nazionale di Studi Verdiani, 1995.

Kambartel, Walter. "Kontrast" I. In *Historisches Wörterbuch der Philosophie*, ed. Joachim Ritter and Karlfried Gründer, vol. 4, coll. 1066–67. Basel, Stuttgart: Schwabe, 1976.

Karbusicky, Vladimir. *Widerspiegelungstheorie und Strukturalismus: Zur Entstehungsgeschichte und Kritik der marxistisch-leninistischen Ästhetik.* Kritische Informationen, no. 3. Munich: Fink, 1973. [German translation from the Czech: *Podstata umění: Sociologický příspěvek do diskuse o gnoseologismu v estetice a teorii umění.* Prague: Horizont, 1969.]

Każyński, Wiktor. *Notatki z podróży muzykalnej po Niemczech odbylej w roku 1844* [1845], ed. Witold Rudziński. Źród ła pami etnikarsko-literackie do dziejów muzyki polskiej, no. 3. Kraków: PWM, 1957.

Kemp, Wolfgang. "Das Bild der Menge (1789–1830)," *Städel-Jahrbuch*, n. s., 4 (1973): 249–70.

———. "Masse—Mensch." In *Der Einzelne und die Masse: Kunstwerke des 19. und 20. Jahrhunderts*, [9]–[16]. Exhibition catalogue. Recklinghausen: Städtische Kunsthalle, 1975.

Kerman, Joseph. "Verdi's use of recurring themes." In *Studies in Music History: Essays for Oliver Strunk*, ed. Harold Powers, 495–510. Princeton, N.J.: Princeton University Press, 1968.

———. "Viewpoint." *19th-Century Music* 2 (1978–79): 186–91.

Kern, Bernd-Rüdiger. "Meister der Verhandlungstaktik: Gioachino Rossinis Verträge mit der Krone Frankreichs." *Neue Zeitschrift für Musik* 153, no. 3 (1992): 13–18.

Kirchmeyer, Helmut. "Die deutsche Librettokritik bei Eugène Scribe und Giacomo Meyerbeer." *Neue Zeitschrift für Musik* 125 (1964): 372–76.

———. "Psychologie des Meyerbeer-Erfolges." *Neue Zeitschrift für Musik* 125 (1964): 471–76.

Kirsch, Winfried. "Carl Maria von Webers Konzertstück f-moll opus 79." In *Studien zur Instrumentalmusik: Lothar Hoffmann-Erbrecht zum 60. Geburtstag*, ed. Anke Bingmann, Klaus Hortschansky, and Winfried Kirsch, 363–94. Frankfurter Beiträge zur Musikwissenschaft, no. 20. Tutzing: Schneider 1988.

Kitchin, Joanna. *Un Journal "philosophique": "La Décade" (1794–1807).* Bibliothèque de littérature et d'histoire, no. 5. Paris: Minard, 1965.

Klotz, Volker. *Die erzählte Stadt: Ein Sujet als Herausforderung des Romans von Lesage bis Döblin.* Munich: Hanser, 1969.

Köhler, Erich. *Der literarische Zufall, das Mögliche und die Notwendigkeit.* Munich: Fink, 1973.

Koon, Helene, and Richard Switzer. *Eugène Scribe*. Boston, Mass.: Twayne, 1980.

Koschorke, Albrecht. "Das Panorama: Die Anfänge der modernen Sensomoto-rik um 1800." In *Die Mobilisierung des Sehens: Zur Vor- und Frühgeschichte des Films in Literatur und Kunst*, ed. Harro Segeberg, 149–69. Mediengeschichte des Films, no. 1. Munich: Fink, 1996.

Koselleck, Reinhart. Introduction to *Geschichtliche Grundbegriffe: Historisches Lexikon zur politisch-sozialen Sprache in Deutschland*, ed. Otto Brunner, Werner Conze, and Reinhart Koselleck, vol. 1, pp. xiii–xxvii. Stuttgart: Klett, 1972.

———. *Futures Past: On the Semantics of Historical Time*, trans. Keith Tribe. Cambridge, Mass.: MIT. Press, 1985. [A translation of *Vergangene Zukunft: Zur Semantik geschichtlicher Zeiten*. Frankfurt am Main: Suhrkamp, 1979.]

Krakovitch, Odile. *Hugo censuré: La liberté au théâtre au XIXe siècle*. Paris: Calmann-Lévy, 1985.

Krauss, Henning. Introduction to the section "Gattungssystem und Gesell-schaftssystem der französischen Literatur des 17. und 18. Jahrhunderts", in *Bildung und Ausbildung in der Romania: Akten des Romanistentages in Gießen 1977*, ed. Rolf Kloepfer et al., vol. 1: *Literaturgeschichte und Texttheorie*, 38–42. Munich: Fink, 1979.

Kunze, Stefan. "Fest und Ball in Verdis Opern." In *Die "Couleur locale" in der Oper des 19. Jahrhunderts*, ed. Heinz Becker, 269–78. Studien zur Musikge-schichte des 19. Jahrhunderts, no. 42. Regensburg: Bosse, 1976.

Labussek, Frank. *Zur Entwicklung des französischen Opernlibrettos im 19. Jahrhun-dert: Stationen des ästhetischen Wandels*. Europäische Hochschulschriften, ser. 13 (Französische Sprache und Literatur), no. 194. Frankfurt am Main: Lang, 1994.

Lahalle, Pierre. *Essai sur la musique, ses fonctions dans les moeurs, et sa véritable expression; suivi d'une bibliographie musicale*. Paris: Rousselon, 1825.

Lajarte, Théodore de. *Bibliothèque musicale du Théâtre de l'Opéra: Catalogue histo-rique, chronologique, anecdotique*. 2 vols. Paris: Librairie des bibliophiles, 1878; reprinted, Geneva: Slatkine; and Hildesheim: G. Olms, 1969.

Lamartine, Alphonse de. *Oeuvres poétiques complètes*, ed. Marius-François Guyard. Paris: Gallimard, 1963.

Lämmert, Eberhard. "Zum Wandel der Geschichtserfahrung im Reflex der Ro-mantheorie." In *Geschichte — Ereignis und Erzählung*, ed. Reinhart Koselleck and Wolf-Dieter Stempel, 503–15. Poetik und Hermeneutik, no. 5. Munich: Fink, 1973.

Lan, Jules. *Mémoires d'un chef de claque: Souvenirs des théâtres de Paris*. Paris: Li-brairie nouvelle, 1883.

Lapauze, Henry. "La Reprise de *Faust* à l'Opéra: Lettres inédites de Gounod— Souvenirs de M. J.-P. Barbier." *Le Gaulois*, 4 December 1893, pp. 1–2.

La Rochefoucauld-Doudeauville, Louis-François-Sosthène de. *Mémoires*. 15 vols. Paris: Lévy, 1861–4.

Lasalle, Albert de. *Les treize salles de l'Opéra*. Paris: Sartorius, 1875.

Laudon, Robert T. *Sources of the Wagnerian Synthesis: A Study of the Franco-German Tradition in 19th-century Opera*. Musikwissenschaftliche Schriften, no. 2. Munich: Katzbichler, 1979.

Le Bon, Gustave. *Psychologie des foules.* Paris: Alcan, 1895.

Legouvé, Ernest. *Eugène Scribe.* Paris: Didier, 1874.

Leich-Galland, Karl. "Pariser Pressestimmen zur Uraufführung von Fromental Halévys *La Juive* (1835)." In *Zwischen tragédie lyrique und Grand Opéra: Französische Oper im 18. und 19. Jahrhundert,* ed. Albert Gier and Jürgen Maehder. Perspektiven der Opernforschung, vol. 3. Frankfurt am Main: Lang, forthcoming.

Lepenies, Wolf. *Das Ende der Naturgeschichte: Wandel kultureller Selbstverständlichkeiten in den Wissenschaften des 18. und 19. Jahrhunderts.* Munich: Hanser, 1976.

———. *Melancholie und Gesellschaft.* Frankfurt am Main: Suhrkamp, 1969.

Le Vacher de Charnais, Jean-Charles. *Costumes et annales des grands théâtres de Paris, en figures au lavis et coloriées.* Troisième année. 4 vols. Paris: Janinet, 1786–89.

Levarie, Siegmund. "A pitch cell in Verdi's *Un ballo in maschera.*" *Journal of Musicological Research* 3 (1979–81): 399–409.

———. "Key relations in Verdi's *Un ballo in maschera.*" *19th-Century Music* 2 (1978–79): 143–47.

Lewald, August. *Ein Menschenleben.* 12 vols. Leipzig: Brockhaus, 1844–46.

Lindenberger, Herbert. *Historical Drama: The Relations of Literature and Reality.* Chicago: University of Chicago Press, 1975.

———. *Opera: The Extravagant Art,* Ithaca, N.Y.: Cornell University Press, 1984.

Lippmann, Friedrich. "Rossinis Gedanken über die Musik." *Die Musikforschung* 22 (1969): 285–98.

———. *Vincenzo Bellini und die italienische opera seria seiner Zeit.* Analecta musicologica, no. 6. Cologne: Böhlau, 1969.

Liszt, Franz. "*Die Stumme von Portici* von Auber" [1854]. In *Sämtliche Schriften,* vol. 5: *Dramaturgische Blätter,* ed. Dorothea Redepenning and Britta Schilling, 27–30. Wiesbaden: Breitkopf & Härtel, 1989.

Locke, Ralph P. *Music, Musicians and Saint-Simonians.* Chicago: University of Chicago Press, 1986.

Longyear, Rey Morgan. "*La Muette de Portici.*" *The Music Review* 19 (1958): 37–46.

———. "Le livret bien fait: The Opéra Comique librettos of Eugène Scribe." *Southern Quarterly* 1 (1962–63): 169–92.

Lo Presti, Fulvio. "*Le Duc d'Albe:* The livret of Scribe and Duveyrier." *The Donizetti Society Journal* 5 (1984): 243–316.

Lotman, Yuri Mikhailovich. "The Stage and Painting as Code Mechanisms for Cultural Behavior in the Early Nineteenth Century," trans. Judith Armstrong. In Ju. M. Lotman and B. A. Uspenskij, *The Semiotics of Russian Culture,* ed. Ann Shukman, 165–76. Michigan Slavic Contributions, no. 11. Ann Arbor: University of Michigan, Department of Slavic Languages and Literature, 1984.

Luhmann, Niklas. *Liebe als Passion: Zur Codierung von Intimität.* Frankfurt am Main: Suhrkamp, 1984.

Luzio, Alessandro, ed. *Carteggi Verdiani.* 4 vols. Reale Accademia d'Italia, Studi e documenti, no. 4. Rome: Reale Accademia d'Italia (vols. 1–2); Accademia Nazionale dei Lincei, 1935–47.

Macdonald, Hugh. "[Nine-eight time, G flat major]." *19th-century Music* 11 (1987–88): 221–37.

———. "*Robert le diable.*" In *Music in Paris in the Eighteen-Thirties/La Musique à Paris dans les années mil huit cent trente,* ed. Peter Bloom, 457–69. Musical Life in 19th-century France/La Vie musicale en France au XIXe siècle, vol. 4. Stuyvesant, N.Y.: Pendragon, 1987.

Maehder, Jürgen. "*Banda sul palco:* Variable Besetzungen in der Bühnenmusik der italienischen Oper des 19. Jahrhunderts als Relikte alter Besetzungstraditionen." In *Alte Musik als ästhetische Gegenwart: Bach, Händel, Schütz. Bericht über den Internationalen musikwissenschaftlichen Kongreß Stuttgart 1985,* ed. Dietrich Berke and Dorothee Hanemann, 2:293–310. Kassel: Bärenreiter, 1987.

———. "Historienmalerei und Grand Opéra: Zur Raumvorstellung in den Bildern Géricaults und Delacroix' und auf der Bühne der Académie Royale de Musique." In *Zwischen tragédie lyrique und Grand Opéra: Französische Oper im 18. und 19. Jahrhundert,* ed. Albert Gier and Jürgen Maehder. Perspektiven der Opernforschung, no. 3. Frankfurt am Main: Lang, forthcoming.

———. "L'opera storica dell'Ottocento e *I vespri siciliani.*" In *Teatro Regio, Città di Parma, Stagione lirica 1986–87,* ed. Claudio Del Monte and Vincento Raffaele Segreto, 93–103. Parma: STEP, 1987.

———. "Verfremdete Instrumentation: Ein Versuch über beschädigten Schönklang." *Schweizer Beiträge zur Musikwissenschaft* 4 (1980): 103–50.

Malakis, Émile. "The first use of 'couleur locale' in French literary criticism." *Modern Language Notes* 60 (1947): 98–99.

Mann, Thomas. *Pro and Contra Wagner,* trans. Allan Blunden. Chicago: University of Chicago Press, 1985.

Marrinan, Michael. "Images and ideas of Charlotte Corday: Texts and contexts of an assassination." *Arts Magazine* 54, no. 8 (1979–80): 58–176.

Marschall, Gottfried R. "L'Opéra et son public de 1848 à 1852." *Revue Internationale de Musique Française* 1 (1980): 376–85.

Marselli, Nicola. *La ragione della musica moderna.* Naples: Detken, 1859.

Martine, Jacques Daniel. *De la Musique dramatique en France, ou, Principes d'après lesquels les compositions lyri-dramatiques doivent être jugées; des révolutions successives de l'art en France, de ses progrès et de sa décadence, des compositeurs qui ont travaillé pour nos spectacles lyriques, et de leurs productions restées au théâtre.* Paris: Dentu, 1813.

Marx, Adolf Bernhard. *The Music of the Nineteenth Century and Its Culture,* trans. August Heinrich Wehrhan. London: Robert Cocks, 1855.

Massmann, Klaus. *Die Rezeption der historischen Romane Sir Walter Scotts in Frankreich (1816–1832).* Studia romanica, no. 24. Heidelberg: Winter, 1972.

Matthes, Lothar. *Vaudeville: Untersuchungen zu Geschichte und literatursystematischem Ort einer Erfolgsgattung.* Studia romanica, no. 52. Heidelberg: Winter, 1983.

Matthews, Brander. "Eugène Scribe." In *French Dramatists of the Nineteenth Century*, 78–104. New York: Scribner, 1881.

Mayer, Arno J. *The Persistence of the Old Regime.* New York: Pantheon, 1981.

Mazzini, Giuseppe. *Scritti editi e inediti (Edizione nazionale).* 94 vols. Imola: Galeati, 1906–43.

Méhégan, Guillaume-Alexandre. *Considérations sur les révolutions des arts: Lettres sur l'éducation des femmes: Dialogue.* Paris: Brocas, 1755; reprinted, Geneva: Slatkine, 1971.

Mémoires pour servir à l'histoire de la révolution opérée dans la musique par le M. le Chevalier Gluck. Paris: Bailly, 1781; reprinted, Amsterdam: Antiqua, 1967.

Mercier, Louis-Sebastien. *De la Littérature et des littérateurs, suivi d'un nouvel examen de la tragédie françoise.* Yverdon: n. p., 1778; reprinted, Geneva: Slatkine, 1970.

——. *Du Théâtre, ou Nouvel essai sur l'art dramatique.* Amsterdam: Van Harrevelt, 1773; reprinted, Hildesheim: G. Olms, 1973.

——. *Mon Bonnet de nuit, ouvrage qui doit servir de suite au "Tableau de Paris."* 4 vols. Neufchâtel: Imprimerie de la société typographique, 1784.

Merle, Jean-Toussaint. *De l'Opéra.* Paris: Baudouin, 1827.

Meyerbeer, Giacomo. *Briefwechsel und Tagebücher,* ed. Heinz Becker and [from vol. 3] Gudrun Becker. Vols. 1–4. Berlin: De Gruyter, 1960–85.

Michelet, Jules. *La Femme.* Paris: Hachette, 1860.

Michotte, Edmond. *Richard Wagner's Visit to Rossini (Paris 1860) and An Evening at Rossini's in Beau-Séjour (Passy) 1858,* trans. from the French and annotated with an introduction and appendix by Herbert Weinstock. Chicago: University of Chicago Press, 1968.

Miller, Norbert. "Große Oper als Historiengemälde: Überlegungen zur Zusammenarbeit von Eugène Scribe und Giacomo Meyerbeer (am Beispiel des 1. Akts von *Les Huguenots*)." In *Oper und Operntext,* ed. Jens Malte Fischer, 45–79. Reihe Siegen, no. 60. Heidelberg: Winter, 1985.

Mitchell, Jerome. *The Walter Scott Operas: An analysis of operas based on the works of Sir Walter Scott.* Birmingham, Ala.: University of Alabama Press, 1977.

Mitscherlich, Alexander. *Society without the Father: A Contribution to Social Psychology,* trans. Eric Mosbacher. London: Tavistock Publications, 1969.

Moeller, Hans. "'Peuple à genoux': Das Volk in Giacomo Meyerbeers *Le Prophète.*" In *"Weine, weine, du armes Volk": Das verführte und betrogene Volk auf der Bühne: Gesammelte Vorträge des Salzburger Symposiums 1994,* ed. Peter Csobádi, Gernot Gruber, Jürgen Kühnel, Ulrich Müller, Oswald Panagl, and Franz Viktor Spechtler, vol. 1, pp. 243–53. Wort und Musik: Salzburger akademische Beiträge, no. 28. Anif/Salzburg: Müller-Speiser, 1995.

Mongrédien, Jean. "A la Découverte des Abencérages," *Les Amis de Luigi Cherubini en France: Bulletin* 3 (September 1986): 5–20.

——. "Aux sources du livret des *Huguenots*: La collaboration entre Scribe et Meyerbeer." In *Giacomo Meyerbeer: Musik als Welterfahrung: Heinz Becker zum 70. Geburtstag,* ed. Sieghart Döhring and Jürgen Schläder, 155–72. Munich: Ricordi, 1995.

————. "Variations sur un thème: Masaniello, Du héros de l'histoire à celui de la *La Muette de Portici.*" *Jahrbuch für Opernforschung* 1 (1985): 90–121.

Montmorency, Louis de Talleyrand-Périgord, duc de, ed., *Lettres sur l'Opéra (1840–1842)*. Paris: Hulin, 1921.

Moscovici, Serge. *L'Age des foules.* Brussels: Éditions Complexe, 1985.

Mozart, Wolfgang Amadeus. *The Letters of Mozart and his Family*, trans. and ed. Emily Anderson; 3d ed. rev. Stanley Sadie and Fiona Smart. London: Macmillan, 1985; reprinted 1990.

Müller, Balthasar. *Getreideversorgung und Mühlenwesen im Westfalen des 16. und 17. Jahrhunderts.* Sassenberg: Zurmühlen, 1989.

Müller, Gerhard. "Ein politischer Stellvertreterkrieg: Heinrich Heines Auseinandersetzung mit Giacomo Meyerbeer." *Musik und Gesellschaft* 39 (1989): 241–44.

Mundt, Theodor. "Ueber Oper, Drama und Melodrama in ihrem Verhältniß zueinander und zum Theater." In *Kritische Wälder: Blätter zur Beurtheilung der Literatur, Kunst und Wissenschaft unserer Zeit,* 79–101. Leipzig: Wolbrecht, 1833.

Muret, Théodore. *L'Histoire par le théâtre, 1789–1851.* 3 vols. Paris: Amyot, 1865.

La Musique à Paris en 1830–1831, a study by Marie-Noëlle Colette, Joël-Marie Fauquet, Adélaïde de Place, Anne Randier, and Nicole Wild, under the direction of François Lesure. Paris: Bibliothèque Nationale, 1983.

Nathan, Michel. "Délinquance et réformisme dans les *Mystères de Paris.*" In *Paris au XIXe siècle: Aspects d'un mythe littéraire,* 61–69. Lyon: Presses Universitaires de Lyon, 1984.

Nectoux, Jean-Michel. "Trois Orchestres parisiens en 1830: L'Académie royale de musique, le Théâtre-Italien, et la Société des concerts du Conservatoire." In *Music in Paris in the Eighteen-Thirties/La Musique à Paris dans les années mil huit cent trente,* ed. Peter Bloom, 471–505. Musical Life in 19th-century France/La Vie musicale en France au XIXe siècle, vol. 4. Stuyvesant, N.Y.: Pendragon, 1987.

Niépovié, Gaëtan [Karol Frankowski]. *Études physiologiques sur les grandes métropoles de l'Europe occidentale: Paris.* Paris: Gosselin, 1840.

Nodier, Charles. Introduction. In René-Charles Guilbert de Pixérécourt, *Théâtre choisi,* 1:i–xvi. Paris: chez l'auteur, 1841; reprinted, Geneva: Slatkine, 1971.

Noske, Frits R. "Verdi and the musical figure of death." In *Atti del III° congresso internazionale di studi verdiani, Milano, Piccola Scala, 12–17 giugno 1972,* 349–86. Parma: Istituto di studi verdiani 1974; also published as "The musical figure of death," in Noske, *The signifier and the signified: Studies in the operas of Mozart and Verdi,* 171–214. The Hague: Nijhoff, 1977; reprinted, Oxford: Clarendon Press, 1990.

Oettermann, Stephan. *Das Panorama: Die Geschichte eines Massenmediums.* Frankfurt am Main: Syndikat, 1980.

Ortigue, Joseph-Louis d'. *De la Guerre des dilettanti, ou de la revolution opérée par M. Rossini dans l'opéra français; et des rapports qui existent entre la musique, la littérature et les arts.* Paris: Ladvocat, 1829.

Ottlová, Marta. "Die französische Grand Opéra in der Entwicklung der tsche-chischen Nationaloper." In *Die Rolle der romantischen Musik bei der Herausbil-dung eines demokratischen Nationalbewußtseins*, part 2: *Die romantische Oper im 19. Jahrhundert = 2. Romantikkonferenz 1982*, ed. Günther Stephan and Hans John, 82–90. Schriftenreihe der Hochschule für Musik Carl Maria von We-ber Dresden, 3. Sonderheft. Dresden: Hochschule für Musik Carl Maria von Weber, 1983.

Ottlová, Marta, and Milan Pospíšil. "Oper und Spektakel im 19. Jahrhundert." *Die Musikforschung* 38 (1985): 1–8.

———. "Zur Problematik der tschechischen historischen Oper des 19. Jahr-hunderts." In *Colloquium "The musical theatre" Brno 1980, Chairman: Jiří Vys-loužil*, ed. Rudolf Pečman, 267–81. Colloquia on the History and Theory of Music at the International Musical Festival in Brno, no. 15. Brno: Meziná-rodní hudební festival, 1984.

Ozanam, Yves. "Recherches sur l'Académie Royale de Musique (Opéra Fran-çais) sous la Seconde Restauration (1815–1830)." Thèse École des Chartes, Paris, 1981.

Pailleron, Marie-Louise. *François Buloz et ses amis: La Revue des Deux-Mondes et la Comédie Française. Correspondances inédites de George Sand, Alfred de Musset, Madame François Buloz, Bocage, Alexandre Dumas, Rachel, etc.* Paris: Calmann-Lévy, 1920.

Palianti, Louis. *Petites Archives des théâtres de Paris: Souvenirs de dix ans, du 1er janvier 1855 au 31 décembre 1864, et des six premiers mois de 1865 . . . Théâtre Impérial de l'Opéra.* Paris: Gosselin, 1865.

Panofsky, Erwin. "'Et in Arcadia ego': Poussin and the Elegiac Tradition." In *Meaning in the Visual Arts*, 340–67. Harmondsworth: Penguin Books, 1970.

Paris, son histoire, ses monuments, ses musées, ses établissements divers, son administra-tion, son commerce et ses plaisirs: Nouveau guide des voyageurs accompagné de 18 plans où l'on trouve en outre les renseignements pour s'installer et vivre à Paris de toutes manières et à tous prix. Paris: Hachette, 1854.

Parker, Roger. "On reading nineteenth-century opera: Verdi through the looking-glass." In *Reading Opera*, ed. Arthur Groos and Roger Parker, 288–305. Princeton, N.J.: Princeton University Press, 1988.

Parker, Roger, and Matthew Brown. "Motivic and tonal interaction in Verdi's *Un ballo in maschera.*" *Journal of the American Musicological Society* 36 (1983): 243–65.

Pascolato, Alessandro. *"Re Lear" e "Ballo in maschera": Lettere di Giuseppe Verdi ad Antonio Somma.* Città di Castello: Lapi, 1902.

Pauls, Birgit. *Giuseppe Verdi und das Risorgimento: Ein politischer Mythos im Prozeß der Nationenbildung.* Politische Ideen, no. 4. Berlin: Akademie Verlag, 1996.

Pendle, Karin. *Eugène Scribe and French Opera of the Nineteenth Century.* Studies in Musicology, no. 6. Ann Arbor: UMI Research Press, 1979.

———. "The Boulevard theaters and continuity in French opera of the 19th century." In *Music in Paris in the Eighteen-Thirties/La musique à Paris dans les années mil huit cent trente*, ed. Peter Bloom, 509–35. Musical Life in 19th-century France/La vie musicale en France au XIXe siècle. vol. 4. Stuyvesant, N.Y.: Pendragon, 1987.

Périgord, C. G. [cadet]. "Dédicace à M. Rossini, le plus illustre des musiciens gourmands." *Almanach des Gourmands* 3 (1829): 1–5.

Petrobelli, Pierluigi. "La fedeltà al testo: Una lettera verdiana." In *Festschrift für Wolfgang Rehm zum 60. Geburtstag am 3. September 1989*, ed. Dietrich Berke and Harald Heckmann, 234–37. Kassel: Bärenreiter, 1989.

Pichois, Claude. *Philarète Chasles et la vie littéraire au temps du romantisme.* 2 vols. Paris: Corti, 1965.

———. *Vitesse et vision du monde: Littérature et progrès: Essai.* Neuchâtel: La Baconnière, 1973.

Pinkney, David H. *Napoleon III and the Rebuilding of Paris.* Princeton, N.J.: Princeton University Press, 1958.

Piot, René. *Les Palettes de Delacroix.* Paris: Librairie de France, 1931.

Pistone, Danièle. "L'Opéra de Paris au siècle romantique." *Revue Internationale de Musique Française* 2 (1981): 7–56.

Pixérécourt, René-Charles Guilbert de [pseud., Le Bonhomme du Marais]. *Guerre au mélodrame!!!* Paris: Delaunay, Barba, Mongie, 1818.

Pizzetti, Ildebrando. "Giuseppe Verdi maestro di teatro." In *Giuseppe Verdi nel cinquantenario della morte,* 14–27. Problemi attuali di scienza e di cultura, no. 26. Rome: Accademia Nazionale dei Lincei, 1952; reprinted in *Verdi: Bollettino quadrimestrale dell'Istituto di Studi Verdiani* 1 (1960): 751–66.

Pizzi, Italo. *Ricordi verdiani inediti (con undici lettere di Giuseppe Verdi ora pubblicate per la prima volta).* Turin: Roux e Viarengo, 1901; part reprinted in Marcello Conati, ed., *Interviews and Encounters with Verdi,* 337–57. London: Victor Gollancz, 1984.

Porter, Andrew. "Don't blame Scribe!" *Opera News* (April 1975): 26–27.

———. "*Les Vêpres siciliennes:* New letters from Verdi to Scribe." *19th-Century Music* 2 (1978–79): 95–109.

Posener, S. *Adolphe Crémieux (1796–1880).* 2 vols. Paris: Alcan, 1933–34.

Pospíšil, Milan. "Der positive Beitrag der französischen *Grand Opéra* zur europäischen Opernentwicklung." In *Die Rolle der romantischen Musik bei der Herausbildung eines demokratischen Nationalbewußtseins,* part 2: *Die romantische Oper im 19. Jahrhundert = 2. Romantikkonferenz 1982,* ed. Günther Stephan and Hans John, 78–81. Schriftenreihe der Hochschule für Musik Carl Maria von Weber Dresden, Sonderheft 3. Dresden: Hochschule für Musik Carl Maria von Weber, 1983.

———. "Die Stellungnahmen zur Revolutionsproblematik, dargestellt an Wandlungen in der Auffassung des historischen Stoffes bei Chénier und Meyerbeer." In *Colloquia musicologica Brno 11/12 (1976–1977),* 498–505. Brno: Mezinárodni hudební festival, 1978.

———. "Dramatická úloha Meyerbeerovy harmonie." *Huděbní věda* 21 (1984): 323–38.

Postman, Neil. *Amusing Ourselves to Death: Public Discourse in the Age of Show Business.* New York: Viking-Penguin, 1985; London: Methuen, 1987.

————. *The Disappearance of Childhood.* New York: Delacorte, 1982; London: W. H. Allen, 1985.

Pougin, Arthur. *Dictionnaire historique et pittoresque du théâtre et des arts qui s'y rattachent.* Paris: Firmin-Didot, 1885.

Powers, Harold S. "'La solita forma' and 'the uses of convention.'" In *Nuove prospettive nella ricerca verdiana: Atti del convegno internazionale in occasione della prima del "Rigoletto" in edizione critica, Vienna, 12/13 marzo 1983,* 74–109. Parma: Istituto di Studi Verdiani; Milan: Ricordi, 1987; also in *Acta musicologica* 59 (1987): 65–90.

————. "*Simon Boccanegra* I.10–12: A generic-genetic analysis of the council chamber scene." *19th-Century Music* 13 (1989–90): 101–28.

Prod'homme, Jacques-Gabriel. "La Musique et les musiciens en 1848." In *Sammelbände der Internationalen Musikgesellschaft* 14 (1912–13): 155–82.

————. "Rossini and his works in France." *The Musical Quarterly* 17 (1931): 110–37.

Radiciotti, Giuseppe. *Gioacchino Rossini: Vita documentata, opere ed influenza su l'arte.* 2 vols. Tivoli: Chicca, 1927–29.

Reckow, Fritz. '"Wirkung' und 'Effekt': Über einige Voraussetzungen, Tendenzen und Probleme der deutschen Berlioz-Kritik." *Die Musikforschung* 33 (1980): 1–36.

Rees, Terence. *Theatre Lighting in the Age of Gas.* London: The Society for Theatre Research, 1978.

Reicha, Antoine. *Art du compositeur dramatique, ou Cours complet de composition vocale, divisé en quatre parties et accompagné d'un volume de planches.* 2 vols. Paris: Farrenc, 1833.

Rétif de La Bretonne, Nicolas-Edme. *Mes Inscripcions: Journal intime de Restif de La Bretonne (1780–1787), publié d'après le manuscrit autographe de la bibliothèque de l'Arsénal,* ed. Paul Cottin. Paris: Plon, Nourrit, 1889; reprinted, Nendeln: Kraus, 1970.

Richer, Adrien. *Essai sur les grand événements par les petites causes, tiré de l'histoire.* 2 vols. Geneva: Hardy 1758–59.

Ridgway, Ronald S. "Voltairian bel canto: Operatic adaptations of Voltaire's tragedies." *Studies on Voltaire and the eighteenth century* 241 (1986): 125–54.

Rieger, Dietmar. "Eugène Scribe et l'anticipation: Essai sur l'idéologie du livret de *Robert le Diable.*" *Romanistische Zeitschrift für Literaturgeschichte* 12 (1988): 103–19.

————. "*La Muette de Portici* von Auber/Scribe: Eine Revolutionsoper mit antirevolutionärem Libretto." *Romanistische Zeitschrift für Literaturgeschichte* 10 (1986): 349–59.

Rienäcker, Gerd. "Wirkung ohne Ursache: Dramaturgie und Ästhetik Meyerbeers im Spiegel von Richard Wagners Kritik." *Musik und Gesellschaft* 39 (1989): 232–38.

Ringger, Kurt. "'Che gelida manina. . .': Betrachtungen zum italienischen Opernlibretto." *Arcadia* 19 (1984): 113–29.

Ritorni, Carlo. *Ammaestramenti alla composizione d'ogni poema e d'ogni opera appartenente alla musica.* Milan: Pirola, 1841.

Ritterman, Janet. "Les Concerts spirituels à Paris au début du XIXe siècle." *Revue Internationale de Musique Française* 6 (1985): 79–94.

Roberti, Giuseppe. "Da autografi di grandi musicisti (spigolature)." *Rivista musicale italiana* 10 (1903): 625–45.

Roccatagliati, Alessandro. "Opera, opera-ballo e *grand opéra:* Commistioni stilistiche e recezione critica nell'Italia teatrale di secondo Ottocento (1860–1870)." In *Opera e libretto,* ed. Gianfranco Folena, Maria Teresa Muraro, and Giovanni Morelli, 2:283–349. Florence: Olschki, 1993.

Rognoni, Luigi. *Gioacchino Rossini.* 2d ed. Turin: ERI, 1968.

Roncaglia, Gino. "Riccardo o Gustavo III?" *Verdi: Bollettino quadrimestrale dell' Istituto di Studi Verdiani* 1 (1960): lv–lvii.

Roqueplan, Nestor. *Les Coulisses de l'Opéra.* Paris: Librairie nouvelle, 1855.

Rosen, David, and Carol Rosen. "A musicological word study: It. *cabaletta.*" *Romance Philology* 20 (1966–67): 168–76.

Rosoi, Barnabé Farmian de. *Dissertation sur le drame lyrique.* Paris: Veuve Duchesne, 1775.

Ross, Peter. "Amelias Auftrittsarie im *Maskenball:* Verdis Vertonung im dramaturgisch-textlichem Zusammenhang." *Archiv für Musikwissenschaft* 40 (1983): 126–45.

Rosselli, John. *The Opera Industry in Italy from Cimarosa to Verdi: The Role of the Impresario.* Cambridge: Cambridge University Press, 1984.

———. "Verdi e la storia della retribuzione del compositore italiano." *Studi Verdiani* 2 (1983): 11–28.

Rossini, Gioachino. *Guillaume Tell,* ed. M. Elizabeth C. Bartlet. Edizione critica delle opere di Gioachino Rossini, sec. 1: Opere, vol. 39. Pesaro: Fondazione Rossini, 1992.

———. *Lettere,* ed. G. Mazzatinti, F. Manis, and G. Manis. Florence: Barbèra, 1902; reprinted, Bologna: Forni, 1975.

Rothe, Arnold. *Der Doppeltitel: Zu Form und Geschichte einer literarischen Konvention.* Akademie der Wissenschaften und der Literatur: Abhandlungen der geistes- und sozialwissenschaftlichen Klasse, Jahrgang 1969, no. 10. Wiesbaden: Steiner, 1970.

———. *Der literarische Titel: Funktionen, Formen, Geschichte.* Frankfurt am Main: Klostermann, 1986.

Rousseau, Jean-Jacques. *A Dictionary of Music,* trans. by William Waring, London [1775]. [*Dictionnaire de musique.* Paris: Veuve Duchesne, 1768.]

Rushton, Julian. "An early essay in *leitmotiv:* J. B. Lemoyne's *Electre.*" *Music and Letters* 52 (1971): 387–401.

Saint-Mars, Anne-Gabrielle de Cisterne de Courtiras, marquise de Poilloüe de [Comtesse Dash]. *Mémoires des autres,* vol. 2, *Souvenirs anecdotiques sur la Restauration.* Paris: Librairie illustrée, 1896.

Sala, Emilio. "Dal *Mélodrame à grand spectacle* verso il teatro musicale romantico." In *L'opera tra Venezia e Parigi,* ed. Maria Teresa Muraro, 1:177–91. Studi di musica veneta, vol. 14. Florence: Olschki, 1988.

———. *L'opera senza canto: Il mélo romantico e l'invenzione della colonna sonora.* Venice: Marsilio, 1995.

———. "'Que ses gestes parlants ont de grâce et de charmes': Motivi *mélo* nella *Muette de Portici.*" In *Transmissione e recezione delle forme di cultura musicale. Atti del XIV° congresso della società internazionale di musicologia, Bologna, 27 agosto–10 settembre 1987, Ferrara-Parma, 30 agosto 1987*, ed. Angelo Pompilio, Donatella Restani, Lorenzo Bianconi, and F. Alberto Gallo, 1:504–20. Turin: EDT, 1990.

Schalk, Fritz. "Der Artikel 'mélancolie' in der Diderotschen Enzyklopädie." In *Studien zur französischen Aufklärung*, 206–20. 2d ed. Frankfurt am Main: Klostermann 1977.

———. "Über Historie und Roman im 19. Jahrhundert in Frankreich." In *Dargestellte Geschichte in der europäischen Literatur des 19. Jahrhunderts*, ed. Wolfgang Iser and Fritz Schalk, 39–74. Studien zur Philosophie und Literatur des 19. Jahrhunderts, no. 7. Frankfurt am Main: Klostermann, 1970.

Schivelbusch, Wolfgang. *Das Paradies, der Geschmack und die Vernunft: Eine Geschichte der Genußmittel.* Munich: Hanser, 1980.

———. *Disenchanted Night, the Industrialization of Light in the Nineteenth Century*, trans. Angela Davies. Oxford: Berg, 1988.

———. *The Railway Journey: Trains and Travel in the Nineteenth Century*, trans. Anselm Hollo. New ed. Leamington Spa: Berg, 1986.

Schläder, Jürgen. *Das Opernduett: Ein Szenentypus des 19. Jahrhunderts und seine Vorgeschichte.* Theatron: Studien zur Geschichte und Theorie der dramatischen Künste, no. 6. Tübingen: Niemeyer, 1995.

Schlaffer, Hannelore. *Dramenform und Klassenstruktur: Eine Analyse der dramatis persona "Volk."* Stuttgart: Metzler, 1972.

Schlegel, August Wilhelm. *A Course of Lectures on Dramatic Art and Literature*, trans. John Black. 2 vols. London: Baldwin, Cradock, and Joy, 1815.

Schnebel, Dieter. "Die schwierige Wahrheit des Lebens: Zu Verdis musikalischem Realismus." In *Giuseppe Verdi*, ed. Heinz-Klaus Metzger and Rainer Riehn, 51–111. Musik-Konzepte, no. 10. Munich: Edition Text + Kritik, 1979.

Schneider, Herbert. *Chronologisch-thematisches Verzeichnis sämtlicher Werke von Daniel-François-Esprit Auber (AWV).* Musikwissenschaftliche Publikationen Hochschule für Musik und Darstellende Kunst Frankfurt/Main 1. Hildesheim: G. Olms, 1994.

———. "Die Barkarole und Venedig." In *L'opera tra Venezia e Parigi*, ed. Maria Teresa Muraro, 1:11–56. Studi di musica veneta, no. 14. Florence: Olschki, 1988.

———. "Drame lyrique." In *Die Musik in Geschichte und Gegenwart: Allgemeine Enzyklopädie der Musik begründet von Friedrich Blume.* 2d rev. edition, ed. Ludwig Finscher, vol. 2, coll. 1436–52. Kassel: Bärenreiter; Stuttgart: Metzler, 1995.

———. Introduction to *La Muette de Portici: Kritische Ausgabe des Librettos und Dokumentation der ersten Inszenierung*, ed. Herbert Schneider and Nicole Wild, 1–8. Erlanger romanistische Dokumente und Arbeiten, no. 11. Tübingen: Stauffenberg, 1993.

Schöning, Udo. *Literatur als Spiegel: Zur Geschichte eines kunsttheoretischen Topos in Frankreich von 1800 bis 1860.* Studia romanica, no. 51. Heidelberg: Winter, 1984.

Schucht, Jean F. *Meyerbeer's Leben und Bildungsgang, seine Stellung als Operncomponist im Vergleich zu den Tondichtern der Neuzeit: Nebst noch ungedruckten Briefen Meyerbeer's.* Leipzig: Matthes, 1869.

Schütze, Stefan. "Ueber die *Stumme von Portici.*" *Caecilia* 12 (1830): 29–34.

Schumann, Robert. *Gesammelte Schriften über Musik und Musiker.* 4 vols. Leipzig: Wigand, 1854.

———. *The Musical World of Robert Schumann: A Selection from His Own Writings,* trans., ed., and annotated by Henry Pleasants. London: Victor Gollancz, 1965.

Scott, Walter. *The Fortunes of Nigel* [1822]. Vol. 14 of The Waverley Novels, centenary edition. 25 vols. Edinburgh: Black, 1870–71.

Scribe, Eugène. *Oeuvres complètes.* 5 sections: 9, 33, 6, 20, and 8 vols. Paris: Dentu, 1874–85.

Second, Albéric. *Les petits mystères de l'Opéra.* Paris: Kugelmann, 1844.

Sennett, Richard. *The Conscience of the Eye: The Design and Social Life of Cities.* New York: Knopf, 1990.

———. *The Fall of Public Man.* New York: Knopf, 1977.

Sibille, Lodoys. "Physiologie du spectateur." *Le Monde dramatique* 2 (November 1835–May 1836): 137–40.

Silvestri, Lodovico Settimo. *Della vita e delle opere di Gioacchino Rossini, Notizie biografico-artistico-aneddotico-critiche compilate su tutte le biografie di questo celebre italiano e sui giudizi della stampa italiana e straniera intorno alle sue opere.* Milan: Privately published, 1874.

Slatin, Sonia. "Opera and revolution: *La Muette de Portici* and the Belgian revolution of 1830 revisited." *The Journal of Musicological Research* 3 (1979): 45–62.

Spector, Jack J. *Delacroix: The Death of Sardanapalus.* London: Lane, 1974.

Staël, Anne-Louise-Germaine de [baronne de Staël-Holstein, née Necker]. *De l'Allemagne* [1810], ed. Comtesse Jean de Pange. 5 vols. Paris: Hachette, 1958–60.

Stanton, Stephen Sadler. "English drama and the French well-made play, 1815–1915." Ph.D. diss., Columbia University, 1955.

Starobinski, Jean. "La Nostalgie: Théories médicales et expression littéraire." *Studies on Voltaire and the Eighteenth Century* 27 (1963): 1505–18.

Steinbeck, Susanne. *Die Ouvertüre in der Zeit von Beethoven bis Wagner: Probleme und Lösungen.* Freiburger Schriften zur Musikwissenschaft, no. 3. Munich: Katzbichler, 1973.

Steiner, George. *In Bluebeard's Castle: Some Notes towards the Redefinition of Culture.* London: Faber and Faber; New Haven, Conn.: Yale University Press, 1971.

Stendhal [Henri Beyle]. *Courrier anglais,* ed. Henri Martineau. 5 vols. Paris: Éditions du Divan, 1935–36.

Strieder, Cornelia. *Melodramatik und Sozialkritik in Werken Eugène Sues.* Erlanger Studien, no. 66. Erlangen: Palm & Enke, 1986.

Strunk, Oliver. *Source Readings in Music History*. 5 vols. London: Faber and Faber, 1981.

Tanguy-Baum, Margrethe. *Der historische Roman im Frankreich der Julimonarchie: Eine Untersuchung anhand von Werken der Autoren Frédéric Soulié und Eugène Sue*. Bonner Romanistische Arbeiten, no. 9. Frankfurt am Main: Lang, 1980.

Temple-Patterson, Helen. "Poetic genesis: Sébastien Mercier into Victor Hugo." *Studies on Voltaire and the Eighteenth Century* 11 (1960): 7–315.

Tetu, Jean-François. "Remarques sur le statut juridique de la femme au XIXe siècle." In *La Femme au XIXe siècle. Littérature et idéologie*, 5–17. Lyon: Presses Universitaires, 1978.

Thiergard, Ulrich. "Schicksalstragödie als Schauerliteratur." Diss. phil., University of Göttingen, 1957.

Tiersot, Julien. *"La Esmeralda*. (Centenaire)." *Revue musicale* 170 (December 1936): 389–405.

Tippkötter, Horst. *Walter Scott, Geschichte als Unterhaltung: Eine Rezeptionsanalyse der Waverley Novels*. Studien zur Philosophie und Literatur des 19. Jahrhunderts, no. 13. Frankfurt am Main: Klostermann, 1971.

Tissot, Claude-Joseph. *De la manie du suicide et de l'esprit de révolte, de leurs causes et de leurs remèdes*. Paris: Ladrange, 1840.

Treille, Marguerite. *Le Conflit dramatique en France de 1823 à 1830 d'après les journaux et les revues du temps*. Paris: Picart, 1929.

[Troplong, Raymond-Théodore]. "Rapport de la commission chargée d'examiner la situation de l'Opéra." *Le Moniteur universel: Journal officiel de l'Empire français*, 2 July 1854, pp. 1–2.

Ubersfeld, Anne. *Le Roi et le bouffon: Étude sur le théâtre de Hugo de 1830 à 1839*. Paris: Corti, 1974.

Ueding, Gert. *Glanzvolles Elend: Versuch über Kitsch und Kolportage*. Frankfurt am Main: Suhrkamp, 1973.

Van, Gilles de. "La notion de *tinta*: Mémoire confuse et affinités thématiques dans les opéras de Verdi." *Revue de musicologie* 76 (1990): 187–98.

———. "Les sources littéraires de *Guillaume Tell* de Rossini." *Chroniques italiennes* 29 (1992): 7–24.

Vander Straeten, Edmond. *La Mélodie populaire dans l'opéra "Guillaume Tell" de Rossini*. Paris: Baur, 1879.

Várnai, Péter Pál. "La struttura ritmica come mezzo di caratterizzazione ne *I Vespri siciliani*." *Studi verdiani* 10 (1994–95): 93–103.

Vauthier, Gabriel. "Le Jury de lecture et l'Opéra sous la Restauration." *Revue musicale* 10 (1910): 13–25, 44–49, 75–80.

Vaux de Foletier, François de. "Les Bohémiens dans la littérature du XIXe siècle." In *Les Bohémiens en France au XIXe siècle*, 193–231. Paris: Lattès, 1981.

Velde, Carl Franz van der. *Die Wiedertäufer: Eine Erzählung aus der ersten Hälfte des 16. Jahrhunderts*. Dresden: Arnold, 1821. [French translation: *Les Anabaptistes: Histoire du commencement du XVIe siècle, d'après les chroniques et les documens du temps*. Romans historiques de C[arl] F[ranz] Van der Velde, traduits de l'allemand et précédés de notices par A[dolphe] Loève-Veimars, no. 4. Paris: Renouard, 1826.]

Vendrix, Philippe. "La Notion de révolution dans les écrits théoriques concernant la musique avant 1789." *International Review of the Aesthetics and Sociology of Music* 21 (1990): 71–77.

Verdi, Giuseppe. *I copialettere di Giuseppe Verdi*, ed. Gaetano Cesari and Alessandro Luzio. Milan: n. p., 1913; reprinted, Bologna: Forni, [1968].

———. *Letters of Giuseppe Verdi*, sel., trans., and ed. by Charles Osborne. London: Victor Gollancz, 1971.

Verne, Jules. "Dr Ox's Experiment." In *Dr Ox's Experiment and Other Stories Translated from the French of Jules Verne*, 1–102. London: Sampson Low, Marston, Low, and Searle, 1874.

Véron, Louis-Désiré. *Mémoires d'un bourgeois de Paris comprenant la fin de l'Empire, la Restauration, la Monarchie de Juillet, et la République jusqu'au rétablissement de l'Empire*. 6 vols. Paris: Gonet, 1853–55.

Viale Ferrero, Mercedes. "Luogo teatrale e spazio scenico." In *La spettacolarità*, ed. Lorenzo Bianconi and Giorgio Pestelli, 1–122. Storia dell'opera italiana, vol. 5. Turin: EDT, 1988.

Viallaneix, Paul. Introduction to *Mémoires de Luther écrits par lui-même*. In Jules Michelet, *Oeuvres complètes*, ed. Paul Viallaneix, 3:227–35. Paris: Flammarion, 1973.

Vier, Jacques. *La Comtesse d'Agoult et son temps, avec des documents inédits*. 6 vols. Paris: Colin, 1955–63.

Villemessant, Hippolyte de. *Mémoires d'un journaliste*. 6 vols. Paris: Dentu, 1867–78.

Vitet, Louis. "Diorama: Vue du village d'Unterseen, par M. Daguerre."—"Vue intérieure de l'abbaye de Saint Vandrille, par M. Bouton" [*signed* L. V.]. *Le Globe* 4 (August 1826–March 1827): 111–12.

———. *Études sur les beaux-arts, essais d'archéologie et fragments littéraires*. 2 vols. Paris: Comptoir des imprimeurs unis, 1846.

Voltaire [François-Marie Arouet]. *Dictionnaire philosophique* [1764–1770]. *Oeuvres complètes*, vols. 51–77. Paris: Baudouin, 1825–26.

Wagner, Hans-Joachim. "Lyrisches Drama und Drame lyrique: Eine Skizze der literar- und musikhistorischen Begriffsgeschichte." *Archiv für Musikwissenschaft* 47 (1990): 73–84.

Wagner, Richard. *Gesammelte Schriften und Dichtungen*. 10 vols. Leipzig: Fritzsch, 1871–83, 2d ed. 1887–88; reprinted, Hildesheim: G. Olms, 1976.

Walsh, T. J. *Second Empire Opera: The Théâtre Lyrique, Paris, 1851–1870*. London: Calder; New York: Riverrun Press, 1981.

Walter, Michael. "'A la recherche de l'histoire perdue.' Scribe, Auber und die historische grand opéra." In *Zwischen tragédie lyrique und Grand Opéra. Französische Oper im 18. und 19. Jahrhundert*, ed. Albert Gier and Jürgen Maehder. Perspektiven der Opernforschung, no. 3. Frankfurt am Main: Lang, forthcoming.

———. "Die Darstellung des Volkes in der französischen Oper von der Revolution bis 1870: Eine Skizze zur Entwicklung des französischen Librettos im 19. Jahrhundert." *Romanistische Zeitschrift für Literaturgeschichte* 10 (1986): 381–98.

————. *"Hugenotten"-Studien.* Europäische Hochschulschriften, ser. 36 (Musikwissenschaft), no. 24. Frankfurt am Main: Lang, 1987.

————. "'Man überlege sich nur Alles, sehe, wo Alles hinausläuft!' Zu Robert Schumanns *Hugenotten*-Rezension." *Die Musikforschung* 36 (1983): 127–44.

Walther, Gerrit. "Bürger zwischen Hof und Hot-Club: Musik und Gesellschaft 1500–1950: Ein Forschungsbericht." *Archiv für Sozialgeschichte* 35 (1995): 377–409.

Wangermée, Robert. "Introduction à une sociologie de l'opéra." In *Critique sociologique et critique psychanalytique,* 59–77. Brussels: Université libre, 1970.

Weaver, William. *Verdi: A Documentary Study.* London: Thames and Hudson, 1977.

Weber, Johannes. *Meyerbeer: Notes et souvenirs d'un de ses secrétaires.* Paris: Fischbacher, 1898.

Weber, William. *Music and the Middle Class: Social Structure of Concert Life in London, Paris and Vienna, 1830–1848.* London: Holmes and Meier, 1975.

Wechsler, Judith. *A Human Comedy: Physiognomie and Caricature in Nineteenth-Century Paris.* Chicago: University of Chicago Press, 1982.

Weiss, Piero. "Verdi and the fusion of genres." *Journal of the American Musicological Society* 35 (1982): 138–56.

Weisstein, Ulrich. "Der Apfel fiel recht weit vom Stamme: Rossinis *Guillaume Tell*, eine musikalische Schweizerreise." In *Der Text im Musiktheater: Romanistische Beiträge zur Libretto-Forschung,* ed. Albert Gier, 147–84. Studia romanica, no. 63. Heidelberg: Winter, 1986.

Welsh, Alexander. *The Hero of the Waverley Novels.* Yale studies in English, no. 154. New Haven, Conn.: Yale University Press, 1963.

Wendorff, Rudolf. *Zeit und Kultur: Geschichte des Zeitbewußtseins in Europa.* Opladen: Westdeutscher Verlag, 1980.

Wentzlaff-Eggebert, Harald. *Zwischen kosmischer Offenbarung und Wortoper: Das romantische Drama Victor Hugos.* Erlanger Forschungen; ser. A: Geisteswissenschaften, no. 32. Erlangen: Universitätsbund, 1984.

Werner, Rudolf. "Die Schicksalstragödie und das Theater der Romantik." Diss. phil., University of Munich, 1963.

Wessel, Matthias. *Die Ossian-Dichtung in der musikalischen Komposition.* Publikationen der Hochschule für Musik und Theater Hannover, no. 6. Laaber: Laaber, 1994.

Wild, Nicole. *Dictionnaire des théâtres parisiens au XIXe siècle: Les Théâtres et la musique.* Paris: Amateurs de livres, 1989.

————. "La Musique dans le mélodrame des théâtres parisiens." In *Music in Paris in the Eighteen-Thirties/La musique à Paris dans les années mil huit cent trente,* ed. Peter Bloom, 589–610. Musical Life in 19th-century France/La vie musicale en France au XIXe siècle, vol. 4. Stuyvesant, N.Y.: Pendragon, 1987.

————. "La Recherche de la précision historique chez les décorateurs de l'Opéra de Paris au XIXe siècle." In *International Musicological Society: Report of the Twelfth Congress, Berkeley, 1977,* ed. Daniel Heartz and Bonnie Wade, 453–63. Kassel: Bärenreiter, 1981.

———. "Le spectacle lyrique au temps du Grand Opéra." In *La Musique en France à l'époque romantique (1830–1870)*, 21–57, 297–99. Paris: Flammarion, 1991.

Williams, Simon. "The well-made play." In *European writers*, ed. Jacques Barzun and George Stade, vol. 7: *The Romantic Century: Charles Baudelaire to the Well-Made Play*, 1909–34. New York: Scribner, 1985.

Willms, Johannes. *Paris: Hauptstadt Europas, 1789–1914*. Munich: Beck, 1988.

Wolff, Stéphane. *L'Opéra au Palais Garnier (1875–1962): Les oeuvres, les interprètes*. Paris: L'Entracte, 1962.

Wood, Caroline. "Orchestra and spectacle in the *tragédie en musique* 1673–1715: Oracle, *sommeil* and *tempête*." *Proceedings of the Royal Musical Association* 108 (1981–82): 25–46.

Wörner, Karl. "Beiträge zur Geschichte des Leitmotivs in der Oper." *Zeitschrift für Musikwissenschaft* 14 (1931–32): 151–72.

Zavadini, Guido. *Donizetti: Vita, musiche, epistolario*. Bergamo: Istituto italiano d'arti grafiche, 1948.

Zimmermann, Reiner. *Giacomo Meyerbeer: Eine Biographie nach Dokumenten*. Berlin: Henschel, 1991.

———. "Komponist extremer Wirkungen. Zum Leben und Schaffen Giacomo Meyerbeers." *Musik und Gesellschaft* 39 (1989): 226–31.

Index of Titles of Operas and Plays

This index comprises not only completed works, including some alternative-language versions, but also titles of unset librettos and other unrealized or unfinished projects. It does not include novels or short stories.

Abencérages, Les, ou L'Étendard de Grenade (Jouy, Cherubini), 43, 55–56

Africaine, L' (Scribe, Meyerbeer), 11–12, 174, 396–97, 403, 438

Aida (Ghislanzoni, Verdi), 62, 174, 205, 231, 323–25, 358, 366, 367, 394, 404, 408, 438–39, 454, 456

Alceste (Calzabigi, Gluck), 320

Alceste (Leblanc du Roullet, Gluck), 55, 319–20

Almaviva, ossia L'inutile precauzione. See *Barbiere di Siviglia, Il* (Sterbini, Rossini)

Alzira (Cammarano, Verdi), 335

Amants magnifiques, Les (Molière, Lully), 261

Anna Bolena (Romani, Donizetti), xvi, 110

Armide (Quinault, Gluck), 2, 44–45, 137

Armide (Quinault, Lully), 44–45, 261

Attila (Solera, Verdi), 151, 299

Attilio Regolo (Metastasio, Hasse), 319

Atys (Quinault, Lully), 261

Ballo in maschera, Un (Somma, Verdi), xxi, 11–12, 194, 205, 324, 366, 407, **409–56**

Barbiere di Siviglia, Il (Sterbini, Rossini), 407

Barbiere di Siviglia, Il, ovvero La precauzione inutile (Petrosellini, Paisiello), 407

Ba-ta-clan (Halévy, Offenbach), xx, 201

Battaglia di Legnano, La (Cammarano, Verdi), 360

Bayadères, Les (Jouy, Catel), 47, 56–57

Belle Hélène, La (Meilhac/Halévy, Offenbach), 245

Belvéder, Le, ou La Vallée de l'Etna (Pixérécourt), 143

Benvenuto Cellini (Wailly/Barbier, Berlioz), xviii, 174

Bohémienne, La, ou L'Amérique en 1775 (Scribe), 417

Boris Godunov (Pushkin/Musorgsky, Musorgsky), 310

Brigands, Les (Meilhac/Halévy, Offenbach), 437

Camille, ou Le Souterrain (Marsollier, Dalayrac), 272

Caravane du Caire, La (Morel de Chédeville, Grétry), 55

Carmen (Meilhac/Halévy, Bizet), 180, 402, 406

Caterina Cornaro (Sacchero, Donizetti), 407

Charles VI (Delavigne/Delavigne, Halévy), xviii, 49, 251, 274, 361, 373

Cheval de bronze, Le (Scribe, Auber), 154

Circassiens, Les, ou Le Prisonnier du Caucase (Scribe), 417

Clemenza di Valois (Rossi, Gabussi), 416

Coelina, ou L'Enfant du mystère (Pixérécourt), *140*

Colinette à la cour, ou La double épreuve (Lourdet de Santerre, Grétry), 55

Colore del tempo (Torelli), 412

Comte de Claros, Le (Delavigne/Scribe), 125

Comte Ory, Le (Scribe/Delestre-Poirson, Rossini), xvi

Contes d'Hoffmann, Les (Barbier, Offenbach), 402

Corsaro, Il (Piave, Verdi), 356

Crociato in Egitto, Il (Rossi, Meyerbeer), 98, 274

Cromwell (Hugo), xv

Cromwell (Lichtenstein, Spontini), 165

Dame aux camélias, La (Dumas), xx

Dame blanche, La (Scribe, Boieldieu), 273–74

Dantons Tod (Büchner), xvii

Dardanus (Le Clerc de la Bruyère, Rameau), 261

Didon (Marmontel, Piccinni), 46, 50

Didone abbandonata (Metastasio, Sarro), 299

Dinorah. See *Le Pardon de Ploërmel*

Dom Sébastien, roi de Portugal (Scribe, Donizetti), xviii, 251

Don Carlos (Méry/Du Locle, Verdi), 11–12, 299, 358, 366, 367, 369–72, 376, 388, 394, 399–400, 404, 405, 439–40, 454, 456

Don Giovanni (Il dissoluto punito, ossia Il Don Giovanni) (Da Ponte, Mozart), xvii, 2, 55, 203, 443–44

Don Juan (Deschamps/Castil-Blaze, Mozart), xvii

Donna del lago, La (Tottola, Rossini), 74, 101, 171

Don Pasquale (Ruffini, Donizetti), xviii

Duca d'Alba, Il (Zanardini, Donizetti/Salvi), 337

Duc d'Albe, Le (Scribe/Duveyrier, Donizetti), 35, 336–37, 346–49, 350, 352–55, 362, 366, 373, 377, 380, 386

Due Foscari, I (Piave, Verdi), 356, 414

Enfant prodigue, L' (Scribe, Auber), 345

Entführung aus dem Serail, Die (Stephanie, Mozart), 2, 318

Ernani (Piave, Verdi), 360, 369–72, 376, 407

Esmeralda, La (Hugo, Bertin), xvii, 22, **215–46**, 453

Esule di Roma, L', ossia Il proscritto (Gilardoni, Donizetti), 355

Étoile du Nord, L' (Scribe, Meyerbeer), xx, 206, 237, 372–73

Euryanthe (Castil-Blaze, Weber), xvi

Falstaff (Boito, Verdi), 413, 428, 454, 456

Faust (Barbier/Carré, Gounod), xxi, 28, 402, 403, 406

Faust (Goethe), xvi

Favorite, La (Royer/Vaëz, Donizetti), xviii, 250–51, 403

Feldlager in Schlesien, Ein (Rellstab, Meyerbeer), 204, 237, 262, 305–7

Fernand Cortez (Jouy/Esménard, Spontini), 43, 47, 49, 56, 74, 101, 203

Fidelio, oder Die eheliche Liebe (Sonnleithner, Beethoven), 2–3

Fin du monde, La, ou Le Jugement dernier (Mirecourt/Gabriel, David), 303

Fledermaus, Die (Haffner/Genée, Strauss), 402

Forza del destino, La (Piave, Verdi), 228, 237, 244, 306, 322, 428, 454, 456

Fra Diavolo (Scribe, Auber), xvi, 235

Freischütz, Der (Kind, Weber), 3, 11, 171

Freyschütz, Le (Pacini, Weber/Berlioz), xviii, 11

Gazza ladra, La (Gherardini, Rossini), 141

Gemmy et Florentine, ou Les Amis fidèlis (Balthazar, Bernal), 341

Gioconda, La (Boito, Ponchielli), 404

Giorno di regno, Un (Romani, Verdi), 406

Giovanna d'Arco (Solera, Verdi), 356, 404

Götterdämmerung (Wagner, Wagner), 298, 299

Government Inspector, The (Gogol), xvii

Grande-Duchesse de Gérolstein, La (Meilhac/Halévy, Offenbach), 361

Guarany, Il (Scalvino/D'Ormeville, Gomes), 404

Guido et Ginevra, ou La Peste de Florence (Scribe, Halévy), xviii, 174

Guillaume Tell (Jouy/Bis, Rossini), xvi, 2, 27, 43, 50, **65–67**, 70, 80, **85–114,** 117, 134, 135, 137, 151, 164, 168–69, 175, 204, 227, 229, 251, 258, 260, 265, 300, 320, 348, 354, 359–60, 365, 367, 372, 384, 403, 407, 434

Guillaume Tell (Sedaine, Grétry), 107, 164

Gustave III, ou Le Bal masqué (Scribe, Auber), xvii, 154–55, 164, 194, 244, 324, 347, 407, 409, 414–18, 419–23, 426–27, 429–31, 433, 435–36, 437–39, 442, 445–47, 450–52

Hamlet (Barbier/Carré, Thomas), 397

Hans Heiling (Devrient, Marschner), xvii

Herculanum (Méry/Hadot, David), 164, 303, 397

Hernani (Hugo), xvi, 21, 369, 371–72, 407

Hippolyte et Aricie (Pellegrin, Rameau), 194

Hoffest von Ferrara, Das (Raupach, Meyerbeer), 258

Horatius Coclès (Arnault, Méhul) 86

Huguenots, Les (Scribe, Meyerbeer), xvii, 9, 37, 39, 61, 87, 110, 138, 142, **158–214,** 220–25, 227–31, 233, 234–35, 237, 244, 250–51, 255–58, 263, 265–66, 270, 277, 283, 304–7, 322, 325–26, 329–33, 348, 349–50, 353–55, 359, 361, 365, 367–68, 372, 373, 393, 396, 402–3, 421, 423, 424, 433, 434, 438, 440, 453

Iphigénie en Tauride (Dubreuil, Piccinni), 55

Iphigénie en Tauride (Leblanc du Roullet, Gluck), 320

Jeanne d'Arc (Mermet, Mermet), 49

Jeanne la folle (Scribe, Clapisson), 345

Jérusalem (Royer/Vaëz, Verdi), xix, 299, 345

Judith (Hebbel), xviii

Juif errant, Le (Scribe/Saint-Georges, Halévy), 303, 345, 400

Juive, La (Scribe, Halévy), xvii, 16, 110, 154–56, 164, 175, 180, 227, 228, 231, 244, 251, 302, 354, 377, 390, 403, 440

Leicester, ou Le Château de Kenilworth (Scribe/Mélesville, Auber), 74

Lohengrin (Wagner, Wagner), xix, 174, 193, 237, 275, 393

Lombardi alla prima crociata, I (Solera, Verdi), 345

Lorenzaccio (Musset), xvii

Louise (Charpentier, Charpentier), 402

Louise Miller (Pacini, Verdi), xx, 395

Lucia di Lammermoor (Cammarano, Donizetti), xvii, 9, 274

Lucrèce Borgia (Hugo), 142

Lucrezia Borgia (Romani, Donizetti), 110, 142

Luisa Miller (Cammarano, Verdi), 328

Lustigen Weiber von Windsor, Die (Mosenthal, Nicolai), xix

Macbeth (Piave, Verdi), xix, 274, 360, 419, 427, 436

Manon (Meilhac/Gille, Massenet), 244, 402

Maometto II (Della Valle, Rossini), 68, 71, 75, 77–78

Margherita d'Anjou (Romani, Meyerbeer), xv

Marguerite d'Anjou (Pixérécourt), 143

Maria Magdalene (Hebbel), xix

Marino Faliero (Delavigne), 436

Martha, oder Der Markt zu Richmond (Riese, Flotow), xix

Martin Luther, oder Die Weihe der Kraft (Werner), 209

Martyrs, Les (Scribe, Donizetti), xviii, 37, 76, 251

Masnadieri, I (Maffei, Verdi), 335, 356

Médée (Hoffman, Cherubini), 46, 53–55

Mignon (Barbier/Carré, Thomas), 401–2, 440

Milton (Jouy/Dieulafoy, Spontini), 43

Mireille (Carré, Gounod), 401–2

Moïse et Pharaon (Balochi/Jouy, Rossini), xv, 70–71, 80, 101, 103, 162, 180, 300

Mort d'Abel, La (Hoffman, Kreutzer), 80

Mort d'Adam, La, et son apothéose (Guillard, Le Sueur), 47, 163

Mort du Tasse, La (Cuvillier/Hélitas, García), 47, 75, 80

Muette de Portici, La (Scribe, Auber), xvi, 2, 70, 81, 84–85, 89–90, 110, **122–57,** 164, 218, 222, 224, 238, 251, 390, 393, 403, 407, 420

Nabucco (Nabucodonosor) (Solera, Verdi), xviii, 325, 360, 414

Nina, ou La Folle par amour (Marsollier, Da-
layrac), 272
Noëma, ou Le Repentir (Scribe/Saint-
Georges, Meyerbeer), 339
Nonne sanglante, La (Scribe/Delavigne,
Berlioz), 251, 400
Nonne sanglante, La (Scribe/Delavigne,
Gounod), 48, 251, 400–401
Norma (Romani, Bellini), xvi, 110

Oberon (Planché, Weber), xv
Oberto, Conte di San Bonifacio (Solera,
Verdi), xviii
Olimpie (Dieulafoy/Briffaut, Spontini), xv,
3, 47, 80, 180
Orphée aux enfers (Crémieux, Offenbach),
xxi
Ossian, ou Les Bardes (Palat-Dercy, Le
Sueur), 261–62
Otello (Berio, Rossini), 9, 251
Otello (Boito, Verdi), 180–81, 376, 408,
413, 454, 456
Othello (Du Locle/Boito, Verdi), 165, 394
Othello (Royer/Vaëz, Rossini), 395

Pardon de Ploërmel, Le (Barbier/Carré,
Meyerbeer), xxi, 275, 340–42, 373
Parsifal (Wagner, Wagner), 2
Pêcheurs de perles, Les (Carré/Cormon,
Bizet), 28
Pelléas et Mélisande (Maeterlinck, De-
bussy), 401
Pharamond (Ancelot/Guiraud/Soumet,
Boieldieu/Berton/Kreutzer), 47
Postillon de Longjumeau, Le (De Leuven/
Brunswick, Adam), xvii
Pré-aux-clercs, Le (Planard, Hérold), 220,
224–25
Prophète, Le (Scribe, Meyerbeer), xix, 2,
11, 35, 37, 148, 151, 165–66, 174, 181,
219, 231, 237, **247–317**, 325–26, 331,
345–46, 348, 355, 365, 372, 379, 396,
403, 405, 421, 427–28, 430, 437–38
Puritani, I (Pepoli, Bellini), xvii, 434
Pygmalion (Rousseau, Coignet/Rousseau),
141

Reggente, Il (Cammarano, Mercadante),
416
Reine de Chypre, La (Saint-Georges, Halévy), xviii, 175, 251, 407

Reine de Saba, La (Barbier/Carré, Gounod), 397, 405
Rheingold, Das (Wagner, Wagner), 5, 151
Richard Coeur-de-lion (Sedaine, Grétry),
170–71, 271–72
Rienzi, der letzte der Tribunen (Wagner,
Wagner), xviii, 299
Rigoletto (Piave, Verdi), xx, 162, 174, 345,
352, 356, 357, 375, 420, 428–29, 441,
443–44
Robert Bruce (Royer/Vaëz, Rossini/Nieder-
meyer), 251
Robert le diable (Scribe/Delavigne, Meyerbeer), xv, xvi, 16, 48, 76, 80, 139, 151–
52, 164–65, 171, 173–74, 182, 207–8,
232–33, 251, 254, 270, 350, 354, 393,
403, 404, 427
Robert Macaire (Saint-Amand/Antier/Le-
maître), xvii
Roi s'amuse, Le (Hugo), xvii, 21, 39, 428
Roland à Roncevaux (Mermet, Mermet),
49, 361, 399–400

Sabinus (Chabanon de Maugris, Gossec),
261
Salammbo (Du Locle, Reyer), 299
Sapho (Augier, Gounod), 397
Sapho (Cournol/Empis, Reicha), 80
Sardanapalus (Byron), 294
Sargino, ossia L'allievo dell amore (Foppa,
Paër), 102
*Seize Ans pour un livre, ou Les Maris ar-
rivent toujours trop tard* (Balthazar), 491
Semiramide (Rossi, Rossini), 98, 108, 354
Semiramide riconosciuta (Metastasio, Mey-
erbeer), 406
Sémiramis (Desriaux, Catel), 47
Sémiramis (Voltaire), 47
Siège de Corinthe, Le (Balochi/Soumet, Ros-
sini), xv, **63–65, 68–85,** 91–92, 106–7,
180, 202, 299, 387, 450, 453
Simon Boccanegra (Piave, Verdi), xx, 360,
366
Sonnambula, La (Romani, Bellini), 273
Struensee (Beer, Meyerbeer), 276

Tancredi (Rossi, Rossini), 98
*Tannhäuser und der Sängerkrieg auf Wart-
burg* (Wagner, Wagner), xix, 22, 174,
233, 393–94
Tête de mort, La (Pixérécourt), 143

Thaïs (Gallet, Massenet), 402

Traviata, La (Piave, Verdi), xx, 5, 180, 228, 375, 441, 452

Triomphe de Trajan, Le (Esménard, Le Sueur), 74

Tristan und Isolde (Wagner, Wagner), xxi, 195, 197, 393

Trouvère, Le (Pacini, Verdi), xx, 395

Trovatore, Il (Cammarano, Verdi), xx, 137, 284, 301–2, 306, 377

Troyens, Les (Berlioz, Berlioz), xxi, 12, 28, 193, 206, 397–99, 401

Undine (Fouqué, Hoffmann), 197

Vampyr, Der (Wohlbrück, Marschner), xvi

Velleda (Jouy, Batton), 56

Vêpres siciliennes, Les (Scribe/Duveyrier, Verdi), xx, 11, 79, 143, 165, 180, 204–5, 244, **342–87**, 388, 393–94, 407, 413, 415, 418, 422, 429, 431, 435, 438, 441, 446, 448, 450, 453–54

Verre d'eau, Le, ou Les Effets et les causes (Scribe), 125, 312–13

Verschwörung des Fiesko zu Genua, Die (Schiller), 435–36

Vestale, La (Jouy, Spontini), 42–43, 47, 137

Virginia, ou La belle Parisienne (Balthazar), 24

Virginie, ou Les Décemvirs (Désaugiers, Berton), 47

Walküre, Die (Wagner, Wagner), 193, 299

Wallensteins Lager (Schiller), 306

Weihe der Kraft, die. See *Martin Luther*

Werther (Blau/Milliet/Hartmann, Massenet), 440

Werther (Kalbeck, Massenet), 448

Wilhelm Tell (Schiller), 94, 113

Zamori, ossia L'eroe delle Indie (Prividali, Mayr), 202–3

Index of Names

Adam, Adolphe, xvii, xix, xx, 300–301
Addison, Joseph, 22
Adorno, Theodor Wiesengrund, 22–23, 309
Aguado, Marie-Alexandre, marquis de la Marismas, 34–35, 93, 250
Aldeguier, J.-B.-Auguste d', 84
Ariosto, Ludovico 46
Armstrong, Alan, 253
Auber, Daniel-François-Esprit, xvi, xvii, xviii, 1–2, 15–16, 70, 84–85, 131, 133–34, 139, 145–47, 164, 194, 329, 390, 407, 409, 416, 418–19, 420–23, 426, 430–31, 436, 437–39, 447, 452
Aubigné, Théodore-Agrippine d', 333
Auden, Wystan Hugh 141
Augustus Octavianus (Roman emperor) 397

Bach, Johann Sebastian, xvi
Balochi, Luigi, xv, 71–72
Balzac, Honoré de, xvi, xx, 15, 19–20, 29 n. 31, 32, 126, 235–36, 244, 413–14
Barbier, Jules, xviii, 340
Barouillet, Marie-Joseph Désiré Martin, 84
Bartlet, M. Elizabeth C., 93 n. 75
Basevi, Abramo, 354, 380, 385, 392, 425
Baudelaire, Charles, xix, xxi, 6, 202, 371
Beaumarchais, Pierre-Augustin Caron de, 332, 407

Becker, Heinz, 172
Beer, Amalia, 120, 279, 298
Beer, Michael, 276
Beethoven, Ludwig van, xv, xvi, 8, 31, 162, 404, 405
Bellini, Vincenzo, xvi, xvii, 116, 156, 353, 355, 364, 374
Benda, Jiří Antonín, 141
Benjamin, Walter, 6, 201–2, 303
Berlioz, Hector, xvi, xviii, xix, xx, xxi, 12, 55, 89, 134, 156, 176–77, 200–201, 203, 205, 220, 221, 251, 270, 303, 320, 327–28, 397–99, 424, 427
Bernal, Moritz, 157
Bertin, Louise-Angélique, xvii, 219–20, 240–42, 246
Bertin, Louis-François, 219–20
Berton, Henri-Montan, xix, 47, 70
Bianconi, Lorenzo, 9
Bis, Hippolyte, xix, 93–94, 320
Bizet, Georges, xxi
Blaze de Bury, Henri, 186, 227, 240–41, 332
Bockelson, Jan. See John of Leyden
Boieldieu, François-Adrien, xvii, 70, 273–74
Boito, Arrigo, 327
Bonald, Louis-Gabriel-Ambroise, vicomte de, 13, 59–60
Bonaparte, Louis. See Napoleon III
Bonaparte, Napoléon. See Napoleon I

Boorstin, Daniel, 154
Brahms, Johannes, xix, xx, xxi
Brandus, Gemmy, 395
Brewster, Sir David, 14–15
Bruckner, Anton, xx
Brüggemann, Heinz, 5–6, 9–10
Brzoska, Matthias, 197–99
Büchner, Georg, xvii
Budden, Julian, 325 n. 13, 337, 367, 419,
    453
Byron, George Gordon Noel, Lord, 294

Calbo, Alvise, 75
Calzabigi, Raniero di, 320
Cammarano, Salvadore, 328, 335, 427
Carafa de Colobrano, Michele, xvii
Carné, Marcel, 21
Caron, Auguste, 77
Carré, Michel, 340
Castil-Blaze (François Henri Joseph
    Blaze), xvi, xvii, 116 n. 123, 170
Catel, Charles-Simon, xvi, 47
Cavour, Camillo Benso, conte di, xxi
Cecchi, Nicola, 431
Cencetti, Giuseppe, 444
Chabanon, Michel-Paul-Guy de, 68
Charles X (king of France), xv, 68, 127
Charles Fernand, duc de Berry, 25
Charpentier, Gustave, 402
Chasles, Philarète, 91–92
Chateaubriand, François-René, vicomte
    de, xix, 163
Chazet, René-André-Polydore de, 129
Cherubini, Luigi, xviii, 11, 43, 46, 53–55,
    320
Chevalier, Louis, 20
Chopin, Fryderyk, xvi, xviii, xix, 31,
    152
Chorley, Henry Fothergill, 240
Cicéri, Pierre-Luc-Charles, 42, 77, 150–
    51, 163–64, 294
Cinti-Damoreau, Laure, 38
Clapisson, Antoine-Louis, xx, 329
Claudon, Francis, 218
Comte, Auguste, xviii
Corday, Charlotte, 292
Corneille, Pierre, 47
Cottrau, Guglielmo, 139
Courbet, Gustave, xix
Crémieux, Isaac-Adolphe, 93

Crosnier, François, 36, 378–79, 394
Cruvelli, Sophie, 38

Daguerre, Louis Jacques Mandé, xviii, xx,
    150–51
Dahlhaus, Carl, 193, 255, 289, 310, 448
Dalayrac, Nicolas-Marie, 272–73
Danuser, Hermann, 200
Da Ponte, Lorenzo, 327
Darwin, Charles, xxi
Daumier, Honoré, xvii
David, Félicien, 299, 303, 397
David, Jacques Louis, 87
Debureau, Jean-Baptiste (Jean Gaspard),
    xvi, xix
Debussy, Claude, 402
Delacroix, Eugène, xv, xvi, xxi, 114, 205,
    294, 349, 372
Delavigne, Casimir, xviii, 339, 436
Delavigne, Germain, xvi, xviii, 125, 128–
    29, 131, 339–40
Delestre-Poirson, Charles Gaspard, xvi
Delfico, Melchiorre (Melchiorre De Fi-
    lippi dei conti di Langano), 391
Delibes, Léo, 453
Delord, Taxile, 435
Dent, Edward Joseph, 69
Deschamps, Émile, 330–331
Deshayes, André-Jean-Jacques, 45 n. 6
Desriaux, Philippe 47
Devrient, Eduard, 225–26
Diderot, Denis, 46, 50, 53, 114, 140, 217
Dieren, Bernard van, 99 n. 84
Döhring, Sieghart, 212, 230, 300, 303, 308
Donizetti, Gaetano, xvi, xvii, xviii, xix, 16,
    37, 194, 328–29, 336–37, 353, 355, 364,
    404
Dostoyevsky, Feodor Mikhailovich, xxi
Dumas, Alexandre *fils*, xx
Dumas, Alexandre *père*, 253
Duponchel, Charles-Edmond, 35, 38,
    250–51
Duveyrier, Charles, xx, 337–39, 346, 362
Dvořák, Antonín, xxi

Engels, Friedrich, xix
Erisso, Paolo, 75
Erkel, Ferenc, 404
Esménard, Joseph Alphonse, 74
Eymieu, Henri, 280

Falcon, Marie Cornélie, 246
Faraday, Michael, xvi
Fénelon, François de Salignac de La
Mothe, 213
Ferdinand, duc d'Orléans, 246
Fétis, François-Joseph, xv, 354
Filippi, Filippo, 186, 392, 419, 423–25,
431–32, 454, 455
Finscher, Ludwig, 139
Flaubert, Gustave, xxi
Flotow, Friedrich, Freiherr von, xix
Foscolo, Ugo, 321
Fould, Achille, 35
Frederick William III (king of Prussia), xv
Frederick William IV (king of Prussia),
xviii
Frese, Christhard, 257, 265–66
Freud, Sigmund, 115–16, 201

Gabussi, Vincenzo, 416
Gail, Jean François, 82
García, Manuel, 47
Garnier, Charles, 17
Gauss, Carl Friedrich, xvii
Gautier, Théophile, 253–54, 284
Gay, Delphine (Mme Émile de Girardin),
231–32
George IV (king of Great Britain and Ire-
land), xv
Géricault, Théodore, 205
Geyer-Kiefl, Helen, 101
Gherardi del Testa, Tommaso, 417
Ghislanzoni, Antonio, 62, 314, 324–26
Gillespie, Patti, 136
Gluck, Christoph Willibald von, 2–3, 11,
68–69, 318–20
Goethe, Johann Wolfgang von, xv, xvi,
130–31, 440
Gogol, Nikolai Vasilyevich, xvii
Gomes, Carlos, 404
Gossec, François-Joseph, xvi
Gounod, Charles, xviii, xxi, 251, 340, 397,
400, 405, 448
Grandville, Jean-Ignace-Isidore Gérard,
232–33, 435
Grétry, André-Ernest-Modeste, 51–55,
58, 80, 164, 170–71, 176, 202–3,
271–72
Griepenkerl, Robert, 61–62
Grillparzer, Franz, 155–56, 186, 243

Grimm, Friedrich Melchior, 46
Guillard, Nicolas François, 320
Guizot, François, 213, 256

Habeneck, François-Antoine, xvi, xix, 31
Habermas, Jürgen, 364, 366
Hachette, Louis, xx
Halévy, Fromental, xv, xvii, xviii, xx, 15–
16, 116, 231, 302, 329, 336, 354, 372–
73, 390, 397, 402–3
Halévy, Ludovic, 155–56, 175, 402
Haller, Albrecht von, 114
Handel, George Frideric, 3, 167
Hanslick, Eduard, xx, 145–46, 323, 329,
407, 434–35, 436–37
Hapdé, Jean-Baptiste Augustin, 140
Hasse, Johann Adolf, 319
Hauser, Arnold, 72, 81, 217
Haussmann, Georges Eugène, baron, xx,
17
Haydn, Joseph, 299
Hebbel, Friedrich, xviii, xix
Hegel, Georg Friedrich Wilhelm, xvi,
61
Heine, Heinrich, xvi, xx, 6, 19, 92, 165,
207–8, 315–16
Henscheid, Eckhard, 448
Héquet, Gustave, 363–64, 430
Hérold, Ferdinand, 70
Hiller, Ferdinand, 61
Hitchcock, Alfred, 199–200, 271
Hittorf, Jacob Ignaz, xix
Hoffmann, Ernst Theodor Amadeus, 43,
197, 314
Hofmannsthal, Hugo von, 327
Hölderlin, Friedrich, xviii
Hugo, Adèle, 240, 245–46
Hugo, Victor, xv, xvi, xvii, xviii, xx, 21, 39,
58–59, 79, 142, 163, 168–69, **215–46**,
371–72, 404, 427–28

Ibsen, Henrik, xxi
Ingres, Jean Auguste Dominique, xvi

John of Leyden (Jan Bockelsen), 259
Join-Dieterle, Catherine, 29
Jouy, Victor-Joseph Étienne de, xv, xvi,
xix, 40, 41–50, 54–58, 59–60, 71, 74,
76, 79, 92–93, 147, 162, 226–27, 320–
21, 327, 361, 435

Köhler, Erich, 245
Körner, Christian Gottfried, 170
Koselleck, Reinhart, 7
Kreutzer, Rodolphe, 5, 70

La Baume, Gile, 250
La Chabeaussière, Ange-Étienne-Xavier-
  Poisson de, 53–54
La Harpe, Jean François de, 58
Lamartine, Alphonse de, 294–95
Lamennais, Hugues-Félicité-Robert, xv
La Rochefoucauld-Doudeauville, Louis-
  François-Sosthène, vicomte de, 33, 36,
  68–69, 128, 233, 251
Laya, Jean-Louis, 129
LeBlanc du Roullet, Marie François Louis
  Gand, 320
Le Bon, Gustave, 288
Legouvé, Ernest, 188
Lemaître, Frédérick, xvii, 21
Lemoyne, Jean-Baptiste, 269
Lemud, François-Joseph-Aimé de, 192
Lenin (Vladimir Ilyich Ulyanov), 13
Lepenies, Wolf, 73
Le Sueur, Jean-François, xvii, 47, 163,
  261–62
Levarie, Siegmund, 449–50
Lewald, August, 146–47
Lewis, Matthew Gregory, 400
Lindenberger, Herbert, 452
Liszt, Franz, xv, xix, xx, 135, 139, 162,
  220, 311, 412
Locatelli, Tommaso, 425
Lotman, Yuri Mikhailovich, 8
Louis, duc de Bourgogne, 213
Louis XIV (king of France), 27
Louis XVI (king of France), 52
Louis XVIII (king of France), 93
Louis-Philippe (king of the French), xvi,
  xix, 127, 213, 253, 256
Louis-Philippe-Joseph, duc d'Orléans
  (Philippe-Égalité), 207
Lubbert, Émile-Timothée, 33
Lully, Jean-Baptiste, 34, 261, 389
Luther, Martin, 165

Macpherson, James, 74
Maehder, Jürgen, 171 n. 37, 176
Maffei, Andrea, 335
Maffei, Clara, 412

Mainzer, Joseph, 211
Mancinelli, Luigi, 406
Mann, Thomas, 329
Manzoni, Alessandro, xv
Marat, Jean-Paul, 292
Marliani, Marco Aurelio, conte, 329
Marmontel, Jean François, 68
Marrast, Armand, 93
Marschner, Heinrich August, xvi, xvii, 269
Marselli, Nicola, 304–5
Marx, Adolf Bernhard, 203–4
Marx, Karl, xix, 13
Massé, Victor, 340
Massenet, Jules, 315
Mayr, Simon, 202–3, 353
Mazzini, Giuseppe, 243
Mehmet II (Turkish sultan), 75
Méhul, Étienne-Nicolas, 269, 320
Meilhac, Henri, 402
Mendelssohn Bartholdy, Felix, xv, xvi, xix,
  61, 228
Mercadante, Saverio, 353, 416
Mercier, Louis-Sebastien, 43, 58, 71, 140,
  170, 217
Mérimée, Prosper, xix, 228, 333
Merle, Jean-Toussaint, 47–48
Mermet, Auguste, 305, 327, 361, 399–400
Mesmer, Franz Anton, 272
Metastasio (Pietro Trapassi), 3, 78, 107,
  319, 321, 398, 406
Meyerbeer, Giacomo, xv, xvi, xvii, xviii,
  xix, xx, xxi, 1–3, 9, 11, 23, 35, 37–40, 55,
  61, 98, 116, 119–21, 141–42, 148, **158–
  214**, 218–20, 227–31, 237, **247–317**,
  318–20, 322, 325–26, 328–35, 339–41,
  345–46, 348, 349–50, 353–55, 367–68,
  372–73, 374, 376, 390, 392, 393–34,
  396–97, 402–3, 404–5, 406, 420–21,
  427–28, 438, 452–53, 454
Meyerbeer, Minna, 332–33
Michelet, Jules, 283, 334
Michotte, Edmond, 92–93, 121
Mitscherlich, Alexander, 364
Moniuszko, Stanisław, 404
Monsigny, Pierre-Alexandre, 202
Moscovici, Serge, 288
Mozart, Leopold, 318
Mozart, Wolfgang Amadé, xvii, 2–3, 203,
  318–19, 327
Mundt, Theodor, 154

Musorgsky, Modest Petrovich, xxi, 310

Musset, Alfred de, xvii

Nadar (Gaspard Félix Tournachon), xx, xxi

Napoleon I (emperor of the French), xviii, 19, 27, 49, 69, 72, 74, 390

Napoleon III (emperor of the French), xvii, xix, xx, xxi, 17, 35, 289, 361, 388, 391, 397–98

Nicolai, Otto, xix

Niedermeyer, Louis, 305

Niépovié, Gaëtan (Karel Frankowski), 185–86

Nodier, Charles, xix, 140

Noske, Frits, 368

Nourrit, Adolphe, xviii, 38, 104 n. 98, 234, 246

Obin, Louis-Henri, 381

Offenbach, Jacques, xvii, xx, xxi, 201, 361, 394, 402, 437, 453

Onslow, Georges, xviii, xx

Orsini, Felice, xxi

Paër, Ferdinando, xvi, xviii, 70

Paganini, Nicolò, xvi, xviii

Paisiello, Giovanni, 272, 407

Parker, Roger, 454

Pendle, Karin, 335

Penthièvre, Marie Louise Adelaïde, du-chesse de, 207

Perrin, Émile, 36

Piave, Francesco Maria, 322, 419–20

Piccinni, Alexandre, 146

Piccinni, Niccolò, 11, 46, 68

Pillet, Léon, 35, 252, 336

Pixérécourt, René-Charles Guilbert de, xv, xix, 140–47

Pizzi, Italo, 346, 413

Planche, Gustave, 304

Poe, Edgar Allan, xviii, xix

Ponchielli, Amilcare, 403

Poussin, Nicolas, 51, 53

Puccini, Giacomo, 314, 408

Puskin, Aleksandr Sergeyevich, xvi, xvii, 310

Quinault, Philippe, 107

Rabelais, François, 456

Racine, Jean, 47

Rameau, Jean-Philippe, 68, 390

Reber, Henri, xx

Reicha, Antoine, xvii, 70, 164, 309

Rétif de la Bretonne, Nicolas-Edme, 5

Reyer, Ernest, 299

Richer, Adrien, 311

Ricordi, Giulio, 406

Rimsky-Korsakov, Nikolai Andreyevich, 404

Ritorni, Carlo, 207

Romanelli, Luigi, 321

Romani, Felice, 331

Ronsard, Pierre de, 398

Roqueplan, Nestor, 35–36, 84, 200, 347

Rosoi, Barnabé Farmian de, 48 n. 13, 58, 71

Rossi, Gaetano, 98, 330

Rossini, Gioachino, xv, xvi, xviii, xx, 1–2, 11, 36, 43, 61, **63–121**, 128, 134, 141, 162, 164, 168–69, 171, 204, 206, 227, 242, 320, 353–54, 384, 387, 404, 407, 421, 437, 450

Roubaud, Benjamin (Benjamin), 338

Rousseau, Jean-Jacques, 46, 51, 114, 141

Royer, Alphonse, xviii, xix, 36, 345

Saint-Georges, Jules Henri Vernoy de, xviii, 339, 407

Salieri, Antonio, 332

Salvi, Matteo, 337

Sand, George (Aurore Dupin), xviii

Sauvo, Étienne, 163

Sax, Adolphe, 291

Schiller, Johann Christoph Friedrich von, 170, 435–36

Schinkel, Karl Friedrich, xviii

Schlegel, August Wilhelm, 304

Schlesinger, Maurice, 37, 395

Schonenberger, Georges, 37

Schöning, Udo, 59

Schreker, Franz, 403

Schubert, Franz, xv, xvi, 269

Schucht, Jean F., 61, 166, 219, 396

Schumann, Robert, xvi, xvii, xviii, xx, 182, 228, 315, 393, 412

Schütze, Stefan, 133

Scott, Sir Walter, xvii, 46, 73–74, 104, 163, 214, 273

Scribe, Eugène, xv, xvi, xvii, xviii, xix, xx, 12, 35, 37–38, 74, 81, 118, **124–57**,

172, 178, 183, 186, 188, 194, 210–11,
212, 218, 228, 235, 244, 251–59, 263,
266, 273, 284, 290–95, 302–3, 306, 310,
312–14, 319–22, 324, 329–41, 345–58,
359, 360–61, 366–67, 373–75, 377–87,
393–94, 397, 400–401, 407, 409, 413–
18, 419–23, 426–27, 430–31, 435–36,
437–39, 442, 445–47, 450–52
Scudo, Paul, 181–82, 347
Séchan, Charles Polycarpe, 196, 282
Second, Albéric, 232
Sennett, Richard, 6–7, 149, 235, 244–45,
361–62
Shakespeare, William, 217, 310, 412–13,
427
Sibille, Lodoys, 30
Smetana, Bedřich, xx
Somma, Antonio, 324, 325, 414–17, 420,
422, 430
Soumet, Alexandre, xv, 71–72
Spontini, Gaspare, xv, xviii, xx, 3, 5, 11,
43, 47, 74, 116, 165, 320, 389, 404
Staël-Holstein, Anne-Louise-Germaine
Necker, baronne de, 55, 230
Stanton, Stephen Sadler, 136–39
Steiner, George, 184
Stendhal (Henri Beyle), xvi, xviii, 58–59,
69, 91, 413
Stephanie, Johann Gottlieb, the younger,
318
Steuben, Carl, 86–87
Stoltz, Rosine Victoire Noël, 35, 252
Strauss, Johann, the younger, xix, 402
Strauss, Richard, 327, 403
Strepponi, Giuseppina, 456
Sue, Eugène, xviii, xxi, 20, 224, 400

Tasso, Torquato, 44, 46
Tchaikovsky, Peter Ilyich, xxi, 404
Thomas, Ambroise, xx, 329, 340
Tissot, Claude-Joseph, 296–97
Titz, Louis, 132

Torelli, Vincenzo, 415
Turgenev, Ivan Sergeyevich, xix

Ueding, Gert, 366

Vaëz, Gustave, xviii, xix, 345
Vatel, Auguste-Eugène, 256
Velde, Carl Franz van der, 333–34
Verdi, Giuseppe, xvi, xviii, xix, xx, xxi, 1–3,
9, 11–12, 37, 40, 62, 79, 162–63, 165,
168, 180–81, 194, 204–5, 206, 231, 284,
303, 304–7, 314, 319, 322–27, 328,
335–39, **342–87**, 388, 391, 393–96,
399–400, 404, 406, 407, **408–56**
Verne, Jules, 189–91
Véron, Louis-Désiré, xvi, xviii, xx, 29–30,
31–32, 34, 147–49, 251, 326
Viardot, Pauline, xix, 252
Victoria (queen of Great Britain and Ire-
land, later empress of India), xvii
Virgil (Publius Vergilius Maro), 397–98
Voltaire (François-Marie Arouet), 43, 47,
98, 311

Wagner, Richard, xviii, xix, xx, xxi, 1–3, 5,
8, 11, 12, 70, 134, 148, 162, 309, 313–
15, 327–29, 393–94, 400–401, 403, 404,
406, 412, 428
Wailly, Léon de, xviii
Walter, Michael, 99, 191, 218, 329 n. 25,
349–50
Weber, Carl Maria von, xv, xvi, xviii, 11,
171, 203, 269
Weber, Gottfried, 208
Weber, Johannes, 292
Weber, Wilhelm Eduard, xvii
Wendorff, Rudolf, 184–85, 193, 206
Werner, Zacharias, 209
William I (king of the Netherlands), 127,
131
William II (king of Prussia, later German
emperor as William I), 62, 286